THE ENCYCLOPEDIA OF
ALFRED HITCHCOCK

THE ENCYCLOPEDIA OF
ALFRED HITCHCOCK

THOMAS LEITCH

Foreword by
Gene D. Phillips

Series Editors
John C. Tibbetts and James M. Welsh

Checkmark Books®
An imprint of Facts On File, Inc.

The Encyclopedia of Alfred Hitchcock

Checkmark Books
An imprint of Facts On File, Inc.
132 West 31st Street
New York NY 10001

Library of Congress Cataloging-in-Publication Data

Leitch, Tom
    The encyclopedia of Alfred Hitchcock / Thomas Leitch ; foreword by Gene D. Phillips.
        p. cm. — (Library of great filmmakers)
    Includes bibliographical references and index.
    ISBN 0-8160-4386-8 (hc: alk. paper) — ISBN 0-8160-4387-6 (pbk.: alk. paper)
        1. Hitchcock, Alfred, 1899—Encyclopedias.   I. Title. II. Series.

PN1998.3.H58 L45 2001
791.43′0233′092—dc21

                                                            2001039293

Text design by Erika K. Arroyo
Cover design by Nora Wertz

Printed in the United States of America

VB Hermitage 10 9 8 7 6 5 4 3 2 1

This book is printed on acid-free paper.

CONTENTS

To David and Judith

PREFACE

□□□

AN IMP OF FORTUNE:
HITCHCOCK AND THE ZEN OF CINEMA STUDIES

No doubt Alfred Hitchcock was a film pioneer. Trained in Britain and Germany, he directed the first talking feature in the United Kingdom, *Blackmail,* in 1929. Working in silent cinema, he had already developed technique. Other pioneers had already worked to develop the grammar of cinema. The Lumière brothers had discovered and developed early examples of miniature cinematic "spectacles" (their "actualities" of scenes from everyday life seemed spectacular on the large screen). Also in France Georges Méliès had invented and introduced cinematic "magic" into the spectacle. William S. Porter first explored the basic components of narrative cinema; then D. W. Griffith took storytelling to another level through his development of crosscutting and parallel montage and greatly expanded the scope of narrative cinema, essentially inventing the feature film. In France, Abel Gance, whose career paralleled Griffith's in America, expanded narrative scope even further, eventually producing his five-hour epic *Napoléon* in 1927, but Gance also made astonishing advances before 1927 in montage effects and utterly inventive and experimental moving camerawork, experimenting with what he would later call polyvision. In the newly formed Soviet Union, Sergei Eisenstein discovered how to shape montage to serve ideology.

Griffith, Gance, and Eisenstein all came to cinema from the theatre, Griffith and Gance as would-be playwrights and actors, Eisenstein as an innovative stage director who quickly realized that cinema could better serve his creative purposes. Hitchcock represented a second generation of pioneering filmmakers. His orientation was not stagebound but entirely visual; not visionary, like Gance; not melodramatic, like Griffith; not political, like Eisenstein. Like all of these predecessors, Hitchcock mastered audience manipulation, but his technique was far subtler and far more adaptable to the new technology of sound. No one by midcentury would have thought of Hitchcock as a silent filmmaker. Rather, he became known as the "master of suspense." His forte was purely commercial filmmaking. He was brought to the United States by David O. Selznick and was quickly recognized as a supremely gifted craftsman, always entertaining and always in control. While Hitchcock was honing his cinematic skills during the 1930s, Orson Welles was still working with stage and radio drama. Welles would be in the first tier of a third generation of directors; like Hitchcock, Welles would develop his own recognizable off-screen persona, but not so amusingly. Hitchcock was better than Welles at working within the industry efficiently and effectively.

Hitchcock was an imp of fortune. Fortune smiled on Alfred Hitchcock, and the cherubic imp winked back. He understood irony, dramatic and otherwise, perhaps better than any other director. During the

1950s he shaped his image as a really big filmmaker as carefully as he had shaped his films—an imposing physical presence, portly and humorous, set apart from the rest of us by his careful and precise elocution and diction, eminently "civilized" as he spoke of murder and mayhem while introducing episodes of his popular television productions of *Alfred Hitchcock Presents.* He became known by his silhouette, which became his "signature," a masterpiece of simple design and his very own logo. He could be imperious, but he was unfailingly amusing. His films were always amusing but also amusingly edgy. One generally knew what to expect but never quite when or how to expect it; therefore, his work was never entirely predictable. There was an impish and wicked slyness that could always turn the tables on his audience, who always suspected that he could be quite perverse, hence, the later obscene interest in Donald Spoto's postmortem disclosures about his alleged "dark side of genius."

Hitchcock *was* a genius, posing as a clown. His image was so ingeniously fabricated that it took years before critics dared to take his work seriously, but once that began to happen, Hitchcock was quickly recognized as the ultimate auteur director, first by the French New Wave architects of the auteur theory, François Truffaut, Claude Chabrol, and Eric Rohmer, who published studies of his work, and then, in America and Canada, by Andrew Sarris and Robin Wood. Hitchcock's films became paradigms of the obsessive and hyperactive auteurism that would follow in the United States. Besides the director's obvious stylistic tics such as what he called the MacGuffin and his sneaky cameo appearances, critics would find thematic patterns as well—how many variants could be worked on the "wrong man" motif, for example? And what about all those blondes and misogynists, such as Uncle Charlie, the "Merry Widow" murderer of *Shadow of a Doubt,* or Norman Bates in *Psycho,* or the necktie murderer in *Frenzy?* How many times did Hitchcock employ doppelgängers, both male and female—Guy haunted by Bruno in *Strangers on a Train,* or Judy haunted by Madeleine and Carlotta in *Vertigo?* The shower murder in *Psycho* and the crop-dusting sequence in *North by Northwest* became textbook examples of excellent storyboarding and montage construction.

Hitchcock created such a widely varied body of work over 50 years of filmmaking that his films could fit into many different critical approaches, once the critics began to take him seriously. At about the same time something called cinema studies was coming into its own as an academic discipline, and its acolytes could communicate about Hitchcock with one another in coded jargon that would lend significance to the work of this most popular of filmmakers. Thus high-minded critics began to refer to his movies as "texts." Those interested in psychology and psychoanalysis could have a field day with Hitchcock, as could those interested in genre studies and film noir. When she wrote her seminal foray into film feminism, "Visual Pleasure and Narrative Cinema," Laura Mulvey turned to Hitchcock to develop her thesis about patriarchy and the "male gaze" in mainstream cinema, designed primarily for the "pleasure" of male spectators. Later Tania Modleski, anticipating Robin Wood's question, "Can Hitchcock be saved for Feminism?," produced *The Women Who Knew Too Much: Hitchcock and Feminist Theory* (1988).

Surveying the shelves of my own modest library, I easily found more than 20 books devoted to Hitchcock. One that I came to appreciate is entitled *Find the Director and Other Hitchcock Games* (1991) by Thomas Leitch, the author of the book you are now reading, and, I hope, will continue to read with pleasure. I have known Professor Leitch for many years and have come to respect him as one of the most insightful, dependable, and thorough contributing editors of *Literature/Film Quarterly,* a periodical I have edited for 30 years. We have published several of his Hitchcock essays, most recently his piece suggesting "101 Ways to Tell Hitchcock's *Psycho* from Gus Van Sant's" odd but competent 1998 remake of Hitchcock's classic thriller (*LFQ* 28:4, 2000).

But my all-time favorite Leitch essay began as a keynote address for a conference on the films of the cold war that I organized for the International Association for Media and History in 1997. That lecture, later published in *Literature/Film Quarterly* (27:1, 1999), entitled "It's the Cold War, Stupid! An Obvious History of the Political Hitchcock," ran a taxonomy of changing opinions about Hitchcock's work, from 1945 to 1969 to 1988 to 1998, ranging from

the "stupid" (what nobody thinks) to the "obvious" (what everybody knows) to the "unimaginable" (what nobody would ever suggest). In 1945 it was obvious, for example, that Hitchcock was "an apolitical entertainer" but unimaginable to consider him "an important humanist artist whose films have universal meanings." By 1969 it was stupid to write Hitchcock off as a "mere entertainer" and obvious that he was a true auteur whose films had "humanistic, universal meanings," but it was unimaginable to consider him a "feminist (or nonfeminist)." By 1988 Hitchcock had obviously become "a touchstone for feminism" and was "worth saving for feminism," but it was stupid to regard him as a "humanist/universalist" and "unimaginable" to consider him as a film-maker with "a conservative political agenda." Ten years later, however, it was obvious that Hitchcock's films were "exactly as political as everybody else's."

As a writer and critic, Tom Leitch is quick, agile, and amusing. He certainly knows the field and many of the major players. I consider him a major player himself, and for that reason asked him to do this book. He couldn't (or wouldn't) say no, out of deference to me, and was therefore coerced into the project. His book avoids jargon (as much as is humanly possible) and is, I believe, eminently readable.

—James M. Welsh, Series Editor
Salisbury, Maryland
May Day, 2001

FOREWORD

THE HITCHCOCK TOUCH

At precisely 9:20 P.M. on the evening of April 29, 1974, Alfred Hitchcock took his place in a special box overlooking the auditorium of Avery Fisher Hall in New York City's Lincoln Center for the Performing Arts. The occasion was a gala tribute sponsored by the Film Society of Lincoln Center, honoring Hitchcock's lifetime achievement as a filmmaker. Several cinema artists associated with his career were on hand to pay tribute, and their remarks on this occasion and on other occasions, such as the American Film Institute's celebration of his career, televised on March 12, 1979, have proved helpful in writing this Foreword. But Hitch himself, as always, was the main attraction.

One of the reasons that the career of Alfred Hitchcock is so fascinating is that he is one of the very few directors in the history of motion pictures whose name was always as important on a movie marquee as that of any actor appearing in one of his films. His perennial popularity with the mass audience, which continues with the availability of his films on videocassette, means that he was discovered by his public as a maker of entertaining films long before movie critics and film scholars got around to realizing that he was also a genuine film artist. That is because Hitchcock firmly believed that his first obligation as a filmmaker was to entertain his audience. For him film was, after all, "life with the dull spots removed," as he affirms in *Hitchcock on Hitchcock* (p. 205).

The very popularity of his movies, however, is reason enough for some critics to write him off as a mere crowd pleaser rather than recognize him as an authentic artist of the cinema. That a director could be both is suggested by the fact that his finest films, for example *The 39 Steps* and *Psycho,* are also among his most popular. Nevertheless, he was not unduly bothered by the fact that his artistry was frequently overlooked by reviewers because, for him, "the mark of good technique is that it is unnoticed," as he says in the same book (p. 208).

I had the pleasure of watching the director work on his next-to-last film, *Frenzy* (1972), in the heart of downtown London, and in conversing with him on the occasion of the Lincoln Center tribute a couple of years later. In studying his work and in speaking with him, I discovered that there are several reasons for Hitchcock's abiding acceptance by the public; these taken together are what comprise the Hitchcock touch.

For a start, his hero is an average person who is thrown into an extraordinary situation. We can easily identify with him: He is not someone who expects trouble because it is his profession, for example, a detective or a secret agent. "My hero," he told me, "is the average person to whom bizarre things happen, rather than the other way round."

Often, the hero cannot go to the police for help because they wrongly suspect him of some crime. Consequently, he is thrown back on his own resources to find the real culprit.

His villains also appear to be average people, rather than obvious criminal types. The reason is that evil can lurk behind the facade of an apparently respectable person. As he indicated to me, "I always make my villains as charming as possible. The really frightening thing about villains is their surface likeableness; they use their charm to attract potential victims."

Not only his central characters, but also the settings of Hitchcock's films are quite ordinary on the surface. Hitchcock does not choose settings where one would expect to encounter evil and violence, such as dark alleys and dives. He prefers to show that evil lurks beneath the surface of apparently harmless settings. His villains commit their mayhem in respectable restaurants and amusement parks, places where the viewers are apt to find themselves.

All of these elements combine to make spectators feel that what is happening to the hero up there on the screen could conceivably happen to them; for Hitchcock aims to make us aware that catastrophe surrounds us all—and can strike when we least expect it—and it is precisely this unsettling reflection that holds one's interest in watching a Hitchcock picture, even after repeated viewings.

One of the reasons that his films continue to involve moviegoers, even on repeated viewings, is that Hitchcock customarily takes the audience into his confidence early in the course of the picture by sharing with them information that other directors might withhold for the sake of a surprise ending. "I believe in giving the audience all the facts as early as possible," he told Pete Martin, because that way a director can "build up an almost unbearable tension" (p. 128). When the viewers know about a danger of which the characters themselves are unaware, they almost want to blurt out a warning to the characters. Surprise lasts only a moment, Hitchcock concluded, but tipping off the audience to what is really going to happen allows the director to nurture excitement that lasts throughout the whole movie. Peter Bogdanovich comments that Hitchcock's famous maxim about the superiority of suspense over surprise "reverberates into every aspect of picture making and is today the single least heeded and most needed" (p. 18).

Still another factor often found as part of Hitchcock's recipe, and one that is similarly calculated to keep the film moving, is what he called the MacGuffin, a term he defined as a device that sets the plot in motion and keeps it going. The MacGuffin (which got its name from an old English music-hall joke) is simply the thing that preoccupies the hero and the heroine, because of which they are thrown into danger, such as a vital secret formula. Because the sole function of the MacGuffin is to keep the story moving, its exact nature is, for all practical purposes, irrelevant to one's enjoyment of the film in question. The characters in the film worry about what they are after, he indicated to me, but the audience does not care about the MacGuffin directly at all "because they only care about the safety of the hero and heroine."

Taken together, then, all of the elements I have elaborated, along with the sardonic bits of black comedy that Hitchcock regularly injected into his movies, serve to define the Hitchcock touch; they are what indelibly and indisputably mark a movie as peculiarly his own, even though most of his pictures are derived from preexisting novels or plays. The sum total of his motion pictures reflects the provocative personal vision and directorial style of the filmmaker who made them all, thereby demonstrating that Alfred Hitchcock is an auteur of the first rank.

Alfred Joseph Hitchcock was born in London in 1899 and was brought up with a rather strict Catholic background, notably at St. Ignatius, a Jesuit preparatory school in London. "The Jesuits," who were strict disciplinarians, "used to terrify me to death," he told me, "and now I'm getting my own back by terrifying other people in my films." After graduating from secondary school, Hitchcock became fascinated with the cinema, and in 1920 he went to work at an American-owned British studio, Famous Players–Lasky (later Paramount Pictures). The aspiring moviemaker gained experience at the studio in all the various phases of film production.

Working in silent pictures, Hitchcock learned to place a great deal of emphasis on telling a story visually. Consequently, at this early point in his career, he began to think primarily in visual terms when mapping out a film, a practice he continued for the rest of his days.

In 1925 the front office promoted Hitchcock to the rank of full-fledged director, and he made his first movie in Munich at Emelka Studios, with which his home studio in London had made a co-production deal. *The Pleasure Garden* (1925) was a tale of madness and murder that presaged the films of his later career. But it was *The Lodger* (1926), which he made after he came back to Britain, that really established Hitchcock as an important film director. The film was based on Jack the Ripper, a subject to which he would return four decades later in *Frenzy. The Lodger* not only demonstrated incontestably Hitchcock's talent for telling a taut suspense tale efficiently, but also marked his first appearance in one of his own films as an extra—such "cameo appearances" would become a trademark of his work. His reason for placing himself in the newspaper office scene in *The Lodger,* however, was purely economic; he needed another person in the foreground of a shot to help give the impression of a crowded office, and his budget would not allow him to hire another extra.

The Lodger found favor with both press and public, and he compounded his good fortune after the film opened by marrying Alma Reville, who had been working with him in different capacities, from script supervisor to assistant director, from his earliest days as a director. She would continue to work on the screenplays for his films for years to come.

In 1929 Hitchcock made *Blackmail,* which has the distinction of being the first major British talking picture. *Blackmail* had been shot silent, but when it became clear that talking pictures were here to stay, Hitchcock went back and reshot several scenes with spoken dialogue. But he was able to incorporate into the finished film a number of action scenes, such as the climactic chase through the British Museum, just as he had originally filmed them, with only the addition of background music and sound effects.

From the very dawn of the sound era, Hitchcock showed that he realized sound should complement image in a movie in an imaginative way. His smooth integration of the techniques of silent and sound pictures, a hallmark of his films from then on, is demonstrated by the fact that some scenes in *Blackmail,* like the British Museum sequence, are essentially visual, while others depend on the creative use of sound.

One scene in the film reflects a shrewd manipulation of the sound track: It takes place after the heroine (Anny Ondra) stabs to death an artist named Crewe with a bread knife when he attempts to rape her in his apartment. The following morning, Alice tries to behave naturally while eating breakfast with her parents. A gossipy neighbor joins them to discuss the murder that is all over the morning papers. As Alice prepares to slice a piece of bread for her father, the chatterbox's voice fades into an incomprehensible babble on the soundtrack, with only the word *knife* clearly audible. The word is repeated a little louder on the soundtrack each time it recurs, until it reaches a crescendo that causes Alice to scream hysterically and throw down the knife she is holding, as if it were the one she had wielded against Crewe the night before. No one present guesses the true import of her behavior. When a seedy blackmailer demands hush money from her, however, the police organize a hunt to track him down. Cornered atop the British Museum, the blackmailer falls to his death through the glass dome of the Reading Room. Later Hitchcock would stage similar scenes of disorder and violence on the top of other symbols of order and culture, such as Mount Rushmore in *North by Northwest.* James Wolcott writes that "no director has shown a greater aptitude for framing and putting actors against architectural surroundings" and for making "classic use of national monuments" (p. 144).

The premiere of *Blackmail* was an unqualified success and formally inaugurated the era of sound pictures in England. During the 1930s Hitchcock continued to make low-budget, high-quality thrillers that still remain exciting cinema, exemplified by *The Man Who Knew Too Much* (1934). Hitchcock was to remake this film two decades later, but this original version deserves attention.

The action begins with Bob and Jill Lawrence (Leslie Banks and Edna Best) as an English couple vacationing with their daughter Betty at a winter resort in Saint Moritz. Bob and Jill inadvertently become enmeshed in international intrigue by associating with a fellow vacationer who is in reality a French secret agent named Louis Bernard.

In the wake of Bernard's death, young Betty Lawrence is abducted by Abbot (Peter Lorre) and his gang of anarchists to silence Bob, who had learned earlier from Bernard about the impending assassination of a foreign diplomat visiting London. The search for Betty takes Bob and Jill from the fashionable vacation resort in Switzerland where they were staying to the slums of London, where danger seems to pounce at every turn. Bob is shut in with the kidnappers temporarily in a scruffy nonconformist chapel, which turns out to be a front for Abbot's mob.

Meanwhile, Jill has gone to the Royal Albert Hall, where the assassination of which Bob had been warned is scheduled to take place during the course of a concert. The featured piece on the program is the "Storm Cloud Cantata," and the assassin is to fire at his target at the precise moment when a cymbal crash will drown out the sound of the gunfire. Jill screams out just when the killer is about to shoot and thus saves the statesman's life. The police then help her to trace Bob and Betty to the anarchists' citadel, where an exciting gun battle brings the film to a close.

The Man Who Knew Too Much was a box office favorite and was followed by *The 39 Steps* (1935), which—as much as any of Hitchcock's films—incorporates all the fundamental elements that constitute the Hitchcock touch.

Richard Hannay (Robert Donat) is the typical Hitchcock hero, an ordinary man drawn against his will into an extraordinary situation. He befriends Annabella Smith (Lucie Mannheim), a young woman he meets at a vaudeville show; she turns out to be a secret agent committed to keeping some vital air-ministry secrets out of the hands of an organization of spies known by the secret code name of the 39 Steps. When Annabella is murdered in Hannay's apartment by emissaries of the 39 Steps, he decides to go after the ringleader of the spy group, who is based in Scotland, and foil his attempt to steal the state secrets.

One of the most celebrated examples of Hitchcock's creative use of sound occurs early in the picture: When the hero's landlady discovers a corpse in his apartment, she opens her mouth to scream in terror. Her scream, as heard on the soundtrack, turns into the screeching of a train whistle, as we see a locomotive barreling out of a tunnel in the next scene. The train is, in fact, carrying the hero away from the scene of the murder—of which he is unjustly accused. The juxtaposition of the screaming woman with the screeching train whistle thus establishes an implicit link between the two scenes.

Richard sets out on the trail of the ringleader of the 39 Steps spy organization. He eventually tracks down the villain in Scotland. The chief of the foreign agents is in fact a charming, highly respected aristocrat, living on a splendid estate in the country.

In a Hitchcock movie the villain, we know, is usually an individual endowed with misleading charm and respectability; Professor Jordan (Godfrey Tearle) is a typical Hitchcock villain in the present film. Moreover, Hannay in due course discovers, with the help of Pamela (Madeleine Carroll), a feisty female with whom he becomes involved along the way, that the classified information that Jordan and his co-conspirators covet is the design of an improved airplane engine. (This vital secret formula is, of course, the film's MacGuffin.) The specifications of the engine have been memorized by a memory expert who calls himself Mr. Memory, whom Hannay had watched perform in the music hall at the beginning of the picture. Hannay's mission comes to an end, then, in what is once more a most unlikely place in which to play out a danger-fraught adventure: a London vaudeville theater, where Mr. Memory is appearing.

In summary, *The 39 Steps* is not only a first-class example of the elements that comprise the Hitchcock touch, but also one of Hitchcock's finest achievements. Like *The Lady Vanishes* (1938), another superb example of the thriller genre, *The 39 Steps* enjoyed considerable popularity in the United States. It is therefore not surprising that Hitchcock was invited to Hollywood to continue his career. Naturally it would take some time for a director accustomed to working in the relatively intimate surroundings of a small British studio to adjust to the factory atmosphere of the larger and more complex Hollywood accommodations. Nevertheless, Hitchcock continued to employ in Hollywood as much as possible his own formal, businesslike method of shooting a scene. His custom was to confer privately with members of the cast and crew about a given scene in advance, all in accordance with the careful plans he had drawn up long before the cameras turned. As Bogdanovich observes, "Would that more filmmakers today had his passion for precision" (p. 18).

I was on hand one day in the summer of 1971 when Hitchcock was shooting a location scene for

Frenzy in the minipark in the center of London's Leicester Square. He tended to stay unobtrusively on the sidelines out of the way of the crew while they set up each shot according to his detailed advance instructions. Then, when all was in readiness, he would come forward and watch the filming. When the day's shooting was completed, the director climbed into his limousine and disappeared from sight, having conducted himself in the same formal, detached manner while shooting in the open air in downtown London that customarily characterized his manner when filming in the controlled atmosphere of a sound stage back in Hollywood.

Looking back on the best thrillers that Hitchcock made during the 1930s in his native Britain, from *The Man Who Knew Too Much* to *The Lady Vanishes,* one can characterize them for the most part as straightforward, fast-moving chase melodramas, with a minimum of plot and character development and a maximum of action and excitement. By contrast, his American movies, starting with *Rebecca* (1940), tended to be longer films that allotted more screen time for a deeper probing into the psychology of the principal characters.

Thus, *Rebecca* presents an in-depth portrait of its key characters, Maxim de Winter (Laurence Olivier), a wealthy, aloof widower, and his youthful bride (Joan Fontaine). Once she takes up residence with Max in the forbidding family castle of Manderley, the disconsolate heroine finds that she is constantly living in the shadow of Rebecca, Max's deceased first wife, with whom, she assumes, he had an idyllic relationship. Max, however, eventually reveals to his second wife that the faithless Rebecca had sadistically sought to make his life a veritable hell, summed up by her attempt to goad him into murdering her by cruelly informing him that she was pregnant with the child of another man. Later the real reason for Rebecca's suicidal death wish is brought to light: She wanted to be spared a prolonged and unglamorous death from cancer by having Max in effect put her out of her misery by killing her.

When Mrs. Danvers (Judith Anderson), the dour, demonic housekeeper who had adored Rebecca, learns the terrible truth about her deceased mistress, the crazed woman puts a torch to the house and is herself burned up in the blaze. Hitchcock adroitly creates the final destruction of Manderley in all its compelling visual detail. When the flames ravaging Rebecca's sumptuous bedroom reach her ornate bed, they devour her monogrammed pillowcase. The embroidered *R* disappears behind a curtain of fire, a visual metaphor that implies that Rebecca's spirit is at last dispelled from the lives of Max and his new wife. The brilliant visual imagery that characterizes the film's final sequence is a vivid reminder of the emphasis that Hitchcock, who joined the motion picture industry long before the movies learned to talk, placed on visual storytelling. He believed that the images should be allowed, as often as possible, to speak for themselves, as they do here in the closing scene of *Rebecca,* a superbly crafted picture that won the Academy Award for Best Picture of the Year.

Shadow of a Doubt (1943) was another highlight of Hitchcock's work in the 1940s; it was one of his personal favorites, largely because he had as his principal collaborator on the script the distinguished playwright Thornton Wilder (*Our Town*), who bestowed on the movie a richness of characterization seldom equaled in Hitchcock's other films. *Spellbound* (1945), with its Freudian dream sequences designed by the esteemed Spanish artist Salvador Dali, turned out to be another superlative psychological thriller in the grand tradition of *Rebecca*. Because of the success of Hitchcock's *Rebecca, Shadow of a Doubt,* and *Spellbound,* movie moguls were willing to concede a greater degree of artistic freedom to Hitchcock than they had accorded him in his first years in Hollywood. Hitchcock proved himself worthy of his increased creative freedom with such films as *Strangers on a Train* (1951), his first major success of the 1950s. It begins with a railway journey, in the course of which Bruno Anthony, a wealthy homosexual (Robert Walker, in an immaculate performance), ingratiates himself with Guy Haines, a handsome tennis champion (Farley Granger), who is unhappily married to a promiscuous wife.

Before they part company at journey's end, Bruno tries to manipulate Guy into agreeing to exchange a murder with him, with Guy killing Bruno's dictatorial father whom Bruno despises, and Bruno doing away with Guy's spouse Miriam. Because neither of them has an ostensible motive for committing the other's crime, they would both, according to Bruno's logic, successfully elude detection. This proposal appeals to Guy more than he is prepared to admit even to himself because he would like to be rid of his hateful wife.

The film's script was coauthored by the great crime novelist Raymond Chandler. One of the tensest scenes in the picture is that in which Bruno strangles Guy's wife in a secluded corner of the amusement park to which he has followed her. The murder is ironically accompanied by the distant music of the merry-go-round's calliope, as it grinds out a cheery tune. We are horrified as we watch the murder, as it is reflected in the victim's glasses, which have fallen to the grass during her struggle with Bruno. Photographing the murder in this distorted fashion, as I have written elsewhere, makes "the strangling look as if it were being viewed in a fun-house mirror, another reminder of the grimly incongruous carnival setting of the crime" (p. 208).

Guy is suspected of slaying his wife, but he is given the chance to redeem himself by pursuing Bruno back to the scene of Miriam's murder and forcing him to confess the truth about her death. As they wrestle each other aboard the carousel, the mechanism suddenly goes berserk, changing what is normally a harmless source of innocent fun into a whirling instrument of terror. The carousel is thus still another reflection of Hitchcock's dark vision of our chaotic, topsy-turvy world. As the runaway merry-go-round continues to spin at top speed, its rendition of "The Band Played On" is also accelerated to a dizzying tempo and mingles with macabre persistence with the screams of the hysterical riders trapped on board. A mechanic at last manages to bring the carousel to a halt, but it stops so suddenly that the riders go sailing off in all directions as the machinery collapses into a heap of smoldering wreckage. As the movie draws to a close, Bruno dies in the debris, unrepentant to the last.

James Stewart starred in three Hitchcock films in the 1950s, *Rear Window* (1954), *The Man Who Knew Too Much* (1956), and *Vertigo* (1958). *The Man Who Knew Too Much* invites examination at this point because it is a remake of the film of the same title

that the director had originally done back in 1934, already discussed. More than 20 years after the release of the original movie, Hitchcock decided that the time was right to film this tried-and-true story a second time.

In this version of the story, Ben McKenna (James Stewart) and his wife Jo (Doris Day) have a son Hank, rather than a daughter, and they go on a vacation to Morocco rather than to Switzerland. But once Hank is kidnapped in the Casbah and his parents pursue the kidnappers back to London, the basic plot line of the first version holds true. The American remake is about 45 minutes longer than the British version because Hitchcock concentrates more on character development this time around and on scrupulously tying up the loose plot strands he had left dangling in the 1934 movie.

To cite one example, in the earlier movie the exact nature of Abbot's curious, emotionally dependent attachment to the woman of indeterminate age called Nurse Agnes, who is his constant companion, is never clarified. In the remake, however, they are established as husband and wife, both of whom have clearly defined personalities. Yet the 1956 film is not automatically a better film because of this and other refinements in its heavily revised, more substantial screenplay.

If the earlier picture left some things unexplained, the filmgoer was kept sufficiently breathless by this fast-moving, 85-minute movie not to notice. In any event, the high point of both films is the almost intolerably suspenseful concert sequence—in which the heroine must decide whether or not to stop the assassination that she knows is about to take place, when it might well mean further imperiling the life of her child, still detained as a hostage by the terrorists.

In Hitchcock's opinion, the remake possessed a professional polish lacking in his earlier attempt. Thus, in the first version, the plot goes into overdrive before the moviegoer really gets a chance to become acquainted with the principals and consequently to sympathize with them to the degree one can in the second movie. On the other hand, because the remake is less tightly constructed than its predecessor, it contains a few slow-paced, talky stretches that may cause the viewer's interest to flag—something that never happens in the original.

The ongoing debate about the relative merits of the British and U.S. periods of Hitchcock's career can be summed up by the comparison of the two versions of *The Man Who Knew Too Much*. Whether one believes that Hitchcock's British thrillers are superior to his U.S. suspense dramas largely depends on whether one prefers fast-paced action movies that have a modicum of plot and character development to longer, somewhat slower, but denser films that reflect a more thorough analysis of the psychology of character. In the last analysis, an individual filmgoer's choice in this matter basically says more about his or her personal cinematic taste than it does about the realative merits of the films themselves.

North by Northwest (1959) was one of Hitchcock's biggest hits and starred Cary Grant, who, like James Stewart, appeared in a number of Hitchcock films. Grant had appeared in *Suspicion* (1941), *Notorious* (1946), and *To Catch a Thief* (1955); *North by Northwest* proved that Grant—and Hitchcock—were still in top form.

In the movie's most renowned sequence, Roger Thornhill (Cary Grant) is lured out into the country by foreign spies, whose leader (James Mason) mistakenly believes that Roger is an undercover agent for the CIA. As Roger stands on a deserted country road, he is unaware that the villain has lured him there to have him liquidated. A crop-dusting plane, which is flying overhead, looks harmless at first. Then, instead of spraying the crops with insecticide, the plane suddenly begins to spray Roger with bullets and then douse him with insecticide. The shot of Roger frantically running for cover is one of the most characteristic images in any Hitchcock film. The hero is totally isolated and vulnerable as he flees across the hot, desolate prairie, pursued by an evil force that has swooped down on him from the sky.

Another celebrated sequence in the film is the cliff-hanging scene on the colossal Mount Rushmore monument. Once again, Hitchcock employs a traditional symbol of culture and stability as the background against which the hero undergoes a death-defying confrontation with hostile forces, just as he did in *Blackmail* and other films. In this instance, Roger and his girl (Eva Marie Saint) are nearly forced by one of the enemy agents to fall down the mountainside, but government agents arrive just in time to save them.

The wide public acceptance of *North by Northwest* was exceeded by *Psycho* (1960). Although *Psycho,* Hitchcock's masterpiece, was to become his biggest blockbuster, it was made on a relatively tight budget. This prompted the director to make the movie with the smaller unit of technicians and with the same modest technical facilities that were employed to turn out the weekly television series he was supervising at the time, rather than to employ the more elaborate and more expensive crew and facilities a big movie studio would have provided for him. The finished film, consequently, has a stark simplicity, to which Bernard Herrmann's spare musical background—scored solely for strings—is the perfect complement.

Marion Crane (Janet Leigh) stops at a motel for an overnight stay. Norman Bates (Anthony Perkins), the motel's proprietor, is ostensibly a mild-mannered young man, who seems devoted to his mother, especially since the death of his father sometime back. Later that same night, Marion is murdered while she is taking a shower.

Marion is savagely stabbed to death by what appears to be a maniacal woman inexplicably possessed of enormous physical strength. All the while, the soundtrack emits a burst of shrill, high-strung music, the notes of the slicing string instruments sounding like the piercing shrieks of some carnivorous bird, clawing at its prey.

The filmgoer is unnerved by the fact that the heroine is eliminated so early in the film. Such an unexpected turn of events, after all, is a notable departure from the usual pattern of thrillers. From this point onward, therefore, the viewer doesn't know what to expect.

In the end, Norman Bates is revealed to be the fiendishly deranged psycho of the title. It transpires that Norman, who had an incestuously possessive love for his mother, poisoned both her and her lover after he discovered them together. Furthermore, Norman dressed up in his mother's clothes when he murdered Marion and his other victims. This disguise indicated that, in his own mind, it was his mother—and not he—who was the real killer. He fantasized that his mother nurtured the same kind of incestuous jealousy toward him that he harbored toward her and that therefore she would kill any girl who "threatened to take her beloved son away" from her.

In addition, because Norman was pathologically shy with women, each of these killings took on the nature of a symbolic rape, giving the dripping knife and the gushing shower nozzle a definite phallic significance. As one critic has put it, Norman begins by enjoying his fantasies, and ends up with his fantasies enjoying him, for by film's end, Norman's frail self-identity has been totally absorbed by the "mother" side of his schizophrenic personality.

As he sits staring into space in a jail cell following his arrest, his complete withdrawal from reality is signaled by the blanket in which he has wrapped himself to insulate himself completely from any further contact with the outside world. A smile gradually creeps over Norman's face, on which for a moment the grinning skull of his mother's corpse is superimposed. In Norman's face, Hitchcock presents an image of humanity clamped in its private trap of frustration and anguish. *Psycho* is not only Hitchcock's greatest film; it is also the most intelligent and disturbing horror movie ever made. Indeed, on the American Film Institute salute to the 100 most thrilling American films, *Psycho* was named the most thrilling American movie ever made. This TV special was televised on June 12, 2001, and included other Hitchcock films in the top 100 thrillers: *Rebecca, Notorious, Strangers on a Train,* and *North by Northwest.*

Hitchcock's next venture was *The Birds* (1963), which portrays a full-scale attack by humankind's erstwhile fine-feathered friends on the population of a small California town. No explanation is offered for the sudden and unexpected hostility toward humanity that prompts flocks of ordinarily pacific creatures to lay siege to this village, but then one is not really required. Hitchcock wishes to examine how human beings react in a crisis, regardless of its cause. If the upheaval that the characters have to contend with in *The Birds* had been an air raid, he told me, with planes rather than birds raining havoc from the heavens, the theme of the movie would have remained the same.

Hitchcock's last vintage thriller was *Frenzy* (1972). The story line recapitulates the Jack-the-Rip-

per plot of his first major motion picture, *The Lodger,* made almost a half-century before. Hence, with *Frenzy,* Hitchcock's professional life in a sense had come full circle. Here once again is the archetypal Hitchcock hero intrepidly chasing down the criminal of whose crimes he is himself falsely accused. Meanwhile the police pursue him because, as one character acridly comments, the cops, as usual, have the whole affair "ass-about-face."

Richard Blaney (Jon Finch) is thought to be the "necktie murderer," a sexual psychopath terrorizing London, because both his estranged wife, Brenda (Barbara Leigh-Hunt), and his girlfriend, Babs Milligan (Anna Massey), have fallen victim to the slayer. The real maniac, however, is none other than Richard's old mate Bob Rusk (Barry Foster), whose amiability marks him as another one of Hitchcock's superficially attractive psychotics—a long line of lunatics that reaches back to Bruno Anthony of *Strangers on a Train.* So *Frenzy* is as clearly marked by the Hitchcock touch as *The 39 Steps* made nearly 40 years before.

Hitchcock wisely depicts only one of Rusk's hideous rape-murders in detail—that of Brenda—because, once the filmgoer has witnessed one of these atrocities, the director need only suggest thereafter that another is taking place off-screen. Thus when Rusk leads the unsuspecting Babs into his flat, the camera stops at the doorway and does not venture to follow them inside. Instead it slowly retreats down the shadowy staircase and out into the bright sunshine of the busy street, as if recoiling from the unspeakable act that is taking place behind curtained windows. Once outside, the camera pauses for a moment to survey the pedestrians going about their business, unaware of what is transpiring inside the building. By means of this briliantly executed shot, Hitchcock once more reminds his audience, perhaps more effectively than ever before, of his disturbing conviction that catastrophe surrounds us all and can strike when we least expect it.

Hitchcock's last film, *Family Plot* (1976), a tale about the pursuit and capture of a master kidnapper, was a good film but not on a par with *Frenzy.* Nevertheless, like every Hitchcock film before it, *Family Plot* reflects the provocative personal vision of the creative artist who made it. Indeed, filmgoers come away from his movies with more than just the satisfaction of having enjoyed a good thriller. If they are reflective, they also take away with them a fresh awareness that people are not always what they seem—for evil and good can bundle together in the same personality like sly lovers. In short, each of us, Hitchcock suggests, is a fascinating bundle of paradoxes, and that observation is a never-ending source of interest for Hitchcock's audience. "If one was brought up by the Jesuits as I was," Hitchcock told me, "these concepts are bound to intrude into one's films."

When I chatted with Hitchcock on the occasion of the Lincoln Center tribute to him, I found him formal but gracious, as befitted his English background. When I was preparing to take leave, I asked him for his autograph. He not only obliged me with his signature, but also drew for me the celebrated caricature of his profile, which had always served to open his TV series. (It is before me as I write.)

Although Hitchcock was nominated five times for an Academy Award as best director, it was never conferred on him. The Motion Picture Academy did, however, somewhat belatedly vote him the coveted Irving Thalberg Award, which he received at the Oscar ceremonies in 1967, in recognition for his lifetime achievement as a film director. He was also knighted by Queen Elizabeth II in 1980. Moreover, his films, which continue to be available on TV and video, continue to fascinate moviegoers. Some films age, some films date. Hitchcock's movies belong to the first category. Perhaps David Sterritt said it all when he affirmed that Hitchcock's "reputation seems to grow more lofty with each passing year" (p. 15).

Sir Alfred Hitchcock died on April 20, 1980; his old friend, Jesuit Father Thomas Sullivan of Loyola-Marymount University, presided at the funeral rites. In eulogizing Hitchcock, screenwriter Ernest Lehman (*North by Northwest*) said that while writing a script for Hitchcock the fact that it was a *Hitchcock* movie made it ultimately memorable. "And there

are no more Hitchcock movies any more, God rest his soul."

Amen to that.

—Gene D. Phillips

Works Cited

Some material in this essay appeared in a completely different form in Gene Phillips's *Alfred Hitchcock* (Boston: Twayne, 1984). In preparing this essay, I have consulted numerous research materials not available when the book was published.

Bogdanovich, Peter. "The Craft and Art of Hitchcock." *New York Times,* April 11, 1999, sec. 2: 15–18.

Hitchcock, Alfred. "Production Methods Compared." In *Hitchcock on Hitchcock: Selected Writings and Interviews,* ed. Sidney Gottlieb (Los Angeles: University of California Press, 1997), pp. 205–09.

Martin, Pete. "I Call on Alfred Hitchcock." In *Filmmakers on Filmmaking,* ed. Harry Geduld (Bloomington: Indiana University Press, 1969), pp. 125–28.

Phillips, Gene. *Creatures of Darkness: Raymond Chandler, Detective Fiction, and Film Noir.* Lexington: University Press of Kentucky, 2000.

Sterritt, David. "Hitchcock's Genius." *Christian Science Monitor,* January 21, 2000, p. 15.

Works Consulted

Film Society of Lincoln Center, The. *A Special Gala in Honor of Alfred Hitchcock.* New York: Lincoln Center for the Performing Arts, 1974. Souvenir program for the tribute to Hitchcock, April 29, 1974.

Freedman, Jonathan, and Richard Millington, eds. *Hitchcock's America.* New York: Oxford University Press, 1999.

Rebello, Stephen. *Alfred Hitchcock and the Making of Psycho.* New York: St. Martin's Press, 1998.

Sloan, Jane. *Alfred Hitchcock: A Guide to References and Resources.* Los Angeles: University of California Press, 1995.

INTRODUCTION

This is one of the volumes that inaugurates Facts On File's Library of Great Filmmakers, and I want to use this introduction to consider why Alfred Hitchcock is an obvious choice for the series, why indeed it would have been downright peculiar to begin with anyone else. Vastly more has been written on Hitchcock than on any other director—so much, in fact, that Gilberto Perez noted several years ago that "he would have to be incomparably the greatest of filmmakers to merit the amount of critical and academic attention bestowed on him."[1] Even filmgoers who have never dipped into this torrent of Hitchcock commentary continue to think of Hitchcock as the exemplary director, the posthumous model for all later directors, not only the person to have given his name to a distinctive film genre, the suspense thriller, but also the person most closely indentified in the public mind with the figure of the movie director. In a book like this, an encyclopedia giving specifics about Hitchcock's films, his collaborators, and his commentators, the first order of business must be to explain why the master of suspense justifies all this fuss once more. How did Hitchcock rise to such singular and unparalleled eminence?

A LIFE IN THE MOVIES

Alfred Joseph Hitchcock was born on August 13, 1899, in Leytonstone, a suburb of East London that would later be annexed as a borough. His family background was in mercantile trade. In addition to siring three chldren, of whom Alfred was the youngest, his father added a second greengrocer's

shop to his first and joined his own brothers in their thriving chain of fishmongers' shops. Hitchcock's Catholic parents sent him briefly to the neighboring primary school and then to St. Ignatius College, a boarding school where he was educated and disciplined by the Jesuits until the age of 14—a place where he was remembered later as quiet, solitary, and fat. Following his father's death in 1914, Hitchcock studied briefly at the School of Engineering and Navigation, went to work as a technical clerk at the W.T. Henley Telegraph Company the following year, and was promoted to Henley's advertising department on the strength of a flair for publicity and graphic design. Spurred by his interest in filmmaking, he applied for work as a title-card designer at the short-lived Famous Players–Lasky's new Islington studio in 1919, and after a brief stint of part-time work there left Henley's for a full-time position.

Born during the infancy of the movies, Hitchcock was present at the birth of Hollywood's attempts to maintain a British production arm. Unlike such earlier filmmakers as Cecil Hepworth and D.W. Griffith, he was a child of the movies who had followed the new medium even as a boy. Yet his interest in film, though intense, was peculiarly limited: The film periodicals he read most closely were not fan magazines but trade and technical journals. He was a more avid theatergoer than moviegoer, and "the contemporary English stage and novel," as Charles Barr has pointed out,[2] were influences as fundamental to his work as they were to Griffith's. From the beginning Hitchcock seemed less interested in watching movies than in making them happen.

Certainly, he seized every chance that came his way to make them happen. In addition to designing intertitles for a dozen Famous Players–Lasky productions, he set out in 1922 to direct *Number 13,* a two-reeler that was left uncompleted by a financial crisis at the studio, and joined the producer Seymour Hicks later that year in completing *Always Tell Your Wife* when director Hugh Croise withdrew from the production. His acquaintance with director Graham Cutts, who sometimes rented space in the Islington studio, brought him to the attention of Cutts's associates, producer Michael Balcon and producer-director Victor Saville, who engaged him in 1923 as assistant director on Cutts's film *Woman to Woman.* The young man, already in charge of intertitles, soon made himself indispensable around the set, volunteering to help Cutts work out the screenplay and taking on the role of art director as well, and he continued to fill all these roles on *The White Shadow* (1923), *The Passionate Adventure* (1924), *The Prude's Fall* (1924), and *The Blackguard* (1925).

By now Hitchcock was eager to direct a film of his own for Balcon's infant Gainsborough Pictures. The project Balcon proposed was *The Pleasure Garden,* to be shot, like *The Blackguard,* at the UFA facilities in Neubabelsberg. Although the production was fraught with difficulties, Hitchcock delighted in describing to later interviewers,[3] it did not prevent him from filming the lost film *The Mountain Eagle* (1926) or *The Lodger* (1926), which he called "the first true 'Hitchcock movie.'"[4] The success of these early films, despite opposition from Balcon's backer C.M. Woolf within the company, encouraged him to marry Alma Reville on December 2, 1926.

His marriage is the purest expression of Hitchcock's life in the movies. He had first met Reville in 1921 when she was an editor at Famous Players–Lasky—a position distinctly above his at the time—but felt unable to approach her until, as assistant director of *Woman to Woman,* he was able to invite her to cut the film. He asked for her hand during a trip scouting locations for *The Prude's Fall* when he felt certain of some degree of financial security, but they were not married until his directorial career had been properly launched. By all accounts she was the only woman in his life except for their daughter Patricia, who was born on July 7, 1928, and the numerous actresses whom he alternately charmed, bullied, and smothered with attention. Hitchcock's romantic life was intimately bound up with a professional partnership with the tiny, tough-minded Reville that continued for more than 50 years. Whether or not she received screen credit, she was not only his wife but also by far his most intimate and influential collaborator.

Lured away from Balcon and Gainsborough after following the success of *The Lodger* with *Downhill* and *Easy Virtue* (1927), Hitchcock settled in for a six-year run of varied projects at John Maxwell's new British International Pictures. Although his first BIP project, a boxing film called *The Ring* (1927), was based on his own original script—the only film he directed in which he would get sole screenplay credit—the farrago of projects that rapidly followed were mostly adaptations of popular plays (*The Farmer's Wife,* 1928; *Blackmail,* 1929; *Juno and the Paycock,* 1930; *The Skin Game,* 1931; *Number Seventeen,* 1932) and novels (*The Manxman,* 1929; *Murder!,* 1930; *Rich and Strange,* 1931), leavened by the occasional original screenplay (*Champagne,* 1928) or "musical without music"[5] (*Waltzes from Vienna,* 1933). But although Hitchcock was Maxwell's star director, he achieved truly national fame only with his return to Balcon's Gaumont-British Pictures for *The Man Who Knew Too Much* (1934). Buoyed by the film's success, he followed it with the even greater international success of *The 39 Steps* (1935) and rounded off his sextet of thirties thrillers for Balcon with *Secret Agent* (1936), *Sabotage* (1937), *Young and Innocent* (1937), and *The Lady Vanishes* (1938), which won him the New York Film Critics Circle Award as Best Director and brought him to the attention of Hollywood producer David O. Selznick, who signed him to an exclusive contract in 1938.

After one final film in England, *Jamaica Inn,* Hitchcock arrived in Hollywood with Alma and Pat in 1939. Although there was considerable indecision about what his first Selznick picture would be, and although Daphne du Maurier, who had written *Jamaica Inn,* was as unhappy with the film as the critics, Hitchcock's first American film, an adaptation of du Maurier's *Rebecca,* was a resounding success, earning Selznick press and profits worthy of *Gone with the Wind*'s producer and winning the Academy Award for Best Picture of 1940. But the following years were more uncertain. The coming of World War II cut Hitchcock off from his family and earned him the sobriquet of deserter from Balcon, and Selznick's businesslike decision to lend Hitchcock out to other studios at tidy (and unshared) profits deprived him of the stable working environment he craved. While such films as *Foreign Correspondent* (1940), *Saboteur* (1942), and *Lifeboat* (1944) grew longer and more expensive than either his British films or a pair of loanouts to RKO, *Mr. and Mrs. Smith* and *Suspicion* (both 1941), so did the time he required to shoot them as he rapidly internalized Selznick's Hollywood conventions of scale and gloss he professed to deplore. The best of Hitchcock's forties films, *Shadow of a Doubt* (1943) and *Notorious* (1946), reveal how hard it is to establish a relation between his success and his ties to Selznick. The first was shot mostly on location for Universal far from Selznick's eye; the second was written, cast, and budgeted under Selznick's close supervision before it was sold to RKO.

Although *Spellbound* (1945), Hitchcock's second film for Selznick, was a critical and financial success, the director, chafing under what he complained was the producer's dictatorial control, yearned for freedom, and after forming his own independent company, Transatlantic Pictures, in partnership with his old friend Sidney Bernstein in 1946, he devoted little attention to *The Paradine Case* (1947), his final Selznick film. The fate of Transatlantic, which folded after only two films, *Rope* (1948) and *Under Capricorn* (1949), suggested however that "the director of things, of negative acting and moving camera, of stories as technical cinematic challenges functioned . . . far better [under Selznick] than he functioned with Bernstein."[6] Hitchcock needed the studio system's guidance and discipline as much as it needed his inventiveness, imagination, and commercial sense.

With *Stage Fright* (1950) Hitchcock settled into the role he was to assume for the rest of his career: a quasi-independent producer/director whose contracts with a succession of studios—Warner Bros., Paramount, MGM, Universal—allowed him substantial creative and often financial control of his films. This new arrangement bore rich fruit in the series of masterpieces Hitchcock released in the following decade: *Strangers on a Train* (1951), *Rear Window* (1954), *Vertigo*

(1958), *North by Northwest* (1959), and *Psycho* (1960). Even his lesser films of the period—*I Confess* (1952), *Dial M for Murder* (1953), *The Trouble with Harry* (1955), *To Catch a Thief* (1955), *The Man Who Knew Too Much* (1956), and *The Wrong Man* (1957)—are accomplished, entertaining, and often penetrating in their scrutiny of psychopathology and American culture. The commercial success of these films was extended by a 1955 arrangement to license Hitchcock's name and image to a monthly magazine of mystery fiction and the debut that same year of the long-running television series *Alfred Hitchcock Presents* (1955–62) and its successor *The Alfred Hitchcock Hour* (1962–65). By the time of *Psycho,* Hitchcock was the only film director who was a household name—and whose image and voice, the portly figure intoning a sepulchral "Good evening" every week in living rooms across America, were as famous as those of his stars.

It was the release of *Psycho,* however, that made Hitchcock wealthy and paved the way for his final years at Universal, at whose studios the film, released by Paramount and financed by Hitchcock himself, had been shot. Under the aegis of his agent Lew Wasserman, Hitchcock signed a contract with Universal, which Wasserman's own company, the Music Corporation of America, was in the process of absorbing, and by exchanging his rights in *Psycho* and his television programs for MCA stock, he became the corporation's third-largest stockholder. Given this wealth, Hitchcock could afford to slow his work pace, and the three years between *Psycho* and *The Birds* (1963), devoted largely to the abortive *No Bail for the Judge,* marked the longest hiatus between releases of his career to date and set a pattern that would continue even though, blessed with remarkably good health considering his great and fluctuating weight, Hitchcock continued to work well into his seventies. Despite the avidity with which the studio publicized its prize director and his investiture by *Cahiers du cinéma,* Andrew Sarris, and a generation of American academics as the preeminent Hollywood auteur, none of his subsequent films—*Marnie* (1964), *Torn Curtain* (1966), *Topaz* (1969), *Frenzy* (1972), and *Family Plot* (1976)—matched the financial or critical success of *Psycho.*

Even as he was slowing down, however, Hitchcock continued to live for his movies. Unlike

Selznick, whose workaholic habits had been complemented by an equally prodigious social and sexual life, none of Hitchcock's few interests outside work—his eye for surrealist painting, his prodigious and legendary appetites for food and drink, his fondness for entertaining a few close friends at his home, his unquenchable interest in practical jokes—took him outside his domestic orbit. Despite the Catholic education that left such a lasting mark on his films, he had not been a regular churchgoer for many years. His nocturnal activities had shrunk ever since his sheltered years at Islington because Los Angeles had no theatrical life to lure him out and because he rarely went to the movies. Whether he was dealing with friends, colleagues, or the press, he seemed never to be comfortable in social situations that he could not dominate. When it became clear in 1978 that his failing health precluded any further activity on his final project, *The Short Night,* he closed his office at Universal. In the absence of any life outside his work, however, he never truly retired but only went into a decline punctuated by retrospective honors—the American Film Institute's Life Achievement Award in March 1979, a knighthood in January 1980—before his death on April 29, 1980.

THE MASTER OF SUSPENSE

By the time he had been directing films for 10 years, Hitchcock was already indelibly identified with a single genre. Even though he had directed an impressive variety of successful films, from the boxing fable *The Ring* to the class-struggle parable *The Skin Game,* the success of the 1934 version of *The Man Who Knew Too Much* and *The 39 Steps* swiftly marked him as the master of suspense. Hitchcock himself seemed eager to embrace this role. True, only four of his first 16 films—*The Lodger, Blackmail, Murder!,* and *Number Seventeen*—could be described as suspense films, and *Murder!* generates as little suspense as a crime film could well do. But the director's discomfort with *Waltzes from Vienna* revealed in his remark that "I hate this sort of stuff. Melodrama is the only thing I can do"[7] evidently confirmed his readiness to identify himself with the thriller. The ubiquity of the Hitchcock thriller has been so pronounced and enduring

that suspense films like *Shallow Grave* (1994) and *With a Friend Like Harry* (2001) are still routinely acclaimed Hitchcockian or dismissed as less-than-Hitchcockian, and Charles Derry's 1988 critical study *The Suspense Thriller* is subtitled *Films in the Shadow of Alfred Hitchcock.*

Hitchcock has become in some ways congruent with the popular perception of the suspense thriller. But what exactly are those ways? Derry's own study, which reveals the number of crime and suspense subgenres in which Hitchcock seldom or never worked—the formal detective story, the police procedural, the gangster film, the caper film, the study of the criminal protagonist—together with Slavoj Žižek's assertion that "Hitchcock's universe is ultimately incompatible with that of the *film noir*"[8]—suggest that Hitchcock's brand of suspense is actually quite distinctive. What is Hitchcockian about Hitchcock's suspense, and why has his name become a trademark for a much broader genre?

Although it would be too easy to dismiss the four suspense films that preceded 1934's *The Man Who Knew Too Much* as early experiments in suspense, it is no wonder that they did not establish their director with a particular genre because their thematic resemblance to each other—three of them are dominated by the theme of the innocent suspect that Hitchcock's U.S. films would define in terms of a "transfer of guilt"[9]—is not matched by any deeper consistency. None of them, not even *Blackmail,* is any more or less Hitchcockian than *The Ring* or *Rich and Strange.* It is only with the Gaumont-British thrillers that Hitchcock is confirmed as the master of suspense. The leading quality of the thirties sextet of suspense films, the films that consolidated his international reputation, is their disconcertingly amusing melding of tones, from doom-laden melodrama to outright farce. The cumulative effect of such abrupt transitions of tone is broadly ironic. When Richard Hannay's perilous search for Professor Jordan in *The 39 Steps* drops him into the middle of a Sunday-morning birthday party, the comedy of his reception punctures the military threat he is supposed to be countering as surely as the unexpected revelation that Professor Jordan is the traitor against whom he has been warned undercuts the comedy. James Naremore, identifying "what most people think of as the Hitchcock 'touch'" with "a feeling of iconoclastic laughter lurking behind classically wrought stories of romance, murder and suspense," concludes that "more than any of his contemporaries, Hitchcock came to be identified with black humor, which he repeatedly packaged as mass entertainment."[10]

Naremore compares Hitchcock's black humor to that of Billy Wilder; an even closer analogy, and one more suggestive about Hitchcock's distinctiveness, is to James Whale, the British-born director of the horror classics *Frankenstein* (1931), *The Old Dark House* (1932), *The Invisible Man* (1933), and *The Bride of Frankenstein* (1935). Like Hitchcock, Whale's injections of perverse humor into gothic horror are understated, civilized, and urbane. The difference is in their mise-en-scene—Whale's Hollywood gothic versus Hitchcock's more subtly stylized everyday reality—and in the pacing of their films. Hitchcock's scenes play faster than Whale's *because of* their wit, which accelerates the melodrama instead of interrupting it with ghoulishly knowing winks. Hence Whale's most characteristic films are elaborately ironic, Hitchcock's deftly and efficiently ironic. Even when Hitchcock adopts the longer, slower Hollywood model of *Rebecca, Shadow of a Doubt,* and *Notorious,* his wit works toward greater velocity because it is more incessant and more unifying. What makes these films witty and blackly comic is not so much isolated details like the cigarette. Mrs. Van Hopper puts out in a jar of cold cream or the inverted point of view shot of Cary Grant's Devlin towering over Ingrid Bergman's reclining Alicia Huberman as an inveterately witty habit of indirect exposition that engages audiences pleasurably in establishing the most fundamental facts and relations of each story of ordinary people caught up in improbable intrigue.

Because Hitchcockian suspense depends more on expository wit and humor than on any specific subject or setting, most of the elements of *Waltzes from Vienna* the director might have been expected to banish from his later thrillers—domestic rivalries, heterosexual romance, broad comedy, even an emphasis on musically expressive soundtracks—are central to them. Only costume drama, which inhibits

his all-important sense of mundane social reality, remains banished, returning only in *Jamaica Inn* and *Under Capricorn.* Hitchcock's ability to engage filmgoers in the process of following his stories can generate intrigue from the most ordinary circumstances as long as they feel ordinary. As the poet of everyday nightmare who engages both the documentary and the oneiric tendencies of filmmaking, he is not only the master of suspense but also the filmmaker whose work best demonstrates why suspense itself occupies a central place in commercial cinema.

THE FIGURE OF THE DIRECTOR

For all his fame, Hitchcock has never enjoyed a reputation as the greatest of all filmmakers. In his own time, his critical reputation was regularly eclipsed by that of such international directors as Ingmar Bergman, Michelangelo Antonioni, and his own disciple François Truffaut. Each of these filmmakers was held up as more intellectually respectable or emotionally sensitive or spiritually resonant than Hitchcock the entertainer. Hitchcock's posthumous reputation, as even his most ardent proponents have noted, has never approached that of Jean Renoir. Like Charles Chaplin and Buster Keaton, John Ford and Stanley Kubrick, he has remained an unrivaled specialist in his own genre whom few admirers would anoint as the greatest filmmaker of all.

Securely and often limitingly as he is identified with the suspense thriller, however, Hitchcock occupies a far more powerful place in contemporary film culture. More than any other single figure—certainly more than such varied and prominent living directors as James Cameron, Woody Allen, Ang Lee, Eric Rohmer, and Steven Spielberg—he incarnates the popular idea of what a film director is and does. The peculiar nature of his eminence can best be appreciated by contrasting it with that of the predecessor who was Hitchcock's closest equivalent: Cecil B. DeMille.

For a generation of audiences who considered the producer, not the director, the most visible creator of a film, DeMille was the most visible of directors. Even though his own career had gone through any number of changes—from his early westerns and melodramas to the naughty post–World War I sex comedies and often risqué biblical spectacles that showed his Hitchcockian grasp of the bottom line— DeMille was identified by the 1950s not only as the director par excellence of epic spectacles like *Samson and Delilah, The Greatest Show on Earth,* and his remake of his own *The Ten Commandments* but also as an all-purpose shorthand figure, a trope for all movie directors. DeMille's trademark costume—his cavalry boots, his jodhpurs, and the megaphone he used to shout orders at the cast of thousands that he consistently maintained he would rather direct than a couple in the most emotionally intense dialogue scene—established the director as a virile manager, an outdoorsman who rode herd on the most over-scaled scenes with the eye and voice of a not entirely benevolent God, the author on whose work DeMille most famously drew. Instantly recognizable from a hundred feet away by his iconic silhouette, DeMille represented the director as general.

What was missing from this figure, of course, was any trace of the director's individual personality. Everyone knew (or thought they knew) what DeMille was like on the set, but except for readers who remembered John Ford's famous rebuke of De Mille's Red-baiting on behalf of the house Un-American Affairs Committee, no one knew what he was like on the town or at home; his individual personality had never been marketed or put on display. There was no reason why it should have been because directors of DeMille's era were not marketable quantities.

Even as DeMille was presenting an image of the director as general, however, Hitchcock, with his unmatched gift for self-promotion, was taking a different tack. Well before he left England, Hitchcock was already giving the interviews that would set the pattern for his later relation to the press. Insisting on speaking with one journalist at a time instead of facing a crowd he could not dominate, he controlled his press through a combination of wit, charm, and storytelling finesse. So great was his prowess as a raconteur that Hitchcock offered a powerful alternative to DeMille's image of the director as manager: the director as storyteller, a figure whose stories resembled each other so closely not only because he preferred to work in a single genre but also because that

genre tapped the deepest springs of his own personal terrors, desires, and fantasies. When the insurgent critics and filmmakers of *Cahiers du cinéma* were looking for standard-bearers against the self-anointed tradition of quality in the French cinema, it was inevitable that they would turn to Hitchcock, who stood as an unrivaled example of a director who could use frankly commercial cinema as a mode of personal expression. And when Andrew Sarris imported the *politique des auteurs* to America in the early sixties, the combination of romantic expressionism and commercial savvy he projected onto Hitchcock made him the supreme auteur.

An irony that was often remarked but seldom analyzed in this enthronement was that Hitchcock was, if anything, an even more private figure than DeMille. Although he incarnated a new aesthetic of personal expression through commercial cinema, he guarded his personal life jealously, living quietly as an outsider in the United States (where he did not take citizenship until 1955, 16 years after his arrival), shunning the obligatory Hollywood social functions, and rarely appearing in public except on occasions he controlled himself. Hitchcock's iconic image—his eight-stroke pencil drawing of his own profile made famous by its appearance at the beginning of each episode of *Alfred Hitchcock Presents* and *The Alfred Hitchcock Hour*—although presented in a close-up that might seem to suggest the revelation of personality, was even more abstract and opaque than the figure of DeMille with jodhpurs and megaphone. The Hitchcock image that replaced DeMille's image as the iconic director was only apparently more personal; what was really replacing DeMille's image was a carefully crafted image of a public personality whose private life, like the actual lives of the stars whose studio-manufactured romances and domestic routines enlivened the pages of *Photoplay,* was finally inaccessible.

Indeed, the opacity of Hitchcock's private life became, like Greta Garbo's, essential to his public image. This new image of the director incarnated by Hitchcock was a cartoon figure whose outline (corpulent figure, unmistakable profile, black suits on set, precise control over every phase of the film, Cockney inflections, heavy drinking at lunch and dinner, avowed distaste for looking through the camera, fondness for practical jokes, aversion to confrontations, fetishistic attachment to professional and domestic routines, availability for endlessly entertaining interviews, ritualistic appearances in throwaway roles in each of his U.S. films) was even more individualistic than DeMille's but whose personality was expressed mainly in a strategic withdrawal from public exposure. Hitchcock and his colleagues sold this new figure of the director not on the basis of the private personality predicated by the director's well-attested work habits but first on the entertainment value of the carefully crafted public personality itself, and ultimately on the promise that there *was* a private personality beneath it all. In the 40 years since Hitchcock was elevated to the status of the exemplary auteur, he has never been displaced or seriously threatened because the instantly recognizable, tantalizingly opaque model he offers is so widely adaptable to observers' hopes and beliefs about the intersection of individual personality and dominant cinema that it has never needed revision.

THE HITCHCOCK INDUSTRY

Just as Hitchcock's life spanned virtually the entire history of commercial cinema from its beginnings through the rise of the Hollywood blockbuster, Hitchcock commentary has spanned the history of academic film criticism and encapsulated most of its leading developments. Together with such genre filmmakers as Howard Hawks, Robert Aldrich, and Nicholas Ray, Hitchcock was among the first directors identified by *Cahiers du cinéma* as Hollywood artists. The 1954 special issue *Cahiers* devoted to his work and the critical study Eric Rohmer and Claude Chabrol published on him in 1957 promoted him still further. But it was Truffaut's book-length series of interviews published in France in 1966 and in the United States the following year that set the seal on his status, though in a paradoxical way. Approaching Hitchcock as a colleague who was frankly an acolyte, Truffaut regularly transformed Hitchcock's answers to questions about individual films and his career as a whole from practiced anecdotes and disquisitions about casting, production design, camera setups,

lenses, and other technical matters to debates about psychology and art, even though a close reading of Truffaut makes it clear that the only psychology Hitchcock is interested in is that of the mass audience.

Supported by a reverential interviewer, a studio eager to publicize its star director, and an impressive backlist of films, many of them still available for rental in 16mm prints, Hitchcock was the first Hollywood filmmaker to enter the academic canon. His films were ideal college texts. Unlike the work of Eisenstein and Godard, which were often so difficult that they cried out for explication, Hitchcock's films wore their heart on their sleeve. They were so entertaining, so easy to watch that every new scholarly intuition came with a thrill of unexpected discovery, as if the commentator had discovered some treasure among the trash. The leading question throughout the first phase of Hitchcock criticism (1954–74), vigorously debated in the essays collected in Albert J. LaValley's *Focus on Hitchcock* (1972), was whether the director was a serious artist or merely a popular entertainer. The former view was upheld by Rohmer and Chabrol, Truffaut, Andrew Sarris, and especially Robin Wood in his influential tour of the fifties films, *Hitchcock's Films* (1965); the latter by Lindsay Anderson, Stanley Kauffman, Pauline Kael, Charles Thomas Samuels, and especially Raymond Durgnat.

Durgnat's *The Strange Case of Alfred Hitchcock* (1974), which pronounced Hitchcock a minor aesthete rather than a universal master of the human soul, turned out to be a transitional volume. Although he lost the battle over Hitchcock's artistic status, Durgnat set the pattern for the studies that would follow over the next decade: variously painstaking, film-by-film studies of the director's entire output by Robert A. Harris and Michael Lasky (1976), Donald Spoto (1976), and Gene D. Phillips (1984) and of his hitherto neglected British films by Maurice Yacowar (1977), together with John Russell Taylor's authorized biography *Hitch* (1978).

But this surveying phase yielded to a more specialized, tendentious phase heralded by two books that might have come from different planets: William Rothman's densely argued *Hitchcock—The Murderous Gaze* (1982) and Spoto's notorious biography *The Dark Side of Genius* (1983). Unlike the earlier critics who had celebrated Hitchcock as the exemplary auteur who could make the academy receptive to film studies, these critics focused on Hitchcock's aptness to more particular tasks. If the hallmark of the first phase of Hitchcock criticism had been Wood's question, "Why should we take Hitchcock seriously?"[11] this new phase might have been defined by the question, "What can we use Hitchcock to do?" Rothman used five Hitchcock films to anatomize the notion of film authorship; Elisabeth Weis, in *The Silent Scream* (1982), used a wider selection of his work to illustrate the importance of film sound; Tom Ryall, in *Alfred Hitchcock and the British Cinema* (1986), argued against the decontextualizing of Hitchcock's British films as auteurist masterpieces by situating them in the social, economic, and industrial contexts of the national filmmaking industry; Leonard J. Leff provided an even more detailed production history of Hitchcock's first American decade in *Hitchcock and Selznick* (1987). The anthologies that best express the flavor of this phase of Hitchcock scholarship are Marshall Deutelbaum and Leland Poague's *A Hitchcock Reader* (1986) and Walter Raubicheck and Walter Srebnick's *Hitchcock's Rereleased Films* (1991).

Specialized studies of Hitchcock entered a new phase in 1988 with the publication of Tania Modleski's *The Women Who Knew Too Much,* which adapted the psychoanalytic semiotics pioneered by Raymond Bellour and Laura Mulvey to a reconsideration of seven key films that dramatize the male subject's—and the director's—radical ambivalence toward the ideals of femininity and bisexuality figured by his heroines. Apart from the influential work of Slavoj Žižek and his fellow contributors to *Everything You Always Wanted to Know About Lacan But Were Afraid to Ask Hitchcock* (1992), Lacanian psychoanalysis has abated as the leading force in Hitchcock studies, but a broader strain of cultural studies has continued to dominate the field despite the persistent auteurism of Lesley Brill's *The Hitchcock Romance* (1988), Thomas M. Leitch's *Find the Director* (1991), David Sterritt's *The Films of Alfred Hitchcock* (1993), and Paula Marantz Cohen's feminist-inflected auteurism in *Hitchcock: The Legacy of Victorianism* (1995). Indeed, Wood suggested that the third edition of his seminal 1965 volume, now titled *Hitchcock's Films Revisited* (1989), might best be framed by the question, "Can Hitchcock be saved for feminism?"[12] Perhaps the most provocative Hitchcock study of the decade was Robert Corber's *In the Name of National Security* (1993), which picked up earlier cues from Theodore Price, D.A. Miller, and Lee Edelman in claiming Hitchcock for Queer Theory. Corber's political-sexual analysis of the fifties films has been followed more recently by Robert Samuels's *Hitchcock's Bi-Textuality* (1998) and, in a broader cultural-studies vein, by Jonathan Freedman and Richard Millington's collection *Hitchcock's America* (1999).

Hitchcock's centennial in 1999 capped a flood of new research in the traditional sense of the term, including production histories of *Psycho* by Stephen Rebello (1990) and of *Vertigo* by Dan Auiler (1998); monographs on *Blackmail* by Tom Ryall (1993), on *Rear Window* by Stefan Sharff (1997), and on *The Birds* by Camille Paglia (1998); and reminiscences of working with Hitchcock by Janet Leigh (*Psycho: Behind the Scenes of the Classic Thriller,* with Christopher Nickens, 1995) and Evan Hunter (*Me and Hitch,* 1997). The 1999 NYU Hitchcock Conference offered the occasion for a new anthology, *Alfred Hitchcock: Centenary Essays,* edited by Richard Allen and Sam Ishii-Gonzalès. Still more important are a pair of indispensable references, Sidney Gottlieb's collection *Hitchcock on Hitchcock: Selected Interviews and Writings* (1995) and Auiler's *Hitchcock's Notebooks* (1999), a treasure trove of production material on the U.S. films. As this volume goes to press, Patrick McGilligan's biography is only the most prominent of the forthcoming volumes on Hitchcock, and the two journals devoted entirely to his work, *The MacGuffin* and *Hitchcock Annual,* continue to flourish.

The single most fascinating development in the history of Hitchcock studies is its survival despite the decline of auteurist notions of romantic aesthetics, individual agency, and intentionalist models of meaning that first made him so attractive to scholars seeking an academic beachhead for film studies. Here the primary exhibit is Robert E. Kapsis's *Hitchcock: The Making of a Reputation* (1992), whose sociological deconstruction of Hitchcock's auteur status, instead of dismissing or diminishing Hitchcock, simply makes him more interesting and posthumously resourceful by illustrating one more use to which his career, his persona, his trademark, and his aura can be put. If Hitchcock has been by far the most analyzed film-maker in the world, that is not so much because his work is richer as because the possibilities of Hitch-cock himself—Hitchcock the career, Hitchcock the persona, Hitchcock the trademark, Hitchcock the aura—are richer, and because having reached a cer-tain critical point some 20 years ago, the industry devoted to his films is now self-sustaining so that ana-lyzing earlier commentators on Hitchcock can be just as illuminating as analyzing the films themselves.

THE DESIGN OF THIS BOOK

Because the Hitchcock literature is already so vast, this book aims to be at once comprehensive, selec-tive, and heuristic. Any Hitchcock encyclopedia should of course present detailed information about his work, placing each of his films in the context of his career and sketching the still broader contexts—the suspense genre, the history of Hollywood film-making practice, the commentary of reviewers and academic critics—it evokes. But because Hitchcock commentary is so copious and often repetitive (nearly every critical study of Hitchcock appends essentially the same filmography listing principal credits for his 53 features), I have tried to avoid sim-ply recycling information readily available elsewhere, indicating instead where such information is to be found. In other words, this book is intended more as a guide to the literature on Hitchcock than as a sub-stitute or epitome of it. Most of my entries fall into four categories:

1. **Individual works.** I have devoted a substantial entry to each of the films and television episodes Hitchcock worked on. Where his contribution was modest (the 12 Famous Players–Lasky silents for which he designed intertitles) or uncertain (his reediting of the U.S. release versions of the British wartime documentaries *Men of the Light-ship* and *Target for Tonight*), the entries are briefest, restricted to lists of credits. In entries on the 20 television segments Hitchcock directed for *Alfred*

Hitchcock Presents and *The Alfred Hitchcock Hour,* I have supplemented credit lists with summaries of the plots, which I take to be unfamiliar to most readers. Although my entries on the theatrical features Hitchcock directed, from *The Pleasure Garden* to *Frenzy,* are still more substantial, they forgo detailed plot summaries because such sum-maries are found in almost every book on Hitch-cock. The briefest and most easily identified and assimilated summaries are given, usually in foot-notes, in François Truffaut's book-length series of interviews with Hitchcock; the most extensive, scene-by-scene summaries are in Jane Sloan's bib-liography. Instead of summarizing the films' sto-ries, I have presented three other kinds of information. First is the most detailed list of cred-its I could find, comparing the films' own credit screens to Charles Barr's *English Hitchcock* for the early films, Sloan's bibliography for the later, and the Internet Movie Database for uncredited per-formers and technicians. This is followed by a brief production history of each film, from the initial proposal or literary property to the final release (or, in a few cases, the rerelease). Each entry concludes with a critical assessment of the film at hand. Like everyone else who has ever written on Hitchcock, I have my favorite Hitch-cock films—*Vertigo, Psycho, North by Northwest; Notorious, Rear Window, Strangers on a Train, Shadow of a Doubt;* 1934's *The Man Who Knew Too Much, The Lady Vanishes, The 39 Steps, Blackmail*—but although my prejudices have certainly flavored these assessments, they are meant to be analytical mainly rather than evaluative and, incidentally, to direct interested readers to more substantial com-mentaries by other hands.

2. **Collaborators.** By far the greatest number of individual entries is devoted to individual per-formers and technicians on Hitchcock's films, ranging from a few lines on up. Many of these entries are of dubious value, whether because the people cited cannot be positively identified (like the mysterious "Campbell and Connolly" who composed the music for *Blackmail*), or because information about them is so hard to come by (hence the large number of entries that omit birth

and death dates for elusive contributors), or because they are so obscure (like the 12 actors and actresses who played members of the jury in *Murder!*). But I have tried to provide the most accurate information possible about every single collaborator who is credited on any Hitchcock film, even if the listing seems to indicate a dead end for later researchers, and have included a smattering of uncredited performers and technicians who seemed especially noteworthy. Because Hitchcock enjoyed an astonishingly long career on both sides of the Atlantic (more than a half-century, he worked for both major studios in England and at every major U.S. studio except Columbia, and his work for each of these studios is accordingly summarized in an entry under the studio's name), his credits include hundreds of collaborators rarely associated with him. Yet the most striking revelation of these credits as a whole is how often Hitchcock returned—early in his career by necessity, later increasingly by choice—to work with the same professional collaborators: not only iconic performers like James Stewart and Grace Kelly but also screenwriters from Eliot Stannard to John Michael Hayes, cinematographers from Jack Cox to Robert Burks, composers from Louis Levy to Bernard Herrmann. I hope, then, that even the briefest of these entries may have some value, as part of a larger picture, in showing with whom Hitchcock returned to work repeatedly and with whom he did not. Although more encyclopedic information is available at the other end of the spectrum, I have not tried in my entries on Cary Grant or Ingrid Bergman to encapsulate the extensive literature on these stars, preferring in each entry on Hitchcock's best-known collaborators to emphasize the specifically Hitchcockian nature of the collaboration.

3. **Commentators.** As the most widely discussed of all filmmakers, Hitchcock has attracted the attention of countless reviewers, interviewers, critics, and theorists whose projects have ranged from popular appreciations of his work to appropriations of it in the service of more general arguments about cinematic practice (of which the most famous is Laura Mulvey's "Visual Pleasure and Narrative Cinema"). Although it is now 10 years old, Jane Sloan's monumental bibliography is still the best guide to this side of Hitchcock. I have made no attempt to duplicate Sloan's careful summaries of hundreds of individual books and essays. My entries on individual commentators, which are restricted almost entirely to the authors of books about Hitchcock (Mulvey, Raymond Bellour, and Andrew Sarris are three obvious exceptions), are again intended to place each commentator's work on Hitchcock in the broader context of the commentator's own career and to send readers back to the books instead of substituting for them.

4. **Themes, motifs, and topics of general interest.** These are the quirkiest of all my entries, their topics often obligatory (who would think of preparing a Hitchcock encyclopedia without entries on Blondes, Catholicism, Eating and Drinking, Eyes, Fetishism, Staircases, and Suspense?) but just as often, no doubt, arbitrary in both their selection and their handling (why Adaptation, for example, and not Theatrical Influences, and why limit myself to just the point I make about adaptation?). There is no point in pretending or aspiring to completeness on such topics; I can only hope I have captured a representative sample of the range of possible subjects for further research and debate. In addition, I have included entries on Awards (the major film and television industry prizes for which Hitchcock's work received nominations and awards), Cameo Appearances (a comprehensive list of Hitchcock's personal appearances in his theatrical films), and Unrealized Projects (a brief and highly selective overview of films ranging from David O. Selznick's planned *Titanic* to the two abortive projects in which Hitchcock invested the most work, *No Flowers for the Judge* and *Kaleidoscope*) on the assumption that no Hitchcock encyclopedia could amount to anything if it were not a reliable reference on these subjects.

It goes without saying, finally, that this volume is meant to be consulted, not read through in alphabetical order. I have therefore tried to make it as easy as possible to find information on particular subjects while maintaining a consistent style. Information about both the literary or theatrical properties on which most of Hitchcock's films are based is found under the original author's name, not the title of the novel, story, or play. So is information about specific writers about Hitchcock. Readers who know the title of the property on which a film is based but not its author are directed to the entry on the film in question; readers seeking the name of a particular commentator are referred to the appended bibliography. Throughout the individual entries, I have used SMALL CAPITALS the first time a given name or topic is mentioned in each entry to mark cross-references to other entries. Readers who ignore these cross-references and attempt to read the book from cover to cover will find that despite my disapproval of such a project, I have made every effort to make the entries as lively and engaging as possible.

NOTES

[1] Perez, Gilbert, *The Material Ghost: Films and Their Medium* (Baltimore: Johns Hopkins University Press, 1998), p. 9.

[2] Barr, Charles, *English Hitchcock* (Moffat: Cameron & Hollis, 1999), p. 14.

[3] See Hitchcock, Alfred, "My Screen Memories" (1936), in Sidney Gottlieb, ed., *Hitchcock on Hitchcock: Selected Writings and Interviews* (Berkeley: University of California Press, 1995), pp. 7–26; and François Truffaut, *Hitchcock,* rev. ed. (New York: Simon & Schuster, 1984), pp. 31–39.

[4] Truffaut, p. 43.

[5] Truffaut, p. 85.

[6] Leff, Leonard J., *Hitchcock and Selznick: The Rich and Strange Collaboration of Alfred Hitchcock and David O. Selznick in Hollywood* (London: Weidenfeld & Nicolson, 1987), pp. 277–78.

[7] Spoto, Donald, *The Dark Side of Genius: The Life of Alfred Hitchcock* (Boston: Little, Brown, 1983), p. 136.

[8] Žižek, Slavoj, "In His Bold Gaze My Ruin Is Writ Large," in Žižek, ed., *Everything You Always Wanted to Know About Lacan (But Were Afraid to Ask Hitchcock)* (London: Verso, 1992), p. 258.

[9] Rohmer, Eric, and Claude Chabrol, *Hitchcock: The First Forty-four Films,* trans. by Stanley Hochman (New York: Ungar, 1979), p. 73.

[10] Naremore, James, "Hitchcock and Humor," *Strategies* 14: 1 (2001): 16, 19.

[11] Wood, Robin, *Hitchcock's Films Revisited* (New York: Columbia University Press, 1989), p. 55.

[12] Wood, p. 371.

ACKNOWLEDGMENTS

My greatest debt, of course, is to all the writers on Hitchcock whose example has been so inspiring. In approaching almost every entry in this volume, I have been daunted by two repeated fears. One is my humbling awareness of the earlier commentators on whom my work depends and from whom I have frequently borrowed. Because this is not a work of original scholarship but a conspectus of Hitchcock's films and Hitchcock scholarship, I hope these borrowings, even when I have failed to note them because they have become so deeply embedded in my own view of Hitchcock, will be forgiven by authors who will accept my profound gratitude for having written so illuminatingly on Hitchcock. My second fear has stemmed from my equally humbling discovery of factual errors in even the most highly regarded books on Hitchcock (Truffaut's classic volume of interviews, for example, is a paradise of misspelled names and misattributed credits). I have tried to correct as many errors as possible, not only in this volume but also, where possible, in my sources. The Internet Movie Database, maintained at <www.imdb.com>, is a miraculously helpful online reference to film credits, but in the weeks I spent with it, I found myself posting additions and corrections to the database far too often to assume that all the online information on which I was relying in the absence of confirming sources was accurate. This is my second and last reference book, and having both times searched out confirmation for thousands of mundane facts and living through night sweats when I could not confirm many of them, I would be disingenuous indeed in offering the assurance that this is the volume that finally gets Hitchcock right. I can only hope that later researchers will find this volume as useful, for all its yet undiscovered errors and inaccuracies, as I have found earlier references and that they will write or post me to call these errors to my attention.

No blame for any of my errors should attach to my editors, John Tibbetts and James M. Welsh, to whom I owe an incalculable debt. Jim insisted from the beginning that I was the right person to tackle this volume, strengthened my resolve whenever it faltered, and was always available to give me practical advice about listings and formatting. John, who supplied the 30 drawings that supplement the obligatory photos illustrating this volume, disagreed with me about any number of procedural matters, patiently explained to me why he was right, and then let me go ahead and do things my way. To both of them I owe the rare privilege of working within the shelter of a well-edited series while being entrusted with the freedom of an inaugural entry that would go far to establish guidelines for later volumes.

ENTRIES A to Z

Acker, Jean (1893–1978)   Blonde lead of Hollywood silent films best known as the first wife of Rudolph Valentino, whom she left on their wedding night in 1919 and divorced in 1921 despite his pleas for her return. Absent from the screen from 1927 to 1935, she returned in a series of bit roles, one of which was the Green Manors matron in SPELL-BOUND.

Ackland, Rodney (1908–1991)   British screenwriter, occasional actor and director, who collaborated on the screenplay of NUMBER SEVENTEEN, which he describes as "a burlesque of all the thrillers of which [J. Jefferson FARJEON's source play] was a pretty good sample"—ignoring the many burlesque elements in the play itself. His autobiographical memoir *The Celluloid Mistress; or The Custard Pie of Dr. Caligari,* written in collaboration with Elspeth Grant (1954), presents Hitchcock as an often malicious practical joker.

Adams, Kathryn (1893–1959)   Hollywood supporting actress whose score of roles in the early forties included the young mother in SABOTEUR.

adaptation   Hitchcock's cavalier attitude toward adaptation is well known. Glossing his deliberate avoidance of such literary classics as *Crime and Punishment* as vehicles for his work, he told François

TRUFFAUT: "What I do is to read a story only once, and if I like the basic idea, I just forget all about the book and start to create cinema"—an attitude amply documented, for example, in SABOTAGE, which extensively reworks themes and motifs from Joseph CONRAD's *The Secret Agent,* and STRANGERS ON A TRAIN, which departs decisively from Patricia HIGH-SMITH's novel to rescue its hero from a fatal moral compromise. Both films, Hitchcock might have argued, are based less on their source novels than on the ideas behind those novels, as he suggested to Truffaut in a remark about PSYCHO: "I think the thing that appealed to me and made me decide to do the picture was the suddenness of the murder in the shower, coming, as it were, out of the blue. That was about all."

Such disdain for close adaptation in the interest of "PURE CINEMA," however, is broadly misleading in several ways. It overlooks the very large proportion of Hitchcock films that depend on source novels or stories or plays for their architecture (and the structural problems of films such as FOREIGN COR-RESPONDENT that are based on original screenplays). It downplays the well-documented closeness between Hitchcock and his screenwriters (the only collaborators with whom he worked so closely), with whom he met daily for weeks or months as they hammered out episodes and dialogue. It also ignores the number of Hitchcock films that follow their sources very closely indeed: not only literal theatrical adaptations from JUNO AND THE PAYCOCK to DIAL M FOR MURDER, which Hitchcock dismissed respectively as "nothing to do with cinema" and "coasting, playing it safe," but also adaptations of other plays and novels from THE SKIN GAME and RICH AND STRANGE to Psycho itself. Hitchcock's entire career, in fact, can be defined in terms of his self-perceived rivalry with the writers whose work he disavowed even as he depended on it.

Addinsell, Richard (1904–1977) British composer, occasionally in Hollywood, but more often a staple of such middlebrow English films as *Fire Over England* (1937), *South Riding* (1938), *Gaslight* (1939), and *Goodbye, Mr. Chips* (1939). His *Warsaw Concerto,* composed for the film *Dangerous Moonlight* (1941), holds a secure place in the light classical repertory. His score for UNDER CAPRICORN dates from about the midpoint of his career.

Addison, John (1920–1998) British composer drawn into film work in 1948 through his friendship with producer/director Roy Boulting. His British scores include those for *Look Back in Anger* (1958), *The Entertainer* (1960), and *A Taste of Honey* (1960). Soon after winning an Academy Award for his music for *Tom Jones* (1963), he replaced Bernard HERRMANN as the composer for TORN CURTAIN when the latter left over Hitchcock's demand that the score include a title song with sales potential. Addison remained in Los Angeles to provide music for a score of films and more than a dozen television series, including the title song for *Murder, She Wrote* (1984).

Adrian (1903–1959) American costume designer, born Adolph Greenberg, who changed his name to Gilbert Adrian when he left New York for Hollywood and landed a job as production designer with Cecil B. DeMille in 1925; he dropped his last name on the hundreds of films on which he received credit as MGM's chief costume designer (1927–42). Despite his great success in helping create the glamorous style of such leading ladies as Norma Shearer, Jean Harlow, and Joan Crawford and despite his wedding to Hollywood star Janet Gaynor (who retired

from the screen on their marriage), he left the studio after being forced to abandon "the MGM look" for Greta Garbo's wardrobe in *Two-Faced Woman*. Opening his own costume-design studio to serve the motion picture industry, he continued to work sporadically on such films as SHADOW OF A DOUBT and ROPE before his retirement in 1952 and his suicide in 1959.

Ahern, Fred (1907–1982) American production manager. He served as unit manager on his first film, THE PARADINE CASE, and as production manager on all three of Hitchcock's Transatlantic films—ROPE, UNDER CAPRICORN, and STAGE FRIGHT. He continued in several Tarzan programmers before landing jobs on the long-running television series *The Fugitive* (1963–67) and *Cannon* (1971–76).

Aherne, Brian (1902–1986) British actor who made his stage debut at the age of eight, returning to the theater after studying architecture at Malvern College. In British films from 1924, he starred as Robert Browning in the 1931 Broadway production of *The Barretts of Wimpole Street* and moved to Hollywood in 1933, stepping outside his tweedy, pipe-smoking persona to play the title roles in *The Great Garrick, Captain Fury,* and *The Man Who Lost Himself,* as well as Emperor Maximilian in *Juarez.* The former husband of Joan FONTAINE, he played Ruth Grandfort's gentlemanly husband Willy Robertson, who prosecuted Father Michael Logan for murder years after Logan's romance with Ruth Grandfort in I CONFESS.

Albertson, Frank (1909–1964) American character actor, in Hollywood from 1922 as prop boy and light leading man but better known for scores of roles as the hero's friend, brother, or sidekick. He appeared in four episodes of ALFRED HITCHCOCK PRESENTS—as Regis in "Disappearing Trick" (1958), Sgt. Kirby in "Out There—Darkness" (1958), George Wyncliff in "You Can't Trust a Man" (1961), and Tom Batterman in "Last Seen Wearing Blue Jeans" (1963)—and returned in a trenchant scene as Cassidy, the Texas oilman whose $40,000 sets the plot of PSYCHO in motion.

Albertson, Jack (1907–1981) Weathered but durable American actor of stage, screen, and television who appeared in more than a hundred features for the large and small screen. One of only three performers to win a Tony (for *The Subject Was Roses,* 1965), an Oscar (for the film adaptation of *The Subject Was Roses,* 1968), and an Emmy (for *Chico and the Man,* 1974–78), he appeared as Harry Crane in "INCIDENT AT A CORNER" in the single FORD STARTIME episode Hitchcock directed.

Alderson, George British actor who plays the first detective on the scene in DIAL M FOR MURDER.

Alexander, James (R.) Hollywood sound technician, veteran of more than 40 films from 1971 to 1989, who headed the sound recording team for FAMILY PLOT.

Alexandre of Paris Hairstylist with occasional Hollywood credits, 1958–86, including Tippi HEDREN's hairstyles in MARNIE.

Alfred Hitchcock Hour, The The hour-long television successor to ALFRED HITCHCOCK PRESENTS premiered on CBS with the episode "A Piece of the Action" on Thursday, September 20, 1962, at 10:00 P.M. On January 4, 1963, the network shifted the program to a new slot Fridays at 9:30 before moving it in its second season into a slot a half-hour later; the program's third and final season aired Mondays from 10:00 to 11:00 on CBS, which had first launched

Hitchcock assumes the role of cheerfully ghoulish drummer in one of his trademark non sequitur introductions for *The Alfred Hitchcock Hour. (National Film Society Archive)*

Alfred Hitchcock Presents in 1955. With the departure of Joan HARRISON in 1962, Norman LLOYD became the program's executive producer, but other credits remained nearly as constant as before, though Hitchcock's trademark entrance each week in heavily backlit silhouette was redesigned. Among the featured performers familiar from Hitchcock's films were Anne BAXTER, Macdonald CAREY, Laraine DAY, Joan FONTAINE, John FORSYTHE, John GAVIN, Margaret LEIGHTON, Vera MILES, and Ray MILLAND; others, like Bruce DERN, moved from the program to Hitchcock's feature films. Hitchcock's own involvement with the program was even more minimal than with *Alfred Hitchcock Presents;* he directed only one of the show's 93 segments, a courtroom drama called "I SAW THE WHOLE THING" that aired as the fourth episode of the first season. Although ratings continued strong, the program's rising costs led to its cancellation after "Off Season" (May 10, 1965), the final program of its third season.

Out of all Hitchcock's films, the programs he directed for television are most neglected. Very little has been written about them, and most of what has steers clear of close analysis. Yet the episodes Hitchcock directed, for all their brevity and modesty, are thoroughly characteristic (although many of the episodes directed by other hands, based on stories chosen to suit his carefully manufactured persona, seem equally Hitchcockian), and a few of them are television classics, as are Hitchcock's drolly matter-of-fact introductions, some of them eerily resurrected to introduce episodes of THE NEW ALFRED HITCHCOCK PRESENTS (1985–89) after the director's death. The best available sources of information about *Alfred Hitchcock Presents* and *The Alfred Hitchcock Hour,* the program, both heavy on lists and anecdotes and light on interpretation, are the invaluable references by John MCCARTY and Brian KELLEHER and by Martin GRAMS, Jr., and Patrik WIKSTROM.

Alfred Hitchcock Presents   Early in 1955, shortly after Hitchcock agreed to license his name to a monthly fiction periodical, *Alfred Hitchcock's Mystery Magazine,* with which (as with the dozens of anthologies with titles like *Stories My Mother Never Told Me* and *Twelve Stories They Wouldn't Let Me Do on TV* that

would be culled from its pages) he was otherwise unconnected, his agent Lew WASSERMAN began discussions with several television executives about another project that would ultimately make Hitchcock the best known of living film directors: a dramatic anthology television series, each episode to be introduced by Hitchcock but most to be directed by other hands. A new company Hitchcock called SHAMLEY PRODUCTIONS engaged Joan HARRISON as the program's executive producer, Norman LLOYD, beginning midway through the second season, as its associate producer, Gordon HESSLER as story editor, and James ALLARDICE as the author of the witty, macabre monologues Hitchcock would deliver every Sunday evening at 9:30. The standing crew, working out of UNIVERSAL's television unit, REVUE PRODUCTIONS, included cinematographers John F. WARREN and John L. RUSSELL, Jr.; art director Martin OBZINA; editors Richard G. WRAY and Edward W. WILLIAMS; and costume supervisor Vincent DEE. Among the many actors familiar from Hitchcock's films to appear on the program were Barbara BEL GEDDES, Patricia COLLINGE, Wendell COREY, Joseph COTTEN, Isobel ELSOM, John GAVIN, Edmund GWENN, Sir Cedric HARDWICKE, Patricia HITCHCOCK, Peter LORRE, Vera MILES, Mildred NATWICK, Claude RAINS, Thelma RITTER, Teresa WRIGHT, and John WILLIAMS. The writers were almost equally numerous, with Henry SLESAR, a prolific contributor to *Alfred Hitchcock's Mystery Magazine,* the most frequent (he eventually amassed 52 credits on the program and its expanded sequel, THE ALFRED HITCHCOCK HOUR). The economies of television allowed only three days for the 23 minutes allotted each episode, one day for rehearsal and two for filming, and the program regularly recycled musical cues by staff composers Frederick HERBERT, Bernard HERRMANN, Lyn MURRAY, and Stanley WILSON. The film's contributing directors ranged from such veterans as John Brahm and Robert Florey to such newcomers as Sydney Pollack and Robert Altman to such sometime actors as Paul Henreid and Lloyd himself, but the episode that premiered on CBS on October 2, 1955, "REVENGE," was directed by Hitchcock, who had already completed a second episode, "BREAKDOWN," before filming "Revenge." Hitchcock went on to direct 15 later episodes with gradually decreasing frequency:

"THE CASE OF MR. PELHAM," "BACK FOR CHRISTMAS," "WET SATURDAY," "MR. BLANCHARD'S SECRET," "ONE MORE MILE TO GO," "THE PERFECT CRIME," "LAMB TO THE SLAUGHTER," "DIP IN THE POOL," "POISON," "BANQUO'S CHAIR," "ARTHUR," "THE CRYSTAL TRENCH," "MRS. BIXBY AND THE COLONEL'S COAT," "THE HORSE-PLAYER," and "BANG! YOU'RE DEAD."

On September 27, 1960, with "MRS. BIXBY AND THE COLONEL'S COAT," the first episode of its sixth season, the program moved from CBS to NBC and from Sunday to Tuesday evening at 8:30. There were additional changes in staff but very few in hallmarks of the program's presentation. Each episode would be introduced by a shot of Hitchcock in silhouette, stepping forward to fill the famous facial profile he had drawn himself, accompanied to Gounod's "Funeral March for a Marionette," a grotesque little tune the director had first heard over the scene in F.W. MURNAU's *Sunrise* in which the husband and wife visit a photography studio; each of Hitchcock's arch, gravely cherubic monologues, most of which had little to do with the specific content of the episode he was introducing, was marked by an edge of condescending disdain for the audience or, more often, toward the sponsors he seemed to regard as sworn enemies. In general, however, the sponsors remained nearly as unchanged as the show's other trappings, despite the director's cavalier attitude toward their participation, presumably because of the program's consistently strong ratings. Both the program and Hitchcock himself were nominated for repeated Emmys, and though neither won any, several technicians were winners for individual segments, including Robert Stevens's Emmy for directing "The Glass Eye" (1957). In all, the program ran for 268 weekly episodes (three of which comprised a single three-part story, "I Killed the Count," running from March 17 through 31, 1957), and one more, "The Sorcerer's Apprentice" (deemed too gruesome for the program's original run, though regularly shown in syndication), before ending with "Where Beauty Lies" (June 26, 1962) and returning the following season in expanded form as *The Alfred Hitchcock Hour.*

Allardice, James (B.) (1919–1966) American writer whose play *At War with the Army* became a

hit vehicle for Dean Martin and Jerry Lewis in 1950. After working on four undistinguished films, he was hired in 1955 to write the introductions and conclusions Hitchcock delivered in each episode of *ALFRED HITCHCOCK PRESENTS,* and later *THE ALFRED HITCHCOCK HOUR.* The often macabre, occasionally outlandish, always witty and deadpan introductions, which showed the director cast in such roles as a victim tied to the railroad tracks and a bubble-blowing Sherlock Holmes, unfailingly in command of his hauteur, repeatedly returned to the running gag of Hitchcock's war with the sponsors he professed to disdain. Building on the persona Hitchcock had cultivated with the press since his earliest interviews, they codified and established that persona in the public mind more firmly than any other single manifestation.

Allen, Jay Presson (1922–) American writer/producer Hitchcock chose to replace Evan HUNTER on MARNIE after reading an advance copy of her first play, *The Prime of Miss Jean Brodie,* in 1963. A self-described novice in screenwriting, the playwright, who had also written the theatrical play on which *Wives and Lovers* was based, was kept ignorant, in violation of ASCAP rules, of Hunter's earlier screenplay. Years after her Oscar nominations for her screenplays for *The Prime of Miss Jean Brodie* (1969), *Cabaret* (1972), and *Prince of the City* (1980), she continued to credit Hitchcock's formative influence in making her think cinematically.

Allen, Patrick (1927–) Tough British actor whose 40-year career playing character roles and tough leads in such films as *Night of the Generals* and *Puppet on a Chain* and the 1971 television series *Brett* was launched with his role as Pearson in *DIAL M FOR MURDER.*

Allen, Richard (1954–) American film scholar, professor of Film Studies at New York University, organizer of the Hitchcock Centennial Conference, and coeditor with Sam Ishii-GONZALÈS of *Alfred Hitchcock: Centenary Essays* (BFI, 1999), to which he contributes an essay on "metaskepticism" in *THE LODGER* and *SUSPICION* that identifies Hitchcock's duplicitous self-presentation as dandy/rogue as the focus of the simultaneous promise and subversion of romance through the ambiguity of appearances throughout his films. The anthology's remaining 20 essays, most of them newly commissioned, were contributed by other conference participants. Compared to the earlier anthologies edited by Albert J. LA VALLEY and by Marshall DEUTELBAUM and Leland POAGUE and aimed at a more general audience, this one is more rigorously grounded theoretically, though no one school predominates. As the editors note in their introduction, most of the contributions implicitly or explicitly take the teasingly "excessive" attention to the figure of Hitchcock, his endurance beyond the passing of auteurism in academic circles, as a point of departure. The anthology is divided into four sections: "The Figure of the Author" (including essays by Paula Marantz COHEN, William ROTHMAN, Susan SMITH, Thomas M. LEITCH et al.); "Hitchcock's Aesthetics" (Peter Wollen, Slavoj ŽIŽEK at al.); "Sexuality/Romance" (Raymond BELLOUR, Lesley BRILL, Richard Allen et al.), and "Culture, Politics, Ideology" (James NAREMORE, Robert CORBER et al.). The volume concludes with an extensive bibliography of books and essays from 1990 to 1999 that is particularly useful as a supplement to the massive bibliography compiled by Jane SLOAN. A second collection, *Hitchcock Past and Present: Essays from the Hitchcock Centennial Conference,* is forthcoming. In 2001 Allen and Sidney GOTTLIEB succeeded Christopher BROOKHOUSE as the coeditors of the *HITCHCOCK ANNUAL.*

Allgood, Sara (1883–1950) Diminutive Irish character actress, a charter member of the Abbey Players from 1904. Beginning in 1929, she alternated her stage work with screen roles, including the heroine's mother in *BLACKMAIL* and the title role in *JUNO AND THE PAYCOCK,* a recreation of her greatest Abbey triumph, in which she played the long-suffering wife of the self-deluded poseur Captain Boyle. Leaving the stage and immigrating to Hollywood in 1940, she was nominated for an Academy Award for her role as the coal-mining matriarch Mrs. Morgan in *How Green Was My Valley* (1941).

Alper, Murray (1904–1984) Balding American character actor whose specialty was chatty cab drivers such as Harold in *MR. AND MRS. SMITH.* He was also cast as the truck driver who gives Robert *CUMMINGS* a lift in *SABOTEUR* and the boat concessionaire who saves Farley *GRANGER* by identifying Robert *WALKER* as the killer in *STRANGERS ON A TRAIN,* and he appears briefly in two segments of *ALFRED HITCHCOCK PRESENTS*—as Lloyd in "BREAKDOWN," and as Sgt. Ed Carmody in "Not the Runaway Type" (1960)—before returning as another cabbie in *THE ALFRED HITCHCOCK HOUR* episode "The Trap" (1965).

Always Tell Your Wife Famous Players—Lasky, 1922. **Producer:** Seymour Hicks; **Director:** Hugh Croise [and Seymour Hicks and Alfred Hitchcock]; **Screenplay:** Hugh Croise, based on the play by Seymour Hicks; **Cast:** Seymour Hicks (the Husband) and Gertrude McCoy (the Wife).

After Hicks dismissed Croise from the film, he and an uncredited Hitchcock, who was serving as the studio's property master, completed the production. Although this short film is almost certainly the first surviving project Hitchcock worked on as director, it is unclear whether any of Hitchcock's work is included in the first half of the film, which is all that remains.

Amann, Betty (1907–1990) Bavarian-born American actress, née Philippine Amann, who began her career in the German silent industry and continued to work mostly in German films except for a period of two years (1931–32) when she went to England, notably as the seductive false Princess who ensnares Henry KENDALL in *RICH AND STRANGE,* and a few later films in Hollywood.

Anderson, John (1922–1992) Rangy American character actor, occasional director and assistant director, a fixture of American movies and television for 40 years, from 1952. He most often played westerners like Virgil Earp in *The Life and Legend of Wyatt Earp* (1955) and Marshal Dana in *Five Card Stud* (1968) before graduating to playing Abraham Lincoln in *The Lincoln Conspiracy* (1977) and Judge Kenesaw Mountain Landis in *Eight Men Out* (1988), a role he reprised in the television movie *Babe Ruth*

(1991). Among his many blunt-spoken roles are California Charlie, the car salesman in PSYCHO; Nicholson in the ALFRED HITCHCOCK PRESENTS episode "The Old Pro" (1961); and two for THE ALFRED HITCHCOCK HOUR: escaped criminal Adam in "Ride the Nightmare" (1962) and threatening husband Luke Smith in "The Second Wife" (1965).

Anderson, (Dame) Judith (1898–1992) Splendidly imperious Australian grande dame of the stage, born Frances Margaret Anderson-Anderson, occasionally in distinguished films like *Laura* (1944) and *And Then There Were None* (1945), more often in forgettable properties or such memorably over-the-top roles as Big Mama in *Cat on a Hot Tin Roof* (1958) and the wicked stepmother in *Cinderfella* (1960). On television, she won Emmies for two different performances (1954, 1960) as Lady Macbeth but is better remembered for her starring stage roles in *Mourning Becomes Electra* (1932) and *Medea* (1947) and her reading of the title role in *Hamlet* (1969). Her performance as Mrs. Danvers, the unsettlingly remote housekeeper in REBECCA, is widely acclaimed as her finest work for the screen.

Anderson, Mary (1921–) Gentle American supporting actress and occasional lead, born Bebe Anderson, whose career extended from *Gone With the Wind* (1939) to the television series *Peyton Place* (1964). Widow of Oscar-winning cinematographer Leon Shamroy. While playing Alice MacKenzie, the second romantic lead in LIFEBOAT, she reportedly asked the director which he thought was her best side, provoking the memorable reply, "My dear, you're sitting on it."

Anderson, Maxwell (1888–1959) Prolific American playwright and screenwriter, former teacher and journalist, especially noted for the literary aspirations of his verse drama. His first success, the World War I play *What Price Glory?* (1924), written with Laurence Stallings, was made into a notable film in 1926, as were *Elizabeth the Queen* (1930/1939), *Winterset* (1935/1936), *Key Largo* (1939/1948), and *Joan of Lorraine* (1946/1948). In Hollywood, he provided dialogue for *All Quiet on the Western Front* (1930) and

worked on the adaptations of *Rain* (1932) and *Death Takes a Holiday* (1934), as well as the adaptations of many of his own plays. Attracted by Anderson's handling of the moral implications of the Sacco-Vanzetti case in *Winterset,* his ghostly satire *High Tor* (1936), and his 1956 Hollywood adaptation of William March's novel *The Bad Seed,* Hitchcock sought Anderson for THE WRONG MAN and VERTIGO but found his draft screenplays on both projects unusable and replaced him, respectively, with Angus MACPHAIL and with Alec COPPEL and Samuel TAYLOR, giving him screen credit for his work on the first film but not the second, which Anderson had titled *Darkling I Listen.*

Andrews, Julie (1935–) Singing British star actress. She made her London debut at age 12 and her New York debut at 19 in *The Boy Friend* (1954). Her performance as Eliza Doolittle in *My Fair Lady* (1956) took Broadway by storm, and she was cast in the television special *Cinderella* (1957) before returning to the stage as Guinevere in *Camelot* (1960). Passed over in favor of the nonsinging Audrey Hepburn for WARNER BROS.' 1964 film version of *My Fair Lady,* she won an Academy Award for her first film, *Mary Poppins,* the same year and gave an acceptance speech thanking "all those who made this possible—especially Jack Warner." But her turn to dramatic roles was more problematic, as she demonstrated in *The Americanization of Emily* (1965) and TORN CURTAIN, in which she played Sarah Sherman, Michael Armstrong's sorely tried fiancée and, eventually, his fellow spy.

Angel, Heather (1909–1986) Delicate leading lady of British stage and screen whose American roles anchoring B-pictures or cast in supporting roles in A-pictures like *Berkeley Square* (1933) and *The Informer* (1935) were generally disappointing. Her greatest popular success was as the dashing hero's girlfriend in five Bulldog Drummond films (1937–39). Hitchcock cast her in two typically undemanding roles, Ethel, the Aysgarths' maid in SUSPICION, and Mrs. Higgins, the bereaved young mother who slips off the boat shortly after LIFEBOAT begins. The latter role, prophetically, marked virtually her final Hollywood appearance.

Anobile, Richard J. (1949–) American writer who began as a film reviewer for *Argosy*, edited a series of popular books on film, and has more recently been active as a television producer. His books, most of them reproducing 1,000 to 1,500 frames of a given film or group of films with the original dialogue, include *Drat! Being the Encapsulated View of Life by W.C. Fields in His Own Words* (1969), *Why a Duck?* (1971), *A Flask of Fields: Verbal and Visual Gems from the Films of W.C. Fields* (1972), *Who's On First? Verbal and Visual Gems from the Films of Abbott and Costello* (1972), *The Marx Brothers Scrapbook* (with Groucho Marx, 1973), *Hooray for Captain Spaulding: Verbal and Visual Gems from* Animal Crackers (1974), *Casablanca* (1974), *Frankenstein* (1974), *John Ford's* Stagecoach *Starring John Wayne* (1975), *Rouben Mamoulian's* Dr. Jekyll and Mr. Hyde *Starring Fredric March* (1975), *The Maltese Falcon* (1974), *Ninotchka* (1975), *Buster Keaton's* The General (1975), *Godfrey Daniels: Verbal and Visual Gems from the Short Films of W.C. Fields* (1975), *A Fine Mess: Verbal and Visual Gems from the Crazy World of Laurel and Hardy* (1975), *The Best of Buster: The Classic Comedy Scenes Direct from the Films of Buster Keaton* (1976), *The Wiz Scrapbook* (1978), and a related series of "photonovels" including Alien: *The Movie Novel* (1979), Battlestar Galactica: *The Photostory* (1979), Popeye: *The Movie Novel* (1980), The Rocky Horror Picture Show: *The Movie Novel* (1980), *Star Trek: The Motion Picture* (1980), and *Star Trek II: The Wrath of Khan* (1982). His Film Classics Library edition of *Alfred Hitchcock's Psycho* (Darien House, 1974), like the other volumes in the series, is a shot-by-shot, word-by-word transcription of the film including more than 1,300 blowups, sketchily introduced but invaluable for close study.

Anthelme, Paul Pseudonym of Paul Bourde (1851–1914), author of the play *Nos deux consciences* (1902), the basis of *I CONFESS*, which presents the dilemma of a priest who hears a confession of murder but, prevented by the seal of the confessional from revealing the murderer to the authorities, comes under suspicion himself.

Anys, Georgette (1909–) Doughty French actress recruited, like so many others in the cast of *TO CATCH A THIEF*, from her native industry to play John Robie's housekeeper Germaine, whose light touch with a quiche lorraine once allowed her to strangle a Gestapo officer without making a sound. She continued to play similar roles in other international productions after 1960.

Appearances Famous Players-Lasky, 1921. **Director:** Donald Crisp; **Assistant director:** Claude Mitchell; **Cinematographer:** Hal Young; **Screenplay:** Margaret Turnbull, based on a story by Edward Knoblock; **Cast:** David Powell (Herbert Seaton), Mary Glynne (Kitty Mitchell), Langhorn Burton (Sir William Rutherford), Mary Dibley (Lady Rutherford), Marjorie Hume (Agnes), Percy Standing (Dawkins).

The third of the 12 silent films for which Hitchcock designed intertitles.

Archibald, William (1917–1970) Trinidadian writer, né John William Wharton Archibald, whose two screen credits, both in collaboration, include *The Innocents* (1961) and *I CONFESS*.

Arginteanu, Judy American author of *The Movies of Alfred Hitchcock* (Scholastic, 1994), an overview designed for readers from 9 to 12.

Armstrong, Anthony Pseudonym for British novelist and playwright George Anthony Armstrong Wills (1897–1976), best known as coauthor with Ian Hay of *Orders Is Orders* (1932) and author of *Ten Minute Alibi* (1933). His infrequent film contributions include collaborating with Charles Bennett and Edwin Greenwood on the very free adaptation of Josephine TEY's novel *A Shilling for Candles* (1936) as *YOUNG AND INNOCENT*. His 1955 story "The Strange Case of Mr. Pelham" served as the basis for the *ALFRED HITCHCOCK PRESENTS* segment "THE CASE OF MR. PELHAM."

Armstrong, Charlotte (1905–1969) American mystery writer who perfected the formula of the female threatened under sunny suburban skies that sent her successor Mary Higgins Clark to the top of the best-seller lists. Her novel *The Unsuspected*

(1946) was adapted for the movies the following year, and *Mischief* (1950) was filmed as *Don't Bother to Knock* (1952). She wrote both the original story and the teleplay adaptation for Hitchcock's FORD STAR-TIME episode "INCIDENT AT A CORNER" and that same year (1960) adapted three stories by other hands for ALFRED HITCHCOCK PRESENTS: "Across the Threshold," "The Five-Forty Eight," and "Sybilla."

Armstrong, David (Dave) American supporting actor who appeared in a half-dozen films (1955–77) and several television programs playing police officers, as in the "FOUR O'CLOCK" episode of SUSPICION, and the ALFRED HITCHCOCK PRESENTS episode "Miss Paisley's Cat" (1957), and as an asylum worker in another segment, "The Dangerous People" (1957).

Arnold, C. Wilfred British art director, later production designer, otherwise billed as C. Wilfred Arnold, C.W. Arnold, W.C. Arnold, and Wilfred Arnold. His first film, THE LODGER, was followed by THE FARMER'S WIFE, THE MANXMAN, BLACKMAIL, RICH AND STRANGE, and NUMBER SEVENTEEN before he went on to design some two dozen films, from *When Knights Were Bold* (1936) to *Walk a Crooked Path* (1969).

Arnold, Norman G. (d. 1964) British art director who worked with C. Wilfred ARNOLD on BLACKMAIL and then continued on JUNO AND THE PAYCOCK and nearly 20 other films through 1963. He directed a single film, *They Met in the Dark,* in 1943.

Arnold, Tom (1896–1969) British producer, widely known as "The Quiet Showman," who began his career as impresario by touring revues and then broke into the London theater with a 1925 production of *Folies Bergere.* A longtime associate of Ivor NOVELLO, he presented many of the actor's shows, as well as musicals, opera, and ice shows. A year after he produced WALTZES FROM VIENNA, he took over the pantomime interests of Julian Wylie and soon became acknowledged as the king of pantomime producers.

Arosenius, Per-Axel (1920–1981) Patrician Swedish actor, rarely seen outside his native country's cinema, who contributes an arrogant cameo as Soviet defector Boris Kusenov in TOPAZ.

Arrigo, Frank American art director and production designer, occasional production manager, assistant director, executive producer, and director of television programs. His hundred films (1946–71) are largely B-westerns and crime programmers, with such occasional big-budget outings as TORN CURTAIN.

"Arthur" 152nd episode of *Alfred Hitchcock Presents,* broadcast September 27, 1959. **Producer:** Joan Harrison; **Associate producer:** Norman Lloyd; **Director:** Alfred Hitchcock; **Assistant director:** Hilton Green; **Teleplay:** James P. Cavanagh, based on "Being a Murderer Myself," a short story by Arthur Williams; **Cinematographer:** John L. Russell; **Art director:** John Lloyd; **Set designer:** James S. Redd; **Costumes:** Vincent Dee; **Editors:** Richard G. Wray and Edward W. Williams; **Music:** Frederick Herbert; **Cast:** Laurence Harvey (Arthur Williams), Hazel Court (Helen Braithwaite), Robert Douglas (Insp. Ben Liebenberg), Barry G. Harvey (Constable Barry), Patrick Macnee (Sgt. John Theron).

The opening program of the show's fifth season stars Laurence Harvey as a chicken farmer driven by his maddeningly importunate on-again, off-again girlfriend to strangle her and hide her body in a manner so ingenious that the local police, certain of his guilt, never find it. Two particularly macabre touches are the murderer's cheerfully confessional direct address to the camera at the program's opening and the name of his character, taken from the name of the source story's author, who had left him nameless.

Arvan, Jan (1913–1979) American film and television actor. A former straight man to comedian Red Skelton, he appeared in more than 40 films, including *The Poseidon Adventure* (1972) and *The Other Side of Midnight* (1977); as Harry in the ALFRED HITCHCOCK PRESENTS segment "THE CASE OF MR. PELHAM"; and as Al in the ALFRED HITCHCOCK HOUR episode "Nothing Ever Happens in Linvale" (1963).

Ashcroft, (Dame) Peggy (1907–1991)
Distinguished British Shakespearean actress, born
Edith Margaret Emily Ashcroft, who made her London stage debut at 20, her New York debut 10 years
later. Though her film performances were at first sporadic—she is credited with no appearances between
1940 and 1959—her long life, her versatility, and the
autumnal glow given her career by her Academy
Award for playing Mrs. Moore in *A Passage to India*
(1984) eventually pushed the number of her film
appearances to more than 30. One of the first of
these was as Margaret, the Scottish crofter's sheltered
wife in THE *39 STEPS*.

Associated British Studios The successor
that emerged from myriad legal transformations of
BRITISH INTERNATIONAL PICTURES in 1933 released
Hitchcock's two wartime shorts, *BON VOYAGE* and
AVENTURE MALGACHE.

Astar, Ben American film and television actor
who appeared as the hotel manager in the *ALFRED
HITCHCOCK PRESENTS* episode "THE CRYSTAL
TRENCH."

Atterbury, Malcolm (1907–1992) Rangy
American character actor, frequently cast as lawmen
on television shows from *Gunsmoke to The Fugitive,*
whose 20-year film career (1954–73) included
appearances as the blackmailer in the *ALFRED HITCH-
COCK PRESENTS* episode "Help Wanted" (1956), the
man Cary GRANT encounters at the prairie bus stop
in *NORTH BY NORTHWEST*, and the stolid deputy Al
Malone in *THE BIRDS*.

Atwater, Edith (1911–1986) Stalwart American character actress, a veteran of film and television,
former wife of actors Hugh Marlowe and Kent
Smith, one of whose last roles was Mrs. Clay in *FAM-
ILY PLOT*.

Auber, Brigitte (1928–) Parisian actress, née
Marie-Claire Cahen de Labzac, whose rare appearances outside her native France include her role as
Danielle Foussard, the marriage-minded daughter of
Cary GRANT's former criminal accomplices, a worldly
ingenue whose spat with Grace KELLY on the Riviera
coast is a highlight of *TO CATCH A THIEF*.

audience Hitchcock always claimed that everything in his films was planned to draw the audience
into his world. But the contractual arrangement he
presumed between himself and his audience—which
made him feel honor-bound, for example, to go on
making cameo appearances in his movies even after
he tired of them—had several remarkable features.
Because he knew the audience expected each of his
nightmares to have a logical core, he was careful to
motivate his most extravagant fantasies and gave up
the cherished idea of having a corpse tumble out of a
car as it rolled off a Detroit assembly line in *NORTH
BY NORTHWEST* when he could not figure out where
it could have come from. Yet he was perfectly content to leave unanswered the question of how
Madeleine Elster could have vanished from the
McKittrick Hotel in *VERTIGO* while Scottie Ferguson was watching the second floor from the bottom
of the stairs, dismissing concerns about such problems as "the plausibles" or "icebox talk." More generally, because he assumed every audience would react
to each film in the same way, he never spoke of ambiguity or resonance in any of his films, not even *THE
BIRDS*, preferring instead to describe *PSYCHO* as a fun
house that would give the audience (presumably
every audience) exactly the same pleasurable thrills.
Hence the excitement of his well-known remark to
Ernest LEHMAN that some day the seats in theaters
would be wired to stimulate the audience directly
and they could quit making movies altogether. The
monolithic audience Hitchcock posited for his
films—an assumption that seemed justified for many
years by his commercial success—is therefore closely
tied to a monolithic notion of film authorship that
depends on the director's and the audience's complete understanding of each other as rational, predictable, individual agents and therefore paves the
way for the version of auteurism that Hitchcock's
defenders were instrumental in establishing. As that
version of auteurism has declined in favor of more
pluralistic critical approaches, Hitchcock's certainty
that he could identify his audience and predict their
reactions, and the dependence of so many of his films

on effecting the "mass emotion" he was so proud of having achieved in *Psycho,* remain a fascinating and little-remarked anachronism.

Auiler, Dan   American film critic and teacher whose first book, *Vertigo: The Making of a Hitchcock Classic* (St. Martin's, 1998), is a detailed production history of the film from Paramount's purchase of Pierre BOILEAU and Thomas NARCEJAC's *D'entre les morts* in the spring of 1956 to its premiere two years later, illustrated with pre-production sketches, production stills, publicity shots, and reproductions of studio memos. Among its revelations are the changes the story underwent as it went from Maxwell ANDERSON to Alec COPPEL to Samuel TAYLOR, the number of titles considered for the film, and the mechanics behind the famous 360° pan around Scottie and the newly transformed Judy, the nightmare sequence, the title sequence, and the two tower sequences. Especially valuable are a chapter on the film's reception and its later reputation and an interview with James C. KATZ and Robert HARRIS, who supervised the restoration of the film in 1996.

Auiler's second book, *Hitchcock's Notebooks: An Authorized and Illustrated Look Inside the Creative Mind of Alfred Hitchcock* (Avon, 1999), is a fascinating, over-sized scrapbook of production materials from every phase of Hitchcock's career from THE MOUNTAIN EAGLE to FAMILY PLOT, including a great deal of information not readily available elsewhere. Despite its eccentric organization (its chapters follow the sequence of a film production, so that the extensive material on the screenplay of SUSPICION comes long before the production stills from THE 39 STEPS and SABOTAGE), its often arbitrary-seeming inclusions and exclusions (because it reproduces draft sections of screenplays, notes, storyboards, interviews, and preview questionnaires as available, the American films loom much larger than the British, and VERTIGO, NORTH BY NORTHWEST, PSYCHO, THE BIRDS, MARNIE and FRENZY in particular get much more attention than *The 39 Steps,* THE LADY VANISHES, NOTORIOUS, or REAR WINDOW), the frequent reticence of its commentary, and its inaccurate title (it does not reproduce any of Hitchcock's notebooks), it is a trove of material for future scholars unrivaled by any other

single volume. Its long chapter on screenplays (which, despite the wealth of illustrations in later chapters, is the most useful and revealing, as it is the most substantial, of all) includes important material on the evolution of SHADOW OF A DOUBT, THE MAN WHO KNEW TOO MUCH (1956), and *Marnie;* its brief concluding chapter on several unrealized projects is properly tantalizing; and its epilogue, presenting a script for a Hitchcock-guided trailer for SPELL-BOUND, is revelatory. It is likely to occupy the same place in Hitchcock studies that François TRUFFAUT's equally flawed, equally indispensable book-length interview did a generation ago.

Ault,   Marie   (1870–1951)   Doughty stage-trained British character actress, onscreen from 1922, mostly in such comic dialect roles as Rummy Mitchens in *Major Barbara* (1941). As the heroine's mother, Mrs. Bunting, she rented a room to the title character of THE LODGER.

Austin, John (P.)   Veteran Hollywood set decorator whose first project, *A Double Life* (1947), led to more than 60 later films and television programs. At first a specialist in westerns and Eastern exotica, he later worked on a wide variety of projects, including TOPAZ, and served as art director on *What's Up, Doc?* (1972).

auteurism   and   authorship   Before the 1950s, the question of who made movies was resolved by a simple answer—movie studios made movies—and for the most part the only widely recognizable figures associated with filmmaking were actors and actresses. The impetus toward establishing directors as the primary makers of movies came from France, where François TRUFFAUT, in his opposition to the French "tradition of quality" represented by literary adaptations that asked to be judged according to their faithfulness to their sources, championed a *politique des auteurs,* a "position of being in favor of creators," that drew attention to the formative role of film directors. As a director who also functioned as a quasi-independent producer who maintained tight control over his projects from the selection and adaptation of properties to the editing and scoring,

Hitchcock was a natural focus for Truffaut's argument, a director whose involvement in his films might be more important than that of any screenwriter or star and one whose films, taken as a body, could dramatize consistent thematic and technical preoccupations that illuminated each other in the same way as a novelist's or playwright's collected work. In October 1954, André BAZIN's influential journal CAHIERS DU CINÉMA ran a special Hitchcock issue including Bazin's interview with Hitchcock, essays by Truffaut, Claude CHABROL, Jean Domarchi, and others, and a preface by the director himself. Hitchcock's reputation as the auteur of his films was further consolidated, as Robert KAPSIS has noted, by the publication of Chabrol and Eric ROHMER's *Hitchcock: The First Forty-four Films* (1957; English translation, 1978) and Truffaut's book-length interview in French (1966) and English; by the appearance of a widely influential series of articles on "the auteur theory" by Andrew SARRIS and by Sarris's annotated list of Hollywood auteurs and nonauteurs, *The American Cinema: Directors and Directions* (1968); and by the publicity buildup UNIVERSAL gave THE BIRDS, which sought to establish it as a work of serious artistic pretensions without abating its claims to entertainment.

Given the pervasive thematic unity virtually guaranteed by the suspense genre with which his mature work was so closely associated and the unblinking gift for self-publicity that had already made him, along with Cecil B. DeMille, virtually the only widely recognized film director in the world, it is not surprising that Hitchcock swiftly rose to become the quintessential Hollywood auteur—always available with anecdotes about his films and always impressively well informed about every technical device behind them, from framing and cutting to lighting for Technicolor—even if his disinclination to analyze his films or himself in close detail left commentators from Bazin to Lindsay Anderson skeptical. What was considerably more surprising was Hitchcock's staying power in the academy even after auteurism had lost its luster as a critical methodology, supplanted by such anti-intentionalist schools as semiotics, deconstructionism, ideological and psychoanalytic critique, feminism, Queer Theory, and identity politics. Even as they agreed on the death of the author, each of

these schools found new uses not only for NOTORIOUS and VERTIGO and PSYCHO but also for Hitchcock, whether he was a pillar of patriarchy to be saved for feminism, an exemplary illustration of the ways Hollywood demonized homosexuality, or the ultimate brand-name auteur ripe for deconstructing. Though he owed his entrance to whatever respectability academic film studies conferred to auteurism, Hitchcock—if not the ideal film author, obligingly visible and voluble, he so neatly incarnated—seems likely to outlive the school of thought that brought him to the attention of film scholars and, through his example, helped justify the discipline of film studies.

Aventure malgache (Alternative titles: *Malgache aventure, Madagascar Landing*) Phoenix Films, 31 minutes, 1944. **Producer:** British Ministry of Information; **Director:** Alfred Hitchcock; **Screenplay:** J.O.C. Orton and Angus MacPhail, based on an original subject by Arthur Calder-Marshall; **Cinematographer:** Gunther Krampf; **Set decoration:** Charles Gilbert; **Cast:** the Molière Players.

The second of Hitchcock's two Ministry of Information shorts in support of the war effort, shot in French, and intended for French distribution but not shown in France or anywhere else until long after the war, shared virtually the same credits (indeed most of the participants were uncredited; even the actors, a French-language troupe called the MOLIÈRE PLAYERS, declined individual billing) as the first, BON VOYAGE. Both were shot between January 20 and February 25, 1944, and remained rarely seen till they were released on video 50 years later.

The film's story comprises a series of flashbacks framed by the Molière Players' contemporary discussion of their characters' motivations. When one actor confesses that he does not understand the role of Michel, the head of Madagascar's secret service, the actor playing Clarus, the defense attorney, offers to explain Michel more fully. His explanation begins in 1940 with Clarus's courtroom accusations that the Vichy sympathizer Michel has framed and cuckolded his client and proceeds to a series of face-offs in which Michel tries to get evidence of Clarus's

Jailed Resistance lawyer Jacques Clarus watches anxiously from his prison cell for the British warships approaching Madagascar as his cellmate, another uncredited member of the Molière Players, looks on in *Aventure malgache*. *(National Film Society Archive)*

efforts on behalf of the resistance, but he repeatedly fails until Clarus is betrayed by the fiancée of a young man whose escape he is organizing. Thrown into prison, Clarus continues to confound his antagonist, eluding the death penalty, listening intently for signs that the British may be approaching, and encouraging them after he is freed to construct a radio transmitter that can broadcast Allied propaganda. But the transparent show of hypocrisy with which Michel tries to ingratiate himself when the liberators land in May 1942 makes the actor playing him recoil from the role as the film ends. The episodic film, lacking the adventure its title promises, is considerably less successful as melodrama than *Bon voyage,* and its

shelving by the French distributor for whom it had been produced made it unsuccessful as propaganda as well.

awards and nominations   Much has been made, occasionally by the director himself, of Hitchcock's relative neglect by the major English-language cinema awards. It should therefore be noted that the British Academy of Film and Television Arts did not begin its BFA awards until 1952, long after Hitchcock had ceased working regularly in the British industry, where he would have been ideally positioned for those awards; that Hitchcock's Best Director Award from the New York Film Critics Circle for

THE LADY VANISHES marked only the third time the award had been presented and was the first victory for a non-Hollywood director; that Hitchcock's first two American films were nominated for Best Picture Oscars (REBECCA winning the 1940 award) and that he himself was nominated for Best Director five times, beginning with his first American film. Hitchcock's Irving Thalberg Memorial Award, presented at the 1967 Academy Awards, was widely viewed as a consolation prize for his persistent snubbing by Academy voters, as was his National Board of Review Award for Best Director two years later for TOPAZ (!). Here is a comprehensive list arranged chronologically by film, followed by awards and nominations for ALFRED HITCHCOCK PRESENTS and THE ALFRED HITCHCOCK HOUR:

The Lady Vanishes: won the New York Film Critics Circle Award for Best Director of 1938.

Rebecca: won Academy Awards for Best Picture and Best Black-and-White Cinematography of 1940; nominated for Best Direction, Best Actor (Laurence OLIVIER), Best Actress (Joan FONTAINE), Best Supporting Actress (Judith ANDERSON), Best Special Effects, Best Screenplay, Best Film Editing, Best Art Direction, and Best Original Dramatic Score.

Foreign Correspondent: nominated for six 1940 Academy Awards: Best Picture, Best Supporting Actor (Albert BASSERMAN), Best Original Screenplay, Best Black-and-White Cinematography, Best Special Effects, Best Art Direction.

Suspicion: won the New York Film Critics Circle Award and Academy Award for Best Actress of 1941 (Joan Fontaine); nominated for Oscars for Best Picture and Best Dramatic Score.

Shadow of a Doubt: nominated for a 1943 Academy Award for Best Writing (Original Story).

Lifeboat: won the New York Film Critics Circle Award for Best Actress of 1944 (Tallulah BANKHEAD); nominated for Academy Awards for Best Direction, Best Writing (Original Story), and Best Black-and-White Cinematography.

Spellbound: won 1945 Academy Award for Best Original Score (Dramatic or Comedy Picture); nominated for Best Picture, Best Direction, Best Supporting Actor (Michael CHEKHOV), Best Black-and-White Cinematography, and Best Special Effects. Ingrid BERGMAN won the New York Film Critics Circle Award for her roles in Spellbound and The Bells of St. Mary's.

Notorious: nominated for Academy Awards for Best Supporting Actor (Claude RAINS) and Best Original Screenplay of 1946.

The Paradine Case: nominated for 1947 Academy Award for Best Supporting Actress (Ethel BARRYMORE).

Stage Fright: nominated for a 1950 Edgar Allan Poe Award for Best Motion Picture.

Strangers on a Train: nominated for a 1951 Academy Award for Best Black-and-White Cinematography.

Dial M for Murder: Grace KELLY was nominated for a 1954 British Academy Award as Best Foreign Actress, and won the New York Film Critics Circle Award and the National Board of Review Award as Best Actress for her work in Dial M for Murder, Rear Window, and The Country Girl. In addition, John WILLIAMS won the National Board of Review Award for Best Supporting Actor for his work in Dial M for Murder and Sabrina.

Rear Window: nominated for four 1954 Academy Awards: Best Direction, Best Screenplay, Best Color Cinematography, and Best Sound Recording. Nominated for a British Academy Award for Best Film from Any Source. Grace Kelly won the New York Film Critics Circle Award and the National Board of Review Award as Best Actress for her work in Dial M for Murder, Rear Window, and The Country Girl, and John Michael HAYES was nominated for a Writers Guild of America Screen Award for the Best Written American Drama and won an Edgar Allan Poe Award for Best Motion Picture.

To Catch a Thief: won the 1955 Academy Award for Best Color Cinematography; nominated for Best Art Direction (Color) and Best Costume Design (Color). Nominated as well for a Writers Guild of America Screen Award for the Best Written American Comedy and the Golden Lion at the 1955 Venice Film Festival.

The Trouble with Harry: nominated for 1956 British Academy Awards for Best Film from Any Source and Best Foreign Actress (Shirley MACLAINE).

The Man Who Knew Too Much: won 1956 Academy Award for Best Original Song ("Que Sera, Sera").

Vertigo: nominated for 1958 Academy Awards for Best Art Direction and Best Sound. Won the Silver Seashell at the 1958 San Sebastián Film Festival, where James STEWART shared the Zulueta Prize for Best Actor with Kirk Douglas. The remastered rerelease won the New York Film Critics Circle Award for Most Distinguished Reissue of 1996.

North by Northwest: nominated for 1959 Academy Awards for Best Original Screenplay, Best Art Direction (Color), and Best Editing. Won the Silver Seashell at the 1959 San Sebastián Film Festival and the Edgar Allan Poe Award for Best Motion Picture. Nominated for a Writers Guild of America Screen Award for Best Written American Comedy.

Psycho: nominated for four 1960 Academy Awards: Best Direction, Best Supporting Actress (Janet LEIGH), Best Black-and-White Cinematography, Best Art Direction (Black-and-White). Leigh won the 1960 Golden Globe Award for Best Supporting Actress. Nominated for a Writers Guild of America Screen Award for Best Written American Drama; won Edgar Allan Poe Awards for both Robert BLOCH and Joseph STEFANO for Best Motion Picture.

The Birds: nominated for a 1963 Academy Award for Best Special Visual Effects and for the Edgar Allan Poe Award for Best Motion Picture.

Topaz: won 1969 National Board of Review Awards for Best Director and Best Supporting Actor (Philippe NOIRET).

Frenzy: nominated for 1972 Golden Globe Awards for Best Dramatic Film, Best Director, Best Screenplay, and Best Original Score, and for an Edgar Allan Poe Award for Best Motion Picture.

Family Plot: Barbara HARRIS was nominated for a 1976 Golden Globe Award for Best Actress in a Musical or Comedy. Ernest LEHMAN won an Edgar Allan Poe Award for Best Motion Picture and was nominated for a Writers Guild of America Screen Award for Best Comedy Adapted from Another Medium.

Five of Hitchcock's films—*Vertigo* (1989), *Shadow of a Doubt* (1991), *Psycho* (1992), *North by Northwest* (1995), and *Rear Window* (1997)—have been selected for preservation by the National Film Registry of the Library of Congress, and four have been named among the American Film Institute's Top 100 Films of the Century: *Psycho* (#18), *North by Northwest* (#40), *Rear Window* (#42), and *Vertigo* (#61).

Alfred Hitchcock Presents won a 1955 Emmy for Edward W. WILLIAMS's editing of "Breakdown" and was nominated the same year for Best Action or Adventure Series, Best MC or Program Host, and Best Director (for "THE CASE OF MR. PELHAM"). Hitchcock won *Look* Magazine's Television Award as Best Director of the year. The program was voted the Television Champion Award for Best Mystery Program by a poll of TV critics conducted by *Television Almanac.*

The following year, the program won an Emmy for Best Teleplay Writing (James P. CAVANAGH for "Fog Closing In") and was nominated for Best Series (Half-Hour or Less) and Best Male Personality (Continuing Performance). *Look* named the program the Best Dramatic Series (One-Half Hour) of 1956, and it won a second Television Champion Award as Best Mystery Program.

In 1957, the program won an Emmy for Best Direction (Robert Stevens for "The Glass Eye") and was nominated for Best Dramatic Anthology Series. The Golden Globe Awards named the series one of the four Best Television Programs of 1957, and *Look* once again named the program television's Best Dramatic Series (One-Half Hour).

The program was nominated for three 1958 Emmies: Best Dramatic Series (Less Than One Hour), Best Direction of a Single Program on a Dramatic Series (Alfred Hitchcock for "LAMB TO THE SLAUGHTER"), and Best Writing of a Single Program on a Dramatic Series (Roald DAHL for "Lamb to the Slaughter").

In 1959, the program was nominated for two Emmies: Outstanding Achievement in Art Direction and Scenic Design (John J. LLOYD) and Outstanding Achievement in Film Editing for Television (Edward W. Williams for "Man from the South").

The following year, Edward W. Williams received an Emmy nomination for Outstanding

Achievement in Film Editing for Television for "Incident in a Small Jail," and the series won its third Television Champion Award as Best Mystery Program of 1960.

James BRIDGES's work on "The Jar" earned *The Alfred Hitchcock Hour's* sole Emmy nomination for Outstanding Writing Achievement in Drama (Adaptation) in 1963, the same year the series won its fourth Television Champion Award as Best Mystery Program.

Ayrton, Randle (1869–1940) Craggy British character actor, in films as performer and director from 1917, whose many portraits of authoritarian patriarchs include the heroine's father, Caesar Cregeen, in THE MANXMAN.

Backes, Alice (1923–) American character actress, in films and (especially) television from 1953. She appeared as Jennifer Gifford in the ALFRED HITCHCOCK PRESENTS episode "Cheap Is Cheap" (1959) and in five segments of THE ALFRED HITCH-COCK HOUR: as a police officer in "The Lonely Hours" (1963), Mrs. Tridden in "The Jar" (1964), Miss Hinchley in "Bed of Roses" (1964), a doctor in "Consider Her Ways" (1964), and Helen Fiske in "The Second Wife" (1965). She was also cast as Aunt Pauline in "INCIDENT AT A CORNER," the Hitchcock-directed episode of FORD STARTIME.

"Back for Christmas" 23rd episode of *Alfred Hitchcock Presents,* broadcast March 4, 1956. **Associate producer:** Joan Harrison; **Director:** Alfred Hitchcock; **Assistant director:** Richard Birnie; **Teleplay:** Francis Cockrell, based on the story by John Collier; **Cinematographer:** John L. Russell; **Art director:** Martin Obzina; **Set designer:** Ralph Sylos; **Costumes:** Vincent Dee; **Editors:** Richard G. Wray and Edward W. Williams; **Music:** Stanley Wilson; **Cast:** John Williams (Herbert Carpenter), Isobel Elsom (Hermione Carpenter), A.E. Gould-Porter (Major Sinclair), Lily Kemble-Cooper (Mrs. Sinclair), Gavin Muir (Mr. Wallingford), Katherine Warren (Mrs. Wallingford), Gerald Hamer (Mr. Hewitt), Irene Tedrow (Mrs. Hewitt), Ross Ford (American partner), Theresa Harris (American maid), Mollie Glessing (Elsie).

The fourth episode Hitchcock directed for the first season of his television program stars the imperturbable John Williams as henpecked Herbert Carpenter, who kills his wife Hermione the day they are to leave for a California trip, buries her body in the cellar of their house, and then makes the trip himself, convinced he has committed the perfect crime, only to be caught by a letter from a construction company promising to begin work on a surprise gift she had arranged for him before her demise: a wine cellar excavated in their basement.

Bacon, Irving (1893–1965) Stage-trained Hollywood character actor, brother of director Lloyd Bacon, specializing in comic rural types. Among his hundreds of film and television appearances from 1927 through 1958, he played the station master in SHADOW OF A DOUBT and the railroad ticket taker whose startled reaction shot is the final image in SPELLBOUND.

Baer, Donald American filmmaker who acted as assistant director on a single film, TORN CURTAIN, and unit production manager on a single television movie, Don Siegel's *Stranger on the Run* (1967).

Bagdasarian, Ross (1919–1972) Singing American bit player and songwriter who appeared in a handful of films between 1952 and 1957, including a role as the composer in *REAR WINDOW*, before conceiving the idea of playing recorded music back at a higher speed to create the figures of Alvin and the Chipmunks, whose cartoon adventures he voiced as David Seville.

Bailey, Raymond (1904–1980) American actor, fired from his first movie job as a laborer when he was caught sneaking into a mob shot. He later went on to become a banker and laborer but returned to Hollywood in 1938 for a long succession of character roles, including Scottie Ferguson's doctor in *VERTIGO*. He appeared in nine segments of *ALFRED HITCHCOCK PRESENTS*—as Ed Johnson in "Breakdown," Dr. Harley in "The Case of Mr. Pelham," Jeff in "Portrait of Jocelyn" (1956), Inspector Braun in "Miss Paisley's Cat" (1957), Dr. Jason in "Sylvia" (1958), Herbert Guild in "Disappearing Trick" (1958), Mr. Harris in "Backward, Turn Backward" (1960), Mr. Watkins in "The Five-Forty-Eight" (1960), and the doctor in "Where Beauty Lies" (1962)—and returned as Allie Saxon in "A Piece of the Action" (1962), the opening episode of *THE ALFRED HITCHCOCK HOUR*, before settling for a long run (1962–71) into the role of Milburn Drysdale, banker to television's Beverly Hillbillies.

Bakaleinikoff, Constantine (1898–1966) Russian-born Hollywood composer and conductor, trained at the Moscow Conservatory, who during a 30-year Hollywood career (1929–57) worked at PARAMOUNT and MGM before rising to become head of RKO's music department (1941–52), where he directed the scores for hundreds of films, including *NOTORIOUS*, and composed three dozen of his own.

Baker, Art (1898–1966) Reassuringly strong-voiced American film, radio, and television actor, born Arthur Shank, in Hollywood from 1937, who played Lt. Cooley, one of the police officers pursuing John Ballantine in *SPELLBOUND*.

Baker, Diane (1938–) Pert American actress, typically in second leads, occasional director and producer. After her debut as the heroine's sister in *The Diary of Anne Frank* (1959), she soon became a staple

of films and television, playing Lil Mainwaring, Mark Rutland's scheming sister-in-law, in *MARNIE*.

Baker, Fay (1894–1954) Hollywood actress, generally cast as the heroine's mother, sister, or confidante, whose relatively brief and late-blooming film career began with the role of Ethel, Ingrid BERGMAN's party guest in the opening of *NOTORIOUS*.

Balcon, (Sir) Michael (1896–1977) Film distributor turned producer, a giant in the British film industry and perhaps the key figure in Hitchcock's early career. He hired Hitchcock as assistant director on his own first film, *WOMAN TO WOMAN*, in 1922 and then watched in amazement as the ambitious neophyte volunteered to contribute to the script and art direction as well. At GAINSBOROUGH (which he founded in 1924) and GAUMONT-BRITISH, he continued to encourage Hitchcock, giving him his first directing job on *THE PLEASURE GARDEN* before producing or executive producing *THE MOUNTAIN EAGLE, THE LODGER, DOWNHILL*, and *EASY VIRTUE*. Soon after Hitchcock departed for BRITISH INTERNATIONAL, Balcon was named head of production for Gaumont-British, where he supervised a massive production schedule that helped ensure the survival of the British industry in the wake of competition from Hollywood. Among the 30 films he produced, often without screen credit, at Gaumont-British between 1934 and 1936 were *THE MAN WHO KNEW TOO MUCH, THE 39 STEPS, SECRET AGENT*, and *SABOTAGE*. He was appointed head of production for MGM-British in 1936 and for Ealing in 1938. After Hitchcock departed for the United States to work for David O. SELZNICK on the eve of World War II, Balcon, who had remained behind, wrote a 1940 newspaper article titled "DESERTERS!" condemning an unnamed "plump junior technician" who had become "one of most famous directors" as a deserter who "prefer[s] to remain in Hollywood instead of returning home to aid [his] country's war efforts." Hitchcock responded with an angry riposte, and the rift between the director and his former mentor continued unmended for 25 years, during which time Balcon produced such varied films as *Dead of Night* (1945), *Nicholas Nickleby* (1947), *Scott of the*

Michael Balcon

last silent, in which she played the nameless hero-ine—a madcap heiress whose ebullient spirit is tested when she loses all her money—before making the transition to occasional talkies, some of which were produced by her own company.

Balmain, Pierre (1924–1982) Parisian coutu-rier who opened his own house in 1945. His designs decorated some 20 films, divided about equally between French and American productions, from 1951. He is credited with fashioning the costumes designed by Edith HEAD and Peter SALDUTTI for *TOPAZ*.

Balsam, Martin (1919–1996) Durable Amer-ican character actor, a familiarly reassuring presence on stage, screen, and television. Trained at the Actors Studio, he made his uncredited film debut in *On the Waterfront* (1954) and his television debut that same year in *The Greatest Gift* (1954–55). Impressed by his performance as Eldon Marsh in "The Equalizer," a 1958 episode of ALFRED HITCHCOCK PRESENTS, the director cast him as Milton Arbogast, the ill-fated private eye in PSYCHO, and he later appeared as Leonard Thompson in the 1961 *Alfred Hitchcock Presents* episode "Final Arrangements." He won an Academy Award for *A Thousand Clowns* (1965) and a Tony for *You Know I Can't Hear You When the Water's Running* (1967).

Bancroft, George (1882–1956) Stalwart Amer-ican character actor with musical stage experience, in Hollywood from 1921, who shot to fame as virile, gentlemanly gangster Bull Weed in *Underworld* (1927) and was nominated for an Oscar when he virtually reprised the same role as Jim Lang in *Thunderbolt* (1929). Familiar to audiences for dozens of perform-ances as manly sheriffs, soldiers, and adventurers, he was equally at home in tough or villainous roles. His one bit in a Hitchcock film is as the second stranger in THE SKIN GAME.

"Bang! You're Dead" 229th episode of *Alfred Hitchcock Presents,* broadcast October 17, 1961. **Producer:** Joan Harrison; **Associate producer:** Norman Lloyd; **Director:** Alfred Hitchcock; **Assistant director:** Wallace Worsley; **Teleplay:** Henry Swanson, based on the story by

Antarctic (1948), and a string of Ealing comedies: *Whisky Galore!* (1949), *Passport to Pimlico* (1949), *Kind Hearts and Coronets* (1949), *The Man in the White Suit* (1951), *The Lavender Hill Mob* (1951), and *The Ladykillers* (1955). In later years, Balcon worked as an independent producer, joining several ex-Eal-ing colleagues to form Bryanston Films, and serving as chairman of British Lion (1964–68) and the Experimental Film Fund of the British Film Insti-tute (1968–72), and it was during this period that he and Hitchcock met again on cordial terms at a din-ner in 1966.

Balfour, Betty (1903–1977) Flapper comedi-enne, onscreen from 1920, who first achieved popu-larity in such British silent films as CHAMPAGNE, her

Margery Vosper; **Cinematographer:** John L. Russell; **Art director:** Martin Obzina; **Set designers:** John McCarthy and Julia Heron; **Costumes:** Vincent Dee; **Editors:** David O'Connell and Edward W. Williams; **Music:** Joseph Romero; **Cast:** Biff Elliott (Fred Chester), Lucy Prentiss (Amy Chester), Billy Mumy (Jackie Chester), Steve Dunne (Rick Sheffield), Kelly Flynn (Stevie), Dean Moray (Gary), Juanita Moore (Cleo), Karl Lukas (mailman), Olan Soulé (Darlene's dad), Joy Ellison, Scott Davey, Craig Duncan (George Webster), Mary Grace Canfield (customer), Thayer Burton (cashier), John Zaremba (supermarket manager), Marta Kristen (Jiffy Snack Girl).

The second episode from the program's seventh season and the final episode Hitchcock directed when he substituted for the ailing director originally assigned the segment, this teleplay traces the path of the loaded gun young Jackie Chester innocently borrows from his visiting Uncle Rick, who has promised him a special present. Frantically pursued by his parents, Jackie wanders around the neighborhood, pointing the gun at his mailman, taking it into a supermarket, and finally firing it at Cleo, the family maid, when she says she's too busy to play with him.

Bankhead, Tallulah (1903–1968) Storied stage actress whose infrequent screen roles include Connie Porter, the hard-bitten reporter who heads the cast of LIFEBOAT. Daughter of the late speaker of the U.S. House of Representatives, she capped her convent education by winning a local beauty contest, moving to New York, and making her Broadway debut at 16. A star in London's West End almost from the moment she arrived in 1923, she took the leading role in the original stage production of *Blackmail* (1928) and made two films in England before returning to the New York stage in 1930, when a PARAMOUNT PICTURES contract led to a brief flurry of indifferent films. A legend in the theater not only for her incisive performances but also for her well-advertised private life, she was noted for her hard drinking and drug use ("Cocaine isn't habit forming," she once memorably said. "I should know—I've been using it for years"), her endless parties, her untrammeled sex life, her penchant for greeting interviewers in the nude, and her trademark foghorn

"Hello, dahling." But although she won the New York Film Critics Circle Award for *Lifeboat,* her success led only to the film role of Catherine the Great in *A Royal Scandal* (1945). None of her film performances made the impression of her work on stage or captured the mercurial, oversized personality her fans loved to be scandalized by.

Banks, Leslie (1890–1952) Veteran stage actor, director, and producer. Despite his casting in a bit part in *Experience* (1921), he was unable to break into the British film industry, and so went to Hollywood, where he made his mark at 42 as General Zaroff in *The Most Dangerous Game* (1932) before returning to success across a broad range of character types in his native land. Equally at home in gentlemanly and character roles, he starred as Bob Lawrence, the ultimate stiff-upper-lip British father whose daughter was kidnapped in THE MAN WHO KNEW TOO MUCH, and returned in the featured role of the smuggler Joss Merlyn, almost unrecognizable beneath his grotesque makeup, in JAMAICA INN, when Charles LAUGHTON, whose company had bought the property, decided he wanted to play the lead villain instead.

"Banquo's Chair" 144th episode of *Alfred Hitchcock Presents,* broadcast May 3, 1959. **Producer:** Joan Harrison; **Associate producer:** Norman Lloyd; **Director:** Alfred Hitchcock; **Assistant director:** Hilton Green; **Teleplay:** Francis Cockrell, based on the story by Rupert Croft-Cooke; **Cinematographer:** John L. Russell; **Art director:** John Lloyd; **Set designer:** George Milo; **Costumes:** Vincent Dee; **Editors:** Richard G. Wray and Edward W. Williams; **Music:** Frederick Herbert; **Cast:** John Williams (ex-Inspector William Brent), Kenneth Haigh (John Bedford), Reginald Gardiner (Major Cooke-Finch), Max Adrian (Robert Stone), George Pelling (butler), Tom P. Dillon (Sgt. Balter), Hilda Plowright (May Thorpe).

For the third time in the television series, Hitchcock directs John Williams, this time as retired Scotland Yard inspector Brent, who, lacking the evidence to convict John Bedford of murdering his aunt for her money, invites Bedford to a party at which actress May Thorpe will impersonate the ghost of his late aunt. The ghost is so compelling that the terrified Bedford bursts out with a confession, but the story ends with the delayed arrival of Thorpe, asking if she is too late for the dinner—and leaving the episode with a rare whiff of the supernatural at work.

Banton, Travis (1894–1958)   Costume designer who began his career in New York before leaving in 1924 for Hollywood. At Paramount he designed the seductive, often outrageous fashions so vital to the allure of Marlene DIETRICH and Mae West. Forced out of the studio by his drinking in 1938, he had no trouble finding other work and was credited by the time of his retirement in 1951 on more than 100 films, including *Intermezzo* (1939), *The Mark of Zorro* (1940), *Blood and Sand* (1941), *Cover Girl* (1944), *A Double Life* (1947), *Letter from an Unknown Woman* (1948), and his single Hitchcock film, THE PARADINE CASE.

Barbour, Joyce (1901–1977)   British supporting actress whose dozen roles (1920–64) included Renee, the ticket-taker in the Verlocs' movie theater in *SABOTAGE*.

Barclay, Jerry   American supporting actor of the later fifties who went from *The Man with the Golden Arm* (1955) to a half-dozen second features and a pair of television credits as George Princey in the *ALFRED HITCHCOCK PRESENTS* segment "WET SATURDAY" and Peters in "I Killed the Count" (1957).

Baring, Norah (1907–)   Delicate British leading lady who began her career in German silents before her brief return as a star in her native country. Her role as Diana Baring, the wrongly accused heroine of *MURDER*!, virtually recapitulates her preceding performance in *Mystery at the Villa Rose* (1930). She retired from the screen in 1934.

Barnes, George (1892–1953)   Veteran American cinematographer noted for the distinguished company he kept. During a 30-year career spanning more than 100 films, he worked with Fred Niblo (*The Haunted Bedroom*, 1919), King Vidor (*Dusk to Dawn*, 1922), Fritz Lang (*The Return of Frank James*, 1940), Frank Capra (*Meet John Doe*, 1941), Ernst Lubitsch (*That Uncertain Feeling*, 1941), Billy Wilder (*The Emperor Waltz*, 1948), Robert Siodmak *The File on Thelma Jordan*, 1949), and Cecil B. DeMille (*Samson and Delilah*, 1949; *The Greatest Show on Earth*, 1952) as well as Hitchcock. He won an Academy Award for his black-and-white cinematography for *REBECCA* and was nominated for five other Oscars, including two in 1946, one for his color photography of *The Spanish Main* (1945), the other for his black-and-white work on *SPELLBOUND*. He was married seven times, once (1932–36) to actress Joan Blondell.

Barr, Charles   British film historian, professor of Film Studies at the University of East Anglia, whose books *Ealing Studios* (1977) and *All Our Yesterdays: 90 Years of British Cinema* (1986) seek to provide an authoritative historical survey of British cinema. His *English Hitchcock* (Cameron & Hollis, 1999), the first volume since Maurice YACOWAR's *Hitchcock's British Films* to be devoted entirely to an analysis of Hitchcock's first 23 films, focuses on two leading arguments, correcting what he sees as the continuing excesses of AUTEURISM and Hollywood universalism: the specific nationalism of the director's early work, which Barr prefers to describe as "English" rather than the more generic "British"; and the close professional relationships Hitchcock developed with the screenwriters on whom he depended throughout his career (despite his customary dismissal of their contributions to the films he preferred to think of as "PURE CINEMA" and his sole creations) to provide his films with a clear sequence of events, an effective dramatic structure, and a core of thematic logic (all features Hitchcock was unable or unwilling to emphasize himself). Although his analysis of the staircase sequence in THE LODGER and his detailed comparison of the silent and sound versions of *BLACKMAIL* show that he can read individual films as closely and persuasively as any earlier commentator, he is more interested in the larger shape of the director's early career, which he divides into periods dominated by successive screenwriting collaborators: Eliot STANNARD, Alma REVILLE, and Charles BENNETT. Noting that critics have often credited Hitchcock for motifs like the incessant theatricality of MURDER! and the innocents-abroad tenor of RICH AND STRANGE that are already present in his screenplays or his literary sources, and contending that such films as THE RING on which Hitchcock is the dominant scenarist are among his weakest, collapsing into a pile of memorable moments without any strong armature that would hold them all together, Barr argues for a reassessment of Hitchcock's collaborators, especially the obscure Stannard, and for a more nuanced conception of film authorship generally. The appended filmography includes many informative asides on screenwriters and other collaborators and the most careful compilations of screen credits to be found in any volume on Hitchcock. Barr's latest book is *Vertigo*, forthcoming from the British Film Institute.

Barrett, Laurinda (1939–) American screen and television actress who first appeared as Constance Willis in THE WRONG MAN. Her relatively few subsequent roles include a bit in *A Perfect Murder* (1998), the remake of DIAL M FOR MURDER.

Barrett, Leslie (1919–) American actor who had made irregular screen appearances, mostly on television, from 1956, for example as Batie on the FORD STARTIME segment "INCIDENT AT A CORNER."

Barron, Marcus (1868–1944) Occasional British actor who debuted as Dreschler in WALTZES FROM VIENNA and returned in two later films, *Loyalties* (1934) and *The Two of Us* (1938).

Barry, Joan (1903–1989) Sweetly appealing British star who had appeared in only two films when Hitchcock, asked to make BLACKMAIL into a talkie, had her dub the speaking voice of his star Anny ONDRA, whose thick Czech accent made her unsuitable for the role of London shopgirl Alice White. Though Barry is never visible in the film, not even on the credits, her presence is often telegraphed by Ondra's emphatic gazes offscreen just before she lip-synchs her lines. Barry's voice was reunited with her face in nine later films, of which RICH AND STRANGE, in which she plays the dazzled middle-class housewife Emily Hill, who discovers some hard

truths about her marriage and herself during a providentially financed cruise, is one of the last.

Barrymore, Ethel (1879–1959) Nonpareil American stage actress, born Ethel Mae Blythe to a distinguished theatrical family. Onstage from 1893, she appeared in her first Broadway starring role in 1900. Indisputably the preeminent American stage actress of her day, she appeared in a dozen films between 1914 and 1919, when, unimpressed by Hollywood, she returned to the stage except for *Rasputin and the Empress* (1932), in which she starred with her brothers Lionel and John, collectively dubbed "the Royal Family of Broadway." Unwilling to submit to the star regimen at MGM, she soon departed again, but in 1944

Ethel Barrymore

she was back in Hollywood as Cary GRANT's Cockney mother in *None But the Lonely Heart,* a performance that won her an Academy Award, and thereafter she settled into a long tenure playing grandes dames, imperious mothers, businesswomen with hearts of gold, and characters of greater vulnerability, among them Sophie Horfield, the endlessly supplicating wife of the sadistic judge in *THE PARADINE CASE.*

Basevi, James (1890–1962) Veteran Anglo-American art director and special effects designer, in Hollywood since 1924. During the transition to sound, he became head of MGM's special effects department, where he created the climactic earthquake sequence for *San Francisco* (1936) before moving over to 20TH CENTURY–FOX PICTURES to design the equally stirring climax for *The Hurricane* (1937). Returning to the Fox art department in 1939, he was responsible for designing many of the studio's most prestigious productions, from *Tobacco Road* (1941) and *The Keys of the Kingdom* (1944), for which he received Oscar nominations, to *The Song of Bernadette* (1943), for which he shared an Academy Award with William Darling. Perhaps his greatest challenge was making the studio tank in which *LIFEBOAT* was shot look interesting and convincing. In addition to his work at Fox, he also served as art director on many other productions, including the Selznick-produced *Duel in the Sun* (1946).

Bass, Saul (1920–1996) American graphic designer and occasional documentary director, long active in Hollywood and industry, who has created logos for many products and displays but is still best remembered for his many innovative film title sequences. Shortly after his first such sequence for *Carmen Jones* (1954), Bass made his mark with the innovatively gritty titles for *The Man with the Golden Arm* (1955) and the decorative endpapers for *Around the World in 80 Days* (1956). For 20 years his title designs for films as different as *Anatomy of a Murder* (1959), *West Side Story* (1961), and *The Age of Innocence* (1993) were unrivaled for their ability to capture the atmosphere of the films they introduced. Among Bass's most celebrated sequences are the three he created for Hitchcock. The haunting titles for *VERTIGO*, discovering a world of revolving spirals inside the heroine's eye, lays the groundwork for two of the film's leading visual and psychological motifs. The witty geometric design of *NORTH BY NORTHWEST*, which turns out to mark a grid for the glass-mirrored skyscraper on which the film's bustling opening tableau is reflected, suggests that even Cary GRANT may be an anonymous man in the crowd, perhaps nothing more than a reflection of someone else. Finally, the stark black-and-white horizontals that race across the screen at the opening of *PSYCHO* establish the turbulent duality of the film's obsession with moral absolutes even as it slyly indicates the difficulty of reducing moral questions to such simplistic terms. Bass was also billed as a pictorial consultant on *Psycho,* as on many of his 50 other films, and he storyboarded the film's shower sequence. To the end of his life, he maintained that he, not Hitchcock, had shot the sequence, but as Stephen REBELLO reports, his memories have been disputed by Janet LEIGH, screenwriter Joseph STEFANO, script supervisor Marshal Schlom, and assistant director Hilton GREEN.

Basserman, Albert (1867–1952) Stage-trained German actor who worked with theatrical director Max Reinhardt between 1909 and 1915 and made his film debut in 1913. His distinguished position in the German industry was threatened by Hitler's rise to power, and he fled to Switzerland in 1933, arriving in Hollywood in 1939. Of his two dozen performances in American films, his signature role is the Oscar-nominated Van Meer, the assassinated diplomat who refuses to stay dead in *FOREIGN CORRESPONDENT.*

Bates, A(lbert) S(idney) (1909–1976) Veteran British editor, also known as Bert Bates. In the later thirties he became supervising editor for WARNER BROS.' English operation; in that capacity he supervised the editing of nearly 50 British and international films, including *UNDER CAPRICORN,* and served as production manager on two more.

Bates, Charles Hollywood child actor of the 1940s who played Charlie Newton's kid brother Roger in *SHADOW OF A DOUBT* but did not mature into adult roles.

Bates, Florence (1888–1954)   American character actress with an unusually forceful line on dowagers. Born Florence Rabe, she studied law and was the first woman admitted to the Texas bar in 1914. Despite her success in law and business, however, she developed an unshakable fascination with the theater and enrolled at the age of 47 as a student at the Pasadena Playhouse. Her minor film roles brought her to the attention of Hitchcock, who chose her to play Joan FONTAINE's formidable employer Edythe Van Hopper in REBECCA—the only American besides Fontaine herself in the cast. Until her death the imposing Bates continued to play matronly types, monstrous or maternal, in more than 50 films.

Bates, Michael (1920–1978)   Mild-mannered British film and television actor, born in India, onscreen from 1954. A specialist in dim police officers like Inspector Reggie Clarke in *Bedazzled* (1967), he played Alec MCCOWEN's deferential subordinate Sergeant Spearman in FRENZY.

Bates, Norman   Shy, boyish, psychotic hero of PSYCHO, keeper of the most famous hotel in all fiction, the one character in Hitchcock's films whose fame has eclipsed the director's. Given the director's success as his own best publicist from early in his career, it is not surprising that Hitchcock's face and figure, at a time of anonymity for the great majority of studio filmmakers, became better known than those of many of his stars, certainly than the names and qualities of the fictional characters they played in his films. Although a few characters like the never-seen Rebecca de Winter (from REBECCA) and the professional rivals Johan Strauss, Sr. and Jr. (from WALTZES FROM VIENNA) arrived in Hitchcock's films already trailing the celebrity conferred by their best-selling literary sources or their historical actuality, and although such stars as Cary GRANT and James STEWART, Ingrid BERGMAN and Grace KELLY, were instantly recognizable, Hitchcock himself was nearly always more memorable than any individual character his films or their stars created. The great exception is Norman Bates. The gangly hotel-keeper/murderer played by Anthony Perkins has long since entered the American popular imagination, and because he is unique among even such notable Hitchcock heroes and heroines as Scottie Ferguson, Alicia Huberman, and Roger Thornhill in achieving such name recognition—even among people who have never seen his movie or its sequels, its prequel, or its remake—it is worth asking why.

Hitchcock has never been known as a creator of particularly memorable characters, and Norman, though his initial pleasantness is deceiving, lacks even the complexity of Scottie or Alicia. Like the two most widely identified characters in English-language fiction, Tarzan and Sherlock Holmes, Norman is iconic rather than psychological, a mythic figure rather than a realistic or compelling character. Except in the film's chilling final sequence, Norman is never presented from inside, only in his interactions with other characters (though his conversations with his mother turn out to be broadly deceptive), and usually characterized through other characters' reactions to him. The film's celebrated surprise—that Norman, driven by guilt at murdering his mother years ago to assume her identity, has killed the victims he blames on her—does not so much deepen or complicate his personality as depersonalize him entirely, suggesting that the smiling youth who asked Marion Crane if she'd like to stay in his parlor a little longer, "just for talk," is actually a bogeyman, a villain/victim whose relation to his postmodern place in history is as iconic as Tarzan and Holmes were to readers hungry for heroes yet suspicious of them in the twilight of the British Empire. In Norman, the split between the heroic status of Tarzan and Holmes, which renders them sympathetic, and their outsider status widens to the point of fracturing. Like his Hollywood successors Michael Corleone and Hannibal Lecter, Norman is a fitting hero for a culture that believes more deeply in villains.

Bath, Hubert (1883–1945)   British composer and music arranger whose first film was BLACKMAIL. He was a staple at GAUMONT-BRITISH, where his work, as on THE 39 STEPS, was frequently uncredited but achieved a compensating measure of fame when parts of his concertante *Cornish Rhapsody* were performed in *Love Story* (1944).

Bau, Gordon (1907–1975)   American makeup artist, born Robert Blau. In Hollywood from 1938, he worked on some 40 films before settling in 1951 at WARNER BROS., where he supervised the makeup for STRANGERS ON A TRAIN, I CONFESS, DIAL M FOR MURDER, and THE WRONG MAN, among more than 100 others through *Dirty Harry*.

Bavier, Frances (1902–1989) American character actress, a specialist in outdoorswomen and Southerners. After extensive stage experience (1925–51), she made her film debut in *The Day the Earth Stood Still* (1951) but remains best known from her work on television, where she played the Spans' neighbor Mrs. Ferguson in the ALFRED HITCHCOCK PRESENTS episode "REVENGE" and several celebrated roles in long-running series, especially Aunt Bee in *The Andy Griffith Show* (1960–68) and *Mayberry RFD* (1968–70).

Baxter, Alan (1908–1976) American actor, combining film work with frequent television appearances. In Hollywood from 1935, he alternated leads in B-pictures with supporting roles in top-drawer productions, as in his portrayal of the soft-spoken Freeman, the second-string Nazi spy in SABOTEUR. Later he appeared as Sheriff Andy Willett in the ALFRED HITCHCOCK PRESENTS episode "Backward, Turn Backward" (1960) and as Mr. Baldwin in THE ALFRED HITCHCOCK HOUR segment "Crimson Witness" (1965).

Baxter, Anne (1923–1985) Demure American leading lady with stage experience who achieved her greatest fame not long after her Hollywood debut in 1940 when, in rapid succession, she was plucked from obscurity to play the ingenue in *The Magnificent Ambersons* (1942), offered the lead role in *The North Star* (1943), and awarded an Oscar for her work in *The Razor's Edge* (1946). Married to actor John HODIAK from 1947 to 1953, she achieved her greatest success as the peerlessly treacherous Eve Harrington in *All About Eve* (1950). Following her Oscar nomination for that film, WARNER BROS. cast her as Ruth Grandfort, Father Michael Logan's former love, in I CONFESS, over the objections of Hitchcock, who had wanted Anita Björk. After her last important Hollywood performance as the Egyptian empress Nefretiri in *The Ten Commandments* (1956), her film roles

began to be outnumbered by her television roles. Among the latter was a star turn as Janice Brandt, the lover inveigled into murder in "A Nice Touch," a 1963 episode of THE ALFRED HITCHCOCK HOUR.

Beaird, Barbara American actress whose brief career (1957–61) in cinema and television included the role of Mary Jane Ryder in the FORD STARTIME segment "INCIDENT AT A CORNER."

Beeding, Francis Joint pseudonym of John Leslie Palmer (1885–1944) and Hilary Aiden St. George Saunders (1898–1951), both graduates of Baliol College, Oxford, who met while working for the League of Nations in Geneva and collaborated on a series of more than 30 mysteries and spy stories, of which the best-known is *Death Walks in Eastrepps* (1931). *The House of Dr. Edwardes* (1927), a wild tale of terror at a mental asylum, became the basis for SPELLBOUND, with a psychoanalytic detective story substituting for its neo-gothic hints of Satanic possession and the supernatural.

Beeson, Paul (1921–) British cinematographer who, soon after serving as a camera operator on UNDER CAPRICORN and two other films, became a lighting cinematographer and second-unit cinematographer on more than 60 films, from *The Cruel Sea* (1953) to *The Lost World* (1992).

Bel Geddes, Barbara (1922–) American actress, née Barbara Geddes Lewis, with theatrical family roots. Her greatest successes were on stage—a New York Drama Critics Circle Award for *Deep Are the Roots* (1945) and Tony nominations for *Cat on a Hot Tin Roof* (1955) and *Mary, Mary* (1961)—and television—her long reign as Miss Ellie, matriarch of the Ewing clan in *Dallas* (1978–84, 1985–90). But her film appearances, though relatively few, were notable. She was proclaimed a star shortly after her Hollywood debut in *The Long Night* (1947) and was nominated for an Academy Award for *I Remember Mama* (1948). Her later films included *Caught* (1949), *Panic in the Streets* (1950), *Fourteen Hours* (1951), and VERTIGO, in which she played Midge Wood, whose quiet devotion to Scottie Ferguson remains unrequited. In addition, she starred in four episodes of ALFRED HITCHCOCK PRESENTS: as Lucia Clay in "FOGHORN" (1958), as Mary Maloney in "LAMB TO THE SLAUGHTER" (1958)—perhaps the most memorable performance in the entire series—as Helen Brewster in "The Morning of the Bride" (1959), and as Sybilla Meades in "Sybilla" (1960).

Bellour, Raymond French film theorist who is director of research at the Centre National de la Recherche Scientifique and a founding coeditor of the journal *Traffic*. His seminal essays on Hitchcock and Fritz Lang, which applied psychoanalytic semiotics to cinema with unprecedented concentration, were collected in *L'analyse du film* (Albatros, 1979; second edition, Calmann-Lévy, 1995). For Bellour, Hitchcock is the supreme enunciator of Hollywood codes whose narrative and visual patterns, from the smallest to the largest, are designed specifically to regulate (and so limit) the audience's awareness of the cinematic apparatus and the "Oedipal trajectory" it obsessively reenacts to inscribe the audience ideologically into the narrative system. Bellour's project is to expose the gaps and inconsistencies each film papers over to restore the audience to a sense of coherence and unity with the narrated world, and he attacks this project with a ferocious attention to detail in essays on PSYCHO, THE BIRDS, MARNIE, and, most notoriously, NORTH BY NORTHWEST in a 100-page essay, half of whose length is an exhaustive shot-by-shot analysis recovering the Oedipal trajectory from the micropatterns of the cornfield sequence. Although he has been one of a handful of commentators from Robin WOOD to Slavoj ŽIŽEK who have moved from close analyses of Hitchcock's work to decisive interventions in film theory, Bellour's more recent work has shifted focus from mainstream Hollywood films to art videos; asserting in "L'analyse flambée" (1985) that film analysis was "an art without a future," he advocated a turn from the analyses of entire films with a view toward explicating their individual projects to a focus on analyzing only those sequences that were important in formulating or resolving specific theoretical problems, and he displayed his own new interest in video in a 1989 exhibition, *Passages de l'image*. Constance Penley has edited an English translation of most of the contents of Bellour's 1980 volume as *The Analysis of Film* (Indiana, 2000), dropping four brief essays, one of them on Hitchcock, and including one slightly more recent essay, "To Alternate/To Narrate." His other books include *Le western* (1966), *Le cinéma américain: Analyses de film* (two volumes, 1980), and *Jean-Luc Godard: Son + Image* (1992), three collections that he edited and to which he contributed, and two collections of his own work, *L'entre-image: Photo, cinéma, vidéo* (1990) and *L'entre-images 2: Mots, images* (1999).

Belton, John American film scholar, professor of English at Rutgers University and author of *Cinema Stylists* (Scarecrow, 1983), *Widescreen Cinema* (1992), and *American Cinema/American Culture* (1994). His *Alfred Hitchcock's* Rear Window (Cambridge University Press, 2000) collects five new essays from different perspectives—Scott Curtis's production history, Elise Lemire's treatment of voyeurism to revisit gender dynamics, Sarah Street's consideration of the part fashion plays in the role's construction of femininity, Michel Chion's analysis of the story's topographical space, and Armond White's discussion of the film in the context of American political culture in the fifties—bracketed by four reviews from 1954 and Belton's own introduction, which emphasizes the film's formal patterning and its many borrowings, documented by Steve Cohen, from the romance between Ingrid BERGMAN and photographer Robert Capa. Belton has published a more detailed analysis of the film as "The Space of *Rear Window*" in RAUBICHECK and SREBNICK.

Benchley, Robert (1889–1945) Portly, amiably dour American humorist and screenwriter who improbably became familiar to American audiences through his roles in nearly 100 films. After long experience as a reviewer, editor, and charter member of New York's Algonquin Round Table, he wrote and starred, generally as a befuddled lecturer, in some 30 short subjects, from the monologue *The Treasurer's Report* (1928) to *Important Business* (1944), including the Oscar-winning *How to Sleep* (1936) and the deathlessly titled *The Romance of Digestion* (1937). Equally well recognized in character roles, usually as fuddy-duddy bosses, he enlivened such comedies as *You'll Never Get Rich* (1941), *Take a Letter, Darling* (1942), *The Major and the Minor* (1942), and FOREIGN CORRESPONDENT, in which he contributed to the screenplay and played the eternally sodden correspondent Stebbins.

Bendix, William (1906–1964) Endearingly hulking American character actor, one-time grocer and New York Yankees batboy, who went on from his Broadway debut in *The Time of Your Life* (1939) to play dozens of Irish cops, thugs, and good-hearted joes onstage, onscreen, and in the long-running radio and television program *The Life of Riley*. His most memorable screen roles include his Oscar-nominated turn in *Wake Island* (1942), his sadistic enforcer in *The Glass Key* (1942), the title roles in *The Hairy Ape* (1944) and *The Babe Ruth Story* (1948), and Gus Smith, the mechanic whose passion for dancing is doomed by his gangrenous leg in LIFEBOAT.

Benjamin, Sir Arthur (1893–1960) Anglo-Australian composer whose 20-year experience in films, which extended from *The Scarlet Pimpernel* (1934) to *Fire Down Below* (1957), was concentrated in three periods: 1934–38, 1947, and 1953–57, bookended by the 1934 and 1956 versions of THE MAN WHO KNEW TOO MUCH, both of which gave special prominence to his *Storm Cloud Cantata*.

Bennett, Charles (1899–1995) British writer for stage and screen, usually in collaboration. A former actor, he left the boards to focus exclusively on writing after his first play, BLACKMAIL (1928), was adapted for Hitchcock's first sound film, signing as a writer with British International, and later working on five successive Hitchcock projects at GAUMONT-BRITISH—THE MAN WHO KNEW TOO MUCH, THE 39 STEPS, SECRET AGENT, SABOTAGE, and YOUNG AND INNOCENT—with occasional breaks for work on *The Clairvoyant* (1935), *King of the Damned* (1936), and *King Solomon's Mines* (1937). Moving to Universal in 1938, he immigrated to the United States, where he worked on *The Young at Heart* (1938), FOREIGN CORRESPONDENT, and some two dozen other properties, including *Madness of the Heart* (1949), which

he wrote and directed, and his only other directorial effort, *No Escape* (1953). Long friendly with Hitchcock even after their collaboration ended, he was working on a script for a remake of *Blackmail* at the time of his death.

Benson, Annette British screen actress of the twenties who plays Mabel, the waitress whose dalliance with his friend Tim Wakeley gets the hero Roddy Berwick expelled from school and launched into "the world of make-believe" and "the world of lost illusion" in DOWNHILL.

Benson, Sally (1897–1972) American journalist, humorist, storyteller, and screenwriter. Her *New Yorker* stories under the byline Esther Evarts established her as a gently witty observer, especially of the domestic milieu, and two collections of her short stories, *Meet Me in St. Louis* and *Junior Miss,* were adapted by Hollywood in 1944 and 1945. In the meantime, she had begun to contribute directly to the screen in SHADOW OF A DOUBT, her first film work, and continued in the Oscar-nominated *Anna and the King of Siam* (1946) and a dozen others, from *Come to the Stable* (1949) and *The Farmer Takes a Wife* (1953) to *The Singing Nun* (1965) and *Joy in the Morning* (1965), her final collaboration.

Beregi, Oscar (Jr.) (1918–1976) Blustering Hungarian-born actor much in demand in the fifties and sixties for playing Teutonic villains and the occasional nonheavy, as in the ALFRED HITCHCOCK PRESENTS episode "THE CRYSTAL TRENCH."

Bergman, Ingrid (1915–1982) Radiant, versatile Swedish-born international star who after her leading role in *Intermezzo* (1936) was signed by David O. SELZNICK to reprise the role in his American remake (1939). Her wholesome good looks and emotional range landed her the star-making roles of Ilsa in *Casablanca* (1942), María (her first Oscar nomination) in *For Whom the Bell Tolls* (1943), and Paula Alquist (her first Oscar) in *Gaslight* (1944), a triptych that made her the toast of Hollywood in the forties and the logical choice to play the title role in *Joan of Arc* (1948). In the meantime, Hitchcock had exploited her range by casting her as the maternally romantic Dr. Constance Peterson in SPELLBOUND and the stoically compromised Alicia Huberman in NOTORIOUS, one of her most accomplished performances. Whether because he respected her rare dedication as an actress or because, like so many other audiences, he fell under the spell of her understated sensuality, Hitchcock designed UNDER CAPRICORN, his third film starring Bergman (the first time a female star had ever dominated so many of his films) as an unabashed showcase for her character Lady Henrietta Flusky's trademark combination of heroism and notoriety. But the film was a critical and financial failure, and shortly after it wrapped, Bergman, hounded by a publicity machine that could not forgive the clash between her public romance with Italian director Roberto Rossellini and her carefully groomed star persona of purity and nobility, left Hollywood and her first husband, Dr. Peter Lindstrom, to make *Stromboli* (1949), the first of a series of commercially unsuccessful films with Rossellini. (Donald SPOTO suggests that the infatuated Hitchcock felt betrayed especially sharply by his star's romantic and professional defection to another filmmaker.) Not until 1956, when her success in Jean Renoir's *Elena et les hommes* and in the London stage production of *Anastasia* led to her casting in the latter's film adaptation, did she return to English-language cinema, winning her second Academy Award as the troubled claimant to the Russian imperial throne. Among her most notable later films were *Indiscreet* (1958); *The Visit* (1964); *Murder on the Orient Express* (1974), for which she received a Best Supporting Actress Oscar; and Ingmar Bergman's *Höstsonaten* (1978), her last film, for which she was nominated for still another Academy Award. For her final role, as Golda Meir on the television miniseries *A Woman Called Golda* (1982), she received a posthumous Emmy. Despite reams of commentary on her films, her trenchant comment on her career has never been excelled: "I've gone from saint to whore and back to saint again, all in one lifetime."

Berkeley, Ballard (1904–1988) Stage-trained British character actor whose 60-year screen career, beginning in 1930, encompassed dozens of profes-

sional men and variously efficient functionaries such as Sgt. Mellish in STAGE FRIGHT. He eventually graduated to the military and nobility before settling into his signature role as Major Gowen in the television series *Fawlty Towers* (1975–79).

Berlinger, Warren (1937–) American character actor, in dozens of films and television programs from 1956, including his performance as Ron Tawley in the FORD STARTIME segment "INCIDENT AT A CORNER."

Berner, Sara American character actress who got her start by providing vocals in WARNER BROS. cartoons (1941–45) and then took bit roles in a dozen Hollywood films, including the woman glimpsed on the fire escape in REAR WINDOW and the unseen telephone operator whose voice informs Roger Thornhill that the killers are on their way up to George Kaplan's Plaza suite in NORTH BY NORTHWEST.

Bernoudy, Edmond F. Veteran American assistant director, active 1923–61, whose 20 films included REBECCA and FOREIGN CORRESPONDENT. In addition, he wrote and directed a single film, *Terra Violenta* (1948), as Edmond Francis Bernoudy.

Bernstein, Sidney Lewis, Lord (1899–1993) British film and television executive. A cofounder of the British Film Society (1924) and a pioneer of movie matinees for children (1927), he founded the Granada chain of movie theaters in 1930 and acted as film adviser to the Ministry of Information during World War II. After the war he formed TRANSATLANTIC PICTURES in partnership with Hitchcock, serving as the business complement to the director's creative contributions. After releasing only two features, ROPE and UNDER CAPRICORN, Transatlantic folded, though Bernstein returned to coproduce I CONFESS before leaving films to found the Granada Television Group in 1954. At the very end of his life, he served as executive producer of a single television film, *Memory of the Camps* (1993).

Bertrand, Robert (R.) American sound engineer of the sixties whose brief career ran the gamut from the television series *McHale's Navy* (1962–66) to *The Sting* (1973), for which he shared an Oscar nomination. With Waldon O. WATSON, he supervised the soundtrack for *TOPAZ*.

Berwick, Ray (d. 1990)   Animal trainer whose first Hollywood assignment, as "Trainer to the Birds" in *THE BIRDS*, led to a half-dozen other films, including *TOPAZ*, in which he trained ravens, dogs, and chimpanzees. He also wrote "Meet Me at the Fair," a 1977 segment of the television program *Little House on the Prairie*.

Beside the Bonnie Brier Bush   (Alternate title: *The Bonnie Brier Bush*) Famous Players-Lasky, 1921. **Director:** Donald Crisp; **Screenplay:** Margaret Turnbull, based on the novel by Ian Maclaren; **Cast:** Donald Crisp (Lachlan Campbell), Mary Glynne (Flora Campbell), Alec Fraser (Lord Malcolm Hay), Dorothy Fane (Kate Carnegie), Jack East (Posty), Langhorn Burton (John Carmichael), Jerrold Robertshaw (Earl of Kinspindle), Adeline Hayden Coffin (Margaret Howe), H.H. Wright (Dr. William MacClure).

Fourth of the 12 silent films for which Hitchcock designed intertitles between 1920 and 1922.

Best, Edna (1900–1974)   Self-effacing star of British stage and screen. Soon after her starring West End role in *The Constant Nymph* (1926), she married actor Herbert MARSHALL and appeared with him in several plays. Onscreen from 1923, she was in the meantime becoming better known in romantic film leads. Her performance as Jill Lawrence, sharpshooting mother of the kidnapped Betty, anchored *THE MAN WHO KNEW TOO MUCH* (1934). Following her success in *South Riding* (1938), she immigrated to the United States, playing character roles on stage and (less often) onscreen in *Intermezzo* (1939), *Swiss Family Robinson* (1940), *The Late George Apley* (1947), and *The Ghost and Mrs. Muir* (1947) and becoming a U.S. citizen in 1950.

Bevans, Clem (1879–1963)   Gangly, white-thatched American character actor, onscreen in more than 100 roles from 1935 to 1957. Most often seen as a kindly old codger, he was cast briefly against type as the Fifth Columnist Neilson in *SABOTEUR*.

Beville, Richard   British codirector of a single feature, *Radio Parade* (1933), who also served as unit production manager for *THE MAN WHO KNEW TOO MUCH* (1934).

Binns, Edward (1916–1990)   Stolid, heavy-featured American character actor, veteran of 100 film and television roles, 1951–89, often as nondescript cops, sheriffs, or military officers. His most recognizable roles are those in *Twelve Angry Men* (1957), *Patton* (1970), and *The Verdict* (1982), and the television series *Brenner* (1959–60), *The Nurses* (1962–65), and *It Takes a Thief* (1969–70). He appeared as Ned Brown in "Heart of Gold," a 1957 episode of *ALFRED HITCHCOCK PRESENTS*, and as Captain Junket of the Nassau County Detectives in *NORTH BY NORTHWEST*.

Birch, Albert (Frederick) (1900–)   British sound recordist, 1934–39, former cinematographer, whose dozen films include *WALTZES FROM VIENNA* (on which he is billed as Alfred Birch) and *THE 39 STEPS*.

birds   A favorite symbol of homicidal impotence as early as *BLACKMAIL*, in which Alice White—returning home after walking the London streets all night, dazed by her killing of the artist who tried to rape her—crawls into bed only to be roused almost immediately by her mother, who uncovers a cage in her bedroom to reveal a noisily chirping bird, like Alice a figure both imprisoned and assaultive. The use of birds as figures both imprisoned and murderous is developed in much greater detail in *SABOTAGE*, in which several of the leading characters are compared to birds: the saboteur Verloc, prevented from planting the bomb that has been sent to him by the vigilant police who have caged him in his house; his courier Stevie, who never knows what it truly is that he has been given to carry; and Stevie's sister, Verloc's birdlike wife. The bomb is accompanied by a note that reads, "Don't forget the birds will sing at 1:45"; later, Stevie's sister stabs her husband to death shortly after watching part of the Disney cartoon *Who Killed Cock Robin?* in which a bird is killed by another bird, both avenging the killing and becoming a killer herself. Far better known, of course, is the imagery of birds as helpless agents of destruction that pervades *PSYCHO*—from the heroine's last name, Crane, and hometown, Phoenix, to Norman's description of his invalid mother as being "as harmless as one of those stuffed birds," indicating that birds are even more dangerous when they are dead and stuffed—and *THE BIRDS*, which presents the suddenly aggressive behavior of its customarily innocuous avian figures as a mystery with no solution. The film might well have ended with the line, "It's just the birds," expressing its despair at the very project of understanding the human agency the birds invariably figure in rational terms.

Birds, The

(Alternative titles: *Die Vögel, Les oiseaux, Gli uccelli*) Universal—Alfred Hitchcock. **Producer:** Alfred Hitchcock, 120 minutes, March 1963. **Director:** Alfred Hitchcock; **Screenplay:** Evan Hunter, based on the short story by Daphne du Maurier; **Cinematographer:** Robert Burks; **Assistant director:** James H. Brown; **Art director:** Robert Boyle; **Set decoration:** George Milo; **Costumes:** Edith Head; **Wardrobe supervisor:** Rita Riggs; **Makeup:** Howard Smit; **Hairstyles:** Virginia Darcy; **Trainer to the birds:** Ray Berwick; **Sound:** Waldon O. Watson and William Russell; **Special effects:** Lawrence A. Hampton and Dave Fleischer; **Special photographic adviser:** Ub Iwerks; **Pictorial design:** Albert Whitlock; **Editor:** George Tomasini; **Production assistant:** Peggy Robertson; **Production manager:** Norman Deming; **Script supervisor:** Lois Thurman; **Titles:** James S. Pollak; **Electronic sound effects:** Remi Gassman and Oskar Sala; **Sound consultant:** Bernard Herrmann; **Cast:** Tippi Hedren (Melanie Daniels), Rod Taylor (Mitch Brenner), Jessica Tandy (Lydia Brenner), Suzanne Pleshette (Annie Hayworth), Veronica Cartwright (Cathy Brenner), Ethel Griffies (Mrs. Bundy), Charles McGraw (Sebastian Scholes), Ruth McDevitt (Mrs. MacGruder), Lonny Chapman (Deke Carter), Joe Mantell (traveling salesman), Doodles Weaver (fisherman), Malcolm Atterbury (Deputy Al Malone), John McGovern (postal clerk), Karl Swenson (doomsayer in diner), Richard Deacon (Mitch's city neighbor), Elizabeth Wilson (Helen Carter), Bill Quinn (man in diner), Doreen Lang (mother in diner), Morgan Brittany and Darlene Conley (schoolgirls).

Hitchcock conceived the idea for his 49th film, and his first for his final return to UNIVERSAL, in the sum-

As Melanie Daniels (Tippi Hedren) enters the pet shop in the opening scene of *The Birds,* she passes Hitchcock, walking his own unbilled dogs. *(National Film Society Archive)*

mer of 1961 when a headline about a mysterious infestation of seabirds in Santa Cruz caught his eye, kindling his interest in Daphne DU MAURIER's short story "The Birds." Recognizing that he would need an experienced writer to develop characters who did not exist in du Maurier's chilling vignette, Hitchcock tried in vain to interest Joseph STEFANO in the project and then asked Evan HUNTER, who also wrote under the pseudonym Ed McBain, to take on the job. At the same time he signed New York model Tippi HEDREN to an exclusive seven-year contract and asked her to star in a new film whose time-consuming special effects would render established stars prohibitively expensive. Hunter's memoir *Me and Hitch* (1997) has detailed the relatively untroubled process by which the writer and the director worked out the screenplay. The shoot itself, however, was Hitchcock's most difficult because of the dangers not only to the performers, especially Hedren, but also to the birds, who were prevented by laws incarnated in an ASPCA representative on the set from being harmed in the production. Because birds do not normally attack people, the film would have to take extraordinary pains to make it look as if they were attacking, so it was planned to include 1,500 shots, including some 400 effects shots (the actual totals turned out to be closer to 1,000 and 300) involving optical overprinting, sodium yellow mattework, and animated effects supervised by longtime Disney associate Ub IWERKS. Shooting, which began in March 1962, ground on until July 1. The climactic sequence in which Melanie Daniels discovers a flock of birds in Mitch Brenner's attic and is nearly pecked to death by them before Mitch rescues her took a week to film—a week that sent Hedren, who spent most of it having terrified birds either attached to her arms and legs with rubber bands or thrown at her in gusts, to the hospital while the production shut down. When shooting ended, the arduous, if less threatening, process of postproduction began, as effects technicians toiled to create the hundreds of composite shots the film required (the final shot alone incorporated elements from 32 different images) and the three composers Hitchcock had chosen to orchestrate the synthetically produced bird sounds that comprised the greater portion of the film's musicless score matched sounds to the rough cut. As Robert KAPSIS has noted, Universal aimed, not entirely successfully, to repackage its new acquisition as both artist and entertainer—an auteur respected by European critics and U.S. academics who was also intent on outdoing the terrors of PSYCHO—and it was during the film's postproduction that Hitchcock, who had coined the film's catchy publicity slogan, "The Birds is coming!" gave his most extensive interviews to date. But the reviews were mixed and the film's business moderate; the studio would have to wait nearly 10 years before FRENZY provided it with anything like a hit from its star director.

The Birds has always been Hitchcock's most problematic film, his only work to generate, from its premiere to the present, radical divergences in interpretation. Unlike Psycho, which had dispelled its chills by providing an extended (perhaps overextended) explanation of its villain's behavior, The Birds put explanations in the characters' mouths without endorsing them. Why do birds without warning begin to attack the citizens of Bodega Bay, California? Their behavior signals the end of the world, one alcoholic prophet indicates; a distraught mother blames their behavior on Melanie's appearance in town; Hitchcock's own trailer, seconded by contemporaneous interviews, implied that their attacks were nature's revenge for humankind's interference. Critics, seizing on Hitchcock's remark to Peter BOGDANOVICH that the film was about Melanie's "complacence," have obligingly joined in the chase, explaining the attacks as punishments directed specifically against the birdlike Melanie, or manifestations of the Brenner family's domestic tensions, or assaults on the tyranny of heteroideology, or indices of the world's or the film's irrationality or unreadability, or portents of black comedy, a generic joke played on viewers who sat through the film's opening scenes expecting a romantic comedy. On one point, however, its commentators agree: The film's unusually artificial atmosphere, which freely combines several different acting styles, often in the same scene (stage-trained Jessica Tandy's clinical emoting, Rod Taylor's underplaying, Veronica Cartwright's uninflected girlish enthusiasm, Hedren's authentically Hitchcockian neutral reactions)—together with an exterior cyclorama as stylized as the cityscape window in Rope and awkwardly expository dialogue Hunter's memoir disavows in embarrassment—encourages interpretive speculation by inhibiting the deceptively straightforward-seeming identifications Hitchcock had manipulated so masterfully in his fifties films. Shorn not only of an answer to its riddle but even of a closing title (it was the first of Hitchcock's films to dispense with the words "The End" over the long fadeout that showed Mitch driving his family in Melanie's little car through an army of thousands of ominously still birds), the film seems likely to generate disagreement for years to come. That it has lost nothing of its power to provoke was dramatized at the Hitchcock Centennial Conference when an exasperated Slavoj ŽIŽEK repeatedly demanded of Evan Hunter, "Why did the birds attack?" only to be met by repeated evasions, capped at last by the smiling reply, "Because Alfred Hitchcock told them to."

Birnie, Richard (Milton) (1924–1986)

American film executive who began at REVUE PRO-DUCTIONS as assistant director on the ALFRED HITCH-COCK PRESENTS episodes "BACK FOR CHRISTMAS" and "MR. BLANCHARD'S SECRET." After retiring from UNIVERSAL as vice president of production, he returned as vice president of television production at MGM in 1980 and later moved to Centerpoint, Stephen J. Cannell, and Viacom as vice president of production.

Bittner, Julius

Coarranger, with Erich Wolfgang KORNGOLD, of the Strauss music for WALTZES FROM VIENNA.

Black, Karen (1945–)

Indefatigable stage-trained American actress, born Karen Blanche Ziegler, who first appeared onscreen at 15, then broke through for her Oscar-nominated performance as the hero's Southern-fried girlfriend Rayette in *Five Easy Pieces* (1970), for which she received a Golden Globe. She went on to play waitresses, hookers, vulgarians, and loyal supporters of strong heroes in such iconic seventies films as *Drive, He Said* (1971), *The Great Gatsby* (her second Golden Globe, 1974), *The Day of the Locust* (1975), and *Nashville* (1975). FAMILY PLOT—in which she was cast over Hitchcock's objections as Fran, the recessive half of the pair of kidnappers the heroes are unwittingly seeking, to offset the nonmarquee value of Barbara HARRIS—turned out to mark the end of her vogue, but she continued to take roles in more than 100 independent, foreign, and low-budget films, occasionally serving as writer, producer, or composer as well.

Blackguard, The

(Alternative title: *Die Prinzessin und der Geiger*) Gainsborough, Wardour & F., 1925. **Producer:** Michael Balcon; **Associate producer:** Erich Pommer; **Director:** Graham Cutts; **Assistant director:** Alfred Hitchcock; **Screenplay:** Alfred Hitchcock, based on the novel by Raymond Paton; **Art director:** Alfred Hitchcock; **Cast:** Jane Novak (Princess Marie Idourska), Walter Rilla (Michael Caviol, the Blackguard), Frank Stan-

more (Pompouard), Bernhard Goetzke (Adrian Levinski), Martin Herzberg (Michael as a boy), Rosa Valetti (grandmother), Dora Bergner, and Fritz Alberti. Filmed at UFA Studios, Neubabelsberg.

The fourth of the five films whose screenplays Hitchcock wrote for Michael Balcon and Graham Cutts, and the only one surviving, is most notable as the project that took him to Germany, where he watched F.W. MURNAU at work and honed his sense of visual design.

Blackmail

(Alternative titles: *Erpressung, Chantage*) British International, Wardour & F., 80 minutes, June 1929 (sound version), August 1929 (silent version). **Producer:** John Maxwell; **Director:** Alfred Hitchcock; **Adaptation:** Alfred Hitchcock, from the play by Charles Bennett; **Dialogue:** Benn Levy; **Cinematographer:** Jack Cox; **Art directors:** C.W. Arnold and Norman Arnold; **Editor:** Emile de Ruelle; **Sound (postsynchronized dialogue):** R.R. Jeffrey; **Music:** Campbell and Connelly, compiled and arranged by Hubert Bath and Henry Stafford, performed by the British Symphony Orchestra, conducted by John Reynders; **Camera assistants:** Ronald Neame and Alfred Roome; **Still photographer:** Michael Powell; **Cast:** Anny Ondra (Alice White), Sara Allgood (Mrs. White), Charles Paton (Mr. White), John Longden (Frank Webber), Donald Calthrop (Tracy), Cyril Ritchard (the Artist), Hannah Jones (the Landlady), Sam Livesey/Harvey Braban (Chief Inspector), Ex-Det. Sgt. Bishop (Detective Sergeant), Percy Parsons (arrested man), Johnny Butt (doorman), Phyllis Monkman/Phyllis Konstam (gossiping neighbors).

Impelled by the notable success of Charles BENNETT's 1928 play *The Last Hour,* John MAXWELL purchased the rights to his preceding play, *Blackmail,* with Hitchcock in mind. Although the playwright would collaborate on the screenplays to many later Hitchcock films, this scenario is credited to the director alone, who wrote it in November 1928, perhaps in collaboration with Bennett, Benn LEVY, or Michael POWELL. Hitchcock's 10th film began shooting in February 1929 as a silent feature, but soon after principal photography was completed in April, Maxwell gave Hitchcock a demonstration of a primitive sound reproduction system and asked him to prepare the film for a limited sound release. It is unclear how much Hitchcock had anticipated this request, but he jumped on it with alacrity, leaving long sequences of the film (especially the first reel detailing the pursuit, arrest, and booking of a criminal suspect) intact except for the addition of music and several sound effects and reshooting others to capitalize on the new possibilities of synch sound, even though the reshoot required him to substitute Harvey BRABAN and Phyllis KONSTAM in roles originally played by Sam LIVESEY and Phyllis MONKMAN. (The recasting of the Chief Inspector's role in particular led to considerable textual complications in the two release versions of the film because, as Charles BARR has noted, not only does the synch-sound version retain a good deal of the silent version's footage, but also the silent version incorporates some of the footage shot for sound.) Hitchcock dealt with another more intransigent problem, the thick Czech accent of his star, Anny ONDRA, by placing British actress Joan BARRY just off-camera and having her dub all Ondra's speeches live as the star lip-synched. The result, though not technically England's first synch-sound film, was exceptionally inventive in its use of sound effects, from the callous whistling of Alice White's police boyfriend Frank Webber as he searches the artist's flat for clues to his murder shortly before finding Alice's glove to the senseless chatter of the caged bird that greets the next morning, from the ghoulish chitchat of the neighbor increasingly emphasizing the word *knife* as she ruminates on the murder last night to the doorbell that resonates as ominously as the voice of doom when it announces the arrival of a blackmailing beggar who saw Alice and the artist enter the flat together. The film was highly successful at its press screening in June 1929 and its general release in November, sparking the release of the embargoed *THE MANXMAN* and confirming Hitchcock's status as Britain's top director.

The film's preeminent status among his early work for latter-day Hitchcockians, however, owes less to its expressionistic handling of sound or indeed to its powerfully idiomatic handling of working-class London or its director's first truly distinctive cameo (he appears as a passenger in the Underground tor-

Alice White (Anny Ondra) and her policeman beau Frank Webber (John Longden) cannot agree how to deal with the witness who can identify her as the killer in *Blackmail.* *(National Film Society Archive)*

mented by a small boy) than to its prophetic feminism. Its central triangle of Alice, Frank, and the artist Crewe amounts to a parody of the romantic triangles of *THE RING* and *The Manxman* because there seems no real love between any two of the principals. Instead, this tale of a curious virgin who abandons her indifferent suitor for an adventurous evening with an artist and ends up fending off his assault by killing him is, as Tania MODLESKI and Robin WOOD point out in their pioneering essays, a fable about power and patriarchy, women's place in a world defined by men's controlling gaze. Hitchcock maintained that he had wanted to change the relatively sunny ending of Bennett's West End melodrama (the police find that the artist died of a heart attack and decide that he fell on the knife only as he was dying, allowing both Alice and the blackmailer to go free) to a more ironic ending (Frank arrests Alice for the crime, and the last reel of the film, in which the police put her through the same dehumanizing procedures as the anonymous suspect pursued in the opening, would be an ironic echo of the first), which Maxwell refused to allow. As it stands, the film proceeds to a technically happy ending (Frank, refusing to submit to blackmail, sets his colleagues on the blackmailer, and they pursue him to his death in the belief that he is the murderer, leaving Alice and Frank to live with their guilty knowledge) that is if anything more ironic. Alice's honor has been vindicated by and for male observers even though she cannot forget what she has done—both silent and sound versions of the film end with a shot of a painting that had snapped Alice's thin control after the murder, a jester that seemed to be pointing accusingly at her, as the jester's painted laughter is echoed by the feeble laughter of Alice and Frank—or tell the story that would surely vindicate her in the eyes of the law. Hence Alice is legally exonerated at the price of fixing moral guilt on her for the rest of her life. From its opening sequence, the film is filled with images showing the intolerable burden of being watched, a series of images that snap abruptly into a pattern when Alice, directly after killing the artist, catches sight of the accusing jester and then leaves the flat in a daze to wander the city streets till dawn, seeing herself accused by a neon sign that seems to show her stabbing hand and a beggar's arm outstretched in the same gesture as the dead artist's. What makes the genteel, seedy blackmailer intolerable is not his demands (he seems to get nothing more than a few pounds and an expensive cigar) but his unbearable knowledge of what Alice has done—a knowledge that drives her to the police station to confess before the timely arrival of Frank, who reveals that the blackmailer is dead and takes her home to what the film's final shots figure as an endless nightmare. Although Hitchcock did not fully embrace the thriller as his chosen genre until the even greater success of THE MAN WHO KNEW TOO MUCH (1934), it is *Blackmail* that points the way most directly to films like *REBECCA, NOTORIOUS, VERTIGO, PSYCHO,* and *MARNIE* that ruthlessly anatomize the fatal costs of men watching women.

Blackwell, Carlyle (1884–1955)   American matinee idol of the twenties, onscreen in nearly 100 silent films from 1909. He directed a handful of films and is credited together with Michael BALCON as producing THE LODGER.

Blancard, René (1897–1965)   French actor, a veteran of some 50 films (1942–65), notably *Quai des Orfèvres* (1947) and *Le plaisir* (1952), a specialist in doughty senior police officers who ventured outside his native cinema, though not outside his customary range, to play Inspector Lepic in TO CATCH A THIEF.

Blas, Samuel   American author who wrote the 1947 story on which the ALFRED HITCHCOCK PRESENTS episode "REVENGE" is based.

Bloch, Robert (1917–1994)   American pulp writer, long active in science fiction and horror fantasy as well as suspense, who sold his first story at 17 and went on to write a dozen novels and some 400 short stories, screenplays, and television and radio scripts, some under the pseudonym Collier Young. Bloch's early work reflected the strong influence of H.P. Lovecraft, but his first novel, *The Scarf* (1947), revealed an equally important debt to Raymond CHANDLER, and most of Bloch's later work combined elements of the occult, psychopathology, or weird horror with criminal premises. Several of Bloch's short stories had already been adapted for ALFRED HITCHCOCK PRESENTS by other hands when his novel PSYCHO (1959), based loosely on the criminal career of Wisconsin mass murderer Ed Gein, came to Hitchcock's attention. Hitchcock's adaptation, entrusted ultimately to Joseph STEFANO, was unusually faithful to the novel. As Bloch proudly maintained for years afterward: "It's all in there—even the fly." He received writing credit for three later episodes of *Alfred Hitchcock Presents*—"The Cuckoo Clock" (1960), "The Changing Heart" (based on his own story, 1961), "The Sorcerer's Apprentice" (based on his own story, 1961)—and four episodes of THE ALFRED HITCHCOCK HOUR—"Annabel" (1962), "A Home Away from Home" (based on his own story, 1963), "The Second Wife" (1965), and "Off Season" (1965).

blondes   In an interview with Richard Schickel, Hitchcock traced his widely acknowledged interest in blonde leading ladies, which became the best known fetish of his later career, back to the iconography of silent films, whose first popular heroine was the girlish blonde Mary Pickford. Even before he began his work in the cinema, Hitchcock evidently associated the sexual reticence of the "cool blonde," a British or northern European type, with hidden sexuality, as against the obvious glamour of women from France, Italy, and the United States. This structuring contrast, of course, is far older than the cinema; it goes back at least to Sir Walter Scott, whose novels from *Waverley* on regularly poise their heroes between a dark, exotic beauty like *Ivanhoe*'s Rebecca, whom the hero must ultimately reject, and a quintessentially English rose like Rowena, whose domesticity represents the promise of his continued line. Certainly the cool blonde—whose reserve provides at once dramatic contrast with the potential, though obscure, sexuality she refuses to flaunt and creates a dramatic obstacle to be overcome, a dramatic air of mystery within which romance may be cloaked, and at least the dramatic promise of unbridled sexual license (encapsulated in Hitchcock's repeated suggestion, "Anything could happen with a woman like that in the back of a taxi")—is more economically useful than her more forthright Mediterranean counterpart in narrative terms and may well have comported more readily with the domestic dreams Lesley BRILL ascribes to the conventionally sentimental filmmaker. Nor did Hitchcock cast the blonde leading ladies of *THE LODGER*, whose opening scenes explicitly establish blond hair as a marker of danger, or of *CHAMPAGNE*, though he evidently had more control over the casting of *THE MANXMAN, BLACKMAIL,* and *RICH AND STRANGE*. Indeed, Hitchcock's silent films feature more dark-haired heroines than blondes.

Soon thereafter, however, the director's own attachment to blonde actresses to whom he played an increasingly masterful Svengali began to merge with and eventually overshadow their narrative functionality as iconic presences. Though he gave no evidence of any untoward attachment to Nova PILBEAM, the child star of *THE MAN WHO KNEW TOO MUCH* (1934) who returned as the ingenue of *YOUNG AND INNO-CENT*, his feelings for Madeleine CARROLL, whom he called "the first blond who was a real Hitchcock type," were different. After casting her as Pamela, the female lead who struck sparks with Richard Hannay in *THE 39 STEPS* despite her relatively brief screen time, he gave her a far more showy role in *SECRET AGENT*, bathing her many closeups with angelic lighting quite at odds with the lighting accorded other characters in the same scene. Carroll returned to Hollywood soon thereafter, but Hitchcock's own arrival in Hollywood brought him together with the first blonde ingenue he could utterly dominate: Joan FONTAINE, whose inexperience and insecurity made her both the logical choice to play the nameless heroine of *REBECCA* and a malleable bit of clay to be molded by the director's taste in food, wine, and especially clothing. But Fontaine, newly married to Brian AHERNE, did not long remain under Hitchcock's spell, and her immediate successor, Carole LOMBARD, was much too strong-willed ever to succumb in the first place. It was not until more than 10 years later that Hitchcock discovered in Grace KELLY the ultimate Hitchcock blonde. Although he did nothing to create Kelly's poised beauty, he did encourage John Michael HAYES to create more humorous and natural characters for her, so that the visual sketch she offers in *DIAL M FOR MURDER* is fleshed out in the coolly seductive heroines of *REAR WINDOW* and *TO CATCH A THIEF*, cocreations of the director (with the help of his screenwriter and costume designer) and his star. Kelly's departure from Hollywood to marry Prince Rainier of Monaco, an echo of Ingrid BERGMAN's abandonment of Hitchcock for Roberto Rossellini five years earlier, left the filmmaker with an iconic heroine he spent the rest of his career trying to cast, with highly variable results, using Shirley MACLAINE, Doris DAY, Vera MILES, Kim NOVAK, Eva Marie SAINT, Janet LEIGH, and, most notoriously, Tippi HEDREN.

In one sense, Hitchcock's infatuation with the blonde actresses on whom he could regularly turn in pain and sadistic outrage is a mark of his deeply neurotic attachment both to impossibly unavailable women and to the powers of filmmaking to create myths (a power explored to devastating effect in *VERTIGO*, which is widely interpreted as a self-portrait of the director's fatal need to choreograph his heroines' every move in an attempt to create what Tania MODLESKI has called "femininity by design"); in another sense, it is an epitome of his status as a director. For all his legendary insistence on controlling every aspect of his films from the screenplay to the final cut and the publicity, Hitchcock was often accused of neglecting his actors on the set because he had already, once the visual design of the movie was complete, lost interest in its realization. The one group of performers he never lost interest in directing—the group that revealed most completely what it meant to be directed by Hitchcock, onscreen and off—were the Hitchcock blondes.

Blythe, John (1921–1993) General-purpose British actor whose starring role as Sgt. John Dougall, the unwary British flier in BON VOYAGE, is socially a cut above most of the lower-middle-class types—barmen, chauffeurs, and village constables—he would play during the next 30 years.

Bogdanovich, Peter (1939–) American filmmaker and journalist best known for the string of genre pastiches he directed, produced, and often wrote, beginning with the low-budget thriller *Targets* (1968) and continuing with the documentary *Directed by John Ford* (1971) and the features *The Last Picture Show* (1971), *What's Up, Doc?* (1972), *Paper Moon* (1973), *Daisy Miller* (1974), *At Long Last Love* (1975), *Nickelodeon* (1976), and *They All Laughed* (1981). His other films include *Saint Jack* (1979), *Mask* (1985), and *Texasville* (1990). Years before entering movies as an assistant director for Roger Corman, the stage-trained Bogdanovich wrote a series of illustrated, film-by-film monographs on directors, typically drawing on interviews he had conducted with the subjects, designed to accompany retrospective screenings of their work at New York's Museum of Modern Art. The third of these, following his volumes on Orson Welles (1961) and Howard Hawks (1962), was *The Cinema of Alfred Hitchcock* (Museum of Modern Art/Doubleday, 1963), the first book on Hitchcock in English and, along with François TRUFFAUT's contemporaneous series of interviews and Robin WOOD's *Hitchcock's Films,* one

of the key documents in establishing the director's unique artistic credentials. In keeping with this mission, Bogdanovich is concerned throughout to indemnify the director against any charges of artistic, as opposed to commercial, compromise. Hence he describes Hitchcock as "the only director worth talking about seriously" in British cinema and notes protectively that "both EASY VIRTUE and DOWNHILL [like THE PLEASURE GARDEN and THE MOUNTAIN EAGLE] were commissioned pictures, and not at all of Hitchcock's choosing." Oddly for an advocate of the director, Bogdanovich, having asked whether Hitchcock had intended "any moral implications" in PSYCHO, never challenges his response: "I don't think you can take any moral stand because you're dealing with distorted people. You can't apply morality to insane persons." A more extensive transcript of the interview, supplemented from material from later interviews, was published in Bogdanovich's interview anthology *Who the Devil Made It* (Knopf, 1997).

Boileau, Pierre (1906–1989) French writer of mystery and suspense novels written in collaboration with Thomas NARCEJAC (1908–98) and published under the pseudonym Boileau-Narcejac. Their novels used mystery plots as the basis for suspenseful stories with corkscrew twists that often extended far beyond the question of whodunit. Many of these novels, little known in English, achieved fame through such frequent film adaptations as *Les diaboliques* (based on *Celle qui n'était plus,* 1955, and remade in 1974, 1993, and 1996), *Les louves* (1957), *Les yeux sans visage* (1959), and *Les visages de l'ombre* (1960, remade in 1984). The pair's novel *D'entre les morts* (1954) served as the basis for VERTIGO.

Bolster, Anita (1895–1985) Irish-American character actress who also worked under the name Anita Sharp-Bolster. Most often seen (1929–66) supporting leading characters as servant or mother, she played the sideshow attraction Lorelei in SABOTEUR.

Bolton, Guy (1885–1979) Prolific Anglo-American playwright, author (sometimes under the name H.B. Trevelyan) of more than 50 plays, generally musicals, often in collaboration with P.G. Wodehouse. Many of his stage plays were adapted in films from *Oh, Boy!* (1919) to *Anything Goes* (1936) and *Rosalie* (1937) to *Anastasia* (1956). In addition, he frequently worked himself on adaptations and original screenplays from *The Love Parade* (1929) and *Transatlantic* (1931) to *Angel* (1937) and *Weekend at the Waldorf* (1945). He collaborated with Alma REVILLE on the adaptation of WALTZES FROM VIENNA.

Bon voyage Phoenix Films, 25 minutes, 1944. **Producer:** British Ministry of Information; **Director:** Alfred Hitchcock; **Screenplay:** J.O.C. Orton and Angus MacPhail, based on an original subject by Arthur Calder-Marshall; **Cinematographer:** Gunther Krampf; **Set dec-**

oration: Charles Gilbert; **Cast:** John Blythe (Sergeant John Dougall) and the Molière Players.

The first of the two French-language propaganda shorts Hitchcock directed for the British Ministry of Information was shot, like its companion piece *Aventure malgache,* between January 20 and February 25, 1944, then shipped to a French distributor and promptly forgotten. Because neither the screenwriters nor any actors besides John Blythe received individual screen credit—the Molière Players, a group of French refugees who had formed an acting troupe in London, preferring to be credited only as an ensemble—the film offered no credits but Hitchcock who

Uncredited members of the Molière Players in the parts of the members of the French Resistance who surround Oscar, the traitor who has just betrayed their friend Jeanne in *Bon voyage*. *(National Film Society Archive)*

might promise a likely home audience, and no one in Britain was eager to title such an instantly dated film for an English audience anyway. So the film languished virtually unseen until its release on videotape some 50 years later.

Its story, though sketchily developed, is framed by a wonderfully Hitchcockian premise. Sergeant John Dougall, an RAF officer who has just escaped from Germany, is debriefed by the Deuxième Bureau about his adventures and recounts the many ways his Polish companion Stefan Godovsky helped him. An extended series of flashbacks illustrates his tale, but at its conclusion his interrogator tells him that Stefan was an impostor, a Gestapo officer who was aiding Dougall's escape so that he could use him to smuggle out a letter to a fellow agent in Paris. When Dougall refuses to believe his helpful companion could have been so treacherous, the film proceeds to a second series of flashbacks, this one emphasizing the complicity Dougall never noticed and ending with Godovsky's execution of a Resistance fighter who had sheltered the two men and his confederate's capture by other members of the Resistance. Although the film is nowhere subtle enough to fulfill the promise of its frame, it contains its share of memorable moments, especially the death of the Resistance fighter Jeanne, and it clearly constitutes an important link in the pattern of unreliably subjective moments in Hitchcock from the misleading daydreams of *Downhill* and *Champagne* to the lying flashback of *Stage Fright.*

Boreo, Emile (1885–1951)   Excitable character actor whose handful of screen roles included the put-upon hotel manager Boris in THE LADY VANISHES.

Bouchey, Willis (B.) (1907–1977)   American character actor whose organlike voice and balding dome made him much in demand from 1951 for such authoritarian roles as one of the most frequent judges to preside over Perry Mason's television courtroom (1960–66). He appeared as the judge in the ALFRED HITCHCOCK HOUR segment "I SAW THE WHOLE THING" and in two later roles in the series, as Mr. Norton in "The Paragon" (1963) and Dr. Bailey in "One of the Family" (1965).

Boulton, Guy Pelham (b. 1890)   British stage actor whose only film appearance was as a juror in MURDER!

Boulton, Matthew (1893–1962)   British actor who played dozens of military officers and police inspectors, including Superintendent Talbot, the hero's boss in SABOTAGE; then he went to Hollywood, where he continued to incarnate British imperturbability.

Bourneuf, Philip (1908–1979)   American character actor in occasional films and more-frequent television roles from 1944. He appeared in two episodes of ALFRED HITCHCOCK PRESENTS, playing the hero's boss Mr. Renshaw in "DIP IN THE POOL" and George Henderson in "A Jury of Her Peers" (1961), and as Mr. Sylvester in THE ALFRED HITCHCOCK HOUR segment "The Photographer and the Undertaker" (1965).

Bouzereau, Laurent   American author, producer, and documentary filmmaker. His films include documentaries about the making of *Jaws* (1995), *Jurassic Park* (1995), *Psycho* (1998), *Marnie* (1998), and *Saving Private Ryan* (1999) produced or excerpted for the DVD releases of these films. His books include *The De Palma Cut: The Films of America's Most Controversial Director* (1988), *The Cutting Room Floor: Movie Scenes Which Never Made It* (1994), *Ultraviolent Movies: From Sam Peckinpah to Quentin Tarantino* (1996), *Star Wars: The Annotated Scripts* (1997), and *Star Wars Episode I: The Phantom Menace: The Making of Episode I* (with Jody Duncan, 1999). He has also taken time out from his work on documentaries to compile *The Alfred Hitchcock Quote Book* (Citadel, 1993).

Boxer, John (1909–1982)   British character actor, a veteran of three dozen roles from 1940 as soldiers, sailors, and gofers, who ripened into Sir George, the distinguished speaker in the opening scene of FRENZY.

Boyd, David (1944–)   Australian film scholar, associate professor of English at the University of Newcastle. He has written *Film and the Interpretive*

Process (1989) and edited *Perspectives on Alfred Hitchcock* (G.K. Hall, 1995), a collection of nine essays, all previously published, to which he adds an introduction that surveys the leading debates in Hitchcock studies (Should Hitchcock be taken seriously? Are his films more concerned with the problems of his characters—guilt, doubling, retribution—or his metafictional relations with his audience? Is he a major artist or an entertainer whose concerns are dictated by his genre? Are his films particularly distinctive from, or typical of, Hollywood product? How can changes in the perceptions of his films since their first release best be theorized?) during a 40-year period. The selections include three "overviews"—Richard Schickel's 1975 interview with Hitchcock and summary essays by Robin WOOD and Thomas M. LEITCH—and essays on *BLACKMAIL, NOTORIOUS, VERTIGO, NORTH BY NORTHWEST, REAR WINDOW,* and *PSYCHO,* and Hitchcock's political films by Tania MODLESKI, Lesley BRILL, and others. The volume concludes with a brief bibliography and filmography and information on 16 mm film rentals. Boyd's latest project is the forthcoming collection *After Hitchcock.*

Boyd, Dorothy (1907–) British actress who worked her way up from such supporting roles as Hilda Whittaker, the hero's sister in *EASY VIRTUE,* to leading roles in second features of the thirties.

Boyle, Robert (F.) (1910–) American art director who began as an associate at UNIVERSAL, where his first credit was *SABOTEUR* was cocredited as art director on *SHADOW OF A DOUBT.* Afterward, he ranged from studio to studio for dozens of films, picking up an Oscar nomination for his shared credit on *NORTH BY NORTHWEST,* before returning to Universal as production designer of *THE BIRDS* and *MARNIE.*

Braban, Harvey (1883–1943) Stiff-upper-lip British actor of the twenties and thirties who played the Chief Inspector in the sound version of *BLACKMAIL.*

Bradin, Jean Continental actor who took a year off from his French and German roles, 1924–32, to star in two 1928 English-language films, *Moulin Rouge* and *CHAMPAGNE.*

Brainville, Yves (1914–) French actor, onscreen from 1947. His infrequent English-language film roles include the Moroccan police inspector in *THE MAN WHO KNEW TOO MUCH* (1956).

Braithwaite, (Dame) Lilian (1873–1948) Commanding British actress of stage (from 1897) and screen (from 1915) who was featured as Lady Berwick, the hero's supplicating mother, in *DOWNHILL.*

Brandon-Thomas, Amy (Marguerite) (1890–1974) British actress whose half-dozen movie chores included serving as Diana Baring's defense counsel in *MURDER!*

brandy Even within the context of eating and drinking that is so frequent and so frequently maligned in Hitchcock's films, the consumption of brandy has a special place. Brandy appears or is mentioned in nearly as many films as the director himself. As Donald SPOTO points out, it takes on a particular association beginning in *MR. AND MRS. SMITH* with medicine that is to be downed in a single gulp. "Just like medicine," Scottie Ferguson urges Madeleine Elster, pressing brandy on her after he has pulled her out of San Francisco Bay in *VERTIGO.* Characters who try to use brandy to create a more socially rarefied atmosphere are usually thwarted, as Lisa Fremont is in *REAR WINDOW* when Tom Doyle spills his snifter down the front of his clothes or Brenda Blaney is in *FRENZY* when the ex-husband she has taken to dinner becomes enraged enough to shatter his snifter in his hand; this suavest of all bottled alcoholic beverages is best taken as a dose of medicine for whatever ails the characters, from a bad chill to possession by the dead.

"Breakdown" 7th episode of *Alfred Hitchcock Presents,* broadcast November 13, 1955. **Associate producer:** Joan Harrison; **Director:** Alfred Hitchcock; **Assistant director:** James Hogan; **Teleplay:** Francis Cockrell and Louis Pollock, based on a short story by Pollock; **Cinematographer:** John L. Russell; **Art director:** Martin Obzina; **Set designer:** James S. Redd; **Editors:** Richard G. Wray and Edward W. Williams; **Costumes:** Vincent Dee; **Music:** Stanley Wilson; **Cast:** Joseph Cotten

(Callew), Raymond Bailey (Ed Johnson), Forrest Stanley (Hubka), Lane Chandler (the sheriff), Harry Shannon (Doc Horner), Murray Alper (Lloyd), James Edwards, Mike Ragan, Jim Weldon, Harry Landers, Richard Newton (convicts), Aaron Spelling (road worker), Elzie Emanuel (Callew's secretary), Ralph Peters.

The first episode of *Alfred Hitchcock Presents* to be filmed, though not the first broadcast, is a tour de force for Joseph Cotten, who stars as Callew, a ruthlessly competitive businessman who has spent a lifetime suppressing any sign of emotion as a weakness. After a back-road auto collision with a road crew's vehicle wrecks his car and leaves him paralyzed, his body is stripped of valuables by the convicts working on the crew and is then discovered and shipped to a mortuary, where a coroner pronouces him dead before a single tear running down Callew's cheek calls attention to the fact that he is still alive.

Brewer, Colin (M.)   British assistant director on a dozen British and international productions from *Tunes of Glory* (1960) to FRENZY and *The Odessa File* (1974).

Brewster, Diane (1931–1991)   American character actress best remembered for such iconic television roles as Miss Canfield, the grade-school teacher in *Leave it to Beaver* (1957–58) and Dr. Richard Kimball's murdered wife in *The Fugitive* (1963). She appeared as a typist in the ALFRED HITCHCOCK PRESENTS episode "THE CASE OF MR. PELHAM."

Brian, Judith   American character actress whose brief career in the fifties included an appearance as a passenger in the ALFRED HITCHCOCK PRESENTS segment "DIP IN THE POOL."

Bridge, Joan (1912–)   British color consultant credited as Natalie KALMUS's assistant on Technicolor films from *Blithe Spirit* (1945) to UNDER CAPRICORN and then became a principal consultant with the lapse of the Technicolor patents on some 40 films, occasionally consulting on costume design as well. She shared an Oscar for the costumes in *A Man for all Seasons* (1966).

Bridie, James (1888–1951)   Scottish physician-turned-playwright, born Osborne Henry Major, a guiding light behind the Glasgow Citizen's Theatre and the Edinburgh Festival. Hitchcock asked that his old acquaintance be brought in to work on the adaptation of THE PARADINE CASE and kept him on for UNDER CAPRICORN. Originally assigned to STAGE FRIGHT, he was not credited on the completed film, but his play *A Sleeping Clergyman* was filmed as *Flesh and Blood* the same year (1950), and he adapted his play *It Depends What You Mean* as *Folly to Be Wise* in 1953.

Brill, Lesley (1943–)   American film scholar, professor of Film Studies at Wayne State University and author of *John Huston's Filmmaking* (1997). His first book, *The Hitchcock Romance* (Princeton, 1988), takes issue with what he sees as the prevailing tendency to characterize the director as a "cynical, macabre trifler with an audience's emotions," arguing instead that his films, generally "happy fairy tales" such as THE 39 STEPS, YOUNG AND INNOCENT, TO CATCH A THIEF, NORTH BY NORTHWEST, and THE TROUBLE WITH HARRY, endorse the redemptive power of romantic love in a fallen world, even when the romance is qualified or complicated in such films as THE LODGER, I CONFESS, STRANGERS ON A TRAIN, and FRENZY. Indeed, Brill suggests, such ironic fables as BLACKMAIL, VERTIGO, PSYCHO, and TOPAZ, though expressing dread that love might not offer a romantic rebirth and grief when it does not, are not simply pessimistic, for they still maintain their faith in redemptive possibilities their particular characters are powerless to achieve or accept. In discussing Hitchcock's affirmative romances, Brill tends to give special weight to the endings that redeem their heroes' and heroines' travails; in considering his ironic romances, by contrast, he emphasizes the yearning developed in the middle of each story, the hope of romantic redemption they hold out until the catastrophes, which are still to be understood in a broader context of descent and return, death and the rebirth promised by love.

Brisson, Carl (1893–1958)   Rugged Danish silent leading man, né Carl Pederson, former middleweight champion with song and dance experience who played the quintessentially English types One-Round Jack, the boxer hero of THE RING, and Pete Quilliam, the sailor husband of Kate Cregeen in THE MANXMAN, before the coming of sound relegated him to Scandinavian ethnic roles in English and American cinema. His son, producer Frederick Brisson, married actress Rosalind Russell in 1941.

Bristol, Howard American set decorator whose three dozen credits, 1933–68, include his interior decoration of REBECCA and a shared credit for the stodgy, but surprisingly mobile, set of ROPE.

British International Pictures GAUMONT-BRITISH's chief rival in the home market throughout the thirties was founded in 1926, as British National, by American entrepreneur J.D. Williams and Scottish solicitor John MAXWELL, who wrested control of the firm from his partner the following year. Maxwell then constructed studios at Elstree ("the British Hollywood"), embarked on an ambitious production schedule, and hired, among others, Hitchcock, who, despite his frequent complaints about Maxwell's autocracy and lack of sympathy, directed 10 films there, more than he would make at any other studio—THE RING, THE FARMER'S WIFE, CHAMPAGNE, THE MANXMAN, BLACKMAIL, JUNO AND THE PAYCOCK, MURDER!, THE SKIN GAME, RICH AND STRANGE, and NUMBER SEVENTEEN—between 1927 and 1932 before the studio mutated into Associated British in 1933.

British Ministry of Information Of the nearly 20 propaganda shorts the ministry financed and released between London Can Take It (1940) and The True Glory (1945), Hitchcock's two wartime shorts, BON VOYAGE and AVENTURE MALGACHE, were among the last.

Britt, Leo British actor, generally in authoritative roles, 1933–69, in his homeland, whose storytelling at Tony Wendice's club nearly distracts Tony from his plan to kill his wife in DIAL M FOR MURDER.

Brodel, Joan (1925–) Hollywood ingenue, onscreen from 1937, who shortly after playing Johnny Jones's kid sister in FOREIGN CORRESPON-

DENT changed her name to Joan Leslie for High Sierra (1941) and under that name played a series of scrubbed second leads including Sergeant York (1941), Yankee Doodle Dandy (1942), This Is the Army (1943), Rhapsody in Blue (1945), and The Revolt of Mamie Stover (1956) before retiring to raise twins.

Brodie, Steve (1919–1992) Fireplug American character actor, born John Stevens. A veteran of nearly 80 films and 40 television segments from 1944, he was often typecast by his dumpling face as the hero's sidekick or sparring partner. He appeared in four episodes of ALFRED HITCHCOCK PRESENTS, as the victim's well-meaning husband Steve Grant in "The Creeper" (1956), the fatally helpful motorcycle cop who dogs Sam Jacoby in "ONE MORE MILE TO GO" (1957), the treacherous thief Maxie in "Enough Rope for Two" (1957), and Al Revnel, the old friend who comes between Norman Frayne and his wife in "Death Sentence" (1958).

Brooke, Hillary (1914–1999) American actress of the forties and early fifties, best known for her continuing roles in the television programs Abbott and Costello (1952) and My Little Margie (1952–54). One of her last roles was as Jo McKenna's friend Jan Peterson in THE MAN WHO KNEW TOO MUCH (1956).

Brookhouse, Christopher American author of novels (Running Out, 1970; Wintermute, 1978; Dear Otto, 1995; Passing Game, 2000), poems (Scattered Light, 1969; The Light Between the Fields, 1998), and stories (If Lost, Return, 1973). From 1992 to 2001 he served as founding editor of the HITCHCOCK ANNUAL, the preeminent American journal on the director's work. With Stanley Gottlieb he has edited the forthcoming Hitchcock Today: Selected Essays from the Hitchcock Annual.

Brough, Antonia (1900–1937) British stage actress whose brief film career was kicked off when she played Thirza Tapper's maid Susan in THE FARMER'S WIFE.

Brown, Bernard R. (1898–1981) American sound technician, a former violinist with the Los

Angeles Symphony at the time it recorded the music for *The Jazz Singer*. Sound supervisor for more than 100 films, 1937–53, including SABOTEUR and SHADOW OF A DOUBT. He was nominated for 10 Oscars—for the soundtracks of *That Certain Age* (1938), *Spring Parade* (1940), *Appointment for Love* (1941), *Arabian Nights* (1942), *The Phantom of the Opera* (1943), *His Butler's Sister* (1944), and *Lady on a Train* (1945), and for his special-effects work on *The Invisible Man Returns* (1940), *The Boys from Syracuse* (1940), and *Invisible Agent* (1942)—and won for his sound recording on *When Tomorrow Comes* (1939). A generation before Robert Altman, he pioneered the use of multiple soundtracks. He shared a technical achievement award in 1945 for the design and engineering of a separate soloist and chorus recording room.

Brown, Bryan Author of *The Alfred Hitchcock Movie Quiz Book* (Perigee, 1986), which attempts to "steer a center course between the profound and the trivial" by posing questions about characters, motives, and themes in Hitchcock's films and collaborators connected with the director.

Brown, James H(armon) American filmmaker who served as assistant director on THE BIRDS, MARNIE, and *Harper* (1966); more recently a producer and occasional writer on such television series as *Dallas* (1985–86).

Brown, John (1904–1957) British-born character actor, onscreen from 1944, most often in stuffed-shirt roles such as Professor Collins, Guy Haines's sozzled alibi witness in STRANGERS ON A TRAIN.

Brown, Wally (1904–1961) Motormouthed American comedian of the forties and fifties who is unusually subdued as Mr. Hopkins in NOTORIOUS.

Browne, Roscoe Lee (1925–) Impish African-American character actor, former track star and literature professor, whose scores of roles in movies and television include Philippe Dubois, the friend of Michael Nordstrom who is nearly killed when he bluffs his way into Rico Parra's New York hotel room in TOPAZ.

Bruce, Nigel (1895–1953) Bluff, genial, imperviously oblivious British character actor, a baronet's son who often played bumbling aristocrats in some 75 films from 1929 until his death. Though he never took a starring role, he often stole films from those who did. Unforgettable as the imperishably obtuse Dr. Watson to Basil Rathbone's canny Sherlock Holmes in the Fox and UNIVERSAL franchise, he took time out from the series to play two utterly characteristic roles for Hitchcock: Max de Winter's brother-in-law Giles Lacey in REBECCA and jolly, doomed Beaky Thwaite in SUSPICION.

Buchan, John (Lord Tweedsmuir) (1875–1950) Scottish novelist, historian, and statesman, whose war experience interrupted a career in law and publishing. He rose rapidly in the armed services to become Britain's director of information in 1917. In 1927 he was named to represent the Scottish universities in Parliament; in 1925 he became governor-general of Canada. In the meantime he had published many volumes of history and several novels of intrigue, most of them starring the reluctant adventurer Richard Hannay. Despite the free-wheeling cinematic flair of this series, which included *Greenmantle* (1916), *Mr. Standfast* (1919), and *The Three Hostages* (1924), only one of them was adapted for the movies: THE 39 STEPS (1915), whose man-on-the-run plot became virtually congruent with the public perception of the Hitchcock thriller (1935) and spawned two remakes in 1959 and 1978.

Bumstead, Henry (1915–) American art director (later production designer), in Hollywood from 1948. He designed the unusually sumptuous visuals for four Hitchcock films—THE MAN WHO KNEW TOO MUCH (1956), TOPAZ, FAMILY PLOT, and VERTIGO, for which he received his first Oscar nomination—and won Academy Awards for his work on *To Kill a Mockingbird* (1962) and *The Sting* (1975).

Burgess, Brian (D.) American producer and occasional director, one of whose first credits is as production manager on FRENZY.

Burks, Robert (1910–1968)   American cinematographer whose background in special-effects photography dates back to 1939. He supervised the effects work for some two dozen features at WARNER BROS., including *The Great Lie* (1941), *Kings Row* (1942), *Arsenic and Old Lace* (1944), *Night and Day* (1946), *The Unsuspected* (1947), and *Key Largo* (1948), and began to work in the meantime as a lighting cinematographer beginning in 1944. Following the success of the moody, stylish black-and-white look he gave his first Hitchcock film, STRANGERS ON A TRAIN, he returned for each of the director's subsequent films for 10 years, at first interspersing his assignments with other shoots like *The Enforcer* (1951), *Hondo* (1953), and *The Desert Song* (1953) but concentrating more exclusively on Hitchcock's films after the director's move to PARAMOUNT PICTURES in 1953. Equally at home in the grim black-and-white Brooklyn of THE WRONG MAN and the picture-postcard Riviera of TO CATCH A THIEF, for which his widescreen VistaVision compositions won him an Oscar, Burks became the core of the team of technicians Hitchcock kept with few changes throughout the fifties. In all, he photographed 12 Hitchcock films—*Strangers on a Train*, I CONFESS, DIAL M FOR MURDER, REAR WINDOW, THE TROUBLE WITH HARRY, *To Catch a Thief*, THE MAN WHO KNEW TOO MUCH (1956), *The Wrong Man*, VERTIGO, NORTH BY NORTHWEST, THE BIRDS, and MARNIE, breaking his streak only when the director decided to shoot PSYCHO with a television crew headed by ALFRED HITCHCOCK PRESENTS veteran John L. RUSSELL—and might have returned to shoot more if he and his wife had not been killed in a house fire in 1968. Asked about his exceptionally long collaboration with a director often noted for his dictatorial habits on set, Burks once said: "You never have any trouble with him as long as you know your job and do it. Hitchcock insists on perfection."

Burr, Raymond (1917–1993)   Grim-featured, heavy-set Canadian leading man who spent 10 years playing heavies, often soulful but nearly always guilty, in some 40 Hollywood films before being cast as the equally emphatic defenders of justice in the long-running television series *Perry Mason* (1957–66) and *Ironside* (1967–75)—in which latter a wheelchair accommodated his increasingly corpulent figure—and returning at the end of his life to play the most famous criminal attorney in fiction in two dozen Perry Mason television movies. Although his hard-set features seemed made for black and white, Hitchcock cast him as the wife-killer Lars Thorwald in REAR WINDOW, one of his first color films, making him up, as he later maliciously explained, to look like his former boss David O. SELZNICK.

Burton, Thayer   American actor who appears as the cashier in the ALFRED HITCHCOCK PRESENTS episode "BANG! YOU'RE DEAD."

Cady, Frank (1915–) American character actor whose three dozen film roles, many of them bits, included the man sleeping on the fire escape in *REAR WINDOW*. Later turning to television, he played the same character, Sam Drucker, on *Petticoat Junction* (1963–70), *The Beverly Hillbillies* (1968–69), and *Green Acres* (1965–71).

Cahiers du cinéma The pioneering cinema monthly, founded in 1951 and coedited by he journalist/theorist André Bazin and the journalist/filmmaker Jacques Doniol-Valcroze, was from its beginnings an amalgam of fans' notes, popular journalism, pamphleteering, and (especially after 1968) high theory. In the midfifties its contributors, many of whom would soon become active in the French New Wave, debated the merits of François TRUFFAUT's *politique des auteurs,* which reacted against the French tradition of quality represented by directors Claude Autant-Lara and Jean Delannoy and screenwriters Jean Aurenche and Pierre Bost—who pegged the merits of such films as *La symphonie pastorale* (1947) and *Le rouge et le noir* (1954) to their fidelity to their highly-regarded literary sources—to champion such American genre directors as Nicholas Ray, Robert Aldrich, and Hitchcock. In particular, the October 1954 issue of the journal (volume 7, number 39), which was devoted entirely to Hitchcock, launched a debate over his stature as a filmmaker represented on the one hand by the enthusiastic endorsements of Truffaut and Claude CHABROL and on the other by the polite skepticism of Bazin himself.

Cain, Syd (Sydney or Sidney) British art director and production designer who began as an assistant in 1955, then took charge of some two dozen productions from *The Road to Hong Kong* (1962) and *Fahrenheit 451* (1965) to *FRENZY*. He worked in various capacities on four James Bond films: *Dr. No* (1962), *From Russia with Love* (1963), *Live and Let Die* (1973), and *Goldeneye* (1995).

Caine, Sir (Thomas Henry) Hall (1853–1931) British popular novelist and playwright. After studying architecture and working as a journalist, he began his series of pietistic melodramas, most memorably about life on the Isle of Man, in 1885. In all, 12 silent films were based on nine of his novels. *THE MANXMAN*, the last of these, was a remake of a 1916 film.

Caine, Henry (1888–1962) British character actor who broke into films with the coming of sound, just in time to play government and military officials and authority figures such as Mr. Ackroyd in *NUMBER SEVENTEEN*. He retired in 1954.

Calder-Marshall, Arthur (1908–) British writer who suggested the subject that served as the basis of BON VOYAGE.

Calhern, Louis (1895–1956) Stage-trained romantic lead of the silents who ripened into an imposing character actor who could be as ineffectual as Ambassador Trentino in *Duck Soup* (1933), as compromised as Alonzo T. Emmerich in *The Asphalt Jungle* (1950), and as imposing as Oliver Wendell Holmes in *The Magnificent Yankee* (1951), even forgoing his trademark pencil mustache for the title role of *Julius Caesar* (1953). His role as Paul Prescott, Devlin's boss in NOTORIOUS, managed to suggest something of all these qualities.

Call of Youth, The Famous Players–Lasky, 1920. **Director:** Hugh Ford; **Screenplay:** Eve Unsell, based on the play by Henry Arthur Jones; **Intertitles:** Alfred Hitchcock; **Cast:** Mary Glynne (Betty Overton), Marjorie Hume (Joan Lawton), Jack Hobbs (Hubert Richmond), Malcolm Cherry (James Agar), Ben Webster (Mark Lawton), Gertrude Sterroll (Mrs. Lawton), Victor Humphrey (Peter Hoskins), John Peachey (Dr. Michaelson), and Ralph Foster (minister).

First of the 12 silent films for which Hitchcock designed intertitles.

Calthrop, Donald (1888–1940) British character actor whose lean and hungry look made him especially well-suited to playing ferrety villains in more than 50 films from 1915. Among his most memorable roles is Tracy, the insinuating blackmailer in BLACKMAIL. But he appeared in three other Hitchcock films, as the actor Ion Stewart in MURDER!, the hanger-on Needle Nugent in JUNO AND THE PAYCOCK, and the criminal Brant in NUMBER SEVENTEEN, and in two burlesque Shakespearean sequences in ELSTREE CALLING that Hitchcock may have directed as well.

cameo appearances Perhaps the very first device that distinguished Hitchcock from other film directors was his ritual appearance in each of his films in wordless walk-ons too brief to be called characters. Apart from his long-running later stint introducing episodes of ALFRED HITCHCOCK PRESENTS and THE ALFRED HITCHCOCK HOUR (and his single appearance in the cover drawing of the issue of *Alfred Hitchcock's Mystery Magazine* Mr. Renshaw is reading in "DIP IN THE POOL"), he appeared on-camera in THE LODGER "to fill the screen," as he said, and soon got into the habit of making equally brief appearances in his films, especially once he moved to Hollywood and was encouraged to promote his image as a marketing device. Of all his post-REBECCA films, only BON VOYAGE and AVENTURE MALGACHE lack the signature cameos; he seems indeed to have taken special pleasure in the challenge of appearing in the four one-set films—LIFEBOAT, ROPE, DIAL M FOR MURDER, and REAR WINDOW—that offered fewest possibilities to a passer-by. The cleverest of Hitchcock's cameos—for example, those in SHADOW OF A DOUBT, STAGE FRIGHT, TO CATCH A THIEF, NORTH BY NORTHWEST, and FAMILY PLOT—are as memorable as any other images in their films. Hitchcock's first truly recognizable cameo, and one of his most characteristic, is in BLACKMAIL; his most trenchant is in *Notorious;* his most hotly disputed, whose location has been resolved only by a search of WARNER BROS.' production records, is in *Rope;* his most ingenious and best-loved is in *Lifeboat.* Thomas LEITCH has suggested that the director's ritual appearances, which bridge the gap between the film's world and the world of filmmaker and audience, indicate the essentially ludic mode of his films; more recently, James VEST has begun a systematic exploration of the thematic significance of individual cameos. The most reliable of many lists of Hitchcock's appearances in his work is the tabulation David Barraclough made for Ken MOGG, on which the following account is based:

The Lodger: in a newsroom early in the film, his back to camera. Many commentators have professed to find him as well in the crowd that taunts the lodger as he is hanging below them, his handcuffs caught on an iron fence.

Easy Virtue: standing beside a tennis court.

Blackmail: a passenger tormented by a small boy in the Underground train carrying Frank and Alice to dinner.

Murder!: passing Sir John and the Markhams on a street as they discuss the investigation.

As Jack Favell (George Sanders) phones Mrs. Danvers in *Rebecca* to tell her of Rebecca's suicide, Hitchcock passes by in one of his hallmark cameo appearances. *(National Film Society Archive)*

The 39 Steps: in the crowd outside the music hall as Hannay prepares to take Annabella back to his flat.

Young and Innocent: as a photographer toying with a tiny camera outside the courthouse Robert Tisdall is escaping.

The Lady Vanishes: passing by in the crowd at Victoria Station at the very end of the film.

Rebecca: passing by a phone booth as Jack Favell phones Mrs. Danvers.

Foreign Correspondent: reading a newspaper as he passes the newly arrived Haverstock on a London street.

Mr. and Mrs. Smith: passing David on the street as David hurls imprecations at Jeff Custer's football prowess.

Suspicion: mailing a letter as Lina emerges from a bookstore.

Saboteur: standing at a New York newsstand.

Shadow of a Doubt: holding 13 spades as he plays bridge on the train that brings Uncle Charlie to Santa Rosa.

Lifeboat: in before-and-after pictures in a newspaper advertisement for the fictional weight-loss product Reduco.

Spellbound: emerging from an elevator in the lobby of the New York hotel to which Constance Peterson has traced the false Dr. Edwardes.

Notorious: drinking champagne at the Sebastians' party just after Devlin has expressed the hope that Alex won't have to go to the wine cellar for more.

The Paradine Case: carrying a cello at the rustic railroad station.

Rope: shown in profile in a small red neon sign that flashes 13 times between Kenneth and Janet just before they leave.

Under Capricorn: standing outside Government House in period costume.

Stage Fright: looking askance at Eve as she passes him on the street tentatively practicing her masquerade as Doris Tinsdale.

Strangers on a Train: carrying a double bass and boarding the train that drops Guy in Metcalf for his meeting with Miriam.

I Confess: crossing a flight of steps at the top of the screen just after the credit sequence.

Dial M for Murder: peering out from a reunion photo in Tony's scrapbook.

Rear Window: winding a mantel clock in the composer's apartment as Jeff waits for Lisa to bring in the dinner she has catered from 21.

To Catch a Thief: sitting next to Robie in the bus he uses to escape the police at the end of the opening sequence—a panning shot invisible in cropped prints but restored to video prints.

The Trouble with Harry: passing a roadside stand as Sam ignores the wealthy patron examining his paintings. Again, the image is missing from cropped prints.

The Man Who Knew Too Much: watching the acrobats in the marketplace at Marrakesh just before Louis Bernard is stabbed.

The Wrong Man: appearing (after excising a more typical cameo from the film as inappropriate) as himself, speaking to the camera to introduce the film before the opening credits.

Vertigo: passing Scottie on the street just before he enters Elster's office at the beginning of the third scene.

North by Northwest: missing a crowded bus at the end of the opening credits.

Psycho: standing outside the realty office at the beginning of the second scene in a five-gallon hat that will be echoed by the oilman Cassidy when he enters a few moments later.

The Birds: leaving a pet shop walking his own two terriers as Melanie enters in the opening scene.

Marnie: standing in a hotel corridor as Marnie goes to her room in the third scene.

Torn Curtain: holding a diapered baby distastefully but delicately above his lap in a lobby of a Copenhagen hotel on Michael and Sarah's arrival.

Topaz: rising from a wheelchair to meet an airline passenger as Michele and François arrive in New York.

Frenzy: shown from overhead as a member of the crowd listening to the political speech in the opening scene.

Family Plot: seen in silhouette behind a frosted window marked "Registrar of Births and Deaths," where Lumley discovers that there is no death certificate for Eddie Shoebridge.

Cameron, A(ngelina)　British sound recordist whose first film, *SABOTAGE*, was followed by only one other, *Dr. Syn* (1937).

Campbell, Kippy　Child actor whose only film role is as Manny Balestrero's son Robert in *THE WRONG MAN*.

Campbell & Connolly　The composers credited with the musical score for *BLACKMAIL* share no other film credits and have never been identified. Two possible candidates are Angela Campbell-MacInnes, whose only credited score is for *Song o' My Heart* (1930), and the American Myles Connolly (1897–1964), whose screen career (1925–52), most often as screenwriter and producer, includes the uncredited score for *Consolation Marriage* (1931).

Canning, Victor (1911–1986)　Prolific British thriller writer, former government clerk. Using both his own name and the pseudonym Alan Gould, he published several successful humorous novels before turning to international thrillers, often taking his latter-day series hero, agent Rex Carver, to exotic locales, with the nonseries *The Chasm* (1947). One of the least globe-hopping of his novels, *The Rainbird Pattern* (1972), was transferred to San Francisco when Hitchcock filmed it as FAMILY PLOT.

Cannon, Adele American continuity coordinator and script supervisor on five UNIVERSAL films of the forties, beginning with SABOTEUR and SHADOW OF A DOUBT.

Cardiff, Jack (1914–) Highly regarded British cinematographer, a specialist in color ever since he served as camera operator for Britain's first three-color Technicolor feature, *Wings of the Morning* (1937). He won an Academy Award for his work on *Black Narcissus* (1946). Immediately after he shot *The Red Shoes* (1948), which color consultant Natalie KALMUS called the perfect Technicolor film, Hitchcock hired him to photograph UNDER CAPRICORN. After another 20 films, including Oscar nominations for *War and Peace* (1956) and *Fanny* (1961), he turned to directing, but except for his Oscar-nominated work on *Sons and Lovers* (1960), this phase of his career was less successful, and after 1976 he returned to lighting and photographing such color spectaculars as *The Dogs of War* (1980) and *Tai-Pan* (1986).

Carey, Leonard (1897–1977) Cadaverous British character actor whose string of more than 80 roles as butlers and valets from 1930 to 1953 was broken by his indelible performance as Old Ben in REBECCA before he returned to his usual form, playing among many others uncredited butlers in SUSPICION and STRANGERS ON A TRAIN.

Carey, Macdonald (1913–1994) Inoffensively handsome American leading man who bounced from PARAMOUNT to other studios, mostly in forgettable films, before finding his niche as Dr. Tom Horton, dependable paterfamilias of the daytime drama *Days of Our Lives* (1965–94). His bland self-assurance made him ideal for the role of Jack Graham, the proudly "normal" detective who falls in love with Charlie Newton in SHADOW OF A DOUBT, and, 20 years later, for the roles of robbery victim John Pittkin in the ALFRED HITCHCOCK PRESENTS episode

"Coyote Moon" (1959) and John Mitchell, head of the equally normal family in the "House Guest" episode of THE ALFRED HITCHCOCK HOUR (1962).

Carlile, David American supporting actor. His sporadic appearances on film and television include six roles in ALFRED HITCHCOCK PRESENTS: as police officers in "The Last Dark Step" (1959), "A Night with the Boys" (1959) "One Grave Too Many" (1960), "Self Defense" (1961), and "The Kerry Blue" (1962), and as a bank teller in "The Horseplayer" (1961).

Carme, Pamela (b. 1902) British stage actress, née the Hon. Kathleen Pamela Boscawen, whose short-lived film career was paralleled by her role as the short-lived Christine Clay in YOUNG AND INNOCENT, the second and last of her films.

Carpenter, Claude (E.) (1904–1976) American set decorator, in Hollywood from 1942 to 1966, who joined Darrell SILVERA in designing the sets for NOTORIOUS.

Carroll, Leo G. (1892–1972) Sepulchral-voiced, stage-trained British character actor whose plummy diction made him a frequent butler and the perfect choice for Marley's Ghost in *A Christmas Carol* (1938). Immigrating to America, he became a leader of Hollywood's British colony and one of Hitchcock's favorite actors, taking a total of six increasingly droll and important roles: Rebecca's physician Dr. Baker in REBECCA; Johnnie Aysgarth's cousin Captain Melbeck in SUSPICION; Dr. Murchison, retiring director of Green Acres, in SPELLBOUND; the Crown Prosecutor in THE PARADINE CASE; Senator Morton in STRANGERS ON A TRAIN; and the Professor in NORTH BY NORTHWEST. He later became familiar to American audiences as the bewildered Cosmo Topper on *Topper* (1953–54) and the avuncular secret agent Alexander Waverly on *The Man from U.N.C.L.E.* (1964–68). When asked why he so often cast the colorless Carroll in his films, Hitchcock replied: "Because he does nothing well."

Carroll, Madeleine (1906–1987) Elegant, university-trained British leading lady, née Marie-

Madeleine Bernadette O'Carroll, whose blonde beauty launched her in the British industry in 1928 and whose immaculate diction made her a natural for sound films. Brought back from America to costar as Pamela in THE 39 STEPS, she was introduced to Robert DONAT on the first day of shooting when they were handcuffed together for a sequence late in the film, and the prop master mysteriously misplaced the key. Hitchcock himself called Carroll "the first blonde who was a real Hitchcock type," and his own revelation of the sexuality beneath her placid surface—especially evident in his often incongruously radiant lighting for her in her role as Elsa Carrington in SECRET AGENT—was consistently matched by his delight in asserting his control over her or making her look ridiculous, for example by his opening shot of Elsa's face covered in cold cream. After the death of her sister in the London blitz shortly after she had completed *My Favorite Blonde* (1942), Carroll returned to England to do war work and made only three more films before retiring in 1949.

Carruth, Milton (1899–1972) Veteran American editor who worked on SHADOW OF A DOUBT and more than 100 other Hollywood films, 1929–66, and directed a half-dozen second features in the thirties.

Carson, Charles (1886–1977) British actor, former civil engineer, onstage from 1919. After making his film debut in 1931, he brought an array of military, aristocratic, and political figures to life in nearly 80 films before his retirement in 1972. He played Ashenden's mysterious superior R in SECRET AGENT.

Carson, Frances (1895–) Mature American actress of the forties who played a half-dozen matronly types, including Mrs. Sprague in FOREIGN CORRESPONDENT, an unnamed society woman in SABOTEUR, and Mrs. Potter in SHADOW OF A DOUBT, her final film role.

Carson, Jack (1910–1963) Rubber-faced Canadian comic actor with vaudeville experience, in Hollywood from 1937. Despite his success in handling dramatic roles like Wally Fay in *Mildred Pierce* (1945),

Matt Libby in *A Star Is Born* (1954), and Jiggs, the airplane mechanic in *The Tarnished Angels* (1957), his raspy tenor and patented double-take cast him more often in comedy, generally as the dumb sharpie or the hero's sidekick. He served both functions in MR. AND MRS. SMITH as Chuck Benson, the fellow club member who takes David Smith on a memorable blind date.

Cartwright, Veronica (1950–) Anglo-American actress, older sister of television child star Angela Cartwright, began her own career early with *In Love and War* (1958) and *The Children's Hour* (1961) and soon thereafter appeared in two episodes of ALFRED HITCHCOCK PRESENTS—as Violet Wellington in "The Schwartz-Metterklume Method" (1960) and Judy Davidson in "Summer Shade" (1961)—and as Mitch Brenner's kid sister Cathy in THE BIRDS. Despite her own television success as the hero's daughter Jemima on *Daniel Boone,* her later career seems to have been haunted by her status as Hitchcockian victim, as witness her performances in *Invasion of the Body Snatchers* (1978), *Alien* (1979), and *Candyman II: Farewell to the Flesh* (1995), as well as her ghoulish/pathetic fate as Felicia Alden in *The Witches of Eastwick* (1987).

"Case of Mr. Pelham, The" 10th episode of *Alfred Hitchcock Presents,* broadcast December 4, 1955. **Associate producer:** Joan Harrison; **Director:** Alfred Hitchcock; **Assistant director:** Jack Corrick; **Teleplay:** Francis Cockrell, based on "The Strange Case of Mr. Pelham," a story by Anthony Armstrong; **Cinematographer:** John L. Russell; **Art director/set designer:** James S. Redd; **Costumes:** Vincent Dee; **Editors:** Richard G. Wray and Edward W. Wilson; **Music:** Stanley Wilson; **Cast:** Tom Ewell (Albert Pelham), Raymond Bailey (Dr. Harley), Kirby Smith (Tom Mason), Kay Stewart (Miss Clement), John Compton (Vincent), Norman Willis (Ray), Jan Arvan (Harry), Tim Graham, Justice Watson (Peterson), Richard Collier (necktie salesman), Diane Brewster (typist), Major Sam Harris.

The third episode Hitchcock directed for his television series, one of the wittiest and most unsettling, stars Tom Ewell as Albert Pelham, a businessman who suspects that someone is impersonating him. In a series of attempts to foil his double, Pelham changes his signature and his style of dress, but during his final confrontation with his double, his butler Peterson pushes him over the edge to madness when he rejects his claims on the grounds that Mr. Pelham would never wear the necktie he has chosen—leaving the false Pelham in complete control of his life. Hitchcock's introduction and conclusion to the program, in which he is led off protesting when his own role is taken over by a double, mirrors the plot of the episode.

Casson, Ann (1915–1993)   British stage actress, daughter of Sir Lewis Casson and Dame Sybil Thorndike, in occasional thirties films such as NUMBER SEVENTEEN, in which she plays the apparent heroine, Rose Ackroyd, who ends by being upstaged by the ostensible bad girl.

Catholicism   Not only the importance of Hitchcock's Catholicism but also its very nature have been the subjects of considerable disagreement. Donald SPOTO surmises that his regular Sunday attendance at Mass through the thirties was undertaken for the sake of his mother and daughter and that his own observance was spotty; Eric ROHMER and Claude CHABROL find Hitchcock's work saturated in the uncompromising Jansenism of Pascal and Racine, in which the mere disposition to sin generates a sense of guilt as overwhelming as sin itself; Neil P. HURLEY sees in it a considerably more positive Catholic spirituality that seeks through identification to mark his audience as well as his characters as "souls in suspense," but most commentators have passed over this side of Hitchcock in silence. It can safely be assumed that the Roman Catholicism of Hitchcock's birth family was one of many factors that isolated their son from his peers, and Hitchcock, who was educated at St. Ignatius College from 1910 to 1913, referred to the formative influence of his Jesuit education for the rest of his life. The elements of this education he most often stressed to interviewers were categorical thinking, an emphasis on strict discipline and corporal punishment for minor infractions, the internalization of guilt, and the ultimate ascendancy of good over evil. His neurotically methodical habits of work and his lifelong love of ritual, from his trademark black

suits on set to his cameo appearances onscreen, if not his generally untrammeled appetite for food and drink, clearly reflect the discipline he was taught. Except for the conventional triumph of right over wrong mandated by the Production Code, however, the scant orthodox, positive Catholic spirituality in Hitchcock's films is dwarfed by the overwhelming emphasis on negative elements: a fear of punishment that becomes internalized as a dread of wrongdoing, a sexual prudishness that represses desires expressed indirectly through a pervasive fetishism, a terror (ironically emphasized by the education that might have given the young Hitchcock a sense of community that compensated for the ways his religion set him apart from his Protestant contemporaries) of alienation. The director's most overtly Catholic gestures in I CONFESS and THE WRONG MAN—the moments when Father Logan is surrounded by a crowd reminiscent of Christ's crucifixion, for example, or when Manny Balestrero prays for deliverance and his prayer is followed immediately by the arrest of the criminal for whom he has been mistaken—both central exhibits for Rohmer and Chabrol—are among his most facile and unconvincing moments. Even the kidnapping of Bishop Wood from Mass in FAMILY PLOT, a scene Hitchcock had long dreamed of filming to show how religious ritual inhibited rational thought or action, is curiously perfunctory. Apart from these few sequences, God and Christ's church are no more obviously present in Hitchcock's world than in Racine's. Both Hitchcock's most anguished descents into spiritual despair—Scottie's breakdown in VERTIGO and the final shot of Norman Bates chastising himself in his mother's voice at the end of PSYCHO—and his most joyous celebrations of transcendence—the love affairs metaphorically consummated at the end of YOUNG AND INNOCENT and THE TROUBLE WITH HARRY—are equally secularized, and it is probably safe to identify the Catholicism of Hitchcock's films, and perhaps of the director himself, as cultural rather than specifically religious.

Cavanagh, James P. (1922–1971)   American film and television writer who adapted many stories for ALFRED HITCHCOCK PRESENTS, among them the

Hitchcock-directed "ONE MORE MILE TO GO" and "ARTHUR," and who wrote an abortive first-draft screenplay for PSYCHO.

Cecil, Henry (pseudonym of **Henry Cecil Leon)** (1902–1976)   British barrister, judge, and crime writer. Of his many books presenting the law as an arena appealing to the sharpest instincts of every player, from criminal defendants to their attorneys to the judges who rule the courtrooms in which their fates are decided, his *Brothers-in-Law* (1955) has reached the widest audience through its adaptations to the stage, the cinema (1957), and a television series. His earlier novel, *No Bail for the Judge* (1952), served as the basis for an abortive film Hitchcock planned to follow NORTH BY NORTHWEST, perhaps the most famous of all his unrealized projects, which was canceled when its prospective star, Audrey Hepburn, whose character went undercover as a prostitute to gather evidence exculpating her jurist father from a murder charge, refused to play a scene in which she was raped. A few years later, Hitchcock chose his story "I SAW THE WHOLE THING," with its typical courtroom maneuvering and its ironic final twist, as the basis for the only television segment he directed for THE ALFRED HITCHCOCK HOUR.

Cellier, Frank (1884–1948)   Britsh character actor whose heavy, deliberate manner and penetrating gaze gave a sour edge to the Scottish sheriff who detains Richard Hannay in THE 39 STEPS and dozens of other roles through the thirties and forties.

Chabrol, Claude (1930–)   French filmmaker and film journalist, first in the publicity department in 20TH CENTURY–FOX's Paris bureau, then as critic for *Arts* and CAHIERS DU CINÉMA. Here, he published an interview with Hitchcock in 1954 and joined François TRUFFAUT for a second interview, whose outcome Truffaut describes in the introduction to his book on Hitchcock, the following year. His feature debut, *Le beau Serge* (1958), is widely acknowledged as the inaugural film of the French New Wave. Chabrol is an analyst of middle-class mores who frequently uses murder, as in *La femme infidèle* (1968), *Que la bête meurt* (1969), and *Le boucher* (1970), to anatomize the stifling petit bourgeoisie of his youth. Indeed, his 40 films, nearly half of them starring his sometime wife Stéphane Audran, have earned him the title of "the French Hitchcock," and apart from their ironic, often dispassionately chilly handling of violent subjects, many of them, like *La femme infidèle* and *Le boucher,* include pastiches that pay explicit homage to Hitchcock. A year before he used an inheritance from his first wife to finance *Le beau Serge,* Chabrol, in collaboration with Eric ROHMER, published *Hitchcock. Classiques du cinéma* (Universitaires, 1957), which surveyed Hitchcock's films through THE WRONG MAN. The study not only established Hitchcock as an artist worthy of serious study but also laid down many arguments about the director that have since become truisms: His films vacillate between moral vision and commercial compromise; the heart of their morality is a "transfer of guilt" that implicates the technically innocent heroes of SHADOW OF A DOUBT and STRANGERS ON A TRAIN in the actions of their demonic doubles; they motivically displace Catholic rituals onto secular iconography (so that the psychoanalyst's couch takes the place of the confessional); their rigorous form "does not embellish content; it creates it." After 20 years of prodigious, though largely indirect, influence on Hitchcock studies, the volume was translated by Stanley Hochman as *Hitchcock: The First Forty-Four Films* (Ungar, 1979).

Champagne   (Alternative titles: *A l'américaine, Tabarin di lusso*) British International, Wardour & F., approximately 86 minutes (U.K.)/88 minutes (U.S.); August 1928. **Producer:** John Maxwell; **Director:** Alfred Hitchcock; **Screenplay:** Eliot Stannard, based on an original story by Walter C. Mycroft; **Adaptation:** Alfred Hitchcock; **Cinematographer:** John J. Cox; **Art director:** C.W. Arnold; **Assistant director:** Frank Mills; **Camera assistant:** Alfred Roome; **Still photographer:** Michael Powell; **Cast:** Betty Balfour (The Girl), Jean Bradin (The Boy), Theo von Alten (The Man), Gordon Harker (The Father), Clifford Heatherley (impresario), Hannah Jones (club servant), Claude Hulbert (club guest on staircase), Balliol and Merton (dancers), Phyllis Konstam.

Hitchcock's eighth film was a labor of love, though the love was not Hitchcock's. It began with production chief Walter MYCROFT's suggestion in February 1928 that because everybody loved champagne, BRITISH INTERNATIONAL ought to make a movie about it. Hitchcock duly responded by sketching out a moral fable about a country girl who works in a wine cellar and watches the trains carrying cases of champagne off to the city. Eventually she makes the trip to Paris herself, loses both her virtue and her taste for champagne, and returns sadder but wiser to watch the departure of the champagne that will doom some other innocent. Mycroft, who was looking for a vehicle for comedienne Betty BALFOUR, Britain's most popular female movie star, demanded something different, and the result, though equally moralistic in outline—a madcap heiress elopes over her father's objections and then has to suffer the humiliation of poverty when he loses all his money, only to be restored to both the father and the lover her behavior has antagonized by the news that the father's impoverishment has all been a hoax—is far broader and more digressive in its treatment. Annoyed at the trite story forced on him by an executive whose involvement in the screenplay remained smothering, Hitchcock refused to cast the usual extras in the crowd scenes aboard the ship the heroine follows in her father's airplane, and then blew up at the novices hired in their places. Nor did contemporary reviewers find the film any more effervescent.

Hitchcock complained to François TRUFFAUT that the film as written had no story to tell, and it is easy to see what he meant. It is no more plotless than Hitchcock's two preceding films THE RING and THE FARMER'S WIFE, but the story seems more weightless, partly because the nameless heroine never makes the convincing transition from lightweight romantic farce to street-sorrow melodrama the film seems to require, partly because the audience is let in on the hoax too soon to generate much sympathy for the heroine's plight, partly because the film is so ill-integrated, not only from its bubbly first half to its allegedly somber second half but also from one sequence to the next. Although nearly every episode even in the glittery opening sequences aboard the ship where the heroine catches up with her swain is marked by petty bickering about who ought to be arranging their marriage or clever bits of business

like the young man's seasickness, the film never places these incidents in a larger frame, and so they undermine the idealized image of comic romance without contributing any ironic new meaning. The film's most serious gesture toward an integrative framework, a mysterious older man who keeps a sinister eye on the heroine throughout her adventures, turns out to be another red herring. Even though a particularly vivid scene shows him assaulting her after she has gone to work in a dance hall before it is revealed as only a scene she has imagined (and just why she has suddenly imagined it is left disturbingly unclear), and even though she agrees to travel with him to America even after this episode because of her anger over her father's hoax, he is simply an old friend her father has asked to keep an eye on her and prevent her marriage. The film seems to embrace an aesthetic of conflict (romantic spats, generational arguments, painful adjustments to apparent poverty or sexual threats, emotional reactions based on jealousy or spite) at any price; the peripheral drama of watching and being watched that, in the end, is no more central to this film than the champagne of its title will have to wait for other films like THE LADY VANISHES, NOTORIOUS, REAR WINDOW, VERTIGO, and PSYCHO for its full development.

Champagne, Clarence Special effects photographer who worked on PSYCHO and *Psycho a Go-Go!* (1965).

Chandler, Joan (1923–1979) American ingenue, born Joan Cheeseman, whose handful of screen roles in the forties and fifties include Janet Walker, successively the girlfriend of Brandon Shaw, Kenneth Lawrence, and David Kentley in ROPE.

Chandler, Raymond (1888–1959) Seminal American hardboiled writer, educated in England, whose extensive business career ended when, fired from his well-paying job for chronic drunkenness, he decided at the age of 45 to become a full-time writer. After a five-year apprenticeship to the pulps, which produced 20 stories, many of which he cannibalized for his later novels, he began his classic series of Philip Marlowe novels with *The Big Sleep* (1939).

A master of dialogue and atmospheric description, Chandler had little patience with the mechanics of plot, and the most successful of the many film versions of his novels, *Murder, My Sweet* (1944) and *The Big Sleep* (1946), freely transform his often rickety stories. (In the most celebrated of many Chandler anecdotes, screenwriter William Faulkner confessed to director Howard Hawks that he couldn't understand who had killed the chauffeur in *The Big Sleep*, and when Hawks, equally uncertain, telephoned the author to ask him, the unconcerned Chandler couldn't remember.) Signed to help Billy Wilder adapt James M. Cain's *Double Indemnity* for the screen in 1944, Chandler pumped up Cain's dialogue with florid running metaphors that sounded a great deal more like Chandler than like Cain. But the film, rather to Hitchcock's envy, was highly successful, and Chandler worked on two other properties and wrote an original screenplay of his own for *The Blue Dahlia* (1946). Signed by Hitchcock to write the screenplay for STRANGERS ON A TRAIN, he suggested that Guy Haines protect his status as hero by only pretending to go through with his plan to kill Bruno Anthony's hated father, but he chafed under Hitchcock's shot-by-shot control of the film, which subordinated problems of motivation to narrative style, and was replaced by Czenzi ORMONDE. The unhappy collaboration was to be Chandler's last Hollywood assignment; though films based on his novels continued to appear for many years after his death, he never worked in the movies again.

Chaplin, Esme V. British actor who played the prosecuting attorney in *MURDER!*

Chapman, Edward (1901–1977) Tall, inexpressive British character actor whose debut performance in the title role of Captain Jack Boyle in *JUNO AND THE PAYCOCK* kicked off a career that lasted 40 years and took him through some 80 roles in the British industry, two more for Hitchcock: Sir John's theatrical liaison Ted Markham in *MURDER!* and the brutish Dawkins in *THE SKIN GAME.*

Chapman, Lonny (1921–) American character actor, in Hollywood from 1954, whose scores of

solid-citizen supporting roles in movies and television include Deke Carter, the sympathetic counterman in *THE BIRDS.*

Chase, Steven (1902–1982) Rugged American film and television actor, born Alden Chase, usually in outdoorsman roles. *ALFRED HITCHCOCK PRESENTS* casts him in one of his rare indoors-only roles as the Colonel, who bids farewell to his longtime inamorata with a mink coat, in "MRS. BIXBY AND THE COLONEL'S COAT."

Chekhov, Michael (1891–1955) Russian-born stage actor and director, nephew of the playwright Anton Chekhov. His success in czarist Russia, where he worked with Konstantin Stanislavski, was confirmed when he played the czar in his first film, *Tercentenary of the Romanov Dynasty's Accession to the Throne* (1913). He worked with Max Reinhardt in Germany and then traveled to England, where he founded a theater and an acting school. In the United States from 1943, he founded a second acting school and appeared in a dozen films in Russian ethnic roles, one of which—Dr. Alex Brulov, Constance Peterson's fatherly training psychiatrist in *SPELLBOUND*—won him an Oscar nomination.

Cheshire, Harry (V.) (1891–1968) American character actor who squeezed more than 100 minor roles into a 25-year period from 1940. Instantly recognizable from his white hair and insinuating voice, he played a bit as Mr. Gorman, Dr. Bixby's dental patient in the *ALFRED HITCHCOCK PRESENTS* episode "MRS. BIXBY AND THE COLONEL'S COAT."

Chesney, Arthur (1882–1949) Balding, stage-trained British actor, younger brother of Edmund Gwenn, who followed his brother into films in 1920 and preceded him in Hitchcock's work when he appeared as the heroine's father Mr. Bunting in *THE LODGER.*

children Given their frequently dark-toned emphasis on violence, guilt, and revenge, it is not surprising that Hitchcock's films were never marketed to children—an anomaly that would doubtless be rectified if they were released today. What is more surprising is the frequency with which children do turn up in these adult stories, nearly always in connection with the adults' regressive behavior. The world of Hitchcock's silents is insulated from children, except for the babies who arrive to complicate the problems in THE MOUNTAIN EAGLE and THE MANXMAN. The children who cause such trouble in THE LODGER, DOWNHILL, and JUNO AND THE PAYCOCK are virtually adults themselves. Soon after showing the heroine of CHAMPAGNE and the entire cast of NUMBER SEVENTEEN acting like children, however, Hitchcock motivically doubles the kidnapped Betty Lawrence, in THE MAN WHO KNEW TOO MUCH (1934), with her often childish captor Abbott from practically her first speech ("I'm not a baby," she tells him indignantly in disclaiming interest in the chiming watch he shows her). This motif disappears from the 1956 remake, though it retains the earlier film's Albert Hall climax, in which, as Elisabeth WEIS notes, the kidnapped child's mother saves the diplomat from shooting by breaking the decorum of a crowded concert hall with her scream, indicating that she is not afraid to act like a child herself. Thereafter, children consistently provide a correlative to the adults' regression to childish irresponsibility, whether this regression is charming (as in YOUNG AND INNOCENT, with the game of blind-man's bluff featured at the birthday party at which Erica tries to hide the police suspect, Robert Tisdall, from the suspicions of Erica's aunt), somber (as in SABOTAGE, with its innocent child sent to do an adult's job), or shocking (as in SHADOW OF A DOUBT, with the psychopathic Uncle Charlie doubled with his teenaged niece and surrounded at the dinner table by his even younger niece and nephew). Children are improbably excluded from the apartments of REAR WINDOW except for the older couple's dog and the sculptress's statuary, but they appear in SPELLBOUND in a flashback that provides a shorthand explanation for John Ballantine's neurotic assuming of guilt in the death of Dr. Edwardes, in STAGE FRIGHT in the person of an innocent emissary who can confront the guilty Charlotte Inwood, in STRANGERS ON A TRAIN to emphasize the ways the amusement park licenses regressive desires, in THE TROUBLE WITH HARRY to provide an oblivious audience to the characters' shenani-

gans and to set the seal of playful inconsequence on them, and in THE WRONG MAN to witness the shame of their wrongly suspected father. Adults are treated like children in THE LADY VANISHES (especially in the sequence in the baggage car), in REBECCA (whose bridegroom tells his bride you "can't be too careful with children"), in SUSPICION (whose heroine marries a man whose suspicious behavior she persistently rationalizes as childlike), in NOTORIOUS (whose adult villain remains firmly under his mother's thumb), in NORTH BY NORTHWEST (whose hero, an hour after he is admonished, "You will wait here," tells the heroine that when he was a little boy he would never let his mother undress him), and in PSYCHO (whose baleful Mrs. Bates tongue-lashes her adult son unmercifully). Perhaps Hitchcock's most memorable sequences involving children, however, are the attacks on the birthday party and the school in THE BIRDS, in which the fragile acculturation represented by adults' rules is shattered by the savagery of the ultimate outsiders to the community.

Chraibi, Abdelhaq Mideastern actor who played bits in *Ali Baba and the Forty Thieves* (1954) and THE MAN WHO KNEW TOO MUCH (1956) and served as well as technical advisor on the latter.

Cianelli, Eduardo (1889–1969) Superlatively villainous Italian actor with experience in opera and onstage. Though he could evoke sympathy, for example as the priest in the ALFRED HITCHCOCK PRESENTS episode "Strange Miracle" (1962), his success as scheming Trock Estrella in the Broadway production of *Winterset* (1935), which he reprised onscreen in 1936, quickly became a signature role that established him as the suavest of Hollywood heavies and led to his typecasting as dozens of ethnic villains such as Krug, the thug whose minions kidnap the diplomat Van Meer in FOREIGN CORRESPONDENT.

Clanton, Ralph (1914–) American character actor of the fifties when he played modest roles in a dozen films. He appeared in four roles in ALFRED HITCHCOCK PRESENTS: Sir Stephen Hurstwood in "The Gentleman from America" (1956), Randolph Burnside in "The Legacy" (1956), Perry Harrison in

"Malice Domestic" (1957), the prosecutor in "Flight to the East" (1958), the pursers in "DIP IN THE POOL" and "The Hero" (1960), and Mr. Saunders in "The Avon Emeralds" (1959).

Clare, Mary (1894–1970) Stage-trained British actress who graduated from playing the pathetic Chloe Hornblower in the silent film version of *The Skin Game* (1920) to dozens of roles during the next 30 years as matrons whose piercing gaze could be counted on to disquiet the principals, as in her performances as Erica's formidable aunt in *YOUNG AND INNOCENT* and the Baroness whose imperiously expressionless "there has been no English lady here" established the menace in the generally lighthearted *THE LADY VANISHES*.

Clark, Carroll (1894–1968) Prolific, versatile American art director, with RKO from the thirties until the studio's closing. After working on the Astaire-Rogers musicals, he went on to design some of the most distinctive black-and-white crime productions of the forties and fifties, from *Murder, My Sweet* (1944) and *NOTORIOUS*, his only Hitchcock film, to *While the City Sleeps* (1956) and *Beyond a Reasonable Doubt* (1957), before hooking up with Disney for *Johnny Tremain* (1957) and some three dozen additional family features. He was nominated for Oscars for his work on seven of his nearly 200 films: *The Gay Divorcee* (1934), *Top Hat* (1935), *A Damsel in Distress* (1937), *Flight for Freedom* (1943), *Step Lively* (1944), *The Absent-Minded Professor* (1961), and *Mary Poppins* (1964).

Clark, Ken (1927–) American supporting actor of the fifties who appeared in a half-dozen Hollywood films, notably *South Pacific* (1958), and took four roles in *ALFRED HITCHCOCK PRESENTS*— the police officers in "The Dangerous Type" (1957) and "The Motive" (1958), Mike in "LAMB TO THE SLAUGHTER," and a firefighter in "Insomnia" (1960)—before moving to Italy and international productions based there.

Clarke Smith, D(ouglas) A. (1888–1959) British character actor, mostly onstage, but a ubiqui-

tous presence in British productions of the thirties, when he played dozens of gruff police inspectors such as Binstead in *THE MAN WHO KNEW TOO MUCH* (1934), returning for an uncredited bit in *SABOTAGE*.

Clatworthy, Robert (1903–1972) Veteran American art director and production designer, in Hollywood from 1944, who graduated from such unsung second features as *Phantom Lady* (1944) to big, nondescript productions such as *The Secret of Santa Vittoria* (1969), with a stop along the way for *PSYCHO*.

Clift, Montgomery (1920–1966) Intense, sensitive American leading man of the fifties, born Edward Montgomery Clift; with Marlon Brando the preeminent film actor of the period. Onstage at the age of 13, he turned down several Hollywood

Montgomery Clift

roles—including Brandon Shaw in ROPE, which he declined because he did not want to play a character whose homosexuality so openly hinted at his own. He preferred to make his debut in the more discreetly homoerotic western *Red River* (1948) and was nominated for an Oscar for *The Search* (1948), the first of his films to be released. *A Place in the Sun* (1951), his second Oscar-nominated lead, catapulted him into the front rank of Hollywood stars, and this time Hitchcock snared him for the role of the chaste, but indubitably heterosexual, Father Michael Logan in *I CONFESS*. Despite his continued professional success, marked by a third nomination for *From Here to Eternity* (1953), Clift's drinking, drug use, and estrangement from his father made him vulnerable to depression, and a near-fatal car crash as he was leaving a party at costar Elizabeth Taylor's home in the middle of filming *Raintree County* (1957) scarred his exceptionally handsome face. His film roles, never frequent, became even fewer, and although he was nominated for a fourth Oscar for *Judgment at Nuremberg* (1961), his career was in decline when he died of a sudden heart attack.

Clive, E.E. (1879–1940)   British character actor, long on stage in England and, after 1912, the United States, where he produced and directed as well as acted, before his Hollywood debut in 1933 led to nearly 100 films crowded into a single decade. A specialist in stiff rectitude, he ranged socially from titled aristocrats to their butlers but is perhaps best remembered as Bulldog Drummond's sidekick Tenny Tennison in a series of B-films beginning with *Bulldog Drummond's Revenge* (1937). His final film appearance was an uncredited bit as Mr. Naismith in *FOREIGN CORRESPONDENT*.

Coburn, Charles (1877–1961)   Portly, crusty American actor of commanding, though sometimes crooked, weight. He became manager of a theater in his hometown of Savannah, Georgia, at 17 and made his stage debut at 24. In 1906 he and his first wife, Ivah Wills, founded the Coburn Shakespeare Players. He turned down many offers from Hollywood, appearing in only two films (his debut was the title role in *Boss Tweed,* 1933) before Wills died in 1937

and he decided at the age of 60 to devote himself to full-time movie work. A specialist in monocled capitalists and politicians in more than 70 films, he scored impressively in *The Lady Eve* (1941) and *The Devil and Miss Jones* (1941) and won an Academy Award for *The More the Merrier* (1943). As Sir Simon Flaquer, Mrs. Paradine's solicitor in *THE PARADINE CASE*, he exuded a characteristic combination of reassuring authority and fussy impotence.

Cockrell, Francis (d. 1987)   American screenwriter, sometimes billed as Frank Cockrell, in Hollywood for a dozen features from 1932, who switched from movies to television in the midfifties. His credits include *Alcoa Presents, Batman, The High Chaparral,* and many episodes of *ALFRED HITCHCOCK PRESENTS*, where he was the director's favorite adapter, writing or cowriting five segments directed by Hitchcock: "REVENGE," "BREAKDOWN," "THE CASE OF MR. PELHAM," "A DIP IN THE POOL," and "BANQUO'S CHAIR." He also wrote the adaptation for "FOUR O'CLOCK," the only episode of *SUSPICION* Hitchcock directed.

Cockrell, Marian (B.) (1909–1999)   American writer, wife of Francis COCKRELL, who wrote the stories used as the basis for *Professor Beware* (1938) and *Dark Waters* (1944). Her later television credits include *Batman* and several episodes of *ALFRED HITCHCOCK PRESENTS*, including one directed by Hitchcock: "WET SATURDAY." She also directed a single episode of the program: "The Rose Garden" (1956).

Cohen, Paula Marantz (1953–)   American film scholar, professor of humanities and communications at Drexel University. She has continued the exploration of "the father-daughter dyad" charted in *The Daughter's Dilemma: Family Process and the Nineteenth-Century Domestic Novel* (1991) with *Alfred Hitchcock: The Legacy of Victorianism* (University of Kentucky, 1995), which considers the waning influence on Hitchcock's career of two forces Cohen associates with Victorianism: a psychological conception of character (as opposed to a conception anchored in physical appearances, such cinematic techniques as shot-reversals, or an appeal to the audience's speculations), and the importance of female subjectivity in provoking and inflecting melodramatic plots by enticing and threatening the male agents. Hitchcock's early films, Cohen argues, seek to balance an essentially feminized culture of emotional subjectivity and introspection with the active male access to the hierarchy of legal power either by moving toward an idealized heterosexual union or by valorizing "the daughter's effect" in providing father figures like Uncle Charlie in SHADOW OF A DOUBT, Commodore Gill in STAGE FRIGHT, or Senator Morton in STRANGERS ON A TRAIN with complementary female figures who can provide the humanity and imagination their founding males lack (and their mother figures cannot supply because they are absent or dead or no longer shrouded in romantic illusion). By the time of PSYCHO, she contends, Hitchcock has lost hope in any such complementarity, and his later films show not only "an unraveling family ideology" but also a lack of interest in psychologically complex characters as such. Her latest book is *Silent Film and the Triumph of the American Myth* (2001).

Cohen, Tom (1953–) American scholar of cultural studies, professor of English at the State University of New York at Albany. He has written *Anti-Mimesis from Plato to Hitchcock* (1994) and *Ideology and Inscription: 'Cultural Studies' After Benjamin, de Man, and Bakhtin* (1998) and edited *Material Events: Paul de Man and the Afterlife of Theory* (2001). Cohen's first two books press Hitchcock, among many other writers and thinkers, into an attack on representational modes of criticism (auteurism, hermeneutics, thematics, mimetics) by focusing on a "black sun"—variously figured in Hitchcock's work as feet, black cats or dogs or birds, excrement, or the blank materiality of writing—that precedes and undercuts any "ocularcentrist" reading that assumes a close correspondence between texts like THE 39 STEPS and SABOTAGE and any clear locus of illumination, meaning, or origin by unmasking the arbitrary codes of all "technologies of the visible" like cinema or tourism. *Hitchcock's Black Sun: Travel Services, Chronographics, and Broken Paroles,* forthcoming from the University of Minnesota Press, extends this argument to a broad range of Hitchcockian texts, culmi-

nating with an exhaustive analysis of TO CATCH A THIEF that seeks to unmask classical aesthetics, whether normative, expressive, or epistemological, as "epistemo-tourism," and replace it with "a new inscriptive model" in which the act and fact of writing in all its materiality takes precedence over any possible meaning it might have.

Colasanto, Nicholas (1924–1985) Beetle-browed, pug-faced American character actor, a natural for ethnic heavies. Most memorable as the mobster Tommy Como in *Raging Bull* (1980), he assumed another nationality to play Constantine, the first kidnap victim in FAMILY PLOT.

Coleman, Herbert (1907–2001) Key Hitchcock collaborator most active in the fifties, 30 years after he began as a script editor at PARAMOUNT and rose to William Wyler's assistant director on *Roman Holiday* (1953). He worked with Hitchcock as assistant director on REAR WINDOW and second-unit director on TO CATCH A THIEF and then served as associate producer on THE TROUBLE WITH HARRY, THE MAN WHO KNEW TOO MUCH (1956), THE WRONG MAN, VERTIGO, and NORTH BY NORTHWEST. Thereupon he left Hitchcock to direct two 1961 features, *Battle at Bloody Beach* and *Posse from Hell,* but returned as associate producer on several episodes of THE ALFRED HITCHCOCK HOUR; directed one episode, "Night Fever" (1965); and several years later served as associate producer on TOPAZ.

Collier, Constance (1878–1955) Grande dame of the British, later the American, theater, born Laura Constance Hardie. A former chorus girl, she made her film debut in *Intolerance,* and during her Hollywood heyday in the thirties and forties played some two dozen imperious, often eccentric dowagers in films from *Anna Karenina* (1935) to *An Ideal Husband* (1947). One of her last films was ROPE, in which she played Anita Atwater, David Kentley's oblivious grande-dame aunt, who smilingly predicted of the pianist who helped strangle her nephew: "These hands will bring you great fame." A sometime playwright and stage director, she collaborated with actor Ivor NOVELLO on several plays, including *Down Hill*

(1926), whose stage run she directed herself before Hitchcock directed its film version as DOWNHILL.

Collier, John (1901–1980) British author whose witty, macabre sensibility was rivaled only by Roald DAHL'S as a match, and perhaps a model, for Hitchcock's. Though his film work was infrequent and generally atypical—he worked on some 10 adaptations, beginning with *Sylvia Scarlett* (1935), over a 30-year period—he wrote many stories from the twenties memorably adapted for ALFRED HITCHCOCK PRESENTS, including "BACK FOR CHRISTMAS" and "WET SATURDAY."

Collier, Richard (1919–2000) American film and television actor, an intermittent supporting presence from 1954 in some 40 films and television segments, including his role as the necktie salesman in the ALFRED HITCHCOCK PRESENTS episode "THE CASE OF MR. PELHAM."

Collinge, Patricia (1892–1974) Gentle Irish-American actress who after long stage experience went to Hollywood to reprise her performance as Aunt Birdie in *The Little Foxes* (1941), won an Oscar nomination, and returned for a half-dozen screen roles, ending with *The Nun's Story* (1959), and a handful of television roles, including four in ALFRED HITCHCOCK PRESENTS—wheelchair-bound Martha Cheney in "The Cheney Vase" (1955), Julia Pickering in "The Rose Garden" (1956), widowed Sophia Winter in "Across the Threshold" (1960), and the title character in "The Landlady" (1961)—and two in THE ALFRED HITCHCOCK HOUR: the unwisely infatuated Naomi Freshwater in "Bonfire" (1962) and the menaced cat fancier Mrs. Snow in "The Ordeal of Mrs. Snow" (1964). A novelist and playwright as well as an actress, she wrote the love scene in the garage between Charlie Newton and Jack Graham in SHADOW OF A DOUBT, in which she plays Charlie's endearingly scatty mother Emma.

Collins, Dale (1897–1956) Prolific Australian novelist and storyteller whose works were occasionally adapted to the screen. A friend of the Hitchcocks, he wrote RICH AND STRANGE (1930), whose story echoes in its early scenes Hitchcock's tales of his 1926 honeymoon, and which Hitchcock's film version follows closely in turn.

color Like synchronized sound, color remained for Hitchcock something added to movies, and therefore not to be added lightly or without pulling its weight. Although his identification with the thriller, the last important Hollywood genre customarily shot in black-and-white, prevented David O. SELZNICK from budgeting any of their forties films for color, Hitchcock insisted on shooting ROPE, his first independent production for TRANSATLANTIC PICTURES, in color, even though the Technicolor camera's fearsome bulk required that the walls be raised to allow it through interior doorways (making so much noise that the direct soundtrack Hitchcock had planned finally had to be replaced with an entirely postsynchronized soundtrack). Yet Hitchcock's use of color in *Rope* is abstemious. Except for Janet Walker's dark red velvet dress and a glimpse of blood on Philip's hand when he nervously smashes his champagne glass on hearing Kenneth misidentified as David, there are no brightly colored objects in the film; its use of color effects is restricted to the light in the killers' apartment as it changes from neutral late-afternoon light to intense orange sunset light to nighttime light punctuated by increasingly expressionistic color lights flashing outside the windows. UNDER CAPRICORN, as befits its period trappings, is more conventionally pictorial, though here again Hitchcock prefers to keep his color palette subdued except to call attention to such details as the red coats of the governor's colonial forces and the ruby necklace Sam Flusky clutches behind his back when Charles Adare airily remarks that rubies would make Lady Henrietta look too washed out. By the time Hitchcock returns to color in DIAL M FOR MURDER and REAR WINDOW, after three further features in black and white, he has settled into a more generally expressionistic use of color, with such lighting effects as *Dial M for Murder*'s midnight lighting and *Rear Window*'s sunsets and twilights rather than objects setting the tone for dramatic scenes, and specific colors like Margot Wendice's red lace dress and Miss Lonelyhearts's green dress used for punctuation and emphasis. TO CATCH A THIEF won a color cinematography Oscar for Robert Burks's more naturalistic approach to color, which generally submerges subjective expressionism in a more decorative, extroverted style. Even here, however, it is obvious—for example when John Robie, wearing a red scarf and a blue pullover, is greeted at Bertani's restaurant by a red-haired woman with a heavily lipsticked mouth and a blue dress—that his use of color is never casual or neutral. THE WRONG MAN and PSYCHO were both shot in black and white, the first for its documentary feel, the second for its dualism (and also ostensibly because Hitchcock hated the sight of blood); with VERTIGO, NORTH BY NORTHWEST, and THE BIRDS, the director showed a new inclination toward specific color associations—green for romantic fantasy and yellow for danger in Vertigo, for example, or earth tones and gray-blue to indicate mother and father figures respectively in North by Northwest, or the red effusions that recall the heroine's childhood trauma in MARNIE, or the contrast between the heroine's warm colors and the barren Leipzig cityscapes in TORN CURTAIN—within a context of continued naturalism. But his screening of Michelangelo Antonioni's Blow-Up in 1966 persuaded him that "these Italian directors are a century ahead of me in terms of technique," and the available footage from his unrealized project Kaleidoscope shows a starker color palette that marks a heightened return to his earlier expressionism. Ironically, Hitchcock's last three completed films are altogether less distinctive in their use of color. TOPAZ, like Torn Curtain, opposes the arid desaturation of its bureaucrats to the full-blooded romanticism of Juanita de Cordoba; FRENZY is dominated by the dull blue-grays of its London exteriors and the red-oranges associated with its killer's red hair; and FAMILY PLOT treats its San Francisco settings a great deal more matter-of-factly, not to say perfunctorily, than the swooningly romantic Vertigo had nearly 20 years before.

Colton, John (1886–1946)   Veteran writer of stage and screen, often in collaboration. His two dozen credits include coauthorship with W. Somerset MAUGHAM of the much-filmed play Rain (1922). His final, posthumous credit is for coauthoring with Margaret LINDEN the dramatic version of Helen Simpson's novel UNDER CAPRICORN, the source of Hitchcock's film.

Colvig, Helen   American costume designer who worked on some 30 films from PSYCHO, her first, to Charley Varrick (1973), her last.

comedy   In his 1995 Introduction to Hitchcock on Hitchcock: Selected Writings and Interviews, Sidney GOTTLIEB expressed surprise that despite various critics' emphasis on the serious Hitchcock (Robin WOOD), the tortured and torturing Hitchcock (Donald SPOTO), the feminist Hitchcock (Tania MODLESKI), and the romantic Hitchcock (Lesley BRILL), there had been no full-length study of the comic Hitchcock. The situation is no better today. Apart from the penetrating, brief overview of Hitchcockian comedy James NAREMORE offered at the Hitchcock Centennial Conference, little has been written directly on Hitchcock's comedy. Yet Hitchcock's work, for all the seriousness of his commentators (and the self-seriousness of the director's own later pronouncements), is in important ways fundamentally comic. Hitchcock frequently noted the persistence of happy endings in his films, and Brill's analysis treats them as comic in construction, if not generally in tone. In addition to having made a handful of unarguable comedies (THE FARMER'S WIFE, CHAMPAGNE, MR. AND MRS. SMITH, THE TROUBLE WITH HARRY) and a rather larger number of thrillers whose prevailing mode is comic (NUMBER SEVENTEEN, RICH AND STRANGE, WALTZES FROM VIENNA, YOUNG AND INNOCENT, THE LADY VANISHES, REAR WINDOW, TO CATCH A THIEF, NORTH BY NORTHWEST, FAMILY PLOT), Hitchcock uses comic moments in nearly every one of his films to defuse tension (as in the byplay between Johnny and Beaky in SUSPICION), to underline ironies (as in the phonograph sequence in JUNO AND THE PAYCOCK), or to complicate or extend the film's dramatic range (as in the Tabernacle of the Sun sequence in 1934's THE MAN WHO KNEW TOO MUCH and the lighthearted banter that will abruptly turn grave after Caypor's death in SECRET AGENT). The filmmaker who complained in 1934 that "a British film is too liable to be one solid chunk of drama or comedy and nothing else" was obviously invested in imitating Hollywood's facility in "switching from grave to gay." The most often-cited result was Hitchcock's early mastery of the comic thriller in THE 39

STEPS and *The Lady Vanishes;* nearly as important was his fondness for black comedy in all shades, from light gray *(The Trouble with Harry)* to dark gray *(ROPE)* to pitch black *(PSYCHO, THE BIRDS)*. These last two examples, which mix baleful violence with shockingly tasteless dialogue jokes ("My mother isn't quite herself today," Norman Bates tells Marion Crane), indicate a third Hitchcock innovation: the film whose tone remains radically ambiguous either because of rapid shifts (like those in *The Man Who Knew Too Much,* 1934, and *STAGE FRIGHT*) or the eruption of comedy into taboo areas (not only in the incorrigible predilection for toilet humor Hitchcock showed, for example, in setting scenes in bathrooms from *Secret Agent* to *Mr. and Mrs. Smith* to *Psycho,* but in the humor associated with the murderer Bruno Anthony, his dotty mother, and outspoken Barbara Morton, but with no one else in *STRANGERS ON A TRAIN*). Apart from the sardonic, often sadistic sense of humor he displayed in his PRACTICAL JOKES on- and offscreen, Hitchcock needed comedy both to make his thrillers more surprising and to relieve the emotional sameness he complained about in 1934. Apart from a few experiments in sustained tone like *THE WRONG MAN,* the Hitchcock films that lack strong comic elements either supply some other contrast to the melodramatic suspense like the brooding fatalism of *BLACKMAIL* or the romantic intensity of *REBECCA, NOTORIOUS,* and *VERTIGO* or remain (like *THE PARADINE CASE, I CONFESS,* and *TORN CURTAIN*) the kinds of monochrome failures that so distressed their director. Also, Hitchcock's puckish public persona, combining elements of archly ceremonious jesting, macabre mischief, and hints of a deeper hostility, was readily adapted to his role as the weekly impresario of *ALFRED HITCHCOCK PRESENTS* and *THE ALFRED HITCHCOCK HOUR.* Hitchcock's characteristic genre is not adequately described as melodrama leavened by comedy; its stylized dramatizations of everyday fears, which not only run but also depend on the entire gamut from tragedy to farce, challenge the distinctions that gamut implies.

Compson, Betty (1897–1974) Brassy blonde leading lady of silent shorts from 1915 who made successful transitions, first to drama, then to sound, and starred in more than 100 films before her retirement in 1948. Having worked as assistant director on three of her silent films, *WOMAN TO WOMAN* (1923), *THE WHITE SHADOW* (1923), and *THE PRUDE'S FALL* (1924), Hitchcock cast her in a memorable cameo as David Smith's blind date Gertie in *MR. AND MRS. SMITH.*

Compton, Fay (1894–1978) British stage actress, born Virginia Lilian Emmeline Compton, who appeared in more than 40 film roles from 1917 to 1970, including the Countess Helga von Stahl, Schani Strauss's romantically minded patron in *WALTZES FROM VIENNA,* and then left an equally strong mark on television in her final years as Aunt Ann in the influential BBC miniseries *The Forsyte Saga* (1967).

Compton, John (1923–) American film and television supporting actor of the fifties who forsook his cowboy boots for his role as Vincent in the *ALFRED HITCHCOCK PRESENTS* episode "THE CASE OF MR. PELHAM" but resumed them for the role of Walt Norton in "The Belfry" (1956).

Condon, Paul British researcher on film and television who collaborated with Jim SANGSTER on *The Complete Hitchcock* (Virgin, 1999), a film-by-film survey aimed at knowledgeable fans rather than scholarly analysts. After a telegraphic treatment of the silent films before *BLACKMAIL,* the authors provide a list of credits (including in many cases uncredited cast members) and extended summary, notes on the casting, a visual description of the opening credits, information on sources and remakes, brief background material on selected performers (including their appearances in other Hitchcock films), quotable lines, the location of Hitchcock's cameo appearance, an identification of the leading MACGUFFIN, a summary of characteristically Hitchcockian themes and motifs, an account of whatever taboos (concerning sex, nudity, suggestive language, or bathrooms) the film broke, information about music and costumes where notable, a list of AWARDS AND NOMINATIONS, a description of marketing devices (slogans, trailers, and so on), a tally of "Ice Maidens" from June TRIPP to Tippi HEDREN, a summary of contemporary reviews, and a final section which assesses the film and rates it from two stars (*NUMBER SEVENTEEN*) to 10 (*VERTIGO* and *NORTH BY NORTHWEST*). Numerous sidebars give more detail about figures from Bernard HERRMANN to Alma REVILLE, and the final sections provide complete lists of each episode of *ALFRED HITCHCOCK PRESENTS, THE ALFRED HITCHCOCK HOUR*, and *THE NEW ALFRED HITCHCOCK PRESENTS*, as well as a brief but useful list of Hitchcock websites. Though the approach is clearly superficial and too much of the volume devoted to summaries most Hitchcockians are likely to find unnecessary, the information is accurate and the style refreshingly impudent and consistently engaging, making this an excellent introduction for fans looking to steer clear of scholarly debates.

Connery, (Sir) Sean (1930–) Brawny, magnetic Scottish leading man, born Thomas Connery, whose adventurous range in romantic, dramatic, and action roles has inevitably been eclipsed in the public imagination by his enduring identification as James Bond. A Royal Navy veteran who later worked as a lifeguard and coffin polisher, he took an interest in body building that led to modeling assignments and a respectable showing in the 1953 Mr. Universe contest. Onscreen in bits from 1955, he shot to stardom in the first Bond film, *Dr. No* (1962), and returned even more successfully in *From Russia with Love* (1963) as the man's man who was also a ladies' man. It was at this point that Hitchcock cast him as Mark Rutland, the zoologist/businessman who marries the kleptomaniac lead in *MARNIE*. Pleased with his performance, Hitchcock attempted to sign him to a multipicture deal, but the restless Connery declined, saying that he wanted to explore a wider range of options, and went on to become identified as the definitive James Bond in five more films, an identification that dogged him well into middle age, when he emerged as a strikingly virile character actor in films from *Robin and Marian* (1976) to *The Untouchables* (1987), in which he won an Oscar as Elliot Ness's Irish cop sidekick Jimmy Malone.

Connolly, Norma (1927–1998) American supporting actress who went from her debut as Betty Todd in *THE WRONG MAN* to a handful of television

appearances before landing the continuing role of Lena Karr Gilroy in the series *The Young Marrieds* (1964–66) and the unending role of Ruby Anderson in *General Hospital* from 1979 to her death.

Conrad, Eddie (1891–1941) American character actor, in Hollywood from 1927, who was much in demand in the later thirties in dozens of ethnic roles, often waiters or barbers. He played the smiling, incomprehensible Latvian diplomat in *FOREIGN CORRESPONDENT*.

Conrad, Joseph (1857–1924) Nonpareil Polish-born novelist, born Józef Teodor Konrad Nalacz Korzeniowski, who, after learning English as an adult, went on to become one of the towering prose stylists

Joseph Conrad

in English fiction. Orphaned as a child by his father's political activities, he went to live with an uncle but preferred the French merchant navy to the discipline of school. He sailed first with French and then, beginning in 1878, with English vessels, using his experiences aboard ships and visiting exotic lands as the basis for his early works *Almayer's Folly* (1895), *An Outcast of the Islands* (1896), "Heart of Darkness" (1899), and *Lord Jim* (1900). Although best remembered as the world's preeminent novelist of the sea, he clung to the shore for his most ambitious novel, the dark South American political fantasy *Nostromo* (1904), and followed it by staying within greater London for his most nihilistic novel, THE SECRET AGENT (1907). The least colorful of all Conrad's novels and therefore one of the least-often filmed, it is set in the shabbiest neighborhoods of an eternally gray city, which it still manages to render as a foreign land that succeeds in disorienting its denizens by calling them—penny-ante spies and their accomplices, victims, and would-be opposites—to actions they cannot accept as their own. The novel became Hitchcock's most distinguished literary source when it was adapted for SABOTAGE; a 1996 remake reverted to Conrad's title and much more of his original plot.

Conrad, Peter (1948–) Tasmanian-born literary scholar, Fellow at Christ Church College, Oxford University. He has written *The Victorian Treasure-House* (1973), *Romantic Opera and Literary Form* (1977), *Shandyism: The Character of Romantic Irony* (1978), *Imagining America* (1980), *The Art of the City: Views and Versions of New York* (1984), *The Everyman History of English Literature* (1985), *The History of English Literature: One Indivisible, Unending Book* (1987), *A Song of Love and Death: The Meaning of Opera* (1987), *Down Home: Revisiting Tasmania* (1988), *Where I Fell to Earth: A Life in Four Places* (1990), *To Be Continued: Four Stories and Their Survival* (1995), and *Modern Times, Modern Places: How Life and Art Were Transformed in a Century of Revolution, Innovation, and Radical Change* (1998) and has edited Jane Austen's *Mansfield Park* (1992). His idiosyncratic, wide-ranging study of Hitchcock, *The Hitchcock Murders* (Faber and Faber, 2000), is an island well off the coast of Hitchcock scholarship that reflects the habits of Conrad's earlier

work in literary and cultural criticism: his eye for the big picture, his gift for epitomizing arguments without resorting to obscurantist jargon, and his serene disdain for such scholarly conventions as chronological ordering and footnotes. After an autobiographical account of Conrad's forbidden, traumatic first viewing of *Psycho* as a schoolboy in Australia, it proceeds to marshal moments and patterns from Hitchcock's films, and often their literary sources, in the service of long sections on the art of murder, the technique of murder, and the religion of murder, all more effective in their trenchant individual aperçus than their larger arguments. The collage portrait of Hitchcock's work that emerges marks the director as at once a willfully eccentric breaker of taboos and a key exemplar of artistic modernism.

Conwell, Carolyn (1933–) Blonde American character actress who graduated in 1980 from such sporadic film roles as her debut, the nameless farmer's wife who helps Michael Armstrong kill his nemesis Herman Gromek in TORN CURTAIN, to the continuing role of Mary Williams on the daytime drama *The Young and the Restless* and has remained ever since.

Cook, Whitfield British playwright and sometime screenwriter. His play *Violet* brought him to Hitchcock's attention in 1944 when Patricia HITCHCOCK starred in its title role, and after three intervening screenplays, he wrote the dialogue for STAGE FRIGHT and the adaptation for STRANGERS ON A TRAIN.

Coolidge, Philip (1908–1967) Mild-mannered American character actor of the fifties and sixties. A mainstay of ALFRED HITCHCOCK PRESENTS, he appeared in six roles—as Henri Tallendier in "The Perfect Murder" (1956), the murder suspect Talbot in "Whodunit" (1956), Lt. Brann in "Decoy" (1956), Bud Horton in "De Mortuis" (1956), Sam Henderson in "The End of Indian Summer" (1957), and bank teller William Tritt in "The Dusty Drawer" (1959). He played Dr. Cross, the police physician who pronounces Roger Thornhill "definitely intoxicated" in NORTH BY NORTHWEST, and returned as Rev. Locke in the ALFRED HITCHCOCK HOUR segment "Night of the Owl" (1962).

Cooper, Charles (D.) American character actor, much on television during the past 50 years, who played Detective Matthews in THE WRONG MAN.

Cooper, (Dame) Gladys (1888–1971) Indomitable British stage actress who dabbled in a dozen films from 1917 to 1934 but essentially settled into a second career at the age of 52, when she appeared as Max de Winter's sister Beatrice Lacey in REBECCA. Among the gallery of gentle autocrats and aristocrats that she made her specialty, she was nominated for three Supporting Actress Oscars for her roles as Charlotte Vale's repressive mother in *Now, Voyager* (1942), Sister Marie Therese in *The Song of Bernadette* (1943), and Henry Higgins's mother in *My Fair Lady* (1964). Her occasional television appearances include the career widow Mrs. Gillespie in the ALFRED HITCHCOCK PRESENTS segment "The End of Indian Summer" (1957), and two matriarchs in THE ALFRED HITCHCOCK HOUR: Mrs. Raydon in "What Really Happened" (1963) and Laura in "Consider Her Ways" (1964).

Cooper, Melville (1896–1973) British character actor who brought his endearingly bullying manner from stage to screen from 1931 to 1958, playing dozens of pompous twits such as the coroner in REBECCA and Mallet, the elevator man in the three-part ALFRED HITCHCOCK PRESENTS segment "I Killed the Count" (1957).

Cooper, Wilkie (1911–) Veteran British cinematographer, former child actor, whose career (1939–71) spanned nearly 70 films, mostly in his native industry, including Hitchcock's return to England, STAGE FRIGHT.

Cooper, Winifred British film editor of the thirties and early forties whose half-dozen collaborative credits include RICH AND STRANGE.

Cope, John Veteran sound recordist, long at PARAMOUNT, whose 20-year career encompassed some 60 films, including REAR WINDOW and TO CATCH A THIEF.

Coppel, Alec (1910–72) Australian-born Anglo-American playwright and screenwriter nominated for an Oscar for adapting his own story for *The Captain's Paradise* in 1953. Hitchcock signed him to replace Maxwell ANDERSON as the lead screenwriter for VERTIGO but replaced him in turn with Samuel TAYLOR, who shares screen credit with him on the completed film.

Corber, Robert J. (1958–) Independent film scholar and scholar of American studies whose influential *In the Name of National Security: Hitchcock, Homophobia, and the Political Construction of Gender in Postwar America* (Duke University Press, 1993) refigured Hitchcock's fifties films as symptoms of a larger U.S. postwar political project: to consolidate a "mainstream" America untainted alike by the fellow-traveling of the thirties, the Red Scare of the fifties, and any marginal or outlaw cultural communities (gays, lesbians, African Americans) to contain the threat of communism. Hence Hitchcock's films from STRANGERS ON A TRAIN through PSYCHO by turns attempt to reclaim the cinematic apparatus for the liberal democracy represented by Jeff and Lisa in REAR WINDOW by rescuing it from the surveillance imperatives of the national security state, and they demonize homosexuality by stigmatizing it as un-American (a security risk in *Strangers on a Train,* a repressed chapter in San Francisco cultural history in VERTIGO) by contrast with the all-American nuclear family figured most directly by the McKennas in THE MAN WHO KNEW TOO MUCH (1956). Corber's project, which he has continued in a later essay on *Vertigo* in ALLEN and GONZALÈS and extended in *Homosexuality in Cold War America: Resistance and the Crisis of Masculinity* (1997), uses Hitchcock's films both as illustrations of this attempt at ideological/sexual consolidation and as a means to expose the contradictions in the version of social reality this consolidation supports.

Corby, Ellen (1911–1999) Spinsterish American character actress, born Ellen Hansen, former script assistant. After a series of 30 bit and character roles, she was nominated for an Oscar as the lovelorn Aunt Trina in *I Remember Mama* (1948), but her career failed to ignite, and 10 years and nearly 50 films later, she could be found putting olive oil on the leaves of her rubber plant as manager of the

McKittrick Hotel in *VERTIGO* and taking minor roles in three segments of *ALFRED HITCHCOCK PRESENTS*—Mrs. McGurk in "Toby" (1956), Samantha in "Bull in a China Shop" (1958), and Emma in "Party Line" (1960)—and appearing as the nurse in the *THE ALFRED HITCHCOCK HOUR* episode "Consider Her Ways" (1964). Fame finally struck with her casting as Grandma Walton in the television series *The Waltons* (1972–76, 1978–79), for which she received three Emmys before suffering a stroke that forced her into semiretirement.

Corcoran, Brian (1951–)   American child actor of the fifties and brother of Disney protégé Kevin Corcoran, mostly on such television programs as *SUSPICION*, in which he appeared as Bobby, the young neighbor who fails to rescue the bomber in "FOUR O'CLOCK," and THE ALFRED HITCHCOCK HOUR, in which he played Eric in "The Magic Shop" (1964).

Corey, Wendell (1914–1968)   Versatile American film actor with stage experience, equally at home in star and character roles. Though he could be duped by Barbara Stanwyck in *The File on Thelma Jordan* (1949) and bullied by Joan Crawford in *Harriet Craig* (1950), he was more comfortable, especially as the years advanced, in the range from genial to hardcase cynic. In *REAR WINDOW* he played Jeff's friend Lt. Tom Doyle, one of Hitchcock's most likeable police officers; in the *ALFRED HITCHCOCK PRESENTS* episode "POISON," he was considerably less sympathetic as the skeptical, playfully sadistic Timber Woods.

Corrick, Jack   Veteran American assistant director, in Hollywood from *Law and Lead* (as Jack Korrick, 1936). He preceded Hilton GREEN as the assistant director on many early episodes of *ALFRED HITCHCOCK PRESENTS*, including "REVENGE," "THE CASE OF MR. PELHAM," and "WET SATURDAY," and returned as unit production manager of *TORN CURTAIN*.

Cosgrove, Jack (R.)   Special effects cinematographer whose 25-year career began with the spectacular *The Garden of Allah* (1936) and three

other SELZNICK films. He was nominated for Academy Awards for *Gone With the Wind* (1939), *REBECCA*, *Pride of the Yankees* (1942), and *SPELLBOUND*.

Costa, Ricardo   Latin American actor whose only Hollywood role was Signor Barbosa, a member of the government agency that sends Alicia Huberman into the Sebastian house in *NOTORIOUS*.

Cotten, Joseph (Cheshire) (1905–1994)   Soft-spoken American leading man of stage and screen, former paint salesman and drama critic, who honed his quiet charm in Orson Welles's Mercury Theater before leaving to create the role of Macaulay Connor in *The Philadelphia Story*. Brought to Holly-

Joseph Cotten

wood to appear in Welles's first two films, *Citizen Kane* (1941) and *The Magnificent Ambersons* (1942), he quickly ripened into the modest, sensitive romantic lead of *Since You Went Away* (1944), *Love Letters* (1945), *The Third Man* (1949), and dozens of other films. It was during this period that Hitchcock cast him twice strikingly against type, first as the charming widow-killer Uncle Charlie in SHADOW OF A DOUBT and then as the unpolished estate owner Sam Flusky in UNDER CAPRICORN. When he aged out of romantic roles, he switched to character parts, often in foreign films or television, including three leads in ALFRED HITCHCOCK PRESENTS: the heartless Callew in "BREAKDOWN" and the ill-fated murderers Tony Gould in "Together" (1958) and Masterton in "Dead Weight" (1959). By the time of his retirement in 1981, he had played more than 100 roles.

Courant, Curt (1899–1968) Distinguished German cinematographer whose work established him as one of the leading stylists in his nation's industry. When Hitler came to power in 1933, he fled the country, beginning an international career in which he collaborated not only with Hitchcock on THE MAN WHO KNEW TOO MUCH (1934) but also with Jean Renoir on *La Bête humaine* (1938), with Marcel Carné on *Le Jour se lève* (1939), with Abel Gance on *Louise* (1939), with Max Ophuls on *De Mayerling à Sarajevo* (1940), and with Charles Chaplin on *Monsieur Verdoux* (1947).

Court, Hazel (1926–) Titian-haired British actress who spent most of her career supporting the stars in dozens of routine films or playing leads such as Lenore in horror extravaganzas like *The Raven* (1963). She played four roles in ALFRED HITCHCOCK PRESENTS: the bereaved Phyllis Chaundry in "The Crocodile Case" (1958), the felonious Lady Gwendolyn Avon in "The Avon Emeralds" (1955), the short-lived Helen Braithwaite in "ARTHUR," and the surprisingly long-married Charlotte Jameson Rutherford in "The Pearl Necklace" (1961).

Cowan, Ashley American actor of the fifties who appeared in *Sorry, Wrong Number* (1948), *The Young Lions* (1958), *Mutiny on the Bounty* (1962), and

the ALFRED HITCHCOCK PRESENTS segment "DIP IN THE POOL," in which he played a shipboard employee.

Coward, (Sir) Noël (1899–1973) Prodigious, omnicompetent British playwright, novelist, screenwriter, actor, producer, composer, wit, and bon vivant. Onstage from 12, he seized the public eye when he starred in his scandalous play *The Vortex* (1924) and retained it till his death. Had he remained only the author of 140 plays, mostly sophisticated drawing-room comedies, he would have been one of the leading figures of the British theater of his time—by the time *Private Lives* opened in 1930, he was the highest-paid author in the world—but his talent and energy led him as early as *Hearts of the World* (1918) to Hollywood, where he acted in a

Noel Coward

dozen films, composed music for a half-dozen more (in addition to his hundreds of songs for the theater), and produced a handful of his own, including the flag-waving *In Which We Serve* (1942), which he produced, codirected, scored, and starred in. EASY VIRTUE is one of the earliest of the many film adaptations of his work.

Cox, John J. (1896–1960) British cinematographer, otherwise J.J. Cox and Jack [E.] Cox, a director of photography from 1920. His decade-long collaboration with Hitchcock began at BRITISH INTERNATIONAL with *THE RING* and continued with *THE FARMER'S WIFE, CHAMPAGNE, THE MANXMAN, BLACKMAIL, MURDER!, MARY, JUNO AND THE PAYCOCK, THE SKIN GAME, RICH AND STRANGE,* and *NUMBER SEVENTEEN*. Hitchcock's departure for GAUMONT-BRITISH effectively ended the relationship, though they were reunited for *THE LADY VANISHES*. Throughout this period, he continued to work with other directors, shooting what would turn out to be a total of 80 films for the British industry through 1958.

Craig, Ian One of the four camera operators who negotiated the intricate long takes of *UNDER CAPRICORN*, he later worked as the Technicolor technician on *Moulin Rouge* (1953) and served as cocinematographer for the television movie *Alternative 3* (1977).

Crain, Earl (N.), Sr. Veteran sound recordist, in Hollywood from 1931 to 1967, who headed the sound team for *THE WRONG MAN*.

Cribbins, Bernard (1928–) British comic actor and recording star, in more than 40 films from 1957, whose lemon-sucking expressions of lower-class distaste enliven his portrait of Felix Forsythe, the pub owner in *FRENZY*.

Croft-Cooke, Rupert (1903–) British novelist whose work has occasionally been adapted to the screen, as in the ALFRED HITCHCOCK PRESENTS episode "BANQUO'S CHAIR," a remake of the film *The Fatal Witness* (1945), based on his 1937 story.

Cronyn, Hume (1911–) Versatile, durable Canadian character actor of stage and screen. After early and extensive experience as a stage actor and director, notably of unremarkable people he still managed to make vivid, he made his screen debut as Herb Hawkins, the Newtons' mousy, murder-minded neighbor in *SHADOW OF A DOUBT* the year after his 50-year marriage to his frequent costar Jessica Tandy began, and returned the following year as the radio operator Stanley Garrett, whose quiet romance with Alice MacKenzie contrasted so dramatically with Constance Porter's histrionics in *LIFEBOAT*. Though not trained as a writer, he wrote the adaptations for *ROPE* and *UNDER CAPRICORN*. He also starred as two unsuccessful murderer, Fritz Oldham and Henry Dow, in the ALFRED HITCHCOCK PRESENTS episodes "Kill With Kindness" (1956) and "The Impromptu Murder" (1958).

"Crystal Trench, The" 153rd episode of *Alfred Hitchcock Presents*, broadcast October 4, 1959. **Producer:** Joan Harrison; **Associate producer:** Norman Lloyd; **Director:** Alfred Hitchcock; **Assistant director:** Hilton Green; **Teleplay:** Stirling Silliphant, based on the short story by A.E.W. Mason; **Cinematographer:** John F. Warren; **Art director:** John Lloyd; **Set designer:** Julia Heron; **Costumes:** Vincent Dee; **Editors:** Richard G. Wray and Edward W. Williams; **Music:** Frederick Herbert; **Cast:** James Donald (Mark Cavendish), Patricia Owens (Stella Ballister), Ben Astar (hotel manager), Werner Klemperer (Herr Ranks), Oscar Beregi (Austrian), Harold (Frederick Brauer), Patrick Macnee (Prof. Kershee), Eileen Anderson, Frank Holmes, Otto Reichow.

The second episode in the program's fifth season, immediately following "Arthur," is a tale of romantic obsession that traces the abortive relationship between Stella Ballister, widowed by her husband's Alpine mountain-climbing accident, and fellow-climber Mark Cavendish, whose attempt to recover the body during a snowstorm ended when it slid away into a deep crevasse and was frozen inside a glacier. Calculating the time before the shifting position of the glacier will make the corpse accessible for one last farewell, Stella and Mark, who have maintained a decorous friendship in the interval, return to the site many years later, having spent their lives waiting for the moment when they find the perfectly preserved body of the husband—complete with a locket containing the photograph of another woman.

Culver, Lillian (1896–)   American actress of the fifties, born Lillian Roberts. She put aside early aspirations of an acting career when she married in 1915 and did not return to the screen until after her husband's death in 1946. Her dozen films and half-dozen television roles include her role as a dental patient in the ALFRED HITCHCOCK PRESENTS episode "MRS. BIXBY AND THE COLONEL'S COAT."

Cummings, Robert (1908–1990)   Eternally boyish, light leading man who broke into the Broadway theater in 1931 by pretending to be an Englishman named Blade Stanhope Conway and began in films four years later as Texan Brice Hutchens. Ironically, his screen persona, once established, varied little over scores of appearances in the next 40 years; in three television series of the fifties and sixties, he continued to play the same girl-chasing scamp. But he was occasionally cast in such dramatic leading roles as Barry Kane, the man on the run in SABOTEUR, and detective-story writer Mark Halliday, Margot Wendice's lover in DIAL M FOR MURDER.

Cunningham, Owen (1902–1983)   American actor, seen mostly on such television programs as ALFRED HITCHCOCK PRESENTS, where he played the auctioneer in "DIP IN THE POOL."

Curtis, Billy (1909–1988)   American actor whose diminutive 4'2" stature ensured that he would spend his career playing midgets. After his debut in *Terror of Tiny Town* (1938), he played the Munchkin city father in *The Wizard of Oz* (1939) and was thereafter instantly recognizable in each of the 40 film and television roles he played through 1986, as in his portrait of the Major who wants to turn Barry Kane over to the police in SABOTEUR.

Curtis, Donald (1915–1997)   Beefy American character actor who interrupted a long career impersonating cops and soldiers to play Harry, the orderly Mary Carmichael tries to seduce in the opening scene of SPELLBOUND.

Curtis, Margaret   American actress who appeared as a ship passenger in the ALFRED HITCHCOCK PRESENTS segment "DIP IN THE POOL."

Curzon, George (1898–1976)   British stage actor of clipped delivery and piercing eye, in occasional films for 30 years beginning in 1930. He played the government agent Gibson in THE MAN WHO KNEW TOO MUCH (1934), Guy in YOUNG AND INNOCENT, and one of Sir Humphrey Pengallan's friends in JAMAICA INN.

Cutts, Graham (1885–1958)   British director of the twenties and thirties, former marine engineer and movie exhibitor, five of whose early films for Michael BALCON—WOMAN TO WOMAN, THE WHITE SHADOW, THE PASSIONATE ADVENTURE, THE PRUDE'S FALL, and THE BLACKGUARD—gave the young Hitchcock, hired as assistant director on all five, an opportunity to contribute to the screenplays, art direction, and editing. He left Balcon in 1927 to join First National–Pathé and continued working on quota quickies through the early forties.

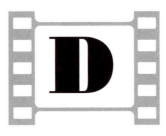

D

D'Agostino, Albert S. (1894–1970) Veteran American art director, sometimes billed as Albert D'Agostini. After working in Hollywood from the 1920s and winning an Oscar nomination for *The Magnificent Brute* (1936), he became head of RKO's art department (1936–58), where his nominations included *The Magnificent Ambersons* (1942), *Flight for Freedom* (1943), *Step Lively* (1944), and *Experiment Perilous* (1944). Credited with designing or supervising hundreds of films, he was largely responsible for the look of velvety menace associated with such crime classics as *Murder, My Sweet* (1944), *The Spiral Staircase* (1946), *Crossfire* (1947), and his single Hitchcock film, NOTORIOUS.

Dahl, Roald (1916–1990) Welsh-born author of Norwegian descent whose fame as an author of variously subversive, often-filmed children's books—*The Gremlins* (the 1943 novel that coined the term *gremlin* for the little saboteurs who hid in bombers and were responsible for all their mishaps), *James and the Giant Peach* (1961), *Charlie and the Chocolate Factory* (1964), *Danny: The Champion of the World* (1975), *The Witches* (1983), *Matilda* (1988)—has overshadowed his occasional contributions as a screenwriter (*You Only Live Twice*, 1967; *Chitty Chitty Bang Bang*, 1968; etc.) and his enduringly macabre short stories, three of which served as the basis for some of the most wittily

Roald Dahl

underplayed episodes of *ALFRED HITCHCOCK PRES-ENTS* directed by Hitchcock: "LAMB TO THE SLAUGHTER" (1953) (for which Dahl also wrote the teleplay), "DIP IN THE POOL" (1954) and "MRS. BIXBY AND THE COLONEL'S COAT" (1948), as well as two of the most memorable non-Hitchcock-directed episodes, "Man from the South" (1960) and "The Landlady" (1961). Noted for his stormy and well-documented marriage to actress Patricia Neal, he also hosted two Hitchcock-inspired television series: *Way Out* (1961) and *Tales of the Unexpected* (1979–80).

Dale, Esther (1885–1961) Formidable, clarion-voiced American character actress, trained as a singer, whose Broadway debut as Carrie Nation (1932) led to nearly a hundred roles as bullying, occasionally sympathetic proletarian matrons such as Mrs. Krausheimer, the heroine's unflinching mother in *MR. AND MRS. SMITH*.

Dalí, Salvador (1904–1989) Flamboyant Spanish artist whose faultlessly precise draftsmanship and fascination with dreams, hallucinations, and psychopathology made him the best-known Surrealist painter. He described such paintings as *The Persistence of Memory* (1931) as "handmade photographs" executed by "the paranoiac-critical method." He collaborated with Luis Buñuel in writing *Un Chien andalou* (1928), in which he also played the seminarian, and *L'Âge d'or* (1930), and later designed sets and costumes for *Don Juan Tenorio* (1952) before dismissing film as a nonart. In between, the eerie clarity of his impossible imagery and his genius for self-promotion made him an obvious choice to design the dream sequence for *SPELLBOUND*.

Dall, John (1919–1971) Saturnine stage-trained American actor, born John Jenner Thompson, in occasional films, mostly in the late forties. Shortly after his Oscar nomination for his first important film, *The Corn Is Green* (1946), Hitchcock cast him as Brandon Shaw, the sinister, joking murderer in *ROPE*. His more memorable later roles included the doomed Bart Tare in *Gun Crazy* (1950) and the

Salvador Dalí

betrayed Marcus Publius Glabrus in *Spartacus* (1960).

Dana, Leora (1923–1983) American character actress, trained at the Royal Academy of Dramatic Art. She made her London stage debut in 1947, her Broadway debut in 1948, and her television debut in 1950. Though she appeared only occasionally in films from 1956 to 1984, she was a favorite of *ALFRED HITCHCOCK PRESENTS*, appearing in the leading roles of the mousy heiress Irene Cole in "The Legacy" (1956), the manipulative wife Vera Brown in "John Brown's Body" (1956), and the deceived wife Naomi Shawn in "Your Witness" (1959) before playing Mrs. Tawley in "INCIDENT AT A

CORNER," the single *FORD STARTIME* episode Hitchcock directed.

Dana, Mark (1920–) American character actor who appeared in some 15 action-adventure films and television episodes, mostly in the fifties, including the *ALFRED HITCHCOCK PRESENTS* segments "The Big Switch" (1956) as Morgan and "THE PERFECT CRIME" as Harrington, returning years later in *The Baby Doll Murders* (1992).

Dane, Clemence (1888–1965) Pseudonym of British novelist and playwright Winifred Ashton, best-known as the author of *A Bill of Divorcement* (1921) and the collaborator of Helen SIMPSON on the West End comedy *Gooseberry Fool* (1929) and a pair of detective novels, *Enter Sir John* (1928) and *Re-enter Sir John* (1932), the first adapted as *MURDER!* Her occasional screen credits for original properties and adaptations extend to 1950.

Dangerous Lies Famous Players–Lasky, 1921. **Director:** Paul Powell; **Screenplay:** Mary H. O'Connor, based on the novel by E. Phillips Oppenheim; **Cast:** David Powell, Mary Glynne.

Fifth of the 12 silent films (1920–22) for which Hitchcock designed intertitles.

Dann, Roger French actor onscreen from 1933 in his native industry. The fourth of his half-dozen English-language roles (1947–74) is Pierre Grandfort, the heroine's Quebecois husband in *I CONFESS*.

D'Annunzio, Lola (1930–1956) Italian-American actress whose film debut as Olga Conforti in *THE WRONG MAN* was her final role; she was killed in a car accident shortly before the film's release.

Dano, Royal (1922–1994) Gaunt American character actor, in nearly 200 films and television programs from 1950 to 1993. His first important role, the tattered soldier in *The Red Badge of Courage* (1951), set the mold for his many later performances as a rube or outdoorsman. He played earnest, ineffec-

tual Deputy Sheriff Calvin Wiggs in *THE TROUBLE WITH HARRY* and returned in two roles in *ALFRED HITCHCOCK PRESENTS*: District Attorney Martin Ross in "My Brother Richard" (1957) and Sheriff Atkins in "Party Line" (1960), and one role in *THE ALFRED HITCHCOCK HOUR*: John Miley in "Change of Address" (1964).

Darcy, Georgine (1931–) Occasional American actress whose screen debut was as Miss Torso, the dancer in *REAR WINDOW*.

Darcy, Virginia Hair stylist active in Hollywood, sometimes as Virginia D'Arcy, mostly in the sixties, whose credits included *THE BIRDS* and *MARNIE*.

Davenport, A(rthur) Bromley (1867–1946) Aristocratic, Eton-educated British character actor who made his stage debut in Siberia in 1892. Onscreen from 1920, he played dozens of statesmen, bureaucrats, and minor functionaries in films from the Hitchcock-produced *LORD CAMBER'S LADIES* to the Hitchcock-directed *JAMAICA INN*, in which he appears as Sir Humphrey Pengallan's friend Ringwood.

Davenport, Harry (1866–1949) Bantamweight, rubicund American character actor from an acting family. In Hollywood from 1912, he directed a dozen silent shorts (1915–17) and appeared in a dozen more, but his career took off when sound came in. From 1930 he played more than 100 benevolent, avuncular figures such as the judge in *You Can't Take It with You* (1938), Arthur Davies in *The Ox-Bow Incident* (1943), and Mr. Powers, the newspaper publisher who sends Johnny Jones to Europe as Huntley Haverstock in *FOREIGN CORRESPONDENT*.

Davenport, Havis (1933–1975) American actress whose first role, as the bride in *REAR WINDOW*, was practically her last.

Davey, Scott American actor whose brief career included a supporting role in the *ALFRED HITCHCOCK PRESENTS* episode "BANG! YOU'RE DEAD."

Dawn, Robert (Lincoln) (1922–1983) American makeup artist. Following distinguished service in World War II, he apprenticed with his father, Jack Dawn, head of MGM's makeup department in the late forties and eventually worked on such projects as *The Ten Commandments* (1956), *Funny Face* (1957), PSYCHO, and MARNIE.

Dawson, Anthony (1916–1992) Ineffably unsavory Scottish-born character actor, onscreen from 1945 to 1987, whose lean, mustachioed features and lower-class inflections made him a specialist in the cringing bravado of treacherous criminal hirelings. His portrayal of C.A. Swann, aka "Captain Lesgate," the small-time crook inveigled into Tony Wendice's plot to kill his wife in DIAL M FOR MURDER, is essentially reprised in *Midnight Lace* (1960) and *Dr. No* (1962).

Day, Doris (1924–) Bubbly, aggressively wholesome American leading lady, born Doris Mary Ann von Kappelhoff, who turned to singing when her dancing hopes were cut short by an auto accident at 15. After success singing with Bob Crosby and Les Brown's bands, she was signed by WARNER BROS. to replace Betty Hutton in *Romance on the High Seas* (1948) and soon became the studio's leading musical star, a reliable audience favorite and one of the highest-paid actresses of the fifties. Her roles in *Storm Warning* (1951) and *Love Me Or Leave Me* (1955) showed that she could handle dramatic roles as well, and Hitchcock sought her to play Jo McKenna, the retired singing star whose son is kidnapped in THE MAN WHO KNEW TOO MUCH (1956). Though she had never before left the United States and found herself so distraught by Hitchcock's remoteness on the set that she offered to leave the film, Day created a paradigmatic portrayal of the American housewife abroad. Famously typed as a perennial virgin in a series of UNIVERSAL sex comedies beginning with *Pillow Talk* (1959), Day turned out, after her mismanaging (or embezzling) agent-husband Marty Melcher's death in 1968, to have been consistently unlucky in marriage, though *The Doris Day Show* (1968–73), the television series Melcher had contracted her to star in without her knowledge, was as successful as her earlier work in Hollywood.

Day, John (1916–1991) American actor, born John Daheim, who started in Hollywood in stunts and outdoorsy roles in 1939 and rounded off his career, which included a cop in the ALFRED HITCHCOCK PRESENTS episode "REVENGE" among his 80 film and television roles, by coordinating stunts for a half-dozen films from *A Man Could Get Killed* (1966) to *Rollercoaster* (1977).

Day, Laraine (1917–) Stage-trained American actress of the forties and after, born into one of Utah's most prominent Mormon families as Laraine Johnson. Onscreen as Laraine Johnson and Lorraine Hayes from 1937, she made her mark in a series of George O'Brien westerns beginning with *Border G-Men* (1938) and then developed into a leading lady employed by several studios. Though she never became a full-fledged star, her 50 roles include the heroines she played opposite Cary GRANT in *Mr. Lucky* (1943), Kirk Douglas in *My Dear Secretary* (1948), and Joel MCCREA in FOREIGN CORRESPONDENT, in which peace-seeking Carol Fisher's love scene with the hero ("I love you and I want to marry you") may be the shortest on record. From 1947 to 1960 she was married to baseball manager Leo Durocher and was so active and visible in her interest for the game that she became widely known as the First Lady of Baseball. Three years after her marriage ended, she appeared as the murderous winery secretary Ruth Hamilton in THE ALFRED HITCHCOCK HOUR segment "Death and the Joyful Woman" (1963).

Deacon, Richard (1921–1984) Balding, stentorian American character actor whose 100 film and television roles include dozens of neighbors, usually more nosey or intrusive than Mitch Brenner's informative San Francisco neighbor in THE BIRDS. A natural for television, he played Fred Rutherford in *Leave It to Beaver* (1957–63), officious boss Mel Cooley in *The Dick Van Dyke Show* (1961–66), and a series of veterinarians, animal psychiatrists, and Martians on *Mr. Ed* (1961–63).

Deane, Darcia British stage actress whose few screen roles include Katharina in *The Taming of the Shrew* (1923), Charlotte Corday in *Simone Evrard*

(1923), and the relatively well-behaved Marion Whittaker, the hero's older sister in EASY VIRTUE. She also appeared in *Passion Island* (1927) and *Dawn* (1928).

death scenes François TRUFFAUT told Hitchcock that he filmed his love scenes like death scenes and his death scenes like love scenes—and idea borne out by the director's rather unrealistic preference for murder by strangulation, which often simulates or parodies a lover's embrace, as in THE LODGER, SHADOW OF A DOUBT, ROPE, STRANGERS ON A TRAIN, FRENZY, and the unfilmed THE SHORT NIGHT. In DIAL M FOR MURDER Margot Wendice is choked nearly to death when she gets out of bed to answer her husband's phone call; in *Strangers on a Train* Bruno Anthony, pretending to strangle a society woman who finds him charmingly naughty, catches sight of Barbara Morton, who reminds him of the late Miriam Haines, and begins to strangle his obliging victim in earnest; and Roger Thornhill, when Eve Kendall dreamily suggests during their long embrace in NORTH BY NORTHWEST that maybe he's the escaped murderer he's advertised as being who's planning to murder her, puts his hands around her throat and asks, "Shall I?" only to encourage the response, "Please do." Stabbings are less common in Hitchcock's world, though he makes use of them in BLACKMAIL, THE 39 STEPS, THE MAN WHO KNEW TOO MUCH (1956), *North by Northwest,* and of course PSYCHO, in which the attacks on Marion Crane and Milton Arbogast must surely be accounted the definitive screen stabbings, the shower scene endlessly imitated ever since the film's release. Hitchcock's occasional poisonings, especially those in NOTORIOUS (whose menacing cups echo the giant glasses in the drugging scene in THE LADY VANISHES and the milk glass lit from within in SUSPICION), are among the most visually inventive in cinema. Shootings, though statistically the most common homicides, are rare in Hitchcock, who despite the inveterate fetishism of his films shows no interest in the ultimate noir fetish, the handgun, preferring to keep his infrequent shootings offscreen or reveal them as fake (as in the apparent murders of Ackroyd in NUMBER SEVENTEEN, Van

Meer in FOREIGN CORRESPONDENT, and Thornhill in *North by Northwest*). A spectacular pair of exceptions are the climactic suicide in SPELLBOUND, shown from Dr. Murchison's optical point of view as he slowly turns the menacing gun (an oversized prop held in an oversized prop hand) from the departing Constance Peterson, who has just revealed him as the killer, to himself, then shoots directly at the camera, and Rico Parra's execution of his treacherous mistress Maria de Cordoba in TOPAZ, a shooting filmed like a love scene.

Except in TORN CURTAIN, in which Michael Armstrong's horrifically strenuous attempts to dispose of his nemesis Herman Gromek are intended to show the difficulty of killing another human being, Hitchcock shows virtually no interest in the mechanics of violent death; he prefers either to eliminate his death scenes altogether, as in the offscreen murders in YOUNG AND INNOCENT, *Spellbound*, THE PARADINE CASE, UNDER CAPRICORN, and I CONFESS, or to turn them into tableaux which are as likely to involve the discovery of a violent death (as in SECRET AGENT and THE BIRDS) as its commission. Among the most theatrically memorable of Hitchcock's death scenes are the literal tableau of MURDER!, in which the camera discovers Diana Baring hovering frozen over the body of Edna Druce, the fatal poker clasped in her hand; the utterly unexpected shot that ends the life of Louis Bernard in the middle of a dance and the middle of a practical joke in *The Man Who Knew Too Much* (1934); the explosions in SABOTAGE and SABOTEUR; the fatal plunges of Madeleine Elster and Judy Barton in VERTIGO; the barely offscreen murders of the artist Crewe in *Blackmail* and the blackmailer Vilette in *I Confess,* and the overheard but unseen murder of Anna Thorwald in REAR WINDOW; and the extended oral accounts of violent death, unadorned by visual flashbacks, in REBECCA, *Under Capricorn*, and *The Birds.*

De Banzie, Brenda (1915–1981) British actress of stage (from 1935) and screen (from 1942), sometimes as Brenda de Banza. Her well-received work as the title character's tart daughter Maggie Hobson in *Hobson's Choice* (1954) seemed at first to mark a breakthrough in her career, but in retrospect simply confirmed her fate: playing the put-upon female relation in *The Entertainer* (1960) and THE MAN WHO KNEW TOO MUCH, whose kidnapper, Mrs. Drayton, Donald SPOTO has called "one of the most emotionally fascinating personalities in any Hitchcock film."

De Casalis, Jeanne (1897–1966) British character actress, née Jeanne De Casalis de Pury, first famous onstage as a revue comedienne and as radio's ditzy Mrs. Feather, then onscreen in 20 roles throughout the thirties and forties, including an unnamed friend of Sir Humphrey Pengallan in *JAMAICA INN*. Married to actor Colin Clive.

De Cordoba, Pedro (1881–1950) Cadaverous stage-trained American actor of Cuban-French background, former operatic bass, in more than 100 Hollywood productions from 1915 to his death. In *SABOTEUR*, he takes a break from aristocratic Latinos to play Bones, the sideshow patriarch who presides over the vote whether or not to turn Barry Kane in to the police.

Dee, Vincent Longtime costume designer who worked mostly on television, notably as costume supervisor for *M Squad* (1957–60), *Thriller* (1960–62), *McHale's Navy* (1962–66), *Dragnet 1967* (1967–70), and the entire 10-year run of *ALFRED HITCHCOCK PRESENTS* and *THE ALFRED HITCHCOCK HOUR*. One of the few Hollywood films he worked on is *MARNIE*, for which he shares a credit with Edith HEAD and others.

Delaney, Maureen (1888–1961) Irish-born character actress, a specialist for 25 years (1935–59, sometimes as Maureen Delany) in tradeswomen and servants such as Flo in *UNDER CAPRICORN*.

Dellar, Mel(vin D.) (1912–1994) American assistant director whose 10 films from *The Babe Ruth Story* (1948) through *New York, New York* (1977) include *DIAL M FOR MURDER*.

De Marney, Derrick (1906–1978) Heavy-lidded, stage-trained British actor, most active in the

later thirties, whose three dozen film roles extended to his death. His portrayal of Robert Tisdall, the man on the run from the police in *YOUNG AND INNOCENT*, is notable for its boyish good humor.

Deming, Norman (W.) (1905–1983) American filmmaker who began as an eight-year-old extra and then graduated from production manager and assistant director at UNIVERSAL (1918–31) and Columbia (1931–45) to producer's assistant (1944–47) at Columbia, directing three 1939 second features along the way, to production analyst at Universal. He produced two Universal vehicles for Burt Lancaster, *Kiss the Blood Off My Hands* (1948) and *The Crimson Pirate* (1952), before serving as unit production manager for another 10 films (1957–66), including THE BIRDS.

Dench, Bertram (1892–1980) British actor of the early 1930s who appears as the fire-engine driver rushing to Ebeseder's Café in the opening scene of *WALTZES FROM VIENNA*.

Dennis, Robert C. (1916–1983) Canadian-born screenwriter who began in radio and then wrote some 500 television scripts, including "DIP IN THE POOL," the *ALFRED HITCHCOCK PRESENTS* episode he cowrote with Francis COCKRELL, and a dozen others for the series. He created the television programs *The New Adventures of China Smith* (1954–55) and *Passport to Danger* (1954–56) and wrote two mystery novels, *The Sweat of Fear* (1973) and *Conversations with a Corpse* (1974).

Denny, Reginald (1891–1967) Polished, veteran British actor, born Reginald Leigh Daymore. Onstage from childhood and onscreen from 1912, occasionally as screenwriter, editor, or director, he moved to Hollywood soon after the arrival of sound and switched from the Douglas Fairbanks roles for which his athletic body and pencil mustache had suited him to a wider range, from George Brown in *The Lost Patrol* (1934) to Benvolio in *Romeo and Juliet* (1935) to a series of comic British types such as Bulldog Drummond's foppish friend Algy Longworth in eight programmers (1937–39), and finally settled into stiff-upper-lip character parts he made as appealing as an old pair of slippers, playing inimitably British types such as Max de Winter's estate manager Frank Crawley in REBECCA. A lifelong aviation enthusiast, he developed the first radio-controlled aircraft to be flown successfully in the United States.

Dent, James American production manager, one-time silent actor, on FOREIGN CORRESPONDENT and three other films, 1931–48.

De Palma, Brian (1940–) American writer/director, a surgeon's son and high school science fair–winning physicist whose checkered career, which has zigzagged between hits and misses, reveals him as the younger filmmaker most clearly influenced by Hitchcock, certainly the most gifted Hitchcock imitator, particularly in the dozen years from 1972 to 1984. *Sisters* (1973) is a virtual remake of PSYCHO, with formerly conjoined twin sisters substituting for the mother-and-son Bates team, and *Obsession* (1976) of VERTIGO, with the addition of a happy ending that prevents the hero from throwing away the love of his life, now reincarnated in his daughter, a second time; both films are scored by Bernard HERRMANN, Hitchcock's favorite composer. De Palma returned to Hitchcockian themes and techniques in *Dressed to Kill* (1980), whose plethora of borrowings from *Psycho,* from its emphasis on voyeurism to its long sequences without dialogue, showed that audiences could be just as shocked 20 years later by the premature death of the female lead. But the influence of Hitchcock is equally strong in the director's later films. De Palma uses Hitchcock mainly as a source of wildly overinflated but detachable moments like the shower-scene parodies that run from *The Phantom of the Paradise* (1974) through *Carrie* (1976) and *Blow Out* (1981)—each of them inventive, suspenseful, and cruelly amusing—and the 360° pan around Scottie Ferguson and the recreated Madeleine Elster in *Vertigo,* which is transformed in *The Untouchables* (1987) into a valentine to male bonding. With his 1983 remake of *Scarface,* De Palma seemed to have moved on to the tempering influence of other models as diverse as Howard Hawks and Sergei Eisenstein, but he returned with a vengeance to his earlier mentor in

Body Double (1984), a fantasia on Hitchcock themes freely drawn from REAR WINDOW and *Vertigo,* with occasional echoes of *Psycho.* The box-office disaster of *The Bonfire of the Vanities* (1990), a clear departure for De Palma, and the failure of the jokey *Raising Cain* (1992), another more modest *Psycho* homage with additional bows to Martin Scorsese, threatened to confirm De Palma's reputation as nothing more than a talented mimic of other filmmakers' styles, but he rebounded strongly with *Carlito's Way* (1993), whose big scenes were stolen mostly from his own earlier work, especially *Scarface,* and the commercial blockbuster *Mission: Impossible* (1996), though he was back in quasi-Hitchcock form again in the tricky thriller *Snake Eyes* (1998).

Dern, Bruce (1936–) American character actor born into a political family whose role as the sailor whom Marnie kills in the climactic flashback of MARNIE (along with his strikingly similar role in *Hush, Hush . . . Sweet Charlotte,* 1964) and his performance as Roy Bullock, the boy falsely accused of obscene phone calls in THE ALFRED HITCHCOCK HOUR episode "Night Caller" (1964) were utterly overshadowed by his key role later the same year in "Lonely Place," another segment of *The Alfred Hitchcock Hour,* as Jesse, the pop-eyed hillbilly drifter. His performance this time was so compelling that it threatened to typecast him as a psychotic or snakelike criminal, particularly in westerns like *Hang 'em High* (1967), *Support Your Local Sheriff!* (1970), and *The Cowboys* (1972). But Hollywood gradually discovered his star potential, though usually in roles that continued to tap his explosive depths: solitary astronaut Freeman Lowell in *Silent Running* (1971), San Francisco detective Leo Larsen in *The Laughing Policeman* (1973), car salesman Big Bob Freelander in *Smile* (1975), and Captain Bob Hyde in *Coming Home* (1978), for which he was nominated for an Academy Award. George Lumley, the raffish driver who partners the fake medium Blanche in FAMILY PLOT, is perhaps his most genial and untroubled role.

De Rosa, Steven British author of *Writing with Hitchcock: The Collaboration of Alfred Hitchcock and John Michael Hayes* (2001).

Derry, Charles American writer and film-maker, professor of film at Wright State University. After serving as assistant director on the 16 mm film *Suspension: A Tribute to Alfred Hitchcock,* he directed *Cerebral Accident* (1986). In addition to his short stories and his one-act play *Joan Crawford Died for Your Sins* (1997), he has published *Dark Dreams: A Psychological History of the Modern Horror Film* (1977) and *The Suspense Thriller: Films in the Shadow of Alfred Hitchcock* (McFarland, 1988). This last volume, though not primarily about Hitchcock, takes his work as establishing the essential norms for the suspense thriller, which Derry, having first subdivided crime films according to their primary emphasis on victims, criminals, or detectives or the various relations possible among these three figures, defines as "a crime work which presents a violent and generally murderous antagonism in which the protagonist becomes either an innocent victim or a nonprofessional criminal within a narrative structure that is significantly unmediated by a traditional figure of detection in a central position"—that is, as films whose heroes are neither detectives nor professional criminals. The ensuing discussion, which assigns central importance to the man-on-the-run formula of THE 39 STEPS, SABOTEUR, and NORTH BY NORTHWEST, is especially valuable in illuminating the ways in which Hitchcock neglects criminal and detective heroes in favor of victims, and figures professionally engaged in crime or punishment in favor of amateur criminals, detectives, and avengers generally.

De Ruelle, Emile (1880–1948) American director, production manager, and editor. He began as an assistant director (1923–28), and his brief career as an editorial supervisor managed to encompass four Hitchcock films at BRITISH INTERNATIONAL: *THE MANXMAN, BLACKMAIL, JUNO AND THE PAYCOCK*, and *MURDER!* He later directed a single film, *L'Indésirable* (1933).

Deutelbaum, Marshall American film historian, associate professor of English at Purdue University. He is editor of *"Image" on the Art and Evolution of Film* (1979) and coeditor with Leland Poague of *A Hitchcock Reader* (Iowa State University Press, 1986), to which he contributed an essay, "Finding the Right Man in THE WRONG MAN," that examined the changes Hitchcock made, despite his film's implicit promise of authenticity, to the true story of Manny Balestrero. By the time this anthology, the second in English, appeared, Hitchcock had been dead for six years, and his place in academic film study was secure enough for the editors to pitch their volume directly to undergraduates and to cite in their introduction the "remarkable series of histories" Hitchcock's name invoked: the history of cinema, of Hitchcock's career, of film criticism and film theory. The 25 pieces they collect, virtually all of them originally intended for a scholarly audience, range from reprintings of seminal essays by Jean DOUCHET, Robin WOOD, Stanley Cavell, and Raymond BELLOUR to selections from books by Wood, Maurice YACOWAR, and Elisabeth WEIS (and from Lesley W. BRILL's forthcoming book) to new essays by Patrice Petro, Marian E. Keane, and Michele Piso. Taken as a whole, they seek to bridge the divide that the editors perceive between formal analysis and film history by providing case studies that will encourage sharper distinctions among different kinds of film, different modes of analysis, and different kinds of history. Except for Bellour's essay, the collection generally eschews the psychoanalytic theories of Jacques LACAN, which the editors find reductive and unhelpful in generating new models of interpretation beyond the motivic exposure of the cinematic apparatus. Each of the volume's five sections ("Taking Hitchcock Seriously," "Hitchcock in Britain," "Hitchcock in Hollywood," "The Later Films," and "Hitchcock and Film Theory: A *Psycho* Dossier") begins with a brief editorial introduction and bibliography; credits for each film follow the essay in which it is discussed; and the volume concludes with a brief chronology of Hitchcock's directorial credits in film and television, though it lacks a more comprehensive filmography and an index.

Devane, William (1940–   ) Wolfish American leading actor of film and television best known for his 10-year stint as Gregory Sumner in the prime-time soap opera *Knots Landing* (1983–93). His earlier roles, many of them suggesting virile untrustworthiness, included Arthur Adamson, the slimy, punctilious kidnapper in *FAMILY PLOT*. He is also notable for having played both Jacqueline Kennedy's husband in one television movie, *The Missiles of October* (1974), and her father in another, *A Woman Named Jackie* (1991).

Devlin, William (1911–1987) Scottish-born stage actor, in occasional films from 1937, who played Pengallan's tenant in *JAMAICA INN*.

DeWeese, Richard American sound recordist who worked on some 20 films between 1945 and 1954—sometimes, as in *SPELLBOUND*, billed as Richard De Weese.

Dewhurst, William (1888–1937) Fussy, perennially disheveled British stage actor whose film career, launched in 1936 with *Toilers of the Sea and SABOTAGE* (in which he played the dotty professor whose storefront workshop supplied Verloc with explosives), was cut short by his early death.

De Wolff, Francis (1913–1984) Brawny British character actor, onscreen from 1935, whose four dozen roles include Major Wilkins in *UNDER CAPRICORN*.

Dial M for Murder (Alternative titles: *Bei Anruf Mord, Le Crime était presque parfait, Il delitto prefetto*) Warner Bros.–First National, 105 minutes, July 1954. **Producer:** Alfred Hitchcock; **Director:** Alfred Hitchcock; **Screenplay:** Frederick Knott, based on his play; **Cinematographer:** Robert Burks; **Assistant director:** Mel Dellar; **Art director:** Edward Carrere; **Set decoration:** George James Hopkins; **Costumes:** Moss Mabry; **Makeup:** Gordon Bau; **Sound:** Oliver S. Garretson; **Editor:** Rudi Fehr; **Music:** composed and conducted by Dimitri Tiomkin; **Cast:** Ray Milland (Tony Wendice), Grace Kelly (Margot Wendice), Robert Cummings (Mark Halliday), John Williams (Chief Inspector Hubbard), Anthony Dawson (C.A. Swann, aka Captain Lesgate), Leo Britt (storyteller), Patrick Allen (Pearson), George Leigh (Williams), George Alderson (first detective), Robin Hughes (police sergeant), Sam Roberts (man in phone booth), Robert Dobson (police photographer), Sanders Clark, Guy Doleman, Thayer Roberts (detectives), Jack Cunningham (bobby).

Hitchcock originally intended that his 39th feature would be based on Francis ILES's *Malice Aforethought* (for whose leading role of the inoffensive physician who poisons his overbearing wife he had hoped to attract Alec Guinness) or David Duncan's *The Bramble Bush*. But when neither of these projects bore fruit, he ran, as he put it, for cover by adapting Frederick KNOTT's stage success of 1952. The playwright himself provided the adaptation—the closest of all Hitchcock's adaptations to its original—based on the unfashionable notion that instead of opening out the one-set play, the film, like *ROPE*, would emphasize its claustrophobia even further. Although the film avoids the uninterrupted long takes of *Rope*, it rarely strays outside the Maida Vale flat in which ex–tennis pro Tony Wendice first induces an old school acquaintance to murder his adulterous wife and then, when the plan ends in the killer's death, methodically frames his wife for the murder. When it does leave the flat's single set, especially in the montage sequence of Margot's trial for murder, the film refuses to establish any distinctive alternative spatial location. The director cast Grace KELLY as a rather subdued Margot in the first of her three Hitchcock films, and John WILLIAMS, a minor player in *THE PARADINE CASE* who had created the stage role of the imperturbable police inspector who brings Tony to book, continued a collaboration with Hitchcock that was scarcely less celebrated and a good deal more durable. Although virtually the entire film was shot on a single interior set, WARNER BROS. complicated the production by demanding that it be shot in 3-D, and reserved the studio, which had already been closed for several months, entirely for this single production from July 30 through September 25, 1953.

Like the earliest synch-sound cameras Hitchcock had used on *BLACKMAIL* and *JUNO AND THE PAYCOCK* and the massive Technicolor camera that would not fit through the doorways in *Rope*, the 3-D camera was so bulky that it restricted both the choice of camera setups and the extent of camera movement, and the opportunity it offered for shock effects seemed to hold no interest for Hitchcock, whose

Tony Wendice (Ray Milland) takes a phone call from the wife whom he has just hired Captain Lesgate, née Swann (Anthony Dawson), to kill in *Dial M for Murder. (National Film Society Archive)*

use of the new technology was characteristically abstemious. He neither followed the fashion of *House of Wax* or *Bwana Devil* or *Kiss Me Kate* (all 1953) by punctuating the film with shots of objects being thrust abruptly toward the audience, as he would very likely have done 20 years earlier, nor treated the three-dimensional space of the Wendices' flat in a consistently realistic way. Instead, each scene began realistically enough before a growing sense of entrapment conveyed by framing characters between or behind layers of looming objects like bottles, knick-knacks, or lamps, and emphasized by a selective use of angled shots, created an increasingly stylized expressionism, particularly at the moment when an over-

head shot shows the unwilling assassin Swann rehearsing the murder as Tony chats with his wife on the phone. (The film's chaste use of color, which apart from Margot's rather showy change of clothing from bright red to muted rust to gray and black, with a white nightgown Kelly suggested herself for the murder scene, recalls the way *Rope* paints with light rather than with bright-hued objects, intensifies this subtly expressionistic effect.) The two most intense moments of the film are both underscored by the use of 3-D but in unexpected ways. When Swann attacks Margot as she gets up in the middle of the night to answer the call by which Tony has lured her to the phone, the film shows her flailing hand thrashing toward the camera with the scissors she plunges into Swann's back in a relatively two-dimensional series of shots, and later, when Inspector Hubbard waits in the flat with Margot and her lover Mark Halliday to see whether Tony will betray himself by using the key Swann had left outside to let himself in, Hitchcock shows Hubbard's hand pivoting slowly toward the camera with the key in a gigantic closeup. The mise-en-scène frames the dialectic of imprisonment and release and betrayal and guilt with far greater subtlety and economy than either Kelly's performance as the guilty victim or Robert CUMMINGS's as her self-righteous avenger. But Williams is memorably understated as the canny inspector, and Ray MILLAND memorably duplicitous as Tony, especially in his snakelike criminal seduction of Swann. The film's modest critical and commercial success made Hitchcock considerably more anxious about his next project, *REAR WINDOW*, his first film for PARAMOUNT PICTURES, but it has remained extremely watchable.

Dick, Douglas (1920–)

Blond, boyish American actor who appeared in some two dozen films and television programs—most memorably as the student whose professor kills him when he assaults her in *The Accused* (1948) and as David Kentley's romantic rival Kenneth Lawrence in *ROPE*—before leaving the industry to become a psychologist.

Dietrich, Marlene (1901–1992)

German-born leading lady, for 30 years the incarnation of seductive continental carnality. Her teenage dream of a career as a violinist dashed by a wrist injury, she looked to the theater, joining a chorus line in 1921 and entering Max Reinhardt's drama school the following year. Her career blossomed on stage and screen, but her international breakthrough came abruptly at the hands of Josef von Sternberg, who by careful lighting and costuming molded the chubby matron (married in 1925 to production assistant Rudolf Sieber, though she lived apart from him most of her life) into the essence of erotic mystery in a series of star vehicles beginnig with *Der Blaue Engel* (1930) and continuing in the United States with *Morocco* (1930), *Dishonored* (1931), *Shanghai Express* (1932), and *Blonde Venus* (1932) and reaching

Marlene Dietrich

an apotheosis in *The Scarlet Empress* (1934). When Dietrich's final collaboration with her Svengali, *The Devil Is a Woman* (1935), proved a critical and commercial failure, she reinvented herself as a comedienne for *Destry Rides Again* (1939) and scored a decisive comeback. Her films banned in Germany ever since she had declined to return to the industry nationalized by Hitler, she became a U.S. citizen in 1939, traveled extensively during the war entertaining U.S. troops, and was awarded the American Medal of Freedom and named a Chevalier of the Legion of Honor. It was at this point, as "the world's most glamorous grandmother," that Hitchcock cast her as Charlotte Inwood, the world-weary prima donna suspected of murdering her inconvenient husband in *STAGE FRIGHT*. Dietrich was the only female star Hitchcock ever allowed to choose her own wardrobe, jewelry, and lighting. Playing a more nuanced version of her mantrap persona, the iconic star delivered one of her last film roles before reinventing herself once again as a cabaret singer and recording artist in the fifties.

Dillon, Tom P. (1895–1962) Irish-American character actor with vaudeville and circus experience, most often seen as a priest or police officer, who appears as Sgt. Balter in the ALFRED HITCHCOCK PRESENTS episode "BANQUO'S CHAIR."

"Dip in the Pool" 111th episode of *Alfred Hitchcock Presents,* broadcast June 1, 1958. **Producer:** Joan Harrison; **Associate producer:** Norman Lloyd; **Director:** Alfred Hitchcock; **Assistant director:** Hilton Green; **Teleplay:** Robert C. Dennis and Francis Cockrell, based on the short story by Roald Dahl; **Cinematographer:** John F. Warren; **Art director:** John Lloyd; **Set designer:** James S. Redd; **Costumes:** Vincent Dee; **Editors:** Richard G. Wray and Edward W. Williams; **Music:** Stanley Wilson; **Cast:** Keenan Wynn (William Botibol), Louise Platt (Ethel Botibol), Philip Bourneuf (Renshaw), Fay Wray (Mrs. Renshaw), Doreen Lang (Emily), Doris Lloyd (Emily's companion), Ralph Clanton (purser), Owen Cunningham (auctioneer), Barry Harvey (steward), Ashley Cowan (ship employee), Michael Hadlow (bidder), Margaret Curtis, Judith Brian (passengers), William Hughes (ship employee).

The third episode Hitchcock directed for the program's third season, and the second consecutive episode he based on a Roald Dahl story, places insecure, loudmouthed vacationer William Botibol and his wife on an ocean liner with a far wealthier crowd. In an effort to keep up socially and economically with his boss Renshaw, whose wife recoils from him in genteel distaste, Botibol bets heavily on the low range of the pool predicting the ship's progress; then, facing humiliation and the loss of his wife's promised European vacation, he plots to slip from the side of the ship in front of a witness who can report his "accident" to the crew, who will lose time recovering him and so slow the ship down enough to make good his bet. Unfortunately, Emily, the simple-minded witness he chooses, has no idea of the consequences of the event he stages, telling her caretaker only that Botibol was "such a nice man. He waved to me."

Disney, Walt (1901–1966) Legendary American animator who began as a commercial artist and cartoonist before introducing Mickey Mouse (whose voice was Disney's own) in *Steamboat Willie* (1928) and producing hundreds of cartoon shorts, dozens of animated features beginning with *Snow White and the Seven Dwarfs* (1937), a series of live action features *(Treasure Island,* 1950, etc.), and a series of films combining live action and animation *(The Three Caballeros,* 1943, etc.). Throughout the thirties and forties, Disney films went from one innovation to the next: the first all-Technicolor Hollywood film *(Flowers and Trees,* 1932); the first use of the Multiplane camera to suggest depth *(The Old Mill,* 1937); and a generally nonnarrative cartoon feature designed to illustrate classical music selections *(Fantasia,* 1940). The debut of the television program *The Mickey Mouse Club* in 1954 and the opening of Disneyland the following year proved Disney the executive to be not only the undisputed king of U.S. family entertainment but also a master of marketing synergy—a status the company he created continues to enjoy and extend years after his death. Hitchcock, who once remarked that "Disney has the best casting. If he doesn't like an actor, he just tears him up," borrows the murder of Cock Robin from Disney's 1935 short *Who Killed Cock Robin?* for a pivotal scene in SABOTAGE just before Mrs. Verloc, overwhelmed with grief by her brother Stevie's death, finds herself laughing at the cartoon murder minutes before she kills the husband who sent Stevie off to plant a bomb.

Dodge, David (1910–1974) American crime and travel writer, former accountant and naval lieutenant commander. Having turned to writing in 1941 to win a five-dollar bet with his wife, he continued, as he said, to raise money to travel to the places he wrote about. Although most of his mystery novels involve one of two series heroes, tax expert Whit Whitney or expatriate private eye Al Colby, he is best remembered as the author of the novel TO CATCH A THIEF (1952), which served as the basis for John Michael HAYES's screenplay.

Dolphe, Hal Composer whose sole film credit is *RICH AND STRANGE.*

Donald, James (1917–1993) Thoughtful, versatile Scottish-born stage actor who has appeared in some three dozen films, generally in introspective roles like that of Vincent Van Gogh's brother Theo in *Lust for Life* (1956) but good company aboard troop ships as well. He appears in leading roles in two episodes of ALFRED HITCHCOCK PRESENTS directed by Hitchcock: alcoholic Harry Pope, convinced a snake is in his bed in "POISON," and mountain climber Mark Cavendish in "THE CRYSTAL TRENCH."

Donat, Robert (1905–1958) Dashing, cultivated British star of stage and screen, whose melodiously expressive voice, coupled with his extensive theatrical experience, soon brought him to the attention of producers on both sides of the Atlantic. He rose to stardom as Anne Boleyn's lover Thomas Culpepper in *The Private Life of Henry VIII* (1933). Recoiling from a brief stint in Hollywood in the title role of *The Count of Monte Cristo* (1934), he returned to England to star as Richard Hannay, the quintessentially cool-tempered man on the run, in THE 39 STEPS. His ability to suggest a man of the people without abating any of his gentility or charm won him many offers, of which his dozen starring roles in other British films represent only a fraction. Though his career was hampered by chronic asthma, he was nominated for an Academy Award for *The Citadel* (1938) and won the following year, beating Clark Gable, for the title role of the beloved schoolmaster in *Goodbye, Mr. Chips.* His celebrated last onscreen words as the Mandarin in *The Inn of the Sixth Happiness,* released after his death in 1958, were "We shall not see each other again, I think. Farewell."

Donath, Ludwig (1900–1967) Viennese-born character actor, onstage from 1924. His film career had barely begun when he left Germany, arriving in 1940 in Hollywood, where he was frequently cast in anti-Nazi films before landing his best-known role, Cantor Yoelson in *The Jolson Story* (1946) and *Jolson Sings Again* (1949). Blacklisted in 1953 after the second wave of hearings by the House Un-American Affairs Committee, he did not return to the screen until *TORN CURTAIN,* in which he played Professor Gustav Lindt, the East German physicist whose mind holds the secrets Michael Armstrong is trying to steal. A year and two films later, he was dead of leukemia.

Dor, Karin (1936–) Tempestuous German-born star of international films, onscreen in her native country from 1954. Among her few English-language films are *You Only Live Twice* (1967) and *TOPAZ,* in which she plays Juanita de Cordoba, the doomed love of both heroic diplomat Andre Devereaux and Cuban strongman Rico Parra.

Dorfman, William (1911–1962) American assistant director, former unit manager at MGM, active in Hollywood mostly during the forties, when he served as Hitchcock's assistant on *NOTORIOUS.*

Dorté, Phillip Sound recordist who received credit for three films (1934–36), third of which is *SECRET AGENT.*

doubles Hitchcock's habit of doubling his heroes and heroines with other characters, typically those who act out the sociopathic impulses the heroes have repressed, extends from his first film, THE PLEASURE GARDEN, which features a pair of mantrap females who change places morally in the course of the film (the veteran Patsy ends up more loyal and loving than the supposedly innocent Jill), to his last, FAMILY PLOT, which doubles Blanche Tyler and George Lumley, the lovers who serve as its unlikely heroes, with villainous Arthur Adamson and his lover and accomplice Fran. Many storytellers before Hitchcock, after all, had dealt with doubles as one of the fundamental patterning devices of narrative. Hitchcock's most memorable doubles, however, display far more intimate relationships than the simple moral alternatives of these films, or of DOWNHILL, whose hero condemns himself to expulsion and rejection by taking the blame for a pregnancy to shield his friend, or THE MANXMAN, which allows its heroine romantic relationships with both of the men who love her only to show the cost of her inadvertent adultery. The nameless hero of THE LODGER, who is set up as the Avenger, the serial killer of young women, turns out to be an amateur sleuth, a bereaved brother on the trail of his sister's killer. Yet the lodger's obsession with the Avenger, whose footsteps he traces and whose crimes he maps on a triangular grid that recalls the Avenger's signature note, both raises questions about the unseen Avenger's own motives and raises suspicions about the lodger that linger even after the happy ending.

This pattern of technical innocence clouded by complicity with a criminal is developed further in Hitchcock's two best-known uses of doubles. SHADOW OF A DOUBT provides a long list of doubled characters and motifs (two pairs of two detectives, two police suspects, two friends for its teenaged heroine, two scenes involving a ring, two taking place in a garage, two on board a train, a pivotal scene at the 'Til Two) organized around the doubling of its heroine Charlie Newton and her beloved Uncle Charlie (introduced in a pair of expository scenes balanced virtually shot by shot that discover the characters lying weary and disillusioned on beds placed in opposite positions on the screen). By the end of the film, all its nominal oppositions have threatened to shade into resemblances that raise questions about Charlie's complicity in her uncle's crimes—at first unwilling to believe him guilty, she then does everything possible to make him leave town instead of turning him in to the police detective pursuing first him, and then her—and about the ways in which social acculturation and maturity are not only produced by encounters with evil but also are evil themselves. STRANGERS ON A TRAIN is scarcely less persistent in its doubles, from the opening sequence that crosscuts between shots of the hero's and villain's legs as they board a train to Bruno Anthony's plan for swapping murders (or, as he dubs it, "crisscross") to its MacGuffin, the cigarette lighter Guy Haines accidentally left with Bruno, a gift from Guy's lover Ann Morton, showing a pair of crossed tennis racquets that Bruno plans to plant at the spot where he killed Guy's wife to incriminate Guy. Like *Shadow of a Doubt, Strangers on a Train* implicates the hero in the evil he has released through the very motifs that originally served to set him apart from the villain. More than any other single film, *Strangers* seems to have inspired Eric ROHMER and Claude Chabrol's Jansenist reading of Hitchcock—a reading widely influential in persuading a generation of viewers that

the director might be up to something more complicated than agreeable thrills.

But doubling plays an equally vital role in many more Hitchcock films. Because every step the second Mrs. de Winter takes in REBECCA is an unwilling echo of her brilliant predecessor, the film has the effect of saddling her with a double who never appears. In the same way, in SUSPICION Lina Aysgarth moves through her marriage never certain whether the man she married is a charming, impecunious scamp or a swindler and killer who is planning to murder her. John Ballantine assumes the identity of the man he neurotically believes he has killed in SPELLBOUND, assuming the guilt for the murder by attempting to conceal it. THE PARADINE CASE doubles its high-minded hero with the murderer who is equally infatuated with the fatal Maddalena Paradine, but the more resonant doubling is of Mrs. Paradine with a potentially guilty version of herself—a theme played out more fully in NOTORIOUS, whose compromised heroine's different roles are indicated by the different ways other characters pronounce her name. By the time of STAGE FRIGHT, doubles have become second nature to Hitchcock, and he returns to the conceit of MURDER!—that the characters are constantly playing versions of themselves, whether or not they are onstage—with a new ease and wit.

In the films that follow, doubles are never far off, whether they shadow the hero's essential innocence, as Jeff's identification with the henpecked murderer does in REAR WINDOW, or plunge him into the Kafkaesque nightmare Manny Balestrero endures when he is mistaken for a robber in THE WRONG MAN. Hitchcock's three greatest films deepen his fascination with doubles in new ways. VERTIGO, which uses an actress playing a role to seduce its hero into an impossible love he prefers to any love a real woman, even the actress herself, could offer him, shows the actress destroyed by her hopeless love for the hero and the hero destroyed by his inability to love anyone but the double who has been tailored to the measure of his desire. The hero of NORTH BY NORTHWEST, mistaken for a secret agent who does not exist, plays out a comic, romantic version of Manny Balestrero's nightmare. And PSYCHO, Hitchcock's most rigorous and pitiless anatomy of doubling, from the opening white-on-black credit sequence that marks it as perhaps the most dualistic film ever made, uses the doubling of Norman Bates with the dead mother he increasingly imagines himself to be to explore the more normal-seeming doubling of Marion Crane, the thief who becomes Norman's logical victim because, unable, like Norman, to accept her crimes as her own, she projects herself into a world in which moral agency is always the responsibility of someone else and so becomes the someone else whom Mrs. Bates imagines is responsible for the threatening sexual arousal of her son. The film, like Hitchcock's work as a whole, could stand as an illustration of the motto *"Je est un autre."*

Doucette, John (1921–1994)   Balding, versatile American character actor who began his film career playing thugs in such films as *Ride the Pink Horse* (1947) and *Criss Cross* (1949) but whose sharp vocal inflections made him suitable for such diverse roles as Hammond, Detective Leslie Hennessey's relief in STRANGERS ON A TRAIN, and the Roman carpenter in *Julius Caesar* (1953). All told, he played more than 100 supporting roles in fifties movies and television programs before tapering off and was still appearing onscreen as late as 1986.

Douchet, Jean   French filmmaker, critic, and historian, former staff writer for *Cahiers du cinéma,* member of the Institute for Advanced Studies in Cinema and teacher at the French Cinémathèque. Along with Eric ROHMER, Jean-Luc Godard, Claude CHABROL, and others, he directed a segment of *Paris vu par . . .* (1964). Thirty years before his sumptuous history *Nouvelle Vague* (1998), he published *Alfred Hitchcock* (Herne, 1967; 2nd edition, 1985), which updates and broadens Rohmer and Chabrol's analysis of the filmmaker's Jansenist moralism through a close examination of three films—REAR WINDOW, NORTH BY NORTHWEST, and PSYCHO—and distinguishes several different varieties of Hitchcockian suspense: esoteric suspense, which stages a battle between conscious and unconscious drives in primal terms; logical suspense, which involves teleology and psychology; quotidian suspense, which involves the conflict between the requirements

of ordinary life and extraordinary situations; aesthetic suspense, Hitchcock's "unique subject," which involves the play of the director's anxiety and imagination over his film; and the suspense of creation, which involves an escape from oppressive impotence to the power of creating films, and which undergirds all the other modes of suspense. Although the volume has never been translated into English, a brief study for it, "Hitch and His Public," is reprinted in DEUTELBAUM and POAGUE.

Douglas, Robert (1909–1999)   Suave British actor, born Robert Douglas Finlayson, equally at home playing stoic military heroes and plausible villains. Onscreen from 1936, he made his Hollywood debut a decade later. But his later career was portended by his experience playing two police officers in ALFRED HITCHCOCK PRESENTS: the wily Charles Tarrant in "The Impromptu Murder" (1958) and the unsuccessful Ben Liebenberg in "ARTHUR," since he became a prolific television producer and director (1957–82) whose early credits included directing several episodes of THE ALFRED HITCHCOCK HOUR: "The Long Silence" (1963), "You'll Be the Death of Me" (1963), and "Sign of Satan" (1964).

Downhill   (Alternative titles: *When Boys Leave Home* [U.S.], *La Pente*) Gainsborough, Wardour & F., World Wide Distributors (U.S.), approximately 80 minutes (U.K.), 74 minutes (U.S.), May 1927. **Producers:** C.M. Woolf and Michael Balcon; **Director:** Alfred Hitchcock; **Screenplay:** Eliot Stannard, based on *Down Hill,* a play by David L'Estrange; **Cinematographer:** Claude McDonnell; **Art director:** Bert Evans; **Assistant director:** Frank Mills; **Editor:** Lionel Rich; **Script/editing associate:** Ivor Montagu; **Cast:** Ivor Novello (Roddy Berwick), Robin Irvine (Tim Wakeley), Isabel Jeans (Julia), Ian Hunter (Archie), Norman McKinnel (Sir Thomas Berwick), Annette Benson (Mabel), Sybil Rhoda (Sybil Wakeley), Lilian Braithwaite (Lady Berwick), Violet Farebrother (the poet), Ben Webster (Dr. Dawson), Hannah Jones (the dressmaker), Jerrold Robertshaw (Rev. Henry Wakeley), Barbara Gott (Madame Michet), Alf Goddard (the Swede), J. Nelson (Hibbert).

Even as THE LODGER opened in February 1927, scenarist Eliot STANNARD was preparing a new screenplay that would reunite the director with his matinee-idol star Ivor NOVELLO. Hitchcock's fourth film went before the cameras in March. The unqualified success of *The Lodger* ensured that *Downhill,* unlike all Hitchcock's earlier films, would not be embargoed by C.M. WOOLF, and it was released in May. Several members of the stage-trained cast in this adaptation of a stage play would work with Hitchcock again, among them Robin IRVINE, Isabel JEANS, Ian HUNTER, and Violet FAREBROTHER. But the film, though apparently well outside the main line of Hitchcock's development, has deeper affinities with his later work as well.

The tale of a boy who allows himself to be expelled from school when he is accused of his sworn friend's romantic infraction is first, as Charles BARR has noted, a story of the price of loyalty. But even before the first of the descents (down a staircase, an escalator, an elevator) that indicate the film's three-part structure ("The World of Youth/The World of Make-Believe/The World of Lost Illusion") by translating the hero's descent from the cloistered environment of his boarding school to the fleshpots of London, Paris, and Marseilles, it has become something else: a nightmare illustration of the principle *esse est percipi,* to be is to be watched. The candy-shop girl Mabel's flirtations with Tim Wakeley and Roddy Berwick, consisting mostly of romantic gestures staged to be watched, darken when they are summoned to the headmaster's office. From this scene onward, Roddy is defined exclusively by his observers rather than his increasingly fatalistic actions. Novello's character had suffered a similar fate in *The Lodger,* but here the camera generally allies itself with him rather than with the observers who found him so opaque in the preceding film. When Mabel points to the wealthy Roddy rather than Tim as the father of her child, her gaze, figured by an atypical shot from her point of view, feels not only menacing but also obtrusive, even assaultive. His brilliant school career abruptly ended by the dismissal he accepts for the friend who needs to keep his character clean to compete for a scholarship, he is tossed out by the minatory father who refuses to accept his pleas of innocence and becomes first the mark who can be fleeced of his £30,000 inheritance by the actress Julia and her unseen but constantly attentive swain Archie, then the gigolo eyed appraisingly by the female clientele of the Parisian music hall when La Patronne has put him on display. A crew of sailors smelling a possible reward return him to London, but only the vindication marked by his father's symmetrical plea for forgiveness restores him to his position at school. The film, which veers abruptly from a setting more insular than the middle-class Hitchcock had ever known to equally unrealistic scenes of stylized squalor, can hardly be called a success. Yet it does have one distinction: It is by far the director's most misogynistic work, overflowing with images of women as harpies and betrayers who prey on helpless young males like Roddy. *Downhill* has never been released on 16 mm prints, videotape, laserdisc, or DVD and therefore has played little role in public awareness of Hitchcock's work. Ironically, his following film, EASY VIRTUE, which has long been available in most of these formats, secures a more lasting place in Hitchcock studies and contemporary film theory by the simple expedient of switching genders so that a woman, not a man, is a victim of the opposite sex's appraising or baleful gaze, a gaze that empowers the observing subject at the price of the person it reduces to a helpless object.

dreams   The revelatory dream that John Ballantine reports to Dr. Constance Peterson, who will use it to solve the murder of which Ballantine has been accused in SPELLBOUND, is the most celebrated of all movie dreams. But in its elaboration and visual stylization (the sequence, which reportedly ran more than 20 minutes in its rough cut, was based on designs by Salvador DALÍ) it represents only one pole of Hitchcock's lifelong interest in dreams. Dreams, daydreams, and nightmares abound in his films, some of them—especially Scottie Ferguson's nightmare linking Madeleine Elster's death with his own death wish in VERTIGO—nearly as stylized as Ballantine's, but most of them so different in their stylistic restraint that it is difficult to tell that they are dreams. Indeed the deceptive daydreams in DOWNHILL and CHAMPAGNE and the heroine's repeated belief that she has encountered her dead brother in the crowds of SABOTAGE, like the notorious lying flashback in STAGE FRIGHT, are presented on exactly the same terms as the stories they interrupt; it is only once they are over that they are revealed as fancies.

But Hitchcock's films are less notable for the self-contained dreams they bracket off, however misleadingly, from the characters' waking lives than for their creation of an oneiric zone that partakes ambiguously of both dream and reality, as when Farmer Sweetland imagines each of the women he is courting occupying his late wife's chair in THE FARMER'S WIFE. Iris Henderson explicitly enters this zone when she is struck on the head by the falling flowerpot aimed at Miss Froy in THE LADY VANISHES, and Charlie Newton lingers in it when she spends all day in bed following her identification of her beloved uncle as the Merry Widow Murderer in SHADOW OF A DOUBT. This oneiric zone is implicitly identified in other films with romance, melodrama, and such departures from normal routine as the initial arrival of the lodger at the Buntings' door in THE LODGER, Lina McLaidlaw's waltz-fueled infatuation with Johnny Aysgarth, the importunate suitor who sweeps her off her feet in SUSPICION, Charlie's initial rising from her bed at the beginning of *Shadow of a Doubt* to send a telegram to her uncle inviting him to come visit, and Marion Crane's descent into nightmare as she catches her boss looking at her and begins to imagine the reactions he and others will have to the news that she has left town with the $40,000 she has stolen. The point of this zone, which can swell to incorporate entire films as different as BLACKMAIL, REBECCA, and *Vertigo,* is to obscure the sharp distinction between waking and sleeping, imagination and reality, desire and action that a photographic medium like cinema might be assumed to preserve unclouded.

Hitchcock's choice of genres associated him with nightmares even before he left England. But the threatening dreams that became one of his hallmarks are regularly counterbalanced by such unlikely wish-fulfillment fantasies as the upper-class pipe dreams of the Whittaker household in EASY VIRTUE, the domestic banter at the ski resort in THE MAN WHO KNEW TOO MUCH (1934), the hero's rapid-fire escapes in THE 39 STEPS, the fairy-tale world *Rebecca*'s modern-day Cinderella moves through, the Riviera locations of TO CATCH A THIEF, and Hitchcock's iconic, picture-postcard treatment of Switzerland in SECRET AGENT,

Holland in FOREIGN CORRESPONDENT, Morocco in THE MAN WHO KNEW TOO MUCH (1956), San Francisco in *Vertigo,* and America writ large in SABOTEUR and NORTH BY NORTHWEST. Hitchcock's people never seem to have a normal day; for better or worse, their every movement and image is charged with the desires revealed only slightly more directly by their dreams.

du Maurier, (Dame) Daphne (1907–1989)

English romantic novelist, daughter of Gerald DU MAURIER and closely related to many other writers, actors, and artists. Following her marriage to Lt. Col. Frederick Arthur Montague Browning II in 1932, she settled into the family tradition of artistic creation. JAMAICA INN (1936), the first of her neo-Gothic romances—whose settings, she said, always formed the basis for her characters and incidents—was immediately successful. But it was the second, REBECCA (1938), that made her the queen of the 20th-century gothic. Both novels were filmed by Hitchcock, the first in an adaptation the author reportedly loathed and the second, much more faithfully under the watchful eye of David O. SELZNICK, who famously told Hitchcock in a monitory memo criticizing a more free-wheeling earlier draft screenplay, "We bought *Rebecca,* and we intend to make *Rebecca.*" Although many of du Maurier's later works, from *Frenchman's Creek* (1941) to *Don't Look Now* (1971), were also adapted to the screen, perhaps the most unexpected adaptation was Hitchcock's reworking of "The Birds," a 1952 short story pitting a nameless Cornish farmer against a series of bird attacks that have evidently been going on for some time before the story opens, into a two-hour widescreen Technicolor film set in the California coastal community of Bodega Bay.

du Maurier, (Sir) Gerald (1873–1934)

Preeminent English stage actor-manager of his time, son of painter-turned-novelist George L. du Maurier and father of peerless romancer Daphne DU MAURIER. Noted as a pioneer of a more natural style of stage acting, he created the roles of Mr. Darling and Captain Hook, Raffles, and Bulldog Drummond. His contempt for movies kept him away from them except when he needed to replace income he had expected from failed theatrical ventures. His handful of film roles (1917–34) include Dr. Napier in the Hitchcock-produced LORD CAMBER'S LADIES.

Duncan, Craig American television actor of the fifties and early sixties who appeared as supermarket clerk George Webster in the ALFRED HITCHCOCK PRESENTS episode "BANG! YOU'RE DEAD" and returned in the three roles in THE ALFRED HITCHCOCK HOUR: the sergeant in "Final Vow" (1962) and police officers in "Bonfire" (1962) and "Blood Bargain" (1963). His film appearance have been infrequent.

Dunn, Emma (1875–1966) British-born character actress, onscreen from 1920, who bided the silent era onstage and then returned to Hollywood after sound came in; personified the sympathetic mother of Dr. Kildare in *Young Dr. Kildare* (1938) and the following series, and settled into a long career playing domestics and housekeepers such as Martha in MR. AND MRS. SMITH before her retirement after 100 films in 1948.

Dunne, Steve (1918–1977) Clean-cut American actor of the fifties who appeared in some 15 films and acted as television emcee for *You're On Your Own* (1956–57) and *Truth or Consequences* (1957–58). He appeared in four episodes of ALFRED HITCHCOCK PRESENTS—as Martian-friendly Tommy Fortnum's father Hugh in "Special Delivery" (1959), as police Lt. Meade in "The Man with Two Faces" (1960), as Rick Sheffield, the uncle whose loaded gun is the MacGuffin in "BANG! YOU'RE DEAD," as the nameless amnesiac hero of "Services Rendered" (1961), and as Jack Wentworth in THE ALFRED HITCHCOCK HOUR segment "What Really Happened" (1963).

Dunnock, Mildred (1901–1991) Inimitably dour American character actress who came to films via *The Corn Is Green* (1945), reprising her 1940 stage role as Miss Ronberry—a feat she repeated with the stage and screen versions of *Death of a Salesman* (1949/1951)—and remained to play three dozen rawboned spinsters and mothers with an edge in movies and television. Nominated for Oscars for *Death of a Salesman* and *Baby Doll* (1956), she was cast

as Mrs. Wiggs in THE TROUBLE WITH HARRY and then returned for three roles in ALFRED HITCHCOCK PRESENTS—the murdered Aunt Muriel in "None Are So Blind" (1956), the long-suffering Louise Tiffany in "The West Warlock Time Capsule" (1957), and the apparently warm-hearted Mrs. Collins in "Heart of Gold" (1957)—and one in THE ALFRED HITCHCOCK HOUR, as the sleuthing paid companion Minnie in "Beyond the Sea of Death" (1964).

Durgnat, Raymond Maverick British academic and critic who teaches at the University of East London. His many books include *Nouvelle Vague: The First Decade* (1963), *Greta Garbo,* coauthored with John Kobal (1965), *Eros in the Cinema* (1966), *Films and Feelings* (1967), *Franju,* (1968), *The Crazy Mirror: Hollywood Comedy and the American Image* (1969), *A Mirror for England* (1970), *Sexual Alienation in the Cinema* (1972), *Jean Renoir* (1974), *Durgnat on Film* (1976), *Luis Buñuel* (1978), *King Vidor, American,* coauthored with Scott Simmon (1988), and *WR—Mysteries of the Organism* (1999). His highly characteristic study *The Strange Case of Alfred Hitchcock; or, the Plain Man's Hitchcock* (Faber and Faber, 1974), attacking the moralistic Hitchcock championed by the CAHIERS DU CINÉMA critics and Robin WOOD, dismisses Hitchcock as a major artist whose moral concerns are no deeper than those of his middle-class audience and pronounces him instead a minor aesthete in the tradition of Oscar Wilde and the Symbolist poets. The extensive film-by-film discussion that follows, the first in English, is most notable for Durgnat's frankly critical attitude toward many of Hitchcock's films and his free-wheeling willingness to plot alternative versions of them (for example, a version of SHADOW OF A DOUBT in which Uncle Charlie seduces his adoring but suspicious niece, who, finding herself pregnant, marries the detective who has been pursuing her) that he would have preferred. More recently, Durgnat has returned to the first Hitchcock film on which he wrote at any length in *Psycho* (BFI, 2001).

Dyall, Franklin (1874–1950) British stage actor who appeared in some two dozen films, mostly after 1927, when he played the husband whose divorce from Larita Filton gave her such a scandalous reputation in the opening minutes of *EASY VIRTUE*.

Dyrenforth, Harold O.   Strong-jawed American actor who made his Hollywood debut as Walter Damrosch in *Carnegie Hall* (1947) and went on to play a dozen scarcely less distinguished-looking gents, including the hero's mountain-climbing companion Frederick Blauer in the *ALFRED HITCHCOCK PRESENTS* segment "THE CRYSTAL TRENCH," in the fifties.

Eagler, Paul E. (1891–1961) American cinematographer of the silent era (1917–21) who returned to Hollywood 15 years later to shoot the special effects shots in *Strike Me Pink* (1936) and South Seas footage in *The Hurricane* (1937) and remained as a special-effects cinematographer in a half-dozen films including *FOREIGN CORRESPONDENT* (in which he is also billed as second-unit cinematographer) and *NOTORIOUS*.

Easton, Robert British actor whose sole film credit is one of the 12 jurors in *MURDER!*

Easy Virtue (Alternative titles: *Le Passé ne meurt pas, Vertù facile*) Gainsborough, Wardour & F., World Wide Distributors (U.S.), approximately 79 minutes, August 1927. **Producers:** C.M. Woolf and Michael Balcon; **Director:** Alfred Hitchcock; **Screenplay:** Eliot Stannard, based on the play by Noël Coward; **Cinematograper:** Claude McDonnell; **Art director:** Clifford Pember; **Assistant director:** Frank Mills; **Cast:** Isabel Jeans (Larita Filton), Franklin Dyall (her husband), Eric Bransby Williams (the co-respondent), Ian Hunter (plaintiff's counsel), Robin Irvine (John Whitaker), Violet Farebrother (his mother), Frank Elliott (his father), Darcia Deane (his elder sister), Dorothy Boyd (his younger sister), Enid Stamp-Taylor (Sarah), Benita Hume (switchboard operator).

Buoyed by the success of *THE LODGER*, Eliot STANNARD began work on the scenario for Hitchcock's fifth film immediately after completing the *DOWNHILL* screenplay in March 1927, and filming began even before additional scenes required for *Downhill* were completed. The new film was rushed into release to capitalize on the popularity of both Hitchcock and Noël COWARD, whose source play, a biting satire of the social hypocrisy revealed by the punitive treatment of a divorcée, had enjoyed great success when it opened in New York in 1925 and in London the following year. But silent cinema was a most unlikely medium for conveying Coward's drawing-room epigrams, and despite (or perhaps because of) Stannard's success in opening out the claustrophobic play to include, among other new locations, two framing courtroom scenes and an idyll in the south of France, the film, Hitchcock's last for Michael BALCON and GAINSBOROUGH until 1938, was a commercial failure.

In discussing the film with François TRUFFAUT, Hitchcock singled out only two details, one of which he was proud of, the other ashamed of. His favorite moment was a tour de force, a shot of a telephone operator alone in the frame that ran for some 60 seconds as her facial expressions and body language reveal the substance of the call she is listening in to: the heroine Larita Filton's acceptance of John Whittaker's proposal of marriage. (The shot launched the film career of Benita HUME, who played the operator in a screen debut lasting just over a minute.) Interestingly, the detail Hitchcock had come to dislike was just as witty and inventive, if more direct in its import: the final title card, in which Larita, emerging from the courtroom where her marriage to John has just ended in her second ugly divorce, tells the ubiquitous press photographers who have hounded her ever since the collapse of her first marriage, "Go ahead and shoot—there's nothing left to kill." Although Hitchcock called this line "the worst title I've ever written," commentators have unanimously praised it as summarizing the film's leading motif: the destruction of a woman by an oppressive male gaze. Coward's play, which kept Larita's scandalous first divorce 15 years earlier as a guilty secret whose revelation through dialogue would shock the Whittakers into closing ranks against her, encloses the primary conflict within John's family circle. The film, though implying Larita's technical innocence of adultery—her husband accused her after an artist painting her portrait committed suicide after a scene with her husband and left her his income—and moving Larita's first divorce to a period only a few months before her romance with John, shows both the original courtroom proceeding and, in flashback, the events that precipitated it. Thus, the center of gravity is shifted from the Whittakers' hypocritical rejection of Larita in the play to the way in which her reputation is irretrievably ruined by professional observers seeking to profit by their image of her, such as the photographers who supply the evidence that ends her marriage to John Whittaker, or to bolster their professional standing by denouncing her, such as the myopic divorce judge who squints at her through spectacles. In casting as Isabel JEANS, who had played Roddy Berwick's faithless actress wife in *Downhill,* as Larita, the film neatly inverts the gender politics of the earlier film (instead of showing a man undone by the poor judgment he shows in a series of relationships with predatory women, *Easy Virtue* shows a woman undone by the iron necessity of living with a reputation foisted on her by men). But this film adds a prophetic new complication to both Coward's play and *Downhill's* gender politics: The leading figure who internalizes the social opprobrium against Larita is a woman, the domineering mother (portrayed by Violet FAREBROTHER, who had played the calculating

older client who had so revolted Roddy during his turn as a gigolo in *Downhill*) before whom John's resolve to defend his wife wilts. The malevolent mother whose hostility is aroused by her son's romance with an unsuitable woman would return with a vengeance in films from NOTORIOUS (a film amounting to a virtual remake of *Easy Virtue* with espionage obbligato) to PSYCHO.

eating and drinking Given Hitchcock's fondness for food and drink—he was notorious for the opulent lunches, invariably accompanied by wine, that often sent him into midafternoon naps as the camera rolled, and his girth, though it fluctuated dramatically in the forties, was always formidable—it is not surprising that eating and drinking, essential human activities in any case and a frequent occasion for social interactions onscreen and off, have special importance in his films. What is surprising is the overwhelmingly negative force they have. Even when a meal is perfect, like the dinner from 21 that Lisa has brought to Jeff's apartment in REAR WINDOW to celebrate what they think will be the final week before the cast comes off his broken leg, it is *too* perfect, a figure for all their simmering disagreements about shared lifestyles, and Lisa's similarly seductive attempt to use brandy to encourage Jeff's police detective friend Tom Doyle to agree that Lars Thorwald has killed his wife merely ends with Doyle spilling his brandy from the snifter. More often, Hitchcock's meals are anything but perfect. After a brief prologue showing the fury of the heroine's father at the news that she has eloped, CHAMPAGNE opens with a shot through the bottom of a champagne glass that shows the point of view of a mysterious man whose gaze will follow the heroine through most of the film. Alice's fatal stabbing of the artist who tries to rape her in BLACKMAIL is bracketed by two unpleasant meals, the supper over which she and her boyfriend Frank Webber quarrel before she leaves with the artist and the nightmarish breakfast with her parents that is interrupted by a neighbor's jarring references to the knife that killed the artist. The offering of food or drink in THE 39 STEPS—Annabella's request of food from Hannay, the tense grace Hannay shares with the crofter and his wife, the drink he is offered at Professor Jordan's party—is typically a sign of danger. Having carved the roast for the husband who sent her brother off to his death in SABOTAGE, Mrs. Verloc proceeds as if in a dream to carve him as well with a single catatonic thrust. The meals in REBECCA all emphasize the alienation of Max de Winter's bride from her husband and his world; toward the end of the film, Jack Favell punctuates his genteel blackmail demands by pinching a drumstick from the picnic basket in the de Winters' car, placidly gnawing on it, and then rolling down the window to toss out the bone. Family dinners become particular ordeals for both Erica Burgoyne in YOUNG AND INNOCENT and Charlie Newton in SHADOW OF A DOUBT because of the guilty knowledge they must conceal from the rest of the family, and the first meal Dr. Constance Peterson shares with the newly arrived Dr. Anthony Edwardes is marred by his neurotic attention to the wavy lines she has marked in the tablecloth.

The conflation of food and drink with danger comes to a head in NOTORIOUS, in which Alexander Sebastian's slow poisoning of his wife is only the latest stage in a dissolution that is regularly marked by her drinking, marking her, like the wine bottle filled with sand that serves as the film's MACGUFFIN, as a vessel to be filled by men. If drinking here is a sign that a woman is being compromised by manipulative males, from Alicia's lover Devlin to her husband Sebastian, eating becomes a sign of men's emotional distance, from the dinner that serves as Alicia's threatening introduction to the Sebastian home to the after-dinner drinks over which her husband and his colleagues coolly plot the death of Emil Hupka to the crackers and cheese Paul Prescott is callously consuming in bed as Devlin reports his grim suspicions about Alicia's appearance. Thereafter, meals in Hitchcock are typically marked as both seductive in intent and repellent in effect. The dinner the Keanes and the Horfields share in THE PARADINE CASE becomes the backdrop for Lord Horfield's crude, bullying come-on to Gay Keane; the party in ROPE is a demonic parody of hospitality, in which dinner is served from the chest containing David Kentley's corpse; in UNDER CAPRICORN, the dinner party Sam Flusky gives to introduce Charles Adare to Australian society, though attended by Sam's business associates, is humiliatingly boycotted by their wives and ruined by the sudden appearance of his wife in an alcholic haze; the meal Guy Haines shares in Bruno Anthony's compartment in STRANGERS ON A TRAIN becomes the scene for Bruno to pitch his plan for the perfect murder.

Meals fare better in the films John Michael HAYES wrote for Hitchcock only because their tension often dissolves into jokes. In THE TROUBLE WITH HARRY, Arnie Rogers swaps his dead rabbit for two of the blueberry muffins Miss Gravely is sharing with Captain Wiles. TO CATCH A THIEF turns its seductive meal—the picnic Francie Matthews has packed for the suspected cat thief John Robie—into a series of double entendres and features the unforgettable shot (a Technicolor echo of *Rebecca*) in which Francie's mother puts out her cigarette in a fried egg. The tension in the dinner scene in THE MAN WHO KNEW TOO MUCH (1956) in which Ben and Jo McKenna see the suspicious Louis Bernard, who has begged off dining with them, and meet the Draytons, the real spies Bernard has mistaken them for, is defused by the running joke of Ben's inability to fold his long legs under the low table. Although the two scenes at Ernie's Restaurant both emphasize the unbridgeable distance between Scottie and Madeleine in VERTIGO, the dinner Roger Thornhill shares with Eve Kendall aboard the train in NORTH BY NORTHWEST returns to this pattern when Eve makes it clear that she has arranged it specifically to lure the unresisting Thornhill into bed.

PSYCHO is the first Hitchcock film to link the appetites for food and sex explicitly. When Marion Crane hears Mrs. Bates forbidding Norman from entertaining a stranger who simply wants to satisfy her appetite for her food and her son, the line implies that eating and drinking are like sex not only because they stem from basic human appetites but also because they reduce their objects to commodities to be consumed—a motif from *Notorious* given an even sharper edge in a film whose heroine ends up swallowed by a swamp that sounds just like a toilet. Except for the dinner at which Sarah Sherman flirts with the tipsy Professor Lindt in TORN CURTAIN, Hitchcock's final films generally subordinate the seductive motive behind shared meals to a growing revulsion from the very idea of eating, from the birds that peck on the schoolchildren just before the waitress at the Tides Café takes an order for two chicken dinners in THE BIRDS to the ceremonious betrayals associated with food and drink (from the defector Kusenov's arrogant domination of a coffee service to the hiding of a spy camera inside a chicken) throughout TOPAZ. The climax of this final pattern is FRENZY, whose repeated scenes of eating and drinking are repeatedly linked to sexual violence, from Richard Blaney's explosive quarrel over the size of his brandy in the pub where two professional men placidly discuss the necktie murders to fruiterer Bob Rusk's rape and murder of Brenda Blaney (to whom he says he is governed by the motto "Don't squeeze the goods until they're yours") in between bites of an apple he has taken from her lunch. The unspeakable Cordon Bleu meals Inspector Oxford's wife serves and Rusk's frantic search for the corpse he has hidden in a sack of potatoes make *Frenzy* among the most revolting treatments of food in all cinema.

It seems clear from this pattern of development that Hitchcock moved from a relatively conventional view of mealtimes as social occasions that could be variously inflected to a more idiosyncratic view of eating and drinking as ambivalent seduction rites, sometimes charmingly witty, sometimes brutally manipulative, and finally to a horrified revulsion from the appetites they represented, as if the price of even the most fundamental human desires was inevitably the destruction of someone else.

Edgar, Hindle (1905–) British actor who played Prince Leopold in WALTZES FROM VIENNA and three other roles (1934–36), then returned 20 years later as producer of four action films (1956–66).

Edington, Harry E. (1890–1949) RKO producer and executive producer, 1940–41, whose last film was MR. AND MRS. SMITH.

Edmunds, William (1886–1981) Italian-born character actor, in Hollywood from 1934. His dozens of minor ethnic roles rounded out the casts of films from *Angels with Dirty Faces* (1938) to *Casablanca* (1942) to *It's a Wonderful Life* (1946, as Bill Edmunds). He played the unexpected proprietor of Mamma Lucie's in MR. AND MRS. SMITH.

Edouart, Farciot (Alexander) (1894–1980) American special effects cinematographer who supervised process photography for more than 200 PARAMOUNT PICTURES films, including TO CATCH A THIEF, THE MAN WHO KNEW TOO MUCH (1956), and VERTIGO, from *Alice in Wonderland* (1933) to *Rosemary's Baby* (1968).

Edwards, James (1918–1970) African-American actor of the fifties, one of the first to break the Stepin Fetchit mold in his performance as Peter Moss in *Home of the Brave* (1949). He appeared briefly in two ALFRED HITCHCOCK PRESENTS segments—in "BREAKDOWN," as a convict set free by the callous Mr. Callew's auto accident who repays the favor by robbing what he thinks is Callew's corpse, and as Ed the bastender in "The Big Switch" (1956).

Ellenstein, Robert (1923–) Balding American actor, son of a Newark, N.J., mayor, in movies and television from 1954, frequently throughout the later fifties—when he played Licht, the less talkative of Roger Thornhill's two kidnappers in NORTH BY NORTHWEST—and more sporadically since.

Elliott, Biff (1923–) Pug-faced American actor who first appeared on television five years before his Hollywood debut as Mike Hammer in *I, the Jury* (1953). A favorite performer in ALFRED HITCHCOCK PRESENTS, he appeared in five roles: as Iggy Kovacs's father in "The Day of the Bullet" (1960), Lt. Bates in "One Grave Too Many" (1960), the conspiratorial detective Phil Ames in "A Crime for Mothers" (1961), Dr. Bob Hudson in "Make My Death Bed" (1961), and Fred Chester, father of the unwittingly well-armed boy Jackie, in "BANG! YOU'RE DEAD."

Elliott, Frank (1880–1970) British actor whose 50-year career (1915–66) included dozens of stiff-upper-lip roles, most in such silents as *EASY VIRTUE*, in which he played the hero's stuffy father Colonel Whittaker.

Elliott, Laura   See ROGERS, KASEY

Ellis, Juney   American character actress, veteran of some two dozen film and television appearances, mostly in the fifties, who appeared as the Steppes' neighbor in the "FOUR O'CLOCK" episode of *SUSPICION* and returned as the barmaid in *FRENZY*.

Ellis, Mollie   British actress, uncredited in her only film role in *THE FARMER'S WIFE*, in which she appears as Sibley Sweetland just long enough in the film's opening scene to leave her eponymous husband widowed.

Ellison, Joy   American actress whose appearances on film and television—such as her role in the *ALFRED HITCHCOCK PRESENTS* episode "BANG! YOU'RE DEAD"—have been brief and sporadic. She returned to Hollywood as a dialogue and dialect coach in 1994.

Elsom, Isobel (1893–1981)   Stage-trained British actress, née Isobel Reed, who appeared in some 60 films before immigrating to Hollywood, where she played increasingly grandes dames from 1941 and was still going strong as Freddy Eynsford-Hill's mother in *My Fair Lady* (1964). She played the frigid innkeeper in *THE PARADINE CASE* and returned to play the inconvenient corpses in three episodes of *ALFRED HITCHCOCK PRESENTS*: "BACK FOR CHRISTMAS," "The Three Dreams of Mr. Findlater" (1957), and "The Diplomatic Corpse" (1957) and nuns in two episodes of *THE ALFRED HITCHCOCK HOUR*: "Final Vow" (1962) and "The Dark Pool" (1963).

Elstree Calling   British International, Wardour & F. 94 minutes; February 1930. **Director**: Adrian Brunel; **Director of sketches and other interpolated items:** Alfred Hitchcock; **Screenplay:** Val Valentine; **Cinematographer:** Claude Friese-Greene; **Ensemble numbers:** staged by Jack Hulbert, Paul Murray, and André Charlot; **Lyrics:** Douglas Furber, Rowland Leigh, and Donovan Parsons; **Music:** Reg Casson, Vivian Ellis, Chick Endor, Ivor Novello, Jack Strachey; **Musical conductors:** Teddy Brown, Sydney Baynes, John Reynders; **Production manager:** J. Sloan; **Sound:** Alec Murray; **Editor:** A.C.

Hammond, under the supervision of Emile de Ruelle; **Cast:** Cicely Courtneidge, Jack Hulbert, Tommy Handley, Lily Morris, Helen Burnell, the Berkoffs, Bobby Comber, Lawrence Green, Ivor McLaren, Anna May Wong, Jameson Thomas, John Longden, Donald Calthrop, Will Fyffe, Gordon Harker, Hannah Jones, Teddy Brown, the Three Eddies, the Balaleika Choral Orchestra, supported by the Adelphi Girls and the Charlot Girls

This Hollywood-style musical revue was rushed into production soon after the success of *Blackmail* to celebrate BRITISH INTERNATIONAL's conversion to synchronized sound, and everyone employed by the studio seems to have been called on to help. Hitchcock was disinclined to talk about a film that was well outside his usual comic/melodramatic range and not primarily his at all, and his contributions have never been definitively established. Charles BARR has identified four episodes (two incorporating brief running gags) Hitchcock is most likely to have directed: a series of framing scenes in which a husband and wife labor to tune in the television transmission of the revue; a series of brief scenes in which Donald CALTHROP is repeatedly interrupted in his attempts to recite some Shakespearean verse; a parody of *The Taming of the Shrew* in which Calthrop also appears; and a sketch in which Jameson THOMAS plays a jealous husband who shoots a couple in rage before realizing that he is in the wrong flat.

Emanuel, Elzie   African-American supporting actor who debuted as a child in *To Have and Have Not* (1945) and returned in *Intruder in the Dust* (1948), *The Sun Shines Bright* (1953), and the *ALFRED HITCHCOCK PRESENTS* segment "BREAKDOWN," playing Callew's secretary.

Emelka Studios   The Munich studio at which, under a coproduction arrangement with Michael BALCON's GAINSBOROUGH PICTURES, Hitchcock directed his first two films, *THE PLEASURE GARDEN* and *THE MOUNTAIN EAGLE*.

Emery, John (1905–1964)   Polished, sometimes oily American second lead in some 30 films (1937–64). Four years after his divorce from Tallulah

BANKHEAD, he played Dr. Fleurot, whose romantic overtures were perfunctorily rebuffed by Dr. Constance Peterson in SPELLBOUND. He returned as the harried murderer Kerwin Drake in the "Servant Problem" segment of ALFRED HITCHCOCK PRESENTS (1961).

Emmett, E.V.H. (1902–1971) Jack-of-all-trades of the British cinema. Best-known for his incisive voiceover commentary in GAUMONT-BRITISH and UNIVERSAL newsreels, he also acted in eight films (1937–64); provided additional dialogue for another half-dozen beginning with SABOTAGE; wrote and directed one film, *Bothered by a Beard* (1945); and served as associate producer on two others, *Passport to Pimlico* (1949) and *Dance Hall* (1950), which he also wrote.

Emmons, Richard One of the four camera operators responsible for negotiating the intricate camera movements in ROPE.

Engelman, Leonard American makeup artist, Bud WESTMORE's uncredited associate on TOPAZ, who has gone on, sometimes as Leonard Engleman, to 40 other films, beginning with *The Magnificent Seven Ride!* (1972).

Esmond, Jill (1908–1990) British leading lady, first wife (1930–40) of Laurence OLIVIER, who made her film debut as Jill Hillcrist in THE SKIN GAME and starred in nine other films on both sides of the Atlantic (1931–33). Following her divorce, she returned to Hollywood, where she appeared in character roles in six films, including *Random Harvest* and *Journey for Margaret,* both in 1942, before her career wound down in the early fifties.

Essen, Robert American child actor whose sole film credit is Manny Balestrero's son Gregory in THE WRONG MAN.

Evans, Bertram British art director who shared billing for THE LODGER, his only film credit, with C. Wilfred ARNOLD.

Evans, Ray (1915–) American lyricist whose long collaboration with his former college room-mate, composer Jay LIVINGSTON, produced such memorable tunes as "Silver Bells," "Dear Heart," "Tammy," and the themes from the television series *Mr. Ed* and *Bonanza*. The team won Academy Awards for three songs: "Buttons and Bows" (from *The Paleface,* 1948); "Mona Lisa" (from *Captain Carey, U.S.A.,* 1950); and, most improbably, "Que Sera, Sera" (from THE MAN WHO KNEW TOO MUCH, 1956).

Evanson, Edith (1896–1980) American character actress who made her debut as one of Jedediah Leland's nurses in *Citizen Kane* (1941) and was a familiar fixture for nearly 50 years thereafter as the vinegary spinsters, nurses, and maiden aunts in such films as *Woman of the Year* (1942), *I Remember Mama* (1948), *The Magnificent Yankee* (1950), and *Shane* (1953). She played the murderers' housekeeper Mrs. Wilson in ROPE and the Rutland Company's cleaning woman Rita in MARNIE, and she appeared in between in two episodes of ALFRED HITCHCOCK PRESENTS, as a pickpocket in "Manacled" (1957) and Mrs. Johnson in "Listen! Listen!" (1958).

Evelyn, Judith (1913–1967) American character actress of the fifties, born J.E. Allen, who appeared as Miss Lonelyhearts in REAR WINDOW and then took roles as husband-killers in two episodes of ALFRED HITCHCOCK PRESENTS that echoed elements of *Rear Window's* central situation: Amelia Verber in "Guilty Witness" (1955) and Mabel McKay in "Martha Mason, Movie Star" (1957).

Ewell, Tom (1909–1994) American comic actor, born S. Eyewell Tompkins, whose long and varied stage career from 1934—he created the roles of Richard Sherman in *The Seven Year Itch* (1952) and Estragon in *Waiting for Godot* (1957)—has largely been eclipsed by his work in movies and television, where he excelled in portraying ordinary men in ludicrous situations. Skulking and cowardly as the philandering husband Warren Attinger in *Adam's Rib* (1949), he soon developed a more likable line in affable neurosis in the film version of *The Seven Year Itch* (1955) and the title role of Albert Pelham in the ALFRED HITCHCOCK PRESENTS segment "THE CASE OF MR. PELHAM" that served him well in three regular television series: *The Tom Ewell Show* (1960–61), *Baretta* (1975–78), and *Best of the West* (1981–82).

Ewing, John F. (1900–1961) American visual artist who served as associate art director on SPELL-BOUND and a half-dozen other Hollywood films from 1938 to 1946.

expressionism The aesthetic movement that arose in German painting and cinema in the early years of the 20th century broke with realistic limitation in favor of stylized visuals representing a subjective, emotionally laden view of the physical world. Its principles united two groups of painters, Die Brücke, active in Dresden from 1905, and Der Blaue Reiter, formed in Munich in 1911, and all the most distinguished Weimar filmmakers, especially Robert Wiene (whose *Kabinett des Dr. Caligari,* 1919, represented the world as seen through the distorting eyes of a madman), F.W. MURNAU, and Fritz LANG. Hitchcock absorbed much of the movement's influence (reflected in his remark to François TRUFFAUT that "the screen rectangle must be charged with emotion") through his observation of Murnau at work in 1924, but the expressionistic elements in his own films more closely paralleled those of Lang. Like Lang's German films, several of Hitchcock's silent films, especially THE RING, are heavily influenced by an expressionist aesthetic that traps the characters in a claustrophobic physical world from which they are hopelessly estranged by their very perceptions. Even in Hitchcock's earliest films, however, this influence is balanced by an interest in such everyday routines as the backstage interludes in THE PLEASURE GARDEN, THE LODGER, and DOWNHILL and the domestic rituals in THE FARMER'S WIFE and THE MANXMAN. Although the dream and daydream sequences in *Downhill,* CHAMPAGNE, and SPELLBOUND and the wedding scene increasingly distorted by drinking in *The Ring* are essentially expressionistic, Hitchcock, again like Lang after he immigrated to America, increasingly aimed for a synthesis of realism and expressionism that would motivate effects of varying intensity within a predominantly realistic framework. Elisabeth WEIS has pointed out, for example, that although the soundtrack of SECRET AGENT is systematically distorted (for example, in the tolling bells close by the trapped Ashenden and the General, or in the nightmarishly repeated folk song as heard by the remorseful Elsa) to represent the characters' tense, frightened, or guilt-ridden perceptions, THE MAN WHO KNEW TOO MUCH (1934) provides a realistic basis for its sound effects.

The contrast between realism and expressionism is more widely noted in Hitchcock's visuals, which typically avoid the extreme stylization of both German silent cinema and its American heir FILM NOIR but still make strategic use of high contrast, deep shadow, and sharply raked angles. But the marriage between realism and expressionism takes many forms in the American films. In the films Hitchcock made for David O. SELZNICK, from REBECCA (photographed by George BARNES) to THE PARADINE CASE (shot by Lee GARMES), expressionistic visuals are subsumed within a romantic aesthetic that softens and glamorizes them. In THE WRONG MAN and the early scenes of PSYCHO, the visuals have a harsher, more documentary look that conveys the protagonists' sense of waking nightmare by indicating the banality of the routines inside which they feel trapped; THE TROUBLE WITH HARRY, by contrast, generates its sense of black comedy by setting a pastoral, scenic handling of the Vermont countryside and its characters' matter-of-fact handling of the nuisance represented by Harry Warp's body against what ought to be the gravity of Harry's death. Most of Hitchcock's later films, however, are broadly flexible in their combination of realistic and expressionistic elements. The generally realistic visuals of NORTH BY NORTHWEST, for example, are enriched by the exoticism of the United Nations as a murder scene, the futuristic design of Philip Vandamm's house in South Dakota, and a pair of high-angle shots—the first a steeply angled shot during Roger Thornhill's initial meeting with Vandamm, the second a birds'-eye shot much later as Vandamm hints at how he plans to dispose of Eve Kendall—that abruptly suggest a danger pointedly at odds with the normalcy of the interior sets. Hitchcock's ultimate achievement in pure cinematic expressionism is VERTIGO, whose hypnotic visuals, soundtrack, performances, and narrative combine to suggest a troubled but unbroken dream from which its hero can never awake.

eyes Despite the enduring importance of looking and being looked at, perhaps the two primary activities in Hitchcock's films, most of his films give little visual attention to the act of looking, emphasizing instead its emotional concomitants and its corrosive effects. Aggressive watching is crucial in THE PLEASURE GAR-DEN, DOWNHILL, EASY VIRTUE, CHAMPAGNE, and BLACK-MAIL, but with rare exceptions like the unfocused shot showing the judge's point of view in *Easy Virtue,* none of them emphasizes eyes as a central visual motif; *Easy Virtue,* for instance, focuses on press cameras rather than eyes, especially in its credit sequence, and *Black-mail's* most searching gaze belongs to the laughing painting of a jester who points accusingly at Alice. Not even THE LADY VANISHES, whose eye-named heroine Iris Henderson's reliability as an observer is the film's central issue, or NOTORIOUS, the first of Hitchcock's films to link spying explicitly to voyeurism, pay any special attention to eyes as such. It is not until REAR WINDOW, a movie about nothing but spying on people, that Hitchcock focuses resolutely on the *look* of people looking, and even here, as he boasted to François TRUF-FAUT, his "PURE CINEMA" depends on intercutting neutral shots of James STEWART looking offscreen with shots of what he is watching that will presumably encourage viewers to supply an emotional freight the shots of Stewart need not bear. Hitchcock's most memorable shots of eyes, then, all show them to be opaque, unseeing, or objectified, from the closeup of Kim NOVAK's masklike face that moves to frame her suddenly, inexplicably frightened eyes over VERTIGO's credits to the two cut-ins to Dan Fawcett's dead, ruined eyes in THE BIRDS. Most memorable of all, of course, are the many shots of eyes in PSYCHO, whose hero refuses to put his mother in a nursing home because she would fall victim to all "the cruel eyes watching" but who has no scruples in spying on his guest as she prepares for her last shower. The extreme closeup of Norman's eye pressed to the peephole in his wall is part of a pattern that runs from the shot of Marion's boss Mr. Lowery doing a double-take as he sees his supposedly sick secretary driving out of town to the closeup of Mrs. Bates's eyeless skull, which Lila Crane finds in her basement, to the shot of the cap-tured Norman peering up from the fly crawling on his hand to smile at the camera as the skull is briefly, chill-ingly superimposed on his face—a pattern epitomized by the most famous ocular closeup in cinema history: the slow dissolve from the bathtub drain carrying away Marion's blood to a rolling shot of her dead eye. Fasci-nated as Hitchcock is with the acts of seeing and being seen, he never lingers over shots of eyes except to deny the identity of the eye as the seat of the soul or even the locus of reliable visual perception.

Falkenberg, C. Actor who played Prince Ivan, the suitor for whom Jill Cheyne rejects her fiancé Hugh Fielding, making him available for the disillusioned Patsy Brand in *THE PLEASURE GARDEN*.

families Families—nuclear, extended, promised, or displaced; supportive, damaged, or lost—supply the social matrix for virtually all of Hitchcock's films. The alternative could hardly be the case, given the importance of family as a locus of value in both England and America, expressing itself in films as different as *Brief Encounter* (1945) and *The Wizard of Oz* (1939). Yet families are far more important in Hitchcock than in most directors of thrillers—so important that the emphasis his forties films give them is a primary distinction between his work and FILM NOIR, so important that their corruption or loss becomes the sign of the greatest danger or disaster as early as Levet's betrayal of his faithful wife in *THE PLEASURE GARDEN*. Hitchcock's British films from *THE LODGER* to *THE MAN WHO KNEW TOO MUCH* (1934) are studded with families whose domestic routine provides both a placid surface the intrigue can disturb and a stable identity for his heroes and heroines. Often, the idea of family is treated with comic affection, as in the portrayal of the unlikely suitor Samuel Sweetland in *THE FARMER'S WIFE* and the Markhams in *MURDER!*; sometimes the family is threatened by intrigue, as in *BLACKMAIL* and *THE SKIN GAME*; often, especially in Hitchcock's early non-thrillers, it is contested by rivalries, from the father-and-son competition in *WALTZES FROM VIENNA* to the escalating hostilities of *THE RING* to the unwitting but ruinous adultery of *THE MANXMAN*, or more generally becomes the site of conflict, its crisis or survival the subject of the film, as in *EASY VIRTUE, CHAMPAGNE, JUNO AND THE PAYCOCK*, and *RICH AND STRANGE*. In *DOWNHILL* and *EASY VIRTUE*, expulsion from the family represents the supreme calamity; in *The Skin Game*, that calamity is represented by the corruption of the family figured by Chloe Hornblower's exposure and attempted suicide, the Hillcrist's connivance at her destruction, and the loss of the land to which the Hillcrists have tied their collective identity. Even *NUMBER SEVENTEEN*, whose old dark house brings together such an ill-assorted collection of strangers, includes in its cast a father and daughter, and parodies such domestic rituals as welcoming guests and house hunting. Families are less central in Hitchcock's British thrillers because their plots require protagonists like Richard Hannay and Iris Henderson to have greater freedom of action. Still the pull of family remains important in *THE 39 STEPS* and *THE LADY VANISHES*, though figured negatively by the sparseness of Hannay's sublet flat and the two variously menacing families he meets, the crofter and his wife and the suavely murderous Jordans, and by the amusing domestic arrangements in the Alpine hotel and Iris's train journey toward her fiancé. The relationship between Elsa and Ashenden in SECRET AGENT might be described as a series of rehearsals for domestic life. More predictably, family is the social unit that is disrupted early on in *The Man Who Knew Too Much*, SABOTAGE, and YOUNG AND INNOCENT and reaffirmed at the end.

After one final British film, JAMAICA INN, which is again a story of family corrupted and lost, Hitchcock's American films show a marked tendency to fetishize the domestic sphere, overvaluing family ties whose endangerment leads such characters as the second Mrs. de Winter and Lina Aysgarth close to hysteria and David Smith to comic despair in REBECCA, SUSPICION, and MR. AND MRS. SMITH respectively. Although Huntley Haverstock and Barry Kane, in FOREIGN CORRESPONDENT and SABOTEUR, attach no more than a conventional importance to family ties past or future, these films continue to provide domestic parodies in Stephen Fisher's household, the grieving Mrs. Mason, and the smiling, grandfatherly saboteur Charles Tobin, and SPELLBOUND, following Freud, roots its hero's neuroses in a family trauma. A pair of films from the forties, SHADOW OF A DOUBT and NOTORIOUS, are Hitchcock's most prescient in large part because of the way they treat families: the first as a suburban arena for anatomizing the American dream and the problem of coming of age within a family, the second as a nest of vipers that, once entered as a convenience, can never be escaped. In both cases the family becomes a trap when family ties are poisoned. Uncle Charlie is figured by turns as his niece's father, lover, and nightmare double in a story whose incestuous overtones undermine any notion of the family as a refuge from danger, and Alicia Huberman, in marrying the German industrialist Alex Sebastian at the behest of her government employers to get inside his house, so dishonors the family ties that these films fetishize that it is eminently logical that her bridegroom and his mother turn on her in coldly murderous fury. These two films mark a crisis in Hitchcock's representation of family. Although he continues thereafter to make films in which families shelter their members from harm, his films become gradually more skeptical of the whole project of assembling and defending a family. Anthony Keane

contemplates leaving his wife in THE PARADINE CASE for a woman who has instigated her husband's murder; Brandon Shaw sets a table in ROPE that violates every domestic taboo imaginable; the interloping Charles Adare finds that neither his adored Lady Hetty nor her marriage to Sam Flusky in UNDER CAPRICORN is what it appears; Father Michael Logan in I CONFESS is prevented by his vows from forming the family ties that would have protected him from blackmail. Families cannot be taken for granted even by the principals of STAGE FRIGHT or STRANGERS ON A TRAIN, and by the time of DIAL M FOR MURDER and REAR WINDOW Hitchcock has returned to the more ruthless anatomy of domestic bliss promised by *Shadow of a Doubt*. Despite the generally sunny tone of the films John Michael Hayes wrote for Hitchcock, domesticity becomes a joke in both TO CATCH A THIEF and THE TROUBLE WITH HARRY, and it is less than a reassuring bulwark against disaster in THE MAN WHO KNEW TOO MUCH (1956) or the non-Hayes film that followed, THE WRONG MAN. Picking up earlier hints from *Notorious* and *Rear Window,* VERTIGO and PSYCHO seem dedicated to insisting in the strongest possible terms that both romance and family ties, fetishized more balefully than ever before in the skillfully manufactured image of Madeleine Elster and the skeletal remains of Mrs. Bates, are rendered impossible by the male paranoia that NORTH BY NORTHWEST treats more comically. THE BIRDS and MARNIE find in their troubled families correlatives or causes for the threats that menace their heroines.

Hitchcock's final films, from TORN CURTAIN to FAMILY PLOT, can be read as postdomestic. Having given up the hope of a sustaining family life the previous films have attacked as fetishistic and self-deluding, his heroes and heroines move through a landscape devoid of domestic love, marked only by the broken families of TOPAZ and FRENZY and the parodistic couples of *Family Plot*. Yet the pairing of *Frenzy* and *Family Plot,* Hitchcock's last two films, together with the screenplay for the unfilmed project THE SHORT NIGHT, suggests that although he expressed his suspicion of the family as a locus of moral value in ever bolder terms, his yearning for the domestic values represented, however improbably, by family ties remained remarkably constant.

Family Plot (Alternative titles: *One Plus One Equals One, Deception, Deceit, Missing Heir* [working titles], *Familiengrab, Complot de famille, Complotto di famiglia*) Universal, 120 minutes, March 1976. **Producer:** Alfred Hitchcock; **Director:** Alfred Hitchcock; **Screenplay:** Ernest Lehman, based on *The Rainbird Pattern,* a novel by Victor Canning; **Cinematographer:** Leonard South; **Assistant directors:** Howard G. Kazanjian and Wayne A. Farlow; **Art director:** Henry Bumstead; **Costumes:** Edith Head; **Makeup:** Jack Barron; **Sound supervisor:** James Alexander; **Sound mixers:** James W. Payne, Robert L. Hoyt, Roger Heman, Earl Madery; **Supervising sound editor:** Roger Sword; **Script supervisor:** Lois Thurman; **Production assistant:** Peggy Robertson; **Production illustrator:** Thomas J. Wright; **Production manager:** Ernest B. Wehmeyer;

Special effects: Albert Whitlock; **Editor:** J. Terry Williams; **Music:** John Williams; **Cast:** Karen Black (Fran), Bruce Dern (George Lumley), Barbara Harris (Blanche Tyler), William Devane (Arthur Adamson), Ed Lauter (Joseph Maloney), Cathleen Nesbitt (Julia Rainbird), Katherine Helmond (Mrs. Maloney), Warren J. Kemmerling (Grandison), Edith Atwater (Mrs. Clay), William Prince (Bishop), Nicholas Colasanto (Constantine), Marge Redmond (Vera Hannigan), John Lehne (Andy Bush), Charles Tyner (Wheeler), Alexander Lockwood (parson), Martin West (Sanger), Louise Lorimer, Kate Murtagh, Clint Young

The subject of Hitchcock's 53rd and final completed film was first announced in October 1973. Ernest *LEHMAN* had already turned down the chance to adapt

Hitchcock prepares to direct George Lumley's mazelike pursuit of Joe Maloney's widow through the graveyard where Maloney is being buried in *Family Plot. (National Film Society Archive)*

Victor CANNING's novel *The Rainbird Pattern* for another studio but agreed to work once more with Hitchcock, who was fascinated with the way the novel's two plots moved inexorably toward each other. Lehman completed a draft of the screenplay the following April, but although Hitchcock returned the script with detailed annotations within a week, he was slow to resume daily work on it, and it was not until August 1974 that Lehman submitted a revised treatment, followed several weeks later by a revised script; the two did not agree on a final screenplay until April 1975. Casting proceeded slowly, with UNIVERSAL PICTURES pushing Liza Minnelli for the role Hitchcock wanted Barbara HARRIS for; eventually, the director accepted the bankable Karen BLACK as the price for casting the less-known Harris. Bruce DERN, who had worked with Hitchcock before, was signed as the male lead, Roy Thinnes as the villain, and Cathleen NESBITT just before shooting began as the catalytic Julia Rainbird. The shoot, which began on May 12, 1975, was closed to the press and public but turned out to be the most closely documented of all his shoots because both Hitchcock's authorized biographer John Russell TAYLOR and his future biographer Donald SPOTO were on the set. Both of them, impressed by Hitchcock's detailed preparation for the film, marked as well the ways his plans, as the crew moved from Hollywood to San Francisco, changed. Hitchcock, who had shifted the story's setting from England to America because he did not want to make another film in his native country, vacillated between giving it a distinctly San Francisco feel and shooting most of it in the studio before ending up shooting at Grace Cathedral and other San Francisco locations. More dramatically, he abruptly replaced Thinnes on July 12 with William Devane—the first time an actor had ever been dismissed from a Hitchcock film so late in the process— requiring considerable reshooting; around the same time it finally acquired the title under which it was released. The choice of the prolific John WILLIAMS, noted most recently for his menacing score for *Jaws*, as composer was not announced until December, some four months after principal photography was completed. The film, which premiered as the opening attraction at Filmex, the Los Angeles International Film Festival, on March 21, 1976, opened nationally to respectful reviews and a healthy profit.

Despite its generally lighthearted tone, the film is one of Hitchcock's most noncommittal and opaque. Its daffy bogus medium Blanche Tyler and her bumptious driver/lover/accomplice George Lumley are constantly swapping insults and bawdy jokes, but their badinage does not, as in earlier films like THE LADY VANISHES and REAR WINDOW, draw audiences into their romance because they do not share a romance or for that matter a direction. Neither does the couple with whom they are paired, Arthur Adamson and his accomplice Fran, who have already been kidnapping prominent citizens and ransoming them for diamonds for some time before the story begins. Neither couple is going anywhere; they both already are where they hope to be, except that Adamson and Fran hope to enrich themselves still further and that Blanche and Lumley hope to claim a $10,000 reward from Julia Rainbird for finding any surviving relatives of her late estranged sister Harriet. The lack of any urgent romantic tension gives the film's trajectory—one couple is feverishly searching for the other, who are first ignorant of their existence, and then desperate to escape their notice—a curiously abstract geometry. Individual characters are almost equally abstract. Although Hitchcock had told Lehman, "This film is going to be made by its characters," he discarded scene after scene Lehman had intended to fill in their background and motivation; Fran in particular turns out to be nearly as enigmatic as Nurse Agnes in THE MAN WHO KNEW TOO MUCH (1934). Even the kidnapping of Bishop Wood during Mass under the baffled eye of Lumley, who has come to question him about the supposedly dead Eddie Shoebridge—a kidnapping whose ironic possibilities had long fascinated the director—turns into something cool and remote. David STERRITT, in his essay on the film in *HITCHCOCK ANNUAL*, sees its ambiguity, coupled with the unreliability of many of the sights and sounds it presents (Fran in heavy disguise, the diamond concealed in a chandelier, the astral voices Blanche fakes during her seances) as a trope for undecidability crystallized by the ŽIŽEKIAN "stain" of the diamond Blanche discovers, with or without the help of her spirit friend Henry, and the wink she tips the audience in the film's valedictory final shot. Considered as a comedy/melodrama in the mold of THE 39 STEPS and TO CATCH A THIEF, the film is too disengaged to be successful; it is probably through such defenses as Sterritt's that it will attract continuing attention as more than the master of suspense's farewell to the cinema.

Farebrother, Violet (1888–1969)
Stage-trained British actress who returned 16 years after her film debut as Queen Elizabeth in *Richard III* (1911) to play Mrs. Whittaker, the hero's mother, in *Easy Virtue*, then returned as the Poetess in DOWNHILL and as one of the 12 jurors in MURDER! before playing increasingly stiff dowagers through 1958.

Farjeon, J(oseph) Jefferson (1883–1955)
British journalist who turned to farcical crime melodrama, producing several plays, including NUMBER SEVENTEEN (1925), and more than 80 novels, several of them resurrecting the play's raffish hero Ben (*Ben Sees It Through,* 1932; *Detective Ben,* 1936). *Number Serventeen,* popular in its original run and a 1930–31 revival, had already been filmed once in Germany (1928) before Hitchcock was assigned to it. Farjeon himself, apart from the film adaptations of his novels and plays, worked on four films directly: *Two Crowded Hours* (1931), *My Friend the King* (1932), *Phantom Light* (1935), and *Lightning Conductor* (1938).

Farlow, Wayne A.
American assistant director, former child actor of the early fifties, who served as second assistant director on FAMILY PLOT and two other films, then found more permanent work as first assistant director of the television series *Quincy* (1976–83) before rounding out his career as production manager and line producer on several television movies.

Farmer's Wife, The
(Alternative title: *Laquelle des trois*) British International, Wardour & F., approximately 100 minutes, March 1928. **Producer:** John Maxwell; **Director:** Alfred Hitchcock; **Screenplay:** Eliot Stannard, based on the play by Eden Phillpotts; **Cinematographer:** John J. Cox; **Art director:** C. W. Arnold; **Assistant director:** Frank Mills; **Camera assistants:** Percy Coe and Alfred Roome; **Cast:** Jameson Thomas (Farmer Samuel Sweetland), Lilian Hall-Davis (Araminta Dench, his housekeeper), Gordon Harker (Churdles Ash, his handyman), Gibb McLaughlin (Henry Coaker), Maud Gill (Thirza Tapper), Louie Pounds (Widow Louisa Windeatt), Olga Slade (Mary Hearne, Postmistress), Ruth Maitland (Mercy Bassett), Antonia Brough (Susan, Thirza's maid), Haward Watts (Dick Coaker), Mollie Ellis (Sibley Sweetland)

Hitchcock's seventh film, his second for BRITISH INTERNATIONAL PICTURES, was shot in October 1927, first on location in Devon and Surrey and then in the studio. When Jack Cox fell ill, Hitchcock was required to shoot much of the film himself, examining the rushes privately to conceal his lack of confidence from the cast. Donald SPOTO reports that Hitchcock celebrated completion of the film by giving a party for the cast and crew at a tiny London restaurant whose waiters were replaced by actors instructed to be as rude and clumsy as possible.

The film, perhaps Hitchcock's most unfairly neglected work, respects the general outlines of its source, a notable stage success about a new widower's comical attempts to replace his late wife by wooing the three least unlikely marital prospects in his little village before realizing that his unassuming housekeeper is the natural choice he has been overlooking all along. The film compresses as usual its time frame and presents directly, as in *Easy Virtue,* events in the play's backstory—here, the death of Farmer Sweetland's first wife, followed immediately in Eliot STANNARD's adaptation by the marriage of his daughter Sibley, which leaves him abandoned (a theme Hitchcock seems to echo from the thematically similar marriage scene in F. W. MURNAU's *Der letzte Mann*) and casting about for female companionship. He methodically lays siege to three likely candidates—the plain-spoken Widow Windeatt, the skittish spinster Thirza Tapper, and the chortling postmistress Mary Hearne—but such is his condescending assurance and insensitivity that even though the first two initially welcome his proposals, they all turn him down, as does the robust barmaid Mercy Bassett in a scene Hitchcock mercifully withholds. Though the humor is rough, it is genuine, sparked by an appealingly vulnerable star turn by Jameson Thomas as Sweetland and a scene-stealing performance by Gordon Harker as his handyman Churdles Ash, who is consistently on hand to comment on Sweetland's every humiliation. He plays a pivotal role as both actor and observer during Thirza Tapper's party, the set piece the film borrows from the play, which Sweetland unwisely arrives at early to make his second abortive proposal. Charles Barr notes the motivic use of sequences based on alternative shots that isolate characters who are sharing the same space (as they will do later on in the opening scene of *Psycho* and throughout *Rear Window*) and the new prominence of camera movement, especially panning or tracking shots that follow the characters. Despite the film's battle-of-the-sexes plot and its unbridled denigration of each sex by the other, it has a warmth and sweetness unprecedented in Hitchcock's work and unrivaled in any of his later films before *The Trouble with Harry*, whose tone is also softened by its rustic setting.

Farr, Patricia (1913–1948)   American character actress of the thirties, usually in lower-class or good-time-girl roles, who returned to play Chuck's blowzy date Gloria in MR. AND MRS. SMITH.

Farrell, Lowell J. (1910–1961)   American assistant director of the forties, former MGM production manager, whose relatively few but glittering credits included *The Jungle Book* (1942), *Since You Went Away* (1944), *Duel in the Sun* (1946), three John Ford movies—*Fort Apache* (1948), *She Wore a Yellow Ribbon* (1949), and *Wagonmaster* (1950), the latter two as associate producer—and three Hitchcock films: SPELLBOUND, THE PARADINE CASE, and ROPE.

fathers   A truism of Hitchcock studies is that his early films revolve around fathers and daughters, his later films around mothers and sons. Certainly the importance of the father-daughter bond in CHAMPAGNE, THE SKIN GAME, WALTZES FROM VIENNA, THE MAN WHO KNEW TOO MUCH (1934), FOREIGN CORRESPONDENT, and especially YOUNG AND INNOCENT seems to bear out this bromide. As Tania MODESKI has pointed out, however, ideals of fatherhood in Hitchcock are complicated by the fact that many of his most important father figures are displaced lovers, as in THE LADY VANISHES, REBECCA, NOTORIOUS, MARNIE, and SHADOW OF A DOUBT, in which Uncle Charlie is more important, more authoritarian, more virile, and more

disturbing than Charlie Newton's biological father. Paula Marantz COHEN, broadening the association of Hitchcock's fathers with the Law of the Father that marks acceptance into the Lacanian Symbolic to include both traditional narrative agency (as opposed to the sustaining, emotionally expressive function of mother figures) and the director's own controlling intelligence, argues that the true importance of Hitchcock's fathers emerges only later in his career, first in the "father-daughter plots" of *Shadow of a Doubt,* STAGE FRIGHT, and STRANGERS ON A TRAIN, then in "the daughter's effect" in REAR WINDOW, which constructs a male subject through a gaze whose efficacy is questioned by his female partner, and THE MAN WHO KNEW TOO MUCH (1956), which brings the female subjectivity represented by Jo McKenna into the realm of narrative agency, linking a Hitchcock father, for the only time in his career, to a mother of comparable strength. If Hitchcock's mothers invite a more direct critique of genetic identity than his fathers, his fathers, less often paired with wives than with the daughters or younger lovers they seek to control, show the fate of patriarchy unmodified by psychological empathy and unwilling to regulate itself.

Faure, John (D.) (1915–1963)   American film editor, in Hollywood from 1943 through 1959, whose dozen credits included THE PARADINE CASE. He later found a secure home on the *Perry Mason* television series from 1957 to his death.

Fawell, John (Wesley) (1959–)   American film scholar, associate professor of humanities at Boston University, and author of *Hitchcock's* Rear Window: *The Well-Made Film* (2001), a meticulous and sometimes critical study of earlier analyses of the film, focusing on technical considerations (the claustrophobic enclosure of the film's single set, its exclusively diegetic soundtrack, the overwhelming predominance of shots from inside L.B. Jefferies's apartment, and its unusually close attention to women's fashion) and thematic concerns (the film's ironic combination of cruelty to women and feminist critique, its evocation of contemporary urban isolation and alienation through sound and image, the complex relationship between Jefferies, Hitchcock, and the audience as voyeurs and manipulators). The paradox that ties these subjects together is Hitchcock's assumption of an exceptionally rigorous formal framework—one that might well have created, in the hands of Fritz LANG, an oppressively schematic film—as the foundation for what is one of his most relaxed and playful works and for whose status as Hitchcock's greatest film Fawell contends, "There is a strong argument to be made."

Fax, Jesslyn (1893–1975)   Fireplug American character actress whose trilling voice, well known from her supporting role in the television series *Our Miss Brooks* (1952–56), was rarely heard in her role as the sculptress in REAR WINDOW. Her 30 later roles include walk-ons in NORTH BY NORTHWEST and the "Four O'Clock" segment of SUSPICION; three parts in ALFRED HITCHCOCK PRESENTS—the hero's battleaxe mother Mrs. Evans in "Coming, Mama" (1961), the liquor store clerk in "Self Defense" (1961), and the motel proprietor in "The Woman Who Wanted to Live" (1962)—and two on THE ALFRED HITCHCOCK HOUR—Mrs. Bates in "The Paragon" (1963) and Miss McGuiness in "The Lonely Hours" (1963).

Fazan, William   British actor of the thirties whose five film roles, all bit parts, include three in Hitchcock films: MURDER! (in which he plays one of the 12 jurors), YOUNG AND INNOCENT, and JAMAICA INN.

fear and pleasure   The founding paradox of Hitchcock's films is that they seek to entertain audiences by frightening them. How can such fear be pleasurable? Hitchcock offered his own explanation in the 1936 essay "Why 'Thrillers' Thrive" when he contended that "our civilization has so screened and sheltered us that it isn't practicable to experience . . . firsthand" the tonic "shake-ups" without which we would grow "sluggish and jellified." Cinema, he argued, was an ideal medium for creating maximally close empathy with characters in dangerous situations while allowing audiences to retain their "subconscious" awareness that "we are safe, sitting in a comfortable armchair, watching a screen." A primary implication of this explantion, that feelings of fear are as healthy as the sense of safety, helps account for the

fact that Hitchcock's films do not follow an invariable recipe for inducing thrills in audiences that generally feel protectively sheltered. Hence MURDER!, except perhaps for its climactic carnival sequence, is almost too sedate to be called a thriller, whereas SABOTAGE, which threatens to blow up a busload of innocents and then, breaking every cinematic taboo, actually does so, seems calculated to prevent audiences from ever trusting Hitchcock's reassurances of ultimate safety again, even though it is still only their fictional surrogates, not audiences themselves, that are endangered and perhaps destroyed.

There are several ways to theorize the distinctive pleasures of Hitchcockian suspense. Because suspense in whatever form is a *sine qua non* of narrative cinema, audiences presumably arrive at theaters prepared to be, if not frightened, at least riven with apprehension, intermittently painful empathy, and the occasional shock; Hitchcock merely intensifies these desirable sensations. Alternatively, Hitchcock's cinema has been described by Eric ROHMER and Claude CHABROL as so rigorously moral, and by Raymond DURGNAT as so formally stylized, that fear and shock alike are either subsumed by audiences' spiritual education or dulled by their pleasure in the films' aestheticism, or their pleasures may be masochistically contractual, as Thomas M. LEITCH has argued, as audiences agree with the director on a narrative contract that prevents them from becoming too secure by changing periodically. Finally, the dialectic of fear and pleasure might be historicized by noting that with the entrance of Hitchcock into academic film studies and the availability of his movies in home-theater media that allow them to be watched repeatedly at a single sitting, the terrors even of a film such as PSYCHO become largely stipulative. For audiences who have not insulated themselves against every surprise by learning Hitchcock's films by heart, however, it seems likely that the intimacy between fear and pleasure will continue to be a piquant problem for Hitchcock studies.

Fehr, Rudi (1911–1999)   German-born editor, who after British experience arrived in 1940 at WARNER BROS., where he edited, among 30 others, *All Through the Night* (1942), *Watch on the Rhine*

(1943), *Devotion* (1946), *Humoresque* (1946), *Key Largo* (1948), *Beyond the Forest* (1949), and two Hitchcock films, *I CONFESS* and *DIAL M FOR MURDER*.

feminism The first important theorist to explore the psychoanalytic import of Hitchcock's films was Raymond BELLOUR. His model, less Freudian than LACANIAN, emphasized acculturation through a family and a male culture designed to contain the threats of Oedipal desire and castration, Bellour's "symbolic blockage" that circumscribes a given text's libidinal energies by an economy designed to produce and protect the heterosexual romantic couple. At the same time, Bellour contended, the Hitchcock "system" makes explicit, at least under sufficiently close examination, the very mechanisms that limit its sexuality to the privileged position of adult heterosexual romance. Bellour's notion of symbolic blockage became the touchstone for such later studies as Laura MULVEY'S essay "Visual Pleasure and Narrative Cinema" (1975), which described Hitchcock's films as organized by a powerfully subjective male gaze that reduced his women to objects to be fetishized and ultimately consumed. By 1990 Hitchcock's work had become a testing ground for feminist theory. In response to critics who attacked or defended Hitchcock on the grounds of his alleged misogyny or the violence his films meted out to women (charges that were galvanized by the graphic rape and murder of Brenda Blaney in *FRENZY*), Tania MODLESKI traced the conflict between Hitchcock's sympathetic identification with female characters, on the one hand, and the patriarchal claims of his controlling male voyeurs and the director himself, on the other. Robin WOOD responded in turn soon after the publication of Modleski's *The Women Who Knew Too Much* by noting admiringly that "the question that haunts contemporary Hitchcock criticism" was: "Can Hitchcock be saved for feminism?" The answer since then has been resoundingly affirmative, though not exactly in the terms Wood envisioned. Hitchcock has been saved for feminism not by being vindicated as a feminist, certainly not by the proto-feminist views that have been ascribed to his films, but in the same way other filmmakers and popular genres have been saved for feminism: by formal or historical analyses that have mined his films for archeological evidence of conflicts that are either gender driven (typically, conflicts that are rationalized and resolved in the romantic couple) or gender inflected (the larger cultural conflicts psychoanalytically minded theorists see as both driven by male anxiety and responsible for the formation of all individual identity and cultural institutions). Continuing feminist critique of Hitchcock's films seems guaranteed by three features that set them apart from most others: the unusual prominence of women as both agents and objects in what appear in outline to be stories of masculine desire and masculine action; Hitchcock's continued fascination with women, both as a storyteller and in his position as director; and the unquestioned range of misogynistic behavior in so many of his films—a set of conflicts figured most economically by the ambiguous status of the Hitchcock BLONDE. If an earlier generation of feminist critics asked to what extent the films approved, for example, of the voyeuristic behavior of two male heroes insulated from intimacy by lacking even first names—Devlin in *NOTORIOUS* and Jefferies in *REAR WINDOW*—latter-day feminists seem more likely to return to Bellour's project by pressing questions that have less to do with the representation of particular characters and conflicts and more to do with issues of representation generally.

Fenby, Eric (1906–   ) British composer whose only film score was for *JAMAICA INN*. The television movie *Song of Summer* (1968) is based on his reminiscence of Frederick Delius, whose secretary he was from 1928 to 1934.

Fennelly,   Parker (1891–1988) American actor whose nasal Down East inflections as Titus Moody, the radio character he played for years on *Allen's Alley,* generally typecast him as New England rubes in his 10 films and allowed Hitchcock to cast him against type but not against region as the millionaire passing through *THE TROUBLE WITH HARRY.*

Ferguson, Perry (1901–1963) American art director, at RKO as associate from 1935. Nominated for four Oscars for *Winterset* (1936), *Pride of the Yan-*

kees (1942), *The North Star* (1943), and *Casanova Brown* (1944), he worked with George Stevens (*Gunga Din,* 1939), Orson Welles (*Citizen Kane,* 1941; *The Stranger,* 1946), Howard Hawks (*Bringing Up Baby,* 1938; *Ball of Fire,* 1941; *A Song Is Born,* 1948; *The Big Sky,* 1952), William Wyler (*The Best Years of Our Lives,* 1946), and Hitchcock (ROPE).

Ferren, John Technician who designed the special effects in VERTIGO, his only film credit, and returned 40 years later as sound re-recording mixer on the television film *Dallas: J.R. Returns* (1996).

fetishism Hitchcock brought to his films three qualities that made them unusually fetishistic: a prudish temperament that repressed sexual desire as fearsome, a Catholic upbringing that repressed his sexual imagination still further, and an interest in a cinematic genre, the thriller, for which objects have always had special importance in conveying desires the characters are too inarticulate or self-deluded to speak. These tendencies crystallized in the director's insistence on "PURE CINEMA," the visual expression of the characters' emotions (and the incitement to audiences' own emotions) that became a fetish itself. Hitchcock's exchange with François TRUFFAUT over his repeated use of handcuffs (which Truffaut calls "the most concrete . . . symbol of the loss of freedom," ignoring Hitchcock's reference to their "sexual connotation") in THE LODGER, THE 39 STEPS, SABOTEUR, and THE WRONG MAN illustrates the director's self-conscious use of objects as sexual fetishes; in the same series of interviews, he explicitly identified the love affairs in NOTORIOUS, VERTIGO, and MARNIE as fetishistic. Fetishism—the repression of desires that are projected onto physical objects because their direct expression is taboo, and the resulting overvaluation of the fetishized object—is not only a leading feature of Hitchcock's cinema; it is its defining condition. Everything in Hitchcock is fetishized, from the smallest physical details—not only handcuffs and stockings in *The 39 Steps,* cups and bottles and keys in *Notorious,* knives and scissors in BLACKMAIL and DIAL M FOR MURDER and PSYCHO, and strangling in more than a dozen films, but also the MACGUFFINS that the director dismissed as inconsequential except for their overvalua-

tion by the characters seeking to possess or protect them—to the largest structures, as the man on the run is pursued by the LACANIAN law of the father and the interdiction on sexual desire leads his heroes and heroines to adventures in which every other goal is fair game. Although this fetishism might be identified with the conventions of commercial cinema under the self-censoring arms of the National Board of Review and the Hays Office, it continues outside the frame in Hitchcock's domination of his leading actresses (especially in his proprietary attention to their wardrobe), his motivic but eternally unacted fantasies of illicit sex (the references to having a woman in the back of a taxi, the shower scene in *Psycho* as interdicted rape visualized in socially acceptable terms as brutal murder, the unfilmed episode showing Mark Rutland catching Marnie robbing a safe and raping her), his work habits legendary for their fastidious consistency (the slow wooing of new screenwriters, the black suits for shooting, the insistence on complete control on the set even on a SELZNICK film), and his everlasting appeal to audiences as voyeuristic and repressed, and perhaps as sociopathic in their fantasy lives, as himself.

Fielding, Edward (1875–1945) Tall, patrician American actor who dabbled in Hollywood twice (1917, 1930) before returning in 1939 to a blizzard of character roles as kindly servants, prelates, and justices of the peace in more than 50 films. He appeared in REBECCA as Frith, the butler at Manderley, and in SHADOW OF A DOUBT as the doctor playing bridge with Hitchcock on the train that brought Uncle Charlie to Santa Rosa. He was cast as the real Dr. Edwardes in SPELLBOUND, but his scenes were cut from the finished film.

film noir A term that translates literally as "black film," first applied by the journalist Nino Frank to five American crime films released in 1944 and first shown in Paris in 1946: *Double Indemnity, Laura, Murder My Sweet, Phantom Lady,* and *The Woman in the Window.* Despite the common ground that such contemporaneous films as SHADOW OF A DOUBT, SPELLBOUND, and NOTORIOUS shared with these films—a high-contrast shooting style, an emphasis on amateur rather than professional criminals, a pervasive romantic fatalism—the term has rarely been applied to Hitchcock's films; indeed Frank himself specifically excepted SUSPICION from the group despite its technical similarities with the other films. The Hitchcock films most often cited in surveys of film noir are *Shadow of a Doubt, Notorious, STRANGERS ON A TRAIN, THE WRONG MAN*, and *PSYCHO*; others are evidently disqualified by their happy endings or their low-contrast or color cinematography or their receptiveness to sympathetic women (as opposed to the femmes fatales who thronged noirs). It is surely no coincidence that the Hitchcock films most often cited as noirs are all in black-and-white and are among the least glossy and glamorous of his American films. Lesley BRILL finds in Hitchcock a more domestic romanticism that seems antithetical to noir's nihilism, though presumably leaving room for *Psycho* as a noir parody with Mrs. Bates as the ultimate femme fatale. More recently, James NAREMORE, arguing in an essay in ALLEN and GONZALÈS that all Hitchcock's American work has close links to both the Hollywood directors of film noir and to the older literary tradition inspired by Poe of fiction noir, has attempted to bring the world's foremost creator of suspense films into America's leading crime genre.

Finch, Jon (1941–) Intense British leading man who enjoyed a brief vogue in the early seventies when he took the title role in *Macbeth* (1971), was top-billed as Richard Blaney in FRENZY, and starred as well in two television series, *Counterstrike* (1969) and *Ben Hall* (1975), that enjoyed limited success. Since then he has continued to work, largely in television and continental feature films.

Finler, Joel W(aldo) British film critic and historian, the first film reviewer for *Time Out*. His books include *Stroheim* (1968), a critical edition of one version of Erich von Stroheim's screenplay for *Greed* (1972), and the nonacademic books *All-Time Movie Favorites* (1975), *All-Time Box Office Hits* (1985), *The Movie Directors Story* (1985), *The Hollywood Story: Everything You Ever Wanted to Know About the American Movie Business* (1988), *Hollywood Movie Stills: The Golden Age* (1995), and *Silent Cinema: World Cinema Before the Coming of Sound* (1998). The first half of his study *Hitchcock*

in Hollywood (1992) covers much the same ground as Leonard J. LEFF but lacks the authority conferred by Leff's close study of archival production material; his later chapters survey Hitchcock's films from 1948 through 1976, emphasizing analytical summary and evaluation. His work is most valuable for its emphasis on the film-by-film economics of Hitchcock's productions, which it places in the broader context of Hollywood economics from 1940 on. An appended table of production details summarizes much of this material. It is more profusely illustrated with production stills than any other small-format volume on Hitchcock.

Fischer, Gisela German actress of the sixties whose one English-language role is as Dr. Koska, the physician who helps Michael Armstrong and Sarah Sherman escape from East Germany in TORN CURTAIN.

Fitzgerald, Barry (1888–1961) Nonpareil Dublin-born character actor, born William Joseph Shields, for many years the quintessence of Hollywood Irish. A former civil servant, he became a star with Dublin's Abbey Players, creating the role of Captain Jack Boyle in JUNO AND THE PAYCOCK (1924), and made his film debut as the Orator in Hitchcock's film version of the O'Casey play. He then returned to the stage until 1936, when John Ford brought him to Hollywood to reprise his role of Fluther Good in another O'Casey drama, *The Plough and the Stars*. He remained to play dozens of diminutive, ferociously twinkling scene-stealers in such films as *Bringing Up Baby* (1938), *The Long Voyage Home* (1940), *How Green Was My Valley* (1941), *None But The Lonely Heart* (1944), *And Then There Were None* (1945), *The Naked City* (1948), and *The Quiet Man* (1952). He was nominated for both a Best Actor and Best Supporting Actor Oscar for the same role, as curmudgeonly Father Fitzgibbon in *Going My Way* (1944); though his costar Bing Crosby won the former award, he took home the latter. A subsequent change in Academy nomination rules ensured that his distinction would remain unique. Among Fitzgerald's last roles was Stretch Sears, the felonious department-store Santa who sees the light in the ALFRED HITCHCOCK PRESENTS segment "Santa Claus and the 10th Avenue Kid" (1955).

Fitzgerald, Edward (1901–1966) American cinematographer, in Hollywood briefly 1931–32, who returned in 1948 as camera operator on *The Babe Ruth Story* and one of the four camera operators on *ROPE*. Beginning in 1954, he became lighting cinematographer for a dozen second features, ending with *Lassie's Great Adventure* (1963).

Fitzsimmons, Thomas Technical adviser on *LIFEBOAT*.

Fleming, Rhonda (1923–) Ravishing red-haired Hollywood star, much beloved of cinematographers who tried in vain to photograph her unbecomingly. A show-business daughter, she went directly from Beverly Hills High School to work as an extra; her first notable role was as the mental patient Mary Carmichael in *SPELLBOUND*. Although most of her subsequent films—including *The Redhead and the Cowboy* (1950), *Cry Danger* (1951), *Tennessee's Partner* (1955)—were forgettable, she provided notably tempestuous support to the heroes of *Out of the Past* (1947), *While the City Sleeps* (1957), and *Gunfight at the O.K. Corral* (1957) before retiring in 1980. Her fifth husband, Ted Mann, owner of Grauman's Chinese Theater, enshrined her handprints in cement there.

Flynn, Joe (1925–1974) Excitable, raspy-voiced American actor, a specialist in apoplectic comedy. In movies and television from 1954, he was a regular on *The George Gobel Show* (1958–59), *The Adventures of Ozzie and Harriet* (1960–62), *The Joey Bishop Show* (1961–62), and *The Bob Newhart Show* (1961–62) but is best remembered as Captain Binghamton on the television series *McHale's Navy* (1962–66). His many other television credits include Dr. Sidney Sinden in the *FORD STARTIME* episode "INCIDENT AT A CORNER" and the murderous cuckold Ken Taylor in the *ALFRED HITCHCOCK PRESENTS* episode "Make My Death Bed" (1961).

Flynn, Kelly American child actor whose half-dozen film and television credits include a role in the *ALFRED HITCHCOCK PRESENTS* episode "BANG! YOU'RE DEAD" as Stevie, one of the friends Jackie almost shoots with his Uncle Rick's gun.

Fonda, Henry (1905–1982) Gangly, self-effacing Hollywood star, the personification of all-American sincerity in more than 100 films from 1935 to 1981. Trained in the theater by Marlon Brando's mother Dorothy, he joined Joshua Logan at the Cape Cod University Players in 1928; the group soon included James STEWART, Mildred NATWICK, and Fonda's future (1931–33) first wife Margaret Sullavan. Called to Hollywood to repeat his role as Dan Harrow in *The Farmer Takes a Wife,* he married socialite Frances Brokaw, who bore him two children who were later to become famous in their own right, Jane (1937–) and Peter (1939–). He rose to fame himself in *The Trail of the Lonesome Pine* (1936)—whose Dan Tolliver was claimed by Al Capp as the model for his hillbilly comic-strip hero Lil' Abner—in *You Only Live Once* (1937), and in *Jezebel* (1938) and expanded his range to sophisticated slapstick in *The Lady Eve* (1941). But it was John Ford, at 20TH CENTURY–FOX, who established his persona as the unaffected young American radiating the strength of his humility in *Young Mr. Lincoln* (1939), *Drums Along the Mohawk* (1939), and *The Grapes of Wrath* (1940), for which he received an Oscar nomination. Following naval service in World War II, he returned to the screen (*My Darling Clementine,* 1946; *The Long Night,* 1947; *Fort Apache,* 1948) and stage (*Mister Roberts,* 1948; *The Caine Mutiny Court Martial,* 1954), but broke off his long professional friendship with Ford over the filming of *Mister Roberts* in 1955, immersing himself instead in a new television anthology series, *Henry Fonda Presents the Star and the Story* (1955) and starring in his first international coproduction, *War and Peace* (1956). It was at this point that Hitchcock offered him the role of Manny Balestrero, the hard-luck Everyman of *THE WRONG MAN*, a part perfectly complemented by his next role, the unruffled Everyman juror in *12 Angry Men* (1957) who prevents another innocent suspect from being convicted. Fonda continued to alternate between stage, screen, and television roles for the next 25 years, playing increasingly elder statesmen such as the U.S. president in *Fail-Safe* (1964) and Admiral Chester Nimitz in *Midway* (1976) and playing one role unforgettably against type as the greedy master-criminal in *Once Upon a Time in the West* (1969). In 1978 he received the American Film Institute's Lifetime Achievement Award, and the Oscar that had so long eluded him—despite his nomination as Tom Joad in *The Grapes of Wrath* (1940) and his honorary Oscar (1980)—was finally awarded for his starring role in his final film, *On Golden Pond* (1981).

Fontaine, Joan (1917–) Delicate, ladylike British film actress, at first known mainly as Olivia de Havilland's younger sister, who later outgrew her persona of the blushing rose to become a more worldly and sophisticated star. Born Joan de Beauvoir de Havilland to British parents living in Tokyo, she struggled in minor roles onstage and screen as Joan Burfield while her sister was starring in *A Midsummer Night's Dream* (1935), partnering Errol Flynn in a series of swashbuckling romances, and landing the role of Melanie Hamilton in *Gone with the Wind* (1939). Unable to rise to the challenge of dancing with Fred Astaire in *A Damsel in Distress* (1937), Fontaine was mired in a series of RKO B-pictures when Hitchcock and David O. SELZNICK cast her as the nameless heroine of *REBECCA*. Both here and in her following film, *SUSPICION*, the characters she played—naïve, impressionable brides who put their fate in the hands of controlling men—uncannily paralleled her own situation, not so much because of her 1939 marriage to Brian AHERNE but because of her willingness to accept Hitchcock as her Svengali. Laurence OLIVIER, who starred opposite her in *Rebecca,* never forgave her for taking the role from his wife Vivien Leigh, and she claimed years later that he went through the film whispering obscenities into her ear, a favor she returned to Cary GRANT in *Suspicion.* Whether because of Hitchcock's overbearing direction or her costars' antipathy, she was nominated for an Oscar for *Rebecca* and won the following year for her performance as Lina McLaidlaw Aysgarth in *Suspicion.* Though she was nominated again for *The Constant Nymph* (1943) and remained a star throughout the forties in such films as *Jane Eyre* (1944) and *Frenchman's Creek* (1944), her career gradually declined after *The Emperor Waltz* (1948) and *Letter from an Unknown Woman* (1948). But she could still be seen in some 25 final films, from *Ivanhoe* (1952) to *Beyond a Reasonable Doubt* (1957), before her retirement from Hollywood in 1966, a few years after her role as Alice Pemberton, the title character in the *ALFRED HITCHCOCK PRESENTS* episode "The Paragon" (1963).

Forbstein, Leo F. (1892–1948) Hollywood musician, long at WARNER BROS. Trained as a violinist, he pioneered the synchronization of orchestral conducting with silent films and then signed as head of Warner Bros.' music department and director of the Vitaphone Orchestra in 1926, just in time to take advantage of the studio's excitement when *The Jazz Singer* set the fashion for sync-sound pictures. As head of Warners' music department, he shared the first Academy Award for music for Erich Wolfgang Korngold's score for *Anthony Adverse* (1936) and was nominated as well for Max Steiner's scores for *The Charge of the Light Brigade* (1936) and *The Life of Emile Zola* (1937). In addition to composing his own scores for nearly 50 films, he was billed as conductor or musical director on all Warners sound films from 1929 to his death—a list of more than 400 films, one of the last of which was *ROPE*, for which he provided arrangements and orchestrations of a musical radio program and Francis Poulenc's *Perpetual Motion No. 1.*

Ford, Ross (1923–1988) American actor of the forties and fifties, often a serviceman, whose television credits include his role as Herbert Carpenter's U.S. coworker in the *ALFRED HITCHCOCK PRESENTS* episode "BACK FOR CHRISTMAS."

Ford, Wallace (1898–1966) Baby-faced British-American actor who matured into a welcomely comfortable character actor. Born Samuel Jones Grundy, he was raised in orphanages in London and Canada and in 17 foster homes; ran off to join the Winnipeg Kiddies, a vaudeville troupe; and hopped freight trains to the United States with Wallace Ford, a friend whose name he took after Ford was crushed in a rail accident. A leading Broadway actor during the twenties, he left for Hollywood in 1930 and appeared in more than 100 films, most often in incisive character roles such as Frankie McPhillip in *The Informer* (1935). A favorite of John Ford, he appeared in a dozen other Ford films. His collaboration with

Hitchcock was briefer but almost equally varied: He played a pillar of civic rectitude, detective Jack Graham's partner Fred Saunders, in SHADOW OF A DOUBT and then returned in SPELLBOUND for a bit as the masher who harasses Dr. Constance Peterson in a New York hotel lobby.

Ford Startime   A one-hour anthology series that ran for a single season (1959–60) on NBC-TV. Unlike dramatic anthologies, the program varied widely in content from week to week. Featured segments included "The Turn of the Screw," in which John Frankenheimer directed Ingrid BERGMAN in her Emmy-winning television debut; musical evenings with Donald O'Connor and Ethel Merman; a performance of the Bach Magnificat; and "INCIDENT AT A CORNER" in which Hitchcock directed a cast headed by Vera Miles, George Peppard, and Paul Hartman in a segment that aired on April 5, 1960.

Foreign Correspondent   (Alternative titles: *Mord, Correspondent 17, Cet homme est en espion, Il prigionero di Amsterdam*) Wanger/United Artists, 120 minutes, August 1940. **Producer:** Walter Wanger; **Director:** Alfred Hitchcock; **Screenplay:** Charles Bennett and Joan Harrison, suggested by *Personal History,* an autobiographical reminiscence by Vincent Sheean; **Dialogue:** James Hilton and Robert Benchley, Harold Clurman, Ben Hecht, John Howard Lawson, John Lee Mahin, Richard Maibaum, Budd Schulberg; **Cinematographer:** Rudolph Maté; **Camera operator:** Burnett Gufffey; **Assistant camera operators:** Frank Bucholtz, Tom Dowling, Norman Freed, James King; **Art director:** Alexander Golitzen; **Associate:** Richard Irving; **Constructor:** Oscar Brodin; **Assistant director:** Edmond F. Bernoudy; **Second assistant director:** Marty Moss; **Set director:** Julia Heron; **Costumes:** I. Magnin & Co.; **Hairstylist:** Carmen Dirigo; **Makeup:** Norman Pringle; **Production manager:** James Dent; **Special effects:** Paul Eagler, William Cameron Menzies; **Special effects cutter:** Louis R. Loeffler; **Special effects assistants:** Paul Wtuliska, Lee Zavitz; **Process photographer:** Ray Binger; **European photographer:** Osmond Borrodaile; **Sound:** Frank Maher; **Sound effects:** James T. Moulton; **Sound film cutter:** Walter Reynolds; **Editorial supervisor:** Otho Lovering;

Editor: Dorothy Spencer; **Music:** Alfred Newman; **Cast:** Joel McCrea (Johnny Jones/Huntley Haverstock), Laraine Day (Carol Fisher), Herbert Marshall (Stephen Fisher), George Sanders (Scott ffolliott), Edmund Gwenn (Rowley), Albert Basserman (Van Meer), Robert Benchley (Stebbins), Eduardo Cianelli (Krug), Harry Davenport (Mr. Powers), Martin Kosleck (tramp), Eddie Conrad (Latvian diplomat), Frances Carson (Mrs. Sprague), Charles Wagenheim (assassin), Charles Halton (Bradley), Barbara Pepper (Dorine), Emory Parnell (*Mohican* captain), Roy Gordon (Mr. Brood), Gertrude Hoffman (Mrs. Benson), Marten Lamont (airplane captain), Barry Bernard (steward), Holmes Herbert (Commissioner ffolliott), Leonard Mudie (Inspector McKenna), Samuel Adams (false Van Meer), Dorothy Vaughan (Johnny's mother), Ferris Taylor (Johnny's father), Joan Brodel (Johnny's sister), Jack Rice (Donald), Meeka Aldrich (Donald's wife), Mary Young (Auntie Maude), Harry Depp (Uncle Buren), Betty Bradley (Cousin Mary), Crawford Kent (toastmaster), Wheaton Chambers (Committeeman), E.E. Clive (Mr. Naismith), Jane Novak (Miss Benson), Hilda Plowright (Miss Pimm), Eily Malyon (hotel cashier), Alexander Granach (valet), Ted Mapes (double for Joel McCrea), Jack Alfred, Bunny Beatty, Frank Benson, Billy Bester, Henry Blair, Rebecca Bohannen, Louis Borel, Barbara Boudwin, Louise Brien, Ronald Brown, Horace B. Carpenter, William Castello, George Cathrey, Ken Christy, Gino Corrado, Jack Dawson, Elspeth Dudgeon, Carl Ekburg, Helena Phillips Evans, Herbert Evans, James Finlayson, Robert Fischer, George B. French, Bill Gavier, John George, Douglas Gordon, Richard Hammond, Otto Hoffman, Billy Horn, Colin Kenny, Gwendolyn Logan, Jackie McGee, John Meredith, Hermina Milar, Thomas Mizer, John T. Murray, Joe O'Brien, George Offerman, Lawrence Osman, Thomas Poague, Loulette Sablon, Harry Semels, Raymond Severn, Frederick Sewell, Ernie Stanton, William Stelling, Donald Stuart, Paul Sutton, Jack Voglin, Hans von Morhart, Bert White, William Yetter, Jr.

Hitchcock's 26th film, and his second American picture, began in his loanout from David O. SELZNICK to Walter WANGER in September 1939, while he was still shooting *Rebecca.* Selznick received a quick infusion of cash to cover publicity expenses for *Gone with the Wind* and REBECCA; Wanger could finally look forward to a film version of Vincent SHEEAN's *Personal*

An apparently occupied Hitchcock passes Huntley Haverstock (Joel McCrea) on his way to interview the diplomat Van Meer in *Foreign Correspondent.* *(National Film Society Archive)*

History, which he had purchased on its publication in 1936; and Hitchcock would get the opportunity to make a stirring propaganda feature with all the resources of a Hollywood studio, though at a salary that would enrich Selznick as quickly as himself. Work on the screenplay began in November, but although a total of 14 writers eventually worked on the project, it remained becalmed until his veteran British collaborator Charles BENNETT was signed to work on it in February 1940. Borrowing little but the Dutch location from Sheean's reminiscence, Bennett and Hitchcock fashioned an episodic story whose contours kept changing as the war came closer to England. Foiled in his attempt to borrow Joan FONTAINE and her husband Brian AHERNE from Selznick as the romantic leads—the leading role was also offered to Gary Cooper, who turned down a thriller as beneath him—Hitchcock and Wanger

agreed on Joel MCCREA, Laraine DAY, and an exceptionally large cast that included the dyspeptic Robert BENCHLEY, one of the film's writers, whose absurdly deadpan short films so clearly presaged Hitchcock's later introductions to *ALFRED HITCHCOCK PRESENTS.* The expensive production, which eventually ran to $1.5 million, proceeded slowly because of the large number of elaborate sets and the number of script changes Hitchcock continued to authorize, contrary to his usual practice, after shooting had begun. The film's enthusiastic reception, especially in Britain, was spoiled for the director by its failure to recoup its initial investment and by Michael BALCON's vitriolic attack on the expatriate director as a traitor to his native land, which appeared just two days before the film's premiere on August 27, 1940.

As the large number of writers would suggest, Hitchcock ended up with a film that was neither a faithful adaptation of Sheean's book (something no one but Wanger seems to have wanted) nor, except in its flag-waving closing scene, the propaganda poster Hitchcock evidently visualized at first. Instead the film is a handsomely overscaled anthology of Hitchcock themes and motifs, each one pitched for maximal individual effectiveness with scant regard for logical or emotional continuity from scene to scene: the insouciant reporter hero Johnny Jones's renaming as the dashing foreign correspondent Huntley Haverstock; his arrival at a peace conference in which, finding himself utterly out of his depth, he promptly falls in love with Carol Fisher, the organizer's daughter; the apparent murder of the Dutch diplomat who alone knows the secret clause to the peace treaty (surely the most confusing of all Hitchcock's MACGUFFINS) on a broad public staircase as the rain beats down; the ominously quiet scene in which the hero realizes that the vanes of the windmill to which he has chased the fleeing assassin have just changed direction; the hero's narrow escape back at his hotel from another pair of assassins; still another murder attempt at Westminster Cathedral by the gruff, lower-class killer whom Stephen Fisher, actually a Nazi agent, sets on Haverstock when he recognizes Fisher's visitor as one of the spies he had seen at the mill; the last-minute rescue of the real diplomat, who has been kidnapped by foreign spies anxious to learn the contents of the secret clause; and—the source of Hitchcock's particular pride—the spectacular (for 1940) crash of the airplane carrying Haverstock and the Fishers from London to New York when the Germans shoot it down. These incidents are unified by the persistent analogy between crime and international intrigue first announced by Haverstock's editor in the opening scene (practically the only moment in Hitchcock's work when the analogy is made explicit), the budding love between Haverstock and Carol Fisher, and the persistent confusion between friends and enemies (whose matrix in romantic comedy is made clear when Haverstock pretends without telling her to kidnap Carol to worm information out of her father, only to have her ruin the plan because she thinks he is trying to seduce her). But none of these unifying factors pulls the film completely together; instead, it remains one of Hitchcock's most rambling works, certainly the most picaresque of his Hollywood films, still more

gripping in its individual scenes, several of which (especially the episode running from the shooting in the rain to Haverstock's escape from the windmill) have an authentically oneiric power of their own, than in the arc of its preposterous story.

Forsythe, John (1918–) Blandly handsome American film and television star of the fifties who won a new following for his television work 20 years later. Born John Lincoln Freund, he moved from the University of North Carolina baseball team to the Brooklyn Dodgers' radio broadcast booth before enlisting in the air force and returning to gradually more prominent stage, screen, and television roles. Apart from his turn as the corrupt Judge Henry Fleming in *And Justice for All* (1979), his best-known film roles are the painter Sam Marlowe in THE TROUBLE WITH HARRY and the American diplomat Michael Nordstrom in TOPAZ. But he is far better-known for his hundreds of television appearances, from his starring role as pianist-sleuth Kim Stanger in "Premonition," the second episode of ALFRED HITCHCOCK PRESENTS to be broadcast in 1955, and as the mystery writer Michael Barnes in THE ALFRED HITCHCOCK HOUR segment "I SAW THE WHOLE THING," to the title role in the television series *Bachelor Father* (1957–62), his unbilled voice as the never-seen Charlie in *Charlie's Angels* (1976–81), and his long-running role as Denver oil tycoon Blake Carrington in *Dynasty* (1981–89).

Foster, Barry (1931–) Red-haired British actor, in films from 1956, whose work in *Twisted Nerve* (1968) showed that he could move outside his customary range—first in smartly military roles, then as comic relief—to play Bob Rusk, the Necktie Murderer who frames his best friend for his crimes in FRENZY. He later made a lasting mark as the Dutch detective Pete Van der Valk in the BBC television series *Van der Valk* (1972–77).

Foulstone, Elsie Dialogue coach on two films presenting French culture to the American market: *Moulin Rouge* (1953) and TO CATCH A THIEF.

"Four O'Clock" Premiere episode of the NBC television series SUSPICION, broadcast September 30,

1957. **Associate producer:** Joan Harrison; **Director:** Alfred Hitchcock; **Assistant director:** Hilton Green; **Teleplay:** Francis Cockrell, based on the short story by Cornell Woolrich; **Cinematographer:** John L. Russell; **Art director:** John Lloyd; **Set designer:** James S. Redd; **Costumes:** Vincent Dee; **Editors:** Richard G. Wray and Edward W. Williams; **Music:** Stanley Wilson; **Cast:** E.G. Marshall (Paul Steppe), Nancy Kelly (Fran Steppe), Richard Long (Dave), Tom Pittman (Joe), Dean Stanton (Bill), Charles Seel (customer), Jesslyn Fax (customer's wife), Vernon Rich (doctor), David Armstrong (police officer), Juney Ellis (neighbor), Brian Corcoran (Bobby), Chuck Webster (gasman).

Although Hitchcock served as executive producer for the entire run of the series, the only episode he directed was this taut hour-long exercise in mounting suspense, focusing on Paul Steppe, a watchmaker who, convinced that his wife is seeing another man, plots to kill her with a homemade bomb. After a rehearsal with a smaller explosive goes off without a hitch, he plants the bomb in his own basement, set to explode at 4:00, but is then prevented from leaving by some young toughs who break into the house to rob it and leave him bound and gagged inches from the bomb that they do not notice. As a series of crosscuts reveals Fran's other man to be her rolling-stone brother Dave, Paul struggles to free himself or to attract the attention of either his wife upstairs or one of several fortuitous passersby as he helplessly watches the hands of the clock timer move toward four. A power outage prevents the bomb from going off as scheduled, but the rescue is too late to save Paul, whose self-inflicted ordeal has driven him mad.

Frampton, Harry British makeup artist, in more than 40 films from 1948, including *Kind Hearts and Coronets* (1949), *The Man in the White Suit* (1951), *The Smallest Show on Earth* (1957), *Our Man in Havana* (1960), *Straw Dogs* (1971), and *FRENZY*.

France, C(harles) V(ernon) (1868–1949) Patrician British character actor, long on stage, whose film career, apart from a few earlier experiments, properly began in the early sound era, when he was

in his sixties. His two dozen film roles are accordingly patriarchal and authoritarian, for example, the beleaguered, aristocratic landowner Hillcrist in *THE SKIN GAME*.

Frankau, Ronald (1894–1951) British comedian of stage and radio whose intermittent film career (1931–47) began when he played the auctioneer in *THE SKIN GAME*.

Franz, Paul American sound recordist of the fifties, first of whose four films was *THE MAN WHO KNEW TOO MUCH* (1956).

Freedman, Jonathan (1954–) American literary scholar, associate professor of English at the University of Michigan and author of *Professions of Taste: Henry James, British Aestheticism, and Commodity Culture* (1990) and *The Temple of Culture: Assimilation and Anti-Semitism in Literary Anglo-America* (2000). With Richard E. Millington, he coedited *Hitchcock's America* (Oxford University Press, 1999), a collection of nine essays, six of them new. The editors' introduction argues that Hitchcock's American films, directed by an émigré filmmaker who never entirely assimilated to his adopted country, constitute a sustained exploration of American culture as their primary project. Comparing Hitchcock to Alexis de Tocqueville and T.W. Adorno, they invite readers to consider him as an "anthropological or ethnographic participant observer" who analyzes rather than embraces the culture through which he moves. Freedman's own contribution to the collection focuses this argument more narrowly by examining Hitchcock's reaction to the "therapeutic culture" figured most prominently in Hitchcock's work by pop psychoanalysis and most persistently by the demystifications of the detective-story formula—both of which, Freeman contends, Hitchcock deconstructs as inadequate to cure or even contain the irrational behavior that inspires them.

Freeman, David (1945–) American journalist, screenwriter, script doctor, and author of the 1972 play *Creeps,* whom Hitchcock hired in 1978 to rework Ernest LEHMAN's screenplay for *THE SHORT NIGHT*, which turned out to be the director's last

unfinished project. His memoir of their collaboration, *The Last Days of Alfred Hitchcock,* includes both his revised script for the unproduced film and a trenchant memoir of Hitchcock in his final decline.

Freericks, Bernard (1898–1985) Veteran American sound recordist, in Hollywood for dozens of films from the Spanish-English feature *La gran journada* (1931) to *M★A★S★H* (1970). Acted as recording director on *LIFEBOAT.*

Frend, Charles (1909–1977) Editor of 15 British films (1934–41), including *WALTZES FROM VIENNA, SECRET AGENT, SABOTAGE,* and *YOUNG AND INNOCENT,* whose eye for adventure led him to become an occasional screenwriter and director of more than 20 films and television segments of his own, most notably *Scott of the Antarctic* (1948) and *The Cruel Sea* (1953).

Frenzy   Universal, 114 minutes, May 1972. **Producer:** Alfred Hitchcock; **Associate producer:** William Hill; **Director:** Alfred Hitchcock; **Screenplay:** Anthony Shaffer, based on *Goodbye Piccadilly, Farewell Leicester Square,* a novel by Arthur La Bern; **Cinematographers:** Gil Taylor and Leonard South; **Camera operator:** Paul Wilson; **Assistant director:** Colin M. Brewer; **Production designer:** Syd Cain; **Art director:** Bob Laing; **Set designer:** Simon Wakefield; **Wardrobe supervisor:** Dulcie Midwinter; **Makeup:** Harry Frampton; **Hairstyles:** Pat McDermott; **Sound recordist:** Gordon K. McCallum; **Sound mixer:** Peter Handford; **Sound editor:** Rusty Coppleman; **Casting:** Sally Nicholl; **Continuity:** Angela Martelli; **Production assistant:** Peggy Robertson; **Production manager:** Brian Burgess; **Special photographic effects:** Albert Whitlock; **Editor:** John Jympson; **Music:** Ron Goodwin; **Cast:** Jon Finch (Richard Blaney), Barry Foster (Bob Rusk), Barbara Leigh-Hunt (Brenda Blaney), Anna Massey (Barbara Milligan), Alec McCowen (Chief Inspector Tim Oxford), Vivien Merchant (Mrs. Oxford), Billie Whitelaw (Hetty Porter), Clive Swift (Johnny Porter), Bernard Cribbins (Felix Forsythe), Elsie Randolph (Gladys), Michael Bates (Sgt. Spearman), Jean Marsh (Monica Barling), Madge Ryan (Mrs. Davison), George Tovey (Mr. Salt), John Boxer (Sir George), Jimmy Gardner (porter at Coburg Hotel), Gerald Sim, Noel Johnson (men at bar), Geraldine Cowper (spectator at open-

ing rally), Juney Ellis (barmaid), Bunny May (barman), Rita Webb (Mrs. Rusk), Jeremy Young (detective), Robert Keegan (hospital patient), Drewe Henley.

Following the financial debacle of TOPAZ, Hitchcock chose to exercise a clause in his UNIVERSAL PICTURES contract that gave him the right to make a film on whatever subject he liked as long as it cost less than $2 million. Purchasing the rights to Arthur LA BERN's novel, he used it to return to the subject of *Kaleidoscope* (also known as *Frenzy*), the abortive project he had shelved in 1966. The subject, which in turn would recycle the basis of his first success, THE LODGER, would be a psychopathic killer of women; the cast would feature theatrical players who would be cheaper than the movie stars whom Hitchcock generally worked with; and the film would mark the first time Hitchcock would take advantage of the passing of the Production Code and the first time in more than 20 years that he would work in England. The production of what turned out to be Hitchcock's 52nd feature mingled triumph with disappointment. After the long and fruitless gestation of the earlier project, which had shocked and horrified executives at Universal, Hitchcock's collaboration with screenwriter Anthony SHAFFER proceeded with little trouble. The director returned to Pinewood Studios as a celebrity, but found that the Covent Garden fruit market where he had hoped to set much of his story had essentially vanished, requiring its rather anachronistic recreation in the film. In the middle of shooting, Alma REVILLE suffered an incapacitating stroke which sent her back to California. Hitchcock, finally able to film a rape and murder with no external constraints, turned the event into the most repulsive scene of his career. Another disappointment remained after the film was shot when Hitchcock pronounced Henry Mancini's score too reminiscent of Bernard HERRMANN and replaced him with Ron GOODWIN. Upon its release, however, the film, brought in for $2 million, was widely reviewed as a return to form for the master of suspense and became his biggest financial success in years—the most successful economically of all his Universal films.

Despite the festive music played over its opening credits and the majestic accompanying vista down the Thames, *Frenzy* is, unlike practically all Hitch-

Fired from his job as a barman, though not yet on the run from the police, Richard Blaney (Jon Finch) unburdens himself to his old friend, Covent Garden fruitseller Bob Rusk (Barry Foster), in *Frenzy*.   *(National Film Society Archive)*

cock's preceding films, exceptionally consistent in sustaining a single tone. That tone is a grimly humorous despair over the characters' moral failings and a corresponding disgust with the physical conditions of their existence, indeed of all human existence. Richard Blaney, the volatile ex-RAF squadron leader turned barman, offers only the most obvious example of an explosive anger he can barely contain as he bounces from the pub from which he has just been dismissed to his pal Bob Rusk's fruit market to the marital bureau his ex-wife runs. Stung by her business success and her habit of surrounding herself with women, from her vinegary secretary to the staff at her club, he focuses his smoldering resentment of his failures on her counterexample, making himself the obvious suspect when she becomes the latest vic-

tim of London's Necktie Murderer. Unlike all Hitchcock's other men on the run, Blaney is clearly capable of murder, of *this* murder in particular, and it is almost incidental that the killer is actually his friend Rusk, whose rage over his sexual impotence so completely reflects his own rage over his social impotence. Instead of representing the innocent suspect's sinister double or opposite, then, the killer this time is his twin, an all-too-normal example of masculine anger at the social emasculation both attribute to women. The uncomfortable intimacy between the villain and the nominal hero is underlined by Hitchcock's portrayal of Chief Inspector Oxford, practically the only sympathetic police officer in Hitchcock's work, whose domestic life, an unbroken series of comically hideous Cordon Bleu meals prepared by his courteously unobliging wife, suggests why even the mildest man could associate his own appetites with a physical revulsion that could be both the correlative and the cause of the Necktie Murderer's behavior. Beginning with the pun in the opening scene, in which the politician's pompous speech about the river's recent freedom from pollutants, industrial effluents, and other "foreign—" is interrupted by the discovery of the latest victim, the film treats the human body as a foreign body, sating its loathesome appetites on revolting food and repellent sexual acts that treat other bodies as so much food to be consumed or thrown away, as Rusk does in the bravura sequence in which he has to crawl into the sack of potatoes in which he has hidden the corpse of his latest victim to retrieve his telltale stickpin from between her fingers, which he breaks with a snapping sound echoed later by Mrs. Oxford's ruminative snapping of a breadstick. In a world in which Covent Garden is conflated with both the garden of Eden and the garden of England, it seems, men are destined to consume and women to be consumed, and the only possible conclusion is the alimentary processes of digestion and excretion. Along with its persistent imagery of repellent eating, drinking, and sexual possession, the film recycles more Hitchcockian motifs than any other Hitchcock film, as bits from *PSYCHO, STRANGERS ON A TRAIN, NOTORIOUS,* and *DIAL M FOR MURDER* surface and subside in the film's brilliantly unpleasant stew. The result is in many respects the ultimate Hitchcock film—the film *The Lodger* might have been if not for the constraints of censorship—but also, for many commentators, an unwitting testimonial to the tonic, formative power of censorship in focusing the fetishes that had carried and transformed the burden of shocked revulsion that surfaced here with horrifying directness. If *Frenzy* is Hitchcock with the gloves off, it has made thousands of viewers thankful for gloves.

Fresnay, Pierre (1897–1975) Dapper French stage actor who found time to appear in more than 50 films. Onstage from the age of 15, he made his film debut in 1915, the same year he first appeared with the Comedie Française, and emerged as a film star for his leading role of Marius in Marcel Pagnol's trilogy (*Marius,* 1931; *Fanny,* 1932; *César,* 1936). His most indelible performances are as Captain de Boieldieu, the doomed aristocrat of *La grande illusion* (1937), and as Dr. Remy Germain, the target of the vicious poison-pen letters in *Le corbeau* (1943). His sole English-language credit is *THE MAN WHO KNEW TOO MUCH* (1934), in which he plays Louis Bernard, whose assassination sets the plot in motion.

Friedhofer, Hugo W. (1902–1981) American composer who came to Hollywood in 1929 as an arranger for Fox, moved over to WARNER BROS. in 1934 as an orchestrator, and eventually composed scores for more than 100 films, including the virtually music-free *LIFEBOAT* and *The Best Years of Our Lives* (1946), for which he won an Academy Award, and arranged the music for more than 50 more, before retiring in 1972.

Fulton, John P. (1902–1965) American special-effects cinematographer who designed the effects for many key UNIVERSAL monster films (*Frankenstein,* 1931; *The Mummy,* 1932; *The Invisible Man,* 1933; *The Black Cat,* 1934)—and incidentally worked uncredited on *SABOTEUR*—then, after several years at Goldwyn, was at PARAMOUNT for *REAR WINDOW, TO CATCH A THIEF,* and *VERTIGO,* among dozens of others.

Furse, Roger (K.) (1903–1972) British stage designer whose long association with Laurence OLIVIER and the Old Vic led him to design the costumes for *Henry V* (1944) and the Oscar-winning sets for *Hamlet* (1948). Except for *Odd Man Out* (1947), his early films are period pieces: *UNDER CAPRICORN* (for which he designed the costumes but not the sets), *Ivanhoe* (1952), *Knights of the Round Table* (1953), *Helen of Troy* (1956), and Olivier's *Richard III.* Eventually, however, he went on to design the variously exotic contemporary sets for *The Prince and the Showgirl* (1957), *Bonjour Tristesse* (1958), *The Roman Spring of Mrs. Stone* (1961), and *The Road to Hong Kong* (1962).

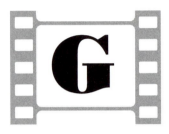

Gabel, Martin (1912–1986) Balding, slope-shouldered American character actor with wide stage experience. He trained at the American Academy of Dramatic Arts, made his Broadway debut in 1933, worked with Orson Welles's Mercury Theater, wrote the novel *I Got a Country* (1944), married actress Arlene Francis (1946), directed several theatrical productions and one film, *The Lost Moment* (1947), and produced a second film, *Smash-Up, The Story of a Woman* (1947) before debuting onscreen in 1951 in the first of 20 roles. His piercing glare and clipped delivery made him equally adept in comic or menacing roles, from Marnie Edgar's smitten victim Sidney Strutt in MARNIE to the psychiatrist Dr. Eggelhofer in Billy Wilder's 1974 remake of *The Front Page*.

Gainsborough Pictures British production company that began when PARAMOUNT PICTURES sold its newly established Islington studio to Michael BALCON and his associates in 1924. Among the infant studio's first releases were THE PASSIONATE ADVENTURE (1924) and THE BLACKGUARD (1925), on both of which Hitchcock served as assistant director, art director, and screenwriter. Gainsborough produced the first five films Hitchcock directed—THE PLEASURE GARDEN, THE MOUNTAIN EAGLE, THE LODGER, DOWNHILL, and EASY VIRTUE—before its merger with GAUMONT-BRITISH in 1928 made Balcon one of the two most powerful producers in Britain. Though

Hitchcock had left Balcon in the meantime to work for his equally influential rival John MAXWELL at BRITISH INTERNATIONAL, he returned to him to make THE MAN WHO KNEW TOO MUCH (1934), and his last British film, JAMAICA INN, once again carried the Gainsborough logo, which was associated by this time largely with costume drama.

Gallaudet, John (1903–1983) American character actor who filled out the casts of more than 100 second features and television segments from 1934, with occasional small roles in such notable films as *Holiday Inn* (1942), *Blue Skies* (1946), *Lonelyhearts* (1959), and *In Cold Blood* (1967), his final film. In television from 1954, he appeared as the doctor in "REVENGE," the premiere episode of ALFRED HITCHCOCK PRESENTS, and later became a fixture as a judge in *Perry Mason* (1959–66).

Galsworthy, John (1867–1933) British novelist and playwright best remembered for his social satires of the upper classes in crisis and decline. Trained as an attorney and admitted to the bar in 1890, he spent little time in practice, instead traveling and writing under the name John Sinjohn. In 1904 he began the series of novels under his own name that were to make his reputation with *The Island Pharisees*. *The Man of Property*, which followed in 1906, established his best-known characters, the

Forsyte family, to whom he returned in *In Chancery* (1920) and *To Let* (1921), as well as a second trilogy, *A Modern Comedy* (1924–28). In the meantime, he wrote and produced a series of problem plays including *The Silver Box* (1906), *Strife* (1909), *The Pigeon* (1912), *The Mob* (1914), and THE SKIN GAME (1920). Although his direct involvement in cinema was limited to acting in two films, *School Days* (1921) and *Island Wives* (1922), more than a dozen films were based on his work, most memorably *That Forsyte Woman* (1947). *The Skin Game* had already been filmed once in Holland (1920) 10 years before Hitchcock filmed it for BRITISH INTERNATIONAL. Galsworthy was awarded the Nobel Prize for Literature shortly before his death.

games Hitchcock's films abound in games, most of them played for high stakes. Boxing and tennis matches provide structuring metaphors in THE RING and STRANGERS ON A TRAIN, allowing the heroes to demonstrate their competitive prowess within a rule-bound arena designed to protect them from their darker impulses. The framing rugby games that symbolize the sheltered world from which Roddy Berwick is expelled represent one pole of DOWNHILL's dynamic. More often, however, Hitchcock uses games, as he uses dreams, to muddle the distinction between unlicensed fantasy and reality. The game of blindman's bluff in YOUNG AND INNOCENT echoes the narrative context in which Erica Burgoyne is trying to keep her inquisitive aunt from finding out that her companion, Robert Tisdall, is a fugitive from the police. When the same game is played in THE BIRDS, it is interrupted by a bird attack. Jill Lawrence's skeet-shooting in THE MAN WHO KNEW TOO MUCH (1934) is a rehearsal for the climactic moment when she kills the assassin threatening her daughter's life. Even the lighthearted interlude in the baggage car in THE LADY VANISHES that brings together the hero and heroine as a romantic couple turns menacing when they are interrupted by the sinister magician, Signor Doppo. More often, Hitchcock's characters engage in games with unwitting accomplices or antagonists, such as the newspaper house that allows Uncle Charlie to conceal the article about the Merry Widow Murderer in SHADOW OF A DOUBT, the theatrical evening Bran-

don Shaw stages for his guests in ROPE, the games Philip Vandamm insists Roger Thornhill is playing on their first meeting in NORTH BY NORTHWEST, or the endless romantic chases in which Francie Stevens entangles John Robie in TO CATCH A THIEF.

By far the most common game Hitchcock's characters play is masquerading. These disguises usually have a specifically playful quality. Richard Hannay's rapid series of impersonations in THE 39 STEPS, though designed to help him elude the police, swiftly assume a comic dimension, as does Eve Gill's masquerade as Doris Tinsdale in STAGE FRIGHT and Roger Thornhill's increasingly accomplished series of performances in *North by Northwest*. But as several key examples of Hitchcockian disguise suggest— John Ballantine's masquerade as Dr. Anthony Edwardes in SPELLBOUND, Judy Barton's masquerade as Madeleine Elster in VERTIGO, Norman BATES's assumption of his mother's identity in PSYCHO, the incessant disguises that allow Marnie Edgar to stay one step ahead of the police and the victims of her thefts in MARNIE—trying on a new role can undermine the fragile identity of the performer. Indeed, many Hitchcock films—MURDER!, NUMBER SEVEN-TEEN, SECRET AGENT, SUSPICION, *Rope, Stage Fright, To Catch a Thief,* THE TROUBLE WITH HARRY, *Family Plot*—can be seen as organized entirely around the quibble between the frivolous and serious aspects of role-playing as characters wonder how seriously to take each other, find themselves trapped in their own games or rituals, parody serious criminal plots in a comic key, or otherwise efface the line between games and social reality to the vanishing point.

Finally, Hitchcock's films themselves can be seen as a series of games between director and audience framed by such provocative remarks as the director's repeated comparisons of *Psycho* to a fun house or moviegoing to riding a roller coaster. Like the games the characters play within the films, these games are designed to license audiences' fantasies in a protected environment that, like the games within the films, frequently turns out to be less than completely protected, inviting audiences, for instance, to overinvest in the fate of Stevie in SABOTAGE or to invest uncritically in Scottie in *Vertigo*. Such examples provide a salutary reminder that for Hitchcock, games are serious business.

Garde, Colin Makeup artist who worked on *STAGE FRIGHT* and five later features through 1969.

Gardiner, Reginald (1903–1980) Peerlessly pompous British character actor, usually in comic roles. A graduate of the Royal Academy of Dramatic Art, he appeared in many London revues and stage plays before debuting on Broadway in 1935 and in Hollywood the following year. His scores of film characters, especially his signature role of Beverly Carlton in *The Man Who Came to Dinner* (1942), wrought changes on the amusingly stuffy Englishman, a role he was still playing as Major Cooke-Finch in the *ALFRED HITCHCOCK PRESENTS* episode "BANQUO'S CHAIR."

Gardner, Ed (1901–1963) American actor, one-time husband (1929–42) of actress Shirley Booth, who rode the role of Archie, the Brooklyn-accented manager of Duffy's Tavern, to radio stardom. Among his rare onscreen appearances are two ruffianly roles on *ALFRED HITCHCOCK PRESENTS*: the horseplayer Sheridan who inveigles Father Amion into backing the ponies in "THE HORSEPLAYER" (1961) and the bargain-hunting murderer Marvin J. Foley in "The Last Remains" (1962).

Gardner, Jimmy (1924–) Perky British character actor whose two dozen screen roles from 1964 include a memorable turn as Bertie, the obliging porter at the Coburg Hotel in *FRENZY*.

Garmes, Lee (1898–1978) Renowned American cinematographer who went directly from high school to Hollywood in 1916, became a lighting cinematographer in 1924, and went on to shoot more than 100 films. His pioneering use of "Rembrandt lighting" to highlight key aspects in the frame while keeping ambient light levels low, influenced a generation of American films, and he was nominated for Academy Awards for his work on *Morocco* (1930), *Since You Went Away* (1944), and *The Big Fisherman* (1959), winning an Oscar for his utterly characteristic lighting of *Shanghai Express* (1932). An occasional director (*Angels Over Broadway*, 1940) and producer (*Specter of the Rose*, 1946), he was most honored as a black-and-white stylist in melodramas like *THE PARA-DINE CASE*, in which his style is almost palpably velvety. Yet he could handle color capably as well, as he showed in shooting the first third of *Gone with the Wind*, for which he received no screen credit.

Garretson, Oliver S. (1900–1967) American sound recordist whose 50 films for WARNER BROS. (1929–55) included *I CONFESS* (1952) and *DIAL M FOR MURDER* (1953).

Garvin, Gene American sound recordist, long at PARAMOUNT. After handling some 50 projects from *My Favorite Blonde* (1942) to *THE MAN WHO KNEW TOO MUCH* (1956), he ended his career as a rerecording mixer in several television series from 1966 to 1981.

Gassman, Remi Sound consultant who, together with Oskar SALA and Bernard HERRMANN, designed the almost entirely musicless soundtrack for *THE BIRDS*.

Gaumont-British Pictures Key British production company of the thirties, formed by the merger of the distributing company Gaumont with Ideal Films and W & F Film Service in the wake of the Cinematograph Films Act of 1927 and enlarged by the incorporation of GAINSBOROUGH PICTURES the following year. Unlike the rival British major, BRITISH INTERNATIONAL, which specialized in "quota quickies" designed as cannon fodder for theaters compelled to guarantee that between 5 and 20 percent of their screenings were British-made films, Gaumont-British, under the creative supervision of Michael BALCON, consistently took more chances with properties and production values and not surprisingly suffered a serious financial crisis in 1936, in the middle of producing the last of five Hitchcock thrillers: *THE MAN WHO KNEW TOO MUCH* (1934), *THE 39 STEPS*, *SECRET AGENT*, *SABOTAGE*, and *YOUNG AND INNOCENT*.

Gausman, R(ussell) A. (1892–1963) Veteran set designer, at Universal from 1931, whose 30-year career encompassed hundreds of films. His early work included the sets for *SABOTEUR* and *SHADOW OF A DOUBT*; his most enduring legacy is his increasingly baroque overdecoration of Douglas Sirk's domestic melodramas *Magnificent Obsession* (1954), *All That Heaven Allows* (1955), *Written on the Wind* (1956), *The Tarnished Angels* (1957), and *Imitation of Life* (1959).

Gavin, John (1928–) Smoothly handsome American leading man, born Jack Golenor, whose diplomatic career, promoted by his service in Naval Intelligence, was derailed by a UNIVERSAL screen test which seemed to mark him as the next Rock Hudson. Groomed as a beefcake gentleman in Universal properties from *Imitation of Life* (1959) and *Spartacus* (1960) to *Romanoff and Juliet* (1961) and *Thoroughly Modern Millie* (1967), he was cast as Marion Crane's lover Sam Loomis in *PSYCHO* largely because his contract with the studio made him affordable and later appeared as the put-upon newlywed Dr. Don Reed in *THE ALFRED HITCHCOCK HOUR* segment "Run for Doom" (1963) and as the trigger-happy cop Johnny Kendall in "Off Season," the program's final episode (1965). Upon his retirement from Hollywood, he resumed his diplomatic career when President Ronald Reagan appointed him ambassador to Mexico. His final role before his appointment, in the television movie *Sophia Loren: Her Own Story* (1980), was as Cary GRANT.

gaze The act of watching is never neutral in Hitchcock from the very beginning of his first film, *THE PLEASURE GARDEN*, to the final shot of his last, *FAMILY PLOT*. Most of his silent films feature variously prominent scenes of men exerting power over women by the ways in which they watch them; when the poles of power are reversed in *DOWNHILL,* the women's gaze is not nearly so prominent. Indeed, Roddy's wife Julia most often displays her power over him by ignoring him, just as the equally important women's gazes in later films like *SUSPICION, SHADOW OF A DOUBT*, and *SPELLBOUND* are consistently undermined by the opacity of the men they are watching. Even the very act of watching a woman, however, can make men who otherwise seem innocuous, for example, the unnamed man constantly watching the heroine of *CHAMPAGNE*, seem sinister. Hitchcock's early films explore many modes of gazing, from the naïvely appraising gaze Samuel Sweetland directs at his matri-

monial prospects in *THE FARMER'S WIFE* to the oppressive gazes under which Alice White wilts in *BLACKMAIL*. But his first film to make the male gaze explicit as the basis for the film's system is *NOTORIOUS*, in which the male gaze (first Devlin's, then Sebastian's) reveals both the visual metaphor at the heart of the activity aptly called spying and the sexual inadequacies of both the noncommittal hero, whose inability to speak his love condemns him to watch his lover from a distance, and the villain, whose betrayal by the bride he so loves leads him to turn on her in cold hatred. *REAR WINDOW* combines these two motifs, spying and male sexual anxiety, with a third, the voyeuristic nature of cinema itself, in the person of L.B. Jefferies, the press photographer who, confined to his apartment by a broken leg, begins to watch his neighbors idly to pass the time; finds himself unwittingly more interested in the neighbors who do not know he exists than in Lisa, the glamorous girlfriend who offers to do the dance of the seven veils in an attempt to keep his eyes from straying outside his apartment; and ends up the victim first of his own voyeurism (his interest in Lisa crests exactly when she becomes the object of his gaze as an intruder in the murderer's apartment and he is powerless to help her) and then of the chilling spectacle of the returned gaze (when the murderer looks back at him, directly into the camera, in one of the most alarming shots in all cinema). The gaze as a link between male anxiety and film spectatorship is equally crucial in *VERTIGO*, in which the male gaze virtually creates the female objects at whom it is directed (as Scottie, making over Judy Barton to resemble Madeleine Elster more closely, finally realizes that Gavin Elster had done exactly the same thing months before) and *PSYCHO*, whose tight closeup of Norman BATES's voyeuristic eye watching Marion undress minutes before he kills her makes starker than any other moment in Hitchcock the masculine insecurity (amounting in this case to Norman's clinical psychosis) that links spying, possessing, and killing, and the female insecurity (here figured as Marion Crane's paranoid neurosis) that encourages women to see themselves as objects to be seen.

Following Jacques LACAN and Raymond BELLOUR, Laura MULVEY has argued that the system of gazes in Hitchcock is central to the whole project of narrative cinema, which is structured by narcissism (the pleasure audiences take in watching figures like themselves) and scopophilia (the fetishistic male drive toward pleasurable voyeurism, which draws male viewers to watch female figures even though their anxiety identifies these figures, which lack the phallus, as sites of castration). The result, Mulvey contends, is that Hitchcock's films are quintessential exemplars of the dominant narrative cinema, whose apparatus is gendered as male in that cinema is designed specifically to facilitate the pleasure of heterosexual male audiences. Although more recent scholars have hotly debated the gender politics of Hollywood cinema, no one has seriously disputed the central role Mulvey's analysis accords the act of watching within Hitchcock's films as a figure for the act of watching films in general.

Gélin, Daniel (1921–) Versatile French leading man whose star persona is a sensitive cosmopolitan type. The veteran of more than 100 films from 1941 in his native country, he has rarely ventured into English-language cinema except to play the assassinated agent Louis Bernard in *THE MAN WHO KNEW TOO MUCH* (1956). He is also the director of *Les Dents longues* (1952), a respected poet, and the father of actress Maria Schneider.

Geraghty, Carmelita (1901–1966) Saucy American actress of the twenties and thirties, in Hollywood from 1923, who costarred in *THE PLEASURE GARDEN* with her friend Virginia VALLI as the initially naïve Jill Cheyne, an ambitious counterpart to Valli's long-suffering Patsy Brand, who abandons her fiancé for a suspiciously wealthy prince.

Geray, Steven (1904–1973) Stage-trained Hungarian-American character actor. Born Istváan Gyergyay, he made his Hungarian film debut in 1932 and was in London two years later. He is best remembered for more than 100 strongly accented Hollywood roles beginning in 1941, ranging from stern (Beethoven in *Heavenly Music,* 1943) to kindly (Uncle Pio in *Gilda,* 1946). He appeared as Dr. Graff in the opening scenes of *SPELLBOUND* and returned unbilled as the hotel desk clerk in *TO CATCH A THIEF.*

Germain, Larry (d. 1981) Hollywood hairstylist, veteran of more than 100 films from *THE PARADINE CASE,* his first, to *TOPAZ,* one of his last.

Giblin, Gary British author of *James Bond's Britain* (2000) and the forthcoming *Hitchcock's London.*

Gielgud, (Sir) John (1904–2000) Formidably articulate British stage actor, with Laurence OLIVIER the leading Shakespearean of his time. He first appeared at the Old Vic at 17 and debuted as Hamlet, his signature role, at 26. Taken like many another theatergoer with his impeccable diction, Hitchcock persuaded him to star as Richard Ashenden in *SECRET AGENT,* which opened at the same time as his first

John Gielgud

Broadway production of *Hamlet,* by telling him that the role was "another Hamlet part." But the film, whose critical reception was mixed, did nothing to allay his reservations about screen acting, and during the next 30 years of a busy stage career he appeared in only a handful of film roles, many of them Shakespearean (*Hamlet,* 1948; *Julius Caesar,* 1953; *Romeo and Juliet,* 1954; *Richard III,* 1955; *Chimes at Midnight,* 1966). But an Academy Award nomination for his role as Louis VII of France in *Becket* (1964) kindled a new interest in the screen, and at a time when most actors think of retiring, he went on to play more than 100 roles in movies and television, ranging from Lord Raglan in *The Charge of the Light Brigade* (1968) to the ruminative novelist Clive Langham in *Providence* (1977), perhaps his favorite screen role, to Hobson, the butler in *Arthur* (1981), for which his drolly frigid hauteur won him an Oscar, to the enchanter Prospero in *Prospero's Books* (1991), a valedictory role the 87-year-old actor essayed when he had only 20 films ahead of him. In between his work for stage and screen, he also found time to write a memoir, *Early Stages* (1939), and two collections of essays, *Stage Directions* (1963) and *Distinguished Company* (1972).

Gilbert, (J.) Charles British art director whose brief career (1942–1950) included uncredited contributions to Hitchcock's two Ministry of Information films, *BON VOYAGE* and *AVENTURE MALGACHE.*

Gill, Maud (1896–1985) British character actress, long onstage, who went to Elstree to reprise her long-running stage success as Thirza Tapper in *THE FARMER'S WIFE* and returned during the following decade for another nine films.

Gillespie, (A.) Arnold (1899–1978) Special-effects cinematographer at MGM for 40 years—first as art director (1924–1936), then as head of special effects—and many more than 100 films. He designed the earthquake in *San Francisco* (1936), the tornado in *The Wizard of Oz* (1939), and dozens of other photogenic disasters, received 10 Academy Award nominations, and won Oscars for his work on *Thirty Seconds Over Tokyo* (1944), *Green Dolphin Street* (1947), *Plymouth Adventure* (1952), and *Ben-Hur*

(1959), the last within months of his one Hitchcock assignment, *NORTH BY NORTHWEST.*

Gilliat, Sidney (1908–1994) British screenwriter, frequent producer and director of his work, usually in collaboration with Frank LAUNDER. His first scenario was produced in 1929, and the screenplay he cowrote with Launder for *THE LADY VANISHES* was acclaimed a model of comic suspense. He survived the poor reception of *JAMAICA INN,* on which Launder did not work, to rejoin him for *Night Train to Munich* (1940), *Kipps* (1941), and *Young Mr. Pitt* (1942), and directed his first film, *Millions Like Us,* in 1943. In 1945 he and Launder formed Individual Pictures, a partnership that allowed them to share writing, directing, and producing credit on films ranging from *The Rake's Progress* (1945) to *Green for Danger* (1946). Their most enduring legacy is their distinctively light touch with suspense films and their farces about the boarding school St. Trinian's.

Gist, Robert (1924–1998) Stage-trained American actor first lured into films by location shooting on *Miracle on 34th Street* (1947) during his Broadway run of *Harvey.* He played some 20 roles, including the companionable police detective Leslie Hennessy in *STRANGERS ON A TRAIN,* and then went behind the camera to direct episodes of *Peter Gunn, The Naked City, The Twilight Zone, Star Trek, Mission: Impossible, Hawaii Five-O,* and others. Formerly married (1953–58) to actress Agnes Moorehead.

Givney, Kathryn (1896–1978) American character actress most frequently seen during the fifties in imperious or eccentric roles. She appeared in some two dozen films from *Follow Thru* (1930) to *Once You Kiss a Stranger,* the 1969 remake of *STRANGERS ON A TRAIN* in which she played the homicidal heroine's inconvenient aunt. Among her television roles are two for *ALFRED HITCHCOCK PRESENTS:* Mrs. Princey, who helps her husband frame their neighbor for the murder of their daughter's straying suitor in "WET SATURDAY," and Mrs. Colton, the inopportune dinner guest in "Servant Problem" (1961).

Glaser (or Glazer), Vaughan (1872–1958) White-haired American character actor whose

Hollywood specialties (1939–44) were such irreproachable moralists as Pat Martin's Uncle Philip in SABOTEUR and genteel authority figures like Dr. Phillips in SHADOW OF A DOUBT.

Glass, Ned (1906–1984) Balding, craggy American character actor whose wisecracking delivery is familiar from more than 100 film and television roles, such as the ticketseller who tries but fails to turn Cary GRANT in to the police in NORTH BY NORTHWEST.

Goddard, Alf(red) (1897–1981) British character actor, former boxer and stuntman, in films from 1926, mostly in Cockney roles. He plays the sailor who rescues Roddy Berwick at his lowest point in DOWNHILL.

Goetzke, Bernhard (1883–1964) German-born actor who, after making his name as Death in *Der müde Tod* (1921) and Dr. Mabuse's nemesis Chief Inspector von Wenck in *Dr. Mabuse, der Spieler* (1922), ventured occasionally outside his homeland to Finland, the USSR, and Britain, where he appeared as Adrian Levinski in *The Blackguard* and as Pettigrew, the old man whose enmity toward Beatrice is the engine driving THE MOUNTAIN EAGLE.

Golitzen, Alexander (1907–) Russian-born art director, in Hollywood from 1935 for FOREIGN CORRESPONDENT and hundreds of other films, mostly at UNIVERSAL. He was nominated 13 times for Academy Awards and won three Oscars, for *The Phantom of the Opera* (1943), *Spartacus* (1960), and *To Kill a Mockingbird* (1962).

Gonzalès, S(am) Ishii American film scholar, doctoral candidate in the Cinema Studies program at New York University, adjunct instructor in the Film and Television division of the Tisch School of the Arts, and coeditor, with Richard Allen, of *Alfred Hitchcock: Centenary Essays* (British Film Institute, 1999) and the forthcoming *Hitchcock Past and Present: Essays from the Hitchcock Centennial Conference*—the first a collection of new essays solicited and collected on the occasion of the Hitchcock Centennial Confer-

ence, the second an anthology of papers from the conference. Essays in the first volume are divided about evenly into neoauteurist studies of Hitchcock's authorship and aesthetics and contextual studies concerning "Sexuality/Romance" and Hitchcock's relation to World War II, cold-war politics, film noir, feminist theory, and cultural history.

Goodman, John (B.) American art director in Hollywood from 1934 to 1967, who worked on SHADOW OF A DOUBT and then shed his middle initial for THE TROUBLE WITH HARRY more than 100 films later.

Goodwin, Bill (1910–1958) Genial, broad-shouldered American character actor of the forties and fifties. A former radio announcer, he invested routine roles such as that of the hotel detective whom Dr. Constance Peterson hoodwinks in SPELLBOUND with a refreshingly engaging gravitas. He reprised his best-known role, Al Jolson's friend Tom Baron in *The Jolson Story* (1946), in the sequel *Jolson Sings Again* (1949).

Goodwin, Ron (1925–) British composer, arranger, and conductor, whose dozens of film and television scores since 1958 have included *Whirlpool* (1958), *I'm All Right Jack* (1959), *The Trials of Oscar Wilde* (1960), and FRENZY, as well as several films featuring Agatha Christie's Miss Marple and Hercule Poirot.

Gordon, Gavin (1901–1983) American character actor in Hollywood from 1929 who appeared briefly as Lord Byron in *The Bride of Frankenstein* (1935) and for scarcely longer in dozens of other film and television roles, from his uncredited Dr. Sedbusk in SUSPICION and Ernest Weylin in NOTORIOUS to his three roles in ALFRED HITCHCOCK PRESENTS: George Brooks in "Our Cook's a Treasure" (1955), a card player in "Crack of Dawn" (1956), and Ernest West in "The Perfect Crime" (1955).

Gorvin, Gloria Actress whose two screen roles were Hippolyta in *A Midsummer Night's Dream* (1966) and a bit in TORN CURTAIN the same year.

Gott, Barbara (1872–1944) Stage-trained Scottish character actress, in occasional films from 1919, who plays Madame Michet, the Parisian "Patronne" who hires Roddy Berwick as a music-hall gigolo in DOWNHILL.

Gottlieb, Sidney American film scholar, professor of English at Sacred Heart University. Long active on the editorial board of HITCHCOCK ANNUAL, to which he has frequently contributed, he is the editor of *Hitchcock on Hitchcock: Selected Writings and Interviews* (University of California Press, 1995). Several of the 46 essays, interviews, dialogues, and stories reprinted—dating from the one-page story "Gas" (1919) to "Surviving," a valedictory 1977 interview with John Russell TAYLOR—are familiar, but most of them appear in book form for the first time; all of them are vastly entertaining; and many of them are revealing, often in ways the director may not have intended. Except in a 1939 lecture at Columbia University and the 1965 "Film Production," originally written for the Encyclopedia Britannica, Hitchcock appears consistently as a playful raconteur. Substantial reminiscences like "My Screen Memories" (1936) and "Life Among the Stars" (1937) and interviews with David Brady of *The New York Times Magazine* (1950) and an anonymous reviewer from *Cinema* (1963) consist largely of strings of anecdotes. Even when Hitchcock is more technical, as in "Some Aspects of Direction" (1938), "My Most Exciting Picture [ROPE]" (1948), and "Hitchcock Talks About Lights, Camera, Action" (1967), he is always eager to illustrate general points with anecdotes. The collection's leading theme might be described as the mechanics of suspense; an important subtheme is the constraints on commercial filmmakers, which the director regularly and rather sadly deplores. Perhaps the most interesting single item is a 1963 dialogue between Hitchcock and Dr. Fredric Wertham in which the comics-baiting psychiatrist repeatedly tries to get Hitchcock to admit that violence in movies is inherently corrupting and the director eludes his doctrinaire accusations with a series of deft counterpunches, noting, for example, that a killer on Death Row had murdered his third victim after seeing PSYCHO and that Hitchcock had asked the names of the movies he had seen before killing the first two. Gottlieb's most recent editorial projects include the forthcoming *Hitchcock Today: Selected Essays from the Hitchcock Annual* (written with Christopher Brookhouse) and *Alfred Hitchcock: Interviews.*

Gould-Porter, A(rthur) E. (1905–1987). Oh-so-British character actor whose 30-year Hollywood career began in 1942. He played bits in some 40 movies and television programs, appearing in ALFRED HITCHCOCK PRESENTS as Major Sinclair in "Back for Christmas," Clifton in "I Killed the Count," Rogers in "The Three Dreams of Mr. Findlater" (1957), the short-lived Herbert Whybrow in "The Hands of Mr. Ottermole" (1957), the hotel man in "The Glass Eye" (1957), the inconvenient husband Arthur Chaundry in "The Crocodile Case" (1957), Tom the bartender in "Relative Value" (1959), and Major Parslow in "The Ikon of Elijah" (1960), and in a bit in TORN CURTAIN, but is best remembered as the Clampett family's butler Ravenswood in *The Beverly Hillbillies* (1962–65).

Grace, Charity American television actress of the fifties who, though she appeared in three roles for ALFRED HITCHCOCK PRESENTS—Mrs. Babford in "The Dusty Drawer" (1959), Gertrude Anderson in "Party Line" (1960), and Amelia Gastell in "Summer Shade" (1960)—and two for THE ALFRED HITCHCOCK HOUR—Sister Jem in "Final Vow" (1962) and Mrs. Weatherby in "Dear Uncle George" (1963)—was directed by Hitchcock himself only once, when she played Elsa Medwick in the FORD STARTIME episode "INCIDENT AT A CORNER."

Grace, Henry (W.) Set decorator at MGM from 1934 for many more than 100 films to 1969, including NORTH BY NORTHWEST.

Graham, Morland (1891–1949) Broad-beamed, versatile Scottish character actor who played some 30 film roles from every class and walk of life, including Merlyn henchman Sea Lawyer Sydney in JAMAICA INN, between 1934 and his death.

Graham, Tim American supporting actor of the fifties, most often in Westerns, who doffed his spurs and Stetson for bits in the ALFRED HITCHCOCK PRESENTS segments "The Long Shot" (1995) and "THE CASE OF MR. PELHAM."

Graham, Winston (1910–) Middlebrow British novelist and occasional screenwriter (*Take My Life,* 1947; *Night Without Stars,* 1951) who wrote the novels MARNIE (1961) and *The Renegade* (1951), *Venture Once More* (1954), and *The Last Gamble* (1955), which served as the basis for the television miniseries *Poldark* (1975) and *Poldark II* (1977).

Grams, Martin, Jr. American author of books on the popular media, including *Suspense: Twenty Years of Thrills and Chills* (1997), *The CBS Radio Mystery Theater: An Episode Guide and Handbook, 1974–1982* (with Gordon Payton, 1999), *Radio Drama: A Comprehensive Chronicle of American Network Programs, 1932–1962* (2000), and, with Patrik WIKSTROM, *The Alfred Hitchcock Presents Companion* (Morris, 2001). This oversized, heavily illustrated reference guide to Hitchcock's television work, authorized by UNIVERSAL PICTURES and introduced by Patricia HITCHCOCK, includes a history of the series; essays by various hands on the program's science fiction elements, the lawsuit concerning imitations and spoofs of the program, and the Hitchcock-directed episodes; a list of the anthologies produced under Hitchcock's byline; a survey of *Alfred Hitchcock Presents* collectables; and information about Hitchcock's other work for television. The core of the volume, however, is a guide to each of the 268 episodes of *Alfred Hitchcock Presents* and *The Alfred Hitchcock Hour,* including the full text (and often alternate texts) of Hitchcock's introductions and conclusions, a cast list, a summary, and remarks from writers, actors, or other participants in the episode.

Granger, Farley (1925–) Soulfully handsome American star, born Farley Earle II, who was signed as a Goldwyn contract player while still in high school, appeared in the propaganda features *The North Star* (1943) and *The Purple Heart* (1944) and then went off to World War II. On his return, he was cast in three key roles: Philip Morgan, the halfhearted murderer in ROPE; Guy Haines, the politically minded tennis player in STRANGERS ON A TRAIN; and, in between, the boyishly sympathetic bank robber Bowie in *They Live by Night* (1949). (Ironically, he won the role in *Rope* because of Montgomery CLIFT'S reluctance to appear in so transparently homosexual a role; screenwriter Arthur LAURENTS has written in his memoir of his own fling with Granger shortly after he met him.) His later Hollywood roles, however, were disappointing, and in 1953 he went to Italy to star as Livia Serpieri's faithless lover Lt. Frank Mahler in *Senso.* Most of his subsequent work has been in Continental films or American television.

Grant, Cary (1904–1986) Irresistibly debonair Anglo-American leading man, the most appealing light comedian of his time. Born Archibald Alexander Leach, he ran away from a poverty-stricken home at 13, ended up in New York, and became in time an acrobat, a lifeguard, and a song-and-dance man before returning to England to appear in stage musicals. Following American stage exposure, he was signed to a contract at PARAMOUNT, where Mae West asked him, in *She Done Him Wrong* (1932), to come up and see her sometime. But it was three other studios that honed his screen persona, carefully burnished with a heterosexual glow that eventually included five marriages, into the perfect romantic comedy lead: Columbia (*The Awful Truth,* 1937; *Holiday,* 1938; *His Girl Friday,* 1940); MGM (*Topper,* 1937, and *The Philadelphia Story,* 1940); and RKO (*Bringing Up Baby,* 1938; *My Favorite Wife,* 1940). By the time Hitchcock, thwarted in his wish to cast him in MR. AND MRS. SMITH, offered him the role of Johnnie Aysgarth in SUSPICION, the screen image fostered by these comedies and the heroic adventure films *Gunga Din* (1939) and *Only Angels Have Wings* (1939) forbade him from killing his wife, as his character had done in the novel under adaptation, and the film suffered a massive case of rewrite jitters. Miraculously, it was a critical and box-office success, and it provided a basis for even more accomplished collaborations between the two intensely private Englishmen who had taken such concern to give their public personas a high gloss. In NOTORIOUS, the two personas seemed

Cary Grant

directors, used his suave urbanity to defang male fears of romantic commitment in order to explore them more searchingly.

Gray, Eve (1904–) British actress who plays the Avenger's blonde showgirl victim in THE LODGER.

Great Day, The Famous Players–Lasky, 1920. **Director:** Hugh Ford; **Screenplay:** Eve Unsell, based on the play by Louis Napoleon Parker and George Robert Sims; **Cinematographer:** Hal Young; **Cast:** Arthur Bourchier (Sir John Borstwick), Mary Palfrey (Lady Borstwick), Marjorie Hume (Clara Borstwick), Bertram Burleigh (Frank Beresford), Adeline Hayden Coffin (Mrs. Beresford), Percy Standing (Paul Nikola), Meggie Albanesi (Lillian Leeson), Geoffrey Kerr (Dave Leeson), Lewis Dayton (Lord Medway), Mrs. L. Thomas (his mother), L.C. Carelli (Semki).

Second of the 12 silent films, 1920–22, for which Hitchcock designed intertitles.

Green, Douglas (Edward) (1921–2000) American assistant director of TOPAZ and a dozen other films in the sixties and early seventies; later a television producer.

Green, Hilton A. (1929–) American film executive first credited as assistant director on *The Desperate Hours* (1955). For years a mainstay of ALFRED HITCHCOCK PRESENTS, he served as assistant director of PSYCHO and unit production manager of MARNIE. UNIVERSAL appointed him vice president of production in 1968 and executive production manager in 1978. Beginning in 1982, he produced a string of films including *Psycho II* (1982), *Sixteen Candles* (1983), *Psycho III* (1985), and *Encino Man* (1992). He was a special visual consultant on the Gus Van Sant remake of *Psycho* (1998).

Greenwood, Edwin British director of silents and early sound films who turned to screenwriting in 1928 and amassed another dozen credits in collaboration, including LORD CAMBER'S LADIES, YOUNG AND INNOCENT, and JAMAICA INN.

to merge, with Grant giving one of his most opaque performances as the fantasy lover T.R. Devlin who prostitutes the woman he loves because he is afraid to admit his love for her. TO CATCH A THIEF treated the same subject comically, with Grant's cat burglar John Robie running amusedly from the marriage-minded Francie Stevens, played by Grace KELLY as the world's most alluring pursuer, and NORTH BY NORTHWEST showed Grant's hero, advertising executive Roger Thornhill, still unable to sever the apron strings and forge a partnership with a woman he does not recreate in the mold of his mother. For this reason, Donald SPOTO's well-known remark that Hitchcock cast Grant in roles that represent himself as he would have liked to be should be supplemented by the observation that Hitchcock, practically alone among Grant's

Greet, Clare (1871–1939)   Stage-trained British character actress, onscreen from 1922, who created the role of Mrs. Bunting in the 1915 production *Who Is He?,* a West End melodrama based on THE LODGER. Signed to play the lead in Hitchcock's abortive first directorial effort NUMBER 13, she returned to annoy the leads of some 20 films as nosey neighbors and meddlesome busybodies, sometimes as Claire Greet. She played the fortuneteller in THE RING, the heroine's mother in THE MANXMAN, one of the 12 jurors in MURDER!, Peach in LORD CAMBER'S LADIES, an intimate of the Tabernacle of the Sun in THE MAN WHO KNEW TOO MUCH (1934), Mrs. Jones in SABOTAGE, and Pengallan's tenant Granny Tremany in JAMAICA INN.

Gregory, Dora (1872–1954)   British character actress who appeared in a handful of film roles, the first of which was Mrs. Jackman, the Hillcrists' tenant in THE SKIN GAME.

Gregory, James (1911–)   American character actor with experience on both Wall Street and Broadway. Following his film debut in *The Naked City* (1948), he went on to play more than 100 roles in film and television, where his heavy, emphatic style made him a natural tough cop or villain. Though his signature role was Inspector Frank Luger on the television series *Barney Miller* (1975–82), his most accomplished performance is as Senator John Iselin, the hero's moronic, witch-hunting stepfather in *The Manchurian Candidate* (1962). He appeared three times in ALFRED HITCHCOCK PRESENTS—as theatrical producer Wayne Campbell in "The Cream of the Jest" (1957), as hectoring defense attorney John Gregory in "THE PERFECT CRIME" (1957), and as Westcott, the reporter who turns out to be an insurance detective in "Post-Mortem" (1958)—and returned to play Fred Kruger, one of the ill-advised safecrackers in THE ALFRED HITCHCOCK HOUR segment "The Dividing Wall" (1963).

Grenfell, Joyce (1910–1979)   Forcefully angular British comedienne, a former journalist and critic, whom Clive James dubbed "St. Catherine of Siena in a sports car." Born Joyce Phipps, she made her stage debut in 1939 and her film debut two years later and traveled the Eastern Hemisphere entertaining British troops at war before settling into a crowded postwar schedule of plays, revues, and films. She made a striking impression in STAGE FRIGHT as the shooting-gallery concessionaire who commanded passersby to shoot at some lovely ducks. In 1954, the same year she created her most memorable screen role of Policewoman (later Sergeant) Ruby Gates in *The Belles of St. Trinian's,* she first performed a one-woman revue of her own sketches and songs, *Joyce Grenfell Requests the Pleasure,* accompanied by Richard ADDINSELL at the piano—a show she subsequently took around the world. From 1957 to her death, she served as vice-president of England's Society of Women Writers and Journalists.

Grey, Anne (1907–)   British leading actress, née Aileen Ewing, who brightened some 40 films of the thirties. After playing the likes of Nora Brant, the apparently mute heroine of NUMBER SEVENTEEN, she finished the decade in Hollywood playing great ladies and retired from the screen, only to return 40 years later in the television movie *No Room to Run* (1978).

Griffies, Ethel (1878–1975)   Craggy British character actress whose stage career, beginning in 1881, was one of the longest on record, and who found time for more than 80 films as well. Long in Hollywood, she played the Governess in *Alice in Wonderland* (1933) and Grace Poole in *Jane Eyre* (1934), returning 10 years later to reprise the latter role without screen credit. By the time she played the ornithologist Mrs. Bundy in THE BIRDS and Lulu in THE ALFRED HITCHCOCK HOUR segment "Bed of Roses" (1964), she was the oldest actress working in the British theater.

Griswold, Claire   American actress, mostly on television, married in 1958 to director Sydney Pollack. Shortly after making her debut that same year, she caught Hitchcock's eye as one more potential replacement for Grace KELLY, but she appeared in only two roles on THE ALFRED HITCHCOCK HOUR: Joanne Dowling in "I SAW THE WHOLE THING" and Natalie Rivers in "A Home Away from Home"

(1962). Following her single feature film appearance in *Experiment in Terror* (1962), she retired to pursue a career as an architect.

Grove, Sybil (b. 1891) Stage-trained British actress, born Syvil Westmacott, who appeared in some three dozen film roles, including Madame Fouchet in *WALTZES FROM VIENNA*, in the 10 years following 1928.

Groves, Sgt. George New York police officer who served as technical adviser on police procedure in *THE WRONG MAN*.

Guffey, Burnett (1905–1983) American cinematographer who soon after coming to Hollywood in 1923 became second-unit cinematographer on John Ford's *The Iron Horse* (1924) and then worked as assistant cameraman until 1928, when he became camera operator on such films as *The Informer* (1935) and *FOREIGN CORRESPONDENT*. Becoming a lighting cinematographer in the midforties, he shot some 80 films from *My Name Is Julia Ross* (1945) to *The Great White Hope* (1970). He won Oscars for his black-and-white photography of *From Here to Eternity* (1953) and his color work on *Bonnie and Clyde* (1967), and was nominated as well for *The Harder They Fall* (1956), *Birdman of Alcatraz* (1962), and *King Rat* (1965).

guilt Perhaps the single factor that first validated Hitchcock, in contrast to dozens of other directors of Hollywood thrillers, to the attention of the *CAHIERS DU CINÉMA* critics was his emphasis on moral guilt, an emphasis shared in his genre only by Fritz LANG. Hitchcock typically treats guilt differently from Lang, however, in that with such rare exceptions as Norman BATES, whose whole psychosis is based on his guilt over killing his mother, his villains rarely experience guilt; instead, as Eric ROHMER and Claude CHABROL noted, the guilt is transferred to the heroes. The immediate practical consequence of this transfer is to double the innocent hero with the criminal who would otherwise be his opposite (for example when Guy Haines, in *STRANGERS ON A TRAIN*, sees a police car at his door

and reflexively hides behind the iron fence that is already concealing Bruno Anthony, who has just murdered Guy's wife). The more general philosophical implication, however, and the one that interests Rohmer and Chabrol more, is that in the unforgiving moral logic of Hitchcock's Jansenist universe, moral agency is a mere accident; everyone is equally guilty, Guy for having wanted his wife's death as well as Bruno for having wished it. Hence Guy's guilt, like that of Father Michael Logan in *I CONFESS*, is not simply neurotic; it is an acknowledgment of his inevitable implication in the world's evil figured by his wife's death, as it is again by Uncle Charlie's victims in *SHADOW OF A DOUBT* or in the death of David Kentley at the hands of two sophistic fellow-students who tell their old teacher in *ROPE* that they are just acting on his Nietzschean moral theories. It is in this severe sense that Manny Balestrero, mistaken for a robber in *THE WRONG MAN*, is guilty—not of the robberies, not even of the breakdown for which his wife at one point blames him, but of "distrust in divine benevolence" until his silent prayer is followed by the apprehension of his criminal double. Rohmer and Chabrol could not know that Hitchcock's very next film, *VERTIGO*, would be his most penetrating study of the corrosive effects of guilt on a well-meaning hero driven to madness by his crippling fear of heights, his failure to save the woman he loved by following her to the top of the tower from which she apparently threw herself, and his domination of the woman who played this role in the name of an idealized woman whose death he can no more accept than her fictional status that made it possible for him to fall in love with her in the first place.

Gwenn, Edmund (1875–1959) Elfin Welsh-born actor equally adept in starring and character roles. Turned out of his father's home at 17 for expressing a desire to act, he made his London debut in 1895 and soon caught the eye of George Bernard Shaw, who sought him for *Man and Superman* (1902) and five subsequent plays. He served with distinction in World War I, rising to the rank of captain, and then returned to the stage. After four preliminary films between 1916 and 1927 (including the 1920 transcript of his stage performance as the parvenu Hornblower in *The Skin Game*), he concentrated more extensively on a film career, appearing in more than 80 roles, mostly in Hollywood from late thirties. He is perhaps best remembered as Mr. Bennet in *Pride and Prejudice* (1940); as Kris Kringle, the Santa Claus claimant of *Miracle on 34th Street* (1947), for which he won an Academy Award; and as Skipper Miller, the well-meaning forger of *Mr. 880* (1950), for which he was again nominated for an Oscar. But he was also a particular favorite of Hitchcock, who cast him in five roles, beginning with a reprisal of his Hornblower in THE SKIN GAME and continuing with Johan Strauss the Elder in WALTZES FROM VIENNA, the pint-sized Cockney assassin Rowley in FOREIGN CORRESPONDENT, Captain Albert Wiles in THE TROUBLE WITH HARRY, and the layabout hero's long-suffering father Joe Saunders in the ALFRED HITCHCOCK PRESENTS episode "Father and Son" (1957).

Haas, Dolly (1910–1994) German leading lady of the thirties who traveled to the U.K. to make two 1936 films, *Spy of Napoleon* and *Broken Blossoms,* in which she played the role created by Lillian Gish in 1919. From 1943 until her death she was married to caricaturist Al Hirschfeld. Hitchcock brought her back to the screen for her third (and last) non-German role as the murderer's wife in *I CONFESS.*

Hagedon, Charles K. (1914–1968) American Technicolor consultant and art director who worked on nearly 60 MGM films, including *NORTH BY NORTHWEST,* from 1955 to 1963.

Haggard, Stephen (1911–1943) British actor, a nephew of romancer H. Rider Haggard who debuted in 1936 as Mozart in *Whom the Gods Love* but—after three later film roles (1939–42), including Willie Penhill, the youngest member of Joss Merlyn's gang, in *JAMAICA INN*—died even younger than Mozart when he was killed in action in the Middle East.

Haigh, Kenneth (1930–) British stage actor who created the role of Jimmy Porter in *Look Back in Anger* and played some two dozen film and television roles from 1954 to 1992, most memorably as Brutus in *Cleopatra* (1963), as Napoleon in *Eagle in a Cage* (1971), and as Joe Lampton in the television series *Man at the Top* (1971–73). He appeared in two 1959 episodes of *ALFRED HITCHCOCK PRESENTS*: "BANQUO'S CHAIR," in which he played the murderer, John Bedford, and "The Specialty of the House," in which he played the hero's friend Costain.

Hale, Jonathan (1891–1966) Canadian character actor, born Jonathan Hatley, who left the diplomatic service to act. Arriving in Hollywood in 1934, he soon found his niche playing such exasperated father figures as the defense counsel in *Fury* (1936) and Dagwood's boss Mr. Dithers in 16 *Blondie* second features and was cast to type as the father Bruno Anthony wants to kill in *STRANGERS ON A TRAIN.* He appeared in more than 200 films and television programs through 1957.

Hale, Robert (1874–1940) British actor of the thirties whose second film role was as the heroine's father, the café owner Ebeseder, in *WALTZES FROM VIENNA.*

Hall Davis, Lilian (or **Lillian)** (1897–1933) British actress, in films from 1918, who appeared in more than two dozen films. Hitchcock, who had first worked with her when he served as assistant director on *THE PASSIONATE ADVENTURE,* cast her as the romantic leads Mabel in *THE RING* and Araminta Dench in *THE FARMER'S WIFE.*

Hallis, A. British composer whose sole film credit is for the score of *NUMBER SEVENTEEN.*

Halton, Charles (1876–1959) Stage-trained American character actor, a veteran of more than 150 films, most memorably as officious small-town bureaucrats such as Carter, the bank examiner in *It's a Wonderful Life* (1946). He appeared as Bradley in FOREIGN CORRESPONDENT, as Harry Deaver, the mild little man who sets the plot of MR. AND MRS. SMITH in motion, and as the sheriff who arrests Barry Kane in SABOTEUR.

Hamer, Gerald (1886–1972) British actor, in Hollywood from 1936 for some 20 film and television roles, two of the last of them for ALFRED HITCHCOCK PRESENTS: Mr. Hewitt in "BACK FOR CHRISTMAS" and the murder witness in "The Hands of Mr. Offermole" (1957).

Hamer, Robert (1911–1963) British filmmaker who began as editor of a half-dozen films (1938–42) including JAMAICA INN and then developed into a stylish director whose most notable credits include the "Haunted Mirror" sequence from *Dead of Night* (1945) and the black comedy *Kind Hearts and Coronets* (1949).

Hamilton, Bernie (1929–) Heavy-set American character actor best known as Captain Dobey in the television series *Starsky and Hutch* (1975–79). Among his 30 other film and television roles are Dawson, the Colonel's butler in the ALFRED HITCHCOCK PRESENTS segment "MRS. BIXBY AND THE COLONEL'S COAT," and a convict in THE ALFRED HITCHCOCK HOUR episode "Final Escape" (1964).

Hamilton, John (Frank) (1893–1967) American actor who moved to England as a child and began his stage appearances shortly thereafter. Soon after working with him in his second film, THE PASSIONATE ADVENTURE (1924), Hitchcock cast him as Edward Pettigrew in THE MOUNTAIN EAGLE. Returning to the United States in 1929, he appeared in occasional second features through 1950.

Hamilton, Patrick (1904–1962) British playwright and novelist whose play *Gas Light,* also known as *Angel Street* (1939), has been filmed twice as *Gaslight* (1939, 1944); whose novel *Hangover Square* (1941) was also filmed twice (1945, 1998); and whose one-set tour de force, *Rope*—also called *Rope's End* (1929)—became the basis for Hitchcock's even more audacious tour de force, ROPE.

Hamilton, William (1894–1942) American editor and occasional director (*Seven Keys to Baldpate,* 1935, and three other films). In Hollywood from 1923, he worked for RKO from its founding to his death, supervising the cutting of *Morning Glory* (1933), *Stage Door* (1937), *The Hunchback of Notre Dame* (1939), and most of the Astaire-Rogers musicals. Among the last of his 60 films were MR. AND MRS. SMITH and SUSPICION.

Hammond, A.C. British editor who cut ELSTREE CALLING under the supervision of Emile DE RUELLE and later edited four films of his own, including NUMBER SEVENTEEN, whose soundtrack he edited as well.

Hampton, Lawrence A. American visual consultant whose only film credit is for his service as part of the special effects team on THE BIRDS.

Handford, Peter British sound technician whose first screen credit was his work on UNDER CAPRICORN and who returned after 20 years and a dozen films from *Night and the City* (1950) to *Tom Jones* (1963) and *The Go-Between* (1971) to serve as sound mixer on FRENZY. He won an Oscar for his work on *Out of Africa* (1985) and was nominated again for *Gorillas in the Mist* (1988).

Hardwicke, Sir Cedric (1893–1964) Urbane, mellifluous British character star. Trained at the Royal Academy of Dramatic Art, he made his stage debut in 1912, returning from war service to ever greater prominence. Soon after being knighted in 1934, he moved to Hollywood, where he played more than 60 roles. Most often cast by his plummy voice as an avuncular sage, he was equally at home as the English kings Charles II (*Nell Gwyn,* 1934) and Edward IV (*Richard III,* 1956) and as the Nazi Col. Lanser in *The Moon Is Down* (1943). He appeared in two Hitchcock films, as the heroine's crusty father General McLaidlaw in *SUSPICION* and the victim's unwitting father in *ROPE*, and in two episodes of *ALFRED HITCHCOCK PRESENTS*, as the conniving Mr. Princey in "WET SATURDAY" and the secretive John Anderson in "A Man Greatly Beloved" (1957).

Hare, (Francis) Lumsden (1875–1964) Irish character actor, in Hollywood from 1916 for more than 100 roles as nobles, colonials, and functionaries such as Tabbs in *REBECCA* and Inspector Hodgson in *SUSPICION*.

Harker, Gordon (1885–1967) Choleric Cockney comedian who made his screen debut as One-Round Jack's trainer in *THE RING* and played Samuel Sweetland's bumptious handyman Churdles Ash in *THE FARMER'S WIFE*, the heroine's millionaire father in *CHAMPAGNE*, and a frustrated watcher of a primitive television set in *ELSTREE CALLING* before going on to appear in some 60 later British films before his retirement in 1961.

Harp, Kenneth American actor who made a handful of film and television appearances beginning in the fifties, for example as two bailiffs in the *ALFRED HITCHCOCK PRESENTS* episode "The Test" (1962) and *THE ALFRED HITCHCOCK HOUR* segment "I SAW THE WHOLE THING."

Harper, Rand American character actor of the fifties best remembered as Harry, the bridegroom in *REAR WINDOW*.

Harris, Barbara (1935–) Pioneering American improvisational actress who rose to fame with Chicago's Second City improv company and went on to become a gamine, versatile star of stage and screen. Soon after her screen debut in *A Thousand Clowns* (1965), she won a Tony for her Broadway performance in *The Apple Tree* (1967) and was nominated for an Oscar for her role as Alison Densmore in *Who Is Harry Kellerman and Why Is He Saying Those Terrible Things About Me?* (1971). Eager to cast her as the ditzy bogus medium Blanche Tyler in *FAMILY PLOT* despite her limited marquee value, Hitchcock

agreed to accept seventies star Karen BLACK as well, and Harris gave one of her most charmingly offbeat performances.

Harris, Robert A. (1945–) American co-author, with Michael S. LASKY, of *The Films of Alfred Hitchcock* (Citadel, 1976), a profusely illustrated period-by-period survey obviously influenced by François TRUFFAUT's book-length interview, which it greatly resembles in format and to which it makes an excellent complement. Following the prevailing fashion, Harris and Lasky give relatively short shrift to the British films before *THE MAN WHO KNEW TOO MUCH* (1934) but then proceed film by film through *FAMILY PLOT*, including (a rarity at the time) a chapter discussing the director's television films for *ALFRED HITCHCOCK PRESENTS* and *THE ALFRED HITCHCOCK HOUR*. The text, which includes an overview of Hitchcock's life and work, frequent excerpts from contemporary reviews, and a list of Hitchcock's cameo appearances, most often recounts plots, describes memorable speeches and tableaus, and notes the immediate impact and lasting influence of the films rather than venturing very far into interpretation. The tone throughout is that of a pair of relaxed fans talking to other fans who share their appreciation of Hitchcock's work. Many of the photographs, both stills and offscreen shots, are not easily available elsewhere. *The Complete Films of Alfred Hitchcock,* revised and updated edition (Carol, 1999), adds a new foreword by Patricia HITCHCOCK and a videography of Hitchcock's work available on VHS and DVD.

In more recent years, Harris has worked more directly in Hollywood as producer of *The Grifters* (1990). But he has become even better known for his work on the reconstruction and restoration of such film classics as *Lawrence of Arabia* (1962/1989), *Spartacus* (1960/1991), *My Fair Lady* (1964/1994), *VERTIGO* (1958/1996), and *REAR WINDOW* (1953/1998).

Harris, (Major) Sam (1877–1969) Australian-born military veteran who served as technical adviser on military drills and tactics in *The Charge of the Light Brigade* (1936) and appeared in mostly uncredited bits in nearly 100 films and television programs from *Dr. Jekyll and Mr. Hyde* (1931) to a half-dozen John Ford films and a sprinkling of Hitchcock's: *MR. AND MRS. SMITH, DIAL M FOR MURDER*—where he is the man who delays Tony Wendice from using the telephone—and the *ALFRED HITCHCOCK PRESENTS* segment "THE CASE OF MR. PELHAM."

Harris, Theresa (1909–1985)   African-American actress usually typecast as a maid in some 50 films from 1930 to 1958 and in such television programs as the *ALFRED HITCHCOCK PRESENTS* episode "BACK FOR CHRISTMAS," in which she plays Herbert Carpenter's U.S. maid.

Harrison, Joan (1911–1994)   British-born Hollywood producer and screenwriter, educated at the Sorbonne and Oxford University, who began in 1933 as Hitchcock's secretary, then a reader of material submitted to him for film consideration, and finally, on his departure for America in 1939, his personal assistant and unofficial member of his household. Collecting credits as a screenwriter on *JAMAICA INN, REBECCA, FOREIGN CORRESPONDENT, SUSPICION*, and *SABOTEUR*, she was signed in 1941 as a screenwriter by MGM and in 1943 as a producer by UNIVERSAL, where she specialized in Hitchcockian thrillers like *Phantom Lady* (1944), *The Strange Case of Uncle Harry* (1945), *Nocturne* (1946), *They Won't Believe Me* (1947), and *Ride the Pink Horse* (1947). She returned to Hitchcock in 1955 as associate producer (later producer) of *ALFRED HITCHCOCK PRESENTS*, where her roles as de facto story consultant and script supervisor made her more than any other single figure the guiding intelligence behind the series until she left the program in 1962. She was married for many years to the spy novelist Eric Ambler.

Hartley, Mariette (1940–)   Vivacious, demure American actress, born Mary Loretta Hartley, who, soon after her debut in *Ride the High Country* (1962), was cast as Susan Clabon, Rutland and Company's gossipy secretary in *MARNIE*. Since then, however, she has enjoyed her greatest success on television, where she has been a regular cast member in *Peyton Place* (1965–66), *The Hero* (1966–67), *WIOU* (1990–91), and *To Have and to Hold* (1998–), as well as making dozens of guest appearances on other programs.

Hartman, Paul (1904–1973)   Weathered American character actor, in Hollywood from 1941 but more familiar from television, where he starred in three episodes of *ALFRED HITCHCOCK PRESENTS*—as the inoffensive bank robber Milton Potter in "Not the Running Type" (1960), the obsessively faithful valet John Ingo in "Gratitude" (1961), and the safecracker Sammy Morrisey in "Burglar Proof" (1962)—and two episodes of *THE ALFRED HITCHCOCK HOUR*—as Trenker in "Death of a Cop" (1963) and Mr. Adams in "The Magic Shop" (1964). He was also featured as James Medwick, the crossing guard accused of molesting schoolchildren, in the *FORD STARTIME* segment "INCIDENT AT A CORNER."

Harvey, Barry (G.)   American actor who appeared in eight episodes of *ALFRED HITCHCOCK PRESENTS*: as Herbert Whybrow's nephew in "The Hands of Mr. Ottermole" (1957), a steward in "DIP IN THE POOL" and again in "The Canary Sedan" (1958) and "The Hero" (1960), Constable Longden in "Relative Value" (1959), Hodges in "The Avon Emeralds" (1959), Constable Barry in "ARTHUR" (1959), and Tom in "The Landlady" (1961).

Harvey, Forrester (1884–1945)   Veteran Irish character actor, onscreen from 1922 in more than 100 films. He appeared as boxing promoter James Ware in *THE RING* and as Chalcroft in *REBECCA*.

Harvey, Laurence (1928–1973)   Coldly handsome British leading man, born Laruschka Mische Skikne in Lithuania, brought up in Johannesburg, and trained at the Royal Academy of Dramatic Art. Onscreen from 1951, he was groomed by Romulus Films head James Woolf for a stardom he finally reached, appropriately enough, as Joe Lampton in *Room at the Top* (1959). That same year he starred as the smilingly lethal title character in the *ALFRED HITCHCOCK PRESENTS* segment "ARTHUR." Throughout the early sixties, he appeared in such notable productions as *The Alamo* (1960), *Butterfield 8* (1960), *Summer and Smoke* (1961), and *Of Human Bondage* (1964). He is perhaps best remembered as the hapless hero Raymond Shaw in *The Manchurian Candidate* (1962).

Harvey, Paul (1882–1955) American character actor who appeared in nearly 200 films from *The Awful Truth* (1929) to *High Society* (1956), usually as a harried executive, functionary, or father. He played the psychiatrist Dr. Hanish in SPELLBOUND.

Hasse, O(tto) E(duard) (1903–1978) Ponderously impressive German character actor who left the law to work with Max Reinhardt and made the first of his 60 film appearances in 1930. After the war, he occasionally ventured outside the German industry, where he enjoyed a distinguished reputation, to take such roles as Otto Keller, the murderous caretaker in *I CONFESS*.

Haste, Jack British technician who served as one of the four camera operators in UNDER CAPRICORN.

Haworth, Edward S. (1917–1993) American art director, often billed as Ted Haworth, whose 40-year career began at WARNER BROS. with STRANGERS ON A TRAIN and I CONFESS. He was nominated for Academy Awards for *Marty* (1955), *Some Like It Hot* (1959), *Pepe* (1960), *The Longest Day* (1962), and *What a Way to Go* (1964) and won an Oscar for *Sayonara* (1957).

Hay, Ian (1876–1952) Veteran British playwright, former schoolmaster and army officer, born John Hay Beith. He began to collaborate directly on screenplays in 1928 and contributed dialogue to THE 39 STEPS, SECRET AGENT, and SABOTAGE.

Haye, Helen (1874–1957) British stage actress, born Helen Hay in colonial India, who made her West End debut in 1898, created the role of Mrs. Hillcrist in THE SKIN GAME (1920), then reprised it in both the original film version (1920) and Hitchcock's film. Hitchcock put her unflappable hauteur to similar use again by casting her in THE 39 STEPS as Professor Jordan's wife, who interrupts Jordan's armed showdown with Richard Hannay to tell them that dinner is served.

Hayes, John Michael (1919–) American screenwriter, with background in newspaper and radio writing. Soon after his first screenplay in 1952, he was thrown together with Hitchcock by the agents they shared at MCA just as Hitchcock was moving from WARNER BROS. to PARAMOUNT, and wrote the Oscar-nominated screenplay for REAR WINDOW and Hitchcock's next three films: TO CATCH A THIEF, THE TROUBLE WITH HARRY, and THE MAN WHO KNEW TOO MUCH (1956). Of all Hitchcock's screenwriters, he had the most distinctive touch with comic dialogue, often depending on bright double-entendres, and the director was reportedly shaken when Hayes refused to return with him to Warners to work on THE WRONG MAN without a fee. Instead, he turned to romance, winning his second Oscar nomination (after *Rear Window*) for *Peyton Place* (1957) and following that with *The Matchmaker* (1958), *Butterfield 8* (1960), *The Children's Hour* (1961), and two Harold Robbins adaptations, *The Carpetbaggers* and *Where Love Has Gone* (both 1965). He retired to teach screenwriting at Dartmouth College.

Head, Edith (1897–1981) Nonpareil Hollywood costume designer, former language and art teacher, at Paramount for hundreds of films from *She Done Him Wrong* (1933). Because she moved from PARAMOUNT to UNIVERSAL in 1967, only a few years after Hitchcock, she remained one of his most frequent collaborators, creating the costume designs for six of his films—REAR WINDOW, THE TROUBLE WITH HARRY, THE MAN WHO KNEW TOO MUCH (1956), VERTIGO, MARNIE, and TOPAZ—and creating wardrobes for the female stars of two more, THE BIRDS and TORN CURTAIN. She is both the most honored costume designer and the most honored woman in Oscar history, having received 34 nominations, including a record eight Academy Awards for *The Heiress* (1949), *Samson and Delilah* (1949), *All About Eve* (1950), *A Place in the Sun* (1951), *Roman Holiday* (1953), *Sabrina* (1954), *The Facts of Life* (1960), and *The Sting* (1973).

Hecht, Ben (1894–1964) Storied Hollywood screenwriter who also directed and produced several important films. A novelist and playwright of the art-for-art's-sake school, he was drawn to Hollywood by the promise of "tremendous sums of money for work that required no more effort than a game of pinochle."

His first screen credit, the original story for *Underworld* (1927), won him one of the first Academy Awards for writing, and he won again for *The Scoundrel,* which he also directed (1935), and was nominated twice more for his work on *Wuthering Heights* (1939) and *Angels Over Broadway,* which he directed and produced as well (1940). He had a special gift for the hard-edged comedy of *Design for Living* (1933), *Twentieth Century* (1934), *Nothing Sacred* (1937), and *His Girl Friday* (1940). Even more important than his 100 screen credits, often shared with Charles MacArthur, were the dozens of films on which he worked without screen credit as Hollywood's highest-paid script doctor, including *What Price Hollywood?* (1932), *The Prisoner of Zenda* (1937), *Stagecoach* (1939), *Gone With the Wind* (1939), *Roxie Hart* (1942), *Gilda* (1946), *Duel in the Sun* (1946), and *Casino Royale* (1967), his final film. He received screen credit for writing what were essentially two original screenplays for Hitchcock, SPELLBOUND and NOTORIOUS, and worked without credit on FOREIGN CORRESPONDENT, LIFEBOAT, THE PARADINE CASE, and ROPE. A pungent raconteur and memoirist, Hecht was not only the quintessential Hollywood writer but one of the great Hollywood characters himself.

Heckroth, Hein (1897–1970) German costume and set designer, formerly of the German national ballet. He entered British cinema as the costume designer on *A Matter of Life and Death* (1946) and continued to collaborate with Michael Powell and Emeric Pressburger, winning an Academy Award for his first credit as production designer, *The Red Shoes* (1948). His final film, and perhaps his least fanciful in conception, was TORN CURTAIN.

Hedgecock, William (W.) (1883–1947) American sound technician whose two dozen films at UNIVERSAL from *Hell's Heroes* (1930) through *The Killers* (1946) included SABOTEUR.

Hedren, Tippi (1931–) American actress, former model, born Nathalie Hedren. Spotting her in a television commercial, Hitchcock signed her to an exclusive contract and launched her career by casting her, billed as "Tippi" Hedren, as Melanie

Daniels in THE BIRDS and Marnie Edgar in MARNIE. But she proved by far the most problematic of the icy BLONDES he had chosen as successors to Grace KELLY, and before *Marnie* wrapped, the Hitchcock-created star and her Svengali were barely speaking—perhaps, as Donald SPOTO has notoriously charged, because she spurned his sexual advances. Since then, she has appeared in some 50 films and television segments, from *A Countess from Hong Kong* (1967) to *Citizen Ruth* (1996) but is still better known as an activist for wild animals and as the mother of actress Melanie Griffith.

Heindorf, Ray (1908–1980) Veteran WARNERS BROS. musical director (as on STRANGERS ON A TRAIN) and music supervisor (as on I CONFESS) who worked on nearly 100 other films from 1931.

Heldabrand, John American character actor of the fifties who is credited as appearing as Mutt in *On the Waterfront* (1954) and as Tomasini in THE WRONG MAN.

Helminger, Florence British stage actress of the twenties whose sole screen role was Mrs. Sidey, the wife of the lecherous patron in THE PLEASURE GARDEN.

Helmond, Katherine (1934–) Twittery American character actress, best known as the hero's vain, pushy mother in *Brazil* (1985) and as Doris Sherman on the television series *Coach* (1995–97), who played Ed Maloney's widow in FAMILY PLOT.

Helmore, Tom (1904–1995) British actor of stage and screen, former accountant, who made some 20 film appearances in the thirties, including his role as Colonel Anderson in SECRET AGENT, before achieving Broadway success in the forties. Soon after understudying Rex Harrison in the original production of *My Fair Lady* (1956), he was cast in two ALFRED HITCHCOCK PRESENTS segments—as the hypnotist Professor Faraum in "Murder Me Twice" (1958) and as playwright Adam Longsworth in "Little White Frock" (1958)—and as Scottie Ferguson's old schoolmate and client Gavin Elster in VERTIGO.

Some viewers have claimed to find him as an extra in *THE RING* as well.

Helton, Percy (1894–1971) Baby-faced, roly-poly Hollywood character actor. In vaudeville from childhood, he scarred his vocal cords screaming in character through the entire run of an early play and switched thereafter to character roles, one of which—the drunken Macy's Santa replaced by Kris Kringle in *Miracle on 34th Street* (1947)—made him instantly recognizable for his hushed, gravelly voice. A television fixture throughout the fifties, he appeared in seven segments of *ALFRED HITCHCOCK PRESENTS*: as Mr. Eaton in "Premonition" (1955), the lawyer in "The Perfect Murder" (1956), George the super in "The Creeper" (1956), Charlie the janitor in "Nightmare in 4-D" (1957), Mr. Bruce in "Disappearing Trick" (1958), Morton the sexton in "THE HORSEPLAYER," and the freeloader Cyrus Rutherford in "Services Rendered" (1961).

Heman, Roger, Sr. (1898–1969) Sound technician at 20TH CENTURY-FOX for 30 years and some 200 films, who served as recording director on *LIFEBOAT.*

Herbert, Frederick (1909–1966) American composer who supplied music for many episodes of *ALFRED HITCHCOCK PRESENTS*, including four directed by Hitchcock—"BANQUO'S CHAIR," "ARTHUR," "THE CRYSTAL TRENCH," and "MRS. BIXBY AND THE COLONEL'S COAT"—and also scored the *FORD STARTIME* segment "INCIDENT AT A CORNER."

Heron, Julia (1897–1977) Veteran American set designer, in Hollywood from 1935, who, 15 years after her work on *FOREIGN CORRESPONDENT*, became one of the staff designers on *ALFRED HITCHCOCK PRESENTS* and later *THE ALFRED HITCHCOCK HOUR*, where she designed sets for (among many others) "THE CRYSTAL TRENCH," "THE HORSEPLAYER," "BANG! YOU'RE DEAD," and "I SAW THE WHOLE THING."

Herrmann, Bernard (1911–1975) American composer who trained as a classical musician, winning a composition prize at 13 and founding his own chamber orchestra at 20, but soon began to mix his traditional compositions—which would come to include the cantata *Moby Dick, Wuthering Heights* and other operas, and a symphony in the mold of Sibelius—with work for Orson Welles's Mercury Theater of the Air. He wrote the music to Welles's 1938 "War of the Worlds" broadcast and followed him to Hollywood to score *Citizen Kane* (1941), which failed to win the Oscar it was nominated for because it was beaten by Herrmann's score for *All That Money Can Buy* (1941). After removing his credit from *The Magnificent Ambersons* (1942) when RKO added music to his score without his or Welles's approval, he moved from studio to studio, providing memorable music for films as different as *Jane Eyre* (1944), *Hangover Square*

Bernard Herrmann

(1945), *The Ghost and Mrs. Muir* (1947), and *On Dangerous Ground* (1951). But his strong opinions, autocratic style, and impatience with filmmakers, most of whom he contended knew nothing about music, kept him from working with any director more than twice until 1955, when he scored THE TROUBLE WITH HARRY, the first of his films with Hitchcock (and one from whose score Herrmann later recorded a suite titled *A Portrait of Hitch*), and signed on as a staff composer on ALFRED HITCHCOCK PRESENTS. The two perfectionists' clash over innumerable details—Hitchcock wanted a jazz score for PSYCHO, with no music at all for the shower scene—did not prevent their collaboration from yielding some of the greatest film music ever written in THE MAN WHO KNEW TOO MUCH, THE WRONG MAN, VERTIGO (along with *Kane* Herrmann's finest score for the cinema), NORTH BY NORTHWEST, *Psycho* (perhaps the most widely known of all film scores), and MARNIE. Impressed by Herrmann's ability to create a wide variety of emotional and psychological tones by different instrumental palettes (e.g., his "black and white" strings-only score for *Psycho*), Hitchcock even engaged Herrmann as auditory consultant in the essentially musicless THE BIRDS, but pressed by Universal executives who wanted a popular title tune instead of Herrmann's grim, gray, no-violins score for TORN CURTAIN, Hitchcock rejected the score, and the two men never spoke again, though Herrmann continued to work on such Hitchcock-inflected films as *Fahrenheit 451* (1965), *The Bride Wore Black* (1968), *Sisters* (1973), and *Obsession* (1975). Hours after finishing recording sessions for his last film, *Taxi Driver* (1976), he collapsed and died, and director Martin Scorsese responded by dedicating the film to him. It was a fitting gesture to the composer who once said, "When Hitchcock finishes a film, it's only 60% complete. I supply the other 40%."

Heslop, Charles (1883–1966)   British stage actor, in occasional films from 1920 to 1962, who played Prince Leopold's valet in WALTZES FROM VIENNA.

Hessler, Gordon (1930–)   German-born British producer/director who cut his teeth as chief reader for ALFRED HITCHCOCK PRESENTS and became

story editor (1960–62) for the series and associate producer (1962–64) and producer (1964–65) for THE ALFRED HITCHCOCK HOUR. When the program was discontinued, he used a story rejected for it as the basis of his directorial debut, *The Woman Who Wouldn't Die* (1965), and followed it with several Poe-tinged horror features, the Ray Harryhausen fantasy *The Golden Voyage of Sinbad* (1974), and several dozen television episodes.

Hichens, Robert (Smythe) (1864–1950) British novelist who never wrote for the cinema but whose work has served as the basis for some 15 international films, most notably *Bella Donna* (1915, 1921, 1934) and *The Garden of Allah* (1916, 1927, 1936). After much 11th-hour fretting over the title—whose candidates included *Mrs. Paradine Takes the Stand, The Lie, Heartbreak, The Grand Passion, A Question of Life and Death, A Woman of Experience, The Dark Hour, A Crime of Passion, This Is No Ordinary Woman, Guilty?, The Indelible Stain, Guilty!, The Woman Who Did the Killing, Hanging Is Easy, The Accused, Bewildered, The Green-Eyed Monster,* and *Woman and Wife*—the Hitchcock film based on Hichens's novel THE PARADINE CASE, a pet project of David O. SELZNICK's ever since the novel's publication in 1933, was released under the novel's own title but without the novel's climactic murder attempt.

Highsmith, Patricia (1921–1995)   Pioneering American novelist of psychological suspense, née Mary Patricia Plangman, whose fascination with neurotic guilt, betrayal, and unexpected violence so exactly mirrors Hitchcock's that it surprised only the author to discover that he had secretly negotiated to purchase the film rights to her first novel, STRANGERS ON A TRAIN (1950). The novel's premise—that two would-be murderers might exchange crimes to avoid suspicion—has often been recycled, notably in *Once You Kiss a Stranger* (1969), *Throw Momma from the Train* (1987), and *Once You Meet a Stranger* (1996). Highsmith's novel *This Sweet Sickness* (1960) was adapted for the ALFRED HITCHCOCK HOUR segment "Annabel" (1962). Several of her later novels and stories have also been filmed, most memorably *The Talented Mr. Ripley* (1955; as *Plein soleil* in 1960 and under its original title in 1999) and *Ripley's Game* (1974; as *Der Amerikanische Freund,* 1977).

Hildyard, Jack (1908–1990) British cinematographer who entered the industry in 1932 and became a lighting cinematographer in 1946. He came to specialize in the lush color effects of *Summertime* (1955), *Anastasia* (1956), and *The Bridge on the River Kwai* (1957), for which he won an Academy Award. His later films include *The Sundowners* (1960), *The V.I.P.'s* (1963), *Casino Royale* (1967), and TOPAZ.

Hill, Paul G. American cameraman who, 15 years after acting as uncredited camera operator on *Imitation of Life* (1934), was one of four camera operators credited on ROPE. He later served as lighting cinematographer on one film, *South Seas Adventure* (1958).

Hill, William Associate producer of FRENZY who went on to assume similar chores for *The Mackintosh Man* (1973) and *Voyage of the Damned* (1973) before turning to television production.

Hilton, James (1900–1954) British novelist and occasional screenwriter who achieved instant fame with *Lost Horizon* (1933) and *Goodbye, Mr. Chips* (1934) and followed his best-known works to Hollywood to work on such films as *Camille* (1936), *Mrs. Miniver* (1942), and FOREIGN CORRESPONDENT.

Hitchcock, Alfred (Joseph) (1899–1980). Nonpareil Anglo-American director whose career spanned a half-century; for many years indelibly associated with stylish, witty thrillers on both sides of the Atlantic; a man whose portly, balding figure and rapidly sketched profile eventually became as well known as any of his stars'. Born to a prosperous East London greengrocer on August 13, 1899, he attended Jesuit schools until the death of his father in 1914 sent him for professional training to the School of Engineering and Navigation and then to a job as a technical clerk. The news that the American film company FAMOUS PLAYERS–LASKY, later PARAMOUNT, was opening a studio in London took him to Islington, where he began in 1919 as a graphic designer of

Alfred Hitchcock

intertitles for 12 films—THE CALL OF YOUTH (1920), THE GREAT DAY (1920), APPEARANCES (1921), BESIDE THE BONNIE BRIER BUSH (1921), DANGEROUS LIES (1921), THE MYSTERY ROAD (1921), THE PRINCESS OF NEW YORK (1921), THE MAN FROM HOME (1922), PERPETUA (1922), SPANISH JADE (1922), TELL YOUR CHILDREN (1922), and THREE LIVE GHOSTS (1922)—tried his hand at directing an uncompleted short, NUMBER 13, and completing Hugh CROISE's ALWAYS TELL YOUR WIFE (both 1922), and served as assistant director, and eventually as co-screenwriter and art director, on WOMAN TO WOMAN (1923), THE WHITE SHADOW (1923), THE PASSIONATE ADVENTURE (1924), THE PRUDE'S FALL (1924), and THE BLACKGUARD (1925). It was during this period that Hitchcock met his future wife, editor Alma REVILLE, whom he married in 1926 after launching his own career as director under the auspices of producer Michael BALCON.

That career began in earnest with THE PLEASURE GARDEN (1925), a melodrama about the romantic entanglements of two roommates who performed at a nightclub, and continued with THE MOUNTAIN EAGLE (1926), a lost film, and THE LODGER (1926), Hitchcock's first thriller. Despite delays in their release attributable to C.M. WOOLF, an executive at GAINSBOROUGH PICTURES who felt that all three were too artsy and obscure for British audiences, all three were successful, and after two more films at Gainsborough, DOWNHILL (1927) and EASY VIRTUE (1927), Hitchcock left the studio to become the star director at John MAXWELL's new BRITISH INTERNATIONAL PICTURES. Here, in frequent collaboration with screenwriter Eliot STANNARD (who had worked on all his Gainsborough films), cinematographer John J. COX, and Alma Reville, he directed a rapid series of varied films: THE RING (1927), THE FARMER'S WIFE (1928), CHAMPAGNE (1928), THE MANXMAN (1929), and his second thriller, BLACKMAIL (1929), first planned and released as a silent, but largely reshot and simultaneously released as one of the earliest and most brilliant British talkies. The following films—MURDER! (1930), THE SKIN GAME (1931), RICH AND STRANGE (1931), NUMBER SEVENTEEN (1932), and especially WALTZES FROM VIENNA (1933)—showed Hitchcock drifting at British International, and he jumped at the chance to rejoin Balcon at GAUMONT-BRITISH PICTURES for THE MAN WHO KNEW TOO MUCH (1934), his fifth thriller, and the one that identified him decisively with the form, an identification promptly confirmed by the international success of THE 39 STEPS (1935). Throughout the later thirties, Hitchcock, often in collaboration with screenwriter Charles BENNETT, cinematographer Bernard KNOWLES, and composer Louis LEVY, strengthened his mastery of the thriller at Gaumont-British in SECRET AGENT (1936), SABOTAGE (1937), YOUNG AND INNOCENT (1937), and THE LADY VANISHES (1938), all but the third, like The Man Who Knew Too Much and The 39 Steps, centering on international espionage. The success of The Lady Vanishes brought Hitchcock to the attention of Hollywood independent producer David O. SELZNICK, who signed the director to an exclusive contract in 1938. After one final British film, JAMAICA INN (1939), Hitchcock immigrated with his wife and their daughter Patricia HITCHCOCK, who had been born in 1928, to America in 1939.

In America, Hitchcock soon settled into a professional and personal routine that became legendary. His experience in so many different areas of filmmaking made him seek involvement in every aspect of his films, from story conferences—which typically began with several hours of conversation or anecdotes every morning—to shooting and postproduction, with which he always professed boredom. His trademark black suits bespeaking self-control, his proprietary behavior toward a series of icy blonde leading ladies, and his desire to control others were but some of his characteristics. He also directed with a methodical efficiency and detachment punctuated by a long series of practical jokes on cast and crew members. He had a horror of scenes or confrontations on the set, preferring to work quietly with performers he could direct and to avoid those he could not. His private life was equally habitual and equally quiet.

Hitchcock's American films departed from the British films that had earned him the sobriquet "the master of suspense" in several striking ways. Both his three films for Selznick—REBECCA (1940), SPELLBOUND (1945), and THE PARADINE CASE (1947)—and the more numerous films he made on loan from Selznick to Walter WANGER (FOREIGN CORRESPONDENT, 1940), RKO (the by now atypical marital comedy MR. AND MRS. SMITH, 1941; SUSPICION, 1941; and NOTORIOUS, 1946), UNIVERSAL (SABOTEUR, 1942, and SHADOW OF A DOUBT, 1943), and 20TH CENTURY−FOX (LIFEBOAT, 1944) were more clearly Hollywood products—longer, slower, more elaborately staged, more expensive, and slower in completion—than anything he had directed in Britain. At the same time, films like Rebecca, Suspicion, Shadow of a Doubt, Spellbound, and The Paradine Case, perhaps influenced by the wartime deaths of Hitchcock's own mother and brother back in England, turned from espionage toward family melodrama as a locus of suspense. By the time Hitchcock signed an independent partnership agreement with businessman Sidney BERNSTEIN to form TRANSATLANTIC PICTURES in 1946, the spy thriller, despite the currency it had been given by World War II—a currency that emerges most clearly in BON VOYAGE and AVENTURE MALGACHE (both 1944), two wartime shorts Hitchcock made for the BRITISH MINISTRY OF

INFORMATION—had become less important to his work than the tale of domestic crime.

Hitchcock's Transatlantic films gave him freedom from what he took to be the interference or financial exploitation of Selznick and freedom to indulge the fascination with the LONG TAKE which had been rekindled by Hitchcock's recent experience supervising the editing of concentration camp footage for the documentary film *Memory of the Camps* (1945). Yet neither of his Transatlantic films, ROPE (1948) and *UNDER CAPRICORN* (1949), duplicated the critical or box-office success of *Rebecca, Spellbound,* or *Notorious,* and Hitchcock returned to work for WARNER BROS., the studio that had distributed the Transatlantic features. Now, however, his contract gave him far more control over properties, cast, and budget, making him a quasi-independent producer within the studio. Although Hitchcock's first film for Warners, STAGE FRIGHT (1950)—shot, like *Under Capricorn,* back in England—met an indifferent reception, his second, *STRANGERS ON A TRAIN* (1951), scored a notable success, ushering in his most triumphant decade.

Continuing to rely on Robert BURKS, the cinematographer who had shot *Strangers on a Train,* Hitchcock began to assemble a core of collaborators who would work with him repeatedly throughout the fifties. Burks continued on *I CONFESS* (1952) and all Hitchcock's films, with a single exception, through MARNIE (1964). Grace KELLY joined Hitchcock for *DIAL M FOR MURDER* (1953), and was partnered by Hitchcock veterans James STEWART in *REAR WINDOW* (1954) and Cary GRANT in *TO CATCH A THIEF* (1955), the first Hitchcock film edited by George TOMASINI. *THE TROUBLE WITH HARRY* (1955) was the first scored by composer Bernard HERRMANN, who more than any single other collaborator came to be identified with the Hitchcock style, and *Rear Window, To Catch a Thief,* and *The Trouble with Harry* were all written by John Michael HAYES, who also wrote the screenplay for Hitchcock's 1956 remake of *THE MAN WHO KNEW TOO MUCH.*

Meanwhile, a new chapter in Hitchcock's professional life had begun in 1955 when he licensed his name to a monthly magazine of mystery fiction and a television program, *ALFRED HITCHCOCK PRESENTS* (1955–62), later expanded to *THE ALFRED HITCH-*

COCK HOUR (1962–65). In addition to directing a total of 20 individual segments for these programs and for SUSPICION (1957) and FORD STARTIME (1960), Hitchcock appeared each week on television to introduce segments of *Alfred Hitchcock Presents.* Such maliciously comic comments as "In each of our stories we strive to teach a lesson or point a little moral. Advice like mother used to give, you know. Walk softly, and carry a big stick. Strike first, and ask questions later," scripted by James ALLARDICE, not only confirmed his fastidiously ghoulish public persona but also vastly enlarged his audience, giving him a personal stardom unique in directorial history.

The greatest of all Hitchcock's films lay just ahead. After directing THE WRONG MAN (1957) for Warner Bros., Hitchcock returned to PARAMOUNT to produce in VERTIGO (1958) his ultimate James Stewart film (and apart from *Rich and Strange* the most revealingly autobiographical of all his films), moved to MGM for NORTH BY NORTHWEST (1959), his ultimate Cary Grant film, and returned one last time to Paramount to work with a television crew on which *Alfred Hitchcock Presents* cinematographer John L. RUSSELL substituted for Robert Burks on PSYCHO (1960), for two generations of viewers the ultimate Hitchcock film, shot on a shoestring during a six-week period and the most financially successful of all his films.

When he followed his longtime agent Lew WASSERMAN to Universal, Hitchcock parlayed the success of *Psycho,* which he had financed himself when Paramount executives expressed reservations about its unsavory story, into a personal fortune by exchanging his ownership of the film and of his television series for a large block of stock in Universal's new owner, Wasserman's Music Corporation of America. His own films for Universal, however, were more problematic. The dauntingly expensive special effects required by THE BIRDS (1963) kept the film from showing a substantial profit; *Marnie* (1964) and TORN CURTAIN (1966) fared no better; and TOPAZ (1969) was Hitchcock's most resounding flop since *The Paradine Case.* Exercising a clause in his contract that allowed him to make a film on any subject of his choice as long as he kept the budget under $2 million, Hitchcock returned to the Jack the Ripper theme of his first notable success, *The Lodger,* for his last, *FRENZY* (1972), and followed it with his unexpectedly lighthearted valedictory film, *FAMILY PLOT* (1976). Gradually worsening health problems forced his retirement while the next film he had planned, *THE SHORT NIGHT*, was still under development. He received the Life Achievement Award from the American Film Institute in 1979 and was knighted by Queen Elizabeth II only three months before his death on April 29, 1980.

Hitchcock's talent as a raconteur and wit made him the most widely quoted of all film directors, from his definition of movies—"Life with the dull bits left out"—to his description of his own work—"Some films are slices of life. Mine are slices of cake"—and from his correction of his reported averral that actors were cattle—"I just said they should be *treated* like cattle"—to his response to a reporter who, told that Hitchcock never attended screenings of his own films, asked if he missed hearing the audience scream—"I can hear them when I'm making the picture." But his most celebrated remark of all is a nonremark. Although *The Lady Vanishes* had won him the New York Film Critics Circle Award as Best Director, Hitchcock, nominated five times for Best Director Oscars (for *Rebecca, Lifeboat, Spellbound, Rear Window,* and *Psycho*), had never won. His perceived snub by the academy may have been responsible for his reaction when as one of the most commercially successful filmmakers in cinema history he received the Irving Thalberg Award for a consistently high level of film production in 1967. As the audience settled back in their seats in expectation of one of the trademark witty speeches Hitchcock had given in virtually every public appearance, the director instead delivered the shortest acceptance speech in Oscar history—"Thank you"—and sat down to let his work speak for itself.

Hitchcock, Patricia (1928–) British-born actress, only child of Hitchcock and Alma REVILLE. She made her Broadway debut at 14 as the star of John VAN DRUTEN's *Solitaire,* studied at the Royal Academy of Dramatic Art, and played three roles in her father's films: as Chubby Bannister, Eve Gill's friend in the garden-party sequence of *STAGE FRIGHT*; Barbara Morton, the heroine's outspoken kid sister in *STRANGERS ON A TRAIN* (a part some commentators, noting her status as a senator's daughter, have found autobiographical); and Caroline, Marion Crane's officemate in *PSYCHO*. In between, she was frequently cast in *ALFRED HITCHCOCK PRESENTS*, appearing as Diana Winthrop, whose mother disappears from their Paris hotel room in "The Vanishing Lady" (1955); Margaret in "The Older Sister" (1956); Ella Marsh, the heroine of "The Belfry" (1956); Count Mattoni's maid Polly Stephens in "I Killed the Count" (1957); the saleslady in "The Glass Eye" (1957); Nancy Mason, the killer's wife in "Silent Witness" (1957); Amy in "The Crocodile Case" (1958); Pat in "The Morning of the Bride" (1959); Ida Blythe's protective daughter Dorothy in "The Cuckoo Clock" (1960); and Rose, the maid in "The Schwartz-Metterklume Method" (1960). Married since 1952 to businessman Joseph E. O'Connell, she retired to raise her two daughters.

Hitchcock Annual The only American periodical devoted entirely to Hitchcock's work first appeared under the founding editorship of Christopher BROOKHOUSE in 1992. Since its inception, it has been a reliable source for substantial, original scholarship on the director, from J. Lary Kuhns's painstaking assembly of information about *THE MOUNTAIN EAGLE* in the 1998–99 issue to James M. VEST's series of articles on the director's cameo appearances. In 2001, Brookhouse turned the editorship of the journal over to coeditors Richard ALLEN and Sidney GOTTLIEB. Subscriptions ($10.00 per annual issue for individuals, $25 for institutions) are available through Sidney Gottlieb, English Department, Sacred Heart University, Fairfield, Connecticut 06432.

Hodges, Horace (1865–1951) Veteran British stage actor and playwright (his play *Grumpy* was filmed three times between 1923 and 1930) whose final screen role was Sir Humphrey Pengallan's faithful butler Chadwyck in *JAMAICA INN*.

Hodiak, John (1914–1955) Virile American leading man of the mid-forties. Classified 4-F because of hypertension, he spent the later war years filling the need for manly Hollywood leads, and his career peaked early in *LIFEBOAT*, in which he played John Kovac, the proletarian hero from the sunken ship's engine room, and in *A Bell for Adono* (1945), *The Harvey Girls* (1946), and *Command Decision* (1948). But the return of competing males from their war service relegated him to increasingly minor roles before his death of a heart attack at 41. He was married to actress Anne BAXTER from 1946 to 1953.

Hoffman, Bud American editor whose first credit is *TORN CURTAIN*; most of the later work in his 10-year career is in television.

Hoffman, Gertrude (W.) (1871–1966) German-born actress who went to Hollywood at 60 after raising two daughters and stayed on to play some 30 generally maternal types and society matrons like Mrs. Benson in *FOREIGN CORRESPONDENT* and Mrs. Wetherby in *SUSPICION*. She is best-known as the title character's elderly confidante Mrs. Odets in the television program *My Little Margie* (1952–54).

Hogan, Dick (1917–1995) Blond American actor who appeared in some two dozen films before retiring at 31, shortly after playing David Kentley, who disappeared from *ROPE* soon after being strangled in its opening moments. The disappearance was more complete than most audiences suspected because the claustrophobic actor had to be released from the bottom of the chest that supposedly held his corpse throughout the film only seconds after being placed there.

Hogan, James Assistant director of the *ALFRED HITCHCOCK PRESENTS* segment "BREAKDOWN," among many others.

Hogan, Michael (b. 1898) British actor and screenwriter who played 20 screen roles from 1928 to 1936. His dozen writing credits (1934–50) include collaborating with Alma REVILLE in adapting *The Passing of the Third Floor Back* (1935) and with Philip MACDONALD in adapting *REBECCA*.

Hokanson, Mary Alan (1916–1994) American character actress who helped fill the frame in some

three dozen films and television programs from 1950 to 1984, often without screen credit, as in *STRANGERS ON A TRAIN*, in which she plays Senator Morton's secretary, and the *FORD STARTIME* segment "INCIDENT AT A CORNER," in which she plays Mrs. Parker.

homes Throughout Hitchcock's career, domestic spaces function as guarantors of the heroes' and heroines' identity. Broadly speaking, homes in Hitchcock's British films are both a locus of safety and security and a teleological goal, like home plate in baseball or home in any number of board games. The Buntings are safe in their own home in *THE LODGER*, endangered only when they leave; Roddy Berwick's dismissal from his own home in *DOWNHILL* has an annihilating force; the hero and heroine of *THE MOUNTAIN EAGLE* evidently spend much of the film repeatedly attempting to create a home worthy of the name. Characters like Samuel Sweetland and the Hills venture forth from their homes for adventure in *THE FARMER'S WIFE* and *RICH AND STRANGE*, though in doing so they risk the sense of drifting or weightlessness that overtakes the unmoored characters of *CHAMPAGNE*. Grave as the Boyles' troubles are in *JUNO AND THE PAYCOCK*, the film's focus on their home shows that they avoid each of the most complete disasters imaginable, as exemplified in other films: the threatening of one's home, as in *THE SKIN GAME*; the invasion of one's home, as in *BLACKMAIL*; or the loss of one's home, as in *EASY VIRTUE* and *THE MANXMAN*. The dialectic of homeyness and homelessness provides a model for the thrillers that followed *THE MAN WHO KNEW TOO MUCH* (1934): the giddy suspension of Richard Hannay, a visitor from Canada, over a homeless abyss in *THE 39 STEPS*, the opposition between the freedom of the road and the responsibilities of domesticity in *YOUNG AND INNOCENT*, the gradual realization that one's home has been turned into a public space (a movie theater, a nest of saboteurs, a murder scene) in *SABOTAGE*, the pull of the intrigue in *THE LADY VANISHES* against the pipe dream of English domesticity with her check-chasing husband, ever closer to whom the speeding train is carrying the heroine.

JAMAICA INN, Hitchcock's last British film, looks forward through its homeless heroine, who moves through a series of false homes, to an American period in which the émigré director casts a far more skeptical light on the power of homes to offer a safe refuge or even a secure genetic identity. Although homes serve variously conventional functions in FOREIGN CORRESPONDENT (the domestic front of the one home shown, the Fishers' house in London, is deceptive), MR. AND MRS. SMITH (a comedy about a man whose wife tosses him out of their home), and LIFEBOAT (which eradicates every trace of individual homes to ask what Americans have in common by virtue of their shared homeland), the homes in REBECCA, SUSPICION, SHADOW OF A DOUBT, NOTORIOUS, and THE PARADINE CASE all serve as traps for visitors, newcomers, or, more often, their nominal hosts. Minyago Yugilla, the Fluskys' sad and mysterious home in UNDER CAPRICORN, could serve as a sketch for Norman BATES's California Gothic house. Perhaps the most claustrophobic of all Hitchcock's homes are the flats in ROPE and DIAL M FOR MURDER because the camera rarely or never leaves a single exterior space that eventually serves as a trap for the killers as well as their victims. At the same time, STRANGERS ON A TRAIN and REAR WINDOW attest to Hitchcock's growing interest in surrogate homes that the heroes find more interesting and compelling than their own. By the fifties, in fact, the American tendency to fetishize the domestic sphere by overidealizing and overvaluing it produces both a yearning for domesticity in films like Rear Window (whose heroine plaintively asks its hero, "Isn't it time you came home?") and THE TROUBLE WITH HARRY and a critique of domesticity in TO CATCH A THIEF (whose final line by the heroine—"So this is where you live! Why, Mother will love it here!"—provokes a reaction of comical shock from the hero) and THE MAN WHO KNEW TOO MUCH (1956). The abiding suspicion of home—now a testing ground or, at best, a temporary shelter rather than a permanent source of refuge and strength—continues in THE BIRDS, MARNIE, and TOPAZ and flavors as well the homelessness of the characters in NORTH BY NORTHWEST (whose only homes are those belonging to Lester Townsend, who has no idea that his gardener has opened it to criminals, and Philip Vandamm's chilly modernist South Dakota eyrie), TORN CURTAIN, and FRENZY (whose hero once again is defined from the opening scene as having no place he can safely lodge). The best known of all Hitchcock's homes, however, and one of the most famous homes in cinema, is the Bates house in PSYCHO, not only because it shelters such a menacing presence as Mrs. Bates but also because Lila Crane, in her search for Mrs. Bates, gives what amounts to a virtual room-by-room tour of it (briefly reprised in Hitchcock's famous trailer for the film). More strongly than any other Hitchcock film, Psycho argues that the most frightful demons are not out there in foggy streets or exotic foreign lands but inside, behind the last door, deep within oneself.

Homolka, Oskar (or Oscar) (1888–1978)

Heavy-set, beetle-browed Austrian character actor whose specialty was menacing villains. A star of Austrian and German stage and screen before he came to England in 1933, he was ideally cast as Karl Verloc, the shabby provocateur in SABOTAGE. Leaving soon after for Hollywood, he gradually broadened his range from the obligatory Slavic wartime heavies and was nominated for an Academy Award for his performance as Uncle Chris in I Remember Mama (1948). Among his later roles—many assumed despite his avowed intention to retire—were three appearances in ALFRED HITCHCOCK PRESENTS: as miserly Carl Kaminsky, who is unlucky enough to find a wallet in "Reward to Finder" (1957); the greedy antique dealer Karpias in "The Ikon of Elijah" (1960); and Jan Vander Klaue in "The Hero" (1960).

homosexuality

Just as Hitchcock delighted in presenting enchanting BLONDE heroines whose sexuality seemed eternally unreachable, he seems to have maintained an enduring fascination with homosexuality, whether the subject was gay men of his acquaintance from F. W. MURNAU to Montgomery CLIFT or the opportunities offered by outlaw modes of love his films, forbidden even to identify explicitly, could fetishize. Although (or because) his own background was sheltered and his temperament prudish, he described the homosexual behavior he encountered on his trips to Germany and France with a combination of dispassionate detachment and candid naïveté, and many of his films, especially *DOWNHILL, MURDER!, REBECCA, ROPE,* and *STRANGERS ON A TRAIN,* present gay males and females as exotica privy to still another range of the sexual fetishes the director cherished. First stigmatized along with other Hollywood films as homophobic because the characters repeatedly marked as gay were villains like Mrs. Danvers, Brandon Shaw, and Bruno Anthony, then singled out by Laura MULVEY and others as exemplary instances of the patriarchal gaze, Hitchcock's films have recently come under reevaluation by theorists considering alternatives to the heterosexual male gaze Mulvey's analysis seems to privilege as normative. D.A. Miller finds the unbroken long takes of *Rope* a fetish that substitutes for the absent fetish of the heroes' homosexuality. Lee Edelman, in his essay in ALLEN and GONZALÈS, figures the bird attacks in *THE BIRDS* as an assault on the grammar of heteroideology. Most influentially, Robert CORBER has persuasively argued that the director's cold-war films systematically link homosexuality to an un-Americanness that must be repressed in the name of national self-interest. Still more recently, Robert SAMUELS has disputed the gendering of Hitchcockian narrative as divided between an enigmatic female object whose role is to be watched and demystified and an authoritarian male voice that watches, controls, and penetrates her mystery and often her body, contending instead that Hitchcock's subjects, men and women alike, are inherently bisexual.

Hopkins, George James (1896–1985) Set decorator who spent most of his career, from *Casablanca* (1942) to *Wait Until Dark* (1967), at WARNER BROS. and so was on hand to design the sets for *STRANGERS ON A TRAIN, I CONFESS,* and *DIAL M FOR MURDER.* He shared Academy Award nominations for *This Is the Army* (1943), *Mission to Moscow* (1943), *Life with Father* (1947), *A Star Is Born* (1954), *Auntie Mame* (1958), *Sunrise at Campobello* (1960), *Days of Wine and Roses* (1962), *The Music Man* (1962), and *Inside Daisy Clover* (1965) and won for *A Streetcar Named Desire* (1951), *My Fair Lady* (1964), *Who's Afraid of Virginia Woolf?* (1966), and *Hello, Dolly!* (1969).

Horning, William A(llen) (1904–1959) American art director at MGM from 1935 for more than 60 films. He was nominated for Academy Awards for *Conquest* (1937), *The Wizard of Oz* (1939), *Quo Vadis* (1951), and *Raintree County* (1957) and won for *Gigi* (1958) and *Ben-Hur* (1959), the last defeating *NORTH BY NORTHWEST,* for which he was also nominated.

"Horseplayer, The" 211th episode of *Alfred Hitchcock Presents,* broadcast March 14, 1961. **Associate producer:** Joan Harrison; **Director:** Alfred Hitchcock; **Assistant director:** James H. Brown; **Teleplay:** Henry Slesar, based on his short story; **Cinematographer:** John L. Russell; **Art director:** Martin Obzina; **Set designers:** John McCarthy and Julia Heron; **Costumes:** Vincent Dee; **Editors:** David O'Connell and Edward W. Williams; **Music:** Joseph Romero; **Cast:** Claude Rains (Father Amion), Ed Gardner (Sheridan), Percy Helton (Morton), Kenneth MacKenna (monsignor), Mike Ragan (Mr. Cheever), William Newell (bank teller), David Carlile (bank teller), Ada Murphy (elderly woman), Jackie Carroll, John Yount (altar boys).

The second episode Hitchcock directed for the program's sixth season and the first time he worked from a script by Henry Slesar, the show's most prolific screenwriter, poses an unusual moral dilemma for Father Amion, the pastor of an inner-city church that is badly in need of a new roof: He realizes that the big contributions from a parishioner named Sheridan come from his winnings at the racetrack in gratitude for his answered prayers about picking winners. Going further, Sheridan gives Father Amion a tip on an upcoming race, urges him to back his pick, and offers to place the bet for him. Desperate for money to repair his church building, the pastor gives Sheridan $500 but then, after his confession to a superior confirms his feelings of guilt, prays for his horse to lose. He realizes his prayers have been answered when Sheridan shows up broke, indicating that their horse had been winning until he suddenly pulled back. Although Sheridan lost his own money, however, he is able to give Father Amion $2,100 because, unwilling to risk the church's money on a risky win bet, he ended up placing a separate bet with the pastor's money for the horse to show.

Horton, Robert (1924–) Smoothly masculine American general purpose actor of the fifties, born Howard Horton, most successful on television, both in his long-running *Wagon Train* role as Flint McCullough (1957–63) and as a regular on ALFRED HITCHCOCK PRESENTS, where he was most frequently cast as two-timing romantic leads. He played Gil Larkin, the ill-used pianist lover in "Decoy" (1956); poker-playing businessman Mason Bridges in "Crack of Doom" (1956); chiding husband John Fenton in "MR. BLANCHARD'S SECRET" (1956); poisoned boyfriend Wally Donaldson in "A Bottle of Wine" (1957); romantically minded tennis partner Walter Richmond in "Disappearing Trick" (1958); two-timing beau Brad Taylor in "The Last Dark Step" (1959); and unfaithful husband Ray Marchand in "Hooked" (1960).

Howitt, Barbara Otherwise uncredited soprano who sang the solo part in the *Storm Cloud Cantata* sequence in THE MAN WHO KNEW TOO MUCH (1956).

Hoyt, Robert (L.) Sound technician who worked on some three dozen films of the seventies and eighties, from *Play Misty for Me* (1971) to *The Breakfast Club* (1985). He served as rerecording mixer on FAMILY PLOT.

Hubert, René (1895–1976) French-born costume designer on more than 100 films from 1927. He began in Hollywood, returned to Europe to work with René Clair on *Sous les toits de Paris* (1930) and *The Ghost Goes West* (1936), was back in America a few years later for dozens of films including LIFEBOAT and Clair's *And Then There Were None* (1945), and enjoyed an international career that lasted into the sixties.

Hughes, Frank E(lmo) (1891–1947) American set decorator who worked on LIFEBOAT and a dozen other Fox films of the forties, serving as production designer on *The Keys of the Kingdom* (1944) and the Oscar-winning *Anna and the King of Siam* (1946).

Hughes, Robin (1920–1989) British character actor, born in Argentina, who appeared in some 40 films and television episodes, most often as police officers, as in DIAL M FOR MURDER.

Hughes, Sally American actress in occasional film and television roles from 1960 to 1993, when she played the president's wife in *In the Line of Fire*. Her far more typical debut role was as Miss Putney, the dental assistant who ends up with Mrs. Bixby's mink in the ALFRED HITCHCOCK PRESENTS episode "MRS. BIXBY AND THE COLONEL'S COAT."

Hughes, William American actor of the fifties whose career was limited to bits like his role as an employee in the ALFRED HITCHCOCK PRESENTS segment "DIP IN THE POOL." He produced one film, *Stakeout!* (1962).

Hull, Henry (1890–1977) Protean American actor of stage and screen who originated the role of Jeeter Lester in the dramatization of Erskine Caldwell's *Tobacco Road* (1933) and transformed himself from a silent lead into a versatile character actor, equally at home playing the convict Magwitch in *Great Expectations* (1934) and the title character of *Werewolf of London* (1935); the sympathetically spluttering newspaper editor of *Jesse James* (1939) and *The Return of Frank James* (1940); and the scheming, becalmed capitalist Charles D. Rittenhouse in LIFEBOAT.

Hume, Benita (1906–1967) British actress; former pianist who changed careers because she wanted excitement. She made a memorable debut as the switchboard operator whose expressions tell the audience Larita Filton has accepted John Whittaker's marriage proposal in EASY VIRTUE and returned a dozen films later to play Janet King, the nurse suspected of poisoning her mistress in LORD CAMBER'S LADIES. Retiring from acting in 1938, she returned in 1954 as costar to her husband, Ronald Colman, in the short-lived television series *The Halls of Ivy*. After Colman's death in 1958 she married another actor, George SANDERS.

Humphries, Patrick British journalist and biographer whose survey *The Films of Alfred Hitchcock*

(Bison, 1986) is a coffee-table book aimed at Hitchcock fans. Although its text, which considers all Hitchcock's features chronologically with briefer nods at his work in television and contemporaneous work by other filmmakers, is unusually full, its proneness to factual errors makes it an unreliable reference. The volume does, however, describe Hitchcock's editing of the war-camps footage first screened in 1985 as *A Painful Reminder*—an episode omitted by most studies of Hitchcock—and its copious illustrations, among the most sumptuous in any book on the director, include the best extant still showing the intended effect of Hitchcock's neon-sign cameo in *Rope.* It concludes with a brief look at a few of the many recent films that pay homage to the Master of Suspense.

Hunt, Grady   Costume supervisor for TORN CURTAIN who went on to design costumes for some 60 productions, mostly in television.

Hunter, Evan (1926–   )   Prolific American writer, born Salvatore Lombino, a man of many pseudonyms (Curt Cannon, Richard Marsten, Ezra Hannon) best known for his crime novels written under the byline Ed McBain. Even before the first of McBain's police procedurals about the 87th Precinct, however, Hunter had achieved fame under his own name for his novel *The Blackboard Jungle* (1954), which was successfully filmed the following year. In 1959 Hunter went to Hollywood to write the screen adaptation of his novel *Strangers When We Meet,* and soon thereafter Hitchcock asked him to write the screenplay for THE BIRDS. According to Hunter's amusing, bittersweet memoir *Me and Hitch* (Faber and Faber, 1996), the relationship between director and writer continued cordial, and Hitchcock invited Hunter to adapt MARNIE for the screen but severed their relationship when Hunter argued vigorously against having Mark Rutland rape his bride on their honeymoon cruise and brought in Jay Presson ALLEN to write a new screenplay that retained the rape.

Hunter, Ian (1900–1975)   Stolid British actor, born in South Africa, who returned from war service in the British army to make his stage debut in 1919 and his screen debut five years later. He played Archie,

Roddy Berwick's rival for Julia's affections, in DOWN-HILL; Australian boxing champion Bob Corby, Jack Sander's rival for his wife Mabel's affections, in THE RING; and the plaintiff's counsel in Larita Filton's divorce proceedings in the opening of EASY VIRTUE. In 1934 he left England for Hollywood, where his reassuringly dependable supporting characters anchored dozens of films before his retirement in 1963.

Huntley Wright, Betty   British character actress who made her film debut as the lady's maid in WALTZES FROM VIENNA and then went on to some 10 other roles in films and television, most in the thirties and forties. She appeared as recently as 1975 in the television series *Fawlty Towers.*

Hurley, Joseph (1914–1982)   American artist and visual designer who was nominated for an Academy Award for his art direction of PSYCHO and then worked as illustrator or staff artist on a half-dozen other Hollywood productions, 1969–83.

Hurley, Neil P., S.J.   American film scholar; professor of Communications at Fordham University; founder and director of Inscape, a policy research institute for "Edu-tainment"; and author of *Toward a Film Humanism: Original Theology Through Film* (1970) and *The Reel Revolution: A Film Primer on Liberation* (1978). His *Soul in Suspense: Alfred Hitchcock's Fright and Delight* (Scarecrow, 1993) makes a case for Hitchcock as a Catholic artist whose films exemplify "the warrior spirit at the heart of Jesuit strategy, a realization that evil will make gains in inverse proportion to our human effort to struggle and strive for something greater than the self, greater than the world." After reviewing the principles behind the director's Jesuit education, he turns to a close examination of Christian motifs in the films— geometric figures, numbers, Christ figures, persecuted innocents—to support his characterization of the "psychospiritual" nature of Hitchcockian suspense, which emphasizes the meliorist power of his heroes' human will to resist the misfortunes, temptations, and adversities that Hurley generally associates with EXPRESSIONISM. Therefore, Hitchcockian suspense is never merely casual or circumstantial: It entails a peculiarly moral, psychological, and spiritual testing ground for each of his souls in suspense and, by implicit analogy to "an Absolute Director," to Hitchcock's audiences. The director's four films for WARNER BROS.—*STRANGERS ON A TRAIN, I CONFESS, DIAL M FOR MURDER,* and *THE WRONG MAN*— are singled out as displaying "a psychospiritual realism not evident in his later PARAMOUNT pictures" that encapsulates Hitchcock's characteristic combination of "balanced realism and restless perfectionism." The appendices include two interviews with Hitchcock collaborators Janet LEIGH and Albert WHITLOCK, three letters from students who attended St. Ignatius at the same time as Hitchcock, and a generously annotated bibliography.

Hutchinson, Josephine (1903–1998)   American actress first cast as a child in *The Little Princess* (1917) who returned to the screen in 1934 after stage success with Eva Le Gallienne's Civic Repertory Company. Her specialty in movies and television was the sympathetic maternal type, a type she deftly parodied as the false Mrs. Townsend in *NORTH BY NORTHWEST.*

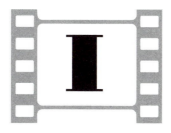

I Confess (Alternative titles: *Ich beichte, La loi du silence, Io confesso*) Warner Bros.-First National, 95 minutes, February 1953. **Producer:** Alfred Hitchcock; **Production associate:** Barbara Keon; **Director:** Alfred Hitchcock; **Screenplay:** George Tabori and William Archibald, based on *Nos deux consciences,* a play by Paul Anthelme; **Cinematographer:** Robert Burks; **Assistant director:** Don Page; **Art director:** Edward S. Haworth; **Set decoration:** George James Hopkins; **Costumes:** Orry-Kelly; **Production supervisor:** Sherry Shourds; **Sound:** Oliver S. Garretson; **Editor:** Rudi Fehr; **Technical advisers:** Father Paul La Couline and Oliver Tangvay; **Music composed and conducted by:** Dimitri Tiomkin; **Music supervisor:** Ray Heindorf; **Cast:** Montgomery Clift (Father Michael Logan), Anne Baxter (Ruth Grandfort), Karl Malden (Inspector Larue), Brian Aherne (Willy Robertson), O.E. Hasse (Otto Keller), Dolly Haas (Alma Keller), Roger Dann (Pierre Grandfort), Charles Andre (Father Millars), Judson Pratt (Murphy), Ovila Légaré (Villette), Gilles Pelletier (Father Benoit), Henry Corden (Farouche), Albert Godderis (night watchman), Nan Boardman (maid), Carmen Gingras, Renee Hudson (schoolgirls).

Hitchcock had dreamed of filming Paul ANTHELME's play *Nos deux consciences* ever since first discovering it in the thirties, but feared that its nexus—a Catholic priest's interdiction from revealing the secrets of the confessional, even a confession of murder that would exonerate himself or his loved ones—would be impossible to make compelling for non-Catholic audiences. One of his first acts on the formation of TRANSATLANTIC PICTURES in 1947 was to purchase the rights to the play and a treatment and screenplay by the playwright's nephew Louis Verneuil, and to prepare with Alma REVILLE a new screenplay. Though the director was not satisfied with his work, he was still intent on filming the property and had commissioned three more draft screenplays by the time Transatlantic dissolved. It was not until early 1952 that Reville suggested he return to the project. Even now there was more difficulty with the screenplay, which Samson RAPHAELSON declined to write. In the end Hitchcock turned to two playwrights, William ARCHIBALD for the scenario and George TABORI for the dialogue. Once the screenplay had been completed, however, the casting presented new problems. Anita Björk, the Swedish actress whom Hitchcock had engaged to play Ruth Grandfort, the former love interest whom the dead man had been blackmailing, arrived in Hollywood with a lover and an illegitimate child, and WARNER BROS., mindful of the public outcry that had driven Ingrid BERGMAN away, insisted she be replaced. Hitchcock chose an old friend, Anne BANCROFT, to play opposite Montgomery CLIFT. But Method star Clift, despite the talent that had made him one of the leading young actors of his day, was a poor fit for Hitchcock because his work was undermined by his heavy drinking and

Because he cannot break the secrecy of the confessional, the finger of suspicion points at Father Michael Logan (Montgomery Clift) in *I Confess*. *(National Film Society Archive)*

his dependence on his acting coach, and despite Hitchcock's zest in scouting and shooting evocative locations in Quebec, his 38th film, shot between August and October 1952, wrapped under a subdued aura. Whatever reservations the filmmakers may have felt about the project were justified by the outcome, which earned mixed reviews and a small profit, though becoming one of the Hitchcock films most highly regarded by the influential Eric ROHMER and Claude CHABROL.

As its title suggests, the film is structured by a series of highly equivocal confessions, beginning with the confession of murder that church sacristan Otto Keller, a frightened European refugee, makes to Father Michael Logan. Urged by his wife Alma to confess to the police, he refuses, citing the seal of the confessional that will keep his secret safe. At first intimidated by Logan's gravely virtuous demeanor

and the friendship he has offered the Kellers, Keller, who had disguised himself as a priest to rob the blackmailing Villette, sees that Logan's former relationship with Villette's married victim Ruth Grandfort has brought him under the suspicion of Inspector Larue and begins to plant evidence against Logan, who is duly arrested for the crime. Keller's behavior thus oscillates between a confession of guilt and a kind of anticonfession that seeks to hide his guilt by placing it on the very person from whom he has sought forgiveness, as if he were more desperate to hide his confession than the crime itself. The film continues to undermine the nominal opposition between confession and concealment by presenting a flashback that leaves it unclear whether Logan and Ruth had been lovers in the strict sense before he took his vows and by having the jury that finds him not guilty announce that they still attach "grave suspicion to the accused." Despite his acquittal, Father Logan leaves the courtroom in the manner of Christ being led off to crucifixion. The real guilt he will have to bear, the film suggests, is not legal but social, the universal assumption that although he has been acquitted, he has not been exonerated. When Alma, horrified at Logan's continuing ordeal, attempts to accuse her husband to the police, Keller shoots her, and she dies in Logan's arms asking forgiveness. Pursued by the police, Keller pours his scorn on Logan, whom he accuses, in a gesture that economically combines confession and anticonfession, of having given him up after all. In a final confrontation, Logan completes the sacrificial pattern of his faith by presenting himself unarmed to Keller, who is shot by the police as he aims his gun at Logan and dies making a final confession to the priest. Rohmer and Chabrol, citing the film's "majesty," take it as central to his career, as does Neil P. HURLEY; Donald SPOTO sees it as Hitchcock's testimonial to his wife of 25 years, another Catholic expatriate named Alma; but once the film had played its role in bringing Hitchcock to the attention of serious thematic analysis, most critics have followed Robin WOOD in ignoring the film in favor of the roughly contemporaneous *STRANGERS ON A TRAIN* and *REAR WINDOW.* The film's neglect may be attributed in large measure to its failure to observe two of Hitchcock's most fundamental rules, the importance of humor and of a strong villain. Its central irony, the way Logan's embrace of his priestly vocation makes him the perfect sacrificial victim, does not lend itself either to comedy (the film's few light-hearted moments, mostly concerning a bicycle-riding fellow priest, seem perfunctory and contrived) or even to the mordant wit Hitchcock had deployed in the otherwise similar NOTORIOUS and *Strangers on a Train*. Keller himself remains a relatively minor figure, never springing fully to life as an external embodiment of Logan's guilty sense of responsibility that provides the hero's true antagonist.

identification   Probably no filmmaker on either side of the Atlantic did as much to promote the importance of identification—audiences' empathetic sense of sharing a character's feelings or situation—as Hitchcock. The notion was central to his storytelling aesthetic, which systematically subordinated emotional displays from his actors and actresses to strategic camera movements and cuts that would encourage audiences to supply each character's emotional reactions by putting themselves in the character's place. In SABOTAGE, for example, he shot the scene in which Mrs. Verloc stabs her husband to death in a series of short, virtually wordless shots that left even his star, Sylvia SIDNEY, feeling certain that the scene was a failure until she saw the rushes. Because he was so dedicated to using the resources of narrative cinema to provoke emotional reactions, Hitchcock had little patience with Method-trained actors such as Montgomery CLIFT and Paul NEWMAN who had been taught to project a specific emotion for each shot and found it difficult to give him the neutral expressions he preferred to use as raw material for the identifications he sought.

In recent years the notion of identification has come under attack from theorists like Noël Carroll who fear that the term is used to cover too broad a range of relations (emotional empathy, situational empathy, wish fulfillment, perception of similarity) to be useful. It is important to note in this connection the special nature of Hitchcockian identification. PSYCHO has often been described as a textbook example of close identification between audiences and characters—in this case, Marion Crane, who is offered as an identification figure early on in the film (her only serious rival for audiences' empathy in the first half of the film, her boyfriend Sam Loomis, is subtly undermined by less-intimate lighting and blocking and greater camera distances throughout the first scene and then disappears until after her death) only to be murdered in a scene doubly shocking, as Robin WOOD and others have pointed out, not only because of its visceral ferocity but also because it deprives audiences of the figure on whom they have relied as their point of contact with the world of the film. Audiences who saw *Psycho* on its premiere in 1960 may have felt this way, but it is unlikely that contemporary audiences, watching the film through their prior experiences of *Scream, Psycho 2,* or Gus Van Sant's remake, identify with Marion in quite the same uncritical way. Instead of *identifying with* Marion, they *identify* her *as* the foreordained victim. But this double mode of identification, though it bars contemporary audiences from the experience presumably available to *Psycho's* original audiences, does not undermine but confirms the double nature of Hitchcockian identification because all Hitchcock's characters, even those closest to audiences' apprehensive solicitude, are types (the naïve innocent, the man on the run, the sinister underling) who are recognized as types from the beginning; though audiences may assign them, on the basis of a story's development, to successively different types (as Eve Kendall appears in NORTH BY NORTHWEST as the fortuitous helper, the love interest, the betrayer, the conflicted agent, and the damsel in distress), they always identify them as members of some type. Hence Hitchcock's films work to combine *identification with* and *identification as,* straddling the line between analytical detachment and uncritical empathy that keeps the audience pleasurably aware, even at the moments of greatest emotional intensity, that what they are involved in is a Hitchcock film.

identity, public and private   A primary reason that Hitchcock's heroes are vulnerable to the intrigues that sweep them up is their insecure fit with the world around them, either because that world does not accept them in the terms they project, as in DOWNHILL and EASY VIRTUE; because their confident sense of their public identities is erroneous, as in THE FARMER'S WIFE; or because the whole notion of a stable public identity is undermined by the ubiquity of theatrical self-presentation, as in MURDER! In Hitchcock's thrillers, this central split between the private identity to which his characters feel entitled and the public identity with which they are saddled is made more urgent by the higher stakes. Richard Hannay, seeking to complete Annabella Smith's secret mission before the police can arrest him for her murder in THE 39 STEPS, risks not only individual unhappiness but also danger to all England; Iris Henderson, frustrated when no one seems to believe her memory of Miss Froy in THE LADY VANISHES, risks not only individual rejection but also the life of Miss Froy and another state secret.

Hitchcock's American films probe this split ever more deeply. After attempting to use psychoanalysis to dramatize the split between conscious and unconscious motives, Hitchcock recast the split in social, moral, and political terms in NOTORIOUS, whose heroine's life depends on her unsavory reputation. Her father's Nazi past makes her attractive to the government agency that enlists her as a spy; her drinking and sexual licentiousness make her the natural prey of the passive-aggressive Devlin; and after her husband discovers her in the wine cellar with Devlin, her marriage and her safety come to depend on Sebastian's belief not only that she is a Nazi sympathizer but also that she is still in love with Devlin. Even her final rescue by Devlin depends on the fact that Sebastian and his mother cannot afford to reveal to their murderous colleagues their knowledge that she has been spying on them. Similarly, NORTH BY NORTHWEST adds a new dimension to the man-on-the-run story of The 39 Steps: The pursued innocent this time is mistaken for a nonexistent person so that he is doubled not only with the murderer he is mistaken for but also with a fictional character. To survive in the film's cold-war world, therefore, Roger Thornhill needs not only to vindicate his technical innocence in the eyes of the police but to establish an independent identity capable of distinguishing him from a nobody. By the time of FRENZY, the split

between public and private identities has assumed a chilling new turn: In a world everywhere marked by loathing and despair, the nominal innocent is just as prone to violent rage as the killer for whom he is mistaken; although Chief Inspector Oxford succeeds in clearing Richard Blaney's name, the final tableau indicates that Blaney is as capable of murder as the actual killer. It is a bleak resolution to a problem that had provided the narrative engine for so much of Hitchcock's work.

ideology During most of his career in England and America, Hitchcock was marked (and occasionally maligned, as by Michael BALCON in 1940) as a nonideological filmmaker, as against directors with overt political sympathies such as Frank Capra, John Ford, and George Stevens. Even though political espionage, one of his two most frequent subjects, implied an obvious political bias, his films were careful to leave their political enemies nameless. Mr. Memory is shot in THE 39 STEPS just as he is at the point of revealing the nationality of his employers; the spies in THE MAN WHO KNEW TOO MUCH (1934) and SABOTAGE never claim allegiance to any particular foreign government; SECRET AGENT is set in the safely closed period of World War I; and THE LADY VANISHES takes place in and near the mythical Central European land of Bandrika. As Sam P. SIMONE and Ina Rae Hark have noted, Hitchcock's films became far more overtly political when World War II broke out shortly after his departure from England. But even FOREIGN CORRESPONDENT and LIFEBOAT, his two most overtly political films apart from BON VOYAGE and AVENTURE MALGACHE, contain brief scenes that make a surprisingly strong case for their anti-Allied villains, and except for his East German thriller TORN CURTAIN, his later cold-war films from STRANGERS ON A TRAIN to TOPAZ seem to regard political ideology as either inconsequential or universally and undiscriminately corrupting. This apparent freedom from ideological bias stood Hitchcock in good stead with the generation of critics who sought to enshrine him as a filmmaker whose concern with universal questions of crime and punishment, good and evil, and the morality of guilt and justice was untainted by transitory partisan politics.

The 1970s saw the first steps in the construction of a new, ideological Hitchcock, an oppositional Hitchcock in the most radical sense of the term. In his pivotal 1976 essay "Ideology, Genre, Auteur: SHADOW OF A DOUBT," Robin WOOD argues both that the film's subversion of the comfortable bourgeois ideology its ending seems to endorse is "everywhere traceable to Hitchcock's presence" and that the film is "much more suggestive and significant a work than Hitchcock the bourgeois entertainer could ever have guessed." In Wood's reading, Hitchcock becomes, like the genre of the thriller, one among several determinants of ideology but not its creator or originator. Throughout the later essays in *Hitchcock's Films Revisited,* Wood struggles to reconcile his earlier auteurism, which prized Hitchcock precisely as the shaper of meanings, with his Marxism, which subordinated individual creators to the ideology that spoke through them. Other critics recreated Hitchcock's films as ideologically charged texts, not by recasting Hitchcock as a consciously partisan ideologue but by recasting the director as ideology's ventriloquist. Laura MULVEY and Tania MODLESKI opened Hitchcock's films to feminist readings by discovering a gender politics deeper than the director's conscious agency; Robert CORBER and Robert SAMUELS have opened the films to Queer Theory in similar ways. It has been left to Slavoj ŽIŽEK to deconstruct Hitchcock's films in the light of his reading of Jacques LACAN at the same time that he maintains the director's authorizing agency over their strategies of meaning. The tendency of recent film theory to find ideology speaking through filmmakers like Hitchcock, rather than vice versa, seems likely to continue.

Iles, Francis Pseudonym of Anthony Berkeley (born Anthony Berkeley Cox, 1893–1970), British mystery author, critic, and theorist. A journalist under his birth name, he first became known as Berkeley for his brainy detective novels starring Roger Sheringham, especially *The Poisoned Chocolates Case* (1929). This explosion of the Sheringham story "The Avenging Chance" turns into a full-blown parody of the detective-story conventions that Berkeley had done so much to institutionalize as the founder of London's Detection Club (which is satirized in the novel as the Crimes Circle Club) the year before. As Iles, he published four novels, beginning with *Malice Aforethought* (1931), submitting the participants in crimes to psychological analysis even as he continued to satirize the conventions of the genre. The second of these novels, *Before the Fact* (1932), was a study of murder from the viewpoint of the victim, Lina Aysgarth, who, as Iles memorably writes in his opening paragraph, "had lived with her husband for nearly eight years before she realized that she was married to a murderer." Growing gradually more certain that her husband Johnny is planning to murder her, Lina, still in love with him, passively allows him to go through with his plan, becoming, in her own words, an accessory before the fact of her own murder. The difficulties Hitchcock and RKO had in transforming this story into the film that became SUSPICION are legendary.

"Incident at a Corner" 27th episode of the NBC television series *Ford Startime,* broadcast April 5, 1960. **Producer:** Joan Harrison; **Associate producer:** Norman Lloyd; **Director:** Alfred Hitchcock; **Assistant director:** Hilton Green; **Screenplay:** Charlotte Armstrong, based on her short story; **Cinematographer:** John L. Russell; **Art director:** John Lloyd; **Set designer:** George Milo; **Editors:** Richard G. Wray and Edward W. Williams; **Music:** Frederick Herbert; **Cast:** Paul Hartman (James Medwick), Vera Miles (Janey Medwick), George Peppard (Pat Lawrence), Bob Sweeney (Uncle Jeffrey), Leora Dana (Mrs. Tawley), Philip Ober (Malcolm Tawley), Jack Albertson (Harry Crane), Alice Backes (Aunt Pauline), Charity Grace (Elsa Medwick), Warren Berlinger (Ron Tawley), Leslie Barrett (Batie), Mary Alan Hokanson (Mrs. Parker), Alexander Lockwood (Mr. Rigsby), Joe Flynn (Dr. Sidney Sinden), Jerry Paris (W.E. Grimes), Eve McVeagh (Georgi Clooney), Barbara Beaird (Mary Jane Ryder), Tyler McVey (Chief Taylor).

Hitchcock's only contribution to FORD STARTIME, a one-hour program that also marks his only television work in color, begins with several views of a scene between an angry mother and an elderly, inoffensive school-crossing guard. When the guard, James Medwick, is fired soon afterward because of a whispering campaign describing him as "a vicious old man," his incredulous granddaughter Janey sets out with her fiancé to clear his name. Making the rounds of the community they thought they had known, they eventually trace the accusations to their surprising source in the incident at the corner.

interviews According to Sidney GOTTLIEB, who has edited the invaluable *Hitchcock on Hitchcock: Selected Writings and Interviews,* Hitchcock gave his first interview in 1929 in connection with the recent release of *BLACKMAIL* and continued to be interviewed throughout the thirties. His persona in these interviews was remarkably consistent. He lamented the slow development of cinema as an art form; proclaimed the proscenium stage its enemy; identified lofty goals for the art of cinema; disclaimed his identification with the thriller genre as accidental and temporary; avowed a wish to film "authentic accounts of incidents in British life" such as the General Strike of 1926 instead of formula fiction; and blamed censors, studios, the public, and the economics of filmmaking for the commercialism of his work and of cinema generally. He presented himself as slightly impatient with the general run of filmed entertainment, including his own, and both eager to undertake and worthy of far more important artistic ventures than he had been entrusted.

Hitchcock the raconteur, the figure who had already dominated the director's published essays and articles for several years, did not emerge as a dominant presence in his interviews until after he came to America, where his lower-class Cockney inflections and his immitigable Englishness gave him a cachet he had lacked in his native land. As his extended association with the thriller made his earlier artistic aspirations ring increasingly hollow, the director, who eschewed press conferences and group interviews in favor of one-on-one settings in which he could charm and dominate his interlocutor, gradually developed a new persona, the ironic and oracular master of suspense who was as masterful an entertainer in interviews as on the screen. In support of this persona, he established a standing repertory of anecdotes about MACGUFFINS, about women in the back of a taxi, about his alleged contempt for actors, and about his delight in courting and resolving tech-

nical problems in his films (and incidentally illustrating his command of film technique) that he recycled from one interview to the next. Endlessly available for interviews on the release of each new film and endlessly amusing, he was endlessly interviewed, and it is no coincidence that the book that set the seal on his reputation as a serious artist was the series of interviews he had given François TRUFFAUT in 1962. The Hitchcock who emerges in conversation with Truffaut is a compendium of earlier Hitchcocks: a supremely commercial filmmaker who continues to blame Hollywood economics for his limited range; a humanist philosopher whose primary interest in his films, particularly his silent films, is narrowly technical; a dictatorial general who rarely speaks of his collaborators without criticism and even more rarely shares credit for any of his films' success (particularly not with screenwriters, whose contributions he passes over in virtual silence); the slyly ironic raconteur who seems intent on shocking the decorous Truffaut as he recounts all his favorite stories for his admiring interviewer. If subsequent writers from Gottlieb to Robert KAPSIS have been less inclined to take Truffaut's book as the definitive study it announces itself to be or indeed to take Hitchcock's word as an interview subject on practically any subject, they have recast the interviews as texts scarcely less intriguing than the films themselves.

Irene (1901–1962) American costume designer, born Irene Lenz-Gibbons. After a brief stint as a silent extra, she studied fashion design and opened a dress shop on the UCLA campus. By 1937, she was an established designer asked to work on such films as *Vogues of 1938* and *Shall We Dance?* In 1942, a year after designing the gowns for *MR. AND MRS. SMITH,* she became head of MGM's wardrobe department and remained there throughout the forties, working on more than 100 films before retiring to open a chain of boutiques.

irony Because Hitchcock's public persona, especially in his playful introductions to each segment of *ALFRED HITCHCOCK PRESENTS* and *THE ALFRED HITCHCOCK HOUR,* is clearly ironic not only in its disingenuousness but also in its contrast with the melodramatic intrigue of his fictions, it may seem unnecessary to suggest that the director has never had his due as an ironist. But although, as Sidney GOT-TLIEB notes, he has been analyzed as a humanist, a romantic, and a sadist, no one has yet produced a comprehensive study of Hitchcockian irony.

Irony is central to Hitchcock's films in ways that have never properly been realized. In a 1934 essay written in connection with *THE MAN WHO KNEW TOO MUCH*, the director condemned most British films as "stodgy" because of their imprudent determination to maintain a single unmodulated tone throughout. American films, he noted by contrast, achieved much broader emotional effects and incorporated many more possibilities for surprise, by mixing drama with comedy, even farce. His new film, he promised, would follow the Americans' lead on this point. Indeed it has become a platitude of Hitchcock criticism that virtually all the director's most successful films except *VERTIGO* depend on incorporating a broad range of tones. There is much merit in this observation, but it makes Hitchcock's films, despite their unmatched narrative pull, sound a bit miscellaneous in their variety. A more positive and more incisive way of describing their special achievement is to recognize their dependence on irony as an organizing trope. Hitchcock's irony begins in motivic contrasts—between comedy and farce, between what characters know and what audiences know, between the routines of the normal world and the melodramatic irruption of intrigue, between Hitchcock's avuncular physical presence and his adolescent sense of fun—but becomes the armature for most of his successful films. A film such as *CHAMPAGNE* is full of small ironies, from the lovers' quarrels aboard the ship that she has commanded her father's airplane to meet to the fantasies it hints about the sinister but ultimately benign older man who is watching the heroine, and is shaped by a single structuring irony: the heroine's false belief that she must support herself and the millionaire father she thinks has gone broke; it fails not because it is insufficiently ironic but because its ironies are insufficiently integrated and thus finally meaningless. The pattern is repeated in *FOREIGN CORRESPONDENT*, which is structured as a series of effectively ironic sequences (the picturesque wind-

mill that hides a nest of spies, the assassinated diplomat who is really alive, the peace organization that is a front for espionage, the hired killer who ends up killing himself) in search of any larger ironic vision consistent with the film's intermittently rousing patriotism. *LIFEBOAT* is more successful in focusing its story on a single powerful irony: the susceptibility of liberal democracies to authoritarian rule by virtue of their very liberalism.

But the ironies that shape Hitchcock's most penetrating films are less often political than moral, psychological, social, representational, or more broadly relational, as in the intimacy first sought, then rejected in horror, between Charlie Newton and her beloved, murderous uncle in *SHADOW OF A DOUBT*, or between the earnest adulterer who wishes his wife were dead in *STRANGERS ON A TRAIN* and the charming villain who is only too happy to oblige. *MURDER!* and *STAGE FRIGHT* both take theatricality as a radical metaphor for the characters' duplicitous or disingenuous behavior; *REAR WINDOW* invites audiences to savor the irony of a man so averse to romantic commitment that he becomes deeply invested in proving that his neighbor has murdered his nagging wife. When later Hitchcock films such as *SPELLBOUND* or *UNDER CAPRICORN* or *I CONFESS* or *TOPAZ* falter, it is not because they are not ironic enough—though all four of these films restrict themselves to a narrower range of tones than most of Hitchcock's work—but because their leading ironies—a man must turn detective to unearth the secrets of his own unconscious; the dissolute aristocrat who ran off to Australia with her own groom is the murderer whose guilt he has taken on himself; a priest cannot save his life by revealing the confession of murder made to him; international politics poison every intimate relationship they touch regardless of particular partisan sympathies—cannot be compellingly visualized or dramatized. When Hitchcock's films succeed most completely, it is because their structuring ironies are powerful enough to pull together many episodes, as in *NORTH BY NORTHWEST*, or because they can motivate two tones as dissonant as the horror and black comedy of *PSYCHO*, or because they can sustain a single, fatally dreamlike mood for more than two hours, as when Scottie

Ferguson falls in love with the woman he is supposed to be protecting, not realizing that she has been manufactured expressly to make him try and fail to save her—or that he is about to repeat the process himself. Hence *Vertigo* is not an exception to the rule of Hitchcockian irony because the contrast of tones the director commended in 1934 is only one possible way of revealing the irreducible inconsistencies that underlie all representation, all desire, and all action.

Irvine, Robin (1901–1933)   British leading man of the twenties who played key roles in *DOWN-HILL*, in which his Tim Wakeley made the pact of loyalty that led his friend Roddy Berwick to be expelled from school for Tim's dalliance with the waitress Mabel, and *EASY VIRTUE*, in which he plays the romantic lead John Whittaker. His subsequent career was cut short by his early death.

"I Saw the Whole Thing"   4th episode of *The Alfred Hitchcock Hour*, broadcast October 11, 1962. **Producer:** Joan Harrison; **Associate producer:** Gordon Hessler; **Director:** Alfred Hitchcock; **Assistant director:** Ronnie Rondell; **Screenplay:** Henry Slesar, based on a short story by Henry Cecil; **Cinematographer:** Benjamin H. Kline; **Art director:** Martin Obzina; **Set designers:** John McCarthy and Glen Daniels; **Costumes:** Vincent Dee; **Editors:** David O'Connell and Edward W. Williams; **Music:** Lyn Murray and Stanley Williams; **Cast:** John Forsythe (Michael Barnes), Kent Smith (Jerry O'Hara), Evans Evans (Penny Sanford), John Fiedler (Malcolm Stuart), Philip Ober (Colonel John Hoey), Claire Griswold (Joanne Dowling), William Newell (Sam Peterson), John Zaremba (Richard Anderson), Barney Phillips (Lt. Sweet), Willis Bouchey (Judge Neilson), Rusty Lane (Judge Martin), Billy Wells (George Peabody), Robert Karnes (police sergeant), Maurice Manson (Dr. Palmer), Ken Harp (bailiff), Anthony Jochim (jury foreman).

The only episode of *The Alfred Hitchcock Hour* Hitchcock directed, dating from its first season, tells the story of Michael Barnes, a mystery writer accused of killing a cyclist in a hit-and-run accident en route to the hospital with his pregnant wife. Though the witnesses all agree on the events surrounding the accident, Barnes, defending himself with some advice from a lawyer friend, leads each of them on cross-examination into fallacies and inconsistencies. His case seemingly won, he takes the stand briefly in his defense, but he mysteriously refuses to answer questions put to him by the prosecutor under cross-examination. A brief sequel after he is acquitted reveals why: Not he but his wife had been driving, and he continued on, taking her to the hospital to have her baby and then taking responsibility for driving to shield her from the trial.

Iwerks, Ub (1901–1971)   American animator, born Ubbe Ert Iwwerks. Working as a commercial artist in Kansas City in 1919, he formed first a friendship and then a company with his colleague Walt DISNEY, and became the principal animator of Disney's early shorts, hundreds of which he produced or directed. He left Disney in 1930 to strike out on his own, but when his characters Flip the Frog and Willy Whopper failed to stir the public, his studio closed in 1936, and he went to work for Columbia, returning to Disney in 1940 to concentrate on the special photographic effects that made possible live-action/animated films like *Song of the South* (1946). On his last film assignment, *THE BIRDS*, he headed the team responsible for the mattework and animation effects that made it look as if the birds were attacking people. He won an Academy Award in 1959 for improvements he had pioneered in optical printing and a second in 1964 for his work in color traveling matte composite cinematography.

Jade, Claude (1948–) Stage-trained French actress who made the transition to films when François TRUFFAUT cast her as Antoine Doinel's lover Christine in *Baisers volés* (1967) (she later played his wife in its two sequels, *Domicile conjugal,* 1970, and *L'Amour en fuite,* 1979). Shortly before he married her in 1968, Truffaut introduced her to Hitchcock, who cast her as Michèle Picard in TOPAZ, one of her few English-language films. She has however gone on to more than 80 roles, mostly in French film and television.

Jamaica Inn (Alternative titles: *Riff-Piraten, La Taverne de la Jamaïque, La taverna della Giamaica*) Mayflower, Associated British, 100 minutes, May 1939. **Producers:** Erich Pommer and Charles Laughton; **Director:** Alfred Hitchcock; **Screenplay:** Sidney Gilliat and Joan Harrison, based on the novel by Daphne du Maurier; **Continuity:** Alma Reville; **Additional dialogue:** J.B. Priestley; **Cinematographer:** Harry Stradling, in collaboration with Bernard Knowles; **Set decoration:** Tom Morahan; **Costumes:** Molly McArthur; **Makeup:** Ern Westmore; **Production manager:** Hugh Perceval; **Special effects:** Harry Watt; **Sound:** Jack Rogerson; **Editor:** Robert Hamer; **Music:** Eric Fenby; **Musical direction:** Frederick Lewis; **Cast:** Charles Laughton (Sir Humphrey Pengallan), Horace Hodges (his butler Chadwyck), Hay Petrie (his groom Sam), Frederick Piper (his agent Davis), Herbert Lomas (his tenant), Clare Greet (tenant Granny Tremany), William Devlin (his tenant); *as Pengallan's friends:* Jeanne de

Casalis, Mabel Terry Lewis (Lady Beston), Bromley Davenport (Ringwood), George Curzon, Basil Radford (Lord George); *Joss Merlyn's household:* Leslie Banks (Merlyn), Marie Ney (Patience, his wife), Maureen O'Hara (Mary Yellan, his niece); *as Merlyn's gang:* Emlyn Williams (Harry the Pedlar), Wylie Watson (Salvation Watkins), Morland Graham (Sea Lawyer Sydney), Edwin Greenwood (Dandy), Mervyn Johns (Thomas), Stephen Haggard (the Boy, Willie Penhill), Robert Newton (Jem Trehearne), Robert Adair (Captain Murray), Aubrey Mather (coach driver), O.B. Clarence, Marie Ault (coach passengers), Mary Jerrold (Miss Black, housekeeper), John Longden (Captain Johnson), Roy Frumkes, Archie Harradine, Harry Lane, Sam Lee, Alan Lewis, Philip Ray, Peter Scott, A. George Smith.

On the eve of departing for America on the 1938 trip that would climax with his signing a contract with David O. SELZNICK to direct a single film that turned out to be *REBECCA,* Hitchcock, despite his aversion to costume pictures, agreed with MAYFLOWER PRODUCTIONS, a partnership between Erich POMMER and Charles LAUGHTON that had already produced two vehicles for Laughton, to direct a film based on Daphne DU MAURIER's previous novel, *Jamaica Inn.* On returning to England, Hitchcock read a screenplay Mayflower had commissioned from Clemence DANE and immediately tried to withdraw from the project, but Laughton, an old acquaintance, insisted that he honor the contract. Other difficulties soon arose. Laughton decided that instead of playing Joss Merlyn, he would give that role to Leslie BANKS and play the story's villain, a Cornish parson who turns out to be the head of a smuggling ring responsible for wrecking and plundering passing ships. Because the Hays Office forbade negative portrayals of clergymen, the role was changed from a parson to the local squire, and because Laughton was clearly the film's star attraction, his part was expanded and his involvement in the smuggling (which could hardly have been kept secret for long) revealed earlier in the story. Although the rewriting offered Hitchcock the opportunity to work with Laughton's old friend J.B. PRIESTLEY, whom he had long admired, the novelist

announced publicly that she was dissatisfied with such a free adaptation, insisting that Selznick treat *Rebecca* with greater circumspection. When shooting began in September 1938, Laughton proved an equally intransigent performer, demanding that Hitchcock shoot only closeups, backgrounds, and scenes without him until he had found the right walk for Squire Pengallan. Although Hitchcock told the press that he expected the film to provide opportunities for the sorts of action sequences he relished, he completed the filming in October with more relief than enthusiasm, and like all his costume dramas, it was an inert piece of filmmaking, as the same reviewers who had rhapsodized over his preceding

Sir Humphrey Pengallan (Charles Laughton, center)is framed by Jem Trehearne (Robert Newton) and Joss Merlyn (Leslie Banks) in this lobby display card for *Jamaica Inn*. *(National Film Society Archive)*

film, *THE LADY VANISHES*, were quick to point out. The film turned a small profit, but it cannot have made Hitchcock more reluctant to leave his homeland behind.

Like du Maurier's novel, Hitchcock's 23rd film is first and foremost a drama of homelessness for its orphaned heroine, sent from Ireland to Cornwall to live with relatives she has never met and finding instead of a proper home a neo-gothic nightmare of intrigue. What the screenplay adds to the novel is a structuring opposition of false homes, as Mary Yellan, en route to the inn kept by her Aunt Patience's husband Joss, stops for help at Squire Pengallan's, where she finds bright company, rich furnishings, and a host suspiciously epicurean in his tastes. From then on she oscillates between the world of Jamaica Inn, which is overrun by lowlife ruffians, to the leering care of the Squire, who treats her, not as the lady she thinks she is but as one more object, like the figurine or the horse he had so highly prized just before her arrival, to add to his collection. In offering her a choice between too little culture and too much, the film seems determined to sever all ties between acculturation and genuinely social behavior and to offer its heroine no alternative to commodity status. The exception to these grim alternatives is Jem Trehearne, the member of Merlyn's gang of smugglers and jackals who is actually an undercover peace officer. After Mary saves Jem from hanging by the gang and they escape the gang together, their romance seems assured. So it is also after further adventures, deaths, and revelations, though the performances of Robert NEWTON, who had not yet found the hammy range that would serve him so well in roles such as Long John Silver, and Maureen O'HARA, whose fighting spirit seems to conceal not demure sexuality but an amateurishly narrow acting range, are completely overshadowed not only by the antics of Laughton but also by Horace HODGES as Pengallan's long-suffering butler and the programmatically colorful gang members who infest Jamaica Inn. Despite occasional touches of gothic atmosphere, the film demonstrates the truth of Hitchcock's dictum that his costume pictures failed because he never knew what the characters inside the costumes were thinking or feeling; because it never creates any sense of normalcy that its quaint horrors might be thought to disrupt,

there never seems to be anything substantial at stake for the orphaned Mary or her blandly roguish lover.

Jarre, Maurice (1924–) French composer. After training at the Paris Conservatoire and directing the orchestra of the Théâtre National Populaire, he began to score short films for Alain Resnais and Georges Franju, working in features from the mid-fifties. Although he won three Oscars for epics he scored for David Lean—*Lawrence of Arabia* (1962), *Doctor Zhivago* (1965), and *A Passage to India* (1984)—his film music is typically intimate rather than grandly scaled, as in his other Academy Award nominations: *Les Dimanches de ville d'Avray* (1963); the song "Marmalade, Molasses, and Honey" from *The Life and Times of Judge Roy Bean* (1972); *The Message* (1976); *Witness* (1985); *Gorillas in the Mist* (1988); and *Ghost* (1990). His score for *TOPAZ* combines both public flourishes, especially in its title music, and reticence.

Jarvis, E(dward) B. British editor who cut more than three dozen films, including *STAGE FRIGHT*, for the home industry from 1930 to 1963.

Jeans, Isabel (1891–1985) British stage actress who made her West End debut in 1909. She appeared in some 30 films from 1917, retiring more than 50 years later. Her early roles were typically aristocratic ingenues, a type she played against as the promiscuous actress Julia in *DOWNHILL* and scandalous divorcée Larita Filton in *EASY VIRTUE*. By the time of *SUSPICION*, she was playing character versions of her earlier star persona like Mrs. Newsham. The best known of her later screen roles was the heroine's imperious Aunt Alicia in *Gigi* (1958). Former wife of actor Claude RAINS.

Jefferson, Ross British actor whose sole screen credit is as one of the 12 jurors in *MURDER!*

Jeffrey, R.E. Dyspeptic British actor who played bits in two films, both for Hitchcock: the jury foreman who can be seen practicing his capital G (for "Guilty") during deliberations in *MURDER!*, and the first stranger in *THE SKIN GAME*.

Jepson, Selwyn (1899–1989) British mystery novelist and screenwriter, a veteran of both World Wars, who published some two dozen detective and suspense novels, which he described as "fairy stories for adults," from 1922 to 1971. The first of his six novels starring amateur sleuth Eve Gill, *Man Running* (1948; U.S. title *Outrun the Constable*) served as the basis for STAGE FRIGHT.

Jewell, Estelle American actress whose only screen credit is Charlie Newton's girlfriend in *SHADOW OF A DOUBT.*

Jochim, Anthony (1892–1978) General-purpose American actor of the fifties and sixties who filled out the casts in some 40 films and television programs, including his role as jury foreman in the ALFRED HITCHCOCK HOUR segment "I SAW THE WHOLE THING."

Johns, Mervyn (1899–1992) Mild-mannered Welsh character actor, onstage from 1923, who appeared as Joss Merlyn's henchman Thomas in *JAMAICA INN* a few years after making his film debut in 1935. Perhaps the most memorable of his 70 film and television roles is Walter Craig, the bedeviled architect in *Dead of Night* (1945).

Johnson, J(oseph) McMillan (1912–1990) American art director who trained as an architect before going to work for David O. SELZNICK in 1938. He served as a sketch artist on *Gone With the Wind* and by 1942 rose to art director on *To Be Or Not to Be,* a capacity in which he continued for some 15 films, including *REAR WINDOW* and the Oscar-nominated *TO CATCH A THIEF.* An Oscar nominee as well for his art direction of *The Facts of Life* (1960), *Mutiny on the Bounty* (1962), *The Greatest Story Ever Told* (1965), and *Ice Station Zebra* (1968), he also designed the visual effects for two dozen other films from 1948 to 1971, sharing a special-effects Oscar for *Portrait of Jennie* (1948).

Johnson, Noel (1916–1999) Authoritative British character actor who usually played distinguished-looking gents in some 30 films and television programs from 1950 to 1995. He gave an aristocratic touch to the unpleasantly sordid conversation about rape and murder that goes on as Richard Blaney drinks his lunch in FRENZY.

Jones, Barry (1893–1981) Stage-trained British actor who graduated from playing Henry Doyle, the junior-grade thief in NUMBER SEVENTEEN, to three dozen later roles, from Aristotle in *Alexander the Great* (1956) and Count Rostov in *War and Peace* (1956) to the voice of Lord Haw-Haw in *Twelve O'Clock High* (1949).

Jones, Carolyn (1929–1983) Versatile American actress with stage experience. Born Carolyn Baker, she worked as a disk jockey before entering films in 1952. Among her early supporting roles were Pamela Waring, the secretary in the ALFRED HITCHCOCK PRESENTS episode "The Cheney Vase" (1955), and Jo McKenna's London friend Cindy Fontaine in THE MAN WHO KNEW TOO MUCH (1956). She was nominated for an Academy Award for her performance as the offbeat existentialist in *The Bachelor Party* (1957), but her signature role was Morticia Addams in *The Addams Family* (1964–65).

Jones, Hannah Fluffy, stage-trained British actress, a specialist in dithering old landladies. Of her seven film credits, four are in Hitchcock films, as Julia's dresser in DOWNHILL, Crewe's determinedly hard-of-hearing landlady in BLACKMAIL, Ted and Doucie Markham's landlady Mrs. Didsome in MURDER!, and Fred and Emily Hill's landlady Mrs. Porter in RICH AND STRANGE.

Jones, Henry (1912–1999) Saturnine American character actor, often in darkly comic supporting roles. Onstage from 1938, he made his film debut in 1943 and television debut in 1949, going on to play hundreds of roles, darkly comic, quietly sinister, or blandly ordinary. He appeared in five episodes of ALFRED HITCHCOCK PRESENTS—as the well-meaning neighbor Wally Long in "De Mortuis" (1956); the innocent patsy Harry Parker in "Nightmare in 4-D" (1957); the put-upon taxidermist George Tiffany in "The West Warlock Time Capsule" (1957); the business executive John Treadwell, whose mother is such a problem in "The Blessington Method" (1959); and the embezzling retiree Miles Cheever in "Profit-Sharing Plan" (1962)—and once in THE ALFRED HITCHCOCK HOUR, as murder-minded philanderer Alex Morrow in "The World's Oldest Motive" (1965). But his most memorable two minutes onscreen are his chilling two-speech performance as the sadistic coroner in VERTIGO.

Jordan, Ted (1924–) American actor whose 50 supporting roles and bits, 1946–80, included the dental patient Mr. Evans in the ALFRED HITCHCOCK PRESENTS episode "MRS. BIXBY AND THE COLONEL'S COAT."

Jourdan, Louis (1919–) Stage-trained French film star, born Louis Gendre. Although he made his screen debut in 1939, his career was interrupted by the outbreak of war, and he and his brothers joined the Underground after their father was arrested by the Gestapo. Stalemated by his refusal to appear in Nazi propaganda films, his career was rekindled by David O. SELZNICK, who cast him as the mysterious valet André Latour in THE PARADINE CASE. His dark, rather inexpressive good looks served him well in similarly opaque romantic roles in other American and international films, from Stefan Brand in *Letter from an Unknown Woman* (1948) to Rodolphe Boulanger in *Madame Bovary* (1949), though he would show more animation in his best-known role, Gaston Lachaille in *Gigi* (1958).

Junge, Alfred (1886–1964) Distinguished German-born art director who designed sets for the Berlin State Theater and State Opera before joining UFA in 1920. In Britain by the end of the decade, he was credited as art director on some two dozen films, including WALTZES FROM VIENNA, THE MAN WHO KNEW TOO MUCH (1934), and YOUNG AND INNOCENT. In the forties he began a fruitful collaboration with Michael Powell and Emeric Pressburger as production designer of such films as *The Life and Death of Colonel Blimp* (1943), *Stairway to Heaven* (1946), and *Black Narcissus* (1947), for which he won an Academy Award. From the late forties to the early fifties, he headed the art department of MGM's British studios.

Juno and the Paycock (Alternative titles: *The Shame of Mary Boyle* [U.S.], *Giuone e il Pavone*) British International, Wardour & F, 85 minutes, December 1929. **Producer:** John Maxwell; **Director:** Alfred Hitchcock; **Adaptation:** Alfred Hitchcock from the play by Sean O'Casey; **Scenario:** Alma Reville; **Cinematographer:** J.J. Cox; **Art director:** J. Marchant; **Assistant director:** Frank Mills; **Editor:** Emile de Ruelle; **Sound:** C. Thornton; **Cast:** Barry Fitzgerald (The Orator), Maire O'Neil (Mrs. Maisie Madigan), Edward Chapman (Captain Jack Boyle), Sidney Morgan ("Joxer" Daly), Sara Allgood (Mrs. Boyle, "Juno"), John Laurie (Johnny Boyle), Dave Morris (Jerry Devine), Kathleen O'Regan (Mary Boyle), John Longden (Charles Bentham), Denis Wyndham (The Mobiliser), Fred Schwartz (Mr. Kelly).

Fond as Hitchcock was of Sean O'CASEY's plays, the extent of his fondness for the project that was to become his 11th film is the subject of some debate: Donald SPOTO says that he was "unenthusiastic about the next job [John] MAXWELL had for him," but John Russell TAYLOR calls the film "something which [Hitchcock] specifically wanted to do." After opening at Dublin's Abbey Theater in 1924, this deeply Irish play had enjoyed two runs between 1925 and 1927 totaling more than 250 London performances, with the cast remaining nearly constant throughout. Hitchcock retained three key members of the London production: Sara ALLGOOD as Juno, her sister Maire O'NEIL as Mrs. Madigan, and Sidney MORGAN as the villainous Joxer Daly. In addition, he invited Kathleen O'REGAN, the first London Mary, to reprise her role and Barry FITZGERALD, who had created the role of Captain Boyle opposite Allgood in 1924, to play the role of the Orator in the new prologue O'Casey wrote for the film. What appealed to him in the film, Hitchcock told François TRUFFAUT, was the "blend of humor and tragedy" in its story of the Boyles, a family headed by an alcoholic husband and a long-suffering wife caught up unwillingly in the Troubles by the political activities of their son Johnny. Though Charles Bentham, a visiting lawyer, brings news of an inheritance that drives Captain Boyle, the "paycock," and his Juno to a rare spending spree, an error revealed in the will drawn up by Bentham (who has meanwhile seduced Mary Boyle away from her swain Jerry

Hitchcock prepares to shoot a scene from *Juno and the Paycock*. Sara Allgood is in the foreground, facing right. Alma Reville stands to the left of the fireplace, cinematographer Jack Cox to the left of the camera. *(National Film Society Archive)*

Devine and impregnated her) leaves Boyle disappointed in his hopes for his daughter and himself and his wife shattered by the news that Johnny is to be executed for informing against the insurgent republicans. Critics were rapturous in their reception—entirely too rapturous for the director, who felt to the end of his life that his literal transcription of the play was winning him praise for someone else's achievement. O'Casey, by contrast, was so pleased by the adaptation that he proposed a second collaboration to Hitchcock, and the screenplay he wrote eventually became the stage play *Within the Gate*.

Despite Hitchcock's dismissal of the film as canned theater, Maurice YACOWAR has noted several

key changes apart from the new prologue, of which the most important are a new ending that aims for pathos instead of black comedy—the film lingers on the grieving Juno instead of showing Boyle returning home too drunk to realize that his son is dead—and a redefinition of Mary Boyle as more conventional and less independent so that her rebellion now seems less a matter of the fresh generational values echoed by her neurotically flawed brother and more an unlucky failure of domestic virtue. The chief success of the film, as its early reviewers realized, was its success, despite these softenings, in preserving so much of the flavor and atmosphere of O'Casey's play. But Hitchcock, who had never sought success as an adapter, did not welcome it when it came, and told Truffaut that "from a creative viewpoint it was not a pleasant experience. . . . It had nothing to do with cinema." In at least one regard he was more accurate than he knew: The film is one of the few Hitchcock adaptations (along with SABOTAGE, SUSPICION, and perhaps REBECCA) that is clearly inferior to its literary source.

Jympson, John British editor, active from 1958 on a wide variety of projects from *A Hard Day's Night* (1964) to FRENZY, and more recently from *A Fish Called Wanda* (1988) to *In and Out* (1997).

Kaganski, Serge French journalist, critic for the weekly *Les Inrockuptibles* and author of the Pocket Archives volume *Alfred Hitchcock* (Art Publishers, 2000), in which an extensive, nontechnical essay surveying Hitchcock's leading concerns serves to introduce 150 pages of stills, publicity photographs, and posters.

Kahn, Florence (1878–1951) British stage actress, widow of Sir Herbert Beerbohm Tree, whose only screen credit is as Mrs. Caypor, wife of the suspected spy in *SECRET AGENT*.

Kalmus, Natalie (1892–1965) First wife, born Natalie Dunfee, of Herbert Kalmus, inventor of the Technicolor process and founder and head of the Technicolor Company. As Technicolor consultant credited on all films using the process from 1933 to the expiration of the patents in 1949, she was listed on hundreds of films. *ROPE* and *UNDER CAPRICORN*, Hitchcock's first two color films, were among her last.

Kapsis, Robert E. American film scholar, professor of Sociology and Film Studies at Queens College, CUNY, and at the CUNY Graduate Center. His study *Hitchcock: The Making of a Reputation* (University of Chicago Press, 1992) focuses on the choreography of the director's transformation from popular entertainer to serious artist at the hands of

François TRUFFAUT, Andrew SARRIS, the UNIVERSAL publicity machine, and the obligingly voluble director himself. Instead of assuming that an artist's reputation is earned through the success of his art, Kapsis argues that the consolidation of a reputation determines the contexts in which an aspiring artist's individual projects are interpreted and evaluated. He traces Universal's delicate attempt to promote the director of *THE BIRDS* to major artistic status without endangering his valuable reputation as a reliable entertainer and the results of this campaign in the popular press, as reviewers responded by reevaluating Hitchcock's career and readjusting their expectations of his newest releases. Instead of closely analyzing specific Hitchcock texts, Kapsis treats his unfolding career as a text to be analyzed, comparing it in turn to the careers, for example, of Fritz LANG (less successfully self-promoting), Brian DE PALMA (not taken seriously until he moved outside thrillers), and, most surprisingly, Vladimir Horowitz (another artist who consolidated his reputation by moving to a new production company that succeeded in promoting his recordings as entries in the artist's own genre, Horowitz recitals rather than Beethoven recordings). Kapsis served as executive producer and director of *Multimedia Hitchcock,* an interactive display of video and audio clips highlighting Hitchcock's life and best-known collaborators, musical cues and clips from many of his films (including Hitchcock's cameo appearances) and television segments and cast and production credits for all of them, articles and essays by Hitchcock and Hitchcock scholars, and marketing materials for PSYCHO and *The Birds.* The display was first installed in the Museum of Modern Art in New York and the Academy of Motion Picture Arts and Sciences in Beverly Hills in conjunction with an exhibition celebrating Hitchcock's centennial in 1999; a DVD version, *Multimedia Hitchcock: The Master and His Legacy—100 Years,* was released the following year.

Karnes, Robert (1917–1979)   Rugged American supporting actor who debuted in *The Best Years of Our Lives* (1946) and went on to play scores of tough or outdoorsy types in films and (more often) television programs. He appeared five times in ALFRED HITCHCOCK PRESENTS—as suspicious café owner Ed Mungo in "A Little Sleep" (1957), Sgt. Henderson in "The Safe Place" (1958), Ted the cop in "Escape to Sonoita" (1960), Mr. Simon in "Coming, Mama" (1961), a police sergeant in "The Right Kind of Medicine" (1961)—and three times in THE ALFRED HITCHCOCK HOUR, as the police sergeants in "I SAW THE WHOLE THING," "How to Get Rid of Your Wife" (1963), and "Change of Address" (1964).

Kaska, Kathleen   American grade-school teacher, author of *The Alfred Hitchcock Triviography & Quiz Book* (Renaissance, 1999), whose general quizzes on the director, along with specific quizzes on each of the films, are laid out in true-false or multiple-choice format. The volume, rife with errors about film titles, actors, and running times, concludes with a brief chronology, filmography, and videography, a bibliography, and information about Hitchcock-related websites.

Kauffer, E. McKnight   British graphic designer who created the decorative intertitle cards for THE LODGER.

Kazanjian, Howard (G.)   Assistant director on a half-dozen films and television programs, the last of them FAMILY PLOT, who graduated to executive producer of *Raiders of the Lost Ark* (1981) and pro-

ducing *Return of the Jedi* (1983), among a dozen other action films and series.

Kedrova, Lila (1918–2000)   Splendidly uninhibited Russian-born character actress whose family fled to France during her childhood. In German and French productions from 1953, she won an Academy Award for her supporting role as Madame Hortense in *Zorba the Greek* (1964), her first English-language film, and was soon thereafter given a showy extended cameo as Madame Luchinska, the gamine, pathetic would-be refugee in TORN CURTAIN. Though she rarely appeared in later Hollywood films, she continued to act into her seventies.

Keen, Malcolm (1887–1970)   Square-jawed British stage actor in occasional films from 1917. He created the role of Charles Hillcrest in John GALSWORTHY's play *The Skin Game* and reprised the role for the 1920 film, though not for Hitchcock's remake. But he had important and varied roles in three Hitchcock silents: as Fear o' God, the spectral hermit who takes in Beatrice in THE MOUNTAIN EAGLE; Joe Betts, the bulldog police detective in THE LODGER; and judge Philip Christian, the tormented adulterer in THE MANXMAN. Sharp-eyed British audiences could still catch him 30 years later in *Francis of Assisi* (1961) and *Life for Ruth* (1962) and as Duncan in a 1960 television *Macbeth.*

Keene, William (J.) (1919–1992)   American television actor on the small screen from 1958 as a police officer in the ALFRED HITCHCOCK PRESENTS segment "LAMB TO THE SLAUGHTER" and dozens of later roles through 1971.

Kelleher, Brian   Sports and entertainment writer, former corporate publicist, who collaborated with John MCCARTY in writing *Alfred Hitchcock Presents: An Illustrated Guide to the Ten-Year Television Career of the Master of Suspense* (St. Martin's, 1985), a segment-by-segment survey of ALFRED HITCHCOCK PRESENTS and THE ALFRED HITCHCOCK HOUR that reviews the background of the two programs, identifies the leading members of their production team (from producer Joan HARRISON to James ALLARDICE, who wrote Hitchcock's opening and closing monologues), and provides a summary and highlights of the cast for each of the series' 266 episodes.

Kelley, (W.) Wallace American cinematographer who did aerial, process, and second-unit work on 16 films through VERTIGO, on which he is credited with the process photography, and then turned lighting cinematographer on another two dozen films from *The Young Captives* (1959) to *Which Way to the Front?* (1970) while continuing some second-unit work.

Kellum, Terry American sound recordist, born Theron O. Kellum. At RKO from 1933 until the studio closed in 1958, he served as sound engineer or recorder for nearly 100 films, including NOTORIOUS.

Kelly, Grace (Grimaldi, Princess of Monaco) (1928–1982) American movie star, best known as Princess Grace and, before that, as the quintessential Hitchcock BLONDE. Onstage from age 10, she became a model while attending the American Academy of Dramatic Arts. Following her adult Broadway debut in 1949, she soon went to Hollywood, where the cool beauty she displayed in *Fourteen Hours* (1951) and *High Noon* (1952) quickly made her a star. Nominated for an Academy Award for her performance as aspiring adulteress Linda Nordley in *Mogambo* (1953), she virtually reprised the role without Clark Gable or the jungle in DIAL M FOR MURDER. When Hitchcock cast her in his next film, REAR WINDOW, he asked screenwriter John Michael HAYES to get to know her to write more congenially for her character, and Hayes, discovering a sense of humor that her earlier films had ignored, allowed it free rein in *Rear Window* (in which she closes the blinds on L.B. Jefferies's inveterate snooping with the remark, "Show's over for tonight," and then adds, displaying the frothy nightgown in her overnight case, "Preview of coming attractions") and TO CATCH A THIEF (in which she ambushes Cary GRANT's reformed cat burglar, whom she had ignored all evening while he chatted with her mother, with a smoldering good-night kiss). Kelly had already given an Oscar-winning performance as the devoted wife of an alcoholic Bing Crosby in *The Country Girl* (1954) when she first heard of Prince Rainier during a break from location shooting on *To Catch a Thief* by asking Hayes whose gardens were in the background. The following year, she met the prince at the Cannes Film Festival, and they were married in 1956, soon after her final film, *High Society*. Hitchcock long cherished the dream that the star he had nurtured would return to the screen, and at least once, considering a comeback in MARNIE, she went so far as to ask the advice of the citizens of Monaco. But a referendum on the subject was soundly defeated, presumably by voters who did not relish the prospect of their prince's wife returning to the screen in the role of a frigid kleptomaniac—which would have been quite a departure for Kelly even before her transformation to Princess Grace.

Kelly, Nancy (1921–1995) American actress, former child model. Onscreen from five, she returned to films via theater, radio, and a brief (1941–42) marriage to actor Edmond O'Brien, reprising her greatest Broadway success, evil little Rhoda Penmark's mother Christine in *The Bad Seed* (1955), in the 1956 film. She appeared the following year as Fran Steppe, the wife whose watchmaker husband wrongly suspects her of infidelity in "FOUR O'CLOCK," the only episode of SUSPICION Hitchcock directed, and returned as the bereaved mother Vera Brandon in THE ALFRED HITCHCOCK HOUR segment "The Lonely Hours" (1963).

Kemble-Cooper, Lily (1892–1977) British stage actress who appeared in some two dozen films from 1916, mostly in uncredited roles after *Gone with the Wind* (1939). Among the last of these was her performance as Mrs. Sinclair in the ALFRED HITCHCOCK PRESENTS episode "BACK FOR CHRISTMAS."

Kemmerling, Warren J. (1928–) American character actor with East Coast stage experience, in films and (mostly) television from 1960, who played Grandison in FAMILY PLOT.

Kendall, Henry (1897–1962) British actor, on stage from childhood and long familiar from London revues. Onscreen from 1921, he played some 50 presentable but variously flawed males, including Fred

Hill, the office drudge who turns into an adulterous cad when a rich uncle gives him enough money to take a trip around the world in RICH AND STRANGE.

Kent, Crauford (or Crawford) (1881–1953) American actor, in Hollywood from 1915, who provided stalwart support, often uncredited, in nearly 200 films as bureaucrats, government officials, and military men. He played the toastmaster at the dinner in which Johnny Jones meets Carol Fisher in FOREIGN CORRESPONDENT.

Keon, Barbara American production assistant. After starting with David O. SELZNICK as continuity supervisor on *The Adventures of Tom Sawyer* and *The Young in Heart* (both 1938), she became scenario assistant on *Gone With the Wind* (1939) and REBECCA and production assistant on SPELLBOUND and NOTORIOUS. When Hitchcock left Selznick to form TRANSATLANTIC PICTURES, she soon followed, serving as production associate on STRANGERS ON A TRAIN and associate producer on I CONFESS, her last film credit.

Kern, Hal (C.) (1894–1985) Veteran Hollywood editor, with David O. SELZNICK from *The Garden of Allah* (1936). He won an Academy Award for cosupervising the editing of *Gone With the Wind* (1939) and was nominated again for REBECCA and *Since You Went Away* (1944). SPELLBOUND and THE PARADINE CASE were also among the 40 other films he edited.

Kieling, Wolfgang (1924–1985) German character actor, onscreen from 1936. His first English-language role, and practically his last, was Hermann Gromek, the bulldog police officer Michael Armstrong has such trouble killing in TORN CURTAIN.

Kilian, Victor (1891–1979) Blustering American character actor with vaudeville and Broadway experience. Onscreen from 1929, he played more than 100 generally choleric roles—one of his more restrained performances was as the sheriff who arrests John Ballantine in SPELLBOUND—before retiring from the screen in 1950 and the stage 10 years later. Only a few years before he was murdered by burglars, his career enjoyed a surprising comeback when he was cast as the heroine's grandfather, aka the Fernwood Flasher, in the farcical television soap opera *Mary Hartman, Mary Hartman.*

Kindem, Gorham Anders American filmmaker and film scholar, professor of Communication Studies at the University of North Carolina at Chapel Hill. His documentary films include *Chuck Davis, Dancing Through West Africa* (1987) and *Hungers of the Soul: Be Gardiner, Stone Carver* (1994). He has written *The Live Television Generation of Hollywood Film Directors: Interviews with Seven Directors* (1994), and *Introduction to Media Production, from Analog to Digital* (1997) and edited *The American Movie Industry: The Business of Motion Pictures* (1982) and *The International Movie Industry* (2000). His 1977 doctoral dissertation at Northwestern University, *Toward a Semiotic Theory of Visual Communication in the Cinema: A Reappraisal of Semiotic Theories from a Cinematic Perspective and a Semiotic Analysis of Color Signs and Communication in the Color Films of Alfred Hitchcock* (Arno/New York Times, 1980), seeks to defend semiotics against the ideological attacks of Fredric Jameson, Julia Kristeva, and Brian Henderson by reconciling the dyadic semiotic theories of Ferdinand de Saussure (signifier/signified) and Umberto Eco (expression/content) with the triadic theories of Charles Sanders Peirce (sign/interpretant/object) through an exhaustive analysis of the use of color as a signifying device in 13 of Hitchcock's color films (all his completed color films except for ROPE and REAR WINDOW). Behind the highly abstract argument and the forbidding use of tables to organize the scenes and characters each film presents lie many sharp observations about specific films (for instance, Blanche Tyler's association with white and Joe Maloney's with green throughout FAMILY PLOT) but several suggestions about Hitchcock's consistent use of color as a signifying system whose authorial or generic associations (red for passion, black for death, green for villains or ghosts) transcend any particular film.

King, Harold (V.) (1907–) British sound recordist whose 30 films, 1936–57, include STAGE FRIGHT, and later *The Magic Box* (1951), *Captain Horatio Hornblower* (1951), *The Master of Ballantrae* (1953), *Moby Dick* (1956), and *The Good Companions* (1957).

Kirkbride, Ronald (1912–) British suspense writer whose novel *A Girl Called Tamiko* (1959) served as the basis of the 1962 film. His thriller THE SHORT NIGHT (1968) was the last property acquired by Hitchcock but never got past preproduction. Screenwriter David FREEMAN's memoir *The Last Days of Alfred Hitchcock* reprints Freeman's draft screenplay.

Klemperer, Werner (1920–) Bald, German-born character actor who left with his father, conductor Otto Klemperer, for the United States upon Hitler's rise to power, only to find himself typecast as a comic or sinister Nazi—most memorably as Colonel Klink in the television series *Hogan's Heroes* (1965–71). He played three minor roles for Hitchcock: Klopa in the ALFRED HITCHCOCK PRESENTS episode "Safe Conduct" (1956), another bit as the mountain-climbing guide Herr Ranks in the episode "THE CRYSTAL TRENCH," and an uncredited bit as Dr. Bannay in THE WRONG MAN.

Kline, Benjamin H. (1894–1974) American cinematographer who moved from hundreds of Hollywood second features (notably *Detour*, 1945) to television (*Thriller, McHale's Navy, Dragnet 1967*). As a staff cinematographer for THE ALFRED HITCHCOCK HOUR, he shot "I SAW THE WHOLE THING," Hitchcock's final film for television.

Knight, Esmond (1906–1987) Welsh actor of stage and screen who made his West End debut in 1925, his film debut three years later. He starred as Schani Strauss in WALTZES FROM VIENNA, but a far more decisive influence on his career was Michael Powell, with whom he worked in nearly a dozen films. Almost completely blinded in World War II during a Royal Navy action against the *Bismarck,* he eventually recovered some sight in one eye and returned to the screen for another 40 roles, including a naval captain in *Sink the Bismarck!* (1960).

Knott, Frederick (1918–) British playwright with a special interest in innocent heroines caught in criminal plots. After studying law at Cambridge and serving in World War II, he set to work as a screenwriter and received screen credit for one film, *The Last Page* (1952; U.S. title *Man Bait*). That same year his original play DIAL M FOR MURDER debuted, first on television, then in the West End. Knott moved to the United States to adapt his work for Hitchcock's film and then remained to produce *Write Me a Murder* (1961) and *Wait Until Dark* (1966), the latter filmed in 1967. His first great success has since inspired two more films, *Dial M for Murder* (television, 1981) and *A Perfect Murder* (1998).

Knowles, Bernard (b. 1900) British cinematographer who first entered the industry in 1929. He shot THE 39 STEPS and all Hitchcock's subsequent Gaumont-British films—SECRET AGENT, SABOTAGE, YOUNG AND INNOCENT—and returned for Hitchcock's last British film, JAMAICA INN, before retiring after some 30 films in 1944.

Koenekamp, H(ans) F. (1891–1992) American cinematographer who worked with Mack Sennett and Larry Semon in silent films before becoming a specialist in the WARNER BROS. special-effects department, where he remained for 30 years, designing the photographic effects for films as different as *A Midsummer Night's Dream* (1935), *The Sea Hawk* (1940), and STRANGERS ON A TRAIN.

Konstam, Phyllis (1907–1976) Stage-trained British actress in occasional films, largely directed by Hitchcock, who cast her first in uncredited bits in CHAMPAGNE and the silent version of *Blackmail* (in which she played the Whites' knife-obsessed neighbor who would be played by Phyllis MONKMAN in the synch-sound version) and then by the more substantial roles of Doucie Markham in MURDER! and Chloe Hornblower in THE SKIN GAME. Though her film roles after 1931 were sporadic, she appeared onscreen as late as *Voice of the Hurricane* (1964).

Konstantin, Leopoldine (1886–1965) Great lady of the German-language stage who appeared with Max Reinhardt's Deutches Theater from 1908 to 1937. In infrequent films from 1913, usually as queens and queenly courtesans like Lola Montez (whom she played in 1918). At the suggestion of

Reinhold SCHÜNZEL, she took the part of Madame Sebastian in *NOTORIOUS*—a role originally designed for Ethel BARRYMORE—and in her only English-language film (and her final work for the screen) created one of the most truly alarming mothers in Hitchcock's oeuvre.

Korngold, E(rich) W(olfgang) (1897–1957) Precociously talented Czech-born musician who together with Julius BITTNER arranged the music of Johann STRAUSS, Sr. and Jr., for the stage production of *WALTZES FROM VIENNA* in 1931—arrangements adapted by Hubert BATH for Hitchcock's film. Immigrating to America in 1935, ahead of the Anschluss, he ended up forsaking his vocation as a classical composer and conductor to become one of the great writers of Hollywood scores, by turns tender and rousing, winning Oscars for *Anthony Adverse* (1936) and *The Adventures of Robin Hood* (1938) and further nominations for *The Private Lives of Elizabeth and Essex* (1939) and *The Sea Hawk* (1940).

Kosleck, Martin (1904–1994) Stage-trained German actor, born Nicolai Yoshkin, who fled the Nazis in 1934 for Hollywood, where he avenged himself on his enemies by portraying Josef Goebbels three times—in *Confessions of a Nazi Spy* (1939), *The Hitler Gang* (1944), and *Hitler* (1962)—and was much in demand, especially during the war, for what one admiring critic described as his portrayal of "the definitive Nazi swine" (as in *FOREIGN CORRESPONDENT*, in which he plays a Dutch tramp with suspiciously clean hands). In all, he played more than 50 roles before his retirement in 1980.

Kove, Kenneth (1893–1965) Stage-trained British actor specializing in Aldwych farces who made his film debut as a juror in *MURDER!* and became one of the four members of that jury to enjoy a substantial film career, playing some three dozen supporting Freddies, Berties, and Reggies through 1965.

Krampf, Günther (1899–1950) Distinguished Viennese-born cinematographer who shot some of the great German silents—*Nosferatu* (1922), *Der Student von Prag* (1926), *Die Büchse der Pandora* (1929)—before settling in England in 1932. Among his many later films are the Ministry of Information shorts *BON VOYAGE* and *AVENTURE MALGACHE*.

Krams, Arthur (1912–1985) American set decorator who cut his teeth on such MGM musicals as *Easter Parade* (1948) and *The Barkleys of Broadway* (1949) and then moved on to a broader range of projects, including the Oscar-nominated *TO CATCH A THIEF* and *THE MAN WHO KNEW TOO MUCH* (1956), before his retirement in 1968. He also shared Oscar nominations for *The Merry Widow* (1952), *The Story of Three Loves* (1953), *Lili* (1953), *Career* (1959), *Visit to a Small Planet* (1960) and won for *The Rose Tattoo* (1955).

Krasna, Norman (1909–1984) American playwright and screenwriter. A specialist in light comedy despite his original stories for Fritz LANG's *Fury* (1936) and *You and Me* (1938), he wrote the screenplays for *Hands Across the Table* (1935), *Wife vs. Secretary* (1936), *Bachelor Mother* (1939), *The Devil and Miss Jones* (1941), and *MR. AND MRS. SMITH*, written for Carole LOMBARD, who persuaded Hitchcock to direct it despite his avowed lack of interest in romantic comedy. Krasna was nominated for Academy Awards for *Fury* and *The Devil and Miss Jones,* and won an Oscar for the original screenplay of *Princess O'Rourke* (1943), the first of three films he directed himself. Later, he produced a few such notable films as *Clash by Night* and *The Lusty Men* (both 1952) before continuing with screenplays for *White Christmas* (1954), *Bundle of Joy* (1956), *Indiscreet* (1958), *Let's Make Love* (1960), and *My Geisha* (1962).

Kristen, Marta (1945–) Norwegian-born American actress, onscreen from 12, who appears in two episodes of *ALFRED HITCHCOCK PRESENTS*: as Marjorie Store in "The Gloating Place" (1961) and as the Jiffy Snack Girl in "BANG! YOU'RE DEAD" (1961). In the latter, she survived the unwitting threat to her character by gun-toting Billy MUMY to play his big sister Judy Robinson in the science-fiction television soap opera *Lost in Space* (1965–68).

Krohn, Bill American-born filmmaker and longtime Hollywood correspondent for *CAHIERS DU*

CINÉMA. He collaborated in writing, producing, and directing *It's All True,* based on Orson Welles's unfinished film, in 1994. His *Hitchcock au travail* (Cahiers du cinéma, 1999), though first written in English, won the Prix de la Critique for the best illustrated film book on its initial publication in France a year before it appeared in English as *Hitchcock at Work* (Phaidon, 2000). Although it is a sumptuous coffee-table book heavily illustrated with photographs often unseen before, Krohn pauses in his survey of Hitchcock's American work long enough for detailed study of 10 films, and the archival material and critical perspective he brings to bear on these films, from SABOTEUR to THE BIRDS, is revelatory. Disputing the characterization of Hitchcock as a "control freak" who planned in advance every step in the production of his films, from dialogue to camera setups to studio sets, and never looked through the camera lens, he uses internal memos, screenplay drafts, and studio schedules to show that for various reasons, Hitchcock regularly sanctioned revisions in screenplays until shortly before shooting began (or even after), shot alternate takes of many key sequences in his films (even filming closeups of the dialogue in ROPE in case his experiment with unbroken long takes did not work), improvised on the set, changed sequences to accommodate absent performers such as Louis CALHERN in NOTORIOUS, dropped ideas (like the trail of blue footprints Louis Bernard would leave in THE MAN WHO KNEW TOO MUCH [1956]) in midshoot, and continued to add unscripted shots even in postproduction. Together with Ken MOGG's *The Alfred Hitchcock Story* and François TRUFFAUT's book-length series of interviews, Krohn's is the indispensable picture book on the director.

Kruger, Alma (1871–1960)   American character actress with long stage experience. Onscreen from 1936, she specialized in authority figures from Princess Maria Theresa in *Marie Antoinette* (1938) to head nurse Molly Byrd in 14 Dr. Kildare films and spinoffs (1939–47), but interrupted her 50-film wallow in Americana long enough to play Bruce Baldwin's hapless mother in *His Girl Friday* (1940) and Mrs. Sutton, the Fifth Column society matron in SABOTEUR.

Kruger, Otto (1885–1974)   American actor who switched from matinee-idol roles on Broadway in the twenties to become the silver-haired smoothie of nearly 100 Hollywood melodramas, most memorably as suave villains such as Charles Tobin in SABOTEUR (a part he took when Harry Carey indignantly rejected it as too anti-American for his image) and Dr. Jules Amthor in *Murder, My Sweet* (1944) and suavely charming cowards such as Judge Percy Mettrick in *High Noon* (1942).

Krumschmidt, Eberhard (1904–1956)   Bespectacled actor and producer who mounted such off-Broadway shows as *Window Panes* (1939) and appeared onstage in *Call Me Madam* (1950) and in many radio and television programs. His only film credit, however, is the ill-fated metallurgist Emil Hupka in NOTORIOUS.

Kuehl, William (L.)   American set decorator, mostly at WARNER BROS. from *Confidential Agent* (1945) to *The Omega Man* (1971), who dressed the sets for THE WRONG MAN.

Kuri, Emile (1907–   )   Mexican-born set decorator, in Hollywood from 1938. Moving frequently from studio to studio, he worked with Hitchcock at SELZNICK *(THE PARADINE CASE),* TRANSATLANTIC *(ROPE),* and PARAMOUNT *(THE TROUBLE WITH HARRY).* He is, however, best remembered for his many Disney films, including *20,000 Leagues Under the Sea* (1954), *Davy Crockett and the River Pirates* (1956), *Darby O'Gill and the Little People* (1959), *Pollyanna* (1960), and *Mary Poppins* (1964).

La Bern, Arthur British suspense novelist, former reporter and feature writer. Soon after his wartime service as Pacific correspondent for the *London Evening Standard,* his drably realistic novel *It Always Rains on Sunday* (1945) became an international bestseller and was filmed by Robert Hamer in 1948. It was immediately followed by *Good Time Girl* (1949; based on *Night Darkens the Streets,* 1947) and *Paper Orchid* (1949). Between 1962 and 1964, La Bern wrote four episodes of the BBC television program *Edgar Wallace Mysteries.* His ninth novel, *Goodbye Piccadilly, Farewell Leicester Square* (1966), was adapted to the screen as FRENZY, with the killer's identity revealed much earlier and the force of the original ending, in which the hero escapes from prison only to incriminate himself in still another murder he has not committed, reversed.

Lacan, Jacques (1901–1981) French clinical psychiatrist whose theories concerning the infantile formation of social identity, like those of his fellow clinician Sigmund Freud 30 years earlier, gave new direction to theories of fictional representation. In "The Mirror Stage as Formative of the Function of the I" (1966) and *The Four Fundamental Concepts of Psychoanalysis* (1978), Lacan posited a "mirror stage" during which a male infant marked by a lack of any sense of physical discreteness recognizes his reflection in a mirror as that of his own body and so identifies himself with his reflection. The narcissistic sense of corporeal unity thus achieved, however, is imaginary and mistaken in its identification of a specular object, the reflected body, as oneself, and the infant does not pass from the imaginary to the symbolic realm of acculturation until he masters (that is, until he is mastered by) the signifying codes of language, which correspond to the power codes of the Law of the Father, the patriarchal realm of culture which thereafter structures one's sense of oneself within the larger realm through one's acceptance of the codes of language and power. Lacan's revisionist psychoanalysis offered to film theory an obvious way out of a theoretical impasse—was the movie screen more like a framed, perfectly composed picture (as the films of Fritz LANG and the theories of Rudolf Arnheim suggested) or more like a window onto a larger world (as the films of Jean Renoir and the theories of André Bazin suggested)?—by offering a third possibility: the screen was a mirror in which viewers regressing to the imaginary realm saw images that invited them to identify both with the characters portrayed and with the camera eye portraying them, thus allowing filmgoers the narcissistically pleasurable illusion of control over both themselves and their world. Feminist theorists such as Laura MULVEY and Tania MODLESKI, interested in exposing the ways in which the power of patriarchal culture had been taken for granted, found in Lacan a useful narrative of male acculturation through infantile narcissism and adult regression, and in Hitchcock an ideal test case of both voyeuristic characters (especially in NOTORIOUS, REAR WINDOW, VERTIGO, and PSYCHO) bent on objectifying, demystifying, or otherwise dominating women and a persistent thematizing of the voyeurism of the cinema and its viewers themselves.

Lacey (or Lacy), Catherine (1904–1979)
British actress of stage and screen, whose film debut as the nun in THE LADY VANISHES marked the first of some 20 roles as spinsters or eccentric mothers before she retired after The Private Life of Sherlock Holmes (1970).

La Couline, Father Paul
Technical adviser on ecclesiastical matters pertinent to I CONFESS.

Lady Vanishes, The
(Alternative titles: Der Dame vershwindet, Une Femme disparait) Gainsborough, MGM, 97 minutes, August 1938. **Producer:** Edward Black; **Director:** Alfred Hitchcock; **Screenplay:** Sidney Gilliat and Frank Launder, based on The Wheel Spins, a novel by Ethel Lina White; **Continuity:** Alma Reville; **Cinematographer:** Jack Cox; **Assistant camera:** Leo Harris; **Location photographers:** Maurice Oakley and Jack Parry; **Set decoration:** [Alex] Vetchinsky; **Assistant set designers:** Maurice Carter and Albert Jullion; **Sound:** S[ydney]. Wiles; **Editor:** R.E. Dearing; **Cutting:** Alfred Roome; **Musical director:** Louis Levy; **Additional music:** Cecil Milner; **Cast:** Margaret Lockwood (Iris Henderson), Michael Redgrave (Gilbert), Paul Lukas (Dr. [Egon] Hartz), Dame May Whitty (Miss Froy), Cecil Parker (Mr. Todhunter), Linden Travers ("Mrs." Todhunter), Mary Clare (Baroness), Naunton Wayne (Caldicott), Basil Radford (Charters), Emile Boreo (hotel manager), Googie Withers (Blanche), Sally Stewart (Julie), Philip Leaver (Signor Doppo), Zelma Vas Dias (Signora Doppo), Catherine Lacey (nun), Josephine Wilson (Madame Kummer), Charles Oliver (officer), Kathleen Tremaine (Anna).

Sidney GILLIAT and Frank LAUNDER had written a screenplay based on Ethel Lina WHITE's 1936 novel the year it was published, and GAINSBOROUGH PICTURES, engaging American director Roy William Neill for the film, had sent a crew to Yugoslavia that summer to shoot exteriors. But when Fred Gunn, the assistant director heading the crew, broke his ankle, a police investigation into the incident disclosed such unflattering implications about the host country in the screenplay that the crew was deported, and the project lay dormant until Hitchcock, looking for a second property to complete the two-picture contract he had begun with YOUNG AND INNOCENT, read it in October 1937, was immediately taken with it, and filmed it with only minor revisions (the addition of the traveling magician and his props in the baggage car, the climactic gunfight on the stopped train). Veteran actress Dame May WHITTY, cast as the grandmotherly secret agent, was joined by Gainsborough contract star Margaret LOCKWOOD, stage actor Michael REDGRAVE—who was amazed at the scant rehearsal time allotted for the baggage-car scene and filmmaking generally—in his first starring role, and Basil RADFORD and Naunton WAYNE, who had never worked together, as an immortally obtuse pair of English dunderheads (a pairing they were to reprise successfully in several later films). Filming was completed in a five-week period on a single 90-foot Islington stage in the fall of 1937—with miniatures prominently featured even in the opening exterior shot and references to central European politics this time discreetly hazy—and postproduction work followed over the winter. By the time of the film's rapturously received premiere in August 1938, Hitchcock had returned from America with a contract with David O. SELZNICK that magnified his fame on both sides of the Atlantic, and the film further burnished his reputation when the film won him the New York Film Critics Circle Award for the Best Director of 1938.

The novel and screenplay, as Hitchcock noted, were a transformation of the old story—later filmed for ALFRED HITCHCOCK PRESENTS as "Into Thin Air" (1955)—about a daughter who, after checking into a hotel at the height of the Paris Exposition, leaves her mother behind to go out and then returns to find that the mother has disappeared and that no one in the hotel will admit having seen her. To the MACGUFFIN of the vanished old lady, White had added a spy plot and a train speeding through exotic European locations, and Gilliat and Launder had

Attempting to reassure Iris Henderson (Margaret Lockwood) about the English lady no one else admits to seeing before she disappeared from the train in *The Lady Vanishes,* Gilbert (Michael Redgrave, left) and Dr. Hartz (Paul Lukas) have the opposite effect. *(National Film Society Archive)*

wrapped the whole story in a comical romance between the heroine Iris Henderson and Gilbert, the insouciant musicologist who is the only person on the train to accept her story and help her get at the truth. What Hitchcock supplied was not so much incisive direction of the actors and actresses—both Lockwood and Redgrave agreed that he seemed bored during filming—but the creation of a casual atmosphere that allowed his performers to relax, and an accelerating onscreen velocity that made the film irresistibly appealing as light entertainment. So successful was the film in its trademark melding of romantic comedy and melodramatic suspense, in

fact, that it was many years before critics who had described the film as a delightfully insubstantial bauble returned to it for a closer look. Gavin Lambert and Raymond DURGNAT have emphasized its internationalist political subtext, Maurice YACOWAR its treatment of the train's ill-assorted passengers as an extended family (whose different approaches to romance and sexuality as well as politics, in a point Yacowar does not make, strikingly anticipate L.B. Jefferies's neighbors in REAR WINDOW), Patrice Petro its unmasking of the patriarchal codes by which "ladies" are constructed to motivate "a female Oedipal (even anti-Oedipal) narrative." More recently,

Charles BARR has analyzed the film's oneiric land-scape, as the flowerpot an unseen hand tips over at Miss Froy strikes Iris instead, propelling her into the center of the spy plot and, by crystallizing Iris's sexual tension through an act of violence, makes explicit the story's status as her dream. Once aboard the train, Iris oscillates uncontrollably between waking and sleeping, investigating and falling in love. Hitchcock characteristically quibbles on the distinction between dream and reality, so that, for example, Iris—who has spoken of marriage to her fiancé back in England in terms less dreamy than resigned before boarding the train—is repeatedly accused of having dreamed Miss Froy, who has been kidnapped and disguised as a brain-surgery candidate immobilized in heavy bandages. When Iris and Gilbert are given a narcotic by the suavely treacherous Dr. Hartz, they only pretend to fall asleep, even though Iris at first thinks she has swallowed the drug. Every attempt Iris makes to stand on her rights—from the episode in which she tips the manager to throw noisy Gilbert out of the hotel room above hers to her self-righteous stopping of the train by pulling the emergency brake—fails; to succeed in her quest of finding the missing lady and her own love, she must surrender to her own unspoken wishes. The film's fairy-tale structure, complete with magical helpers, exotic villains, and a romantic ending, reveals a remarkable economy of unconscious desire.

Laing, Robert W. (Bob) Art director on some two dozen international films from *On Her Majesty's Secret Service* (1969) and FRENZY to *Rules of Engagement* (2000).

"Lamb to the Slaughter" 104th episode of *Alfred Hitchcock Presents,* broadcast April 13, 1958. **Producer:** Joan Harrison; **Associate producer:** Norman Lloyd; **Director:** Alfred Hitchcock; **Assistant director:** Hilton Green; **Teleplay:** Roald Dahl, based on his short story; **Cinematographer:** John L. Russell; **Art director:** John Lloyd; **Set designer:** James S. Redd; **Costumes:** Vincent Dee; **Editors:** Richard G. Wray and Edward W. Williams; **Cast:** Barbara Bel Geddes (Mary Maloney), Harold J. Stone (Lt. Noonan), Allan Lane (Patrick Maloney), Ken Clark (Mike), Robert C. Ross (grocer), William Keene (police officer), Thomas Wild (doctor), Otto Waldis (police officer).

The second episode Hitchcock directed for the third season of ALFRED HITCHCOCK PRESENTS is perhaps his most characteristic and best-known work for television. Mary Maloney is a long-suffering policeman's wife who greets the news that her husband is leaving her for another woman by catatonically beating him to death with the nearest object at hand, which happens to be a frozen leg of lamb. Realizing the probable sentence she will receive for killing a police officer, she methodically covers up her involvement in the crime, pretending her husband had still been alive when she went out to the grocery to pick up last-minute items for his supper. As a crowning touch, she cooks the leg of lamb and serves it to the police detectives headed by Lt. Noonan, who questions her solicitously, vows to find the missing murder weapon, and joins the other investigating officers in a late supper as Bel Geddes stifles her hysterical laughter behind the kitchen door.

Landau, Martin (1931–) Lean American character actor, former cartoonist (1948) with the *New York Daily News,* who of 2,000 applicants for Lee Strasberg's Actors Studio in 1955 was one of only two accepted (the other was Steve McQueen). Following his Broadway debut in *Middle of the Night* (1957), he went on to play more than 100 roles in films and television, often variants of his smoothly sinister villain Leonard in NORTH BY NORTHWEST, occasionally inversions of it, as in his role as the conscience-stricken lawyer Ned Murray in the THE ALFRED HITCHCOCK HOUR episode "Second Verdict" (1964). Though he was Gene Roddenberry's choice to play Mr. Spock in *Star Trek,* he lost the role to Leonard Nimoy, who replaced him when he left the television series *Mission: Impossible* (1966–69). He was nominated for Oscars for his performances in *Tucker: The Man and His Dream* (1988) and *Crimes and Misdemeanors* (1989) and won the Best Supporting Actor award for playing the aging Bela Lugosi in *Ed Wood* (1994).

Landis, Jessie Royce (1904–1972) Delight-fully fluttery American stage actress, born Jessie

Royce Medbury. Onstage from 1924, she took time out from her theatrical engagements in New York and London to play some 30 roles in film and television, mostly from 1949. She is best known for playing Jessie Stevens, Cary GRANT's prospective mother-in-law, in TO CATCH A THIEF, and Grant's mother Clara Thornhill in NORTH BY NORTHWEST despite being nearly a year younger than Grant. She played William Shatner's equally indomitable mother Claire Crane in the ALFRED HITCHCOCK PRESENTS segment "Mother, May I Go Out to Swim?" (1960).

Landry, Bob (1914–1960) American photographer who covered the Pearl Harbor attack and then worked as a staff photographer for *Life* magazine and a still photographer for numerous movies. He served as technical adviser concerning photographic matters on *REAR WINDOW*.

Lane, Allan (Rocky) (1904–1973) American character actor, former football player, who appeared sporadically in Hollywood from 1929 before finding his metier as a B-western hero, most often as Red Ryder or playing a hero named after himself, in the mid-forties. He appeared in more than 100 films and television roles, including the ill-fated Patrick Maloney in the ALFRED HITCHCOCK PRESENTS episode "LAMB TO THE SLAUGHTER" before television killed second features in the fifties, and returned from 1961 to 1966 as the voice of television horse *Mr. Ed*.

Lane, Priscilla (1917–1995) American actress, née Priscilla Mullican, youngest of the three Lane sisters (the others were Lola, 1909–81, and Rosemary, 1913–74) to forge Hollywood careers. A former singer with Fred Waring's band, she signed a contract with WARNER BROS. in 1937, appearing in four films with her sisters—*Four Daughters* (1938), *Daughters Courageous* (1939), *Four Wives* (1939), and *Four Mothers* (1941)—branching out meanwhile to support James Cagney in *The Roaring Twenties* (1939) and Cary GRANT in *Arsenic and Old Lace* (1942, released 1944). Unable to secure Barbara Stanwyck for the role of Patricia Martin in SABOTEUR, Hitchcock instead accepted Lane, by now a UNIVERSAL contract

star who looked like Stanwyck but lacked her worldly savvy and wit. It was one of her last roles before she retired in 1948.

Lane, Rusty (1899–1986) American character actor who played an admiral in his film debut (*The House on 92nd Street,* 1945) and went on to play some 50 similarly authoritarian roles—sheriffs, judges, and police chiefs—in movies and television. He appeared in seven episodes of ALFRED HITCHCOCK PRESENTS—as the detective in "None Are So Blind" (1956), the train conductor in "Manacled" (1957), the police detective in "Martha Mason, Movie Star" (1957), Matt the cop in "The Young One" (1957), Father Rafferty in "Listen, Listen!" (1958), Mr. Ivers in "A Very Moral Theft" (1960), and the judge in "The Test" (1962)—and twice in THE ALFRED HITCHCOCK HOUR, as Judge Martin in "I SAW THE WHOLE THING" and Otto Brandt in "The Dividing Wall" (1963).

Lang, Doreen (1915–1999) American character actress who made her film debut as Ann James, one of the witnesses against Manny Balestrero in THE WRONG MAN, and then returned as Roger Thornhill's secretary Maggie in NORTH BY NORTHWEST and the distraught mother in the Tides Café who accuses Melanie Daniels of having brought the birds to Bodega Bay in THE BIRDS. Her casting as Emily, the simple-minded witness to William Botibol's leap from the side of the ship in the ALFRED HITCHCOCK PRESENTS segment "DIP IN THE POOL," looks forward to her later roles, which are almost entirely in television.

Lang, Fritz (1890–1976) Towering German director, for many years Hitchcock's principal competitor in the creation of cinematic suspense. He briefly trained as an architect at the Technische Hochschule in his native Vienna but left in 1910 to study painting in Munich and Paris. He returned to Austria for wartime service and became interested in acting and screenwriting while convalescing from wounds. He then joined Decla as a script reader and editor. Following the first film he wrote and directed, *Halbblut* (1919), he was sought to direct *Das Kabinett des Docktor Caligari* (1919) but was prevented from doing so by his commitment to write and direct the two parts of *Die Spinnen* (1919, 1920).

International success came with *Der müde Tod* (1921), which confirmed Lang's status as one of the leading expressionist filmmakers in the German industry. In 1922 he married actress/screenwriter Thea von Harbou, who collaborated with him in writing most of his German films: the gangser epic *Dr. Mabuse de Speiler* (1922); the two part Wagnerian epic *Die Niebelungen* (1924); the futuristic dystopia *Metropolis* (1927); the global espionage thriller *Spione* (1928); the science-fiction fantasy *Die Frau in Mond* (1929); and his trademark film, *M* (1931), an unsparing study of a compulsive child-killer. When Lang put Nazi slogans into the mouth of the archcriminal hero of *Das Testament des Dr. Mabuse* (1933), Joseph Goebbels banned the film, then shocked Lang by offering to appoint him head of production at Universum Film, AG, Germany's largest studio, even though Lang's mother had been Jewish. That same night, Lang left his wife, von Harbou, and fled alone to Paris, where he directed *Liliom* (1934) before immigrating to America.

In Hollywood, Lang's paranoid vision of a doom-laden world whose citizens devised laws and institutions specifically designed, but often failing, to repress their darkest urges—a visually hyperstylized world whose every shopwindow expressed the torment of the soul who peered into it—became gradually more naturalized. Following the searing *Fury* (1936), a study of lynch-mob mentality, and *You Only Live Once* (1937), the prototypical saga of a criminal couple on the run, he alternated between explorations of criminal guilt (*Hangmen Also Die,* 1943; *The Woman in the Window,* 1944; *Scarlet Street,* 1945; *The Big Heat,* 1953; *Human Dsire,* 1954; *While the City Sleeps,* 1956) and westerrns (*The Return of Frank James,* 1940; *Western Union,* 1941; *Rancho Notorious,* 1952), for which he had an exceptional visual flair. The themes of these films are strikingly similar to Hitchcock's: the world as a trap for the unwary, the doubling of innocence with guilt, crime and punishment as radical metaphors for human morality. But Lang's films are colder and less consistently thrilling than Hitchcock's, more geometric in their visual design, more schematic in their moralizing, more sociological in their approach to psychology. Monocled, curt, and imperious, Lang never achieved Hitchcock's popular success because of his reputation for being difficult to work with and his remoteness from the press. He left a memorable self-portrait in Jean-Luc Godard's *Le Mépris* (1963), in which he plays himself.

Lang, Irene   American actress who appeared as the Princeys' maid in the ALFRED HITCHCOCK PRESENTS episode "WET SATURDAY."

Lang, Julia   British actress whose five screen roles (1948–49) include the servant Susan in UNDER CAPRICORN.

Langley, Bryan   British cinematographer who shot some 40 films beginning with *No Exit* (1930) and NUMBER SEVENTEEN and then supervised the photographic special effects on another half-dozen from *The Weaker Sex* (1948) through *1984* (1956).

Larabee, Louise (1914–1988)   American theatrical actress, onstage from 1941, whose infrequent film and television roles included two for ALFRED HITCHCOCK PRESENTS, as the short-lived wives of antique dealer Mr. Appleby in "The Orderly World of Mr. Appleby" (1956) and of Sam Jacoby in "ONE MORE MILE TO GO" (1957).

Lasky, Jesse (L.), Jr. (1908–1988)   American screenwriter, son of pioneer producer Jesse L. Lasky, who came to work for Michael BALCON in 1934 to rewrite the dialogue for American characters to make GAUMONT-BRITISH's films more acceptable to the American market, succeeding so well with Robert Marvin, the American in SECRET AGENT, that he was given screen credit for additional dialogue. Soon after, he returned to the United States, where he worked on some 30 films, many of them, from *The Buccaneer* (1938) through *The Ten Commandments* (1956), with Cecil B. DeMille.

Lasky, Michael   American journalist, senior associate editor at *PC World* and coauthor, with Robert A. HARRIS, of *The Films of Alfred Hitchcock*

(Citadel, 1976), an oversized, film-by-film review of the director's career notable for its detailed summaries of all the thrillers beginning with *The Man Who Knew Too Much* (1934), its many brief citations of contemporary reviews, and its appended list of Hitchcock's cameo appearances. A revised and updated edition retitled *The Complete Films of Alfred Hitchcock* (Carol, 1999) includes a new foreword by Patricia HITCHCOCK O'Connell and a filmography of all Hitchcock's films and television programs available on video and DVD.

Latham, Louise (1922–) American character actress whose 30-year career playing nearly 100 variously snoopy and eccentric old ladies, usually on television, began with her roles as the title character's mother, Bernice Edgar, in MARNIE, and as the tippling housekeeper Maude Isles in THE ALFRED HITCHCOCK HOUR episode "An Unlocked Window" (1965).

Laughton, Charles (1899–1962) Protean, ungovernable, often gloriously hammy British star of stage and screen whose talent was as outsized as his ego. After returning from war service, he attended the Royal Academy of Dramatic Art. Soon after making his West End debut in 1926, he played the first theatrical Hercule Poirot in *Alibi* (1928), the year he met actress Elsa Lanchester, who married him the following year and often played character roles in his films. Onscreen from 1929, he made his Hollywood debut in *Payment Deferred* (1932) but left a more immediate mark in several key British films of the thirties, especially in the title roles of *The Private Life of Henry VIII* (1933) and *Rembrandt* (1936). Awarded an Oscar for the first of these roles—the first actor in a non-Hollywood production to be so honored—he was nominated again for his withering performance as Captain Bligh in *Mutiny on the Bounty* (1935). In 1937 he joined the producer Erich POMMER to form his own film company, MAYFLOWER PRODUCTIONS; it was Mayflower that produced *JAMAICA INN*, in which he played the monstrously epicurean squire Sir Humphrey Pengallan, in between some of his characteristic roles, the dogged Inspector

Charles Laughton

Javert in *Les Miserables* (1935) and the pathetically deformed Quasimodo in *The Hunchback of Notre Dame* (1939). Despite Hitchcock's difficulties with Laughton on the set—he complained to François TRUFFAUT that he had been restricted to closeups of his star for the first 10 days of shooting because Laughton had not yet found the right walk for his character—he worked with him again in THE PARADINE CASE, where Laughton played Lord Thomas Horfield as the sort of lecherous sadist that, despite his exceptionally wide range, had become his trademark role. After directing the nightmare fairy tale *Night of the Hunter* (1955), perhaps the most striking one-shot film in Hollywood history, Laughton ended his screen career with unforgettable roles as the barrister Sir Wilfrid Robarts in *Witness for the Prosecution* (1957), his third Oscar nomination; the Roman Sempronious Gracchus in *Spartacus* (1960); and Senator Seabright Cooley in *Advise and Consent* (1962). Hitchcock's verdict on his most willful collaborator apart from David O. SELZNICK was telling: "One doesn't direct Charles Laughton. The best you can hope for is to referee."

Launder, Frank (1906–1997) British screenwriter, later director and producer, often in collaboration with Sidney GILLIAT. Beginning with *Seven Sinners* (1936), the pair soon established a reputation for mixing comedy and suspense that crested with THE LADY VANISHES. Their writing partnership continued through *Night Train to Munich* (1940), *Kipps* (1940), and *Young Mr. Pitt* (1941) before Launder, who had meantime made his directorial debut, joined Gilliat in 1944 to form Individual Pictures, the most notable of which were the series of farces about St. Trinian's, the boarding school for England's most madcap girls—from *The Happiest Days of Your Life* (1950), which Launder directed, through *The Wildcats of St. Trinian's* (1980).

Launer, S. John (1919–) American supporting actor, onscreen from 1955 for some three dozen roles, most often on television. Best known for his portrayal of a judge on television's *Perry Mason* (1958–66) and elsewhere, he played Ed Rutherford in THE ALFRED HITCHCOCK HOUR segment "Starring the Defense" (1963) and Sam Ward in *MARNIE*.

Laurents, Arthur (1918–) American playwright and screenwriter who first made his mark on Broadway with *Home of the Brave* (1945). It was adapted by other writers for the screen—like his later plays *The Time of the Cuckoo* (1952) (which became *Summertime,* 1955) and *West Side Story* (1957/1961)—but Laurents was soon brought to Hollywood himself to adapt Patrick Hamilton's play *Rope's End* to the screen as *ROPE*, and he returned for another eight films, from *Caught*

(1949) to *The Turning Point* (1977), for which he was nominated for an Academy Award.

Laurie, John (1897–1980) Dour Scottish character actor, onstage from 1921, who made his film debut as Johnny Boyle, the ill-placed hope of the Boyle family in JUNO AND THE PAYCOCK, and proceeded to nearly 100 screen roles through 1979, often—as when he played the crofter who takes in Richard Hannay in THE 39 STEPS—ethnic types who seemed to be nursing some deep grievance against the world.

Lauter, Ed (1940–) Balding, sharp-featured American character actor in many more than 100 film and television roles from 1972, often as a sheriff or military man. He played Arthur Adamson's unsavory coconspirator Joe Maloney in FAMILY PLOT.

LaValley, Albert J. American academic, professor of English at Livingston College, Rutgers University, whose anthology *Focus on Hitchcock* (Prentice-Hall, 1972) is still valuable as an historical overview of Hitchcock criticism circa 1970. The editor's introduction seeks to locate a Hitchcock between the popular entertainer briskly dismissed by *Sight and Sound* critics such as Penelope Houston and the stern moralist canonized by CAHIERS DU CINÉMA critics such as Eric ROHMER, Claude CHABROL, and François TRUFFAUT. Beneath the doubles of SHADOW OF A DOUBT and STRANGERS ON A TRAIN, he finds a more general attempt "to release a kind of absurdist logic in life. . . . [Hitchcock] makes life seem dreamlike, its surface a thin crust over a substratum of fear, insecurity, unconscious anxiety, and guilt." Finding in the director's fifties work the fullest expression of this penetration from social reality to revelatory psychosexual dream, he emphasizes essays by Ronald Christ, Rohmer and Chabrol, Leo Braudy, and Raymond DURGNAT that discuss *Strangers on a Train*, REAR WINDOW, THE WRONG MAN, VERTIGO, and PSYCHO. The anthology also includes Hithcock's 1937 essay "Direction," excerpts from Peter BOGDANOVICH's interviews with the director and other interviews on *Rear Window* and *TORN CURTAIN*, a pair of brief essays on Hitchcock's television work, and a shot-by-shot visual summary of the cornfield sequence in *NORTH BY NORTHWEST*. Perhaps the most valuable section today, however, is "Hitchcock Controversy," which shows the battle for Hithcock's reputation between such auteurist champions as Robin WOOD and Andrew SARRIS and such naysayers as Lindsay Anderson (who, writing in 1949, pronounces the American films disappointing) and Durgnat (who finds Hitchcock "too mediocre to be diabolical"), with André Bazin, in "Hitchcock versus Hitchcock," occupying a politely skeptical middle ground in describing an interview conducted during the shooting of *TO CATCH A THIEF*. The annotated bibliography, which includes several defenses of such problematic late films as *Torn Curtain* and *TOPAZ*, is the most complete for its time, and the whole collection, which is rounded out with brief reviews by James Agee and Pauline Kael and excerpts from Raymond CHANDLER's exasperated notes on his work for *Strangers on a Train,* is an exceptionally useful account of the battle to enshrine Hitchcock's reputation—the choice of a privileged canon of work, the debate over the relation between art and entertainment, the search for a single governing viewpoint, whether moralistic, aesthetic, or nihilistic, that would armor the director against his inveterate puckish evasiveness in discussing his own work.

Lawrence, Gertrude (1898–1952) Irrepressible British revue star, born Gertrude Alexandria Dagmar Lawrence-Klasen. Long associated onstage with Nöel COWARD, she made 10 screen appearances between 1929 and 1950. She played Lady Camber, née Shirley Neville, in *LORD CAMBER'S LADIES* and was in turn played herself by Julie Andrews in *Star!* (1968) and lampooned as actress Lorraine Sheldon by Ann Sheridan in *The Man Who Came to Dinner* (1942).

Lawton, Frank (1904–1969) Genteel British leading man of stage and (after 1930) screen who began in such romantic leads as Rolf Hornblower in *THE SKIN GAME* and then, increasingly

after playing the adult David in *David Copperfield* (1935), in character roles.

Leaver, Philip (or Phillip) (1904–) British character actor, onstage from 1924, who made his screen debut as Signor Doppo, the smilingly sinister magician in *THE LADY VANISHES*, and played another 20 film roles running the gamut from Harelip Murphy in *This Man Is News* (1938) to Pope Leo X in *Martin Luther* (1953).

Leavitt, Norman (1913–) General-purpose American actor who filled out the casts of more than 100 films and television segments from *The Spider Woman Strikes Back* (1946) to *The Day of the Locust* (1975). He appeared in four episodes of *ALFRED HITCHCOCK PRESENTS*—as Elmer in "The Belfry" (1956), the accountant in "John Brown's Body" (1956), the gas station attendant in "ONE MORE MILE TO GO," and Burns the painter in "Where Beauty Lies" (1962)—and three in *THE ALFRED HITCHCOCK HOUR*—as Ben Kaylor in "Night of the Owl" (1962), Kyle Sawyer in "You'll Be the Death of Me" (1963), and the gasman in "The Gentleman Caller" (1964).

Le Blanc, Lee American special-effects expert who worked on two dozen MGM films, including *NORTH BY NORTHWEST*, from 1957 to 1962.

Le Deaux, Marie American actress who played Tatania, the fat lady in *SABOTEUR*.

Lee, Auriol (1881–1941) Monocled British character actress and director. She made her London stage debut in 1900 and her New York debut three years later but stayed away from films for many years. Shortly after completing her second screen role as Isobel Sedbusk, the mystery novelist in *SUSPICION*, she was killed in an auto accident on her way from Hollywood to New York, where she was to direct Patricia HITCHCOCK in her Broadway debut in John Van Druten's *Solitaire.*

Lee, Canada (1907–1952) African-American actor, born Leonard Lionel. Onscreen from 1939, he played increasingly important parts in a half-dozen films, including the porter George ("Joe") Spencer in LIFEBOAT, ending with *Cry the Beloved Country* (1951), in which he was cast in the lead, the grieving father Stephen Kumalo.

Leff, Leonard J. American film historian, professor of English and Norris Chair in the Humanities at Okalahoma State University, and author of *Film Plots: Scene-by-Scene Narrative Outlines for Feature Film Study* (1983), *The Dame in the Kimono: Hollywood, Censorship and the Production Code from the 1920s to the 1960s* (with Jerrold L. Simmons, 1990), and *Hemingway and His Conspirators: Hollywood, Scribners, and the Making of American Celebrity Culture* (1997). His study *Hitchcock and Selznick: The Rich and Strange Collaboration of Alfred Hitchcock and David O. Selznick in Hollywood* (Weidenfeld and Nicolson, 1987), taking exception to the largely self-created myth that Hitchcock was an independent artist constantly undermined by unhelpful interference from SELZNICK, notoriously the most activist of his producers, argues that the two men, despite their contrasting personal styles (Selznick was a volcanic workaholic, Hitchcock an imperturbable creature of habit), depended on each other both as filmmakers and as careerists (each using the other to foster his own power and independence) throughout a collaboration that included not only the three Hitchcock films that Selznick produced (REBECCA, SPELLBOUND, and THE PARADINE CASE) but NOTORIOUS, on which Selznick worked with Hitchcock for a year before selling the package of screenplay, stars, and director to RKO in July 1945. Noting that neither ROPE nor UNDER CAPRICORN, the films he directed for TRANSATLANTIC PICTURES after his hard-won independence from Selznick in 1947, approaches the achievement of his best Selznick films, Leff concludes that it was not until Hitchcock and Sidney BERNSTEIN began to negotiate distribution deals for their own independent productions with studios that demanded sizeable percentages of the gross and approval of everything from the story and script to the title that the director realized that Hollywood studios "never defined 'independent' as 'not subject to control by others.'" His incisive study of the ways the odd-couple collaboration flourished despite the collaborators' incessant battles for control and the director's pursuit of a chimerical independence, well illustrated throughout and including an unusually detailed list of credits for their films together and extensive credits for the films they made separately, won a British Film Institute Award.

Légaré, Ovila (1901–1978) French stage actor, onscreen from 1945 in a dozen films. His first English-language role is as the murdered blackmailer Villette, briefly glimpsed in flashback in I CONFESS.

Lehman, Ernest (1920–) Versatile American screenwriter, former financial editor. Though the first film based on his work was *The Inside Story* (1948), he did not receive any screenwriting credits until 1954, the year he wrote the boardroom melodrama *Executive Suite* and the romantic comedy *Sabrina,* his first Oscar nomination. He followed these with the musical *The King and I,* the boxing memoir *Somebody Up There Likes Me,* and the Hollywood confidential *The Sweet Smell of Success* before Hitchcock asked MGM, to whom he was under contract, to secure his services for *The Wreck of the Mary Deare.* Both director and screenwriter soon lost interest in the project and set out, unbeknownst to MGM, to make the film that became NORTH BY NORTHWEST, which won Lehman an Oscar nomination for Best Original Screenplay. Fifteen years later, after his most financially successful film (*The Sound of Music,* 1965), two more Oscar-nominated screenplays (*Who's Afraid of Virginia Woolf?,* 1966; *Hello, Dolly!,* 1969)—both of which he produced—and his directorial debut, *Portnoy's Complaint* (1972), Lehman came back to work with Hitchcock in adapting Victor CANNING's *The Rainbird Pattern* for a film to be called first *One Plus One Equals One,* then *Deception,* and finally FAMILY PLOT.

Lehne, John American character actor, onscreen from 1972 in some 40 roles, mostly for television. He played Andy Bush in FAMILY PLOT.

Leigh, Janet (1927–) American actress, born Jeanette Helen Morrison. She was discovered while still a teenager by Norma Shearer, who, staying at a ski resort at which Leigh's parents worked, saw a photograph of her on her father's desk. She was soon signed to play the female lead in *The Romance of Rosy Ridge* (1947) and continued as a peaches-and-cream ingenue, gradually broadening her range in *The Naked Spur* (1952), *Houdini* (1953), *Touch of Evil* (1958), and PSYCHO; in the last, cast as the cheapest big star whose early death in the film could be guaranteed to shock the audience, she landed an Academy Award nomination. Although she appeared in some 60 films as various as *The Manchurian Candidate* (1962), *Bye Bye Birdie* (1963), and *Harper* (1966), Marion Crane became the role with which she was thenceforth indelibly associated, and in traveling the country to publicize her memoir, *There Really Was a Hollywood* (1984), her production history, *Psycho: Behind the Scenes of the Classic Thriller* (1995), and her novel, *House of Destiny* (1995), she repeatedly confirmed reports that since the week she spent dripping wet while shooting Hitchcock's most famous scene, she has never taken a shower. Formerly married to *Houdini* star Tony Curtis, she is the mother of actress Jamie Lee Curtis, with whom she appeared in *Halloween: H$_2$O* (1998).

Leigh-Hunt, Barbara (1935–) British stage actress who made her feature film debut as the ill-fated Brenda Blaney in FRENZY and then shifted immediately (beginning with her work as Catherine Parr in *Henry VIII and His Six Wives,* 1973) to playing great ladies and other character roles, many for the BBC.

Leighton, Margaret (1922–1976) Demure British actress, onstage from 16. Best known for her work in the theater—for example, her Tony-winning role in *Separate Tables* (1956)—she made some 40 film and television appearances, usually in such leading roles as Catherine Winslow in *The Winslow Boy* (1948) and Marguerite Blakeney in *The Elusive Pimpernel* (1950) but occasionally in such character parts as Milly, the treacherous servant in UNDER CAPRICORN. An Oscar nominee for her supporting role as

Mrs. Maudsley in *The Go-Between* (1971), she starred as Iris Teleton, whose husband's girlfriend presses her too hard to divorce him, in the ALFRED HITCHCOCK PRESENTS episode "Tea Time" (1958), and as the frightened aunt Nell Snyder in THE ALFRED HITCHCOCK HOUR episode "Where the Woodbine Twineth" (1965). Her second husband was actor Laurence HARVEY, her third actor Michael WILDING.

Leitch, Thomas M. (1951–) American academic, professor of English at the University of Delaware and author of *What Stories Are: Narrative Theory and Interpretation* (1986), *Lionel Trilling: An Annotated Bibliography* (1992), and *Crime Films* (2002). His *Find the Director and Other Hitchcock Games* (University of Georgia Press, 1991) uses the games Hitchcock's characters play in the course of his films and the director's trademark cameo appearances, which challenge mimetic theories of narrative by encouraging audiences to search for the figure of the director even as they believe their attention is enclosed within the frame of the story, as figures for the films themselves. Not only Hitchcock's cameos but his films, Leitch contends, are games the director plays with his audience by establishing himself as the shaping presence of "Hitchcock films"; offering a promise of pleasure, beginning with THE MAN WHO KNEW TOO MUCH (1934), based on a series of rules governing what Hitchcock films will be like (witty, fast-paced, suspenseful, ranging in rapid succession over a broad variety of tones); and periodically changing the rules in subsequent periods of his work beginning with such rule-breaking films as REBECCA, ROPE, REAR WINDOW, THE WRONG MAN, and THE BIRDS. These changes affirm the Hitchcockian status of the director's work by challenging audiences to find new pleasures in place of the pleasures with which earlier films had made them perhaps too familiar and suggest that Hitchcock's status as an exemplary storyteller has broader implications for conceiving stories as games between authors and audiences.

Lerner, Goodhart, and Hoffman The three composers credited with writing songs for

YOUNG AND INNOCENT, notably "No One Can Like the Drummer Man," over which Hitchcock traverses the entire length of a ballroom in a mesmerizing single crane shot to frame the murderous drummer's twitching eyes.

Leslie, Joan   See BRODEL, JOAN.

L'Estrange, David   The pseudonym under which Ivor NOVELLO and Constance COLLIER collaborated on several plays, including *Down Hill* (1926), filmed by Hitchcock the following year as *DOWNHILL*.

Leverett, Winston (H.) (1908–1960)   American sound recordist of the fifties, most often at PARAMOUNT, as for *THE TROUBLE WITH HARRY* and *VERTIGO*.

Levy, Benn W. (1900–1973)   British playwright and stage director, much in demand as a screenwriter in the early years of synchronized sound. He cowrote *Kitty* (1928), the first British film with dialogue sequences; provided additional dialogue for *BLACKMAIL*; and directed *LORD CAMBER'S LADIES*, which Hitchcock produced. His proficiency sent him to Hollywood to work on *The Old Dark House* (1932), but he was soon back for *Loves of a Dictator* (1935), his final film. In 1945 he was elected to Parliament, where he served until 1950.

Levy, Louis (1893–1957)   British composer, in films from 1916, longtime supervisor of musical production at GAUMONT-BRITISH and GAINSBOROUGH. His billing as "musical director" in 100 films from 1932 is often ambiguous. He evidently composed the music for Hitchcock's early British thrillers—*THE MAN WHO KNEW TOO MUCH* (1934), *THE 39 STEPS, SECRET AGENT, SABOTAGE, YOUNG AND INNOCENT,* and *THE LADY VANISHES*—although Arthur BENJAMIN is credited for the only substantial piece of music heard during *The Man Who Knew Too Much,* and LERNER, GOODHART, AND HOFFMAN are credited with the songs in *Young and Innocent*. By contrast, *UNDER CAPRICORN* and *STAGE FRIGHT*, the last two Hitchcock films on which he is billed as

musical director or music supervisor, credit Richard ADDINSELL and Leighton LUCAS respectively as composers.

Levy, Weaver (1925–)   Chinese-American actor typecast in ethnic bit parts from 1945. Best known as the costar of the television series *Adventures in Paradise* (1959–61), he appeared in two episodes of *ALFRED HITCHCOCK PRESENTS*, as the chauffeur Chang in "The Canary Sedan" (1958) and the native servant sent to fetch the doctor in "POISON."

Lewis, B.M.   British stage actor who appears as Domeyer in *WALTZES FROM VIENNA*.

Lewis, Frederic (or Frederick)   British composer who wrote the music for *Storm in a Teacup* (1937) and served as musical director on 10 later films, including *JAMAICA INN*.

Lewis, Harold (1901–1966)   American sound recordist and designer, with PARAMOUNT with minor exceptions from *A Farewell to Arms* (1932) to *The Last of the Secret Agents* (1966). An occasional composer and production manager, he supervised the sound recording on *TO CATCH A THIEF, THE TROUBLE WITH HARRY*, and *VERTIGO*.

Lifeboat   (Alternative titles: *Das Rettungsboot, I Prigionieri dell'oceano*) 20th Century-Fox, 96 minutes, January 1944. **Producer:** Kenneth MacGowan; **Director:** Alfred Hitchcock; **Screenplay:** Jo Swerling and Ben Hecht, based on an original subject by John Steinbeck; **Cinematographer:** Glen Mac Williams; **Art directors:** James Basevi and Maurice Ransford; **Set decoration:** Thomas Little and Frank E. Hughes; **Costumes:** Rene Hubert; **Makeup:** Guy Pearce; **Sound:** Bernard Freericks, Roger Heman; **Special effects:** Fred Sersen; **Technical adviser:** Thomas Fitzsimmons, National Maritime Union; **Editor:** Dorothy Spencer; **Music:** Hugo Friedhofer; **Cast:** Tallulah Bankhead (Constance Porter), William Bendix (Gus Smith), Walter Slezak (Willie), Mary Anderson (Alice MacKenzie), John Hodiak (John Kovac), Henry Hull (Charles D. Rittenhouse), Heather Angel (Mrs. Higgins), Hume Cronyn (Stanley Garrett), Canada

Lee (George ["Joe"] Spencer), William Yetter, Jr. (German sailor).

On loan to 20TH CENTURY-FOX for what was to have been a two-picture deal beginning in 1942, Hitchcock considered the possibility of shooting an entire film in a single location—in this case, aboard a lifeboat carrying the surviving passengers whose ocean liner had just been sunk by a German U-boat. The first screenwriter Fox producer Kenneth MACGOWAN considered was A.J. Cronin, whose novel *The Keys of the Kingdom* was to serve as the basis for Hitchcock's second Fox film, but Hitchcock, invigorated and perhaps star-struck by his recent collaboration with Thornton WILDER, suggested first Ernest Hemingway, who declined with thanks, and then John STEINBECK, whose treatment failed to ignite enthusiasm. MacKinley KANTOR was likewise dismissed after two weeks, and the screenplay was largely written by Hollywood veteran Jo SWERLING, with Ben HECHT serving again as script doctor. The cast, headed by the inspired choice of Tallulah BANKHEAD as the person least likely to be found sitting in a lifeboat in the North Atlantic, did not have the inconvenience of traveling to remote locations because the entire film was shot in the SERSEN tank at Fox, with the background skies and the rolling horizon line sup-

The most famous of all Hitchcock's cameo appearances is in *Lifeboat*: before-and-after photographs memorializing his recent weight loss in a newspaper Gus Smith (William Bendix) is reading. *(National Film Society Archive)*

plied by back projection. But actors did suffer the discomfort of the wind and water-spraying machines constructed to add atmosphere to the shots, the repeated indignity of falling into the tank, and in most cases the trials of illness. The restricted set posed another problem as well: How would the director make his ritual cameo appearance? At first he thought of being a body floating past the lifeboat, but then his recent weight loss suggested the idea of his appearance in before-and-after poses for a fictional weight-loss product called Reduco advertised in a newspaper the radio operator Gus is reading.

Hitchcock's 30th film was greeted in January 1944 by reviews often as stormy as the film's weather. Dorothy Thompson gave it 10 days to get out of town, and Bosley Crowther complained that its fable of would-be allies swayed by their passivity and bickering to follow a stronger survivor, captain of the U-boat that sank their ship, "sold out democratic ideals and elevated the Nazi superman." Ironically, later critics have had precisely the opposite reaction, neglecting the film's judicious warnings about Allied weaknesses and Axis strength and its formal austerity (a single set, no music between the opening and closing, severely limited opportunities for variety in blocking and lighting), emphasizing instead the film's preachiness, and it has attracted little sustained critical attention. Although Hitchcock, Steinbeck, and cinematographer Glen MACWILLIAMS were nominated for Oscars for their work on the film, and Bankhead won the New York Film Critics Circle Award for Best Actress, *Lifeboat* lost nearly $1 million—the first of Hitchcock's American films to post such a significant loss—and Hitchcock's promised second feature for Fox never materialized. The film's major legacy has been its status as an unusually fair-minded example of wartime propaganda (even if its political complexity is not matched by psychological nuance)—its portrait of hardbitten reporter Constance Porter as perhaps the strongest woman ever subjected to the Hitchcock treatment (not only does the character lose her camera, her typewriter, her incongruous fur coat, and finally her beloved diamond bracelet, sacrificed as bait to catch a fish for her starving companions, but the tough-

minded actress who played her during those weeks in the studio tank came down with pneumonia)—and as the first fruits of the director's enduring passion for the possibilities of one-set films, which later bore the fruits of *ROPE, DIAL M FOR MURDER,* and *REAR WINDOW.*

Linden, Margaret British playwright who with John COLTON coauthored the play *UNDER CAPRICORN,* based on Helen SIMPSON's novel.

Lindgren, Harry (M.) American sound recordist at PARAMOUNT from the early days of synch sound for more than 50 films, including *REAR WINDOW.*

Linn, James (I.) American wardrobe designer specializing in men's fashions who worked on the costumes for *MARNIE* and seven later films.

Lion, Leon M. (1878–1947) British playwright, comedian, and producer, often the star of his own waggish farces. Onstage from 1895, he produced more than 100 West End entertainments. His 10 film credits include the starring role in both versions of his play *The Chinese Puzzle* (1919, 1932) and the joking, feckless Ben in *NUMBER SEVENTEEN,* whose stage run he had produced in 1925.

Livesey, Sam (1873–1936) Stalwart stage-trained Welsh actor, onscreen for more than 40 roles from 1917, often as a police officer, as in *BLACKMAIL,* in which he plays the Chief Inspector in two scenes of the silent version and one scene of the sound version.

Livingston, Jay (1915–) American composer and songwriter, at PARAMOUNT from 1943. With his frequent collaborator, lyricist Ray EVANS, he turned out a series of hit film songs during the next 20 years, earning seven Oscar nominations and winning Academy Awards for "Buttons and Bows" (from *The Paleface,* 1948), "Mona Lisa" (from *Captain Carey, U.S.A.,* 1950), and "Que Sera, Sera" (from *THE MAN WHO KNEW TOO MUCH,* 1956) before turning to television and writing the theme songs for *Bonanza* (1959–73) and *Mr. Ed* (1961–66).

Lloyd, Doris (1896–1968)   Stage-trained British actress, born Hessy Doris Lloyd, onscreen from 1920. During a 50-year career that included roles in more than 100 films and television programs, she ripened from such roles as the socialite Miss Wetherby in *SUSPICION* to starchy servants and spinsters. She appeared five times in *ALFRED HITCHCOCK PRESENTS*—as Emily's shipboard companion in "DIP IN THE POOL," Miss Wilkinson in "The Impromptu Murder" (1958), Mrs. Crawpit in "Safety for the Witness" (1958), the Wellington maid in "The Schwartz-Metterklume Method" (1960), and the housekeeper Mrs. Boyd in "The Silk Petticoat" (1962)—and four more in *THE ALFRED HITCHCOCK HOUR*—as Andrina Gibbs in "The Dark Pool" (1963), Martha in "Isabel" (1964), the Dailey maid in "One of the Family" (1965), and the mother in "Thou Still Unravished Bride" (1965).

Lloyd, Frank (1886–1960)   Proficient Scottish-born writer-director, in Hollywood from 1913, first as actor in some 40 films and then as writer and director of wide and prodigious experience in more than 100 films, including *The Divine Lady* (1929) and *Cavalcade* (1933), which won him Best Director Oscars, and *Mutiny on the Bounty* (1935), which won for Best Picture. Beginning in 1920, he turned to producing some two dozen films, most of them his own, but a few, such as *SABOTEUR*, written and directed by other hands.

Lloyd, John (J.)   Longtime art director for *ALFRED HITCHCOCK PRESENTS* and *THE ALFRED HITCHCOCK HOUR* and dozens of later television programs and such feature films as *Animal House* (1978) and *The Naked Gun* (1988). Among scores of other episodes of Hitchcock's series, he designed the visuals for the Hitchcock-directed "MR. BLANCHARD'S SECRET," "ONE MORE MILE TO GO," "THE PERFECT CRIME," "LAMB TO THE SLAUGHTER," "DIP IN THE POOL," "POISON," "BANQUO'S CHAIR," "ARTHUR," and "THE CRYSTAL TRENCH," as well as the *SUSPICION* segment "FOUR O'CLOCK."

Lloyd, Norman (1914–)   Stage-trained American character actor, a charter member of Orson Welles's Mercury Players who came to Hollywood to play Frank Fry, the colorless title role in *SABOTEUR*. Cast again as the suicidally neurotic patient Garmes in *SPELLBOUND*, he continued over the next 10 years in 20 supporting film roles before joining *ALFRED HITCHCOCK PRESENTS* in 1957 as associate producer. During the next six years he served with Joan HARRISON as the series' producer and script supervisor. In addition, he acted in several episodes—"Nightmare in 4-D" (1957), "Design for Loving" (1958), "The Little Man Who Was There" (1960), and "Maria" (1961)—and directed several more, most notably "Man from the South" (1960). Upon Harrison's departure from *THE ALFRED HITCHCOCK HOUR* in 1963, he was named executive producer, and remained in that status until the series ended two years later. Retired from film and television production since 1979, he continues to make occasional acting appearances, most recently as the president of Wassamotta U in *The Adventures of Rocky and Bullwinkle* (2000).

Lockwood, Alexander (1902–1990)   Polish-born American actor in 40 film and television roles from 1938. Cast in uncredited bits in *SABOTEUR* and *THE WRONG MAN*, he returned as the judge (still uncredited) before whom Roger Thornhill pleads not guilty to drunk driving and car theft in *NORTH BY NORTHWEST* and as the parson who gives George Lumley information about Eddie Shoebridge in *FAMILY PLOT*. He also appeared as Mr. Rigsby, the principal in the *FORD STARTIME* episode "INCIDENT AT A CORNER"; twice on *ALFRED HITCHCOCK PRESENTS*, as Henry Willet in "Self Defense" (1961) and the sheriff in "Make My Death Bed" (1961); and as Dr. Campbell in *THE ALFRED HITCHCOCK HOUR* segment "Day of Reckoning" (1962).

Lockwood, Margaret (1916–1990)   Stage-trained British leading lady, born Margaret Day to a British family in Pakistan. Onstage from 12, she made her film debut in 1935, soon graduating from such ingenues as Iris Henderson, the heroine of

THE LADY VANISHES—a role she virtually reprised in *Night Train to Munich* (1940)—to such sleek schemers as Barbara Worth in *The Wicked Lady* (1945) before returning to the theater in the fifties in character parts. Her final film role, as Cinderella's wicked stepmother in *The Slipper and the Rose* (1976), fit her like a glass slipper.

Loder, John (1898–1988) British romantic lead, born John Muir Lowe into a military family. He served in Gallipoli in World War I and ended as a prisoner of war before returning to England to begin an acting career. Onscreen from 1926, he rose to stardom in such roles as John Ridd in *Lorna Doone* (1935) and Ted Spencer, the bland undercover police sergeant in SABOTAGE, and then departed for Hollywood when World War II broke out but failed to duplicate his stardom in America, where he was most memorable for playing Elliot Livingston, the suitor Charlotte Vale so briskly dismissed in *Now, Voyager* (1942). After marrying actress Hedy Lamarr in 1943 (they divorced in 1947), adopting U.S. citizenship in 1947, and appearing on Broadway in 1947 and 1950, he made the last of his 80 films in England before retiring to his fifth wife's cattle ranch in Argentina.

Lodger, The: A Story of the London Fog

(Alternative titles: *The Lodger, The Strange Case of Jonathan Drew* [U.S.], *Les cheveux d'or*, *Il Pensionante*, *Le Locataire*) A Gainsborough Picture, Wardour & F., Amer-Anglo Corporation (U.S.), approximately 75 minutes (U.K.), 83 minutes (U.S.), September 1926. Presented by Michael Balcon and Carlyle Blackwell, by arrangement with C.M. Woolf; **Director:** Alfred Hitchcock; **Screenplay:** Eliot Stannard, based on the novel by Mrs. [Marie Adelaide] Belloc Lowndes; **Cinematographer:** Baron [Gaetano] Ventimiglia; **Assistant director:** Alma Reville; **Art directors:** C. Wilfred Arnold and Bertram Evans; **Editing and titling:** Ivor Montagu; **Title designs:** E. McKnight Kauffer; **Cast:** Marie Ault (the landlady [Mrs. Bunting]), Arthur Chesney (her husband), June [Tripp] (Daisy, a mannequin [their daughter]), Malcolm Keen (Joe [Betts], a police detective), Ivor Novello (the Lodger), Eve Gray (showgirl victim), Maudie Dunham, and Daisy Campbell.

Michael BALCON chose the property on which Hitchcock's third film would be based—Marie Belloc LOWNDES's novel about a landlady who gradually realizes that her new lodger is Jack the Ripper but protects him from the police until he departs—in April 1926, and by the following month Eliot STANNARD had completed the adaptation and the director had prepared shot-by-shot sketches for the film. The uneventful shoot was completed in July, but Graham CUTTS persuaded C.M. WOOLF to withhold the film, like THE PLEASURE GARDEN and THE MOUNTAIN EAGLE, from distribution. Balcon, however, eager to capitalize on his star Ivor NOVELLO's success in Cutts's *The Rat* and to recoup his £12,000 investment in the production, called in Ivor MONTAGU, who suggested reshooting several scenes, reducing the 300 title cards by three-quarters, and periodically inserting titles designed by E. McKnight KAUFFER, whose triangular pattern echoed the notes left at the scene of each murder by the self-styled Avenger. The trade screening in September 1926 was so successful that it not only overcame Woolf's objections but persuaded him to release the two embargoed earlier films as well.

One price of this success was fidelity to Lowndes's novel, whose shadowy hero had been revealed as Jack the Ripper. As in SUSPICION 15 years later, the male star's immense romantic popularity forbade him from playing a killer, so a psychological study of a woman's dawning realization that she has grown attached to an irredeemable criminal became in both cases a more melodramatic and problematic tale of false suspicions and their cost. In adapting *The Lodger,* Stannard further (and predictably) shifted dramatic interest from the landlady Mrs. Bunting, who becomes a relatively minor character, to her daughter Daisy, whose relationship with her mother's lodger is more conventionally romantic, and made the Lodger himself, even before he is unmasked as the would-be avenger of his sister's murder, a more romantic figure. The result is paradoxically both more conventional and richer than the source novel. By framing her story from the landlady's increasingly suspicious but acutely limited point of view, Lowndes had achieved the sort of single-minded intensity that would later often and rather misleadingly be described as Hitchcockian. The director's own treatment is much more uneven in its details: The elder Buntings' domestic jocosity and the risible self-confidence of Daisy's fatuous police fiancé Joe Betts ("Great news! They've put me on the Avenger case") comport incongruously with the Lodger's imperious behavior toward the parents and his mournful romance with their daughter. Yet the film's calculated ambiguities have a power the novel lacks. William ROTHMAN's exhaustive analysis of the film notes the ways Hitchcock quibbles on the relation between perception and imagination, as when he illustrates the Buntings' awareness of the Lodger pacing in the room above by showing him walking back and forth on a glass ceiling installed above their chandelier, or when he cuts between Mrs. Bunting sitting up in bed and the spectral Lodger descending the stairs, leaving it unclear whether the film is showing his actual departure or his landlady's imaginings. In the same way, the film, in doing everything it can to show the Lodger in a gratuitously suspicious light only to clear him in the end, is logically unconvincing and yet psychologically compelling because it doubles him with the never-seen Avenger as an avenger himself, raising nagging questions about the purity of his own motives and the unguessed motives of his criminal quarry in ways that endure long after the film's happy fadeout, which bookends its opening two shots—a closeup of a blonde victim screaming, then a cut to a flashing neon sign announcing "To-Night Golden Curls"—with a track-in from a shot of Daisy snuggled safely in the Lodger's arms as the same sign is seen flashing outside the window to a facial closeup that leaves both the sign and Novello's face outside the frame. Although the director forever after described *The Lodger,* with its criminal plot and the first of his cameo appearances, as "the first true Hitchcock film," it would be eight years before he settled once and for all into the niche marked by its suspense formula. Yet the film's melding of domestic routine and oneiric melodrama would be both deeper and more immediately pervasive, as he showed the following year in *DOWNHILL* and *EASY VIRTUE.*

Lomas, Herbert (1887–1961) Cadaverous British character actor with stage experience.

Onscreen from 1931, he appeared in nearly 40 films, mostly in the thirties, in roles ranging from the artist's father in *Rembrandt* (1936) to Sir Humphrey Pengallan's tenant in *JAMAICA INN.*

Lombard, Carole (1908–1942) American leading lady, born Jane Alice Peters, the doyenne of thirties screwball comedy. Discovered playing baseball on a California street, she was cast in her first film, *A Perfect Crime* (1921), at 12 and then returned reluctantly to school, leaving at 15 to pursue an acting career. In 1925 she signed a contract with Fox, but after a few films, the studio canceled it when an auto accident the following year left her face scarred. Signing with Mack Sennett, she appeared in a dozen two-reel slapstick comedies in 1927–28 and then returned to dramatic roles with Fox and PARAMOUNT, the studio that changed her screen name from Carol to Carole Lombard in 1930. But her real breakthrough was at Columbia, playing actress Lily Garland opposite John Barrymore's megalomaniac star/producer Oscar Jaffe in the frantically paced *Twentieth Century* (1934). Her unlikely combination of giddy humor, earthiness, and sophisticated glamour in such films as *My Man Godfrey* (1936)—in which she costarred with her ex-husband William Powell and won an Oscar nomination—and *Nothing Sacred* (1937), in which she played a small-town girl determined to milk the rumor that she was dying to take advantage of a newspaper-sponsored trip to New York, made her Hollywood's leading comedienne of the thirties. Her friendship with the Hitchcocks ever since their first trip to America (they rented her house in Bel-Air when she went to live on her new husband Clark Gable's ranch in Encino) made her and the director eager to work with each other on *MR. AND MRS. SMITH,* in which she enlivened the breaks from her performance as the loving, battling Ann Krausheimer Smith by matching Hitchcock joke for practical joke; she responded to his oft-repeated remark that "actors are cattle" by arranging for three heifers to be delivered to the set, labeled Robert MONTGOMERY, Gene RAYMOND, and Carole Lombard. It was the last time she would see herself onscreen; before the release of her final film,

To Be Or Not to Be (1942), she was killed in an airplane crash during a war-bond tour.

Long, Richard (1927–1974)

American actor who went directly from high school to a Universal contract and soon worked his way up from such juvenile leads and character roles as Ma and Pa Kettle's son Tom to leads in second features. He is best-known, however, for his work on television, from his roles as Fran Steppe's apparent lover (actually her brother Dave) in the SUSPICION segment "FOUR O'CLOCK," the scheming store manager Paul De Vore in the *Alfred Hitchcock Presents* episode "Golden Opportunity" (1962), and the adulterous bookie Eddie Breech in the *Alfred Hitchcock Hour* segment "Blood Bargain" (1963) to his starring roles in the series *77 Sunset Strip* (1960–61), *The Big Valley* (1965–69), and *Nanny and the Professor* (1970–71).

Longden, John (1900–1971)

Starchy, reliable British leading man, a paragon of stiff-upper-lip romance, who entered movies just in time to survive the transition to sound. He played Alice White's coldly solicitous detective fiancé Frank Webber in BLACKMAIL, Charles Bentham in JUNO AND THE PAYCOCK, and Charles Hornblower in THE SKIN GAME; he then gradually ripened into a character actor in some 50 later roles, from Inspector Kent in YOUNG AND INNOCENT and Captain Johnson in JAMAICA INN to the narrator in *Stairway to Heaven* (1946) and Leodogran in *Arthur and Guinevere* (1963).

long takes

"As you can see, the best way to do it is with scissors," Hitchcock told a crowd gathered at a gala reception in his honor at the Film Society of Lincoln Center in April 1974. The reference was not only to his short speech and to the killing of Swann in DIAL M FOR MURDER but also to his dedication to efficient editing, whose locus classicus is the shower scene in PSYCHO. Yet Hitchcock did not always favor scissors. Charles BARR has found long takes, some lasting as long as four minutes, as early as JUNO AND THE PAYCOCK, THE SKIN GAME, and WALTZES FROM VIENNA. *The Skin Game* especially anticipates the rhythmic aesthetic that would come to be associated with Orson Welles: an alternation between long, static shots and rapidly cut sequences. In these early sound films, Hitchcock's camera is severely restricted in movement. But his most celebrated long take of the thirties is marked by audacious, mesmerizing, and inexorable movement as the camera, cutting from Erica Burgoyne's despairing comment in YOUNG AND INNOCENT that the murder suspect she and Old Will are seeking (a man who can be identified only by his twitching eyes) must be somewhere in the Grand Hotel, glides high over the dividing wall to the ballroom of the hotel, framing the bandstand at the far end of the room, and finally comes to rest only a few inches from the eyes of the drummer, which obligingly start to twitch. This alarming shot is so motivic, though so out of keeping with the rest of the film, that William ROTHMAN took it as the inspiration for his title *Hitchcock—The Murderous Gaze.*

According to Leonard J. LEFF, Hitchcock's interest in the long take was revived by his use of them in editing documentary footage of Nazi atrocities to preserve them from any suspicion of fakery. When the director returned to gradually more pronounced long takes in the late forties, he used them in ways that owed less to Welles and William Wyler than to *Young and Innocent*—not only as the logical extension of unbroken dramatic moments that would preserve their unity as long, and ideally as suspensefully, as possible but also as visual narratives virtually complete in themselves. Lacking the great leaps in time of *Citizen Kane,* he saw no reason to adopt Welles's rhythmic alternation; Hitchcock's most notable long takes in the forties, like Alicia and Devlin's monumental kiss in NOTORIOUS or the crane-in from the second floor landing to Alicia's hand secretly clutching the key to the wine cellar, are embedded in films that are already slow moving. He began to experiment with complex camera movements hat would travel up staircases, following characters or linking conversations, in THE PARADINE CASE. Though he gave most of these shots up when David O. SELZNICK objected to them as needlessly time consuming, he returned to the long-take aesthetic with a vengeance in his two TRANSATLANTIC films. The more widely noted of these is *ROPE*, 10 of whose 11 shots are not only exceptionally long in duration (averaging between seven and eight minutes each) but also spliced together in ways often designed to make them seem even longer to suit the continuous action of the story by creating an uninterrupted flow of space. The film is occasionally breathtaking in its use of sustained dramatic moments to build suspense, most notably when it frames the oblivious Mrs. Wilson methodically clearing off the chest in preparation for opening it. Yet André Bazin clearly had a point when he remarked that Hitchcock was not using long takes at all but simply cutting the film according to orthodox rules of continuity editing, except that he was joining his shots by camera movements instead of cuts. The space of the apartment interior is not especially interesting, and most of the camera movements simply follow characters from place to place or from group to group. More important, the absence of cutting works forbids unobtrusive cut-ins to material clues and works as well against segmentation, leaving the story to be broken down, in the manner of a play, by the characters' entrances and exits.

Although it is both less well known and less successful than *Rope*, UNDER CAPRICORN is far more interesting as an example of the long-take aesthetic because, as John BELTON has pointed out, "Hitchcock is free to cut at any time in the film [but] . . . for the most part, he doesn't." The latter film, running almost two hours, includes fewer than 170 shots, some of them far more elaborate than anything in *Rope,* and because Hitchcock is not bound by the restriction of a single continuous space or an unbroken visual field, the most striking of the film's many long takes open up startling new possibilities. The shot that takes Charles Adare from the dark exterior of Minyago Yugilla to a close approach to the house, where he can look in the windows and get glimpses of the mysterious Lady Hetty, then to the interior, where the camera marks the entrance of each male guest without his wife before cutting on the dramatic moment of Hetty's entrance, dramatizes the ambiguity of Adare's status as outsider and Hetty's as insider with extraordinary power, and the single long take in which Hetty confesses to the murder of her brother

is mesmerizing. With these two films, however, Hitchcock seems to have gotten his infatuation with long takes out of his system. "No doubt about it; films must be cut," he ruled soon afterward, and although the rhythm of later films like *VERTIGO* is more languorous than anything in *Rope* or *Under Capricorn,* he never returned to such striking long takes again.

Lord Camber's Ladies An Alfred Hitchcock Production for British International, 80 minutes, November 1932. **Producer:** Alfred Hitchcock; **Director:** Benn W. Levy; **Screenplay:** Edwin Greenwood and Gilbert Wakefield, based on *The Case of Lady Camber,* a play by H.A. Vachell; **Additional dialogue:** Benn W. Levy; **Cinematographer:** James Wilson; **Art director:** David Rawnsley; **Assistant director:** Frank Mills; **Sound recordist:** Alec Murray; **Special stage dresses:** British Celanese Ltd; **Cast:** Gerald du Maurier (Dr. Napier), Gertrude Lawrence (Shirley Neville), Benita Hume (Janet King), Nigel Bruce (Lord Camber), Clare Greet (Peach), A. Bromley Davenport (Sir Bedford Slufter), Betty Norton (Hetty), Hal Gordon (stage manager), Molly Lamont (actress), Hugh E. Wright (old man), and Harold B. Meade.

This quota quickie, which represents Hitchcock's last work for BRITISH INTERNATIONAL, was planned in 1932 as the first of a number of projects on which he would mentor young directors working under him. Although it gave a meatier role to Hitchcock discovery Benita HUME, the telephone operator of EASY VIRTUE, as the nurse wrongly suspected of poisoning the new Lady Camber, the adaptation of H.A. VACHELL's play—the only film Hitchcock ever produced without directing—was certainly unsuccessful in its avowed goal. Not only was it not followed by any later such projects, but the mentoring relationship between Hitchcock and Benn LEVY, who had collaborated with him on *BLACKMAIL,* was subverted when Levy told a grip to whom Hitchcock was speaking to ignore the sometime director. The two former collaborators did not speak again for 30 years.

Lorne, Marion (1883–1968) Inimitably dotty American character actress, born Marion Lorne

MacDougal. She trained at the American Academy of Dramatic Arts, made her Broadway debut in 1905, and married playwright/theater manager Walter Hackett, who wrote many roles for her before his death in 1944. At that point she contemplated retirement but was tempted back to the stage to play Veta Louise Simmons in the National Road Company's production of Mary Chase's play *Harvey* (1945–48). She made her screen debut at 68 as Bruno Anthony's hilariously oblivious mother in STRANGERS ON A TRAIN. Though she appeared in only two later films (once in a priceless cameo in *The Graduate* [1967]), she achieved her greatest fame on television, playing twittery Aunt Clara in *Bewitched* from 1964 until her death.

Lorre, Peter (1904–1964)   Diminutive, popeyed Hungarian-born character actor, né László Löwenstein, equally unforgettable in sinister or pathetic

Peter Lorre

roles. He ran away from home at 17 to join a theater, worked for a time as a bank teller, and found gradually more substantial roles on the German, Austrian, and Swiss stages before Fritz LANG cast him as Hans Beckert, the psychopathic child murderer in *M* (1931). Lorre was so successful at conveying both the killer's menace and his self-loathing vulnerability that the part vaulted him to international fame and became his signature role. Fleeing the Nazis in 1933 after 10 more film roles, he stopped in England long enough to appear as Abbott, the provocateur who kidnaps little Betty Lawrence in THE MAN WHO KNEW TOO MUCH (1934), before continuing on to Hollywood for *Mad Love* and *Crime and Punishment* (both 1935), both of which continued to play on this mixture of menace and pathos. The following year, however, Hitchcock persuaded him to return to play the General, the lighthearted, bloodthirsty assassin in SECRET AGENT. Lorre achieved his widest English-language audience five years later, in a series of nine WARNER BROS. films beginning with *The Maltese Falcon* (1941) in which he was bookended in character roles with the broad but equally sinister Sidney Greenstreet. Although a weight gain largely restricted his later roles to burlesques like O'Hara in *Beat the Devil* (1954), Brankov in *Silk Stockings* (1957), and his two roles in ALFRED HITCHCOCK PRESENTS—the conniving Mexican detective Tomas Salgado in "The Diplomatic Corpse" (1957) and the high-stakes gambler Carlos in "Man from the South" (1960)—he gave one last nuanced performance as Skeeter the Clown in *The Big Circus* (1959). He died the same day his wife was appearing in court to seek a consent decree to their divorce.

Lovell, Roderick   British actor whose brief film career (1948–52) spanned just five film roles, including a bit in UNDER CAPRICORN.

Lovering, Otho (or Otto) (1889–1968) American film editor, a specialist in westerns and other action-filled properties who worked on more than 100 films from 1928 until his death. He is credited as editorial supervisor on FOREIGN CORRESPONDENT.

Lowndes, Marie Belloc (1868–1947) British novelist and playwright, née Marie Adelaide Belloc. Born into a distinguished family (her great-great-grandfather was pioneering chemist Joseph Priestley, her brother essayist Hilaire Belloc), she claimed to have sat down to write every day since she was 16. Her success was both direct and indirect. Her novel *The Chink in the Armor* (1912), a tale of murder presented from the viewpoint of the intended victim, anticipates the work of Francis Iles; *Lizzie Borden: A Study in Conjecture* (1939) sandwiches a fictionalized account of the famous murder case in between factual endboards; *The Story of Ivy* (1927) and *Letty Lynton* (1931) were both filmed (as *Ivy*, 1947, and *Letty Lynton*, 1932), and her story "What Really Happened" was adapted for THE ALFRED HITCHCOCK HOUR in 1963. But she is best remembered for THE LODGER, her 1913 novelization based on her 1911 short story that presents a mysterious killer as his landlady might have seen him. It has been filmed four times, every version but Hitchcock's 1926 film—the 1932 remake again starring Ivor NOVELLO, the 1944 version with Laird Cregar, and the 1954 *Man in the Attic* with Jack Palance—following the novel closely.

Lucas, Leighton (1902–1983) British composer and conductor, former ballet dancer. In the 12 years following 1949 he composed scores for nine films (including STAGE FRIGHT, his second) and served as musical director or conductor for two more.

Ludwig, Otto (1903–1983) Film editor who worked on both sides of the Atlantic before settling in 1939 at UNIVERSAL, where he edited SABOTEUR and some 50 other films.

Lukas, Karl (1919–1995) Stocky American character actor, born Karol Louis Lukasiak. Most of his roles before 1970 were in such television series as ALFRED HITCHCOCK PRESENTS—where he appeared as Otto in "Gratitude" (1961), the mailman in "BANG! YOU'RE DEAD," Uncle Ben in "Services Rendered" (1961), and prizefighter Soldier Fresno in "Ten O'Clock Tiger" (1962)—and THE ALFRED HITCHCOCK HOUR, where he appeared as Mel Tanner in "Last Seen Wearing Blue Jeans" (1963). Afterward he moved to supporting roles in feature films from *Tora! Tora! Tora!* (1970) to *Memories of Me* (1988).

Lukas, Paul (1887–1971) Immaculately polished Hungarian actor, born Pál Lukács. After training at the Hungarian Actors' Academy, he made his stage debut in 1916 and soon became a matinee idol famous throughout central Europe and was cast in three Hungarian films. But his English-language roles, beginning in 1928, were consistently less sympathetic, casting him as a genteel seducer or, increasingly as war loomed, a Teutonic villain such as the courteous, treacherous Dr. Egon Hartz in THE LADY VANISHES. Of his 90 films, his finest performance was in the Oscar-winning role of Kurt Muller, the Nazi-fighting husband and father in *Watch on the Rhine* (1943), based on the role he had created in Lillian Hellman's 1941 play—one of the most compelling dramatizations of moral conviction in Hollywood history. He died shortly after his final television appearance on a trip to Tangier to look for a retirement home.

Lummis, Dayton (1903–1988) American character actor with stage experience. Most at home in a wagon train or a toga (*Julius Caesar,* 1953; *Demetrius and the Gladiators,* 1954; and *Spartacus,* 1960), he also played a wide variety of contemporary roles, including three for ALFRED HITCHCOCK PRESENTS: Tom Ackley in "Crack of Doom" (1956), the mysterious title character in "MR. BLANCHARD'S SECRET," and Sgt. Oliver in "Listen, Listen!" (1958). He also appeared as Judge Groat in THE WRONG MAN.

Lynch, Ken (1910–1990) American film and television actor, a staple of the series *Bonanza* (1959–72) and *The Big Valley* (1965–69), who played a police lieutenant in the ALFRED HITCHCOCK PRESENTS episode "Man with Problem" (1958) and one of the two Chicago police officers who pick up Roger Thornhill in NORTH BY NORTHWEST.

Lyon, Therese (1887–1975) American character actress who came to the screen in middle age in
1945 and rapidly aged into a dozen elderly roles in film
and television such as the housekeeper in the *ALFRED
HITCHCOCK PRESENTS* segment "THE PERFECT CRIME."

Lytton, Herbert (C.) (d. 1981) American character actor, born Herbert Lytton Cress, most often in
military and western roles. He appeared as the hotel
porter in "REVENGE," the premiere episode of
ALFRED HITCHCOCK PRESENTS.

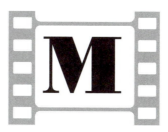

Mabry, Moss American wardrobe designer, in Hollywood from 1953, who went from *DIAL M FOR MURDER* to design costumes for some 75 films, from *Rebel Without a Cause* (1955) to *King Kong* (1976).

MacDonald, Philip (1899–1980) Scottish-born mystery writer who created the facetious detective Anthony Gethryn in *The Rasp* (1920), spent the next decade producing a series of fictional tours de force—from the wartime suspense novel *Patrol* (1927), filmed as *The Lost Patrol* (1934), to *Murder Gone Mad* (1931), which essentially invented the serial-killer genre—then traveled to Hollywood to work on original screenplays for Charlie Chan and Mr. Moto and adapt his own and other writers' work to the cinema, as in *REBECCA*, on which he collaborated on the treatment approved by David O. SELZNICK. His final Gethryn novel, *The List of Adrian Messenger* (1959), was filmed by John Huston in 1963.

Macgowan, Kenneth (1888–1963) American producer, former drama critic and stage producer, who started as a story editor at RKO, became an associate producer in 1931, and then moved in 1936, after 20 films, to 20th Century-Fox, where he produced, among two dozen others, *Young Mr. Lincoln* (1939), *Man Hunt* (1941), and *LIFEBOAT*. Upon his retirement in 1947, he became chair of Theater Arts at UCLA and wrote *Behind the Screen,* a history of the movies, published posthumously in 1965.

MacGregor, Hector (1916–1951) Suave British stage actor who appeared in a half-dozen films from 1936 to 1952. He played Charlotte Inwood's factotum Freddie Williams in *STAGE FRIGHT.*

MacGuffin According to Donald SPOTO, Angus MACPHAIL coined this term for the item that *Kiss Me Deadly* (1955) refers to as "the great whatsit"—the talismanic object that provides the pretext for every thriller, leading to battles between the heroes and villains who struggle to find and possess it. In *THE 39 STEPS*, the MacGuffin is the military secret that is about to be smuggled out of England; in *FOREIGN CORRESPONDENT* it is the secret clause to the peace treaty that only the diplomat Van Meer is privy to; in both 1934 and 1956 versions of *THE MAN WHO KNEW TOO MUCH* it is the information that a foreign ambassador is about to be assassinated. These examples suggest that MacGuffins are more common in spy thrillers than in domestic mysteries and that they need not be concrete objects like the Crown Jewels. Indeed the point of a MacGuffin, as Hitchcock frequently averred, is that it need not be or mean anything at all, except of course to the characters who are chasing it. In support of this point, he often defined the term by reciting the following exchange:

> Two men were traveling by train from London to Edinburgh. In the luggage rack overhead was a wrapped parcel.
> "What have you there?" asked one of the men.
> "Oh, that's a MacGuffin," replied the other.
> "What's a MacGuffin?"
> "It's a device for trapping lions in the Scottish Highlands."
> "But there aren't any lions in the Scottish Highlands!"
> "Well, then, that's no MacGuffin."

Compared to those of other filmmakers, Hitchcock's MacGuffins can be imaginative and even elegant: John Ballantine's locked unconscious in SPELLBOUND, the wine bottle filled with sand in NOTORIOUS, the chest containing David Kentley's body in ROPE. But Hitchcock repeatedly disclaimed any importance for the MacGuffin, and some of his most successful films include MacGuffins that are as broadly misleading as the stolen $40,000 in PSYCHO or, like the undefined "government secrets" Philip Vandamm is smuggling out of the country on microfilm in NORTH BY NORTHWEST, literally nothing at all.

MacGuffin, The   A quarterly newsletter devoted to Hitchcock's films. Its founding editor, Ken MOGG, formerly taught film studies at Melbourne University's College of Advanced Education, but the tone for which he aims is less formal than that of his American counterpart, the HITCHCOCK ANNUAL. Each issue, which typically focuses on a particular film, aims to strike a balance between academic criticism and fans' notes, both of whose excesses it regularly criticizes. Its emphasis is less on reinterpretations of the films than on new scholarship about their collaborators, their connections to other films, and the circumstances of their production, and reviews of new books on Hitchcock and rereleases of his films on videotape, LaserDisc, and DVD. The mailing address of the journal, which is available in the United States at $17 for four issues, is *The MacGuffin*, 18 Twyford Street, Box Hill North, Victoria 3129,

Australia. It maintains an active, informative, and frequently updated Web presence at <http://www.labyrinth.net.au/~muffin/index.html>.

MacKenna, Kenneth (1899–1962)   American actor, born Leo Mielziner, Jr. The brother of stage designer Jo Mielziner, he made his theatrical debut in 1919, and then moved to California in 1925 to play some 20 romantic leads and direct a half-dozen early sound features before returning to the stage in 1934. By 1960, however, he was back in Hollywood as a script editor and occasional actor in distinguished-looking roles such as the president in *High Time* (1960), Judge Kenneth Norris in *Judgment at Nuremberg* (1961), and Bishop Cannon, Father Amion's superior in the ALFRED HITCHCOCK PRESENTS segment "THE HORSEPLAYER."

MacLaine, Shirley (1934–)   Enduringly gamine American actress, born Shirley MacLaine Beatty, the sister of actor Warren Beatty. A dancer from childhood, she was plucked from the chorus line of *The Pajama Game* when Carol Haney, the star she was understudying, broke her leg, and producer Hal Wallis, who was in the audience, signed her to a contract. She made her film debut starring as Jennifer Rogers, the matter-of-fact widow in THE TROUBLE WITH HARRY. As Hitchcock's first successor to Grace KELLY, she was offbeat, humorous, and direct to the point of bluntness but with hints of passion beneath it all (when Sam Marlowe offers to seal their sudden engagement with a kiss, she tells him, "Gently, Sam. I have a short fuse"). The multiply talented actress went on to fame in such musicals as *Can-Can* (1959) and *Sweet Charity* (1968) as well as comic and dramatic roles and her own television series, *Shirley's World* (1971–72). A celebrated member of Frank Sinatra's Rat Pack, she managed at her best to combine a sense of starchy, even driven, rootedness with the sensibility of an impish sprite. Nominated for Academy Awards for her leading roles in *Some Came Running* (1958), *The Apartment* (1960), *Irma La Douce* (1963), and *The Turning Point* (1977), she won for *Terms of Endearment* (1983). In recent years she has published best-selling memories, self-help books, and speculations about reincarnation.

Macnee, Patrick (1922–) Whimsically understated British leading man. Best known as television's imperturbable John Steed of *The Avengers* (1960–68), he has also appeared in more than 100 other films and television roles, including two for ALFRED HITCHCOCK PRESENTS: Sgt. John Theron in "ARTHUR" and Prof. Kersley in "THE CRYSTAL TRENCH." He has played both Sherlock Holmes (in the television film *The Hound of London,* 1993) and Dr. Watson (in *Incident at Victoria Falls,* 1991, and the television film *Sherlock Holmes and the Leading Lady,* 1990).

MacNeilly, David One of the four camera operators on UNDER CAPRICORN.

Macollum, Barry (1889–1971) Irish character actor in sporadic movies from 1923, usually in menial walk-ons. He plays the tramp who steals the late Harry Warp's shoes in THE TROUBLE WITH HARRY and the vendor in THE ALFRED HITCHCOCK HOUR segment "The McGregor Affair" (1964).

MacPhail, Angus (1903–1962) British screenwriter and executive, long associated with Michael BALCON. A founding member of Britain's Film Society in 1925, he wrote intertitles before becoming script supervisor at GAINSBOROUGH (1927–31); at GAUMONT-BRITISH (1931–37), where he produced or coproduced three films; and at Ealing (1937–48). Virtually all of his 50 film credits are for collaborative work; in addition to working informally with Hitchcock on his Gaumont-British films, he is credited with cowriting BON VOYAGE and coadapting SPELLBOUND and THE WRONG MAN, his final film. Donald SPOTO credits him with coining the term "MACGUFFIN."

Macrorie, Alma (Ruth) (d. 1970) Veteran Hollywood editor, at PARAMOUNT from 1938, who cut THE TROUBLE WITH HARRY.

MacWilliams, Glenn (1898–1984) American cinematographer, in Hollywood from 1918, who shot nearly 100 films on both sides of the Atlantic, from *His Majesty, the American* (1919) to the television series *My Living Doll* (1964–65). His films in between include *The Front Page* (1931), *King Solomon's Mines*

(1937), and two Hitchcocks, WALTZES FROM VIENNA and LIFEBOAT.

Magnin, I., & Co. American department store that provided costumes for several productions of the early forties, including FOREIGN CORRESPONDENT.

Maher, Frank American sound technician who worked on some 30 films from 1930 to 1943, including *Nana* (1934), *You Only Live Once* (1937), *Gone With the Wind* (1939), and FOREIGN CORRESPONDENT.

Maitland, Ruth (1880–1961) British stage actress, née Ruth Erskine, who made her film debut as Mercy Bassett in THE FARMER'S WIFE and then appeared in a dozen other character roles through 1942.

Malden, Karl (1912–) Likeable, iconically virtuous American actor, born Mladen Sekulovich. Onstage from the midthirties and onscreen from 1940, he gradually rose to substantial parts in Arthur Miller's *All My Sons* (1947) and Tennessee Williams's *A Streetcar Named Desire* (1948). When Elia Kazan filmed the latter in 1951, he reprised his role as Mitch and won an Oscar. Since then he has appeared in more than 60 films and television programs, most recognizably as Lt. Mike Stone in the television series *Streets of San Francisco* (1972–76) and as the indefatigable American Express pitchman who enjoined audiences, "Don't leave home without it." Only a few film roles have allowed him the shadings of which he is capable; more often, he plays straight man to more volatile characters, as in *On the Waterfront* (1954), *Baby Doll* (1956), *One-Eyed Jacks* (1961), and *Patton* (1970). He plays a similar role as Inspector Larue in *I CONFESS.*

Malleson, Miles (1888–1969) Versatile British actor and writer who appeared onstage from 1911, often in plays he wrote or directed, before turning to cinema with the coming of sound. He played character roles in nearly 100 British films, sometimes as Miles Malieson, often leaving a strong impression in only a few seconds, as in his appearance as Mr. Fortescue, the drunk who tries to pick up Eve Gill while she is trying to pick up Wilfred Smith in STAGE FRIGHT. In addition, he wrote or cowrote 30 screenplays for such films as *Nell Gwyn* (1934), *Lorna Doone* (1935), and *The Thief of Baghdad* (1940).

Maltby, H(enry) F(rancis) (1880–1963) Prolific and versatile British man of the theater, onstage from 1899. The first of his 50 plays was produced in 1905, and thereafter he alternated between acting and writing for the stage and, from 1933, the screen. In all, he wrote or cowrote nearly 40 screenplays and appeared in more than 60 more films, usually in such blustery supporting roles as Sergeant Ruddock in YOUNG AND INNOCENT.

Malyon, Eily (1879–1961) Gaunt British character actress, born Eily S. Lees-Craston. In Hollywood from 1931, she played nearly 80 maiden aunts, domestics, and fussy functionaries such as the hotel cashier in FOREIGN CORRESPONDENT and the public librarian in SHADOW OF A DOUBT.

Mander, Miles (1888–1946) British actor, screenwriter, producer, and director, a man of a thousand roles in the theater. Born Lionel Mander, he was a farmer, novelist, and playwright before going into film exhibition. Onscreen from 1920, he played such plausible but untrustworthy males as Sir Neville Moreton in THE PRUDE'S FALL and Levett in THE PLEASURE GARDEN, broadening his range to such character roles as the actor Gordon Druce in MURDER! before departing in 1935 for Hollywood. There, he specialized in brass hats and politicos but could play the hero's treacherous guardian Ebenezer Balfour in *Kidnapped* (1938) or the sorely used millionaire Mr. Grayle in *Murder, My Sweet* (1944) with equal aplomb. He produced two films of his own, wrote the screenplays for eight, directed nine, and appeared in nearly 100.

Man from Home, The Famous Players–Lasky, Release date: 1922. **Director:** George Fitzmaurice; **Screenplay:** Ouida Bergére, based on the play by Booth Tarkington and Harry Leon Wilson; **Cinematographer:** Roy [F.] Overbaugh; **Cast:** James Kirkwood (Daniel Forbes

Pike), Anna Q. Nilsson (Genevieve Granger-Simpson), Geoffrey Kerr (Horace Granger-Simpson), Norman Kerry (Prince Kinsillo), Dorothy Cumming (Princess Sabina), José Ruben (Ribière), Annette Benson (Faustina Ribière), John Miltern (the King), Clifford Grey (his secretary).

Eighth of the 12 silent films, 1920–22, for which Hitchcock designed intertitles.

Manley, Nellie (1984–1976) American hair stylist who worked with George Westmore and then Vilma Banky, at PARAMOUNT from 1928. For 25 years (1943–68), she worked as head of the studio's hairdressing department on some 75 films, including VERTIGO.

Mannheim, Lucie (1899–1976) German-born character actress, onscreen from 1923. A principal at the Berlin Theater, she came to England when she was expelled by the Nazis in 1933, played the secret agent Annabella Smith in THE 39 STEPS, and then embarked on a varied mix of stage and screen roles, usually in accented roles. She was married to the actor Marius Goring from 1941 until her death.

Manson, Maurice (1913–) American character actor, born Moritz Levine. After extensive stage experience, he made his film debut in 1948, soon settling into a round of such paternal authority figures as the district attorney in THE WRONG MAN. He returned for four episodes of ALFRED HITCHCOCK PRESENTS—as the postman in "Anniversary Gift" (1959), Captain Harvey Ellison in "Not the Running Type" (1960), the hunter in "Craig's Will" (1960), and Arthur in "O Youth and Beauty!" (1960)—and once in THE ALFRED HITCHCOCK HOUR, as Dr. Palmer in "I SAW THE WHOLE THING."

Mantell, Joe (1920–) American character actor onscreen since 1949 in roles from Angie in *Marty* (1955) to J.J. Gittes's dim operative Walsh in *Chinatown* (1974). He appeared twice in ALFRED HITCHCOCK PRESENTS, as snoopy grocer Stanley Crane in "Guilty Witness" (1955) and lodge brother Harry Brown in "The Indestructible Mr. Weems" (1957). He also played the irritable traveling salesman who set fire to the gas station in THE BIRDS.

Man Who Knew Too Much, The   (Alternative

titles: *Der Mann, der zuviel wusste, L'homme qui en savait trop, L'uomo che sapeva troppo*) Gaumont-British, General Film Distributors Ltd., 84 minutes, December 1934. **Producer:** Michael Balcon; **Associate producer:** Ivor Montagu; **Director:** Alfred Hitchcock; **Screenplay:** A.R. Rawlinson and Edwin Greenwood, based on an original subject by D.B. Wyndham Lewis and Charles Bennett; **Additional dialogue:** Emlyn Williams; **Cinematographer:** Curt Courant; **Art director:** Alfred Junge; **Assistant director:** Penrose Tennyson; **Unit production manager:** Richard Beville; **Sound:** F. McNally; **Editor:** H.St.C. Stewart; **Music:** Arthur Benjamin; **Musical direction:** Louis Levy; **Cast:** Leslie Banks (Bob Lawrence), Edna Best (Jill Lawrence), Peter Lorre (Abbott), Nova Pilbeam (Betty Lawrence), Frank Vosper (Ramon), Hugh Wakefield (Clive), Pierre Fresnay (Louis Bernard), Cicely Oates (Nurse Agnes), D.A. Clarke Smith (Inspector Binstead), George Curzon (Gibson), Henry Oscar (George Barbor, dentist), S.J. Warmington (gang member), Frederick Piper and Frank Atkinson (police officers), Charles Paton (shopkeeper), Joan Harrison (secretary), Celia Lovsky.

Unhappy with the shooting of WALTZES FROM VIENNA, Hitchcock was more than receptive when Michael BALCON, visiting his old employee on the set, asked if he might like to return to the reorganized GAUMONT-BRITISH company, where Balcon was now head of production. Hitchcock replied that the property he had in mind, a kidnapping tale featuring the dashing amateur sleuth Bulldog Drummond, might be hard to secure because BRITISH INTERNATIONAL owned the rights to the character. When Balcon pressed him, Hitchcock purchased the rights for £250 and then sold them to Balcon for £500 (though, guilt-stricken at the transaction, he commissioned a bust of the producer by the sculptor Jacob Epstein and presented it to him as a gift), as the basis for the first of the five films he would make under his new contract with Gaumont-British. Story conferences with Charles BENNETT, Ivor MONTAGU, and sometimes Angus MACPHAIL, freed from the interference of John MAXWELL and Walter MYCROFT, went far more smoothly than at British International, and the shooting of Hitchcock's 17th film proceeded from May 29 through August 2, 1934, with postpro-

duction work complete by the end of September. The National Board of Review's objection that the final shootout, which was based on Winston Churchill's handling of the 1910 Sidney Street siege as Home Secretary, featured police officers armed with guns was met by a telegraphic new series of shots showing them requisitioning the weapons they were normally forbidden to carry. A more serious objection came from C.M. WOOLF, who was now in charge of distribution for Gaumont-British. As he had with THE PLEASURE GARDEN, THE MOUNTAIN EAGLE, and THE LODGER, Woolf announced his refusal to release the film unless it were reshot by Maurice Elvey. When he relented far enough to permit a weeklong public screening at the bottom of a double bill, however, critics were ecstatic, and the major phase of Hitchcock's career—his well-nigh exclusive association with THRILLERS—began, appropriately enough, with his independence from the kind of egregious interference Woolf represented.

   The film's story of a vacationing family whose daughter is kidnapped from St. Moritz to keep them from revealing a plot they have uncovered to assassinate a foreign diplomat established a pattern for the Gaumont-British thrillers that followed. An unas-

Perhaps the most unobtrusively complex moment in a film full of such moments: the death of Nurse Agnes (Cicely Oates), the ambiguous companion of the kidnapper/spy Abbot (Peter Lorre) in *The Man Who Knew Too Much* (1934). *(National Film Society Archive)*

suming set of heroes is plunged into international intrigue (of all the Gaumont-British thrillers, only YOUNG AND INNOCENT forgoes espionage for the intimacies of domestic homicide) by a chance encounter (only in SECRET AGENT are the heroes spies themselves, and even then their lack of professional background is central to the film) that places them in danger from powerful enemies and beyond the aid of the authorities. Equally important, it established Hitchcock's reputation for rapid tempo—in all his previous work, only the madcap chase sequence of NUMBER SEVENTEEN matches it for sheer velocity—and for lightning-fast, often disconcertingly abrupt, shifts between radically different tones. The meeting of a pair of innocuous men who will turn out to be the doomed Louis Bernard and Abbott—the criminal mastermind who will shortly order his murder, when Bernard, frantic to avoid the dog that has escaped Betty Lawrence's arms and leaped onto his ski run, plows into Abbott on the sidelines and knocks him down—is so quick a piece of exposition that many audiences miss not only the ironies of the meeting but its significance as a catalyst for the story. The scenes that follow, bringing Betty together with her parents and the flirtatious Bernard in what seems to be a frivolously witty mode of domestic comedy, is unexpectedly shattered together with the windowpane through which the assassin shoots Bernard to death, beginning the Lawrences' odyssey through a world in which their hometown of London turns out to be just as dangerous and just as full of disconcerting shifts from comedy to menace and back again as the exotic Alps. Bob Lawrence demonstrates his comical inability to make his English understood in Switzerland moments before he gets the news that Betty has been kidnapped; a visit back home to Wapping dentist George Barbor, identified on a cryptic note Bob has removed from Bernard's shaving brush, teeters between the serious dangers of international intrigue and the comical dangers of dentistry; a visit to a second neighborhood landmark, the Tabernacle of the Sun, is punctuated by farcical details (Bob takes cover in a hymn to sing a warning to Clive, the family friend who has accompanied him); Bob, prevented from leaving by a decorous old lady who holds him at gunpoint, interrupts his ensuing battle

with the spies who have infested the tabernacle with his attempts to rouse the stupefied Clive from his hypnotic trance; the gun-toting lady, eager to get home to her husband, is herself prevented from leaving when the conspirators confiscate her skirt. Not until the film's big set piece, a long, wordless sequence at Albert Hall—the site of the planned assassination—which Jill, despite a renewed threat to her daughter, interrupts by a timely scream, does the film settle into sustained melodrama; even the shootout that follows is complicated by a series of jokes, including the chiming watch that identifies Abbott's hiding place to the police officers who kill him. Though it has been largely overshadowed by its more elaborate 1956 remake, the film has decisive importance not only for its deft balancing of adult responsibilities (saving the foreign ambassador) and childish outbursts (screaming in the middle of a concert) but also for the rapid range of tones it handles with such virtuosity.

Man Who Knew Too Much, The

(Alternative titles: *Der Mann, der zuviel wusste, L'Homme qui en savait trop, L'uomo che sapeva troppo*) Paramount-FilWite, Paramount, 120 minutes, May 1956. **Producer:** Alfred Hitchcock; **Associate producer:** Herbert Coleman; **Director:** Alfred Hitchcock; **Screenplay:** John Michael Hayes, based on a story by Charles Bennett and D.B. Wyndham Lewis; **Cinematographer:** Robert Burks; **Assistant director:** Howard Joslin; **Art directors:** Hal Pereira and Henry Bumstead; **Set decoration:** Sam Comer and Arthur Krams; **Costumes:** Edith Head; **Makeup:** Wally Westmore; **Sound:** Paul Franz and Gene Garvin; **Technicolor consultant:** Richard Mueller; **Special effects:** John P. Fulton; **Process photography:** Farciot Edouart; **Editor:** George Tomasini; **Technical advisers:** Abdelhaq Chraibi and Constance Willis; **Music:** Bernard Herrmann ("Storm Cloud Cantata" by Arthur Benjamin and D.B. Wyndham-Lewis, performed by the London Symphony Orchestra, conducted by Bernard Herrmann, with Barbara Howitt, soprano, and the Covent Garden Chorus); **Songs:** Jay Livingston and Ray Evans ("Whatever Will Be [Que Sera, Sera]" and "We'll Love Again"); **Cast:** James Stewart (Dr. Ben McKenna), Doris Day (Jo McKenna), Brenda De Banzie (Mrs. Drayton), Bernard Miles (Mr. Drayton), Ralph Truman (Buchanan), Daniel Gélin (Louis Bernard),

Mogens Wieth (Ambassador), Alan Mowbray (Val Parnell), Hillary Brooke (Jan Peterson), Christopher Olsen (Hank McKenna), Reggie Nalder (Rien, the assassin), Richard Wattis (assistant manager), Noel Willman (Woburn), Alix Talton (Helen Parnell), Yves Brainville (police inspector), Carolyn Jones (Cindy Fontaine), Berry Bascomb (Edna), Leo Gordon (chauffeur), Patrick Aherne (handyman), Lewis Martin (detective), Louis Mercier, Anthony Warde (French police officers), Richard Wordsworth (Ambrose Chappell, Jr.), George Howe (Ambrose Chappell, Sr.), Gladys Holland (Bernard's girlfriend), Barbara Burke (assassin's girlfriend), Abdelhaq Chraibi, Lou Krugman, Mahin S. Shahrivar (Arabs on bus), Elsa Palmer (cook), Edward Manouk (French waiter), Peter Camlin (head-waiter), Donald Lawton (desk clerk), Clifford Buckton (Sir Kenneth Clarke), Enid Lindsey (Lady Clarke), Harry Fine (Edington), Barry Keegan (Patterson), Eric Snowden, Patrick Whyte (Special Branch officers), Peter Williams (police sergeant), Frank Atkinson, John Barrard, Mayne Lynton, Liddell Peddieson (taxidermists), Janet Bruce, Alma Taylor (box-office women), John O'Malley (uniformed attendant), Arthur Ridley (ticket collector), Naida Buckingham, Janet Macfarlane (members of Albert Hall audience), Pauline Farr (ambassador's wife), Lloyd Lamble (general manager of Albert Hall), Allen Zeidman (assistant manager), Leslie Newport (Inspector at Albert Hall), Alexi Bobrinskoy (foreign prime minister), Wolf Priess (his aide), Milton Frome, Walter Gotell (guards), Harold Kasket, John Marshall (butlers), Guy Verney (footman), Ralph Neff (henchman), Alex Frazer.

Hitchcock had planned as early as 1941 to remake his 1934 film THE MAN WHO KNEW TOO MUCH for David O. SELZNICK, using American settings in a story that moved from Sun Valley, Idaho, to New York—a story whose eastward movement echoed that of SABOTEUR, the project he had in preproduction at the time. After the indifferent reception of Saboteur, however, he put the idea aside until 1954, when his agents purchased the rights to the story from Selznick and he began to work out a new foundation for which Angus MACPHAIL supplied the story—capitalizing on the impending visit of Hungary's prime minister Imre Nagy to London and transposed from Switzerland to Marrakesh and London—and John Michael HAYES the characters and dialogue. The cast of Hitchcock's 43rd film was anchored by James STEWART, who, as in REAR WIN-DOW, shared in its profits, and Doris DAY, whom Hitchcock cast in her first dramatic role; Hitchcock paid Arthur BENJAMIN, the composer of the "Storm Cloud" cantata, $1500 for an additional 90 seconds of music for the Albert Hall sequence. The film went into production in May 1956 without a completed screenplay, and the shoot, as Bill KROHN has reported, fell steadily behind because of script changes and delays in location shooting (not only in Marrakesh, but also at the Albert Hall, which could be used only during the day because concerts had been booked there every night) before wrapping in July. Hitchcock lavished far more care on the Albert Hall sequence than he had in 1934, revising the sequence of its 134 shots, readjusting the sound levels of the music from shot to shot, adding and deleting an outside observer who watches the heroine's distress, and clarifying her emotional turmoil. Day was unhappy because Hitchcock seemed more attentive to her wardrobe than her performance and disliked "Whatever Will Be," the song PARAMOUNT had insisted over the director's objections that she sing to her son. But she still managed to film her most demanding scene, the moment when her husband refuses to tell her what has happened until she takes a sedative, in a single take, and the song she so disliked became a hit and eventually her signature tune. Hitchcock's collaboration with Hayes ended less happily when he insisted that MacPhail be credited on the film. Hayes submitted the matter to the Writers Guild for arbitration, and MacPhail's name was removed, cooling the relationship between the director and one of his most gifted writers. Hayes's refusal to follow Hitchcock to WARNER BROS. and work on THE WRONG MAN for a share of the profits rather than a salary confirmed the split.

None of these problems are evident in the completed film, whose production in Technicolor and VISTAVISION has a visual splendor worlds apart from the 1934 version. The remake is longer, slower, more richly detailed, and far less subversive in its shifts in tone than its progenitor. The new screenplay removes the scene of ambiguous menace at the dentist's office and recasts the murder of Louis Bernard and the discovery of spies in Ambrose Chapel in more measured terms; its principal additions—a long prologue bringing the McKenna family together with the mysterious Bernard for the first time and a briefer sequence that takes Ben McKenna, hunting back in London for Ambrose Chapel, on a wild-goose chase to the taxidermy shop of Ambrose Chappell— change keys less often and less abruptly; the nightmare dilemma of the McKennas, an Indianapolis physician and a professional singer who sacrificed her career for her marriage, is presented in more straightforwardly melodramatic terms; and the submerged domestic problems revealed when Jo McKenna presses her husband just before Bernard's catalytic

murder if they can talk about having a second child and when he considers it necessary to drug her before sharing the news of their son Hank's kidnapping—are no longer played as light comedy but as an anatomy of marital compromise and resentment. Both leads, especially Day, find in the roles of frantically bereft parents a heartfelt anguish that could not be further from the stiff-upper-lip responses of their predecessors, Bob and Jill Lawrence. Indeed the two major scenes involving Jo and her son Hank, both of which depend on her singing "Whatever Will Be" to him, seem to fetishize family life itself in peculiarly American terms, idealizing and inflating the relationship between mother and son (which Hitchcock

Hitchcock prepares to film the murder in the Marrakesh marketplace in *The Man Who Knew Too Much* (1956). *(National Film Society Archive)*

normally represented in far more repressive, conflictual, or predatory terms) to the point of self-parody. Most commentators on the film have followed the director's lead in pronouncing "the first version . . . the work of a talented amateur" who had by then directed 16 earlier films in a period of nearly 10 years "and the second . . . made by a professional"; certainly its version of fifties domestic Americana has provided material for much more frequent political analysis than its quicksilver older sibling.

Manxman, The   (Alternative title: *L'Isola del Piccato*) British International, approximately 100 minutes, January 1929. **Producer:** John Maxwell; **Director:** Alfred Hitchcock; **Screenplay:** Eliot Stannard, based on the novel by Sir Hall Caine; **Cinematographer:** Jack Cox; **Assistant director:** Frank Mills; **Art director:** W. Arnold; **Editor:** Emile de Ruelle; **Cast:** Carl Brisson (Pete Quilliam), Malcolm Keen (Philip Christian), Anny Ondra (Kate Cregeen), Randle Ayrton (Oscar Cregeen), Clare Greet (Mrs. Cregeen), Harry Terry (wedding guest).

Hitchcock's ninth film, his final all-silent film, began life as an adaptation of a best-selling novel. Shooting commenced in September 1928, with Polperro and other spots on the Cornish coast doubling for the Isle of Man locations the story stipulates. The project proceeded smoothly, but John MAXWELL took such a dislike to the film that after its trade screening he held up its theatrical release, as C.M. WOOLF had done with several of Hitchcock's GAINSBOROUGH films, until after the successful premiere of *BLACKMAIL*. Hitchcock seems to have shared his producer's low opinion of the film, dismissing it as a project that smacked more of Hall CAINE than of Hitchcock, and it has attracted little attention among Hitchcock scholars despite strong endorsements from Maurice YACOWAR and Charles BARR. This neglect is a pity, for despite its remoteness from the thriller genre with which Hitchcock would become synonymous, the film is one of the director's finest silents. In outline, the story is no more than another romantic triangle involving innkeeper's daughter Kate Cregeen; Pete Quilliam, the poor fisherman who loves her; and Pete's boyhood friend Philip Christian, the lawyer who has long fought for the fishermen's way

of life against the steamships that have increasingly crowded even this wild island. When Pete, gone to seek his fortune in Africa, is presumed lost at sea, Philip and Kate, who have fallen in love, begin an affair that is doomed first by Philip's social position—he expects to follow the family tradition of becoming a judge who cannot afford a lower-class wife—and then by Pete's sudden return to claim his fiancée. Concealing her affair from Pete, she agrees at Philip's urging to marry him and to pass her unborn daughter off as his. Eventually, however, she cracks under the strain, throws herself into the sea, and is brought before Philip, in his first session as judge, to be tried as an attempted suicide; the hearing brings out Philip's feelings for her, and he resigns his new post under a cloud and, under the minatory eyes of the villagers, marches out of the village with Kate and her baby, leaving the bewildered Pete to return to the sea.

The film follows this story closely but intensifies it in three ways. The casting of the frankly sensual Anny ONDRA—who, unlike the heroines Lilian HALL DAVIS had played in *THE RING* and *THE FARMER'S WIFE*, is no passive prize to be won but a spirited, tempestuous participant in the triangle, a woman in whose emotions and psychology the film takes an unprecedentedly direct interest—gives the romantic rivalry between Pete and Philip, whose sufferings never eclipse her own, a sense of gravity and yearning unique in Hitchcock's silents. The recurring visual motifs—the millstone to indicate the grinding passage of time, the lighthouse's revolving beam for romantic indecision, and above all the striking exterior landscapes that entrap the characters even when they think they are most free—both express the three leads' often suppressed emotions and integrate them into a firmer pattern. Finally, the film develops the playful or baleful hints of subjectivity in Hitchcock's earlier films—the point-of-view shots marking the power of the gaze in *THE PLEASURE GARDEN* and *EASY VIRTUE*, the glass ceiling to represent the lodger's tread overhead and the stylized staircase sequence to show his nocturnal departure, the vividly horrific daydreams of *DOWNHILL* and *CHAMPAGNE*, the hallucinatory wedding reception in *The Ring*—into an extended nightmare represented by Kate's sinking into catatonic passivity as she feels the pressures of her false marriage closing in on her. It is the first Hitchcock film to be posed unequivocally in the no-woman's-land between waking and dreaming, but it inaugurates a long series of later films from THE LADY VANISHES and NOTORIOUS to VERTIGO to MARNIE—a series that would continue with *Blackmail,* the very next film Ondra would make for Hitchcock.

Marfield, Dwight (1908–1978) American character actor and producer, mostly on stage. After long Broadway experience, including his own one-man revue, *Dwight Night,* he appeared in a handful of films, from THE TROUBLE WITH HARRY, in which he played the oblivious Dr. Greenbow, to *One Flew Over the Cuckoo's Nest.*

Marianne British costume designer of the thirties who designed the wardrobe for THE 39 STEPS, SABOTAGE, YOUNG AND INNOCENT, and more than a dozen other films.

Marischka, Ernst (or Ernest) (1893–1963) Austrian playwright and filmmaker who cowrote the 1931 Alhambra musical WALTZES FROM VIENNA on which Hitchcock's film is based. He was extraordinarily active in German-language cinema, contributing to the screenplays of 60 films from 1931 on and often directing or contributing song lyrics as well, before contributing directly to his first English-language film, *Forever My Love* in 1962.

Marlowe, Nora (1915–1977) Matronly American character actress, onscreen from 1955, who graduated from playing occasional film bits such as Philip Vandamm's formidable housekeeper Anna in NORTH BY NORTHWEST and television roles like the Scotland Yard officer in the ALFRED HITCHCOCK PRESENTS episode "I Killed the Count" (1957) and the landlady in THE ALFRED HITCHCOCK HOUR segment "Final Vow" (1962) to television success as Flossie Brimmer in *The Waltons* (1972–77).

Marmont, Percy (1883–1977) Courtly British actor who made his stage debut in 1900. He appeared in his first film, *Die Vortrekkers,* while touring South Africa in 1913 and returned to play nearly 80 gentlemanly film roles, first in Hollywood—most notably the title character in *Lord Jim* (1925)—then, after 1928, back in England. Hitchcock consistently cast him as decent chaps who received a bad shake: as Commander Gordon, Emily Hill's disappointed lover in RICH AND STRANGE; as Caypor, the wrongly suspected enemy agent murdered by the General in SECRET AGENT; and as the heroine's father, Colonel Burgoyne, driven to resign from his position by his daughter's efforts on behalf of a fugitive suspect in YOUNG AND INNOCENT.

Marnie (Alternative title: *Pas de printemps pour Marnie*) Universal—Geoffrey Stanley, 120 minutes, June 1964. **Producer:** Alfred Hitchcock; **Director:** Alfred Hitchcock; **Screenplay:** Jay Presson Allen, based on the novel by Winston Graham; **Cinematographer:** Robert Burks; **Assistant director:** James H. Brown; **Camera operator:** Leonard South; **Art directors:** Robert Boyle and George Milo; **Costumes:** Edith Head, Vincent Dee, Rita Riggs, James Linn; **Costume supervisor:** Vincent Dee; **Makeup:** Jack Barron, Howard Smit, Robert Dawn; **Hairstyles:** Alexandre of Paris and Virginia Darcy; **Sound:** Waldon O. Watson and William Russell; **Production assistant:** Peggy Robertson; **Script supervisor:** Lois Thurman; **Unit manager:** Hilton A. Green; **Editor:** George Tomasini; **Special effects:** Albert Whitlock; **Music:** Bernard Herrmann; **Cast:** Tippi Hedren (Marnie Edgar), Sean Connery (Mark Rutland), Diane Baker (Lil Mainwaring), Martin Gabel (Sidney Strutt), Louise Latham (Bernice Edgar), Bob Sweeney (Cousin Bob), Milton Selzer (man at track), Mariette Hartley (Susan Clabon), Alan Napier (Mr. Rutland), Bruce Dern (sailor), Henry Beckman (first detective), S. John Launer (Sam Ward), Edith Evanson (Rita), Meg Wyllie (Mrs. Turpin), Louise Lorimer (Mrs. Strutt), Melody Thomas Scott (young Marnie).

Almost as soon as he read Winston Graham's 1961 novel, Hitchcock wanted to entice Grace KELLY back to Hollywood to star in it. But when Princess Grace, who was interested in the proposal, submitted it in a referendum to the citizens of Monaco, they resoundingly rejected it, presumably unable to see their princess as the frigid compulsive thief who

Hitchcock offers suggestions to Tippi Hedren about how to submerge her role of Marnie Edgar in the guise of Mary Taylor, the secretary who is too good to be true in *Marnie*. *(National Film Society Archive)*

version without the rape. But Hitchcock, who had made no secret from the beginning that this was a film about a man who would have preferred to catch his quarry in the act and ravish her on the spot, would not be gainsaid; under the pretext of taking time away from the film, he engaged Jay Presson ALLEN to write the screenplay instead, and on May 1 Hitchcock's office notified Hunter that he had been removed from the project. Nor did he ever show Hunter's draft screenplay to the new writer, a playwright who had never worked on a film before. Filming, which began in September, was scarcely less fraught with tension between the director and his protégée. In January 1964, already planning to star her in the romantic melodrama *Mary Rose* after *Marnie* wrapped, he refused her permission to travel to New York to accept the Photoplay Award as the year's most promising new actress, provoking an embarrassing scene on the set. Soon thereafter—whether or not because of the sexual overture Donald SPOTO ascribes to the director—Hitchcock and Hedren stopped speaking to each other, and the film was completed in an arctic atmosphere, its postproduction effects the subject of only the most cursory efforts. On its release, the film was universally panned, even by such Hitchcock admirers as Andrew SARRIS.

Ever since its first release, in fact, Hitchcock's 49th film has continued to polarize his commentators, some damning it for its amateurish special effects (particularly the process shots of Marnie riding her horse—her subliminal release from the tensions of masquerade and theft—and the shots of the Baltimore harbor at the end of the street where her mother lives), others praising it as a masterly example of fetishism made visually manifest, and a few, like Spoto, arguing first one side and then the other. Like *The Birds,* the film has attracted few critics prepared to accept its story within a realistic mode. But many others have defended its intense expressionism, which Ken MOGG compares to that of *VERTIGO,* or its analysis of sexual politics, which Michele Piso, in her essay in DEUTELBAUM and POAGUE, finds far more prescient than the smugness of the reviewers who originally dismissed it. Although the film's tale of a crippling neurosis resolved by a confrontation

is tamed by a husband who blackmails her into marriage, rapes her on their honeymoon, and draws her out by a word association test. Considering younger actresses for the role, Hitchcock at length offered it to Tippi HEDREN, still under contract to him following *THE BIRDS*, and engaged that film's screenwriter, Evan HUNTER, to write this screenplay as well. Hunter's memoir *Me and Hitch* recounts the typically lengthy sessions during which the writer and director mapped out the film and their clash in April 1963 over the pivotal scene in which Philadelphia businessman Mark Rutland, who has caught Marnie Edgar after she robbed his company safe and knows that she has robbed before, breaks his promise to leave his reluctant bride alone and forces himself on her. Hunter, strongly objecting to the scene, submitted both a version written according to Hitchcock's prescription and an alternate with the childhood trauma that led to the adult's guilt follows the narrative pattern of SPELLBOUND, Hitchcock is far more skeptical of the curative powers of psychoanalysis 20 years later, and the film, for better or worse, is riven by unresolved internal contradictions (Mark as loving husband or predatory rapist, an ending that promises domestic bliss or female subjugation, the director's continued fascination with the fetishism his film sets itself to cure) that go far to determine different viewers' attitudes toward it; along with *The Birds,* it is perhaps Hitchcock's most obviously postmodern film. The director's failure to sign Sean CONNERY, on the cusp of his fame as James Bond, to a multipicture deal is only one way in which *Marnie* marks the end of an era: Soon after its completion, both cinematographer Robert BURKS and editor George TOMASINI died, and Bernard HERRMANN, although he went on to compose a score for *TORN CURTAIN,* was replaced by John ADDISON and was never again credited on a Hitchcock film.

Marrison, Rene   British editor whose only two film credits are *MURDER!* and *RICH AND STRANGE.*

Marsh, Garry (1902–1981)   Mustached, balding British character actor, born Leslie March Geraghty. Although he appeared in more than 100 roles in British films from 1930 to 1960, his essential character, physically imposing yet modestly self-effacing, was already well established by the time he played Sheldrake, the crooks' ringleader in *NUMBER SEVENTEEN.*

Marsh, Jean (1934–)   Vinegary British character actress, born Jean Lyndsay Torren Marsh. Onscreen from 1953 sporadically in film and more frequently in television appearances, she is best known for her role as Rose Buck, the Bellamys' maid in the BBC series *Upstairs, Downstairs* (1971–75), which she cocreated with actress Eileen Atkins. Shortly after its debut, she was cast in *FRENZY* as Monica Barling, the secretary who finds Brenda Blaney's corpse and blames her ex-husband for her murder—a role originally intended for Anna MASSEY, who ended up playing Barbara Milligan.

Marshall, E(dda?) G(unnar?) (1910–1998)   Bald-pated American character actor whose gamut of recititude runs from the severe to the prissy. An alumnus of the Actors' Studio, he mixed his many stage roles in the later forties with a long stint as host of the *CBS Radio Mystery Theater* and a few walkons in films and graduated in the fifties to playing cerebral politicians and military officers. Perhaps his best-known film role is Harold Horn, the district attorney who traps the two killers in *Repulsion* (1959). He is more celebrated, however, for his television work, from his nerve-shredding performance as the watchmaker/bomber Paul Steppe in the SUSPICION segment "FOUR O'CLOCK" to his gullible clerk Ronald Grimes in the ALFRED HITCHCOCK PRESENTS episode "The Mail-Order Prophet" (broadcast just two weeks later in 1957) to his long-running roles as Lawrence Preston, the father of the father-and-son lawyer team in *The Defenders* (1961–65), and Dr. David Craig in *The Bold Ones: The Lawyers* (1969–73). Throughout his career, he insisted that he had been born in 1914, not 1910 (as public records indicated), and refused to divulge the names his given initials stood for.

Marshall, Herbert (1890–1966)   British actor, born Herbert Brough Falcon Marshall, the last word in British gentility for Hollywood audiences for more than 30 years. A former accountant and business manager, he made his stage debut in 1911. Though he lost a leg in service during World War I, he returned to an ever more crowded slate of bookings. Blessed with a matinee-idol profile and a caressing voice, he soon established himself as an urbane romantic lead in both London and New York and in 1928 married actress Edna BEST, his frequent theatrical costar thereafter. Immediately following his first important film role, the adulterer Geoffrey Hammond in *The Letter* (1929), he was cast as Sir John Menier, the courtly juror-turned-detective in *MURDER!,* while still maintaining a busy theatrical schedule. He retired from the stage in 1932 to work exclusively in such films as *Trouble in Paradise* (1932), *The Good Fairy* (1935), *The Letter* (1940)—now taking the role of Robert Crosbie, the betrayed husband—and *FOREIGN CORRESPONDENT,* in which he played the treacherous pacifist

Stephen Fisher. His portrayal of the ailing Horace Giddens in *The Little Foxes* (1941) set the seal on his development from romantic lead to character actor, a development confirmed by his roles in the Somerset MAUGHAM adaptations *The Moon and Sixpence* (1942) and *The Razor's Edge* (1946), playing the world-weary Maugham himself in the latter. Still later he starred in two episodes of *ALFRED HITCHCOCK PRESENTS*, playing the overingenious Judge Condon in "A Bottle of Wine" (1957) and the spellbinding old actor Colin Bragner in "Little White Frock" (1958).

Martelli, Angela Continuity supervisor for *FRENZY* and 16 other films from *Mogambo* (1953) through *Superman* (1978).

Martin, Charles British cinematographer whose work on Hitchcock's films as assistant cameraman on *THE SKIN GAME* and cocinematogapher (with J. J. COX) on *RICH AND STRANGE* account for most of his film credits.

Martinelli, Jean (1910–1983) Fearsomely tall Parisian actor, onscreen from 1933 in two dozen French films, whose only English-language appearance was the nonspeaking role of Danielle Foussard's father, the waiter at Bertani's, in *TO CATCH A THIEF*.

Martini, Ferd(inand) (d. 1931) Italian actor with New York stage experience who made his film debut as Mr. Sidey, the lecherous patron in *THE PLEASURE GARDEN*, and played a half-dozen other roles, mostly in German films.

Mary German-language version of *Murder!* (Alternative title: *Sir John greift ein!*) British International, Wardour & F., 1931. **Producer:** John Maxwell; **Director:** Alfred Hitchcock; **Screenplay:** Alma Reville, Herbert Juttke, and Dr. Georg C. Klaren, based on *Enter Sir John,* a novel by Clemence Dane and Helen Simpson; **Cinematographer:** Jack Cox; **Art director:** John Mead; **Editing:** Rene Marrison, under the supervision of Emile de Ruelle; **Music:** John Reynders; **Cast:** Alfred Abel, Olga Tschechowa, Paul Graetz, Lotte Stein, Ekkehard Arendt, Jack Mylong-Münz, Louis Ralph, Hermine Sterler, Fritz Alberti, Hertha von Walter, Else Schünzel, Julius Brandt, Rudolph Meinhardt-

Jünger, Fritz Grossman, Lucie Euler, Harry Hardt, Eugen Burg, Heinrich Gotho, and Miles Mander.

Although silent films had routinely and easily been sold on foreign markets by the simple expedient of substituting foreign-language intertitles for the original dialogue, the coming of sound made such economies impossible, and BRITISH INTERNATIONAL arranged to shoot a foreign-language version of Hitchcock's third talkie at the same time as the original, using the same sets and lighting setups on the same London sound stage—a version that would follow the original closely but with a German cast. As Hitchcock's biographers have noted, the changes were more extensive than anyone had expected. Alfred Abel, in the role of the playwright/juror/sleuth played in the English-language version by Herbert MARSHALL, insisted on wearing formal attire to visit Diana Baring, the woman he had unwillingly voted to condemn, in her prison cell and refused to endure the indignities of a comic scene in which Sir John, visiting a shabby boarding house in his search for evidence that will exonerate Diana, is beset by children who climb all over his bed. Although he first resisted such changes, Hitchcock, whose working knowledge of German would have seemed to make him a logical candidate for the project, eventually capitulated to the wishes of his German cast and screenwriters because he sensed that they would understand their audience better than he would.

masculinity Although even the films Hitchcock directed at the height of FILM NOIR have resisted simple identification with that genre, they share at least one concern—masculinity—which they define and defend in the same terms, as the opposite of antimasculinity. Men are manly in Hitchcock, as in films noir, not only because they are unlike women (as T.R. Devlin refuses to copy Alicia Huberman's openness and vulnerability in *NOTORIOUS* by telling her that he loves her and L.B. Jefferies staunchly maintains that his rough-and-ready lifestyle is incompatible with Lisa Fremont's Park Avenue refinement in *REAR WINDOW*) but also because they are unlike unmanly men like the comically sterile momma's boy Herb Hawkins in SHADOW OF A DOUBT, the more sinister momma's boy Alexander Sebastian in *Notorious,* or the psychotic momma's boy Norman BATES in PSYCHO. Although the Production Code prevented Hitchcock from presenting any openly homosexual characters, many of his villains, from Handel Fane in MURDER! to Brandon Shaw and Philip Morgan in ROPE, Bruno Anthony in STRANGERS ON A TRAIN, Leonard (and the presumably bisexual Philip Vandamm) in NORTH BY NORTHWEST are presented in the visual terms by which Hollywood conventionally figured homosexuality, so that the films intertwine their defense of morality with a defense of male heterosexuality. The definition of masculinity in opposition to femininity has been studied by such feminists as Laura MULVEY and Tania MODLESKI; the defense of masculinity as a heteroideology challenged by homosexuality has been analyzed by such proponents of Queer Theory as Robert J.CORBER, D.A. Miller, Lee Edelman, and Amy Lawrence; and Robert SAMUELS has proposed a radically bisexual reading of Hitchcockian desire.

Mason, A(lfred) E(dward) W(oodley)

(1865–1948) British novelist and playwright, former actor, who published his first novel, *A Romance of Wastdale,* in 1895 and his most famous, *Four Feathers,* in 1902. The latter story has been filmed six times, in 1915, 1921, 1929, 1939, 1955 (as *Storm over the Nile*), 1977, and 2001. Following his retirement from Parliament in 1910, he wrote *At the Villa Rose,* first in a series of mystery novels about Inspector Gabriel Hanaud; it too has often been filmed (in 1920, twice in 1930, and in 1939). Stirling SILLIPHANT adapted his 1917 story "THE CRYSTAL TRENCH" for *ALFRED HITCHCOCK PRESENTS* in 1959.

Mason, James

(1909–1984) Volcanic British actor who ripened into one of Hollywood's most thoughtful, durable leading men. A former architecture student and stage actor, he made his screen debut in 1933 and within 10 years had become the top box-office star in England, typically as black-browed Byronic villains irresistible to women in such films as *The Man in Grey* (1943). His acclaimed performance as Johnny McQueen, the dying terrorist in

Odd Man Out (1947), sent him to Hollywood, where the studios smoothed his rougher edges. His villains—Field Marshall Erwin Rommel in *Desert Fox* (1951), the valet/spy Cicero in *Five Fingers* (1952), Rupert of Hentzau in *The Prisoner of Zenda* (1952)—became more introspective. His tormented heroes—Brutus in *Julius Caesar* (1953); Norman Maine in *A Star Is Born* (1954), his first Oscar nomination; Ed Avery in *Bigger Than Life* (1956), which he also produced—were more well rounded. He hosted and starred in a short-lived television series, *The James Mason Show* (1956); played Phillip Vandamm, suavest of all Hitchcock heavies, in NORTH BY NORTHWEST; and returned to play the murderous mystery novelist Warren Barrow in THE ALFRED HITCHCOCK HOUR segment "Captive Audience" (1962) the same year he created an indelible portrait of sexual panic in *Lolita.* Though he was now old enough to play the leering James Leamington in *Georgy Girl* (1966), his second Oscar nomination, he still had 70 film performances left in him, from his mild-mannered British agent Charles Dobbs in *The Deadly Affair* (1967) to his warmly good-hearted Dr. Watson in *Murder by Decree* (1979) to his Oscar-nominated Prince of Darkness defense attorney Ed Concannon in *The Verdict* (1982) to Sir Randolph Nettleby, the courtly host of *The Shooting Party* (1984), his last important role.

Massey, Anna

(1937–) British character actress, daughter of actor Raymond Massey. She made her film debut as the title character's daughter in *Gideon's Day* (1958), but her first real chance to show her acting talent came in her second film, *Peeping Tom* (1960), in which she played the killer's friend Helen Stephens. The film was a box-office disaster, however, and thereafter she alternated between supporting roles in features such as FRENZY, in which she played starchy, ultimately poignant barmaid Barbara Milligan, and more extensive television work in such buckram-bound roles as Mrs. Danvers (in *Rebecca,* 1962 and 1978), Jane Murdstone (in *David Copperfield,* 1970), and Queen Victoria (in *Around the World in 80 Days,* 1989).

Maté, Rudolph

(1898–1964) Polish-born cinematographer of international films and reputation, born Rudolf Mayer. Hired in 1919 as Alexander Korda's assistant cameraman, he worked with Karl Freund and Erich POMMER before shooting second-unit footage for Carl Dreyer's *Mikaël* (1924) that so impressed the director that he hired him as lighting cinematographer on his pioneering films *The Passion of Joan of Arc* (1928) and *Vampyr* (1932). In 1935 he arrived in Hollywood, where he shot some three dozen films, including *Stella Dallas* (1937), *The Adventures of Marco Polo* (1938), *To Be Or Not to Be* (1942), *Gilda* (1946), and FOREIGN CORRESPONDENT, before taking up directing in 1947. His 30 films as director were proficient but unexceptional, though films such as *D.O.A.* (1950) and *When Worlds Collide* (1953) show how exciting his visual sense could make routine projects. He also produced two films, *The Return of October* (1948) and *The 300 Spartans* (1962), his final work as director.

Mathers, Jerry (1948–)   Child star of movies and television, onscreen from age six, who appeared as Jennifer Rogers's son Arnie, the young discoverer of the body of an unknown man who turns out to be his father, in THE TROUBLE WITH HARRY and then achieved stardom a few years later playing Theodore Cleaver, the title character of the television series *Leave It to Beaver* (1957–63). More recent appearances have been spotty.

Mathieson, Muir (1911–1975)   Scottish conductor and musical director, born Murray Mathieson. Educated at London's Royal College of Music, he began in the film industry as Alexander Korda's assistant musical director in 1931. Beginning with *Catherine the Great* (1958), he was credited as musical director on some 250 films, including 20 in 1958, the year he conducted Bernard HERRMANN's score to VERTIGO. Instrumental in persuading Arthur Bliss, Benjamin Britten, Ralph Vaughn Williams, and Sir William Walton to write for the cinema, he orchestrated Walton's music for *Henry V* (1944) and *Hamlet* (1948), composed scores to 20 films of his own, and appeared as Sir Arthur Sullivan in *The Magic Box* (1951).

Matthews, Jessie (1907–1981)   Celebrated star of British musical revues and films who enjoyed her greatest vogue in the thirties. Born into a large, poor Soho family, she made her stage debut at 10 and her first film at 16. By 1933 when she starred as Rasi Ebeseder in WALTZES FROM VIENNA, she was Britain's most popular musical star, dubbed "the Dancing Divinity," anticipating her greatest success the following year when she recreated the role in Hitchcock's film, and when her husband, Sonnie Hale, appeared with her in the film of her greatest stage triumph, *Evergreen* (1934). But she refused to leave Hale behind to work with Fred Astaire in America; the next two films in which Hale directed her, *First a Girl* (1935) and *It's Love Again* (1936), failed at the box office; she found herself mired in abortive film projects; and her advancing age and weight problems stalled her comeback after the war, though she did enjoy a successful stint in the sixties radio drama *Mrs. Dale's Diary*. Only thanks to *Catch a Fallen Star*, a BBC documentary of her life, was her body removed from an unmarked grave and properly interred.

Maugham, W(illiam) Somerset (1874–1965)   British playwright and novelist, one of the most popular English storytellers of the 20th century. Orphaned at 10, he qualified as a physician and surgeon, but never practiced, pursuing instead the writing career he had begun as a medical student. He soon followed his first successes (1908–14) in stage comedy with his most popular novel, the autobiographical *Of Human Bondage* (1915), the same year that *The Explorer*, first of some 60 films to be based on his work, was released. Although Maugham never worked in Hollywood until 1948—when, abandoning fiction and drama for essays, he appeared to introduce his own stories in the anthology films *Quartet* (1949) and *Trio* (1950)—stories such as "Rain" and "The Letter" were adapted many times by other hands, and *The Moon and Sixpence* (1919) and *The Razor's Edge* (1944) were made into notable films (1942, 1946). Perhaps the most curious of all Maugham adaptations was SECRET AGENT, which, according to Hitchcock, combined and freely transformed elements from two chapters—"The Traitor" and "The Hairless Mexican"—in Maugham's episodic novel *Ashenden; Or, The British Agent* (1928) together with a 1933 dramatization of the novel by

Campbell Dixon that has never, according to Maugham experts, been published or performed.

Maxwell, John (1875–1940)   Scottish solicitor who began as a film exhibitor, became head of Wardour Films in 1923, joined American J.D. Williams to form British National Pictures (the British wing of the American film company First National) in 1926, and then took control of the enterprise when his partner was ousted the following year. As head of BRITISH INTERNATIONAL PICTURES, aiming to balance the studio's production of middlebrow literary (usually theatrical) adaptations with low-budget programmers, he signed Hitchcock away from Michael BALCON's GAINSBOROUGH PICTURES to an exclusive contract and became executive producer, usually without screen credit, of 10 of the director's films: *THE RING, THE FARMER'S WIFE, CHAMPAGNE, THE MANX-MAN, BLACKMAIL, JUNO AND THE PAYCOCK, MURDER!, THE SKIN GAME, RICH AND STRANGE*, and *NUMBER SEVENTEEN*. Relations between the hard-nosed producer and his star director, who went from choosing his own subject and writing his own screenplay for *The Ring* to drifting from one adaptation to the next and producing a quota quickie of his own in *LORD CAMBER'S LADIES*, were never cordial, and Hitchcock professed himself happy to return to Balcon at GAUMONT-BRITISH in 1933, the same year British International became Associated British Pictures. Though he remained a potent force in the British industry—as late as 1937 he was trying unsuccessfully to purchase the financially ailing Gaumont-British—Maxwell's name appeared on only one more film, *On Secret Service* (1936), before his death.

Mayflower Productions   A corporation formed by Charles LAUGHTON and Erich POMMER to finance films starring Laughton and produced by Pommer. After releasing only two films, *Sidewalks of London* (1938) and *JAMAICA INN*, it quietly folded, anticipating Hitchcock's later experience with his own equally short-lived production company, TRANSATLANTIC PICTURES.

McArthur, Molly   British costume designer whose only film credit is *JAMAICA INN*.

McCarthy, John (Jr.)   Veteran American set designer on hundreds of films and television programs from 1943. He designed sets for many episodes of *ALFRED HITCHCOCK PRESENTS* and *THE ALFRED HITCHCOCK HOUR*, including the Hitchcock-directed "THE HORSEPLAYER," "BANG! YOU'RE DEAD," and "I SAW THE WHOLE THING."

McCarty, John (1944–)   Coauthor with Brian KELLEHER of *Alfred Hitchcock Presents: An Illustrated Guide to the Ten-Year Television Career of the Master of Suspense* (St. Martin's, 1985), a survey of all 266 episodes of *ALFRED HITCHCOCK PRESENTS* and *THE ALFRED HITCHCOCK HOUR* that also provides background information on Lew WASSERMAN's 1955 suggestion that "we ought to put Hitch on the air," the roots of the series' witty, macabre tone in *THE TROUBLE WITH HARRY*, and the principal creators and collaborators who kept the programs profitable and Hitchcockian, usually in Hitchcock's absence, for 10 years.

McCauley, Daniel (J.)   American assistant director, at PARAMOUNT from 1953 for such films as *TO CATCH A THIEF* and *VERTIGO*. He followed Hitchcock briefly to WARNER BROS. for *THE WRONG MAN*.

McCowen, Alec (1925–)   British stage actor who has also found time to appear in 40 films, from *The Cruel Sea* (1953) to *FRENZY*, in which he plays self-effacing Chief Inspector Tim Oxford, the most sympathetic of all Hitchcock's police officers largely because of the unspeakable haute cuisine his wife foists on him in counterpoint to the film's leading image of a serial rapist-killer who consumes his victims like so many pieces of fruit.

McCrea, Joel (1905–1990)   Virile American leading man, a former extra whose dream was to star in westerns. In Hollywood from the early days of sound, he was actively promoted by his friend Will Rogers, who shared his interest in riding and roping, and he soon graduated to athletic roles in *The Most Dangerous Game* (1932) and *Barbary Coast* (1935) and romantic leads in *These Three* and *Come and Get It* (both 1936) but was cast only rarely in such westerns as *Wells Fargo* (1937) and *Union Pacific* (1939). In the meantime, however, he had built a reputation as a dependable, versatile lead, and when Gary Cooper turned down the title role of Huntley Haverstock, né Johnny Jones, in FOREIGN CORRESPONDENT, Hitchcock sought McCrea for the role. Soon thereafter he proved himself equally adept as the exasperated straight man in the comedies of Preston Sturges (*Sullivan's Travels,* 1941; *The Palm Beach Story,* 1942) and George Stevens (*The More the Merrier,* 1942). By 1944 his power and wealth, amassed through canny investments in livestock and real estate, allowed him to devote himself almost exclusively to westerns, from *Buffalo Bill* (1944) and *The Virginian* (1946) to his valedictory film, *Ride the High Country* (1962). He was married for more than 50 years to actress Frances Dee.

McDermot, Betty   British actress whose sole film credit is the servant Martha in UNDER CAPRICORN.

McDermott, Pat(ricia)   American hair stylist whose work in entertainment began on the television series *Alcoa Presents* (1959–61) and then continued in 20 features (FRENZY; *Superman,* 1978; *Raiders of the Lost Ark,* 1981; *Return of the Jedi,* 1983) and television programs.

McDevitt, Ruth (1895–1976)   American character actress, born Ruth Shoecraft, in Hollywood from 1951, usually playing older than her age. Best known to two generations of television audiences as Mom Peepers in *Mr. Peepers* (1953–55) and Jo Nelson of *All in the Family* (1973–75), she also played two dozen grandmotherly types in other projects, from Mrs. MacGruder in THE BIRDS to two roles for THE ALFRED HITCHCOCK HOUR: Mrs. Fister in "The Cadaver" (1964) and Emmy Rice in "The Gentleman Caller" (1964).

McDonnell, Claude (L.)   British cinematographer who shot BESIDE THE BONNIE BRIER BUSH (1921), on which Hitchcock designed intertitles, and three films on which he served as assistant director: WOMAN TO WOMAN, THE WHITE SHADOW, and THE PASSIONATE ADVENTURE. Hitchcock was reunited with him at GAINSBOROUGH for EASY VIRTUE and DOWNHILL.

McDonnell, Gordon   American writer who is credited with the original stories for three films: *Lucky Days* (1935), *His Lordship Goes to Press* (1939), and SHADOW OF A DOUBT.

McGilligan, Patrick   American interviewer and biographer. His many books include *Cagney: The Actor as Auteur* (1975), *Robert Altman: Jumping Off the Cliff: A Biography of the Great American Director* (1989), *George Cukor: A Double Life: A Biography of the Gentleman Director* (1991), *Backstory: Interviews with Screenwriters of Hollywood's Golden Age* (1986), *Backstory 2: Interviews with Screenwriters of the 1940s and 1950s* (1991), *Backstory 3: Interviews with Screenwriters of the 1960s* (1997), *Tender Comrades: A History of the Hollywood Blacklist* (with Paul Buhle, 1997), *Fritz Lang: The Nature of the Beast* (1997), *Clint: The Life and Legend* (2000), and *Film Crazy: Interviews with Hollywood Legends* (2000). He has also edited the screenplays for *Yankee Doodle Dandy* (1981) and *White Heat* (1984) and *Six Screenplays by Robert Riskin* (1997). His biography *Alfred Hitchcock: Shadow and Light* is forthcoming from HarperCollins.

McGovern, John (1912–1985)   Genial, rubicund American character actor who appeared in nine roles from 1946, the last of them being the postal clerk in THE BIRDS.

McGraw, Charles (1914–1980)   Hard-faced American character actor, one of the screen's most reliable heavies, who came from stage and radio to Hollywood to play more than 70 instantly recognizable tough guys (with William Conrad, he was one of the two title characters in *The Killers,* 1946) and hard-charging authority figures such as the Los Angeles county health physician Dr. Oliver in THE ALFRED HITCHCOCK HOUR episode "Diagnosis: Danger" (1963). His appearance that same year as the sodden Sebastian Scholes who prophesies the end of the world in THE BIRDS marks perhaps his most laid-back performance.

McIntire, John (1907–1991)   Rough-voiced American character actor with stage and radio background who played more than 100 cops, medicos, and avuncular types from 1948. The best known of his early roles, Police Commissioner Hardy in *The Asphalt Jungle* (1950), was eclipsed in popularity by his continuing television roles as Lt. Dan Muldoon, the Barry Fitzgerald role, in *The Naked City* (1958–59) and Christopher Hale in *Wagon Train* (1961–65), sometimes opposite his wife of many years, actress Jeanette Nolan. In between these two series, he appeared in two ALFRED HITCHCOCK PRESENTS segments, as Sylvia Leeds's possessive father in "Sylvia" (1958) and paranoid businessman Charles Underhill in "Hitch Hike" (1960), and as Sheriff Chambers in PSYCHO.

McKelvy, Frank (R.) American set decorator who started with PARAMOUNT in 1955, worked on 10 films through VERTIGO, and then followed Hitchcock to MGM for NORTH BY NORTHWEST and continued on 30 films during the next 20 years for a variety of studios.

McKinnel, Norman (1870–1932) British stage actor who made his screen debut as early as *King John* (1899) and played a handful of later roles, including Sir Thomas Berwick, the hero's imperious father, in DOWNHILL.

McLaughlin, Gibb (1884–1960) Gaunt British character actor, formerly the star of theatrical monologues, whose spectral, mutable features graced nearly 100 films from 1921, from THE FARMER'S WIFE, in which he played Henry Coaker, to *The Lavender Hill Mob* (1951) and *Hobson's Choice* (1954).

McNally, F. British sound recordist on THE MAN WHO KNEW TOO MUCH (1934) and three later films through 1936.

McNaughton, Gus (1881–1969) Bespectacled British comic actor with extensive revue experience. Born Augustus Howard, he was onstage from 1899 but did not make his film debut until 30 years later, when sync sound created a demand for his understated patter in some 60 roles such as the commercial traveler in THE 39 STEPS, who extols the virtues of his firm's lingerie as a nervous Richard Hannay looks on.

McVeagh, Eve (1919–1997) American character actress whose 40 roles in movies and television from 1946 include four in ALFRED HITCHCOCK PRESENTS— the diner attendant in "Coyote Moon" (1959), the reporter in "The Gloating Place" (1961), Mrs. Archer in "The Test" (1962), Dr. Cullen in "What Frightened You, Fred?" (1962)—two more in THE ALFRED HITCHCOCK HOUR—Rose Cates in "Last Seen Wearing Blue-jeans" (1963) and Sylvia Boggs in "The Second Wife" (1965)—and the part of Georgie Clooney in the FORD STARTIME segment "INCIDENT AT A CORNER."

McVey, Pat(rick) (1910–1973) Burly American character actor, in Hollywood from 1941, best known for playing reporter Steve Wilson in the television series *Big Town* (1950–54). He appears as the more exasperated of the two Chicago police officers who rescue Roger Thornhill from the auction in NORTH BY NORTHWEST and returns as the police chief in THE ALFRED HITCHCOCK HOUR segment "A Matter of Murder" (1964).

McVey, Tyler (1912–) Rugged American character actor who impersonated dozens of cowboys, cops, and soldiers in the fifties and sixties then graduated to doctors and generals. He interpreted six roles for ALFRED HITCHCOCK PRESENTS—Mac, the store detective in "Santa Claus and the Tenth Avenue Kid" (1955), Cargan, the Martian news editor in "Human Interest Story" (1959), Prentiss, the accountant in "Dry Run" (1959), the referee in "Man from the South" (1960), Sgt. Dugan in "One Grave Too Many" (1960), and Sgt. Steve Morton in "The Gloating Place" (1961)—two for THE ALFRED HITCHCOCK HOUR—District Attorney Driscoll in "Hangover" (1962) and the police chief in "A Matter of Murder" (1964)—and one more as Chief Taylor in the FORD STARTIME episode "INCIDENT AT A CORNER."

McWilliams, Glen (1898–1984) American cinematographer, in Hollywood from 1918, who crisscrossed the Atlantic shooting nearly 100 films from *His Majesty, the American* (1919), photographed two wildly disparate Hitchcock films, WALTZES FROM VIENNA and LIFEBOAT. He ended his career in television, shooting Steve McQueen in *Wanted: Dead or Alive* (1958–61) and Bob Cummings in *My Living Doll* (1964–65).

Mead, J(ohn) F.   British art director whose only film credits are *MURDER!* and its German-language sister *MARY*.

Meader, George (F.) (1888–1963)   American character actor who played such minor roles, often uncredited, as the railroad clerk in *SPELLBOUND* in more than 40 movies and television shows from 1940 to 1958.

Meadows, Audrey (1924–1996)   American actress, born Audrey Cotter. The sister of actress Jayne Meadows, she was born to a missionary family stationed in China and trained as a soprano before turning to acting. Although her film appearances were few, she is instantly identifiable from her many television roles, from Alice Kramden in *The Honeymooners* (1955–56) to the brightly adulterous Mrs. Bixby in the *ALFRED HITCHCOCK PRESENTS* segment "MRS. BIXBY AND THE COLONEL'S COAT."

Meeker, Ralph (1920–1988)   Tall, booming-voiced American leading man, born Ralph Rathgeber. Onstage from the early forties, he understudied Henry FONDA in *Mister Roberts* (1947) and took over the role of Stanley Kowalski when Marlon Brando left the stage run of *A Streetcar Named Desire* (1948). Making his screen debut in 1951, he took a succession of Brandoesque roles, playing such physically imposing heroes or villains, variously troubled or untrustworthy, as Roy Anderson in *The Naked Spur* (1952) and his signature role, Mike Hammer in *Kiss Me Deadly* (1955). He starred as the tormented hero Carl Span, desperate to avenge his wife's assault in *REVENGE*, the premiere episode of *ALFRED HITCHCOCK PRESENTS*, and returned to the program to play three more roles: domestic poisoning victim Carl Borden in "Malice Domestic" (1957), arson-minded boyfriend Mel Reeves in "Total Loss" (1959), and murderous used-car salesman John Forbes in "I'll Take Care of You" (1959). He ended his career playing a long succession of television police chiefs.

Mendl, Sir Charles   British diplomat featured as the commodore who offers to take Alicia Huberman away from the plot complications of *NOTORIOUS* and then was cast the following year in his only other role, as Sir Charles Gage in *Ivy* (1947).

Men of the Lightship   British Ministry of Information, 1941, 20th Century–Fox. **Director:** David MacDonald; **Editor (U.S. version):** Alfred Hitchcock:

Though his name does not appear in its credits, Hitchcock reportedly supervised the reediting and dubbing of this wartime documentary for American audiences.

Menzies, William Cameron (1896–1957)   Nonpareil American art director whose example went far to promote the importance of visual stylists in Hollywood. He served as production designer on his first film, *The Naulahka,* in 1918; won his first Academy Award, for *The Dove* and *Tempest,* in 1928; and was nominated again in 1929 for *Alibi* and *The Awakening,* and still again the following year for *Bulldog Drummond*. A year after *Gone With the Wind* (1939), for which he won a special Oscar for his expressive use of color in production design, he designed the special production effects on *FOREIGN CORRESPONDENT* and five years later directed the dream sequence Salvador DALÍ designed for *SPELLBOUND*, refusing screen credit because he disliked the sequence. In addition to his vastly influential work as a visual designer, he also directed 15 films of his own, of which the most important was the visionary British science-fiction epic *Things to Come* (1936).

Merchant, Vivien (1929–1982)   British stage actress, born Ada Thompson. Onstage from 14, she appeared sporadically in films from 1966, when her debut performance as Lily in *Alfie* won her an Oscar nomination. Of her later 10 screen roles, the most gently forceful is Mrs. Oxford, the Cordon Bleu cooking student who delights in preparing revoltingly inedible meals for her husband, Chief Inspector Oxford, in *FRENZY*.

Merivale, Philip (1886–1946) British stage actor, born to a family of Indian colonials, who after a few movie credits going back to 1914 moved to Hollywood in the midthirties to play such imperturbable elders as Jeff Custer's father in MR. AND MRS. SMITH. He was married until his death to actress Gladys COOPER.

Merritt, George (1890–1977) Stolid British character actor, veteran of more than 100 films from 1931, who seemed most at home in a provincial police station, as when he played Detective Sergeant Miller in YOUNG AND INNOCENT.

Metro–Goldwyn–Mayer Pictures For many years the preeminent Hollywood production company, MGM traced its lineage to a series of mergers beginning in 1920 when Marcus Loew's theater chain bought a share of Metro Pictures. In 1924, Metro merged with Samuel Goldwyn Productions (though Goldwyn left almost immediately) and Louis B. Mayer supplied the third name in the logo the following year. Advertising "more stars than there are in the heavens," the studio specialized for years in the kind of glossy middlebrow productions represented in 1939 alone by *Goodbye, Mr. Chips, Northwest Passage, Ninotchka, The Shop Around the Corner, The Women, At the Circus, The Wizard of Oz,* and *Gone With the Wind.* Leonard J. LEFF, in his essay "Hitchcock at Metro," in DEUTELBAUM and POAGUE, has described how the studio, hurt by the departure of so many of its former contract stars, approached Hitchcock early in 1957 to produce and direct a film based on Hammond Innes's *The Wreck of the Mary Deare,* a novel to which the studio owned the rights, but ended up with NORTH BY NORTHWEST instead. The film, though long, expensive, and devoid of any MGM stars (Hitchcock dickered with the studio about the final cut as well as the casting), was a substantial hit. But Hitchcock, despite the unusual degree of control he had been granted at every stage of the project, departed for UNIVERSAL, never making *The Wreck of the Mary Deare,* or indeed any other film, at MGM.

Miles, (Lord) Bernard (1907–1991) British actor, former schoolteacher, who made his stage debut in 1930 and his first film two years later. Though he continued to work onstage, and founded London's Mermaid Theatre in 1959, he appeared in some 50 films, often as slow-spoken regional types. Occasionally, as on *The Tawny Pipit* (1944), *The Guinea Pig* (1948), and *Chance of a Lifetime* (1950), he wrote the screenplays as well. His portrait of the gentlemanly kidnapper Drayton in THE MAN WHO KNEW TOO MUCH (1956), in contrast to Peter LORRE's dangerously mercurial Abbott in the 1934 film, is a study in deepening menace. He was knighted in 1969 and given a life peerage in 1979, the first actor to be so honored.

Miles, Vera (1929–) American actress, born Vera June Ralston. A former Miss Texas of 1948, she appeared in several minor film roles beginning with *Two Tickets to Broadway* (1951), but her big break came through a 1955 television appearance on *Pepsi-Cola Playhouse.* Seeing the broadcast, Hitchcock was struck by her face and within a few days had signed her to a five-year contract and set about molding her into the new Grace KELLY through carefully chosen parts in his films and his new television series, wardrobe consultations with Edith HEAD, and highly directive advice about her public behavior. He introduced his new star in the premiere episode of ALFRED HITCHCOCK PRESENTS, "REVENGE"—shot shortly after "BREAKDOWN" but pushed ahead of it in the broadcast schedule—in which she played Elsa Span, the fragile ex-dancer whose assault leads her husband to exact a bloody revenge. In THE WRONG MAN, her first Hitchcock feature, she played the remarkably similar role of Rose Balestrero, the disintegrating wife who blames herself and her husband when he is misidentified as a thief. In the meantime, *The Searchers* (1956), in which she played the tomboy ingenue Laurie Jorgenson, was released, sending her stock soaring. But the relationship between the new star and her Svengali was soon soured by her marriage to screen Tarzan Gordon Scott and her subsequent announcement of her pregnancy, which precluded her taking the role of Madeleine Elster/Judy Barton in VERTIGO. Although Hitchcock cast her as Marion Crane's sister Lila in PSYCHO and featured her in three other television roles—once as Janey Medwick, determined to clear her grandfather of vicious rumors, in the FORD STARTIME segment "INCIDENT AT A CORNER," and twice in THE ALFRED HITCHCOCK HOUR, as Daphne Grey, the fiancée staked out as bait for the killer in "Don't Look Behind You" (1962), and as the surprisingly resourceful ingenue Nicky Revere in "Death Scene" (1965)—the disappointed director soon moved on to other BLONDE leading ladies. Nor did Miles's career ever fulfill her early promise: Although she appeared in more than 30 films, by the end of the sixties she was working almost entirely on television, where she remained an active guest star for another 20 years.

Milland, Ray (1907–1986)   Welsh leading man, born Reginald Alfred Truscott-Jones. A former Royal Guardsman, he made his film debut in 1929 and went the following year to Hollywood, where he played a long succession of light romantic second leads, occasionally starring as John Ball in *Easy Living* (1937) and Philip Kirby in *The Major and the Minor* (1942) and taking occasional dramatic leads such as Roderick Fitzgerald in *The Uninvited* and Stephen Neale in *the Ministry of Fear* (both 1944). It was in another dramatic role, the Oscar-winning alcoholic Don Birnam in *The Lost Weekend* (1945), that he achieved his greatest success. His later film work was highly variable. He could be properly sinister as the Devil in *Alias Nick Beal* (1949), suavely accomplished as the globe-trotting private detective in the television series *Markham* (1959–60), and master of an old-fashioned range of emotions as the philandering editor George Stroud in *The Big Clock* (1948). But many of his properties, including the half-dozen he directed himself beginning in 1955, were routine. Perhaps the most interesting of his later characterizations was Tony Wendice, a part that seemed to draw on the actor's own earlier romantic persona as the washed-up tennis pro who methodically plots his wife's death in DIAL M FOR MURDER and then just as methodically frames her for murder when his plan goes awry. Hitchcock cast him again in THE ALFRED HITCHCOCK HOUR episode "A Home Away from Home" (1963) as Dr. Fenwick, the homicidal mental patient whose takeover of an asylum strikingly recalls the plot of SPELLBOUND. In 1970, after

a few years of relative inactivity, he returned to the screen in *Love Story* in the character role of Oliver Barrett's disapproving father and appeared in another 50 films and television programs before his death.

Miller, John   British character actor who helped fill the screen in a dozen films from *The March Hare* (1919) to *The £20,000 Kiss* (1963). He played a police constable in YOUNG AND INNOCENT.

Millington, Richard H. (1953–)   American academic, associate professor of English at Smith College, and author of *Practicing Romance: Narrative Form and Cultural Engagement in Hawthorne's Fiction* (1992) and coeditor, with Jonathan FREEDMAN, of *Hitchcock's America* (Oxford University Press, 1999), a collection of nine essays that combines reprints by Paula Marantz COHEN, Robert J. CORBER, and Amy Lawrence with new essays on such touchstones of American culture as romance as the arena for nationalistic skepticism (Debra Fried), the ideology of domesticity (Elsie B. Michie), the flaneur from Poe to Hitchcock (Dana Brand), and the double plot as the figure for an American "excess of order" (Michael Wood). Millington's own essay traces the ways *North by Northwest* uses the promises of love, performance, and the movies as "a strategy for the reclamation of 'American character'" by rescuing both Roger Thornhill and his viewers from a peculiarly American imperative to social conformity despite (or largely, it turns out, because of) the celebrated national emphasis on "American independence."

Mills, Frank   British assistant director who worked on EASY VIRTUE and then followed Hitchcock to BRITISH INTERNATIONAL for all nine of his films there—THE RING, THE FARMER'S WIFE, CHAMPAGNE, THE MANXMAN, BLACKMAIL, MURDER!, THE SKIN GAME, RICH AND STRANGE, and NUMBER SEVENTEEN. His only other screen credit is as production manager on *The Amazing Quest of Ernest Bliss* (1936).

Mills, Mort (1919–1993)   American character actor whose flat voice made him an obvious choice to play cowboys or cops during the fifties and sixties. His longest-running, but well-nigh invisible, role as

Sergeant Ben Landro in the *Perry Mason* television series (1961–65) is bracketed by his roles as Al Schwartz, the American police officer who befriends Mike Vargas in *Touch of Evil* (1958), and his two performances for Hitchcock, as the anonymous highway patrolman whose innocuous questions terrorize Marion Crane in *PSYCHO* and the farmer/spy who helps Michael Armstrong escape East Germany in *TORN CURTAIN*.

Milo, George American set decorator who, after 10 years at Republic, moved to UNIVERSAL, where he worked on *PSYCHO, MARNIE, THE BIRDS*, and *TORN CURTAIN* before retiring in 1974.

Milton, Frank(lin E.) American sound recording supervisor who went from *Some Came Running* (1958) and *NORTH BY NORTHWEST* to some 80 later films at MGM. He won Oscars for *Ben-Hur* (1959), *How the West Was Won* (1963), and *Grand Prix* (1966) and was nominated for *Cimarron* (1960), *The Unsinkable Molly Brown* (1964), and *Doctor Zhivago* (1965).

Minciotti, Esther (1888–1962) Italian-born actress in a half-dozen ethnic roles, including Manny Balestrero's mother in *THE WRONG MAN*, from 1949.

mirrors The symbolic value of mirrors is hardly exclusive to Hitchcock; they are used in hundreds of films from *Double Indemnity* (1944) to *Snow White and the Seven Dwarfs* (1937) to reveal the double or fractured identities of the characters who look into them. The convention of Hollywood mirrors is that they reflect the true identity the watcher is unable to acknowledge, a notion the director flirts with when he cuts from the discovery of the Necktie Murderer's latest victim in *FRENZY*, to a shot of Richard Blaney knotting his necktie in front of a mirror. Curiously, however, Hitchcock's most celebrated films about doubles—*SHADOW OF A DOUBT* and *STRANGERS ON A TRAIN*—make scant use of mirrors, preferring, like *THE PARADINE CASE* and *THE WRONG MAN*, to double their characters visually with each other rather than with themselves. Most of the Hitchcock films that make extensive use of mirrors, such as *STAGE FRIGHT*, use them in quite different ways—as here to emphasize the narcissism of Charlotte Inwood, who is constantly looking into mirrors even while she is talking to other people, forgoing the role of watcher for the paradoxically powerful role of object-to-be-watched.

But all this changed in *VERTIGO*, in which Hitchcock told art director Henry Bumstead: "Try to use a lot of mirrors." The mirrors Bumstead placed prominently in Ernie's Restaurant, in the flower shop to which Scottie Ferguson trails Madeleine Elster, in Ransohoff's Department Store, and in Judy Barton's room at the Empire Hotel all emphasize not only the female lead's duality but also her genesis in a romantic fantasy the hero is only too eager to adopt and internalize (as the disconcerting shot of Madeleine walking up and down in the flower shop in front of a full-length mirror Scottie is hiding behind, doubling her body with his, is echoed later on by the tableau at the Palace of the Legion of Honor in which she stares raptly at the portrait of Carlotta Valdes while he stares equally raptly at her). Even the window in Midge Wood's apartment can provide a strategic reflection of her unhappy desperation when she throws the palette knife at it after defacing the painting in which she had represented herself in Carlotta's pose. Hitchcock continued to exploit the possibilities of mirrors to reveal characters' latent fears and desires in *NORTH BY NORTH-WEST*, when Roger Thornhill tries on the nonexistent George Kaplan's suit in front of a mirror at the Plaza Hotel, draws an inquisitive look when he shaves with Eve Kendall's tiny razor in the men's room at the Chicago train station, and is discovered by Philip Vandamm's sinister housekeeper when his stealthy image is reflected in a television screen that turns him—not for the first time in the film—into a parody of a public figure. The most important mirrors in Hitchcock, however, appear in *PSYCHO*, which begins with a scene in which Marion Crane dresses while watching herself in an off-screen mirror (by the time Hitchcock shows the mirror, she is standing with her back to it), allows her a long moment to appraise her image in her bedroom mirror as she is deciding to steal the Texas oilman's $40,000, and then follows her through a landscape of prominent mirrors in which she never once sees her reflection: the rear-view mirror in which she watches the police officer who had questioned her, the ladies-room mirror at the used-car lot, the mirror placed at the end of the check-in counter at the Bates Motel, and the mirror in her motel room (as well as the unseen mirror presumably placed over the sink in the motel bathroom). Later, first the detective Arbogast, then Sam Loomis and Lila Crane will also be reflected in the mirror at the end of the check-in counter, which reveals the duality even of characters who cannot recognize it in themselves. After the departing Arbogast has questioned Norman, a dissolve from a smiling Norman to a shot of Arbogast emerging from his car to use a public telephone momentarily seems to reflect Arbogast's body reflected in the window behind Norman as the two men's bodies are doubled. But the climactic mirror shot in the film, and in Hitchcock's career, comes when Lila, searching the Bates house for Norman's mother, is startled at a movement reflected in the mirror before her and whirls in terror to confront another mirror behind her, reflecting her own frightening image and portending the gravest threat the film, and the body of Hitchcock's work, unmasks.

Mr. and Mrs. Smith (Alternative titles: *No for an Answer* [working title], *Joies matrimonials, M. et Mme. Smith, Il Signore e la Signora Smith*) RKO, 95 minutes, January 1941. **Executive producer:** Harry E. Edington; **Director:** Alfred Hitchcock; **Screenplay:** Norman Krasna; **Cinematographer:** Harry Stradling; **Assistant director:** Dewey Starkey; **Art director:** Van Nest Polglase [and Albert S. D'Agostino]; **Associate:** L[awrence].P. Williams; **Set director:** Darrell Silvera; **Costumes:** Irene; **Sound:** John E. Tribby; **Special effects:** Vernon L. Walker; **Editor:** William Hamilton; **Music:** Edward Ward [**Musical director:** Roy Webb]; **Cast:** Carole Lombard (Ann Krausheimer Smith), Robert Montgomery (David Smith), Gene Raymond (Jeff Custer), Jack Carson (Chuck), Philip Merivale (Mr. Custer), Lucile Watson (Mrs. Custer), William Tracy (Sammy), Charles Halton (Mr. Deaver), Esther Dale (Mrs. Krausheimer), Emma Dunn (Martha), Betty Compson (Gertie), Patricia Farr (Gloria), William Edmunds (Mamma Lucie), Adele Pearce (Lily), Emory Par-

nell (Conway), Barbara Woodell (David's secretary), Beatrice Maude (Jeff's secretary), Murray Alper (Harold, taxi driver), Frank Mills (dining taxi driver), Ronald R. Rondell (waiter), Ralph Brooks (captain of waiters), Alec Craig (Thomas, club clerk), Ralph Sanford (store checker), Robert Emmett Keane (store manager), Francis Compton (Mr. Flugle), Ralph Dunn (police officer), Georgia Carroll (silent girl at Florida Club), James Flavin (her escort), James Pierce (doorman), Stanley Taylor (lodge clerk), Ernie Alexander (bellhop), Allen Wood (bellhop), Jack Gardner (elevator boy), Sam Harris, Bess Flowers, D. Johnson.

Though Hitchcock maintained to the end of his life that he directed his 26th film only as a favor to his friend (and absentee landlady) Carole LOMBARD, Leonard J. LEFF persuasively argues that he was probably attracted to the project not only because he liked Lombard and the script but because, facing the threat of suspension by David O. SELZNICK, he was eager for another loan-out over which he could have greater control and more than willing to accept the studio's budgetary restrictions to prove his discipline. Norman KRASNA's screenplay presented a married couple long given to settling their marathon domestic disputes by agreeing not to leave the room where the fight has broken out with the news that their marriage is technically void. Instead of informing his wife Ann of the complication, stockbroker David Smith attempts to withhold it from her until after sleeping with her one more time, but she finds out anyway, throws him out of their apartment, and begins to date his partner Jeff Custer. Lombard had agreed to star in the film for RKO if it could be shot in five weeks; when Cary GRANT was unavailable to play David, the studio considered a wide variety of leading men before settling on Robert MONTGOMERY a week before shooting began in September 1940. The production was perhaps the only time Hitchcock was matched with an equally inventive connoisseur of PRACTICAL JOKES. Hearing Hitchcock's remark that actors should be treated like cattle, Lombard had three calves labeled Carole Lombard, Robert Montgomery, and Gene RAYMOND delivered to the set; every morning she pasted a new set of Roosevelt stickers onto Montgomery's bumper, forcing the Willkie supporter to remove them every

After they have discovered their marriage is technically illegal, David Smith (Robert Montgomery) tries in vain to woo back his sometime wife Ann Krausheimer Smith (Carole Lombard) in *Mr. and Mrs. Smith.* *(National Film Society Archive)*

night; and when a photographer from *Life* arrived to shoot what proved to be the second of three versions of Hitchcock's ritual CAMEO APPEARANCE, she insisted on take after take. The production ran over schedule, wrapping after eight weeks but not seriously over budget, giving Hitchcock proof that he could bring in a modest film with an efficiency he had never shown Selznick.

The story, by far the most unlikely of all Hitchcock's American vehicles, marks an extreme contrast with the scale and sprawl of his previous loan-out, FOREIGN CORRESPONDENT. It fits comfortably, however, into what Stanley Cavell has called the comedy of remarriage—a cycle that

includes *It Happened One Night* (1934), *The Awful Truth* (1937), *The Lady Eve* (1941), and *His Girl Friday* (1940). Hitchcock maintained that because he did not understand romantic comedy, he simply shot Krasna's screenplay, and a comparison between script and film reveals few changes or additions. If there is anything particularly Hitchcockian about the finished product, it is in the sadistic exaggeration with which it embarrasses its romantic leads. Both Smiths are chastened by the romantic dinner they plan at the quaint little restaurant where David proposed to Ann; she can no longer get into the same outfit, and he is suspicious of the restaurant's seediness and finally of its food. Later, David is humiliated when he accosts his estranged wife in the department store where she has taken a job, and again at the Florida Club, where she spots him with a blowsy blind date he is trying to ignore, and Ann, in the film's most memorable sequence, is marooned with Jeff at the top of a stalled Ferris wheel in the rain. Such humiliations are the stuff of all romantic comedy, but even Cavell has noted the relative chill of this entry in the genre. It is hardly surprising that, of all Hitchcock's American films, it remains the most neglected.

"Mr. Blanchard's Secret"
52nd episode of *Alfred Hitchcock Presents,* broadcast December 23, 1956. **Associate producer:** Joan Harrison; **Director:** Alfred Hitchcock; **Assistant director:** Richard Birnie; **Teleplay:** Sarett Rudley, based on a short story by Emily Neff; **Cinematographer:** John L. Russell; **Art director:** John Lloyd; **Set designer:** James Walters; **Costumes:** Vincent Dee; **Editors:** Richard G. Wray and Edward W. Williams; **Music:** Stanley Wilson; **Cast:** Mary Scott (Babs Fenton), Robert Horton (John Fenton), Dayton Lummis (Charles Blanchard), Meg Mundy (Mrs. Blanchard).

The second episode Hitchcock directed for his television program's second season stars Mary SCOTT as Babs Fenton, a mystery writer whose hyperactive imagination persuades her, over her husband's objections, that their new neighbor, Charles Blanchard, has murdered his wife. Her theories confounded when Mrs. Blanchard appears at her door to introduce herself, she concludes instead from her missing cigarette lighter that Mrs. Blanchard must be a kleptomaniac whose husband is struggling to keep her condition secret. But this theory is exploded as well when the presumed kleptomaniac returns with the lighter, which she had given to her husband to fix when she discovered that it wasn't working. The abrupt shifts in tone throughout the episode and its rickety logical foundation broadly parody *Rear Window* and make it at once Hitchcock's lightest and his most problematic work for television.

"Mrs. Bixby and the Colonel's Coat"
190th episode of *Alfred Hitchcock Presents,* broadcast September 27, 1960. **Producer:** Joan Harrison; **Associate**

producer: Norman Lloyd; **Director:** Alfred Hitchcock; **Assistant director:** James H. Brown; **Teleplay:** Halsted Welles, based on the short story by Roald Dahl; **Cinematographer:** John L. Russell; **Art director:** Martin Obzina; **Set designer:** James S. Redd; **Costumes:** Vincent Dee; **Editors:** David O'Connell and Edward W. Williams; **Music:** Frederick Herbert; **Cast:** Audrey Meadows (Mrs. Bixby), Les Tremayne (Dr. Fred Bixby), Stephen Chase (the Colonel), Sally Hughes (Miss Putney), Madie Horman (Eloise), Harry Cheshire (Mr. Gorman), Howard Caine (pawnbroker), Lillian Culver (patient), Ted Jordan (Mr. Evans), Bernie Hamilton (butler).

The opening episode in the program's sixth season follows Mrs. Bixby as she leaves her dentist husband for a trip to her mother that actually takes her to the home of her secret lover, the Colonel. The following morning, the Colonel leaves a note informing her that he is breaking off their long-term affair, together with the parting gift of an opulent mink coat. Realizing that she cannot return to her husband in the coat without arousing his suspicions, she pawns the coat for a nominal sum; returns home with the claim ticket, which she says she found on the train; and sends him off to the pawnshop to redeem the pledge, whatever it might be. When she stops by her husband's office the next day to see the pledge that has so excited him, he presents her proudly with a scrawny mink neckpiece instead. On the way out, she glimpses Miss Putney, his dental assistant, modeling the coat.

Modleski, Tania
(1949–) American scholar of film and popular culture, Florence R. Scott professor of English at the University of Southern California, and author of *Loving with a Vengeance: Mass-Produced Fantasies for Women* (1982), *Feminism Without Women: Culture and Criticism in a "Postfeminist" Age* (1991), and *Old Wives Tales and Other Women's Stories* (1998). Her critical study *The Women Who Knew Too Much: Hitchcock and Feminist Theory* (1988), taking issue with Laura MULVEY's claim that Hitchcock's films, as exemplary Hollywood films, reduce their female characters to passive objects to foster voyeuristic pleasures for male characters and viewers, maintains instead that identifications in

Hitchcock are irreducibly bisexual, that male characters even at their most patriarchal routinely identify themselves with suffering or oppressed female characters as well as with other males, but that they protect their sense of their masculinity by disavowing these identifications. Through an examination of BLACKMAIL, MURDER!, REBECCA, NOTORIOUS, REAR WINDOW, VERTIGO, and FRENZY, Modleski argues that this oscillation between empathy and objectification produces in Hitchcock's films, which are "anything but exemplary of Hollywood cinema," an unresolved ambivalence toward female subjectivity, ruthlessly demystifying and punishing the very females for whom they feel the greatest solicitude, and holding the scopophilic pleasures Mulvey takes as normative up to close and critical scrutiny. Her ultimate goal is to provide a less fatalistic, better informed position from which female spectators may consider the possibilities open to them.

Mogg, Ken Australian film scholar, formerly with the College of Advanced Education, Melbourne University. As founding editor of the journal THE MACGUFFIN, a quarterly newsletter devoted to Hitchcock scholarship, he has attracted a readership of both academics and fans through the journal and its Web page at <http://www.labyrinth.net.au/~muffin/index.html>. Many of his columns for the journal have been collected in The Alfred Hitchcock Story (Titan, 1999), a copiously illustrated oversized book surveying Hitchcock's career film by film, each entry including a brief synopsis, background material on the filming and Hitchcock's collaborators, and analytical and evaluative comments. Behind the running commentary is a view of Hitchcock as a vitalist in the tradition of Arthur Schopenhauer, who sees the world as the expression of a powerfully ambivalent will to "life-or-death" Mogg also finds in Dickens, whom he takes to be Hitchcock's most important literary influence. The discussion is enriched by sidebars on such diverse subjects as BRITISH INTERNATIONAL PICTURES, the segment cut from SPELLBOUND's dream sequence, and the British cut of STRANGERS ON A TRAIN, as well as interpolated essays on Hitchcock's writers (by Steven L. DEROSA), the director's radio programs and short story

anthologies (by Martin GRAMS, Jr.), ALFRED HITCHCOCK PRESENTS and THE ALFRED HITCHCOCK HOUR (by J. Lary Kuhns), Hitchcock's leading collaborators, famous locations, technical innovations, and icy blondes (all by Philip Kemp), his leading men, his cameo appearances, and "remakes, sequels, and homages" of his work (all by David Barraclough), and a survey of Hitchcock's unrealized projects (by Dan AUILER, who also contributes several summary essays that divide the book into historical periods). An American abridgment was published by Taylor the same year.

Molière Players A troupe of French actors and actresses who fled to England during World War II. They comprised the ensemble cast for the two short films Hitchcock directed for the BRITISH MINISTRY OF INFORMATION, BON VOYAGE and AVENTURE MALGACHE.

Monkman, Phyllis (1892–1976) Stage-trained British character actress with a nice line in working-class vanity, as the knife-obsessed neighbor in the sync-sound version of BLACKMAIL and 10 other films, 1919–49.

montage and decoupage Hitchcock's repeated definition of PURE CINEMA in terms of montage requires some clarification. Even though the director equated montage with "cutting" when he told Peter BOGDANOVICH that "pure cinema is complementary pieces of film put together, like notes of music to make a melody," it would be more accurate to say that he was speaking of precutting (decoupage)—that is, of planning a given film in terms of a sequence of images to be composed, photographed, and then assembled in sequence—than of the actual cutting (montage) that took place after principal photography was completed. Hence Hitchcock's well-attested boredom during his shoots, his insistence that he never looked through the camera, and his avowed wish that he didn't have to shoot the picture because he had already completed the creative part, planning the decoupage that would unfold his story in a way that would provoke strong emotional reactions in his viewers. Recently, however, Bill KROHN has disputed the force of this distinction, demonstrating that films as different as DIAL M FOR

MURDER, THE MAN WHO KNEW TOO MUCH (1956), and *THE BIRDS* underwent important changes during and after shooting that belie Hitchcock's self-portrait as the sole creator who planned every effect of his films before they ever went before the camera.

Montagu, Ivor (1904–1984) British Renaissance man of the cinema, variously a writer, editor, producer, director, critic, and theorist. Born Ivor Goldsmid Samuel Montagu, he was educated as a zoologist but soon turned to film, becoming a founding member of London's Film Society in 1925. The following year, Michael BALCON, recognizing his interest in new films from the continent, asked him for suggestions about *THE LODGER*, whose distributor, C.M. WOOLF, had shelved it. Montagu recommended some reediting, cutting the title cards from 300 to 80, and hiring E. McKnight KAUFFER to design decorative title cards emphasizing the film's triangular motif. When the resulting version was successful, Montagu returned as script and editing consultant on *DOWNHILL* and *EASY VIRTUE*, and directed four films of his own in 1928. A longtime devoté of Soviet cinema who translated Pudovkin's *Film Technique* and Eisenstein's *Film Form* into English, he traveled through Europe and Hollywood with the director in 1929–30 but was back in England to direct three more films and to serve as associate producer on *THE MAN WHO KNEW TOO MUCH* (1934), taking the same job without screen credit in *THE 39 STEPS, SECRET AGENT,* and *SABOTAGE*. He later made propaganda films for the Spanish Republicans and the BRITISH MINISTRY OF INFORMATION and co-wrote the screenplay for *Scott of the Antarctic* (1948). The first film critic for *The Observer* and *New Statesman and Nation,* he was also author of the 1964 textbook *Film World.*

Montgomery, Ray (1919–1998) Stalwart American character actor in more than 70 supporting roles, most notably Professor Howard Ogden in the television series *Ramar of the Jungle* (1952–54) and its sequels. He appeared as the short-lived man in Room 321 in "REVENGE," the first episode of *ALFRED HITCHCOCK PRESENTS*, and returned as the intern in "PenPal" (1960) and the even more short-lived gas station attendant in "The Woman Who Wanted to Live" (1962).

Montgomery, Robert (1904–1981) Ebullient, dependable American romantic lead, for years the king of smart comedy at MGM. Left impoverished by his wealthy father's death in 1920, he tried writing and then acting, making his stage debut in 1924 and his screen debut five years later. Though occasionally straying from studio drawing rooms for his acclaimed performances in the prison melodrama *The Big House* (1930) and the psycho-shocker *Night Must Fall* (1937), he was still best known as a light comedian when Hitchcock cast him as a substitute for Cary GRANT as David Smith in *MR. AND MRS. SMITH*. Ironically, his genial image would be darkened soon afterward, not by his association with Hitchcock but by his distinguished war service, his direction of several sequences of the Pacific-war drama *They Were Expendable* (1945), and his first film as director, *The Lady in the Lake* (1946), a much-disputed hardboiled tour de force shot almost entirely from the offscreen shamus hero's point of view. He went on to direct four more films from 1947 to 1960; to direct, produce, host, and occasionally star in a long-running television series, *Robert Montgomery Presents* (1950–54); and to win a Tony for his direction of Joseph Hayes's play *The Desperate Hours*. Long active in politics, he served in the Eisenhower administration as a special consultant to the president on television and public communications. His daughter, actress Elizabeth Montgomery, rivaled her father's popularity as Samantha, the heroine of the television series *Bewitched* (1964–71).

Moore, Brian (1921–1999) Irish-born novelist, long resident in Canada, whose screen adaptation of his 1960 novel *The Luck of Ginger Coffey* (1964) made UNIVERSAL and Hitchcock seek him out to write the original screenplay for *TORN CURTAIN*. Despite his misgivings about the project and his suitability for it, he agreed. But the process was beset by such difficulties that he was eventually removed from the project by Hitchcock and, in response, offered to remove his name from the credits in favor of rewriters Keith Waterhouse and Willis Hall. The offer was declined, and Screen Writers Guild arbitrators awarded Moore sole screenplay credit, even though he maintained that the only ideas he had contributed to the film were the MACGUFFIN of secret information buried in a scientist's mind, the difficulty of killing another person, and the dramatic possibilities of a would-be defector who battens on the heroes as potential saviors. Several of Moore's other novels have since been adapted for television (*Catholics,* 1972/1973) and film (*The Lonely Passion of Judith Hearne,* 1955/1987); he adapted his own novel *Black Robe* (1985) to the screen in 1991.

Moore, Juanita (1922–) African-American actress, onscreen from 1949. By far the best known of her three dozen screen roles is Lora Meredith's life-long friend Annie Johnson in *Imitation of Life* (1959), for which she was nominated for an Oscar. She played the Chesters' maid Cleo in the ALFRED HITCHCOCK PRESENTS segment "BANG! YOU'RE DEAD" and returned for three segments of THE ALFRED HITCHCOCK HOUR, as Mrs. McFarland in "The Lonely Hours" (1963), Mrs. Jones in the "The Gentleman Caller" (1964), and Suse the maid in "Where the Woodbine Twineth" (1965).

Morahan, Thomas (N.) (1906–) British art director whose film career began in 1938 with credits for "settings" on *Vessel of Wrath* and, the following year, JAMAICA INN. Following 10 other films, notably *On Approval* (1944), he served as art director on THE PARADINE CASE and production designer on UNDER CAPRICORN and another dozen films on both sides of the Atlantic through 1968. He served as associate producer on one of these films, *Sons and Lovers* (1960), and produced two more.

Moray, Dean American child actor whose brief list of film and television credits includes Gary in the ALFRED HITCHCOCK PRESENTS episode "BANG! YOU'RE DEAD,"

Morell, André (1909–1978) Stage-trained British actor, born André Mesritz, who joined the Old Vic repertory company in 1938, the same year he made his first film. Onscreen for more than 70 roles, often as aristocrats, judges, and such senior police officers as Inspector Byers in STAGE FRIGHT, he is best known for his title role in the television series *Quatermass and the Pit* (1958). Formerly married to actress Joan Greenwood.

Morgan, Sidney (1873–1946) Veteran producer/director of some 30 British silents, often from his own screenplays, who ventured before the camera to play Joxer Daly in JUNO AND THE PAYCOCK and two other roles.

Morris, Christopher D. American film scholar, professor of English at Norwich University, author of *Models of Misrepresentation in the Fiction of E.L. Doctorow* (1991) and editor of *Conversations with E.L. Doctorow* (1999). *The Hanging Figure: On Suspense and the Films of Alfred Hitchcock*, which traces the nature of Hitchcockian suspense, as exemplary of Hollywood cinema, to the undecidability arising from the inescapably figural conditions of representation in cinematic narrative, is forthcoming from Praeger/Greenwood Press.

Morris, Dave (1897–1960) British character actor, in films from 1914, who played Jerry Devine in JUNO AND THE PAYCOCK.

mothers Mothers are conspicuously absent from Hitchcock's early films. THE PLEASURE GARDEN and THE RING have no room for parents of any kind, and fathers rule their families with varying success in THE MOUNTAIN EAGLE, THE MANXMAN, THE FARMER'S WIFE, CHAMPAGNE, and NUMBER SEVENTEEN (in families defined by the mother's absence) and DOWNHILL (in which Lady Berwick defers to her irate husband). The most prominent mother in these films is the long-suffering Juno Boyle in JUNO AND THE PAYCOCK; the most interesting are the troubled mother in THE LODGER (a far less complex character than in Marie Belloc Lowndes's source novel) and the scheming mothers in EASY VIRTUE and THE SKIN GAME. In *The Farmer's Wife,* BLACKMAIL, and MURDER!, Hitchcock begins to conflate father figures with romantic leads—a pattern he parodies in SABOTAGE, and one that continues even today in Hollywood's May-December pairings—and figures fathers as authoritarian rivals in WALTZES FROM VIENNA and YOUNG AND INNOCENT. But mothers do not undergo any similarly problematic reconfiguration until his arrival in America, where REBECCA figures the heroine's late romantic rival in terms of the forbiddingly maternal Mrs. Danvers. FOREIGN CORRESPONDENT and SUSPICION both rehearse the central father-daughter relationship, and MR. AND MRS. SMITH treats its mother-daughter pairing as conventional Hollywood comedy, but SHADOW OF A DOUBT, balancing its villain's fate on the emotional pain his arrest would cause his sister, the heroine's mother, examines the link between maternal authority and female suffering more closely, and SPELLBOUND presents its romantic heroine for the first time implicitly in maternal terms, as the nurturing therapist who will return the helplessly delusional hero to the comfort of the family romance that was poisoned when he accidentally killed his brother.

If Emma Newton, in Shadow of a Doubt, is comically and pathetically ineffectual, Madame Sebastian is the first of a new breed of mothers who scheme against their sons' romances from a viewpoint explicitly informed by an Oedipal sexual rivalry figured in NOTORIOUS by the bride's battle with her mother-in-law, duly mediated by the embattled bridegroom Alex Sebastian, over closets and keys. Despite the prevalence of what Paula Marantz COHEN has called "the father-daughter plot" in Shadow of a Doubt, STAGE FRIGHT, and especially STRANGERS ON A TRAIN and "the daughter's effect" in REAR WINDOW and THE MAN WHO KNEW TOO MUCH (1956)—this last film Hitchcock's only example of a mother presented in unequivocally positive terms—Hitchcock's families are thereafter increasingly dominated by threatening mothers. Sometimes their menace is purely comic, as in Mrs. Gill's erratic behavior toward Wilfred Smith in Stage Fright or the mixture of ridicule and overprotectiveness Mrs. Thornhill lavishes on her son in NORTH BY NORTHWEST or the implication of Francie Matthews's final line to John Robie when she finally tracks him to his lair in TO CATCH A THIEF: "So this is where you live. Why, Mother will love it here!" Sometimes it is grotesquely or disarmingly comic, as in Mrs. Bruno's bland assurances to Ann Morton in

Strangers on a Train that although her son may sometimes get carried away, he would never murder anybody, or Jennifer Rogers's in The Trouble with Harry his late father's corpse: "Thank Providence! . . . Let's run home and get some lemonade." By the time of THE BIRDS and MARNIE, however, the traumatic sexual jealousies and disavowals of mothers have made them as much the enemies of family as the commitment-shy males of Notorious and Rear Window; or, to put it more accurately, Hitchcock's films, looking inward for the threats they once found outside, identify mother's family as a psychosexual battleground rather than a locus of security, stability, and emotional nurturing.

Commentators long saw the rough treatment of mothers in Hitchcock's later films through the lens of the director's alleged misogyny, a pattern feminist theorists have complicated by reference to his heroes' fear of loss, their need to maintain the power established by the male gaze, the bisexual nature of the identifications he fostered, or the rise of what Philip Wylie called the American fetish of "momism." Still another reason Hitchcock's mothers become so menacing is his loss of faith in the project of genetic identity and with it in the power of narrative to restore a sense of imaginary union with the world. Roddy Berwick and Richard Hannay can survive their vicissitudes to return to the identities with which they began, but Charlie Newton and Lina Aysgarth have no such option; minutes after SUSPICION presents Lina packing to return to her mother, the sequel shows that she can't go home again because it is impossible to unlearn or retreat from the experience of Johnny or Uncle Charlie. These motives come together in Hitchcock's most monstrous mother, Mrs. Bates in PSYCHO. Prefigured by the absent mother of Marion Crane's officemate Caroline (played, interestingly enough, by Patricia Hitchcock), who prepared Caroline for her wedding night by giving her tranquilizers, Norman's mother is presented as spitefully jealous and homicidally possessive, an unmoving figure who, though rarely seen or heard, anchors the iconography of the Bates house both indoors and out, and whose dictates her son has internalized so completely that he refuses to have her committed or even cultivate outside friendships, believing that "a boy's best friend is his mother." Yet

Mrs. Bates, at least in the sense in which the film presents her, does not exist; far from dictating her son's deepest loyalty, she functions purely to externalize his own psychosis. As James NAREMORE has pointed out, the film's final scene leaves it chillingly unclear whether the voice speaking over a long track-in to Norman's face indicates his projection of what his mother would say or his final, absolute possession by his dead mother. In either case, the mother whom *Psycho* and other Hitchcock films take to be smothering the hero is indistinguishable from the hero's unresolved attempt to separate himself from her for good.

Mountain Eagle, The (Alternative titles: *Fear o' God* [working title], *Der Bergadler, L'Aigle de la montaigne*) Gainsborough-Emelka, Wardour & F., approximately 85 minutes, October 1926. **Producer:** Michael Balcon; **Director:** Alfred Hitchcock; **Screenplay:** Eliot Stannard (based on an unpublished story by Charles Lapworth); **Cinematographer:** Baron (Gaetano) Ventimiglia; **Assistant director:** Alma Reville; **Art directors:** Wily and Ludwig Reiber; **Cast:** Bernard Goetzke (Pettigrew), Nita Naldi (Beatrice), Malcolm Keen ([John Fulton, known as] Fear o' God), John [F.] Hamilton (Edward Pettigrew).

The Mountain Eagle, the second complete film Hitchcock directed, has assumed legendary status as his most sought-after rarity, a film at one time extant in at least three versions—an English print, a German-language print, and an abridged American print—none of which has survived. The story, as summarized in contemporary reviews in the *Bioscope* and *Kinematograph Weekly,* concerns the village schoolteacher Beatrice, who antagonizes Pettigrew, the local justice of the peace, by the professional attention she has given his son Edward and her rejection of his own advances. Driven away, she is befriended by a hermit named Fear o' God, who defuses accusations of scandal by having Pettigrew marry them, giving her the option of divorce when she leaves him. In the meantime, however, Pettigrew has Fear o' God jailed for killing the missing Edward. After languishing in prison for a year, Fear o' God, hearing that his wife has borne a child, escapes with them to the mountains but returns for a doctor when the child falls

sick. The climactic confrontation between Fear o' God and Pettigrew is defused when a bystander fires a gun that wounds Pettigrew, and Edward suddenly returns, paving the way for Pettigrew to renounce his enmity.

Because the film has been missing, along with any of its scripts, for many years, information about it is spotty and largely conjectural, both because the film cannot be consulted as an authoritative source and because its absence has diminished the enthusiasm of most commentators. Maurice YACOWAR, in his survey of the director's British films, confines himself to quoting and paraphrasing earlier summaries, and Charles BARR omits it altogether. Hitchcock himself told François TRUFFAUT simply that "it was a very bad movie." A primary source of information about the film's production is Hitchcock's 1937 essay "Life Among the Stars," reprinted by Sidney GOTTLIEB. Describing the vagaries of location shooting in Obergurgel, a German village standing in for the hills of Kentucky, the filmmaker recounts how a snowstorm drove him from the location he had spotted to Umhaus, a neighboring village struck by another snowstorm; how he persuaded the local fire brigade, after four days' wait, to clear enough of the snow to permit filming; and how he overcame his initial reservations about his star—the American vamp Nita NALDI, cast as a Kentucky schoolteacher—whom he came to respect professionally and to cherish as a friend.

In the absence of a rediscovered print of the film, J. Lary Kuhns's long essay on the film in the 1998–99 *HITCHCOCK ANNUAL*, which reprints 28 stills (evidently frame enlargements) from the film together with three on-set production stills and nine off-set stills showing Hitchcock and his crew at work in the Tyrol, is likely to remain the most judicious and authoritative gathering of information about it. Kuhns reports that the film was in production by November 1925, completed the following month, screened in Berlin in May 1926, and exhibited to the British press in October 1926 before being scheduled for public release on May 23, 1927. Unless a print surfaces, a possibility that fades with each passing year, questions about how the film fits into Hitchcock's career—its handling of the male gaze, its emphasis on homelessness, its analysis of families in crisis—or what it reveals about his working methods will probably remain subordinate to speculations about exactly what sort of film it was.

Mowbray, Alan (1896–1969) British-born character actor, born Ernest Alan Mowbray, with extensive stage experience from 1923. He made his screen debut in 1931. Soon after his arrival in Hollywood two years later, his aristocratic bearing and faultless diction won him the first of more than 150 supporting roles as butlers, majordomos, doctors, and their noble employers, with occasional departures from his type such as the crass Rawdon Crawley in *Becky Sharp* (1935). In 1956, as his career was slowing down, he starred in the television series *The Best in Mystery* and played roles in three films: the British ambassador in *The King and I,* the British consul in *Around the World in 80 Days,* and Jo McKenna's friend Val Parnell in THE MAN WHO KNEW TOO MUCH.

Moyer, Ray (1898–1986) American set decorator, at PARAMOUNT for more than 60 films from 1943. A specialist in color, he was nominated for Academy Awards for *Lady in the Dark* (1944), *Love Letters* (1945), *Kitty* (1946), *Red Garters* (1954), *The Ten Commandments* (1956), *Funny Face* (1957), *Summer and Smoke* (1961), and *The Greatest Story Ever Told* (1965) and won for *Sunset Boulevard* (1950) and *Cleopatra* (1963). He decorated the single set for REAR WINDOW—the largest and most complex set in Hollywood history to that date.

Mueller, Richard Color consultant who started with 20TH CENTURY–FOX in the forties and then settled in the fifties at PARAMOUNT, where he worked on REAR WINDOW, TO CATCH A THIEF, THE TROUBLE WITH HARRY, and THE MAN WHO KNEW TOO MUCH (1956), among 60 others. He retired in 1964 with the decline of Technicolor but returned in 1987 as a television writer and script consultant.

Muir, Gavin (1900–1972) American character actor, born Gaven Muir. Educated in England, he played British characters almost exclusively and was especially effective as aristocratic villains such as Lord

Haw-Haw in *Passport to Destiny* (1944). He appeared in three episodes of ALFRED HITCHCOCK PRESENTS: as Mr. Wallingford in "BACK FOR CHRISTMAS," the priest in "Miss Bracegirdle Does Her Duty" (1958), and Mr. Thompson in "The Canary Sedan" (1958).

Mulcaster, G.H. (1891–1964) British character actor, mainly onstage, whose 30 film roles from 1920 most often cast him as such upper-class or professional types as Dr. Macallister in UNDER CAPRICORN.

Mulvey, Laura British filmmaker and academic, equally well known for her avant-garde film *Riddles of the Sphinx* (codirected with Peter Wollen, 1977) and her pioneering essay "Visual Pleasure and Narrative Cinema" (1975). This last argues that mainstream cinema is aimed at a regressive male heterosexual audience whose primary desires, by turns voyeuristic and narcissistic, create conflicts (men enjoy looking at images of women, whom the cinema positions as figures-to-be-looked-at, but see them as potentially castrating) that it resolves by either fetishizing the female figure, breaking it down into an appealing but depersonalized aesthetic spectacle (as in Josef von Sternberg's films), or reenacting the original trauma of castration by investigating the female and demystifying her threat (as in Hitchcock's). Although Mulvey's discussion of the power of the male gaze as "patriarchal superego" to anatomize and disempower threatening women and install male viewers in Jacques LACAN's symbolic order in Hitchcock's films (REAR WINDOW, MARNIE, and especially VERTIGO) is brief, her essay, a milestone in film theory, effected a fundamental reorientation in Hitchcock studies.

Mumy, Billy (1954–) American child actor, born Charles William Mumy, Jr. Shortly after his 1961 debut in *The Twilight Zone,* he was cast in the ALFRED HITCHCOCK PRESENTS episode "BANG! YOU'RE DEAD" as Jackie Chester, the boy whose toy gun is more real than he or the people he threatens with it know. The following year he returned to series as Mickey Hollins, the lost boy in "The Door Without a Key" (1962), and the year after that he turned up in THE ALFRED HITCHCOCK HOUR to play Tony Mitchell, the son providentially saved from drowning in "House Guest" (1962). He achieved his widest fame, as Erasmus Leaf in the film *Dear Brigitte* (1965) and Will Robinson in the television series *Lost in Space* (1965–68), while still a teenager but has continued to make film and television appearances as Bill Mumy in adult character roles.

Mundy, Meg (1923–) British-born actress best known from her appearances on American television, from Martha Sturgis and Mrs. Blanchard in the ALFRED HITCHCOCK PRESENTS episodes "The Orderly World of Mr. Appleby" (1956) and "MR. BLANCHARD'S SECRET," to her long-running roles as Mona Croft on *The Doctors* (1972–82) and as Eugenia von Voynavitch on *All My Children* (1997–).

murder   There is no logical reason why thrillers must revolve around murder rather than blackmail, rape, or robbery. Yet Hitchcock's films always do. Even the sunniest of them, like TO CATCH A THIEF, entangle the hero in homicide sooner or later—this time, ironically, to provide the evidence that will vindicate him. More often, his films begin with a murder (YOUNG AND INNOCENT, FRENZY) or work up to it as the climax of their first movement (both versions of THE MAN WHO KNEW TOO MUCH, NORTH BY NORTHWEST). A convention of detective fiction established early in the 20th century (in contrast to the 19th-century practice of Wilkie Collins and Arthur Conan Doyle) rules that murder, the only crime whose effects can neither by reversed nor avenged by its victim, is worthy of readers' attention. Surprisingly, however, not only domestic mysteries such as SHADOW OF A DOUBT but also espionage films such as SECRET AGENT and FOREIGN CORRESPONDENT include murder—often the incongruous killing of a minor character, as in THE LADY VANISHES—as if the threat of war itself were not substantial enough to hold viewers' attention.

There are several reasons why murder is essential to Hitchcock's thrillers. The most obvious is that it raises the stakes for his characters because the peril of a heroine such as Alicia Huberman in NOTORIOUS becomes more urgent once her husband has assented to the death of the inoffensive Emil Hupka. A second is that it provides him with an occasion for staging many memorable DEATH SCENES that can be made more intense than the transfer of funds from one custodian to another. Although movie audiences may well acknowledge greed as a wellnigh universal motive, they are far less likely to admit to the desire to kill. The single act of murder can therefore be used to distinguish several disparate types as characterized by such thrill-killers as the General in *Secret Agent,* such doughty professionals as Rowley in *Foreign Correspondent,* such psychopaths as Uncle Charlie in *Shadow of a Doubt,* such ordinary souls driven to desperate measures as Lars Thorwald in REAR WINDOW, psychotics like Norman BATES in PSYCHO, and inept amateurs like Michael Armstrong in TORN CURTAIN. In films like ROPE and STRANGERS ON A TRAIN, murder is the ultimate exercise of power; and as Hitchcock agreed with François TRUFFAUT in quoting Oscar Wilde's line "each man kills the thing he loves," his films closely link love and death so that the drive toward possession, self-sacrifice, and even self-annihilation can end in death, as in VERTIGO. Finally, murder can provide the basis for a newly invigorated community whose social order is based on mutual protection, as in THE TROUBLE WITH HARRY. It is no wonder, then, that the ultimate social and moral outrage is the normal state of affairs in Hitchcock.

Murder!   (Alternative titles: *Meutre, Omicidio!*) British International, Wardour Films Ltd., British International (U.S.), 92 minutes, August 1930. **Producer:** John Maxwell; **Director:** Alfred Hitchcock; **Adaptation:** Alfred Hitchcock and Walter Mycroft from *Enter Sir John,* a novel by Clemence Dane and Helen Simpson; **Scenario:** Alma Reville; **Cinematographer:** J.J. Cox; **Art director:** J.F. Mead; **Assistant director:** Frank Mills; **Editor:** Rene Marrison, under the supervision of Emile de Ruelle; **Sound recordist:** Cecil V. Thornton; **Musical director:** John Reynders; **Cast:** Herbert Marshall (Sir John Menier), Norah Baring (Diana Baring), Phyllis Konstam (Doucie Markham), Edward Chapman (Ted Markham), Miles Mander (Gordon Druce), Esme Percy (Handel Fane), Donald Calthrop (Ion Stewart), Esme V. Chaplin (prosecuting counsel), Amy Brandon-Thomas (defending counsel), Joynson Powell (judge),

Handel Fame (Esme Percy) agrees to read through a scene from a new play by Sir John Menier (Herbert Marshall) in *Murder!*—unaware that it is a thinly disguised version of his murder of Edna Druce. *(National Film Society Archive)*

S.J. Warmington (Bennett), Marie Wright (Miss Mitcham), Hannah Jones (Mrs. Didsome), Una O'Connor (Mrs. Grogram), R.E. Jeffrey (jury foreman), Alan Stainer, Kenneth Kove, Guy Pelham Boulton, Violet Farebrother, Clare Greet, Drusilla Wills, Robert Easton, William Fazan, George Smythson, Ross Jefferson, Picton Roxborough (members of the jury), and Harry Terry (stage doorman).

The adventurous premise behind Hitchcock's 12th film—that an entire novel could be successfully adapted to a synchronized-sound film—was presumably softened by the novel's limited status within the genre of detective fiction and by its leitmotif of theatricality, which at times makes it seem more play than novel. When the film went before the cameras in 1930, however, Hitchcock and

BRITISH INTERNATIONAL production chief Walter MYCROFT had not yet finished the screenplay. Accordingly, the director tried several scenes in which he discussed the requirements of the dialogue beforehand with the performers and then allowed them to improvise their lines on-camera. Although this method worked well for directors like Howard Hawks, the experiment proved a disaster for Hitchcock's cast, confirming his faith, if any confirmation were needed, in meticulous preproduction preparation. Even as he was directing the film, Hitchcock, who had already made a trip to Berlin to discuss possible script changes, was simultaneously shooting *MARY*, a German-language version of the film for which a German cast headed by Alfred Abel had been brought to the studio. Both versions of the film followed the source novel in installing the aristocratic playwright/impresario Sir John Saumerouz/Menier first on a jury in which he reluctantly votes to convict Diana Baring of the murder of her fellow actress Edna Druce, then as an amateur sleuth determined to clear the name of the woman he helped sentence to death. The film is therefore customarily described as one of Hitchcock's few whodunits. But like other such alleged whodunits (STAGE FRIGHT, THE TROUBLE WITH HARRY, even PSYCHO), it is not adequately described by the term. In *Stage Fright* and *Psycho,* the detectives and the audience think they know from the beginning who is guilty; in *The Trouble with Harry,* the interest in discovering who killed Harry Warp, who turns out to have died of natural causes, is incidental to the question of what to do with his corpse. *Murder!* is more orthodox in its construction but not in its proportions because only the middle third of the film, in which Sir John follows the clues that lead to the real killer, can fairly be described as a detective story that foregrounds the mystery of who killed Edna Druce; the first third follows the case from the discovery of the body as Diana stands over it, clutching the murder weapon, to the trial that ends in Sir John's being browbeaten into joining his fellow jurors in a guilty verdict, to his certainty, as he muses to himself while shaving to the strains of the Prelude to Act I of *Tristan and Isolde*— a tricky use of live sound made possible by playing back a tape recording of Herbert MARSHALL's voice and having an orchestra play Wagner just off-camera—that Diana must be innocent after all. The film is therefore better described as an expanded whodunit or a whodunit sandwiched between a truncated courtroom drama and what mystery writer Philip MACDONALD has called a howcatchem.

At any rate, the leading interest of the film, as commentators have unanimously recognized, is not in its posing of the mystery or its investigation of the evidence but in its exploration of theatricality among professional actors (another similarity it shares with *Stage Fright* and one that throws an interesting light on the proper New England amateurs of *The Trouble with Harry*). Hitchcock's retracing of the deductive steps Sir John takes in the novel is no more than dutiful. But his anatomy of acting as a metaphor for the public staging of private desire, an equally important motif in the novel, releases a torrent of memorable images: the stage manager Ted Markham and his wife, roused from bed by the news of calamity, struggling into their clothes (and Markham into the false teeth that alone make his speech intelligible); the misleading tableau in which the murder is presented; the formal decorum of the courtroom dissolving into the mob rule in the jury room; the oppressively static blocking of Sir John's visit to Diana in prison; the repeated scenes wringing comedy out of the class differences between tactful, dignified Sir John and the ingratiating, uncertain Markhams; the backstage sequence contrasting the farcical roles taken by members of Diana's acting troupe with their apparent nonacting as themselves; the scene in which Sir John asks the transvestite half-caste killer, Handel Fane, to read through a scene in his new play only to discover that the crucial murder scene is a blank page designed to invite his improvisation; the glittery, gloomy circus sequence, imitated from *Variety,* in which Fane acknowledges his guilt by hanging himself in the middle of his trapeze act in drag; and the final shot, in which the camera tracks back to enclose Sir John's confession of love to Diana within a proscenium arch, revealing it as another scene in his new play. None of these moments grows out of the whodunit plot, which implies a single duplicitous actor within a generally sincere community; instead, they join to raise questions about the relation between the inveterate acting both novel and film show going on both onstage and off and, ultimately, the relation among different kinds of performance (epitomized by Fane's status as openly transvestite in his onstage performances, secretly half-caste, and perhaps homosexual). William ROTHMAN, in the most extended reading of the film to date, speculates further that the film's emphasis on both theatricality and the cinematic apparatus draws attention to the status of the film as film and ultimately to the mysterious authority of its camera, which represents both "a passive viewing presence and a godlike agency," and the shaping power of its director as well.

Murnau, F. W. (1888–1931) German film director, born Friedrich W. Plumpe. A former student of art and literary history, he became an assistant to Max Reinhardt, then a combat pilot during World War I, ending the war in Switzerland after his plane strayed off course and landed there, and finally entering the cinema in 1921. Towering over his colleagues literally—he was nearly seven feet tall—he achieved a similar eminence metaphorically with his formative vampire film, the darkly expressionistic *Nosferatu: Eine Symphonie des Grauens* (1922), and his tour de force *Der letzte Mann* (1924) which presented its story of an old man's heartbreaking decline with only a single intertitle announcing his surprising reversal. It was while shooting *Der letze Mann* in Berlin that Murnau

F. W. Murnau

met Hitchcock, who was working in an adjoining studio on THE BLACKGUARD, and gave him through example and explanation a crash course in visual design for the cinema. Following two striking literary adaptations, *Tartüff* and *Faust* (both 1926), Murnau departed for Hollywood, where his first film for Fox, *Sunrise: A Song of Two Humans* (1927), uniting his mastery of majestically unbroken long takes with the predominantly sunlit visuals and happy ending demanded by the studio system, won an Oscar at the first awards ceremony as the most "unique and artistic picture"—the only such honor any film has ever received. Following two more films, Murnau left Fox to collaborate with documentarist Robert Flaherty on a lightly plotted South Seas idyll *Tabu* (1932) but was killed in an auto accident before the film's successful release. His prodigious influence on later filmmakers has been summarized by one of Hitchcock's rare acknowledgments of artistic indebtedness: "My models were forever after the German filmmakers of 1924 and 1925. They were trying very hard to express ideas in purely visual terms."

Murphy, Ada (1888–1961) American actress who was in Hollywood from 1915 for some 300 film and television appearances, of which one of the very last is as an elderly woman in the ALFRED HITCHCOCK PRESENTS episode "THE HORSEPLAYER."

Murray, Alec British sound recordist on THE SKIN GAME and RICH AND STRANGE.

Murray, Lyn (1909–1989) American composer, in Hollywood from 1947, who wrote music for some 40 films and television productions. Soon after composing the score for TO CATCH A THIEF, he was signed as a staff composer for ALFRED HITCHCOCK PRESENTS and remained with the series and its successor, THE ALFRED HITCHCOCK HOUR, through 1964, earning a musical credit for Hitchcock's last television film, "I SAW THE WHOLE THING."

Muse, Clarence (1889–1979) African-American actor. A law-school graduate who worked in vaudeville and theater, appearing in concerts and on the radio, he cofounded the Lafayette Players of

Harlem before coming in 1929 to Hollywood, where he was swiftly typecast in well more than 100 such backwoods or menial roles as the porter on the train that brings Uncle Charlie to Santa Rosa in SHADOW OF A DOUBT. Only occasionally did he find more substantial roles, as in *Broken Strings* (1940), a black-targeted film in which he plays the crippled concert violinist Arthur Williams, and to whose screenplay he contributed as well.

Mycroft, Walter C. (1891–1959)   British film executive, former film critic for the *Evening Standard,* whom John MAXWELL hired in 1927 as scenario editor at BRITISH INTERNATIONAL. Although he wrote the original story for CHAMPAGNE and joined Hitchcock in adapting the novel *Enter Sir John* for the screen as MURDER!, his cavalier attitude toward the logic of the first project and his generally literary sensibilities put him at odds with Hitchcock from the beginning. Hitchcock's departure from the studio was evidently a source of satisfaction for both the director and the producer, who rose to the post of chief of production in 1933 and remained with the studio and its successors as the producer of nearly 100 films, a handful of which he directed himself.

Mystery Road, The   Famous Players–Lasky, 1921. **Director:** Paul Powell; **Screenplay:** Mary Hamilton O'Connor, based on the novel by E. Phillips Oppenheim; **Cinematographer:** Hal Young; **Cast:** David Powell (Gerald Dombey), Nadja Ostrovska (Myrtile Sargot), Pardoe Woodman (Christopher Went), Mary Glynne (Lady Susan Farrington), Ruby Miller (Vera Lypashi), Percy Standing (Luigi), Lewis Gilbert (Jean Sargot), Irene Tripod (Widow Dumesnel), Lionel d'Aragon (Pierre Naval), Arthur M. Cullen (Earl of Farrington), R. Judd Green (the vagabond), Ralph Forster (the priest).

Sixth of the 12 silent films for which Hitchcock designed intertitles between 1920 and 1922.

Nalder, Reggie (1911–1991)   Balding Viennese-born actor, né Alfred Reginald Natzler. Though he played more than two dozen film roles during a 30-year career, his set Eurasian features and cold eyes typecast him as a killer soon after *Impasse des deux anges,* his 1948 debut, and he played similar roles in THE MAN WHO KNEW TOO MUCH (1956), *The Manchurian Candidate* (1962), and *The Bird with the Crystal Plumage* (1970). He took the name Detlef van Berg to play the uncharacteristically heroic role of Dr. Van Helsing in *Dracula Sucks* (1979).

Naldi, Nita (1897–1961)   Storied vamp of Hollywood silents, born Anita Donna Dooley. A former Ziegfeld Girl, she made her film debut as the seductive Gina opposite John Barrymore in *Dr. Jekyll and Mr. Hyde* (1920) and soon cornered the American market in screen sirens. Especially notable were her Doña Sol, Rudolph Valentino's temptress in *Blood and Sand* (1922), and Sally Lung, the adventuress in the modern section of *The Ten Commandments* (1923). She was cast dramatically against type as the village schoolteacher Beatrice in THE MOUNTAIN EAGLE. Two years later, she retired when the coming of sound unmasked her New York accent as broadly incongruous with the exotic roles in which she specialized.

Napier, Alan (1903–1988)   British character actor, born Alan Napier-Clavering. He studied at the Royal Academy of Dramatic Art, made his stage debut in 1924 and his screen debut six years later, and moved in 1939 to Hollywood, where he played nearly 100 staunchly imperturbable British types in films from *Random Harvest* (1942) to *Hangover Square* (1945) to *A Connecticut Yankee in King Arthur's Court* (1949). Although he is best remembered as Alfred Pennyworth, the butler in the television series *Batman* (1966–68), he also appeared in several episodes of ALFRED HITCHCOCK PRESENTS, playing Sir Everett in "Into Thin Air" (1955), Wilfred the obliging angel in "Whodunit" (1956), Lord Sorrington in all three installments of "I Killed the Count" (1957), and Charles Harrington in "The Avon Emeralds" (1959); in two segments of THE ALFRED HITCHCOCK HOUR, as Mr. Hodges in "An Out for Oscar" (1963) and Mr. Gurney in "Thou Still Unravished Bride" (1965); and as the hero's bemused, horsey father Mr. Rutland, the American aristocrat of MARNIE.

Narcejac, Thomas (1908–1998)   French mystery novelist, born Pierre Ayraud, who with Pierre BOILEAU coauthored the thrillers published under the pseudonym Boileau-Narcejac, several of which became famous as the basis of films: *Celle qui n'était plus* (1955), which was transformed into *Les diaboliques* (1955, 1974, 1993, 1996); *Les louves* (1957), *Les yeux sans visage* (1959), and *Les visages de l'ombre* (1960, 1984). Hitchcock used the Boileau-Narcejac novel *D'entre les morts* (1954) as the basis for VERTIGO. Narcejac also wrote on his own for three French television series, *Les survivantes* (1965), *Le train bleu s'arrête 13 fois* (1965), and *Témoignages* (1973).

Naremore, James American film scholar, chancellors' professor of communication and culture at Indiana University. He has written *The World Without a Self: Virginia Woolf and the Novel* (1973), *The Magic World of Orson Welles* (1978), *Acting in the Cinema* (1988), *The Films of Vincente Minnelli* (1993), and *More Than Night: Film Noir in Its Contexts* (1998) and edited *The Treasure of the Sierra Madre* (1979), *Modernity and Mass Culture* (with Patrick Brantlinger, 1991), and *Film Adaptation* (2000). His *Filmguide to* Psycho (Indiana University Press, 1973), the first book on a single Hitchcock film, frames its scene-by-scene analysis by an introduction on the "aesthetics of repression," a brief account of the film's production, a "summary critique," and a bibliography. By far the most interesting of these is the introduction, which emphasizes the importance of strategic, unconscious, or externally mandated omissions, elisions, and understatements to Hitchcock's brand of suspense and the very possibility of a Hitchcock aesthetic. Noting that "repression not only has its dramatic uses for Hitchcock, it is also an extension of his personality," Naremore argues that his personal repressions and repressiveness make his filmmaking orderly and ritualistic, and his films fetishistic, detached, oneiric, and often subversively satiric. In his conclusion, he generalizes this proposition to describe Hitchcock as a paradoxical combination of artist and entertainer whose witty, disturbing movies generate pleasurable fear and PSYCHO itself as marking a transitional moment in American popular film "midway between the conventional Hollywood narrative and the self-conscious style of the art film." More recently, Naremore has edited a critical edition of the screenplay for *North by Northwest: Alfred Hitchcock, Director* (Rutgers University Press, 1993) that appends contemporaneous reviews, an interview with Jean Domarchi and Jean DOUCHET, and critical essays by Luc Moullet, Marian Keane, Slavoj ŽIŽEK, and others.

Natwick, Mildred (1905–1994) Rawboned American actress, a specialist in civilized eccentrics and starchy aunts. She made her Broadway debut in 1932 and was soon in much demand as a character actress, usually playing older than her own age. In 1940 she appeared in her first film role as Freda in *The Long Voyage Home;* thereafter she alternated between stage and screen, adding savor to more than 30 films from *The Court Jester* (1956) to *Barefoot in the Park* (1967), for which, repeating her Broadway role as the heroine's long-suffering mother Mrs. Banks, she was nominated for an Oscar. She played Helen Hayes's sister Gwendolyn Snoop in the television movie *The Snoop Sisters* (1972) and the series it spun off (1973–74) and Aunt March in the 1979 television series *Little Women*. In THE TROUBLE WITH HARRY, her delicately comic Ivy Gravely unbent far enough from her maidenly reserve to accept the quirky autumnal advances of Captain Wiles, and in the even more blackly comic ALFRED HITCHCOCK PRESENTS episodes "The Perfect Murder" (1956) an "Miss Bracegirdle Does Her Duty" (1958), her widowed Aunt Rosalie proves surprisingly durable and her spinsterly Millicent Bracegirdle develops unexpected resources when she is locked in a hotel room with a murderer.

Neff, Emily American author who wrote several stories adapted for ALFRED HITCHCOCK PRESENTS, including the one that served as the basis for MR. BLANCHARD'S SECRET.

Nesbitt, Cathleen (1888–1982) Twinkling British character actress. The fiancée of British poet Rupert Brooke, killed in World War I, she had already made her stage debut in 1910. Though best known for her work in theater, she appeared in some 40 films in a 50-year period beginning in 1910, increasingly as such grand ladies as La Principessa in *Three Coins in the Fountain* (1954) and Grandmother Janou in *An Affair to Remember* (1957). Ten years after she played the congressman hero's mother Agatha Morley in the television series *The Farmer's Daughter* (1963–66), Hitchcock cast her as wealthy, gullible Julia Rainbird, whose guilty need to make peace with her sister's heirs sets FAMILY PLOT in motion.

New Alfred Hitchcock Presents, The A television series based on the original ALFRED HITCH-

COCK PRESENTS that began in 1985. Though the director had been dead four years, he was still on hand to introduce each episode, courtesy of colorized footage of the introductions he had filmed 30 years earlier. After a two-hour pilot comprising four remakes of episodes from the original program ("Incident in a Small Jail," "Man from the South," "BANG! YOU'RE DEAD," "The Unlocked Window"), the series ran for 76 episodes, many of them color remakes of series originals (such as "REVENGE," which, like its progenitor, launched the first season of the series after the pilot, and "FOUR O'CLOCK," which had originally aired on SUSPICION rather than *Alfred Hitchcock Presents*), others based on new properties (including "VCR—Very Careful Rape," the first episode in the program's second season, which was released only on videotape). The series ran through the 1988–89 season.

Newcom, James E. (1905–1990)   American film editor, in Hollywood from 1933, who supervised the cutting of the SELZNICK productions *The Prisoner of Zenda* and *Nothing Sacred* (both 1937) and served as associate editor on *Gone With the Wind* (1939) and REBECCA. He supervised the editing of some 30 more films before retiring after *Tora! Tora! Tora!* (1970).

Newell, William (1894–1967)   American character actor who provided well-nigh invisible support in bits as friends, bystanders, orderlies, receptionists, waiters, and occasional drunks in more than 150 films and television episodes. Most noticeable in four Little Rascals features beginning with *Alfalfa's Aunt* (1939), as Alfalfa's father, he receded into the background in three roles for ALFRED HITCHCOCK PRESENTS—as Charlie in "Momentum" (1956), Mr. Fescue in "A Very Moral Theft" (1960), and a bank teller in "THE HORSEPLAYER"—and two for THE ALFRED HITCHCOCK HOUR—the intoxicated Sam Peterson in "I SAW THE WHOLE THING" and Mr. Jones in "Terror at Northfield" (1963).

Newman, Alfred (1901–1970)   Much-honored American film composer and conductor, former child pianist, whose 250 original Hollywood scores and arrangements from 1930 include 45 Academy Award nominations (four from 1939 alone) and nine Oscar winners: *Alexander's Ragtime Band* (1938), *Tin Pan Alley* (1940), *The Song of Bernadette* (1943), *Mother Wore Tights* (1947), *With a Song in My Heart* (1952), *Call Me Madam* (1953), *Love Is a Many Splendored Thing* (1955), *The King and I* (1956), and *Camelot* (1967). The 15 films he scored in 1940 (in addition to uncredited work on two others) included FOREIGN CORRESPONDENT. He is best known, however, for a much briefer piece of music still heard around the world every day: the fanfare that introduces all 20TH CENTURY FOX films.

Newman, Paul (Leonard) (1925–)   Charismatic, versatile American actor who emerged from Marlon Brando's shadow to become the most bankable star of the sixties. Determined to escape his family's sporting-goods franchise, he attended the Yale Drama School and the Actors Studio, made his television debut in 1951, his Broadway debut in William Inge's *Picnic* (1953), and his film debut the following year in *The Silver Chalice,* giving a performance for which he took out a full-page advertisement in *Variety* to apologize. But his second film role, as boxer Rocky Marciano in *Somebody Up There Likes Me* (1956), made him a star, a status confirmed by his work in *The Left-Handed Gun, The Long Hot Summer,* and *Cat on a Hot Tin Roof* (all 1958). Oscar-nominated for this last role and again for *The Hustler* (1961) and *Hud* (1963), Newman was at the top of his profession when UNIVERSAL pressed Hitchcock to cast him as the defecting American physicist/spy Michael Armstrong in TORN CURTAIN. The Method-trained star and his dictatorial director, however, clashed from the first (when Newman asked what his motivation was in a particular shot, Hitchcock replied, "Your salary"), and the result was a dispirited, atypically unhumorous performance in an underwritten and unconvincing role, memorable only for the grim sequence in which Armstrong, bent on killing his nemesis, Hermann Gromek, without making any noise that would call attention to the murder, demonstrates just how difficult it is to kill someone. Newman survived the film to give Academy Award-nominated performances in *Cool Hand Luke* (1967),

Paul Newman

Absence of Malice (1981), *The Verdict* (1982), and *The Color of Money* (1986), for which he finally received the Oscar a year after an Honorary Award for his entire career. He is also noted as an occasional director (his first film, *Rachel, Rachel,* 1968, a showcase for his actress wife, Joanne Woodward, was nominated for a Best Picture Oscar), a stock-car driver, the entrepreneur of the Newman's Own food line, and a philanthropist who has repeatedly noted that his foodstuffs, whose profits he donates to charity, often gross more than his films.

Newton, Richard American character actor sporadically in films and (especially) television from 1938. Best known as Judge Cooksey in the television series *Matlock* (1986–90), he appeared as one of the escaping convicts in the *ALFRED HITCHCOCK PRES-*

ENTS segment "BREAKDOWN" and later served as producer or associate producer on a half-dozen television series and episodes of his own.

Newton, Robert (1905–1956) British character whose rolling eye stole many a scene from his costars and made him a star soon after his film debut in 1932. His performance as Jem Trehearne, the romantic lead in *JAMAICA INN,* marked one of the few occasions he was upstaged himself, this time by the even hammier Charles LAUGHTON. The most memorable roles of his later career were such overripe villains as Bill Sikes in *Oliver Twist* (1948), Inspector Javert in *Les Miserables* (1952), the title role in *Blackbeard the Pirate* (1952), and his signature role of Long John Silver in *Treasure Island* (1950) and its television spinoff, *The Adventures of Long John Silver* (1955). His performance as the blackmailing Goodfellow in the *ALFRED HITCHCOCK PRESENTS* segment "The Derelicts" (1956) was one of his last.

Ney, Marie (1895–1981) British stage actress, born Marie Fix, who appeared in some 20 British films from 1919, often in staid or authoritarian character roles. She suffers the weight of male authority herself as Mary Yellan's ill-used Aunt Patience in *JAMAICA INN.*

Nicholl, Sally (1900–1981) British casting director credited on a half-dozen films from *Alfie* (1966) to *FRENZY*, which was released the year she retired.

Nicholson, Nick (1919–1982) American radio talk-show host and character actor who appeared as a reporter in the *ALFRED HITCHCOCK PRESENTS* episode "THE PERFECT CRIME" and a half-dozen other television segments (1960–64).

Noiret, Philippe (1930–) Stage-trained French actor in many more than 100 French and international films from 1952. He first came to wide notice as the heroine's Uncle Gabriel in *Zazie dans le métro* (1960) and won the Venice Festival Award for his performance as Bernard Desqueyroux in *Thérèse Desqueyroux* (1962). Twenty-five films later, Hitchcock cast him as the jittery spy Henri Jarre, another Emil Hupka type, in *TOPAZ*. He is best known to American audiences as Alfredo, the sage film projectionist in *Nuovo cinema Paradiso* (1988).

normalcy The director who once said that "movies are life with the dull bits left out," and, more grandly, that "some films are slices of life. Mine are slices of cake" might seem to have little investment in representing everyday life in his films. Yet all of Hitchcock's best films are deeply rooted in the rhythms of normal life, from the seedy music hall row that suddenly erupts in gunfire in *THE 39 STEPS* to the scrubbed yet unsatisfying small-town idyll of *SHADOW OF A DOUBT* to the dreary adultery of Marion and Sam and her return to her boss's realty office in *PSYCHO*. Indeed, though no one would claim that Hitchcock has anything like Yasujiro Ozu or Mike Leigh's interest in the ordinary, it provides both an indispensable starting point and a thematic counterpoint for all his most melodramatic nightmares, and with rare exceptions such as *VERTIGO* that unspool like a dream from beginning to end, the success or failure of his films is directly proportional to their grasp of normalcy. Hence *THE PLEASURE GARDEN* is sharply observed as long as it sticks to its chorines' everyday routine of working at the club and trolling for men, and it falters as soon as it leaves London for the outer reaches of the Empire, whereas *DOWNHILL* runs into trouble much earlier because the public-school world in which its intrigue is rooted never seems convincingly inhabited in the first place. Hitchcock's costume pictures, from *WALTZES FROM VIENNA* to *UNDER CAPRICORN*, are invariably undermined by their director's self-confessed ignorance of what the corseted characters eat for breakfast or what goes on inside their bewigged heads when they are not plotting against each other.

Hitchcock is never more effective than in evoking the first inklings of suspicion in early scenes that depend on an almost imperceptible slide from normalcy to apprehension, increasingly lubricated by viewers' generic expectations of Hitchcock's films. When Mrs. de Winter first arrives at Manderley in *REBECCA*, it is easy to put down her fears to awkwardness and ignorance; it is only gradually that the film reveals how justified her feelings are. The long dialogue scene in which Tony Wendice virtually hypnotizes C.A. Swann into homicide in *DIAL M FOR MURDER* is a tour de force that begins as a negotiation over the price of a used car and ends in a murder plot. Scenes like these explain Raymond DURGNAT's remark that in all Hitchcock's films, "the richness of experience lies not so much in the vision from which one penetrates, so much as in the process of penetration."

The normal world is more than a foundation for Hitchcockian melodrama; it is constantly invoked to deflate expectations, modulate the tone toward comedy, structure and so warrant the most outrageous fantasies, and recall the basis or the stakes of the characters' struggles. *THE MAN WHO KNEW TOO MUCH* (1934) and *The 39 Steps* both show violence erupting with shocking suddenness in unexpected surroundings—settings where people have gone specifically to enjoy themselves—but then return repeatedly to quibble on the distinction between dream and reality, as when Clive's scream from the sinister dentist's office turns out to be the result of his having had a tooth pulled, or when the master criminal Abbott jokes with the captured hero Bob Lawrence, or when Richard Hannay, leaping through a window to escape the police, finds himself first in a parade and then addressing a political rally for a candidate he has never heard of. In *YOUNG AND INNOCENT* and *THE LADY VANISHES* the tension is punctured by comic scenes of a child's birthday party and a search through a magician's properties; in *SABOTAGE*, the corresponding sequence, in which Stevie, unwittingly carrying a bomb to Piccadilly Station, is held up by a quack salesman who wants to demonstrate his grooming aids on the hapless boy, has fatal consequences. In each case the interludes, though just as improbably stylized as the intrigue they interrupt, are so sharply observed and so contrasting in tone that they come across as realistic.

As early as *BLACKMAIL*, Hitchcock had planned to use the police routine of arrest, questioning, and booking detailed in the prologue as both the setup line and the punch line to the melodrama sandwiched in between; the film was to end with Frank Webber's arrest of his girlfriend Alice White for murdering the artist who tried to rape her. The projected film thus would have ended by inscribing Alice's horrific ordeal as simply another routine in her boyfriend's professional life. As it was actually completed, though, the film departs early on from normalcy and maintains a steady trajectory outward into an ever-deepening nightmare, never returning except for quotidian touches like her caged bird's song and the door chime announcing the blackmailer's entrance that mock Alice's guilty secret. Throughout the forties and fifties, Hitchcock frequently followed the Hollywood practice of indicating a happy ending by returning his characters to a tense earlier scene replayed as a joke: the lovers' nongoodbye kiss at the railroad station in SPELLBOUND, the chance recognition in STRANGERS ON A TRAIN, the playful rescue in the upper bunk of NORTH BY NORTHWEST. In darker films from NOTORIOUS to Psycho, however, his endings confirm the sense of a decisive, irreversible departure from normalcy. THE WRONG MAN provides two glaringly dissonant endings, a final title card reassuring the audience that the Balestreros were returned to normal when Rose Balestrero emerged from the asylum completely cured two years after the harrowing scene of her apathetic breakdown the film has just shown. Two late films take as their subject the false opposition between normalcy and intrigue: THE BIRDS, which begins as romantic comedy before veering off abruptly into horror, and TOPAZ, whose every betrayal, even the most intimate, is business as usual for its well-dressed spies of every stripe. Films like these suggest that Hitchcock's true subject was the normalcy of melodramatic intrigue and the intrigue implicit in the normal.

Norman, Maidie (1912–1998) African-American actress who, following her debut in *The Burning Cross* (1947), played more than 50 screen roles, often as domestics, the most memorable being the ill-fated Elvira Stitt in *What Ever Happened to Baby Jane?* (1962). The first of her many television parts was playing the colonel's maid, Eloise, in the ALFRED HITCHCOCK PRESENTS episode "MRS. BIXBY AND THE COLONEL'S COAT."

North by Northwest (Alternative titles: *In a Northwesterly Direction, The CIA Story, Breathless, The Man on Lincoln's Nose* [working titles], *Der unsichtbare Dritte, Das Erbe des Grauens, La Mort aux trousses, Intrigo internazionale*) Metro-Goldwyn-Mayer, 136 minutes, July 1959. **Producer:** Alfred Hitchcock; **Associate producer:** Herbert Coleman; **Director:** Alfred Hitchcock; **Original screenplay:** Ernest Lehman; **Cinematographer:** Robert Burks; **Assistant director:** Robert Saunders; **Storyboard artist:** Mentor C. Huebner; **Production designer:** Robert Boyle; **Art directors:** William A. Horning and Merrill Pye; **Set decorators:** Henry Grace and Frank McKelvey; **Makeup:** William Tuttle; **Hairstyles:** Sydney Guilaroff; **Sound:** Frank Milton; **Special effects:** A. Arnold Gillespie and Lee LeBlanc; **Technicolor consultant:** Charles K. Hagedon; **Editor:** George Tomasini; **Titles:** Saul Bass; **Music:** Bernard Herrmann; **Cast:** Cary Grant (Roger Thornhill), Eva Marie Saint (Eve Kendall), James Mason (Phillip Vandamm), Jessie Royce Landis (Clara Thornhill), Leo G. Carroll (the Professor), Josephine Hutchinson ("Mrs. Townsend"), Martin Landau (Leonard), Adam Williams (Valerian [assassin]), Robert Ellenstein (Licht [assassin's companion]), Edward Platt (Victor Larrabee, Esq.), Les Tremayne (auctioneer), Philip Coolidge (Dr. Cross), Ed Binns (Captain Junket), Patrick McVey, Ken Lynch (Chicago police officers), Doreen Lang (Maggie), Tommy Farrell (elevator operator), Harvey Stephens (stockbroker), Jimmy Cross (first taxi driver), Frank Wilcox (Mr. Weltner), Robert Shayne (Larry Wade), Carleton Young (Fanning Nelson), Ralph Reed (bellhop), Nora Marlowe (Anna, housekeeper), John Beradino (Sgt. Emile Klinger), Alexander Lockwood (Judge Anson B. Flynn), Maudie Prickett (Elsie, Plaza maid), James McCallion (Plaza valet), Sara Berner (telephone operator), Barnes Barron (second taxi driver), Sally Fraser (attendant), Doris Singh (Indian attendant), Walter Coy (reporter), Ned Glass (ticket seller), Howard Negley (conductor on 20th Century), Harry Strang (assistant conductor), Stanley Adams (Lt. Harding), Ernest Anderson (porter on 20th Century), Bobby Johnson, Harry Seymour (waiters), Jack Daly (steward), Bill Catching, Maura McGiveney, Susan Whitney (attendants), Taggart Casey (shaving man), Malcolm Atterbury (man at Prairie Crossing), Andy Albin (farmer), Carl Milletaire (hotel clerk), Olan Soulé (assistant auctioneer), Helen Spring (bidder), Dale Van Sickel (ranger), Madge Kennedy (housewife), Paul Genge (Lt. Hagerman), John Damler, Len Hendry (police lieutenants), Robert Williams (Patrolman Waggoner), Frank Marlowe (South Dakota taxi driver), Patricia Cutts, Jesslyn Fax, Tom Greenway.

Hitchcock's 46th film grew out of one of the great bait-and-switch stories in Hollywood annals. Approached by MGM in 1957 to produce and direct *The Wreck of the Mary Deare,* Hitchcock, attracted by the prospect of independence within a studio in disarray, set about his work in story conferences with Ernest LEHMAN, a screenwriter to whom Bernard HERRMANN had introduced him. Within a month, however, the two decided that the project was untenable and agreed to abandon it. Without telling anyone at the studio, they began instead to write an original spy thriller based on a little-known incident from World War II: the creation of a fictitious master spy whom the Nazis mistakenly attempted to track down. Imagining the fate of an innocent man mistaken for such a nonexistent spy in contemporary peacetime, they called the developing saga *In a Northwesterly Direction.* When Hitchcock reported to MGM that he was "temporarily putting

Their mutual deceptions and posturing at an end, Roger Thornhill (Cary Grant) and Eve Kendall (Eva Marie Saint) enjoy a brief reunion in *North by Northwest* as the patriarchal figures on Mount Rushmore look on from the background. *(National Film Society Archive)*

aside" *The Wreck of the Mary Deare* in favor of this new project, the studio, delighted by the prospect of getting two films instead of one and secure in their knowledge that although Hitchcock had approval over the film's final cut, they could insist on budgetary ceilings for the production and the negative costs, agreed. Given the story's episodic construction, which took it at one point from New York to Mount Rushmore and at another to a missile base in Alaska, Lehman felt free to scout memorable locations while Hitchcock finished shooting VERTIGO; at different points, the story was planned to include a sequence in Yankee Stadium and another in a Detroit auto assembly plant where a corpse would tumble from a newly completed car just rolling off the line. Urged by MGM to cast contract stars Gregory PECK and Cyd Charisse in the leads, Hitchcock responded by casting the film entirely from outside the MGM ranks, allowing the 54-year-old Cary GRANT, in his final film for Hitchcock, to bare his chest in a beefcake sequence at the hospital, and casting 54-year-old Jessie Royce LANDIS, who had already played Grant's prospective mother-in-law in TO CATCH A THIEF, as his mother. In his essay "Hitchcock at Metro," in DEUTELBAUM and POAGUE, Leonard J. LEFF has pointed out the importance of Hitchcock's final contract with the studio, which gave him control over a project with a studio for whom he had never worked. The contract was as complete as he had won over five years of working at PARAMOUNT and implied that this control was now immutable and transferable at the director's discretion and served as an example for Hitchcock's UNIVERSAL contract and eventually for those of other independent filmmakers as well. Leff also notes the range of problems the production encountered as its budget ballooned from $2.3 million to $3.3 million. The Production Code forbade direct references to the villainous Leonard's homosexuality or Roger Thornhill's sexual dalliance with Eve Kendall; the United Nations refused permission to shoot in the General Assembly building; the National Park Service insisted that the carved faces on Mount Rushmore could not be used as the setting for either violence or low comedy; and MGM, worried at the length of Hitchcock's longest film, demanded that he cut the scene in which Thornhill and Eve, who has just shot him with

blanks, are reunited in the woods behind the monument. Hitchcock, citing his control over the film's final cut, agreed to all these requirements but the last, and the film was a critical and financial success, the sixth biggest moneymaker of 1959.

In the years since then, it has become something more: the ultimate Hitchcock film for audiences who find *Vertigo* too slow-moving and PSYCHO too schematic or dated. This exhilarating tale of advertising executive Roger O. Thornhill, who begins by being kidnapped from Manhattan's Plaza Hotel when he is mistaken for a nonexistent spy and takes him from one improbable adventure to the next—a mad pursuit by his killers as the thoroughly inebriated hero pilots a stolen Mercedes, an attempt to question a United Nations diplomat that ends in Thornhill's being sought for his murder, a whirlwind romantic fling with an obliging stranger aboard the 20th Century Limited, a lunatic pursuit by a crop-dusting plane at the edge of an Indiana cornfield in the middle of nowhere, a hairsbreadth escape from an auction turned menacing, a perilous descent between the faces of Mount Rushmore—with a brio unexcelled in Hitchcock's American work. The film marries the man-on-the-run plot of THE 39 STEPS and SABOTEUR to the story of the hero's struggle to outgrow his crippling attachment to his mother, the host of father figures (from the suavely threatening Philip Vandamm to the noncommittal CIA agent the Professor to the impassive presidential faces on Mount Rushmore) the film supplies, and the infantile dependence these attachments project. The combination of an episodic travelogue, the hero's series of comic but increasingly controlled theatrical performances, and his tensely romantic dance with an enigmatic heroine produced a tale that was not only a compendium but also a purification of motifs from earlier Hitchcock films, as if the director were now giving them definitive final form. Critics observing Thornhill's psychological development have been divided between celebrants of his new maturity like Robin WOOD and skeptics of its costs like Raymond BELLOUR, but no one has disputed the importance of the film itself, which remains, for all its complexity and apparent aimlessness, the most probing, as it is the most generous, of all Hitchcock's comedies of peril.

Norton, Betty British stage actress who took character roles in half a dozen thirties films, including Hetty in LORD CAMBER'S LADIES, then retired from the screen except for *El juramento de lagardere* (1955).

Notorious (Alternative titles: *Berüchtigt, Weisses Gift, Les Enchaînés, Notorious—l'amante perduta*) RKO, 101 minutes, July 1946. **Producer:** Alfred Hitchcock; **Production assistant:** Barbara Keon; **Director:** Alfred Hitchcock; **Screenplay:** Ben Hecht (based on a subject by Alfred Hitchcock); **Cinematographer:** Ted Tetzlaff; **Second unit cinematographer:** Gregg Toland; **Assistant director:** William Dorfman; **Art directors:** Carroll Clark and Albert S. D'Agostino; **Set decoration:** Darrell Silvera and Claude Carpenter; **Miss Bergman's gowns:** Edith Head; **Sound:** John E. Tribby, Terry Kellum (and Clem Portman); **Special effects:** Vernon L. Walker and Paul Eagler; **Editor:** Theron Warth; **Music:** Roy Webb; **Orchestrations:** Gil Grau; **Musical direction:** F. Bakaleinikoff; **Cast:** Ingrid Bergman (Alicia Huberman), Cary Grant (T.R. Devlin), Claude Rains (Alexander Sebastian), Louis Calhern (Paul Prescott), Leopoldine Konstantin (Mme. Sebastian), Reinhold Schünzel (Dr. Anderson), Ivan Triesault (Eric Mathis), Alex Minotis (Joseph), Wally Brown (Mr. Hopkins), Eberhard Krumschmidt (Emil Hupka), Sir Charles Mendl (commodore), Moroni Olsen (Walter Beardsley), Ricardo Costa (Senor Barbosa), and Fred Nurney (Huberman), Warren Jackson (district attorney), Harry Hayden (defense counsel), Charles D. Brown (judge), Dink Trout (court clerk), Tom Coleman (court stenographer), Howard M. Mitchell (bailiff), George Lynn, Frank Marlowe, Howard Negley (photographers), Eddie Bruce, Paul Bryan, Ben Erway, Donald Kerr, James Logan, Emmett Vogan, John Vosper, Alan Ward (reporters), Frank Wilcox (FBI agent), Gavin Gordon (Ernest Weylin), Fay Baker (Ethel), Luis Serrano (Dr. Silva), Antonio Moreno (Senor Ortiza), Patricia Smart (Mrs. Jackson), Frederick Ledebur (Knerr), Peter von Zerneck (Rossner), Herbert Wyndham (Mr. Cook), Alfredo DeSa (Ribero), William Gordon (Adams), Lester Dorr, Garry Owen (motorcycle cops), Bernice Barrett, Bea Benaderet, Virginia Gregg (file clerks), Candido Bonsato, Ted Kelly (waiters), Tina Menard (maid), Aileen Carlyle (woman at party), Lenore Ulric (scenes deleted), Beulah Christian, Richard Clarke, Almeda Fowler, Leota Lorraine, Frank McDonald, Sandra Morgan, Lillian West.

As her husband Alexander Sebastian (Claude Rains, right) and his mother (Leopoldine Konstantin) watch impotently, T. R. Devlin (Cary Grant) helps the poisoned Alicia Huberman (Ingrid Bergman) down the staircase to safety in the final scene of *Notorious*. *(National Film Society Archive)*

According to David O. SELZNICK story editor Margaret McDonnell, writing in August 1944, the idea for *Notorious* originated in Hitchcock's wish to follow *SPELLBOUND* with a film in which Ingrid BERGMAN "could play the woman who is carefully trained and coached in a gigantic confidence trick which might involve her marrying some man. He is fascinated by the elaborateness with which these things are planned and rehearsed." Selznick and Hitchcock quickly agreed to retain *Spellbound* scriptwriter Ben HECHT to write the screenplay, but as the story went through draft after draft over the following year (Leonard J. LEFF has described four distinct drafts, the first two beginning in Brazil, the third ending with the hero's death, before the "temporary screenplay" that was actually sold to RKO), whatever emphasis Hitchcock may have planned on the business of training and coaching patriotically duplicitous Alicia Huberman for the masquerade that would send her into a former Nazi suitor's house and eventually into his bed, would be subordinated to the emotional ups and downs of her relationship with the American agent T.R. Devlin, her recruiter and handler. Not until the final draft did Hecht and Hitchcock come up with the film's MACGUFFIN, the possibility that Alexander Sebastian's friends were building an atomic bomb. Curious about the size and power of such a device, Hitchcock and Hecht paid a visit to physicist Robert Milliken at the California Institute of Technology to ask details about its operation. According to Hitchcock, Milliken ridiculed the idea, sent them on their way, and then phoned the FBI, which had them shadowed for the next six months. In the meantime, Selznick, faced with cost overruns on *Duel in the Sun* (1946), a steady stream of objections about Alicia's loose morals from the Production Code Administration and her dubious American virtue from the Office of War Information, continued delays in the preproduction of what he already called "the most expensive script in the history of my career," sold the entire package—screenplay, stars, and director—to RKO for $800,000 and 50 percent of the net profits. Rejecting a rewritten screenplay by Clifford Odets, Hecht turned out still another revision himself in August 1945. The film's production from October 1945 through January 1946 was considerably smoother—Hitchcock skirted the Production Code's injunction against "lustful and prolonged kissing" during Devlin and Alicia's celebrated embrace while he calls his hotel for messages by having the stars' lips break contact at strategic points throughout the long take—and postproduction was completed by April. Hitchcock's 32nd film, boosted by its prophetically topical MACGUFFIN as well as its marquee stars, earned impressive profits for both RKO and Selznick; the director would have to wait several years before earning comparable sums himself.

The film's subject is aptly announced by both its title (it is one of the rare Hitchcock films whose title never changed from the first story conferences to the release prints) and its opening framing of a news photographer's camera: the scandalous reputation of Alicia Huberman, whose apparent closeness to her father, convicted of treason, combines with her well-known penchant for drinking and dissolution to make her just the sort of loose woman best equipped to go undercover to battle America's enemies. Although it presents only a single scene in which her cold-hearted handler Devlin explicitly defends her to the colleagues who accept her at face value, *Notorious* clearly relishes the dissonance not only between Alicia's public image and her private virtue but also between that image and Ingrid Bergman's wholesome established image, which the star was eager to expand. As usual, the censors who might have trammeled another film served as helpful collaborators on this one because the substitution of uncensored onscreen drinking for the sexual licentiousness the film could not show helped release and diffuse the unspoken secret of her desperately needy sexuality. The use of such obviously Freudian symbols as glasses, cups, and closets to represent Alicia's status as a vessel for male desire, the stolen key to represent the villain's emasculation, and the wine bottle filled with sand as the ambiguously sexualized object of every character's pursuit gave the imagery a focus the more explicitly and ambitiously psychoanalytic *Spellbound* had lacked. Hecht's pungent dialogue, often written as if for Tallulah BANKHEAD; the pairing of the uncommonly warm Bergman with Cary GRANT at his most suavely remote; and the sparkle of Ted TETZLAFF's visuals, which find something romantic in the drabbest betrayals—all combined to make the film Hitchcock's biggest moneymaker until *REAR WINDOW*. Also, its portrayal of "Mrs. Sebastian" as a woman whose marriage is nothing more than legal prostitution uneasily endorsed by the man who loves her (Tania MODLESKI aptly calls Alicia "the woman who was known too much") raises lasting questions about the moral valence of such seemingly transparent terms as *love, marriage, loyalty, principle, heroine,* and the film's own favorite—*nice.*

Novak, Jane (1896–1990) British star of 60 silent films, including *THE PRUDE'S FALL* (1924) on which she worked with Hitchcock, who brought her back for one of her few sound roles as the proper Miss Benson in *FOREIGN CORRESPONDENT*.

Novak, Kim (1933–) American movie star of the fifties, born Marilyn Pauline Novak. A former model groomed by Columbia as the studio's answer to Marilyn Monroe, she made promising appearances in *Phffft!* (1954), *Picnic* (1955), *The Man with the Golden Arm* (1956), and *Pal Joey* (1957), and by the time Vera MILES's pregnancy sidelined her from *VERTIGO*, her classic profile and blonde beauty had made her the highest-paid actress in Hollywood. Once she was cast as Miles's replacement in the dual roles of Madeleine Elster and Judy Barton, her relationship with Hitchcock, who responded to her bewildered request for information about her character's emotions by telling her it was only a movie, soon began to echo the pattern of the film itself. Despite her misgivings, her lack of experience, and her well-attested fear of the director, she was magically ethereal as Scottie Ferguson's doomed love but seemed considerably less believable as the shopgirl whose love for him is equally hopeless, perhaps demonstrating that Scottie is not the only audience to prefer a simulacrum to the real thing. Playing the witch Gillian Holroyd, she was paired again with James STEWART in *Bell, Book, and Candle* (1959), the film Stewart owed Columbia in return for her loanout to PARAMOUNT for *Vertigo*, and with Fredric March for *Middle of the Night* (1959), but reviewers found her cast beyond her talents in her later performances, most notably as the heroines of *Of Human Bondage* (1962) and *The Legend of Lylah Clare* (1968). Her most visible work since the sixties has been her season on *Falcon Crest* (1986–87) playing Kit Marlowe, the name Columbia had originally wanted her to use as her own.

Novello, Ivor (1893–1951) Welsh-born actor, composer, playwright, producer, and stage manager, the first of the British matinee idols. Even before his film debut in 1919, his patriotic wartime song "Keep the Home Fires Burning" had made him famous; by the time he starred as the mysterious title character in *THE LODGER* and the unwilling adventurer Roddy Berwick in *DOWNHILL* (based on his own play), he was the most popular film star in Britain, an actor whose

Kim Novak

classic good looks, flavored with a pervasively melancholy screen persona, made him especially irresistible to female audiences. Soon after working as lyricist on the songs for *ELSTREE CALLING* (1930) and starring in Maurice Elvey's 1932 remake of *The Lodger,* he tried his luck as a screenwriter at MGM but returned soon after with few credits, and after working briefly in the British industry, returned to his first love, the theater, where he achieved his greatest popular success as the writer and star of stage musicals.

Noyes, Jack American sound recordist on *REBECCA* and eight other Hollywood films of the thirties and early forties.

Number Seventeen (Alternative titles: *Nummer siebzehn, Numéro 17*) British International, Wardour Films Ltd., 65 minutes, July 1932. **Producer:** John Maxwell; **Director:** Alfred Hitchcock; **Screenplay:** Alma Reville,

Alfred Hitchcock, and Rodney Ackland, based on the play by J. Jefferson Farjeon as produced by Leon M. Lion; **Cinematographers:** John J. Cox and Bryan Langley; **Art director:** Wilfred Arnold; **Sound recordist:** A.D.Valentine; **Film and sound editor:** A.C. Hammond; **Music:** A. Hallis; **Cast:** Leon M. Lion (Ben), Anne Grey (Nora Brant), John Stuart (Fordyce, subsequently revealed as Detective Barton), Donald Calthrop (Brant), Barry Jones (Henry Doyle), Garry Marsh (Sheldrake), Anne Casson (Rose Ackroyd), Henry Caine (Mr. Ackroyd), Herbert Langley (guard).

For many years Rodney ACKLAND's account of this film's genesis was accepted as gospel. Although Hitchcock and Ackland, an actor recently turned playwright, had expressed an interest in a film adaptation of John Van Druten's *London Wall* and BRITISH INTERNATIONAL contract director Thomas Bentley in

Fordyce (John Stuart) and Rose Ackroyd (Ann Casson) are left dangling when the railing to which the villains have tied them in the spooky house at *Number Seventeen* collapses. *(National Film Society Archive)*

J. Jefferson FARJEON's old-dark-house thriller *Number Seventeen,* John MAXWELL assigned the former to Bentley and the latter to Hitchcock and Ackland. In revenge, Hitchcock planned his film as a parody of the source play, though one so sly that Maxwell would never see the joke. Charles BARR has recently disputed this anecdote by pointing out the serio-comic, often farcical nature of the play itself, which, rather than being the serious melodrama Ackland's account implies, is more clearly pitched in the vein of the film *The Old Dark House* (1932). Drastically stripped down to just more than an hour and making do without any stars except for Leon M. LION, the gleeful scene-chewer who had created the role of Ben onstage, the film marks Hitchcock's closest approach to a quota quickie. Withheld from distribution until after the release of *RICH AND STRANGE*—so that although it was the 14th feature Hitchcock directed, it was the 15th to be released—it attracted little notice from reviewers or the general public, and its reputation is still eclipsed by those of Hitchcock's three other early thrillers, *THE LODGER, BLACKMAIL,* and *MURDER!*

This neglect is a shame, since the film, despite the amateurishness of its writing and acting, is full of interest, particularly for viewers whose idea of the last word in self-conscious sophistication in genre films is *Scream* (1996). The keynote of the film, established as early as the hero Fordyce's accidental entrance to spooky Number Seventeen when a gust of wind carries his hat to the doorstep, is that not one of its events or people has any basis in everyday reality. So Fordyce's discovery of a body a floor above him on the same winding staircase most of the film is set on and around is staged in the most stylized way imaginable, and the entrance of each new character—as, for example, the moment when Rose Ackroyd falls through a skylight—is the signal for another round of questions about what everybody is doing in this deserted house and who they really are. At least three characters are unmasked as pretenders to the identities they claim—even the corpse disappears so that this turns out to be Hitchcock's only thriller except for *THE TROUBLE WITH HARRY* without a murder—but even the characters who end the film with the same nominal identity they had at the beginning display very few emotions apart from an intense skepticism about each other and a ceremonious bewilderment about what they ought to be doing. The film, which starts off very slowly, gradually speeds up as it goes along, and the departure of the conspirators from the house by means of a secret train station directly beneath acts like a starter's gun to open the last phase of the film: an extended chase, via bus, train, and boat, all represented by insouciant miniatures, that becomes so rapid and nonsensical that it transcends its particular motivations to become a platonic form of the chase. Commenting on the resolutely oneiric quality of the film, Barr adds that what Hitchcock added to his original—the joke, for example, of the dumb gangster's moll who for once is literally dumb, though her inability to speak turns out to be only "a cheap crook's trick"—is less important than what he took from it: the idea of the MACGUFFIN, in this case the diamond necklace both the crooks and the police are pursuing: "No

Hitchcock film before *Number Seventeen* has contained a MacGuffin, and the Farjeon play certainly seems to be where he gets it from." Everything about Hitchcock's exceptionally abstract treatment of this MacGuffin, which makes its pursuers obsessive while leaving viewers bemused until it is displayed for the first time in all its glory in the film's startling final shot, looks forward to the cavalier handling of MacGuffins that would become the trademark of even such a mature film as NORTH BY NORTHWEST.

Number 13 (Alternative title: *Mrs. Peabody*) Famous Players-Lasky, 1922. **Producer:** Alfred Hitchcock; **Director:** Alfred Hitchcock; **Screenplay:** Anita Ross; **Cinematography:** Rosenthal; **Cast:** Clare Greet, Ernest Thesiger.

Hitchcock's directorial debut, this two-reel film was incompletely funded and left uncompleted when its American parent studio went out of business.

Oakland, Simon (1922–1983) Stage-trained American character actor, a former violinist most at home playing police officers who became less oily and more sympathetic as they aged. His Dr. Richman, the psychiatrist who explains away Norman BATES at the end of *PSYCHO*, is little more than a variation on the cops he plays in *The Rise and Fall of Legs Diamond* (1960), *Murder, Inc.* (1960), and *West Side Story* (1961). By the time of *Bullitt* (1968), his grizzled look and deepening voice give him more moral authority than his opposite, the even more oleaginous Robert Vaughn. His many television appearances include two telemovies as Tony Vincenzo and a costarring role on the ensuing series *Kolchak: The Night Stalker* (1974–75) as well as the featured roles of General Thomas Moore in *Baa Baa Black Sheep* (1977–78) and Police Lieutenant Abrams in *David Cassidy—Man Undercover* (1978–79).

Oates, Cicely (1889–1934) British character actress whose brief film career was cut short by her early death. She appeared in eight films beginning in 1931, most memorably as the enigmatic "Nurse Agnes," whose relation to the villainous Abbott is never made clear, in *THE MAN WHO KNEW TOO MUCH* (1934).

Ober, Philip (1902–1982) Balding American character actor, former advertising executive, who appeared in some 50 films and television episodes, mostly from 1950. Though he generally played mild-mannered fellows, his best-known role, Captain Dana Holmes in *From Here to Eternity* (1953), is a tyrant who tries to force Pvt. Robert E. Lee Prewitt into his regiment's boxing team even while Prewitt's friend, Sgt. Milt Warden, is sleeping with Karen Holmes. He played the short-lived Lester Townsend in *NORTH BY NORTHWEST*, Wilton Stark in the *ALFRED HITCHCOCK PRESENTS* segment "Burglar-Proof" (1962), and the eyewitness Colonel John Hoey in *THE ALFRED HITCHCOCK HOUR* episode "I Saw the Whole Thing," before reaching his widest audience as the hero's commanding officer, General Stone, in the opening year of the television series *I Dream of Jeannie* (1965–66).

Obzina, Martin (1905–1979) Veteran Hollywood art director who, after a brief stint as a film editor in 1929, settled at UNIVERSAL beginning with *Destry Rides Again* (1939) and *My Little Chickadee* (1940) and remained for 10 years and 30 films, from undistinguished second features to sleepers such as *The Killers* (1946), on which he served as Jack OTTERSON's associate. After freelancing on a dozen low-budget productions in the early fifties, he became one of the staff art directors for *ALFRED HITCHCOCK PRESENTS*, where he designed the visuals for many episodes, including the Hitchcock-directed "REVENGE," "BREAKDOWN," "THE CASE OF MR. PELHAM," "WET

SATURDAY," and "BACK FOR CHRISTMAS." He left the program in 1957 to become art director on the television series *M Squad* (1957–60), but returned when that series ended for "MRS. BIXBY AND THE COLONEL'S COAT," "THE HORSEPLAYER," and "BANG! YOU'RE DEAD." Continuing in the same capacity with THE ALFRED HITCHCOCK HOUR, he is credited on Hitchcock's "I SAW THE WHOLE THING" and many others.

O'Casey, Sean (1880–1964) Irish playwright, a key figure in the Irish Literary Revival. Born John Casey, he worked as a laborer, journalist, trade union secretary, and provocateur before the Abbey Theatre produced *Shadow of a Gunman* (1923), JUNO AND THE PAYCOCK (1924), and *The Plough and the Stars* (1926). After the last of these touched off nationalist riots in the theater, the author exiled himself to England, where he spent the rest of his career writing poems, stories, a six-volume autobiography, and theatrical tragicomedies shot through with melancholy fantasy, most of them fated to be published before they were staged. Hitchcock's grim 1930 film version of *Juno*, which retained Sara ALLGOOD, her sister Maire O'NEIL, Sidney MORGAN, and Kathleen O'REGAN from the play's first London run, was the first adaptation of O'Casey's work to the cinema; John Ford's RKO version of *The Plough and the Stars* followed in 1936; and *Juno* was remade for television in 1960.

O'Connell, David J. (1916–1996) American television producer who began as an editor on ALFRED HITCHCOCK PRESENTS and THE ALFRED HITCHCOCK HOUR, coediting, among other episodes, the Hitchcock-directed "MRS. BIXBY AND THE COLONEL'S COAT," "THE HORSEPLAYER," "BANG! YOU'RE DEAD," and "I SAW THE WHOLE THING." In 1962 he became head of the editorial department on the television series *McHale's Navy* and earned his first producing credits on the telemovie *Marcus Welby, M.D.* (1969) and the ensuing series (1969–76) before moving on to a dozen later television films and the science-fiction series *Buck Rogers in the 25th Century* (1979–81) and *Galactica 1980* (1980).

O'Connell, Patricia Hitchcock See HITCHCOCK, PATRICIA.

O'Connor, Frank D. New York district attorney who served as technical adviser on THE WRONG MAN—a task for which he was uniquely well qualified because, as an attorney in private practice, he had defended the real-life Christopher Emmanuel Balestrero.

O'Connor, Una (1880–1959) Diminutive, spirited, stage-trained Irish character actress, born Agnes Teresa McGlade, with an especially pungent line in lower-class domestics. One of her earliest film roles was the birdlike Mrs. Grogram in MURDER! Shortly thereafter she went to Hollywood, where she created more than 60 roles in films as different as *The Bride of Frankenstein, David Copperfield,* and *The Informer* (all 1935) before capping her career by playing Janet McKenzie, the cook in *Witness for the Prosecution* (1957).

O'Dea, Denis (1905–1978) Irish stage actor who appeared in some 20 films, initially in broadly ethnic roles like the street singer in *The Informer* (1935) and the young covey in *The Plough and the Stars* (1936). By the time he played Richard Corrigan, the attorney general of Australia, in UNDER CAPRICORN, he was ready for deracination in such roles as Rear Admiral Sir Rodney Leighton in *Captain Horatio Hornblower* (1951), though he still took such occasional Irish roles as Father Murphy in *Darby O'Gill and the Little People* (1959).

O'Donoghue, A.(C.) Sound recordist on YOUNG AND INNOCENT and 10 other British films of the thirties.

O'Hara, Maureen (1920–) Spirited Irish actress, born Maureen Fitzsimmons, who trained at the Abbey School, performed on radio programs while still a child, and appeared with the Abbey Players before her film debut in 1938. Signed to a contract by Erich POMMER and Charles LAUGHTON, she appeared opposite Laughton as the plucky orphan Mary Yellan in Pommer's production of JAMAICA INN, then departed with him for Hollywood, and co-starred with him in *The Hunchback of Notre Dame.* Cast as Angharad in John Ford's *How Green Was My*

Valley (1941), she gave a particularly effective performance as a helpmeet who was as tough and combative as the men among whom she lived, and returned to Ford in *Rio Grande* (1950), *The Quiet Man* (1952), *The Long Gray Line* (1955), and *The Wings of Eagles* (1957). After making some 60 films, she retired in 1971 but came back to the cinema 20 years later in an even more striking turn as the hero's impossible mother in *Only the Lonely* (1991).

Oliver, Charles British character actor in some 20 films of the later thirties, equally at ease playing Squire Montague Pennington in *Ask a Policeman* (1939) and such questionable foreigners as Pierre in *Beloved Imposter* (1936), the sheik in *Crooks Tour* (1939), and the sleekly treacherous officer in THE LADY VANISHES who tries to get the English passengers to surrender by assuring them that he was at Oxford. (The hero's riposte, after he knocks the officer out: "I was at Cambridge.")

Olivier, Sir Laurence (Lord Olivier) (1907–1989) Accomplished British actor/director/producer, the most celebrated stage actor of the 20th century. A clergyman's son, Olivier made his debut at 15 playing Kate in a schoolboys' performance of *The Taming of the Shrew* at the Shakespeare Festival; a few years thereafter he made his professional debuts in London and New York and his screen debut in *The Temporary Widow* (1930). Handsome, graceful, and well spoken, with what Charles BENNETT called a rare gift for speaking Shakespeare's lines as if he were actually thinking them, he was a natural romantic lead, although his early screen career was so spotty that Greta Garbo refused to accept him as her romantic partner in *Queen Christina* (1934). In 1935, however, he scored a personal stage triumph, alternating with John Gielgud in the roles of Romeo and Mercutio in a West End production of *Romeo and Juliet*. A year later he appeared as Orlando in Paul Czinner's screen version of *As You Like It,* and in 1939 William Wyler selected him to star as Heathcliff in *Wuthering Heights,* during which Olivier said he learned how to act for the screen. Oscar-nominated for this role and again the following year for his performance as Maxim de Winter in

REBECCA—an experience that, despite his storied failure to secure the role of Mrs. de Winter for his actress bride, Vivien Leigh, he summarized in five bland words, "happy with Hitchcock in *Rebecca*," in his extremely candid 1982 autobiography *Confessions of an Actor*—Olivier returned to England, joined the Fleet Air Arm of the Royal Navy, and served until 1944, when he and Ralph Richardson were appointed codirectors of the Old Vic Theatre. That same year he directed himself in *Henry V*, the first of a distinguished series of starring-directing stints that came to include *Hamlet* (1948), *Richard III* (1955), and the non-Shakespearean *The Prince and the Showgirl* (1957).

Knighted in 1947, Olivier continued, despite notable success in such films as *Carrie* (1952) and *The Beggar's Opera* (1953), to work mostly in the theater until Tony Richardson's screen version of *The Entertainer* (1960), which allowed him to reprise his starring role as the seedy dance-hall performer Archie Rice, paired him again with stage costar Joan Plowright (who became his third wife), and rekindled his interest in the screen. Emerging in his later years as a character actor of unsurpassed range, he created indelible portraits in such wildly different roles as Sir John French in *Oh! What a Lovely War* (1969), cuckolded mystery writer Andrew Wyke in *Sleuth* (1972), and Nazi dentist Christian Szell in *Marathon Man* (1977). He was nominated for nine more Oscars and won as Best Actor for *Hamlet* (which also won Best Picture). He received honorary awards for *Henry V* and, in 1979, for the whole body of his filmwork. Other honors for his work on stage and in films and television were legion, and he was created a life peer in 1971. His last important performance, which won him his fifth Emmy, was as King Lear (for a television production in 1983).

Olsen, Christopher American child actor, veteran of a half-dozen films, who retired two years after playing the kidnapped Hank McKenna in THE MAN WHO KNEW TOO MUCH (1956).

Olsen, Moroni (1889–1954) Heavy-set American character actor, veteran of 100 films from 1931, who could be as corrupt as Ralph Henry in *The Glass Key* (1942) or MacDonald in *Cobra Woman* (1943) or as upstanding as General Robert E. Lee in *The Santa Fe Trail* (1940) or Colonel Blake in *Air Force* (1943). His brief appearance as Walter Beardsley, the bureaucrat who looks down his nose at Alicia Huberman's morals in NOTORIOUS, draws on both strains.

O'Malley, Lillian   American stage actress who occasionally appeared in films and television programs, most often as a domestic. She played maids, housekeepers, and cleaning ladies in the ALFRED HITCHCOCK PRESENTS episodes "BREAKDOWN," "A True Account" (1959), "Invitation to an Accident" (1959), and "The Twelve Hour Caper" (1962), stepping outside her customary range to play the Williamses' neighbor in "The Percentage" (1958) and the replacement nurse in "A Woman's Help" (1961).

Ondra, Anny (1902–1987)   Polish-born leading lady, née Anna Sophie Ondrakova, with long experience in the Czech, Austrian, and German cinemas before she came to England in 1927. Her burgeoning English-language film career, nurtured by such starring roles as Kate Cregeen in THE MANXMAN, was ended by the coming of sound. She appeared in one English sound film, BLACKMAIL, though her character's voice was provided by Joan BARRY, who stood just out of camera range. After completing the film, she returned to Europe, where she made another 46 films, mostly in German, before retiring in 1957.

O'Neil, Maire (1885–1952)   Irish stage actress, born Maire Allgood, sister of Sara ALLGOOD. After long experience with the Abbey Theatre, she made her film debut as Mrs. Madigan in JUNO AND THE PAYCOCK, a part she had taken in the play's London run, and went on to alternate her theatrical roles with some 40 Milligans, Finnegans, and O'Sheas in the British cinema.

"One More Mile To Go"   65th episode of *Alfred Hitchcock Presents,* broadcast April 7, 1957. **Associate producer:** Joan Harrison; **Director:** Alfred Hitchcock; **Assistant director:** Hilton Green; **Teleplay:** James P. Cavanaugh, based on the short story by F.J. Smith; **Cinematographer:** John L. Russell; **Art director:** John Lloyd;

Set designer: Ralph Sylos; **Costumes:** Vincent Dee; **Editors:** Richard G. Wray and Edward W. Williams; **Music:** Stanley Wilson; **Cast:** David Wayne (Sam Jacoby), Louise Larabee (Martha Jacoby), Steve Brodie (police officer), Norman Leavitt (gas station attendant).

The third episode Hitchcock directed for the program's second season tracks Sam Jacoby from his home, where he murders his wife during an all-but-unseen-and-unheard opening argument. Bundling the corpse into his car's trunk, Sam drives off to dispose of it but finds himself followed and bedeviled by a cherubically helpful police officer who notices a taillight out, accepts Sam's argument that he does not have the trunk key with him, but eventually drives with the haggard, resigned killer to the police station, where tools to open the trunk await, along with detection and punishment. Hitchcock's framing speeches are notable for being delivered entirely in rhymed couplets.

Opatoshu, David (1918–1996)   Smooth, versatile American character actor, onstage in Yiddish theater from adolescence. He made his film debut in 1939 but did not work steadily in movies until 10 years later, beginning shortly thereafter his extensive list of television credits, including two in ALFRED HITCHCOCK PRESENTS—the store detective Mr. Cooney in "On the Nose" (1958) and the fake paralytic Pedro Sequiras in "Strange Miracle" (1962)— and one in THE ALFRED HITCHCOCK HOUR—the mysterious shopkeeper Mr. Dulong in "The Magic Shop" (1964). He returned to play Michael Armstrong's inoffensive but ultimately threatening East German minder Jakobi in TORN CURTAIN.

O'Regan, Kathleen (1903–)   Stage-trained Irish actress who made her film debut as Mary Boyle in JUNO AND THE PAYCOCK and appeared in four other films through 1942.

Ormonde, Czenzi (1913–)   American screenwriter, an assistant to Ben HECHT who was hired to provide dialogue for STRANGERS ON A TRAIN and ended up sharing screen credit with Raymond CHANDLER, but was credited on only two later films, the SHADOW OF A DOUBT remake *Step Down to Terror*

(1958) and *1001 Arabian Nights* (1959). Her book *Solomon and the Queen of Sheba* was published in 1954.

Orry-Kelly (1897–1964) Australian fashion designer, born Jack Kelly, who came to New York in hopes of becoming an actor but ended designing titles for Fox's east coast studios. In Hollywood from 1923, he worked on hundreds of films, first at WARNER BROS. and later principally at Fox. He designed gowns for Katharine Hepburn, Ingrid BERGMAN, Rita Hayworth, and (some 20 times) Bette Davis. Soon after sharing an Oscar for *An American in Paris* (1951), he designed the costumes for *I CONFESS*. He later won Academy Awards for *Les Girls* (1957) and *Some Like It Hot* (1959) and was nominated for *Gypsy* (1962).

Orton, J.O.C. British screenwriter who worked on some 30 films between *After the Ball* (1933) and *BON VOYAGE*, his last, which he cowrote with Angus MACPHAIL, both of them forgoing screen credit.

Otterson, Jack (1881–1975) American art director, a former architect who collaborated on designs for the Empire State Building. At Fox from 1932 as a sketch artist, he moved in 1936 to UNIVER-SAL, where he served as supervising art director from 1937 to 1943, working with everyone from Abbott and Costello to Sherlock Holmes. He was nominated for Academy Awards for *The Magnificent Brute* (1936), *You're a Sweetheart* (1937), *Mad About Music* (1938), *First Love* (1939), *The Boys from Syracuse* (1940), *Flame of New Orleans* (1941), *The Spoilers* (1942), and *Arabian Nights* (1942). Among the most distinctive of his 150 films are *Son of Frankenstein* (1939), *SABOTEUR*, and *The Killers* (1946).

Owens, Patricia (1925–) Canadian-born leading lady who moved to England as a child and launched her career as an ingenue on both stage and screen in the early forties. Arriving in Hollywood in 1956, she became a contract player at 20TH CENTURY–FOX and then freelanced. Although she occasionally appeared in A-list films like *Sayonara* (1957), she was more often stuck in such routine properties as *No Down Payment* (1957) and *The Fly* (1958). Her role in this last film as the dutiful wife of an unwisely adventurous husband is echoed in her performance in the ALFRED HITCHCOCK PRESENTS segment "THE CRYSTAL TRENCH" as Stella Ballister, widowed by a mountain-climbing accident but determined to wait most of her life for a last reunion with her husband's body.

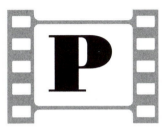

Page, Don (1904–1967) Mexican-American actor, born José Paige, who as Don Alvarado came to Hollywood in 1924 and played a succession of more than 50 Latin lovers. When his acting career petered out in the forties, he changed his name to Don Page and moved behind the camera as assistant director on a half-dozen films, including *I CONFESS*, *Rebel Without a Cause* (1955), and *East of Eden* (1955) and the television series *Maverick* (1957–62).

Paglia, Camille American scholar of popular culture, professor of Humanities at the University of the Arts, Philadelphia, and self-styled counterfeminist and scourge of academia. Her distinctively provocative brand of cultural commentary first attracted widespread attention in *Sexual Personae: Art and Decadence from Nefertiti to Emily Dickinson*(1990), which she followed with *Sex, Art, and American Culture* (1991) and *Vamps and Tramps: New Essays* (1994). Her monograph *THE BIRDS* (British Film Institute, 1998) links the film's presentation of "destructive, rapacious nature" to the glamorous but dangerously unbridled female sexuality incarnated by Melanie Daniels. Taking sharp exception to commentators who have dismissed Tippi HEDREN's performance as Melanie as mannered and pronounced the film inferior to *PSY-CHO*, Paglia's chatty, scene-by-scene analysis hails Hedren in all her cool artifice as "the ultimate Hitchcock heroine" and the film, marking in its uncanny

wholesale assaults a return of repressed sexual power, as Hitchcock's most ambitious work technically, linking it to both the apocalyptic violence of *Suddenly Last Summer* (1959) and the tradition of British romanticism going back to the *femmes fatales* of Coleridge. Although she sees Hedren as the ideal expression of Hitchcock's powerful ambivalence toward female sexuality, she applauds her for having "actively confronted Hitchcock's challenges" by founding a nature preserve in the years following the film, eventually pawning the fur coat the director had given her to support its work.

Palmer, John (1916–1991) British producer who rose from production supervisor on *UNDER CAPRICORN*, his first credit, and 15 other films, mostly in the fifties and sixties, to associate producer on a half-dozen films from *Bonjour tristesse* (1958) to *A Bridge Too Far* (1977).

Paradine Case, The (Alternative titles: *Der Fall Paradin, Le Procès Paradine, Il caso Paradine*) Selznick International–Vanguard, 132 minutes, December 1947. **Producer:** David O. Selznick; **Director:** Alfred Hitchcock; **Screenplay:** David O. Selznick (James Bridie and Ben Hecht), based on the novel by Robert Hichens, **Adaptation:** Alma Reville; **Cinematographer:** Lee Garmes; **Assistant directors:** Lowell J. Farrell (and Joel Freeman); **Production designer:** J. McMillan Johnson; **Art direc-**

tor: Thomas Morahan; **Set decoration:** Emile Kuri; **Interiors:** Joseph B. Platt; **Gowns:** Travis Banton; **Hairstyles:** Larry Germain; **Scenario assistant:** Lydia Schiller; **Unit Manager:** Fred Ahern; **Sound director:** James G. Stewart; **Sound recordist:** Richard Van Hessen; **Editor:** Hal C. Kern; **Associate:** John Faure; **Special effects:** Clarence Slifer; **Music:** Franz Waxman; **Cast:** Gregory Peck (Anthony Keane), Ann Todd (Gay Keane), Charles Laughton (Lord Thomas Horfield), Charles Coburn (Sir Simon Flaquer), Ethel Barrymore (Lady Sophie Horfield), Louis Jourdan (André Latour), [Alida] Valli (Maddalena Paradine), Joan Tetzel (Judy Flaquer), Leo G. Carroll (Sir Joseph Farrell), Isobel Elsom (innkeeper), John Williams, John Goldsworthy, Lester Matthews, Patrick Aherne, Colin Hunter.

David O. SELZNICK had wanted to film Robert HICHENS's stately, fact-based legal thriller *The Paradine Case* ever since its publication in 1933, and Hitchcock agreed to the project early in 1946, even though he was already planning to leave Selznick to join Sidney BERNSTEIN in TRANSATLANTIC PICTURES. The adaptation, which had run afoul of the Production Code Administration when Selznick had submitted earlier versions in 1933, 1936, and 1940, continued to pose problems even after the PCA was satisfied, largely because its center shifted from Maddalena Paradine, the frigid society woman arrested for poisoning her husband, to Anthony Keane, the barrister who falls in love with his client, to Keane's long-suffering wife Gay. Casting was marked by a series of compromises.

Smitten barrister Anthony Kane (Gregory Peck) consults with Maddalena Paradine (Alida Valli), the mysterious client accused of poisoning her husband in *The Paradine Case*. *(National Film Society Archive)*

Selznick envisioned Laurence OLIVIER or Maurice Evans as Keane; Hitchcock argued for Joseph COTTEN and Gregory PECK. When Greta Garbo and Ingrid BERGMAN both declined the role of Mrs. Paradine, Selznick recruited Alida VALLI, an Italian actress unknown in America. Even Charles LAUGHTON, whose over-the-top antics as the sadistic judge Lord Thomas Horfield represent virtually the only exception to Hitchcock's rule of "negative acting," was a second choice to Selznick's preference, Claude RAINS. But the final cast, mixing veteran British character actors with potent younger box-office draws and the future stars Valli and Louis JOURDAN, was one of Hitchcock's most illustrious. Shooting, which began in December, ran wildly over schedule. Leonard J. LEFF has detailed the reasons for the delays: bad weather at the Cumberland locations; elaborate sets (which eventually cost more than those for *Gone With the Wind*); the decision to shoot the film in continuity; Hitchcock's preparation, with cinematographer Lee GARMES, of elaborate long takes that Selznick arrived on the set to veto or cut out in the editing room; the producer's constant rewrites (he eventually took sole screen credit for the script) as shooting continued; and the need to keep the expensive cast on salary as the shoot stretched out to 92 days, a Hitchcock record—even though the director had managed some economies by abandoning his commitment to decoupage and filming the climactic Old Bailey sequence with four cameras running simultaneously, cutting the footage afterwards. Hitchcock's rough cut of the film ran three hours; it was Selznick who edited it down to two hours and, before the film premiered, rejected all the alternate titles he had considered—*Mrs. Paradine Takes the Stand, The Lie, Heartbreak, The Grand Passion, A Question of Life and Death, A Woman of Experience, The Dark Hour, A Crime of Passion, This Is No Ordinary Woman, Guilty? The Indelible Stain, Guilty!, The Woman Who Did the Killing, Hanging Is Easy, The Accused, Bewildered, The Green-Eyed Monster, Woman and Wife*—including several that that had outpolled Hichens's—*Fascination, Bewitched, Under Oath, The Lawyer's Secret*—to return to the novel's original title, which was added to release prints in bold capitals in stark contrast with the rest of the credits' ornate lettering.

The results were predictable. Though it opened on December 31, 1947, in hopes of qualifying for that year's Academy Awards, Hitchcock's 33rd film, and his last for Selznick, was an unqualified disaster at the box office. Adjusted for inflation, the film, despite coming in under budget at $4 million, was the most expensive of his career and apart from *TOPAZ* his biggest flop. No matter how much they admired the glacially elegant production, contemporary reviewers found the film static, talky, and profoundly undramatic. Everyone connected with it could fairly be demonized—the novelist for his interminable and diffuse property, the producer for his stiff adaptation, the performers for their emotional reserve, the director for his lack of attention to the cost and quality of the production. Unlike *SHADOW OF A DOUBT* and *VERTIGO*, which took years to find a substantial audience, *The Paradine Case* has never won a favored reputation. Both Peck and Hitchcock attempted to disavow it, and more recent critics have been no kinder. Certainly very few films have inspired academic analysis in exclusive terms of *unpleasure,* the word Michael Anderegg used to describe its effect in his *Cinema Journal* essay on the film. Although Leff and others have explained the film's failure by noting Hitchcock's distraction with the business of setting up his own independent company, it seems more judicious to conclude that *The Paradine Case* warrants the complaints that James STEWART and Ingrid Bergman made about their own films for Transatlantic: the director, more interested in the camera than the performers, produced a film as visually splendid as it is dramatically inert. Because the rough cut was destroyed in a 1980 flood, restoration of the original footage, whatever its merits, seems unlikely.

Paramount Pictures This Hollywood production company was the descendant of Famous Players in Famous Plays, a motion-picture company founded in 1912 by Adolph Zukor, who emerged as the firm's head after Paramount Pictures' agreement to distribute both Famous Players and Lasky Productions in 1914 led to a series of mergers and shakedowns. Saved from bankruptcy in the early thirties by the code-baiting comedies of Mae West, the studio was particularly hospitable to émigré filmmakers like Maurice Chevalier, Ernst Lubitsch, and Billy Wilder, whose contributions gave it a more Continental flavor than its competitors, and it became the only major studio ever run, however briefly, by a filmmaker when Lubitsch was named head of production from 1936 to 1937. In 1953, having fulfilled the terms of his WARNER BROS. contract, Hitchcock signed a deal brokered by his agent Lew WASSERMAN to make nine films with Paramount, five of which would revert to his ownership after a period of eight years, four to belong to the studio. As the deal worked out, however, Hitchcock made five films for himself—*REAR WINDOW, THE TROUBLE WITH HARRY, THE MAN WHO KNEW TOO MUCH* (1956), *VERTIGO,* and *PSYCHO*—and only one, *TO CATCH A THIEF,* for the studio. In 1962 he exchanged his proprietary rights in *Psycho* for a block of stock in UNIVERSAL, the new studio to which Wasserman had moved; in 1973, the other four Paramount films were withdrawn from circulation while attorneys for the director, and eventually for his estate, negotiated new terms for their redistribution. The Paramount films were finally rereleased in theaters and on videotape in 1983–84.

Paris, Jerry (1925–1986)   American general-purpose actor of the fifties and sixties. Best known as Rob Petrie's next-door television neighbor Jerry Helper in *The Dick Van Dyke Show* (1961–66), he also played, among 50 other roles, two for ALFRED HITCHCOCK PRESENTS—Wally Benson, the lover who cuckolds Arthur Arlington in "Whodunit" (1956), and the felonious Fred Piper in "The Safe Place" (1958)—and returned as the lawyer W.E. Grimes in the *FORD TARTIME* episode "INCIDENT AT A CORNER." Beginning with *The Dick Van Dyke Show,* he became a prolific director of television and occasional features.

Parker, Cecil (1897–1971)   Aristocratic British actor, born Cecil Schwabe. He returned from war service to make his stage debut in 1922 and his film debut in 1929. The quintessence of the stiff-upper-lip school, he specialized in flinty authority figures with a touch of insecurity, such as the uncomfortable adulterer Todhunter in *THE LADY VANISHES.* Toward the end of the forties he interrupted a series of starring

roles in *Captain Boycott* (1947), *The Weaker Sex* (1948), *The Chiltern Hundreds* (1949), *Dear Mr. Prohack* (1949), *Tony Draws a Horse* (1950), and *I Believe in You* (1952) to play Charles Adare's uncle, the governor, in *UNDER CAPRICORN.* Among his handful of television roles is Captain Morgan, the husband convinced his estranged wife is having an affair, in the *ALFRED HITCHCOCK PRESENTS* episode "I Spy" (1961).

Parker, Charles (E.)   Makeup artist on some 30 films from *UNDER CAPRICORN,* his first, to *Star Wars* (1977), his last. After retiring, he cowrote the story and screenplay for *Breakin'* (1984).

Parnell, Emory (1892–1979)   Portly, booming-voiced American character actor with vaudeville experience. Most familiar as Bill Reed in four Ma and Pa Kettle movies and as Hank Hawkins in the television series *The Life of Riley* (1953–58), he played more than 200 cowboys, laborers, bank officials, police officers, and next-door neighbors. A favorite of Preston Sturges, he also appeared in three Hitchcock films: as the ship's captain who rescues the survivors of the airplane shot down at the end of *FOREIGN CORRESPONDENT,* as the uncredited Conway in *MR. AND MRS. SMITH,* and as the homicidal husband on the Radio City movie screen whose gunplay covers up the sound of the gunfire in the theater in *SABOTEUR.*

Passionate Adventure, The   Gainsborough, Gaumont, 1924. **Producer:** Michael Balcon; **Director:** Graham Cutts; **Assistant director:** Alfred Hitchcock; **Screenplay:** Alfred Hitchcock and Michael Morton, based on the novel by Frank Stayton; **Cinematographer:** Claude L. McDonnell; **Art director:** Alfred Hitchcock; **Cast:** Alice Joyce (Drusilla Sinclair), Clive Brook, Lillian Hall-Davies, Marjorie Daw, Victor McLaglen, Mary Brough, John Hamilton, J.R. Tozer.

The third of the five Graham Cutts films (1923–25) on which Hitchcock served as assistant director, screenwriter, and art director was the first film to be released under the Gainsborough imprint.

Paton, Charles (1874–1970)   Balding, stage-trained British character actor who played Alice

White's tobacconist father in BLACKMAIL and then continued in nearly 70 film roles, variously avuncular and eccentric, over the next 20 years.

Patrick, Lee (1901–1982)   American actress who came to Hollywood with the coming of sound and played dozens of brassy blondes before ripening into the hard-edged but likeable character actress who appears briefly in VERTIGO as the purchaser of Madeline Elster's Rolls-Royce whom Scottie briefly mistakes for Madeleine. She is most fondly remembered as Sam Spade's secretary Effie Perrine in *The Maltese Falcon* (1941)—a role she reprised in her final film, *The Black Bird* (1975)—and as haunted banker Cosmo Topper's imperious, flustered television wife Henrietta in *Topper* (1953–55).

Payne, James W.   American set decorator, in Hollywood from 1959, whose three dozen credits include *In Like Flint* (1967), *The Sting* (1973), and *FAMILY PLOT*.

Pearce, Adele (1918–)   American actress who came to Hollywood in 1937 and landed 15 small roles such as the uncredited Lily in MR. AND MRS. SMITH. In 1942 she changed her screen name, and as Pamela Blake appeared in supporting or occasional starring roles in some three dozen B-pictures.

Peck, Gregory (1916–)   Durable, likeable American movie star, born Eldred Gregory Peck, who left his pre-medical studies at Berkeley to pursue acting. A back injury he had suffered in a college rowing match proved a boon to his career because it kept him out of the war at a time when many young American leads were overseas. Soon after his stage debut in 1942, he was signed to a film contract, and his second role, as Father Chisholm in *The Keys to the Kingdom* (1944), earned an Oscar nomination and made him a star. At once boyish and virile, he was much in demand for a wide variety of heroic roles, and he shortly appeared in two Hitchcock films, as the amnesiac John Ballantine in SPELLBOUND (a role for which David O. SELZNICK had first wanted Joseph COTTEN) and the romantically smitten barrister Anthony Keane in THE PARADINE CASE (a part Selznick had first envisioned for John Bar-

rymore and one that Hitchcock's candidate, Ronald Colman, had already turned down). Neither collaboration was happy. The inexperienced Peck wanted more direction from Hitchcock, who, although happy, when he professed an ignorance of wine, to send him a case as a gift, simply advised him on the set to empty his face of all emotion, courting François TRUFFAUT's criticism years later that Peck's eyes were inexpressive. The real problem, however, was that both the troubled amnesiac and the morally compromised attorney were outside Peck's most comfortable range. As his later Oscar nominations for Pa Baxter in *The Yearling* (1946), Phil Green in *Gentleman's Agreement* (1947), and General Frank Savage in *Twelve O'Clock High* (1950)—and his award-winning performance as Atticus Finch in *To Kill a Mockingbird* (1962)—attested, he was at his best in portraying decent men capable of seizing the high moral ground to fuel their outrage, and his most notable experiments outside this range—as the lowdown Lewt McCanles in *Duel in the Sun* (1946), the tragically obsessed Captain Ahab in *Moby Dick* (1956), and the Nazi physician Josef Mengele in *The Boys from Brazil* (1978)—were among his least successful roles. Long active in Hollywood politics, Peck served as president of the Academy of Motion Picture Arts and Sciences from 1967 to 1970.

Pelletier, Gilles (1925–)   French-Canadian actor who made his film debut as Father Benoit in I CONFESS and has since played some 15 French-language roles. A favorite of Canadian television, he anchored the casts of *R.C.M.P.* (1960) and *L'Héritage* (1987), and appeared as a regular on several programs in between.

Pelling, George   American character actor whose few film and television appearances between 1947 and 1965 included five on ALFRED HITCHCOCK PRESENTS—as Johnson, the elevator man in "I Killed the Count" (1957), a police officer in "Father and Son" (1957), the gateman in "The Impromptu Murder" (1958), Lein the butler in "BANQUO'S CHAIR," and Bert in "The Ladlady" (1961)—and two on THE ALFRED HITCHCOCK HOUR—the train conductor in "See the Monkey Dance" (1964) and the police sergeant in "Thou Still Unravished Bride" (1965).

Pember, Clifford British art director who first worked in Hollywood on *Way Down East* (1920) and then returned to England for EASY VIRTUE and two other films through 1931.

Peppard, George (1928–1994) Easygoing American leading man with stage experience. Shortly after his film debut in *The Strange One* (1957), he appeared as the harried Evan Wallace in the ALFRED HITCHCOCK PRESENTS segment "The Diplomatic Corpse" (1957) and as Janey Medwick's sleuthing fiancée Pat Lawrence in the FORD STARTIME segment "INCIDENT AT A CORNER." His similar pairing with Audrey Hepburn in *Breakfast at Tiffany's* (1962) seemed to presage an important career, but he appeared mostly in routine action films, making his most lasting mark on television, as Tom Banacek in *Banacek* (1972–74) and as Hannibal Smith in *The A-Team* (1983–87). In 1978 he directed himself in *Five Days from Home.*

Perceval, Hugh British producer of some 20 films, 1933–69, who served as production manager on JAMAICA INN. He cowrote two features, *A Man of Mayfair* (1931) and *Raising a Riot* (1955).

Percy, Esme (1887–1957) Distinguished British stage actor, born Saville Esme Percy, closely associated from 1904 with the work of George Benard Shaw. He made his screen debut as the cross-dressing half-caste Handel Fane in MURDER! His storied good looks, which won him many screen roles in the thirties, were later spoiled by his broken nose and loss of an eye.

Pereira, Hal (1905–1983) American art director, former stage designer, at PARAMOUNT from 1942. After working for several years on such films as *Double Indemnity* and *The Ministry of Fear* (both 1944), he was promoted to an executive position in 1947 and named the studio's supervising art director in 1950—a status that placed his name on more than 200 films. He supervised the art direction on all Hitchcock's Paramount films except PSYCHO: REAR WINDOW, TO CATCH A THIEF, THE TROUBLE WITH HARRY, THE MAN WHO KNEW TOO MUCH (1956), and VERTIGO, the lat-ter one of his 19 Oscar nominations. He shared the 1955 Academy Award for *The Rose Tattoo*. He retired in 1968 to become a design consultant for his brother's architectural firm.

"Perfect Crime, The" 79th episode of *Alfred Hitchcock Presents,* broadcast October 20, 1957. **Associate producer:** Joan Harrison; **Director:** Alfred Hitchcock; **Assistant director:** Hilton Green; **Teleplay:** Stirling Silliphant, based on the short story by Ben Ray Redman; **Cinematographer:** John L. Russell; **Art director:** John Lloyd; **Set designer:** James S. Redd; **Costumes:** Vincent Dee; **Editors:** Richard G. Wray and Edward W. Williams; **Music:** Stanley Wilson; **Cast:** Vincent Price (Charles Courtney), James Gregory (John Gregory), Marianne Stewart (Alice West), Gavin Gordon (Ernest West), Mark Dana (Harrington), John Zaremba (newspaper photographer), Charles Webster, Nick Nicholson (reporters), Therese Lyon (housekeeper).

The first episode Hitchcock directed for the program's third season is a battle of wits between arrogant criminologist and devoted amateur potter Charles Courtney, who boasts that he has never made a single professional mistake, and attorney John Gregory, who comes forward with conclusive proof vindicating a suspected killer whom Courtney's evidence helped convict and send to his execution. Realizing that he cannot count on his nemesis to protect his own reputation by keeping silent about his mistake, Courtney turns on him, kills him, and conceals his body by baking it in a kiln with his most recent creations—though Hitchcock returns in an epilogue to reassure the audience that he was caught in the end.

performance Hitchcock's attitude toward the whole notion of performance seems fraught with contradictions. On the one hand, he was from all accounts an inveterate ham who enjoyed shocking actresses with off-color stories, dominating interviewers he met in the role of seasoned raconteur, and playing practical jokes on eveyone who crossed his path. Many of his collaborators described the florid way he acted out roles for them or mouthed the lines of favored performers as he watched them on the set.

On the other, he is more closely associated than any other Hollywood filmmaker with what he called "negative acting," summarized in his dicta that "actors are cattle" or that Leo G. CARROLL was an effective actor because "he does nothing well." The obvious way to reconcile these positions would be to conclude that Hitchcock was himself a scene-stealing performer who brooked no competition, and this may well have been as true in his closely guarded private life as it clearly was in his assiduously tended public persona. As a film director, Hitchcock's constant competition with his performers (as against the actor-friendly direction of Elia Kazan) made him an anomaly because, instead of focusing on the traditional task of directing the *actors,* he typically acted as if he wanted to dominate, bully, or bypass them entirely to direct the *audience,* hence his remark to Evan HUNTER, "there will be no stars in [*THE BIRDS*]. I'm the star, the birds are the stars—and you're the star" and the enthusiasm he expressed to Ernest LEHMAN for the day when theater seats could be wired to administer jolts of electricity directly to the audience and they could skip making movies entirely.

Hitchcock's contradictory attitude toward performance, which made every professional actor a potential rival, gave him a preference for what Andrew SARRIS has called "iconic" performers like Cary GRANT and Grace KELLY and meant, despite the nominations and awards garnered by Laurence OLIVIER, Joan FONTAINE, Judith ANDERSON, Albert BASSERMAN, Tallulah BANKHEAD, Michael CHEKHOV, Claude RAINS, Ethel BARRYMORE, and Janet LEIGH, that audiences rarely looked to Hitchcock films as showcases for acting. Instead the films both foreground and undermine performances, as if the characters as well as the actors were playing roles. This is particularly true in man-on-the-run stories such as *THE 39 STEPS,* in which Richard Hannay is required to play a rapid series of roles, and *NORTH BY NORTHWEST,* in which Roger Thornhill often seems, as in his attempt to buy a train ticket in Grand Central Station, to be playing Cary Grant, and in movies about acting such as *MURDER!* and *STAGE FRIGHT,* which contrast the mannered performances given within the confines of the proscenium stage with the riskier, more problematic, well-nigh incessant performances given offstage—or

in spaces that quibble on the distinction between artifice and sincerity, acting onstage and off. For much of the running time of *North by Northwest,* for example, the characters accuse each other of giving performances, and it gradually becomes obvious that none of the leading characters in *Stage Fright* is ever entirely offstage—certainly not the guileless heroine Eve Gill, an acting student who is trapped at the moment of unmasking her nominal opposite, accomplished actress and femme fatale Charlotte Inwood, when she herself is caught in two incompatible roles at once. The best brief treatment of performance and performativity in Hitchcock remains William ROTHMAN's chapter on *Murder!;* a more extended treatment that explores the director's contradictory attitude toward performance remains to be written.

Perkins, Anthony (1932–1992) Gangly American actor with stage experience, son of stage and screen actor Osgood Perkins, whose budding film career as a fresh-faced juvenile in roles such as the Oscar-nominated Josh Birdwell in *Friendly Persuasion* (1956) and the baseball player Jimmy Piersall in *Fear Strikes Out* (1957) was forever changed when he accepted the role of the shy motelkeeper Norman BATES in *PSYCHO.* A commitment to appear in the Broadway play *Greenwillow* required his absence from the film's most famous scene, in which stunt double Margo Epper wielded the butcher knife that killed Marion Crane, and he never spoke in Mrs. Bates's voice, which was supplied by mixing the voices of actresses Jeanette Nolan (whose husband, John MCINTIRE, played Sheriff Chambers), Virginia Gregg (who also voiced Mrs. Bates in two *Psycho* sequels), and mimic Paul Jasmin. But he did contribute one bit of business for the boyish Norman—his fondness for candy—which creates a particularly macabre moment as he is watching Marion's car sink in the swamp and stops chewing when the car suddenly stops sinking. The role transformed Perkins's career, fueling a demand for his services in European films and providing him an indelible screen persona many of his later roles played off, some cleverly (his fake government agent Dennis Pitt in *Pretty Poison,* 1968), some clumsily (his incongruously mother-obsessed secretary Hector MacQueen in *Murder on* the *Orient Express,* 1974). Indeed, although Perkins appeared in a wide variety of later roles and cowrote the screenplay for *The Last of Sheila* (1973), it is hard to think of another performer whose 60-film career has been so utterly defined by a single performance. Inevitably, he returned to his signature role in *Psycho II* (1983); *Psycho III* (1986), which he also directed; and the television film *Psycho IV: The Beginning* (1991), which aired only a year before his death.

Perpetua (Alternative title: *Love's Boomerang*) Famous Players–Lasky, 1922. **Directors:** John S. Robertson and Tom Geraghty; **Screenplay:** Josephine Lovett; **Cast:** Ann Forrest (Perpetua), Bunty Fosse (Perpetua as a child), David Powell (Brian McCree), John Miltern (Russell Felton), Roy Byford (Monsieur Lamballe), Florence Wood (Madame Lamballe), Geoffrey Kerr (Saville Mender), Lillian Walker (Stella Daintry), Lionel d'Aragon (Christian), Ollie Emery (Madame Tourterelle), Amy Willard (Jane Egg), Tom Volbecque (Auguste), Frank Stanmore (Corn Chandler), Ida Fane (Mrs. Bugle), Sara Sample (Perpetua's mother).

Ninth of the 12 silent films for which Hitchcock designed intertitles between 1920 and 1922.

Perry, Dennis American academic, assistant professor of English at Brigham Young University. His book *Hitchcock and Poe: The Legacy of Delight and Terror,* forthcoming from Scarecrow Press, considers Edgar Allan Poe as offering both a series of suggestive individual analogies to Hitchcock—individual chapters, for example, compare *The Birds* to "The Masque of the Red Death," *Rear Window* to "The Man of the Crowd," and *Marnie* to "Berenice"—and a decisive general influence on Hitchcock's visual and psychological world, especially through the "master cosmological narrative" Poe adumbrates in the leading topological features—oscillation, a vortex, an invisible center—of Poe's *Eureka.*

Perry, George (1935–) British journalist and reviewer, former film editor of the Sunday London *Times.* He has coedited *The Victorians: A World Built to Last* (with Nicholas Mason, 1974) and written, among many other books, *The Penguin Book of Comics: A Slight History* (with Alan Aldridge, 1971),

The Great British Picture Show (1974; 2nd edition, 1985), *Movies from the Mansion: A History of Pinewood Studios* (1976; 2nd edition, 1986), *The Life of Python* (1983), *The Complete* Phantom of the Opera (1987), *Steven Spielberg* (1998), and *Magic Movie Moments* (2000). His monograph *Hitchcock* (Macmillan/Doubleday, 1975), a volume in the Movie Makers series, is an extended essay, beautifully illustrated in black-and-white and color, tracing the director's career period by period through FRENZY by means of capsule summaries and evaluations, usually adding some background information and ranging in length from a paragraph to a page. Although nearly half the volume is devoted to the British films, the analysis throughout is less rewarding than the stills.

Persoff, Nehemiah (1920–) Jerusalem-born American character actor. A former subway electrician, he trained at the Actors Studio, made his stage debut in 1940, and played more than 100 heavies in movies and television beginning in 1948. Most memorable as the comically treacherous crime lord Little Bonaparte in *Some Like It Hot* (1959), he appeared as Gene Conforti in THE WRONG MAN and in two roles in ALFRED HITCHCOCK PRESENTS: deceptive householder Ralph Collins in "Heart of Gold" (1957) and wronged husband Jeff Jensen in "The Cure" (1960).

Peters, Ralph (1902–1959) American character actor familiar from more than 100 films, mostly westerns, from 1936. His rare television appearances include two for ALFRED HITCHCOCK PRESENTS: a bit in "BREAKDOWN" and the cab driver in "The Rose Garden" (1956).

Peterson, Dorothy (1899–1979) Maternal American character actress, a veteran of some 80 film roles, best known as the mother of the Five Little Peppers in four features (1939–40), the wife Professor Wanley unwisely packs off to the country in the opening minutes of *The Woman in the Window* (1944), and the grieving mother of Barry Kane's murdered friend Ken Mason in SABOTEUR.

Petrie, Hay (1895–1948) Stage-trained Scottish character actor, born David Hay Petrie, who entered the cinema with the coming of sound and played more than 70 eccentric supporting roles such as Sam, Sir Humphrey Pengallan's groom in *JAMAICA INN*, in the thirties and forties, with breaks for the occasional featured role such as the villainous Daniel Quilp in *The Old Curiosity Shop* (1934).

Phillips, Gene D., S.J. American film scholar, professor of English at Loyola University, Chicago. His many books include *The Movie Makers: Artists in an Industry* (1973), *Evelyn Waugh's Officers, Gentlemen, and Rogues: The Fact Behind His Fiction* (1975), *Stanley Kubrick: A Film Odyssey* (1975), *The Films of Tennessee Williams* (1979), *Ken Russell* (1979), *Hemingway and Film* (1980), *John Schlesinger* (1981), *George Cukor* (1982), *Fiction, Film, and F. Scott Fitzgerald* (1986), *Fiction, Film, and Faulkner: The Art of Adaptation* (1988), *Major Film Directors of the American and British Cinema* (1990), *Conrad and Cinema: The Art of Adaptation* (1995), *Exiles in Hollywood: Major European Film Directors in America* (1998), and *Creatures of Darkness: Raymond Chandler, Detective Fiction, and Film Noir* (2000). His *Alfred Hitchcock* (Twayne, 1984), a volume in the same series as his books on Russell, Schlesinger, and Cukor, is an illustrated overview of the director's career divided into period chapters that provide brisk analytical summaries and evaluations of each of his features. It is distinguished from other surveys by the thoughtfulness of its humanistic framework; its extended consideration of the British films, which comprises a third of the volume; its useful chapter on *ALFRED HITCHCOCK PRESENTS*; and the highly critical annotations of its bibliography of earlier Hitchcock scholarship.

Phillpotts, Eden (1862–1960)   British novelist and playwright who in the course of an immensely long career (1888–1959) produced more than 150 novels, many under the pseudonym Harrington Hext, in addition to poems, plays, essays, and short stories. It is ironic that despite his impressive credentials as an author of such mystery classics as *The Grey Room* (1921), *The Red Redmaynes* (1922), and *The Marylebone Miser* (1926), and as the mentor who encouraged Agatha Christie in her first mysteries, his sole contribution to Hitchcock's career was

the nonmystery play *THE FARMER'S WIFE* (1917), adapted by Hitchcock and Eliot STANNARD and filmed again in 1941.

Phoenix Films   The production company that released *BON VOYAGE* and *AVENTURE MALGACHE*.

Piccoli, Michel (1925–)   Balding, versatile French actor, born Jacques Daniel Michel Piccoli. Onstage and onscreen from the midforties, he first attracted international attention as the self-lacerating screenwriter Paul Javal in *Le mépris* (1963); he was equally effective 20 films later as the sinister family friend Henri Husson in *Belle de jour* (1967). Since then he has brought his suavely ironic intelligence to many more than 100 films, mostly French, with such occasional forays into English-language cinema as *TOPAZ*, in which he plays the master spy Jacques Granville.

Pilbeam, Nova (1919–)   Child star of the thirties who made her film debut as the kidnapped Betty Lawrence in *THE MAN WHO KNEW TOO MUCH* (1934) and returned to star in the ingenue role of Erica Burgoyne, the chief constable's daughter, in *YOUNG AND INNOCENT*. Like other Hitchcock heroines of the period, she accepted her femininity matter-of-factly (in her first scene with her future love Robert Tisdall, the murder suspect her father's police have in custody, she helps bring the fainting Tisdall around by slapping his face and twisting his ears) but with more asperity and less romantic intensity than the heroines played by Madeleine CARROLL and Margaret LOCKWOOD; perhaps as a result, little has been written about her, despite her obvious affinity with other inexperienced BLONDE actresses he directed. She was announced as the star of *THE LADY VANISHES* and a Hitchcock film for MAYFLOWER called *Another World,* but the first role went to Lockwood, and the second went nowhere. She married the director Penrose TENNYSON in 1939 and retired after a dozen further films in 1948.

Piper, Frederick (1902–1979)   Stage-trained, whippet-faced British character actor who played policemen and passersby in nearly 100 films through 1971, most of them in the thirties and forties. He is credited for only one Hitchcock role, Sir Humphrey Pengallan's agent Davis in JAMAICA INN, but he appears as well in THE MAN WHO KNEW TOO MUCH (1934) as the policeman whose mate is shot as they crouch behind a mattress, in THE 39 STEPS as the milkman who lends his uniform to the escaping Richard Hannay, as the conductor who unwittingly allows Stevie to bring the bomb aboard a London bus in SABOTAGE, and in a bit in YOUNG AND INNOCENT.

Pittman, Tom (1932–1958)   American actor who appeared in eight films and a dozen television episodes, including his role as the burglar Joe in the SUSPICION segment "FOUR O'CLOCK" before his death in an auto accident.

Platt, Edward (C.) (1916–1974)   Bald, fatherly American character actor, former big-band vocalist. Ten years after his film career properly began with *Rebel Without a Cause* and *The Shrike* (both 1955), he had appeared in 50 films and 25 television segments, from *Written on the Wind* (1956) to *Cape Fear* (1962), with a brief stop to play Roger Thornhill's lawyer in NORTH BY NORTHWEST and District Attorney Henshaw in the ALFRED HITCHCOCK PRESENTS episode "Museum Piece" (1961). He was better known by far, however, as Thaddeus, the Chief of Control on the television spy spoof *Get Smart!* (1965–70).

Platt, Joseph B. (d. 1968)   American production designer whose half-dozen Hollywood credits include the art direction of interior sets for *Gone With the Wind* (1939) and REBECCA and set decoration for THE PARADINE CASE.

Platt, Louise (1915–)   American actress of the thirties. After Broadway success, she made her Hollywood debut in *I Met My Love Again* (1938), but only three years after her definitive performance as sheltered, pregnant, coldly minatory Lucy Mallory in *Stagecoach* (1939), she returned briefly to the stage. Fifteen years later she appeared in three television roles, including two wronged wives in ALFRED HITCHCOCK PRESENTS: murderous Marcia Hendrix in "One for the Road" (1957) and long-sufering Ethel Botibol in "DIP IN THE POOL."

Pleasure Garden, The   (Alternative titles: *Irregarten der Leidenschaft, Le jardin d'agrément*) Emelka (in association with Gainsborough) Wardour & F., Aymon Independent, approximately 75 minutes, March 1926. **Director:** Alfred Hitchcock; **Presented by** Michael Balcon; **Screenplay:** Eliot Stannard, based on the novel by Oliver Sandys; **Cinematographer:** Baron [Gaetano] Ventimiglia; **Assistant Director:** Alma Reville; **Cast:** Virginia Valli (Patsy Brand), Carmelita Geraghty (Jill Cheyne), Miles Mander (Levet), John Stuart (Hugh [Fielding]), Ferd[inand] Martini (Mr. Sidey), Florence Helminger (Mrs. Sidey), George Snell ([Oscar] Hamilton), C. Falkenburg (Prince Ivan).

The Pleasure Garden did not mark Hitchcock's first experience as a movie director; he had begun work on the uncompleted short NUMBER 13 just as Famous Players–Lasky was closing down its British operation in 1922 and had completed ALWAYS TELL YOUR WIFE the following year after the withdrawal of director Hugh Croise from the project. But it did mark his first assignment to direct a substantial film. Michael BALCON, watching Hitchcock's rise from intertitle designer to art director and screenwriter, offered him the job of directing his first complete film early in 1925, when Graham CUTTS, Hitchcock's jealous superior at GAINSBOROUGH, indicated that he did not want the upstart working on his new film, *The Rat*. Under a new agreement between the fledgling Gainsborough and EMELKA, the film's exteriors, though the story was set in England and the Far East, would be shot in Italian locations—Genoa, San Remo, and Lake Como—and its interiors in Emelka's Munich studios. To the end of his life Hitchcock delighted in recounting the comical misfortunes that befell the production even before the crew arrived in Italy. Eager to avoid Italian duties, the cinematographer, Baron VENTIMIGLIA, had hidden the camera under the unwitting director's bunk; customs authorities, though they missed the camera, found the unexposed film and duly confiscated it, then returned it several days later after the crew had paid for fresh film and assessed a duty and penalty that dangerously depleted the production's budget; the actress cast as Miles MANDER's native wife refused to act her drowning scene in San Remo because it was the wrong time of the month. Hitchcock and his assistant director, to whom he had just become engaged, arrived in Munich thoroughly disenchanted with the vagaries of location shooting and eager to complete the film in a studio setting he could control far more completely—a prejudice that was to endure for the rest of his career. Finally, the film's commercial release was delayed for nearly a year after its initial trade screening; only the success of THE LODGER persuaded C.M. WOOLF, who had embargoed the film at Wardour, to approve it for general release early in 1927.

For all but the most dedicated Hitchcock scholars, these cautionary anecdotes have tended to substitute for any direct experience of a film that has rarely been seen and even more seldom analyzed. Yet the film deserves a closer look because of its fascinatingly selective prevision of the later Hitchcock. Most obvious, of course, is the florid melodramatic strain of its later scenes, a strain he pointedly did not pursue. The stories of Patsy Brand and Jill Cheyne, two dancers at the Pleasure Garden Theater whose quest for fame and love leads the newcomer Jill to a romance with Hugh Fielding that she dishonors at every opportunity and the more seasoned, but surprisingly faithful, Patsy to a sudden marriage to Hugh's friend Levet before he returns to the eastern colonies to betray her with a native wife, lead to a sequel that seems a compendium of features Hitchcock would specifically exclude from his later work: exotic settings, overscaled emotions, humorless intensity, and improbable motivations, especially Patsy's superhuman devotion to the treacherous, ultimately murderous Levet, whose timely death leaves her free to accept the love of the sadly abandoned Hugh. Shorn of the humorless Far Eastern settings, however, these are exactly the ingredients of Hitchcock's most successful films from BLACKMAIL to VERTIGO. The early scenes of the film, set in and around the calculatingly demiprofessional Pleasure Garden, reveal not only many of the director's most characteristic preoccupations—the fondness for childish jokes (Hugh is announced as Jill's "fiasco") and visual wit (the dog that licks Jill's feet as she kneels in prayer), the incessant sexualizing of everyday behavior by means of fetishes from wigs to stockings, the institutional exploitation of women by men and their frequent personal revenge on

their exploiters, the resulting intrigue that drives the most innocuous social relations, the emergence of melodrama from most ordinary corners of the urban jungle—but also the ways in which he would and would not succeed in developing these concerns into powerfully involving melodramas in a mode all his own.

Pleshette, Suzanne (1937–) Good-natured, unpretentious American actress with stage experience who made her film debut opposite Jerry Lewis in *The Geisha Boy* (1958) and despite her Ava Gardner looks continued to be upstaged throughout much of her career, for instance by Troy Donahue, the heartthrob husband to whom she was briefly married in 1964, and by both Tippi HEDREN and the avian cast of THE BIRDS, in which she played lovelorn schoolteacher Annie Hayworth. She had already appeared as business executive Charles Underhill's niece Anne in the ALFRED HITCHCOCK PRESENTS episode "Hitch Hike" (1960), and her 20 films made less of an impact than her television work as the title character's wife Emily Hartley on *The Bob Newhart Show* (1972–78), the star of *Suzanne Pleshette Is Maggie Briggs* (1984), and featured roles in dozens of other programs.

Plowright, Hilda (1890–1973) British character actress who made her uncredited film debut as Lady Melville in *You Can't Take It with You* (1938) and played nearly 40 nurses, librarians, and female dependents, many unbilled, through 1965, including the unbilled Miss Pimm in FOREIGN CORRESPONDENT and the duly credited postmistress in SUSPICION.

Poague, Leland A(llen) (1948–) American film scholar, professor of English at Iowa State University, author of *The Cinema of Frank Capra: An Approach to Film Comedy* (1975), *Howard Hawks* (1982), *Film Criticism: A Counter Theory* (with William Cadbury, 1982), *Another Frank Capra* (1994), and *Susan Sontag: An Annotated Bibliography, 1948–1972* (2000), and editor of *Conversations with Susan Sontag* (1995). *A Hitchcock Reader* (Iowa State University Press, 1986), which he coedited with Marshall DEUTELBAUM, is a collection of 25 essays that offers itself as a more theoretically informed successor to Albert J. LA VALLEY's 1972 anthology *Focus on Hitchcock* designed specifically as a core resource for college courses on Hitchcock's films. The editors' introduction to the first of their five sections—"Taking Hitchcock Seriously"—identifies two questions as fundamental to Hitchcock scholarship: "How are we to understand the relationship between Hitchcock's camera . . . and the world it inhabits and takes views of?" and "How far does Hitchcock's apparent willingness to impose his views on film entail a corollary desire to impose those views on the members of his audience?" and prophetically notes the narrowing analytical or diagnostic gap between Hitchcock's staunchest defenders and his severest critics. The remaining sections—"Hitchcock in Britain," "Hitchcock in Hollywood," "The Later Films," and "Hitchcock and Film Theory: A *PSYCHO* Dossier"—combine seven new essays with 18 reprints by such figures as Jean DOUCHET, Maurice YACOWAR, Leonard J. LEFF, Lesley W. BRILL, William ROTHMAN, Elisabeth WEIS, Robin WOOD, and Raymond BELLOUR. Poague's own contributions to the volume, apart from coauthored introductions and bibliographies to each section, are "Criticism and/as History: Rereading *BLACKMAIL*," which uses the film's landmark status to confront the problems raised by reading it in terms of both the historical moment within which it was first produced and the ever-advancing present it occupies for the analyst, and "Links in a Chain: *Psycho* and Film Classicism," which emphasizes the engulfing threat figured in the film by corporate capitalism and the characters' obsession with money.

"Poison"   116th episode of *Alfred Hitchcock Presents,* broadcast October 5, 1958. **Producer:** Joan Harrison; **Associate producer:** Norman Lloyd; **Director:** Alfred Hitchcock; **Assistant director:** Hilton Green; **Teleplay:** Casey Robinson, based on the short story by Roald Dahl; **Cinematographer:** John L. Russell; **Art director:** John Lloyd; **Set designer:** James S. Redd; **Costumes:** Vincent Dee; **Editors:** Richard G. Wray and Edward W. Williams; **Cast:** Wendell Corey (Timber Woods), James Donald (Harry Pope), Arnold Moss (doctor), Weaver Levy (messenger).

The opening episode of the program's fourth season focuses on Harry Pope, the alcoholic colonial who awakens convinced that a poisonous snake is asleep under the bedclothes with him, and Timber Woods, the sardonic partner and unsuccessful romantic rival who thinks he is only imagining it. Overcoming his amusement at what he takes to be Harry's hallucinations, Timber summons the closest doctor to help, and together they attempt to anesthetize the snake so that they can lift the covers. But when no snake is disclosed, the doctor leaves in high dudgeon and Timber dissolves in laughter on the bed, a perfect target for the snake, which leaps from behind a pillow to strike at his face now that the doctor cannot be reached in time to help.

Polglase, Van Nest (1898–1978)   Prodigiously influential American production designer, a former architect who came to Hollywood in 1919, became head of RKO's art department in 1932, and supervised the design team responsible for more than 200 films from *Topaze* and *King Kong* (both 1933) to *MR. AND MRS. SMITH* and *SUSPICION*. Best remembered for the Art Deco look of the Astaire-Rogers Bakelite interiors, he was also credited for the design of films as different as *Morning Glory* (1933), *The Hunchback of Notre Dame* (1939), and *Citizen Kane* (1941). Dismissed from RKO for alcoholism, he worked at Columbia on *The Fallen Sparrow* (1943), *Gilda* (1946), and a dozen others.

police   "I don't dislike the police, I'm just afraid of them," Hitchcock told François TRUFFAUT. Certainly the director's fear of the police was legendary. Despite his long association with the crime film, he never made a movie with a police hero; with rare exceptions, police officers in his films are always menacing presences seen from outside. Apart from Hitchcock's personal fears, there are several reasons why this should be so. He began to make films before the police hero rose to prominence in such movies as *G-Men* (1935) and *Laura* (1944), inheriting instead the portrayal of the police as witless foils to such master detectives as Sherlock Holmes (who typically runs rings around police officers even dumber than Dr. Watson), a type evoked by the incompetence of the officers tailing

John Robie in TO CATCH A THIEF and by Joe Betts's fatuous remark in THE LODGER: "Great news—they've put me on the Avenger case." The episode in which Joe playfully shows off his authority by handcuffing his girlfriend Daisy Bunting, however, shows a darker and more characteristic side of Hitchcock's police officers, who regularly use their institutional power as a pretext for personal bullying, as Frank Webber does in BLACK-MAIL and Scottie Ferguson, a retired police officer, does at the McKittrick Hotel in VERTIGO. Such figures reveal a double distrust of institutional authority as such (represented by figures such as the headmaster in DOWNHILL, the judge in EASY VIRTUE, and the coroner in REBECCA) and the power of the male gaze to objectify, categorize, and ultimately dehumanize its objects (as in NOTORIOUS and REAR WINDOW). Broadly speaking, Hitchcock's most sympathetic police officers are his least effective professionally: Ted Spencer in SABOTAGE, Colonel Burgoyne in YOUNG AND INNOCENT, Jack Graham in SHADOW OF A DOUBT, the hotel detective Constance Peterson hoodwinks in SPELLBOUND, Wilfred Smith in STAGE FRIGHT. Occasionally the requirements of the plot will bring the solitary heroes into an accord with the police, as in both versions of THE MAN WHO KNEW TOO MUCH, or galvanize heretofore ineffectual police officers into action, as in REAR WINDOW. More generally, police officers are humanized when they are protecting the heroes from still more devastating threats, as in DIAL M FOR MURDER, or when they are beset by problems themselves, as is the long-suffering Chief Inspector Tim Oxford in FRENZY. Usually, however, the police function less as independently conceived characters than as projections of the heroes' paranoia. Very few of the police officers who are pursuing Richard Hannay in THE 39 STEPS, Barry Kane in SABOTEUR, or Roger Thornhill in NORTH BY NORTHWEST leave a strong impression as individuals, and none of them rivals the villains' charismatic power. Nor are any of the fearsome detectives in THE WRONG MAN, Hitchcock's most unrelenting ode to the power of the police, as memorable as the power they represent to force Manny Balestrero into the role of accused criminal. Hitchcock's police, then, are at their most human precisely when they stop acting like the police; their official function is by definition as dehumanizing to them as to their prey.

Pollak, James S. American artist who designed the titles for *The Wheeler Dealers* (1963) and THE BIRDS.

Pollock, Louis (1904–1964) American writer whose career was halted in 1954, when he was mistaken for an author with a similar name and blacklisted. His few credits include the original 1947 story for the ALFRED HITCHCOCK PRESENTS segment "BREAKDOWN," whose screenplay he cowrote with Francis Cockrell. His legal exoneration in 1959 came too late to restart his career.

Pommer, Erich (1889–1966) Pioneering German producer, with GAUMONT-BRITISH in Paris from 1907, who became director of the company's central European operations. In 1915 he founded his own production company, Decla, which merged with Bioscop before being absorbed by UFA in 1923. Even a selective list of films he produced at Decla-Bioscop and UFA is astonishing: *Die Spinnen* (1919), *Das Kabinett des Doktor Caligari* (1919), *Der müde Tod* (1921), *Dr. Mabuse, der Spieler* (1922), *Der letzte Mann* (1924), *Variete* (1925), *Faust* (1926), *Metropolis* (1927). In 1924 Michael BALCON arranged with Pommer for Graham CUTTS's film THE BLACKGUARD, on which Hitchcock was assistant director, to be shot at the UFA studios at Neubabelsberg, an arrangement that was repeated for THE PLEASURE GARDEN. More than 10 years later, after Pommer had fled his homeland after Hitler's rise, settled first in France and then in England, formed MAYFLOWER PRODUCTIONS in partnership with Charles LAUGHTON, and directed a Mayflower film of his own (*Vessel of Wrath,* 1938), Hitchcock directed the Mayflower property JAMAICA INN. Hardly had the film been completed than the peripatetic Pommer was in Hollywood to produce *They Knew What They Wanted* and *Dance, Girl, Dance* (both 1940), When the war ended, he returned to Germany to help rebuild the crippled industry before returning in 1956 to Hollywood, where he died 10 years later.

Potevin, Jim (1899–1989) American electrician on sporadic Hollywood productions from 1935. He served as lighting technician on ROPE and ended his career as chief electrician for the television series *The Fugitive* (1963–67).

Poulenc, Francis (1899–1963) French composer. A largely self-taught composer and pianist, he became a member during the twenties of the Groupe des Six, musicians united in their opposition to the romantic excesses of the prevailing Wagner-Strauss orthodoxy. Of all the original group, he remained the most consistently faithful in his modesty and satirical wit to this antiromantic creed despite the lyricism of much of his music, for example the *Mouvements perpètuels* (1918), which first became the piano tune Philip Morgan plays repeatedly but is unable to finish in ROPE and which, in the absence of other music composed for the film, became the basis for its title music as well. Poulenc also wrote four scores for French films himself; a fifth, for *Voleur de vie* (1998), is based, like that of *Rope,* on his nonfilm music.

Pounds, Louie British stage actress whose sole film credit is the Widow Windeatt in THE FARMER'S WIFE.

Powell, Joynson British actor whose only film credit is the judge who presides over Diana Baring's trial in MURDER!

practical jokes Hitchcock was a lifelong joker on and off the set. Even at school, he had a reputation for bullying smaller boys, and as he grew into an adult, his penchant for jokes at other people's expense continued. John Russell TAYLOR relates several of Hitchcock's most elaborate jokes—giving a dinner party for Gerald DU MAURIER in which every item served had been colored blue; exiting a hotel elevator on the pregnant line, "I didn't think one shot would cause so much blood," and betting a grip that he could not spend overnight in the studio handcuffed to a camera and then spiking the brandy he left him with a laxative—as examples of "the workings of an active fantasy and an almost surrealistic sense of the incongruous and bizarre." When Donald SPOTO recounts the same jokes, they sound sadistic and cruel. It is certainly possible to see Hitchcock, who was fond of recycling the same jokes over and over again—he was still trying the

elevator line with Peter BOGDANOVICH in 1964—as a sadist intent on using his films as sardonic practical jokes designed to demonstrate his superiority to viewers by manipulating them into vulnerable and perhaps unpleasant emotional states, while at the same time remaining above them as a disinterested aesthete. But Hitchcock the sadist is surely overshadowed by Hitchcock the fantasist whose films, if not his jokes in private life, explore nightmare fantasies he shares with his viewers (a range that extends from his often-remarked fear of the police to more-comic nightmares such as the repeated immurings and exhumations in THE TROUBLE WITH HARRY and the improbably romantic fantasies in TO CATCH A THIEF) rather than inflicting nightmares he does not share. At the very least, viewers who feel hoodwinked by the lying flashback of STAGE FRIGHT, the deceptive presentation of Mrs. Bates in PSYCHO, or the bird attacks in THE BIRDS always have the option of watching the films again in the light of the dramatic irony afforded by hindsight.

Pratt, Judson (1916–) Burly American character actor who made his film debut as Murphy in I CONFESS and then went on to play some 60 roles in films and television, including the postmaster in the ALFRED HITCHCOCK PRESENTS episode "Mail Order Prophet" (1957), before retiring after *F.I.S.T.* (1978).

Prentiss, Lucy American actress who plays Jackie Chester's frantic mother Amy in the ALFRED HITCHCOCK PRESENTS episode "BANG! YOU'RE DEAD."

Press, Marvin (1915–1968) American character actor whose 10 film and television appearances, 1947–65, include Chessy in the ALFRED HITCHCOCK PRESENTS segment "BREAKDOWN."

Previn, Charles (1888–1973) American composer and conductor who served as musical director on SABOTEUR and some 200 UNIVERSAL films, composing the scores for many of them as well.

Price, Theodore (1924–) American literary scholar, professor of English and Comparative Literature at Montclair State College. His *Hitchcock and Homosexuality: His 50-Year Obsession with Jack* the Ripper and the Superbitch Prostitute—*A Psychoanalytic View* (Scarecrow, 1992) advances three leading arguments: (1) that the "homosexual triptych" of MURDER!, ROPE, and STRANGERS ON A TRAIN, identified by Eric ROHMER and Clsude CHABROL, be joined by a fourth film, THE PARADINE CASE, whose hero he compares to the heroine of Strindberg's play *Miss Julie;* (2) that most of Hitchcock's films have homosexual overtones signaled by the involvement of homosexual writers or performers, homosexual situations, male characters with a pathological hatred for women (or the reverse, as in MARNIE), or the feminizing of the heroes through passivity, transvestism, physical weakness, or bondage; and (3) that Hitchcock's interest in homosexuality is only part of a deeper misogyny that runs throughout his films, emerging in particular in the "Supertheme" of Jack the Ripper as the hero who avenges himself on the superbitch prostitute who deserves to die. After a detailed examination of REBECCA, *The Paradine Case,* I CONFESS, VERTIGO, PSYCHO, *Marnie,* and TORN CURTAIN, he turns to German silent cinema, especially *Anders als die Anderen* (1919) and *Mikael* (1924), as models for Hitchcock's handling of homosexuality.

Price, Vincent (1911–1993) Towering, cultivated American character actor forever identified with Grand Guignol. After studying art and literature at Yale and the University of London, he made his West End debut in 1935 and his film debut three years later. Although his cultivated voice and sculpted features initially seemed to destine him for such costume roles as Sir Walter Raleigh in *The Private Lives of Elizabeth and Essex* (1939), the Duke of Clarence in *Tower of London* (1939), and Clifford Pynchon in *The House of the Seven Gables* (1940), he made the most lasting impression of his 200 film and television appearances in such horror films as *House of Wax* (1953) and Roger Corman's Poe cycle (*House of Usher,* 1960, etc.), in which he served as an urbane, self-mocking guide to dozens of creaky manses. A noted expert on food and the visual arts, he satirized both interests when he was cast in the ALFRED HITCHCOCK PRESENTS episode "THE PERFECT CRIME" as Charles Courtney, the detective whose

arrogant pride in his own powers is so great that he strangles the man who threatens to unmask his one mistake and bakes his body in a pottery kiln.

Priestley, J(ohn) B(oynton) (1894–1984) Prodigiously prolific British novelist, essayist, playwright, and producer often cited by Hitchcock as a personal influence. Returning from war service, he soon established himself as a journalist, reviewer, and essayist, turning to fiction with the picaresque, characteristically digressive *The Good Companions* (1929; filmed 1933). Long fascinated by the philosophical problem of time, he wrote not only *Man and Time* (1964), a long essay on the subject, but also two plays, *Dangerous Crossing* (1932; filmed in 1934) and *An Inspector Calls* (1946; filmed in 1954) that openly play with dramatic time to explore the characters' natures. He staged more than a dozen of his own plays in theaters he managed during the thirties, and in addition to seeing many of his own works adapted to the screen—his comic horror novel *Benighted* (1927), for example, was the basis for two films titled *The Old Dark House* (1932, 1963)—worked intermittently

J.B. Priestley

between 1934 and 1950 on five films himself, supplying additional dialogue in *JAMAICA INN* for Charles LAUGHTON, who had starred in the first version of *The Old Dark House.*

Prince, William (1913–1996)

Stage-trained American character actor who after an uncertain Hollywood start in the forties achieved his greatest success in television soap operas, playing Dr. Jerry Malone in *Young Dr. Malone* (1958–59), Ken Baxter in *Another World* (1964–65), Senator Ben Travis in *The Edge of Night* (1968–69), and Russell Barry in *A World Apart* (1970–71). He made one of his rare returns to the big screen to play the kidnapped Bishop Wood in *FAMILY PLOT* before settling into another 50 television roles.

Princess of New York, The

Famous Players–Lasky, 1921. **Director:** Donald Crisp; **Screenplay:** Margaret Turnbull; **Cast:** David Powell (Geoffrey Kingsward), Mary Glynne (Helen Stanton), Saba Raleigh (Mrs. Raffan), George Bellamy (Sir George Meretham), Dorothy Fane (Violet Meretham), Ivo Dawson (Allan Meretham), Philip Hewland (Colonel Kingsward), R. Heaton Gray (Mr. Greet), Wyndham Guise (Eardley Smith), Jane West (Mrs. Eardley Smith), H. Lloyd (moneylender), Lionel Yorke (Reddish), William Parry (magistrate).

Seventh of the 12 silent films (1920–22) for which Hitchcock designed intertitles.

Pritchard, Robert (1893–1959)

American sound technician, at UNIVERSAL for *SHADOW OF A DOUBT* and more than 60 other films from 1939 to 1959, who died just before Hitchcock returned to the studio for *THE BIRDS.*

Prude's Fall, The

Balcon-Saville-Freedman, Wardour & F.; 1924. **Producer:** Michael Balcon; **Director:** Graham Cutts; **Assistant director:** Alfred Hitchcock; **Screenplay:** Alfred Hitchcock, based on the play by Rudolph Besier; **Art director:** Alfred Hitchcock; **Cast:** Jane Novak (Beatrice Audley), Julanne Johnson (Sonia Roubetsky), Warwick Ward (Andre le Briquet), Hugh Miller (Marquis de Rocqueville), Gladys Jennings (Laura Westonry), Miles Mander (Sir Neville Moreton), Henry Vibart (Dean Carey), Marie Ault (Mrs. Masters), Betty Compson.

Fourth of the five Cutts films (1923–25) on which Hitchcock served as assistant director, scenarist, and art director.

Psycho

(Alternative titles: *Wimpy* [fake working title], *Psychose, Psyco*) Paramount-Shamley, 109 minutes, June 1960. **Producer:** Alfred Hitchcock; **Director:** Alfred Hitchcock; **Screenplay:** Joseph Stefano, based on the novel by Robert Bloch; **Cinematographer:** John L. Russell; **Assistant director:** Hilton A. Green; **Art directors:** Joseph Hurley and Robert Clatworthy; **Set decoration:** George Milo; **Costumes:** Helen Colvig; **Wardrobe supervisor:** Rita Riggs; **Makeup:** Robert Dawn and Jack Barron; **Hairstyles:** Florence Bush; **Special pictorial consultant:** Saul Bass; **Sound:** William Russell and Waldon O. Watson; **Unit manager:** Lew Leary; **Editor:** George Tomasini; **Titles:** Saul Bass; **Music:** Bernard Herrmann; **Cast:** Anthony Perkins (Norman Bates), Janet Leigh (Marion Crane), Vera Miles (Lila Crane), John Gavin (Sam Loomis), Martin Balsam (Milton Arbogast), John McIntire (Sheriff Chambers), Lurene Tuttle (Mrs. Chambers), Simon Oakland (Dr. Richman), Frank Albertson (Cassidy), Patricia Hitchcock (Caroline), Vaughn Taylor (George Lowery), Mort Mills (highway patrolman), John Anderson (California Charlie), Frank Killmond (Bob Summerfield), Helen Wallace (customer in Sam's store), George Eldridge (chief of police), Francis De Sales, Sam Flint (officials), Ted Knight (prison guard), Margo Epper (Mother's stand-in), Marli Renfro (Janet Leigh's stand-in), June Gleason, Myra Jones, Paul Matthews, Frank Vinci, John Drake, Ann Dore (stand-ins), Virginia Gregg, Paul Jasmin, Jeanette Nolan (Mother's voice).

Hitchcock's most famous film began when—eager to compete with imitators from William Castle to Henri-Georges Clouzot who were rivaling his reputation for shockers, alerted by Peggy ROBERTSON to an enthusiastic review of Robert BLOCH's novel *Psycho,* and undeterred by a PARAMOUNT reader's report that labeled it "too repulsive for films"—he purchased the film rights anonymously for $9,000 in April 1959 and presented the property to the studio. When they refused to finance it, despite a contract

Norman Bates (Anthony Perkins), doubled by one of *Psycho's* many strategic reflecting surfaces, meeting Marion Crane (Janet Leigh) outside Cabin 1 of the Bates Motel. *(National Film Society Archive)*

that gave the director carte blanche on every film he could bring in under $3 million, he proposed to finance the film himself if they would distribute it, exchanging his $250,000 fee for 60 percent ownership of the negative, and keeping costs down by shooting the project with a television crew at UNIVERSAL's Revue Studios. Unable to resist such a low-risk deal despite their reservations about the novel's unsavory qualities—its lack of sympathetic characters or glamorous locations, its abrupt violence, its candid portrayal of sexual fetishes—the studio agreed, and Hitchcock asked James P. CAVANAGH, who had written several episodes of ALFRED HITCHCOCK PRESENTS, for a screenplay. Disappointed with Cavanagh's earnest, moralizing treatment of the story, however, he replaced him with Joseph STEFANO, another relative newcomer, who, hired on a weekly contract in

September, conceived the idea of extending the film's first act to build viewers' identification with the heroine who steals $40,000 from her boss and runs off to her boyfriend. In the meantime, Hitchcock had begun to cast his most cost-conscious production from among the thinning ranks of Hollywood contract players. Three of the four leads were quickly cast because Anthony PERKINS was under contract to Paramount, John GAVIN to Universal, and Vera MILES to Hitchcock himself. For the key role of Marion Crane, Hitchcock wanted the biggest star he could afford to kill off, increasing the shock of her death. After considering Eva Marie SAINT, Piper Laurie, Martha Hyer, Hope Lange, Shirley Jones, and Lana Turner, he settled on Janet LEIGH, who, like Perkins, had never before been associated with thrillers. The film, budgeted at $800,000, began to shoot on November 30, 1959 and wrapped on February 1. Of this schedule, an entire week was devoted to the 70 shots of the shower scene—described at length in Stephen REBELLO's *Alfred Hitchcock and the Making of Psycho* and Leigh's own *Psycho: Behind the Scenes of the Classic Thriller*—and another week to the sequence immediately following in which Norman BATES discovers Marion's body and cleans up the bathroom. Finding it impossible to backlight Perkins strongly enough to pass as Mrs. Bates in the shower scene, Hitchcock cast stuntwoman Margo Epper in the role, with Ann Dore doubling her in turn in several shots; her offscreen voice was supplied by a soundtrack combining the voices of mimic Paul Jasmin and actresses Virginia Gregg and Jeanette Nolan. Both Stephen REBELLO and Leigh have disputed the claims of Saul BASS, the visual consultant who designed the film's titles and storyboarded the shower sequence, to have shot the sequence himself. The film's critical reception was marked by distaste, but its commercial release, bolstered by a shrewd, Clouzot-inspired publicity campaign asking the audience not to reveal the ending and forbidding entrance once the film had begun, was phenomenally successful, giving it one of the best profit-to-cost ratios in Hollywood history and making its director a wealthy man.

Ironically, the very features that made *Psycho* repellent to so many early reviewers—its brusquely efficient direction, its refusal to glamorize its story in conventional Hollywood terms, its breaching of a powerful convention by killing off its leading lady without warning, its unprecedented violence whose ferocity seems an attack on the audience along with the heroine, its avoidance of a happy ending—helped secure its status as the classic Hitchcock film even for audiences who never saw it. Even more ironically, most of those features are impossible to recover today for viewers who (often well acquainted with the film's three sequels or its literal 1998 remake by Gus Van Sant) know perfectly well what is going to happen in the story long before it does. The surprise of Marion's murder, which breaks the director's cardinal rule prescribing suspense instead, has been weathered by familiarity and imitation, leaving only the suspense of watching Marion escape from her hometown of Phoenix and hurtle toward her doom—and the careful pattern of imagery that predicts that doom from the opening scene. As her lover Sam Loomis complains that he's "tired of sweating for people who aren't there," Marion gently reminds him, "Hotels of this sort aren't interested in you when you come in, but when your time is up —." Later, despite her assurance to her officemate Caroline that "you can't buy off unhappiness with pills" like the tranquilizers Caroline's mother gave her on her wedding day, Marion follows the advice of her victim, Texas oilman Tom Cassidy, by attempting to buy off her own unhappiness with his money, looking forward to the shopper in Sam's hardware store who, looking at poisons, maintains, in the film's first speech since Norman discovered Marion's body: "Insect or man, death should always be painless." Even the windshield wipers in Marion's car foretell the scene of her death, as the thief who wanted to buy off unhappiness is brutally wiped out of Norman's life. Similarly, Norman's fatal passive-aggressiveness is signaled by two images: murderous eyes (which link Norman's fear of being watched, the extreme closeup of his spying on Marion shortly before he kills her, the dissolve from a closeup of Marion's blood swirling down the bathtub drain to a closeup of her dead eye, the climactic shot of the dead eye sockets in Mrs. Bates's skeleton) and birds (which indicate, from Marion's last name and hometown to Mrs. Bates's final voiceover comment, "As if

I could do anything but just sit and stare like one of his stuffed birds," that the most dangerous agents are those who do not think of themselves as agents at all). *Psycho* has been the most widely discussed of all Hitchcock's films. Twenty years before Rebello's production history and Leigh's third-person reminiscence appeared, James NAREMORE had already published his *Filmguide to* Psycho. The two most influential essays on the film remain Robin WOOD's discussion of the ways it manipulates viewers' sympathies and Raymond BELLOUR's analysis of the patterns that link Norman's psychosis to Marion's more statistically normal neurosis.

psychoanalysis Hitchcock's work has been closely associated with psychoanalysis for more than a half-century. It is hardly surprising that SPELLBOUND is, with *Lady in the Dark* (1944), one of the first Hollywood films to use the terms and situations of psychotherapy to drive the plot; the Freudian dialogue, which encourages patients under the direction of a trusted therapist to recall traumatic memories that have crippled the subconscious and weave them into a more curative conscious narrative, might well serve as a basis for the ideal relationship the director prescribed for the viewers he proposed to expose to the therapeutic shocks a deadening culture denied them. For years after Constance Peterson lovingly interrogates John Ballantine in *Spellbound,* Hitchcock's lovers ask each other probing questions in films as different as NOTORIOUS, THE PARADINE CASE, UNDER CAPRICORN, I CONFESS, REAR WINDOW, TO CATCH A THIEF, VERTIGO, and MARNIE designed not only to uncover their hidden motives but also to urge them to act differently.

Although the psychoanalytic attention the films have attracted from theorists has been less explicitly therapeutic than diagnostic, it maintains in every instance some vestige of the therapeutic motive. Raymond BELLOUR, whose minutely detailed analysis of the crop-dusting sequence from NORTH BY NORTHWEST is motivated by his attempt to map the economy of an inscription of Oedipal desire onto the categories of the LACANIAN symbolic, is constantly concerned to dramatize the costs of such a patriarchal, heteroideological inscription. Laura MUL-

VEY harbors a still more therapeutic attitude toward her audience in the intention she ascribes for her analysis of the exemplary power of the male gaze in Hitchcock: to make the traditional scopophilic pleasures of narrative cinema impossible by analyzing and demystifying them. Tania MODLESKI's discussion of the mechanisms by which Hitchcock's films repress, for example, the male hero's formative relationship with his mother leads even more forthrightly to "the crucial question facing feminist theory . . . 'What are the consequences *for women* of this repression?'" And Robert SAMUELS's use of Lacan's theory of ethics to disentangle "the bi-textual Real" from "the main mechanisms of control that the dominant heterosexist Symbolic order employs in order to contain and silence diverse forms of desire and identification" points just as clearly to a culturally therapeutic alternative understanding of the Real. It is reassuring to think that, however roughly Hitchcock's films may treat both their characters and their viewers, the director and his commentators are united in their desire to cure the culture from which they all spring.

Purdom, Tita American actress who played two roles in *ALFRED HITCHCOCK PRESENTS*: the decorously murderous Millicent Princey in "WET SATURDAY" and Maude in "Miss Bracegirdle Does Her Duty" (1958).

pure cinema The reputation Hitchcock established as a film artist in the early sixties depended largely on his advocacy of *pure cinema,* a term that appears most prominently in three contexts in interviews he gave in 1962 and 1963. Asked for a definition of the term by Peter BOGDANOVICH, he replied: "Pure cinema is complementary pieces of film put together, like notes of music make a melody. There are two primary uses of cutting or montage in film: montage to create ideas—and montage to create violence or emotions." An action sequence, he added, "is much more effective if it's done in montage because you involve the audience much more. . . . And the other, of course, is the juxtaposition of imagery relating to the mind of the individual." He glossed this second variety of montage in his series of interviews with Françcois TRUFFAUT by referring to the intercutting of event

shots and reaction shots in *Rear Window* as "the purest expression of a cinematic idea," one that allowed him to make "a purely cinematic film." Both these formulations seem to echo V.I. Pudovkin (whom Hitchcock cites) and Sergei Eisenstein (whom he does not) and emphasize editing as the foundation of pure cinema. In discussing PSYCHO with Truffaut, however, Hitchcock defined this notion more broadly in terms of audience engagement: "I don't care about the subject matter; I don't care about the acting; but I do care about the pieces of film and the photography and the sound track and all of the technical ingredients that made the audience scream. . . . It wasn't a message that stirred the audiences, nor was it a great performance or the enjoyment of the novel. They were aroused by pure film." Although the elements Hitchcock enumerates here begin with editing, they are less notable for what they include than what they exclude: the subject matter, the performances, the message, the source novel—all the elements over which the director has no control. Whether it is defined in terms of the specific technique of montage or the more general goal of engaging or moving or scaring the audience, then Hitchcock's concept of pure cinema seems to have been calculated to efface everyone but himself and the audience from the cinematic apparatus and to have succeeded as a recipe for exactly the kind of auteurism that would establish film as the art form his practice exemplified. Dated, self-aggrandizing, and inconsistent as this concept may have grown to seem, its importance in establishing the artistic pretensions of both Hitchcock and cinema in general can hardly be overstated.

Pye, Merrill (1901–1975) Veteran American art director, in Hollywood from 1925, who came to MGM in 1933 and stayed to design the visuals for more than 50 films, to earn credit for musical presentation in another dozen, and to direct a single film, *Musical Masterpieces* (1946), that combined both his interests. After working on NORTH BY NORTH-WEST, he spent the next several years on several television series—*The Twilight Zone* (1959–65), *Outlaws* (1960–62), *Combat* (1962–67), and *The Man from U.N.C.L.E.* (1964–68)—before concluding his career with another half-dozen films.

Quayle, (Sir) Anthony (1913–1989) British stage actor, born John Anthony Quayle. After studying at the Royal Academy for the Dramatic Arts, he made his theatrical debut in 1931. From 1948 to 1956 he directed the Shakespeare Memorial Theatre in Stratford-upon-Avon, alternating his many roles onstage with occasional work in films. One of his first film roles after relinquishing his post was Frank O'Connor, Manny Balestrero's earnest, inexpert lawyer in THE WRONG MAN. He went on to play more than 60 film and television roles, sometimes Shakespearean or classical, but more often stiff-upper-lip Hollywood Englishmen from Major Roy Franklin in *The Guns of Navarone* (1961) to Inspector Hubbard in the television remake of DIAL M FOR MURDER (1981).

Quinn, William (1912–1994) Doughty American character actor in more than 100 roles, mostly as television outdoorsmen or authority figures, from 1958. Although he appeared as Mr. Dutton in the ALFRED HITCHCOCK PRESENTS segment "You Can't Be a Little Girl All Your Life" (1961), as Mr. Penny in THE ALFRED HITCHCOCK HOUR segment "How to Get Rid of Your Wife" (1963), and as the man in the Tides Café in THE BIRDS, he is much better known for his regular roles in *The Rifleman* (1958), *McHale's Navy* (1962–65), *McMillan and Wife* (1976–77), and *All in the Family* (1978–83).

Radford, Basil (1897–1952) Mustachioed British character comedian who made his stage debut in 1922, his film debut in *Barnum Was Right* (1929). Already memorably browbeaten as Erica Burgoyne's uncle in YOUNG AND INNOCENT, he rose to character stardom when he was paired with Naunton WAYNE as the chauvinistically oblivious Englishmen abroad in THE LADY VANISHES. The two were reunited for similar roles in *Night Train to Munich* (1939), *Crooks' Tour* (1941), *Millions Like Us* (1943), *Dead of Night* (1945), and *Passport to Pimlico* (1949). In the meantime, Radford, who had also played Sir Humphrey Pengallan's friend Lord George in JAMAICA INN, closed out his career by starring as Captain Waggett in *Whiskey Galore!* (1949) and writing the story for his final film, *The Galloping Major* (1951).

radio   Scholars have yet to ascertain the full extent of Hitchcock's work for American radio. The fullest accounts to date are by Martin GRAMS, Jr., (in the opening section of his book coauthored with Patrik WIKSTROM and in a section of Ken MOGG's book) and by Charles Huck (also appearing in Grams and Wikstrom's publication); both include air dates and program and cast credits for much of the radio programming associated with Hitchcock. The director was interviewed by Otis Ferguson on radio as early as August 1937, when he was visiting Holly-

wood at the invitation of David O. SELZNICK, and again on *The Royal Gelatin Hour* on April 13, 1939, to promote REBECCA. His later interviews, quiz-show panels, and guest appearances included segments on *Information Please* (June 27, 1941, and January 22, 1943), *The Texaco Star Theater* (January 24, 1943), *The Charlie McCarthy Show* (March 21, 1948), and *Screen Directors' Playhouse* (January 30, 1949, and November 11, 1950).

In the meantime, *The Lux Radio Theatre* had presented "The 39 Steps," the first of many abridged adaptations of a Hitchcock film, on December 13, 1937; three further adaptations of the story would follow. Most of Hitchcock's contemporaneous films similarly aired in several different versions. *Rebecca* was adapted at least 10 times (including a 1938 version released more than a year before Hitchcock's film); MR. AND MRS SMITH and SHADOW OF A DOUBT eight times each; SUSPICION six times; SPELLBOUND, NOTORIOUS, and STRANGERS ON A TRAIN twice each; and THE LADY VANISHES, JAMAICA INN, FOREIGN CORRESPONDENT, LIFEBOAT, THE PARADINE CASE, and I CONFESS once each. Except for being mentioned as the director of whatever forthcoming film he had in hand or, less often, for interpolating comments on the action, Hitchcock generally had nothing to do with these projects nor the many adaptations of THE LODGER—by far the most popular of all Hitchcock-directed film properties, especially after the release of

John Brahm's 1944 remake. The very first of these *Lodger* adaptations, however, is notable for three reasons. As part of the July 22, 1940, broadcast of CBS's *Forecast* anthology series, it inaugurated the long-running radio anthology *Suspense*; the "Hitchcock" who hosted the segment was actually voiced by Joseph Kearns; and the episode omitted the story's ending, allowing Herbert MARSHALL, the rest of the cast, and Kearn's Hitchcock to debate how it ought to end. The real Hitchcock took a single acting role in radio—his only true acting credit in any medium—costarring with Peter LORRE and Boris Karloff in "O Is for Old Wives' Tales," a 1958 episode of *As Easy as A.B.C.*

In addition to providing an outlet for recycling his stories, radio proved a potent influence on Hitchcock as well. Several of his own television episodes—the "FOUR O'CLOCK" segment of *Suspicion,* the *ALFRED HITCHCOCK PRESENTS* episodes "Alibi Me" "The Long Shot," and "Salvage" (the last originally titled "The Long Wait"), and *THE ALFRED HITCHCOCK HOUR* episode "The Evil of Adelaide Winters"—began life as radio broadcasts on *Suspense*, and Hitchcock first heard "BREAKDOWN" in a 1949 broadcast of the *Prudential Family Hour of Stars*. The 1951 *Suspense* segment "Death on My Hands" drew his attention to its scriptwriter, John Michael HAYES, who would later write the screenplays for four of his films at PARAMOUNT PICTURES. And years before Hitchcock's film *THE BIRDS*, the story was dramatized for radio in 1953 and in 1954.

Although he was seldom heard in radio broadcasts and never directed them, Hitchcock twice attempted to kindle interest in a radio program he could host himself. In 1945 he hosted an audition segment based on Francis ILES's novel *Malice Aforethought* for a series to be called *Once Upon a Midnight*, and two years later he hosted yet another audition based on the same novel but with a different script, cast, and crew for a program titled *The Alfred Hitchcock Show*. Since no director credit survives for either pilot, Hitchcock may have directed either or both. But ABC, the network to which both pilots were submitted, expressed no interest in either series, and Hitchcock would have to wait nearly 10 years for success in his own weekly programs, *Alfred Hitchcock Presents* and *The Alfred Hitchcock Hour*, in the rival medium of television. His final (posthumous) television appearances introducing segments of THE NEW ALFRED HITCHCOCK PRESENTS from 1985 through 1989 were anticipated by his resurrection to introduce segments of a South American radio series title *The Hitchcock Half Hour* just a few years after his death.

Ragan, Mike (1918–1995)   American character actor, also known as Holly Bane. Following his debut in *Wake Island* (1942), he played more than 100 film and television roles, often as western outlaws. He appeared in seven episodes of ALFRED HITCHCOCK PRESENTS—as an escaping convict in "BREAKDOWN," the cab driver in "Momentum" (1956), the firefighter in "Kill with Kindness" (1956), an unidentified bit in "On the Nose" (1958), Alfredo in "Madame Mystery" (1960), the robbery victim Pete in "The Little Man Who Was There" (1960), and Mr. Cheever, the plumber in "THE HORSEPLAYER"—and one in THE ALFRED HITCHCOCK HOUR, the bartender in "Goodbye, George" (1963).

Rains, Claude (1889–1967)   Suavely accomplished British character actor, onstage from 11, who made his film debut in *The Invisible Man* (1933) when Bela Lugosi turned down the role because he would not be seen in it. He made the part his own through the expressive use of his voice—trained by elocution lessons for which Sir Herbert Beerbohm Tree had paid when he found Rains's elocution inexact—and went on to featured and occasional starring film and television roles. Short and nondescript, he provided effective antiromantic foils to many other more handsome leads. Rains was especially impressive in providing mild support to the strong-willed Bette Davis in *Now, Voyager* (1942), *Mr. Skeffington* (1944), and *Deception* (1946) and playing charming villains like the Nazi industrialist Alexander Sebastian in NOTORIOUS and morally compromised heroes like Father Amion, the comically tormented gambler in the ALFRED HITCHCOCK PRESENTS episode "THE HORSEPLAYER." He was nominated for Academy Awards for his roles as Jefferson Smith's corrupt mentor Senator Joseph Blaine in *Mr.*

Smith Goes to Washington (1939), the weathervane police prefect Captain Louis Renault in *Casablanca* (1942), the determinedly unglamorous Job Skeffington in *Mr. Skeffington* (1944), and the hopelessly smitten Sebastian in *Notorious,* a role for which Hitchcock had wanted Clifton Webb. The first of his five wives was actress Isabel JEANS.

Randolph, Elsie (1901–1982) British actress with extensive revue experience, often as the partner of Jack Buchanan. By the time she made her film debut in RICH AND STRANGE, her comically predatory manner already made her appropriate to cast as the old maid Miss Imrie; 40 years and a scant 10 films later, she played Gladys, the leering, minatory desk clerk at the Coburg Hotel in FRENZY.

Ransford, Maurice (1896–1963) American art director, former architect, who worked on nearly 50 20TH CENTURY-FOX films of the forties and fifties, often in collaboration with Lyle WHEELER, head of the Fox art department. His first important assignment was LIFEBOAT; a year later he was nominated for an Oscar for *Leave Her to Heaven* (1945) and received further nominations for *The Foxes of Harrow* (1947) and *Titanic* (1953).

Raphaelson, Samson (1896–1983) American screenwriter who came to the theater by way of advertising and journalism and then to Hollywood when his play *The Jazz Singer* (1925), based on his 1922 story "Day of Atonement," was adapted as the first feature film with synchronized dialogue. He contributed to many of the effervescent comedies filmed by Ernst Lubitsch (*The Smiling Lieutenant,* 1931; *One Hour with You,* 1932; *Trouble in Paradise,* 1932; *The Merry Widow,* 1934; *Angel,* 1937; *The Shop Around the Corner,* 1940; *Heaven Can Wait,* 1943; *That Lady in Ermine,* 1948) but worked on several dramatic projects as well. The most problematic of these was SUSPICION. Though Hitchcock, who admired Raphaelson's work, had asked RKO to hire him, their sensibilities never meshed, and the screenplay, contrary to Hitchcock's usual practice, became a textbook example of the wrong kind of collaboration, filled with additions by Joan HARRISON and

Alma REVILLE and so uncertain in its direction that the studio could not even decide on a title for the project. Miraculously, the film was a commercial success, winning Joan FONTAINE the Oscar she had been denied for REBECCA.

Raubicheck, Walter (1950–) American academic, associate professor of English at Pace University and coeditor with Walter SREBNICK of *Hitchcock's Rereleased Films: From* Rope *to* Vertigo (Wayne State University Press, 1991), a collection of 15 papers from a 1986 Pace conference celebrating the rerelease, after 10 years of unavailability, of ROPE, REAR WINDOW, THE TROUBLE WITH HARRY, THE MAN WHO KNEW TOO MUCH (1956), and VERTIGO. The essays, together with an appended talk and discussion led by Samuel TAYLOR on the screenplay of *Vertigo,* are prefaced by a brief foreword by Andrew SARRIS and a substantial introduction by the editors that reviews the legal circumstances under which the films were withheld from and returned to release, places Hitchcock scholarship within the broader currents of contemporaneous film theory, discusses the range of approaches represented by the essays—from the auteurism of Thomas M. LEITCH and Lesley BRILL to the psychoanalysis of Robin WOOD to the technological narratology of John BELTON—and notes their shared assumption that all five of the rereleased films are central to any assessment of Hitchcock's career, and two of them, *Rear Window* and *Vertigo,* crucial to establishing his place within film history generally.

Rawlinson, A.R. (b. 1894) British screenwriter who collaborated on more than 40 screenplays beginning in 1932. His most important projects included THE MAN WHO KNEW TOO MUCH (1934), *Jew Süss* (1934), and *Gaslight* (1939), and he served as an uncredited script doctor on *King Solomon's Mines* (1937).

Raymond, Gene (1908–1998) Blond, bland American leading man of the thirties, born Raymond Guion. Onstage from five years of age, he made his film debut in 1931 and soon settled into a round of earnest would-be romantic leads and second leads, upstaged by the likes of Clark Gable (in *Red Dust,*

1932), Fred Astaire (in *Flying Down to Rio,* 1933), and Robert MONTGOMERY (in *MR. AND MRS. SMITH,* in which he played David's partner–turned–Ann's imperturbable suitor Jeff Custer). Long married to musical star Jeanette MacDonald, he spent much of his later years traveling with her and nursing her in her final illness, but he found time to direct one film, *Million Dollar Weekend* (1948), and to host *Fireside Theater* (1953–55) and two other television programs.

Rear Window (Alternative titles: *Das Fenster zum Hof, Fenêtre su cour, La finestra sul cortile*) Paramount, 112 minutes, July 1954. **Producer:** Alfred Hitchcock; **Director:** Alfred Hitchcock; **Screenplay:** John Michael Hayes, based on "It Had to Be Murder," a short story by Cornell Woolrich; **Cinematographer:** Robert Burks; **Camera operator:** William Schurr; **Assistant camera:** Leonard South; **Assistant director:** Herbert Coleman; **Art directors:** Hal Pereira and Joseph MacMillan Johnson; **Set decorators:** Sam Comer and Ray Moyer; **Costumes:** Edith Head; **Makeup:** Wally Westmore; **Sound:** Harry Lindgren and John Cape; **Technical adviser:** Bob Landry; **Editor:** George Tomasini; **Technicolor consultant:** Richard Mueller; **Special effects:** John P. Fulton; **Special visual effects:** Irwin Roberts; **Music:** Franz Waxman; **Cast:** James Stewart (L.B. Jefferies), Grace Kelly (Lisa Fremont), Wendell Corey (Tom Doyle), Thelma Ritter (Stella), Raymond Burr (Lars Thorwald), Judith Evelyn (Miss Lonelyhearts), Ross Bagdasarian (songwriter), Georgine Darcy (Miss Torso), Sara Berner (woman on fire escape), Frank Cady (man on fire escape), Jesslyn Fax (sculptress), Irene Winston (Anna Thorwald), Rand Harper (Harry, newlywed man), Havis Davenport (his wife), Alan Lee (landlord), Ralph Smiley (Carl, the waiter), Iphigenie Castiglioni (woman with bird), Jerry Antes (dancer), Barbara Bailey (choreographer), Marla English, Kathryn Grant (party girls), Bess Flowers (woman with poodle), Anthony Warde (detective), Len Hendry, Mike Mahoney (police officers), Benny Bartlett (Miss Torso's friend), Fred Graham (stunt detective), Harry Landers, Dick Simmons.

Hitchcock's 40th feature—his first at PARAMOUNT, his first written by John Michael HAYES, and his final, most elaborate, and most successful one-set film—began in a 1942 Cornell WOOLRICH story whose rights were sold to Patron, Inc., a produc-

tion company formed by Hitchcock and James STEWART in 1953, while Hitchcock was still working on *DIAL M FOR MURDER.* Introduced to Hayes by the MCA agent they shared, he asked him to write a treatment, which he submitted to Paramount in September. Donald SPOTO reports that the director did not even send Grace KELLY a treatment; he merely summoned her for wardrobe fittings, leading her to drop the role she had been offered as Evie in *On the Waterfront.* Given the benefit of working with two stars with whom he felt so comfortable and with his veteran cinematographer Robert BURKS and costume designer Edith HEAD, Hitchcock felt more free than usual to develop the characters in what had been a very short story, and he asked Hayes to meet with Kelly so that he could tailor the character of Lisa Fremont more closely to her. Discovering that Kelly had a sense of humor none of her earlier projects (certainly not *DIAL M FOR MURDER*) had tapped, Hayes, with little initial input from Hitchcock, fashioned a skein of romantic byplay for her character and Stewart's, providing Hitchcock with perhaps the wittiest of all his scripts. The director seemed to revel in the difficulties of shooting on the enormous single set constructed to mimic a block of 31 apartments (the largest set ever constructed on the Paramount lot, and one that promptly became an attraction for visitors to the studio), particularly the occasional challenge of directing both foreground action in the photographer hero L.B. Jefferies's apartment and distant action in the background apartments in perfect synchronization through an intercom that allowed the unseen director to communicate with the distant actors, who ranged from Ross BAGDASARIAN, the future voice of Alvin and the Chipmunks, to Raymond BURR, the suspected murderer made up to look like Hitchcock's old boss David O. SELZNICK. Shooting proceeded from November 1953 through January 1954 in a state of relaxed optimism, and the film, which set the seal on Kelly's stardom, proved a substantial hit, garnering enthusiastic reviews and earning in its first run more than $5 million on a production budget of little more than $2 million. Although a lawsuit by

Wheelchair-bound photographer L.B. Jefferies (James Stewart) and his girlfriend Lisa Fremont (Grace Kelly) enjoy a rare moment of harmony in *Rear Window,* with neither of them looking out Jefferies's window. *(Literature/Film Society Archive)*

the Woolrich estate kept it out of circulation for many years, the film, a favorite of both François TRUFFAUT and the director himself, was rereleased in 1983 to equal enthusiasm.

In conversation with Truffaut, Hitchcock referred to the film as a stellar example of "PURE CINEMA" detached from performance by virtue of its rigorous alternation between shots from the fixed point of view of its hero and facial closeups that allow viewers to supply his reactions without the actor's registering them. But the film is much more than the technical experiment Truffaut hailed. Hitchcock himself, in the same conversation, noted the sexual fetishism of the Peeping Tom Jefferies (whose last name, although it never appears in the credits, is presumably correctly spelled on the plaster cast that keeps him wheelchair-

bound throughout the film), and the film has become a case study for feminist theorists of the male gaze. At the same time, the generous, if superficial, cross-section of neighbors Jefferies spies on establish the film, like *SHADOW OF A DOUBT* and Hayes's *THE MAN WHO KNEW TOO MUCH* (1956), as an anatomy of Americana that focuses on the hero's ritual reluctance to settle down with his impossibly glamorous fashion-model girlfriend and live the American Dream. At the root of Jeff's unwillingness to marry the impassioned, importunate Lisa, the film, like *NOTORIOUS,* finds a male fear of commitment that expresses itself in a voyeuristic desire for romantic idealism and emotional distance. Eventually Jeff, fearing the clash between his gadabout lifestyle and Lisa's cool refinement and irritated by his confinement to his wheelchair, justifies his fear of marriage by persuading himself that the salesman Lars Thorwald has killed his invalid wife. He is outwitted, however, by Lisa, who first resists his theories, then comes to share them, and finally acts on them, crossing over, as Jeff cannot, from his apartment into the dream space he has been watching: a courtyard plot where a neighbor's dog was digging before someone killed it and Thorwald's apartment, where she is nearly killed before the police Jeff has summoned rescue her moments before her telltale gesture—displaying Mrs. Thorwald's wedding ring on her own finger, thus demonstrating both that Mrs. Thorwald is dead and that Lisa, in proving herself a worthy partner for Jeff, has won the right to his marriage proposal—alerts Thorwald to the fact that she is signaling someone outside his apartment and inexorably draws his returning gaze to Jeff. Following Jeff's own rescue by the police, a wordless epilogue shot in a single long take surveys the background characters, whose problems it briskly solves (Miss Lonelyhearts tells the composer how much his music has meant to her, Miss Torso welcomes her boyfriend Stanley home from the service, the couple whose dog was killed are shown training a new dog), then pans to show Jeff sleeping peacefully in two full-leg casts and Lisa, carefully dressed in a casual outfit, putting down the volume *Beyond the High Himalayas* and picking up an issue of *Harper's Bazaar* just before the apartment's shades, finally visible again in Robert A. HARRIS's 1998 restoration, are lowered in a final echo of the film's opening. The film, one of Hitchcock's most widely discussed, has been the subject of three books—Stefan SHARFF's formalist study *The Art of Looking in Hitchcock's* Rear Window, John BELTON's collection of five original essays, and John FAWELL's *Hitchcock's* Rear Window: *The Well-Made Film.*

Rebecca (Alternative titles: *Rebekka, Rebecca, la prima moglie*) Selznick International, United Artists, 130 minutes, March 1940. **Producer:** David O. Selznick; **Director:** Alfred Hitchcock; **Screenplay:** Robert E. Sherwood and Joan Harrison, based on the novel by Daphne du Maurier; **Adaptation:** Philip MacDonald and Michael Hogan; **Cinematographer:** George Barnes; **Art director:** Lyle Wheeler; **Interior designer:** Joseph B. Platt; **Interior decorator:** Howard Bristol; **Assistant director:** Edmond Bernoudy; **Special effects:** Jack Cosgrove and Arthur Johns; **Sound:** Jack Noyes; **Supervising film editor:** Hal C. Kern; **Associates:** James E. Newcom (and W. Donn Hayes); **Scenario assistant:** Barbara Keon; **Music:** Franz Waxman; **Musical associate:** Lou Forbes; **Cast:** Laurence Olivier (Maxim de Winter), Joan Fontaine (his wife), George Sanders (Jack Favell), Judith Anderson (Mrs. Danvers), Gladys Cooper (Beatrice Lacey), Nigel Bruce (Giles Lacey), Reginald Denny (Frank Crawley), C. Aubrey Smith (Colonel Julyan), Melville Cooper (coroner), Florence Bates (Mrs. Edythe Van Hopper), Leonard Carey (Ben), Leo G. Carroll (Dr. Baker), Edward Fielding (Frith), Philip Winter (Robert), Lumsden Hare (Tabbs), Forrester Harvey (Chalcroft), Billy Bevan (police officer), Leyland Hodgson (chauffeur), Edith Sharpe.

Soon after Hitchcock signed a one-picture contract with David O. SELZNICK on July 14, 1938, Selznick announced that the film in question would be *The Titanic,* and both producer and director spoke of the project with enthusiasm. Even before Hitchcock signed an amended two-picture contract with Selznick the following March, however, he had already been assigned to film Daphne DU MAURIER's book, which he had read in galleys and brought to Selznick's attention. The project, which Selznick originally considered a backup to *The Titanic,* gradually took priority, despite the disapproval du Maurier had registered concerning the liberties Hitchcock's previous film, *JAMAICA INN,* had taken with her first novel. Even before signing Hitchcock, Selznick, with typical enthusiasm, began to fire off cables to him concerning the casting of the two leads ("Can sign Leslie Howard for it . . . Bill Powell has been absolutely wild about role and anxious to do it, but I turned him down on expectation of getting [Ronald] Colman"). Mindful of his success in generating publicity for *Gone With the Wind* by testing actresses from Joan Bennett to Bette Davis for the role of Scarlett O'Hara, Selznick cast his net equally wide this time, suggesting in turn Nova PILBEAM, Margaret Sullavan, and Anne BAXTER; Laurence OLIVIER, once cast as Maxim de Winter, championed his wife Vivien Leigh, who had won the O'Hara competition; and Hitchcock responded by requesting an American actress and testing some 30 candidates before the two men settled on dark-horse Joan FONTAINE, who left her bridegroom Brian AHERNE behind on their honeymoon when she was offered the part. The screenplay provided an even more hotly contested battleground. An early treatment developed by Hitchcock that had broadened du Maurier's story and introduced more humor was dismissed by Selznick in a long, intemperate memo of June 12, 1939, that announced his own position: "We bought *Rebecca* and we intend to make *Rebecca*." Even more than the clashes of casting, this memo drew the battle lines between director and producer that were to persist throughout their eight-year relationship: Each had his own idea of mass entertainment (Selznick's allegiance to an American tradition of quality based on fidelity to acknowledged literary classics and popular successes, Hitchcock's to the generic formulas that subordinated character to situation and the flair for witty visual exposition that had served him so well in England), and each was convinced the shaping intelligence of their collaborative project should be his own. Hitchcock resented Selznick's constant rewrites and interference on the set; Selznick could not understand why one of his contract employees could not bend more gracefully to his authority. The film that

Colonel Julyan (C. Aubrey Smith, second from right) announces the news of an inquest on the late Rebecca de Winter to Maxim de Winter (Laurence Olivier), Frank Crawley (Reginald Denny), Maxim's wife (Joan Fontaine), and Rebecca's smirking cousin Jack Favell (George Sanders) in *Rebecca*. *(National Film Society Archive)*

emerged after 10 expensive weeks of shooting, four weeks over schedule, marked a compromise between the two men's visions, one that charmed reviewers, filmgoers, and the academy—which nominated the film for 11 Oscars, including Best Actor, Best Actress, Best Supporting Actress (Judith ANDERSON), and Best Director, and won two, Best Black-and-White Cinematography and Best Picture—but one that did nothing to make them more eager to work together.

Though Hitchcock persistently dismissed his 24th film as a "novelette" that was "not a Hitchcock picture," its combination of telling details, from the cigarette the heroine's vulgar employer Mrs. Van Hopper puts out in a jar of cold cream to the final closeup of Rebecca's embroidered pillowcase consumed by the flames that are destroying Manderley, with a strong story with unapologetically psychological overtones—another Hitchcock fairy tale but one with a far more high-toned pedigree—became a model for Hitchcock's films, in and out of Selznick's employ, throughout the forties. (A close look at the TRANSATLANTIC production of UNDER CAPRICORN, made far from Selznick's control, shows how much of Selznick's Hollywood aesthetic Hitchcock internalized.) It also adapted from du Maurier a leading motif Hitchcock would borrow for most of these films that would persist beyond them: the fascination with an enigmatic central character whose personality became not only the MACGUFFIN of the story but also the touchstone for a second, observing hero or (more often) heroine, as in the relation between Kurtz and Marlow in Joseph CONRAD's "Heart of Darkness." The enigmatic character here is the dead Rebecca de Winter, never seen even in photos or flashbacks, whose suffocatingly accomplished example the second Mrs. de Winter tries and repeatedly fails to imitate, finding her salvation and the way to her husband's heart only through the revelation that he detested the unfaithful Rebecca, whom he accidentally killed and whose body he concealed when she revealed her pregnancy, presumably by the sinister Jack Favell, to him. (In the novel, written without the collaboration of the Hays Office, Rebecca's death had been no accident, and the climactic conflagration at Manderley, together with the aimless, dreamlike wandering the narrator-heroine chronicles in her prophetically listless

opening chapters, had been the price exacted for his murder.) Rebecca, figured only by her example, her presumed effect on her grieving husband—"They say he simply adored her!" Mrs. Van Hopper casually tells the heroine—her taste in dress and furnishings and domestic habits, and her ubiquitous initial, becomes the romantic ideal that the heroine wanly condemns herself for not achieving until she realizes that the ideal is unattainable because it had been manufactured by the de Winters to satisfy an avid public and conceal her adulteries and his trapped unhappiness. Just as du Maurier's novel, in updating the moody, unsociable Byronic hero as a figure of irresistible sexual attractiveness whose antisocial habits turned out to be emotional scars that concealed a nature just as sensitive, empathetic, and hungry for affection as the heroine's, had a decisive impact on the modern gothic romance, Hitchcock's spin on the formula, which turned personal relationships and glamorous interiors alike into traps for the homeless heroine, set the course for such disparate later films as SUSPICION, SHADOW OF A DOUBT, SPELLBOUND, NOTORIOUS, and still later I CONFESS, DIAL M FOR MURDER, VERTIGO, and PSYCHO.

Rebello, Stephen   American journalist, contributing editor for *L.A. Style,* frequent interviewer of Hollywood stars and filmmakers, coauthor with Richard Allen of *Reel Art: Great Posters from the Golden Age of the Silver Screen* (1988), with Edward Margulies of *Bad Movies We Love* (1993), and with Jane Healey of *The Art of* Hercules: *The Chaos of Creation* (1997), and author of *The Art of* Pocahontas (1995) and *The Art of* The Hunchback of Notre Dame (1996). His production study *Alfred Hitchcock and the Making of* Psycho (December 1990), the first book on the production of any Hitchcock film, traces the development of the film from its roots in Ed Gein's criminal outrages to the pulp novel Robert BLOCH based on them to PSYCHO's several draft screenplays, the controversies surrounding its shooting, and the aftermath of its release. Basing his reconstruction on archival material and two dozen interviews with performers and technicians who worked on the film, Rebello traces its ritual dance around the censors, agrees with Janet LEIGH and Hilton GREEN that Hitchcock rather than Saul BASS shot the shower scene, reviews the often outlandish ploys to which Hitchcock and PARAMOUNT went to publicize the film, and provides an appendix indicating what became of each of the film's leading collaborators after *Psycho.*

Redd, James S. (1904–1973) American set decorator, at Republic from 1945, who worked on 40 Poverty Row films, including *Macbeth* (1948), before joining REVUE PRODUCTIONS in 1953 and becoming a staff art director on *ALFRED HITCHCOCK PRESENTS* in 1955. He decorated the sets for many episodes of the series, among them "REVENGE," "BREAKDOWN," "WET SATURDAY," "THE PERFECT CRIME," "LAMB TO THE SLAUGHTER," "DIP IN THE POOL," "POISON," "ARTHUR," and "MRS. BIXBY AND THE COLONEL'S COAT," as well as for the *SUSPICION* segment "FOUR O'CLOCK." He retired from UNIVERSAL in 1970.

Redgrave, (Sir) Michael (1908–1985) Distinguished British actor of stage and screen, former journalist and schoolmaster. Soon after making his stage debut in 1934, he played an uncredited bit as the army captain in *SECRET AGENT,* and John GIELGUD, in whose company he had just performed in three plays in repertory, persuaded him to make his starring debut in *THE LADY VANISHES.* Although he agreed with his costar Margaret LOCKWOOD that Hitchcock was not an actor's director, Hitchcock's relative indifference to actors perfectly complemented his own condescendingly casual approach to film acting, and his resulting performance as Gilbert, the insouciant musical researcher who takes Iris Henderson under his wing when no one else believes her story of an elderly lady vanishing from a speeding train, launched him on a triumphant cinematic adjunct to his work as stage actor, director, producer, and occasional playwright. His first early film roles were romantic and dramatic leads. Then, beginning with his Oscar-nominated performance as Orin Mannion in *Mourning Becomes Electra* (1947), he created intellectual, emotionally repressed, unattractive figures like the heroes of *The Secret Behind the Door* (1948) and *The Browning Version* (1952). But he could still summon his old ebullience for the Jack Worthing role in *The Impor-*

tance of Being Ernest (1952) before disappearing into a fog of elder-statesman roles, concluding with the title character in *The Rime of the Ancient Mariner* (1976). All three of his children—Vanessa (1937–), Corin (1939–), and Lynn (1943–)— are notable actors.

Redmond, Marge (1926–) Down-to-earth American character actress in Hollywood from 1960, mainly on television. She played the helpful clerk Vera Hannagan in *FAMILY PLOT* but is much better known as Sister Jacqueline in the television series *The Flying Nun* (1967–70).

Reichert, Heinz (1878–1940) Coauthor of the Alhambra play *WALTZES FROM VIENNA* that served as the basis for the screenplay by Guy BOLTON and Alma REVILLE.

Reichow, Otto (1904–) Beefy German-born actor who came to Hollywood in 1940, just in time to play a string of more than 20 Gestapo officers, and then settled after the war into a series of ethnic roles. Among his few television credits is the *ALFRED HITCHCOCK PRESENTS* segment "THE CRYSTAL TRENCH."

remakes and premakes The best known of all Hitchcock remakes is of course the 1956 version of *THE MAN WHO KNEW TOO MUCH,* directed by Hitchcock himself 22 years after the original film. But just as Hitchcock occasionally took on projects that had already been filmed, many of the properties he filmed, their value often inflated by his association with them, were remade by other hands. Here is a comprehensive listing of earlier and subsequent versions chronologically in the order of the Hitchcock films:

The Lodger: remade in the U.K. as *The Lodger* (Twickenham, directed by Maurice Elvey, with Ivor NOVELLO, Miles MANDER, Paul Rotha, and H. Fowler Mear) in 1932, and in the United States as *The Lodger* (20TH CENTURY–FOX, directed by John Brahm, with Laird Cregar, Merle Oberon, George SANDERS, Cedric HARDWICKE, and Sara ALLGOOD) in 1944, and as *Man in the Attic* (20th Century–Fox, directed by Hugo Fregonese, with Jack Palance,

Frances BAVIER, and Rhys Williams) in 1953. Hitchcock often spoke of remaking the film and often incorporated motifs from the story in such later films as FRENZY but never directed a remake himself.

The Farmer's Wife: remade in the U.K. (Associated British, directed by Norman Lee and Leslie Arliss, with Basil Sydney, Wilfred Lawson, and Nora Swinburne) in 1940.

The Manxman: previously filmed in the U.K. (directed by George Loane Tucker, with Harry Ainley, Fred Groves, Edward O'Neill, Elisabeth Risdon) in 1916.

Juno and the Paycock: remade for American television (directed by Paul Shyre, with Liam Clancy, Hume CRONYN, Evans Evans, Pauline Flanagan, Luella Gear, Walter Matthau) in 1960.

The Skin Game: previously filmed in the Netherlands (directed by B.E. Doxat-Pratt, with Edmund GWENN, Mary CLARE, Helen HAYE, Dawson Millward, Malcolm KEEN, Meggie Albanesi) in 1920; remade for British television with Judy Geeson in 1974.

The Man Who Knew Too Much (1934): remade for PARAMOUNT PICTURES by Hitchcock himself.

The 39 Steps: remade in the U.K. in 1959 (Rank, directed by Ralph Thomas, with Kenneth More, Taina Elg, Barry Jones, Faith Brook, Brenda DE BANZIE) and again in 1978 (Rank/Norfolk, directed by Don Sharp, with Robert Powell, Karen Dotrice, John Mills, Eric Porter, David Warner).

Sabotage: remade in the United States as *Joseph Conrad's The Secret Agent* (directed by Christopher Hampton, with Bob Hoskins, Patricia Arquette, Gérard Depardieu, Jim Broadbent, Robin Williams, Christian Bale) in 1996.

The Lady Vanishes: remade in the U.K. (Rank/Hammer, directed by Anthony Page, with Cybill Shepherd, Elliott Gould, Angela Lansbury, Herbert Lom, Arthur Lowe, Ian Carmichael) in 1979.

Jamaica Inn: remade for British television (directed by Lawrence Gordon Clark, with Jane Seymour, Trevor Eve, Patrick McGoohan, Billie WHITELAW, John McEnery) in 1985.

Rebecca: remade three times for British television: in 1962 (with James MASON and Anna MASSEY), in 1978 (directed by Simon Langton, with Jeremy Brett, Joanna David, Anna Massey (now graduated from Mrs. de Winter to Mrs. Danvers), Julian Holloway), and in 1997 (directed by Jim O'Brien, with Emilia Fox, Charles Dance, Diana Rigg, Jonathan Cake).

Suspicion: remade for British television (directed by Andrew Grieve, with Anthony Andrews, Jane Curtin, Jonathan Lynn, Betsy Blair, Michael Hordern) in 1987. Despite its identical title, the film has no connection to the television series for which Hitchcock directed "FOUR O'CLOCK."

Shadow of a Doubt: remade in the United States as *Step Down to Terror* (UNIVERSAL-International, directed by Harry Keller, with Charles Drake, Coleen Miller, Rod TAYLOR, Josephine HUTCHINSON, Jocelyn Brando) in 1958, and as *Shadow of a Doubt* for American television (directed by Karen Arthur, with Mark Harmon, Margaret Welsh, Norm Skaggs, William Lanteau, Dianne Ladd, Tippi HEDREN) in 1991.

Lifeboat: remade for American television as the science-fiction thriller *Lifepod* (directed by Ron Silver, with Silver, Robert Loggia, Adam Storke, Kelli Williams) in 1993.

Notorious: remade for American television (directed by Colin Bucksey, with John Shea, Jenny Robertson, Jean-Pierre Cassel, Marisa Berenson) in 1992.

Strangers on a Train: remade in the United States as *Once You Kiss a Stranger* (directed by Robert Sparr, with Paul Burke, Carol Lynley, Martha Hyer, Peter Lind Hayes) in 1969 and for American television as *Once You Meet a Stranger* (WARNER BROS., directed by Tommy Lee Wallace, with Jacqueline Bisset, Theresa Russell, Andi Chapman) in 1996, and parodied in *Throw Momma from the Train* (Orion, directed by Danny DeVito, with DeVito, Billy Crystal, Anne Ramsey, Kim Greist, Kate Mulgrew) in 1987.

Dial M for Murder: remade for American television (NBC, directed by Boris Sagal, with Christopher Plummer, Angie Dickinson, Anthony QUAYLE, Michael Parks, Ron Moody) in 1981 and for Hollywood as *A Perfect Murder* (Warner Bros., directed by Andrew Davis, with Michael Douglas, Gwyneth Paltrow, Viggo Mortensen, David Suchet, Sarita Choudhury) in 1998.

Rear Window: remade for American television (ABC, directed by Jeff Bleckner, with Christopher Reeve, Daryl Hannah, Robert Forster, Ruben Santiago-Hudson) in 1998.

"Banquo's Chair": this 1959 episode of *Alfred Hitchcock Presents* was a remake of the 1945 feature film *The Fatal Witness* (Republic, directed by Lesley Selander, with Richard Fraser, Evelyn Ankers, George Leigh, Frederick Worlock).

Psycho: generated two Hollywood sequels: *Psycho II* (Universal, directed by Richard Franklin, with Anthony PERKINS, Vera MILES, Meg Tilly, Robert Loggia, Dennis Franz, Claudia Bryar) in 1983 and *Psycho III* (Universal, directed by Anthony Perkins, with Perkins, Diana Scarwid, Jeff Fahey, Roberta Maxwell, Robert Alan Browne) in 1986; a prequel, *Psycho IV: The Beginning,* for American television (Universal, directed by Mick Garris, with Anthony Perkins, Henry Thomas, Olivia Hussey, CCH Pounder, Warren Frost, Donna Mitchell) in 1990; and a theatrical remake widely but erroneously described as following the original shot-by-shot (Universal, directed by Gus Van Sant, with Anne Heche, Vince Vaughn, Viggo Mortensen, Julianne Moore, William H. Macy, Robert Forster) in 1998.

The Birds: hatched a sequel, *The Birds II: Land's End* for American television (Showtime, directed by Alan Smithee [Rick Rosenthal], with Brad Johnson, Chelsea Field, James Naughton, Jan Rubes, Tippi HEDREN) in 1994.

"Revenge"   Premiere episode of *Alfred Hitchcock Presents,* broadcast October 2, 1955. **Associate producer:** Joan Harrison; **Director:** Alfred Hitchcock; **Assistant director:** Jack Corrick; **Teleplay:** Francis Cockrell and A.I. Bezzerides, based on the story by Samuel Blas; **Cinematographer:** John L. Russell; **Art director:** Martin Obzina; **Set designer:** James S. Redd; **Costumes:** Vincent Dee; **Editors:** Richard G. Wray and Edward W. Williams; **Music:** Stanley Wilson; **Cast:** Ralph Meeker (Carl Span), Vera Miles (Elsa Span), Frances Bavier (Mrs. Ferguson), Ray Montgomery (man in Room 321), Ray Teal (police lieutenant), John Gallaudet (doctor), Norman Willis (sergeant), John Day (police officer), Lillian O'Malley (cleaning woman), Herbert Lytton (porter).

Although he directed this episode after "BREAK-DOWN," Hitchcock asked that it lead off the series to showcase his new star, Vera MILES, who plays Elsa Span, a ballet dancer forced into retirement by a nervous breakdown. Her husband Carl, returning home one evening to the trailer park where they live, finds her hysterical, barely able to tell him that she was attacked by an intruder. When the police come up empty, Carl decides to look for the intruder himself. Driving along a city street with Elsa, he is excited when she identifies her assailant: "That's the man." Following the man into a hotel room, Carl kills him. Moments after they drive off, however, Elsa points to another man and says in exactly the same affectless voice: "That's the man." The episode, the most brutal and baleful of all Hitchcock's television films, ends with the sound of a rising police siren.

Reville, Alma (Lucy) (1899–1982)   British editor, screenwriter, and continuity supervisor who worked in a dozen capacities, almost always without screen credit, on Hitchcock's films before and espe-

Alma Reville

cially after becoming his wife. Born the day after Hitchcock, the daughter of a Nottingham ironsmith who had moved to the London suburb of Twickenham, she had been interested in movies from an early age. She landed a job as a cutter for the London Film Company at the age of 16 and soon became a continuity supervisor as well, even appearing as an actress in one film, *The Life Story of David Lloyd George* (1918). She was already a seasoned veteran when she met her future husband, a part-time employee at Famous Players–Lasky, in 1921. Two years later, Hitchcock, as assistant director on WOMAN TO WOMAN, engaged Reville to edit the film, and later in 1923, on a return trip from scouting German locations for THE PRUDE'S FALL, he asked her to marry him. The marriage was not celebrated until December 1926, by which time Hitchcock had directed three films and achieved a position that was both financially secure and superior in the industry hierarchy to that of Reville, who served as assistant director and continuity supervisor on THE PLEASURE GARDEN and assistant director on THE LODGER. After the wedding, she soon established herself as a scenarist, working on the adaptations of the GAINSBOROUGH productions of *The First Born* and *The Constant Nymph* and taking sole screen credit for writing *After the Verdict* (all 1928). Taking scarcely any time off for her pregnancy and the birth of her daughter PATRICIA, the Hitchcocks' only child, on July 7, 1928, she was soon back at work cowriting *The Romance of Seville* (1929). Throughout the thirties her screenwriting work alternated between Hitchcock's films (she is credited as scenarist on JUNO AND THE PAYCOCK, MURDER!, and THE SKIN GAME, as coscenarist on NUMBER SEVENTEEN, RICH AND STRANGE, and WALTZES FROM VIENNA, and as in charge of "continuity"—presumably as script editor—on THE 39 STEPS, SECRET AGENT, SABOTAGE, YOUNG AND INNOCENT, THE LADY VANISHES, and JAMAICA INN) and those of other directors (*Sally in Our Alley*, 1931; *The Outsider*, 1931; *The Water Gipsies*, 1932; *Nine Till Six*, 1932; *Forbidden Territory*, 1934; *The Passing of the Third Floor Back*, 1935). On their immigration to America, she readily adapted to life in her new home, applying for citizenship at the earliest possible opportunity and accepting it in 1945, 10 full years before her husband. Although her name

appeared on fewer and fewer shared continuity credits—Hitchcock's SUSPICION, SHADOW OF A DOUBT, THE PARADINE CASE, and STAGE FRIGHT, as well as the Fred Allen–Jack Benny comedy *It's in the Bag!* (1945), her last non-Hitchcock credit—she continued to serve as her husband's most active and trusted collaborator, excising a shot of Madeleine Elster from the first tower sequence in VERTIGO because it made Kim NOVAK's ankles look fat and shortening a shot of the dead Marion Crane in PSYCHO when, alone of all the rough cut's viewers, she could see that Janet LEIGH had blinked. As Charles BARR concludes in summarizing her extensive and enduring contributions to her husband's work, "The testimony both of others and of Hitchcock himself suggests that throughout his career he consistently referred, and often deferred, to her judgment, whether or not she had credit on a given film." It seems likely, despite Hitchcock's repeated tendency, in essays and interviews, to downplay the importance of his many collaborators, that she was the collaborator whose impact on his work was most decisive. A more detailed account of her role in that work is promised in her daughter's forthcoming biography of her.

Revue Productions The television production arm UNIVERSAL PICTURES acquired in 1955 under whose supervision ALFRED HITCHCOCK PRESENTS and THE ALFRED HITCHCOCK HOUR were produced. In accord with his distribution agreement with PARAMOUNT, Hitchcock shot PSYCHO at Revue as well.

Reynders, John British musician with a few movie credits, most of them on Hitchcock films. He directed the music for BLACKMAIL and RICH AND STRANGE and composed the score for MURDER!

Rhoda, Sybil British actress whose second and last film role was Tim Wakeley's sister Sybil in DOWNHILL.

Rhodes, Leah (1902–1986) American costume designer, at WARNER BROS. from 1939 for some 50 films, including *Saratoga Trunk* (1945), *The Big*

Sleep (1946), and *STRANGERS ON A TRAIN*. She shared an Oscar for *The Adventures of Don Juan* (1949).

Rich, Lionel British film editor who cut *DOWNHILL*.

Rich, Vernon (1905–1978) American character actor who played some 20 film and television roles, many uncredited, between *The Sellout* (1952) and *One Man's Way* (1964). He appeared as the doctor in the *SUSPICION* episode "FOUR O'CLOCK."

Rich and Strange (Alternative titles: *East of Shanghai* (U.S.), *Endlich sind wir reich, A l'est de Shanghai*) British International, Wardour & F., 87 minutes, December 1931. **Producer:** John Maxwell; **Director:** Alfred Hitchcock; **Adaptation:** Alfred Hitchcock, from the novel by Dale Collins; **Scenario:** Alma Reville and Val Valentine; **Cinematographers:** John Cox and Charles Martin; **Art director:** C. Wilfred Arnold; **Assistant director:** Frank Mills; **Editors:** Rene Marrison and Winifred Cooper; **Sound:** Alec Murray; **Music:** Hal Dolphe; **Musical direction:** John Reynders; **Cast:** Henry Kendall (Fred Hill), Joan Barry (Emily Hill), Percy Marmont (Commander Gordon), Betty Amann (the Princess), Elsie Randolph (Miss Imrie), Hannah Jones (Miss Porter).

The genesis of Hitchcock's 14th film is a subject of disagreement among Hitchcock scholars, who do not even agree whether it should count as his 14th film. Maurice YACOWAR, John Russell TAYLOR, Jane SLOAN, and Charles BARR all note that it was released in 1931 before *NUMBER SEVENTEEN*; yet Donald SPOTO places *Number Seventeen* first, observing that it was shot earlier and then shelved, like *THE PLEASURE GARDEN* and *THE MOUNTAIN EAGLE* six years earlier at GAINSBOROUGH. A more fundamental disagreement concerns the film's relation to its source. Most commentators have taken the film as a fantasia on themes drawn from the Hitchcocks' honeymoon in 1926, citing especially the similarity of its heroes' names, Fred and Emily Hill, to Alfred and Alma Hitchcock and the way that their comic misadventures in Paris recall the innocents-abroad stories Hitchcock told about himself and Alma. Recently, however, Barr has argued that the film, identified in the credits as "by" the author of its original property, Australian novelist Dale COLLINS, follows Collins's 1930 novel *Rich and Strange* closely—so closely, in fact, that at least two incidents Hitchcock identified in the film that do not appear in extant prints (the moment when Fred, swimming underwater, is trapped between his inamorata's legs and nearly drowns, and the episode when the enthusiastic Hills tell their story to a shipboard companion—Hitchcock, allegedly, in the film, Collins in the novel—who dismisses it as not worth fictionalizing) do appear in Collins's novel. Considering the film's curiously unacknowledged closeness to the novel and Hitchcock's apparently false memories of the novel as if it were the film, Barr considers whether Collins, a friend of the Hitchcocks, might in fact have written a novelization of the film and whether the Hitchcocks might have supplied him with material for the novel or even collaborated on it, but he finds no evidence to support either proposition. If the film represented the sort of personal testament Hitchcock wanted to make when he was given a free hand, its fate is revealing because John MAXWELL's decision to delay its release was justified by the film's disappointing reception by reviewers and the public.

This is hardly surprising because the film, which shows the folly of the middle-class Hills' wish for money by showering it on them through a providential uncle's gift and watching their marriage disintegrate under the pressure of temptation, lacks the one feature audiences would have confidently associated with Hitchcock by 1931: a story with a strong sense of direction. Despite Taylor's apt description of the film as "an adventure story in which all the adventures turn out badly," Fred and Em's antiromance is unadventurous in at least one respect: It has a strong beginning—the extended, wordless comic-opera prologue in which Fred battles his way home from his assembly-line office through the London crowds to a depressingly predictable domestic evening—but no particular end in sight. As early as the couple's inebriated attempt to cross their hotel lobby in Paris, it seems clear that the ordeals inflicted by their sud-

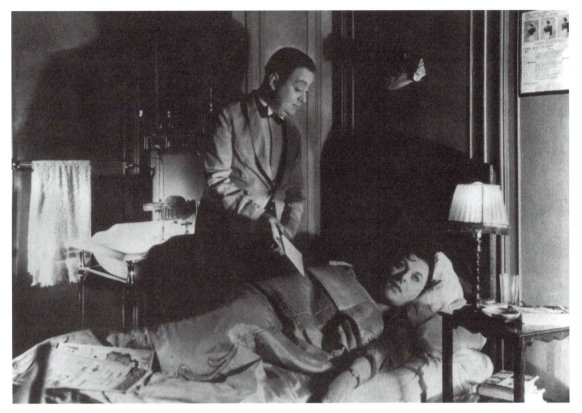

Fred Hill (Henry Kendall) suffers a well-earned bout of seasickness in *Rich and Strange*. *(National Film Society Archive)*

den wealth comprise simply a series of amusing but ever more threatening tableaux—from their shipboard flirtations with other partners to their impending separation to a shipwreck that will threaten their lives and a rescue by Chinese sailors that will threaten their insularity—from which they will learn nothing. The film is therefore less interesting as a story than as an experiment in style and in the proprieties of self-revelation. The alternation between dialogue scenes shot in the studio (an unusually low proportion of the film) and stylized musical scenes without dialogue reminiscent of René Clair, shot on location and often introduced by anachronistic subtitles, not only marks Hitchcock's most sustained attempt to combine the aesthetics of sound and silent film, implicitly identified here with realist and antirealist aesthetics respectively, but also looks forword to his deliberate courting of technical difficulties through the one-set restrictions of LIFEBOAT, ROPE, DIAL M FOR MURDER, and REAR WINDOW and the long takes in *Rope* and UNDER CAPRICORN. The unraveling of the Hills' marriage, which survives despite their travails unchanged in a brief epilogue as they bicker safely back in their cookie-cutter London home, offers a passionless, oddly depersonalized look at the Hitchcocks' marriage for what is supposedly such a personal film. In addition, the casting of sharp-witted, edgy music hall star Henry KENDALL opposite the warmer, more charming Joan BARRY, who had voiced Anny ONDRA in the sync-sound version of BLACKMAIL, seems a piece of self-portraiture at once narcissistic and self-lacerating. Like THE MAN WHO KNEW TOO MUCH (1934), the film is perhaps best described as a nightmare of domestic relationships that is also a joke on domestic relationships, with money this time providing access to the adventures the later film would make more urgent, if no more plausible, in motivating them by menace.

Richards, Addison (1887–1964) Stage-trained American character actor who radiated competence and authority in more than 300 film and television roles, often as physicians, police chiefs, district attorneys, and military brass, from 1933. In 1945, at the height of his career, he appeared as a police captain in *SPELLBOUND* and in 22 other films; in 1960, the year he played a bar patron in the *ALFRED HITCHCOCK PRESENTS* episode "Outlaw in Town," he appeared in two films and eight other television programs in addition to playing Martin Kingsley in the television series *Cimarron City* (1958–60) and Dr. Gamble in the series *Fibber McGee and Molly* (1959–60). The following year he returned to *ALFRED HITCHCOCK PRESENTS* to play Crandall Johnson in "A Secret Life."

Rigby, Edward (1879–1951) British character actor with long theatrical experience. Onstage from 1900, he dabbled briefly in silent films early in his career and then returned to the screen in 1935 to play the first of 70 variously whimsical old men in the manner of Edmund Gwenn. In addition to playing Old Will, the reluctant witness (and even more reluctant ballroom dancer) in *YOUNG AND INNOCENT*, he appeared in *A Yank at Oxford* (1938), *The Stars Look Down* (1939), *Kipps* (1941), and the 1941 remake of *THE FARMER'S WIFE* and was still at work when he died.

Riggs, Al American sound recordist, in Hollywood for five films, 1932–50. As the recordist on *ROPE*, he was unable to record any live sound on the one-room studio set because the frequent movement of furniture and walls required by the film's unbroken takes was too noisy; the entire soundtrack, including all dialogue, music, and effects, consequently had to be recorded separately and postsynchronized, an experience that may well have hastened his retirement two years later.

Riggs, Rita American costume designer who has worked on some three dozen films since her uncredited debut in *PSYCHO*. Her later films include

THE BIRDS, MARNIE, Cinderella Liberty (1973), *An Officer and a Gentleman* (1982), and *Texasville* (1990).

Ring, The (Alternative titles: *Le masque de cuir, Le ring, La piste, L'arène, Vinci per me*) British International, Wardour & F., approximately 110 minutes, September 1927. **Producer:** John Maxwell; **Director:** Alfred Hitchcock; **Screenplay:** Alfred Hitchcock; **Cinematographer:** John J. Cox; **Assistant director:** Frank Mills; **Art director:** C.W. Arnold; **Cast:** Carl Brisson ("One Round" Jack Sander), Lilian Hall Davis (The Girl [Mabel]), Ian Hunter (Bob Corby), Forrester Harvey (The Promoter [James Ware]), Harry Terry (The Showman), Gordon Harker (Jack's trainer) Clare Greet (fortune teller), Eugene Corri (himself: boxing referee).

When Hitchcock left GAINSBOROUGH for the higher budgets of the newly organized BRITISH INTERNATIONAL PICTURES in the summer of 1927, studio owner John MAXWELL and Walter MYCROFT, his chief of production, were so preoccupied with consolidating the business that they allowed Hitchcock to choose the subject for his first production. The result was the only film based on an original screenplay by the director, written, according to Donald SPOTO, in two weeks in July, perhaps in consultation with Eliot STANNARD. The choice of subject might seem unusual for Hitchcock, who told Peter BOGDANOVICH more than 30 years later that he had been attracted to it by the extreme formality of boxing rituals in England, where the spectators wore formal clothes and poured bottles of champagne over the contenders after the 13th round. Urged on by the businesslike atmosphere at his new studio, Hitchcock completed the film in time for a trade premiere at the end of September and received his strongest notices to date. An anonymous reviewer in *Bioscope* called the picture "the most magnificent British film ever made."

In concept, the film could not be simpler: a romantic triangle involving two rival boxers and the woman they both love; in fact, the outlines of the story are predictable and often banal from the moment "One Round" Jack Sanders's ticket-seller sweetheart gazes attentively at his latest challenger, who promptly knocks Jack out, reveals that he is Australia's heavyweight champion Bob Corby, and uses his purse from the fight to buy Jack's girl a serpentine bracelet. The rest of the film, proceeding from Jack's wedding through his gradual rise to the top and his gradual alienation from his wife to his climactic rematch with Corby, with his estranged wife sitting in his rival's corner, is structured by the relations among three rings: the wedding ring that seals the newlyweds' union, the bracelet that secretly declares Mrs. Sanders's continuing attachment to Corby, and the boxing ring within whose laws the men will be forced to fight. Although each ring represents a ritual that not only expresses an affiliation but also claims to govern the behavior of its affiliates, the competing claims of the three rings dramatize the fragility of those claims, as love is repeatedly set against loyalty and the rituals of the boxing ring set against the brutality it licenses. Beneath the new metaphor of these interlocking rings, the film closely resembles several of Hitchcock's earlier films about divided loyalty and social breakdown, especially THE PLEASURE GARDEN and THE LODGER, and looks forward to future films from SHADOW OF A DOUBT to VERTIGO. It is best remembered, however, not for its place in the director's development but as the most expressionistic of all his films. The opening shots of the fairground are obviously Germanic in their inspiration, as is the extended wedding sequence halfway through that begins with the absurd but logical behavior of the guests from the carnival where Jack has worked and becomes increasingly hallucinatory as it moves from the ceremony to the reception. Some of the individual touches of which Hitchcock was so proud, such as the montage of fight bills showing Jack's name closer and closer to the top to indicate his growing fame, now seem dated; others, such as producing a brand-new Round 2 sign, clearly never before needed, when Jack first fights Corby, still pass virtually unnoticed. Nor are the dialogue intertitles in which the characters speak their love and pain ever as expressive as the visuals that allow viewers to infer those feelings for themselves. Even so, the film represents more than a road-not-taken in Hitchcock's career, more even than a fascinating indication of his strengths and weaknesses as a screenwriter (clever set pieces, continually inventive composition and editing, a powerfully unified sense of visual style, a fond-

ness for obvious metaphors, stilted dialogue, cardboard characters). It shows both his preference for conceiving films as well-wrought artifacts rather than imitations of life and his enduring attachment to the schematic sorts of melodrama and romance whose resonance the conventions of the thriller would extend in unimagined ways.

Ritchard, Cyril (1897–1977)   Australian song-and-dance man of the British stage, actor who made two dozen film and television appearances beginning in 1929. His performance as Mr. Crewe, the carefree, calculating artist whom Alice White kills when he tries to rape her in BLACKMAIL, assured him a footnote in the history of the talkies; American audiences are more likely to remember him as Mr. Darling and Captain Hook in the 1955 television production of *Peter Pan.*

Ritter, Thelma (1905–1969)   Unquenchable American character actress, one of the cinema's great scene-stealers. After years of indifferent success on stage, she made her film debut in 1947 and was nominated for an Academy Award as Birdie, Margo Channing's acid-tongued dresser in *All About Eve* (1950). An astonishing five further nominations followed during the next 12 years, the most frequent run for any supporting actor or actress, for her work in *The Mating Season* (1951), *With a Song in My Heart* (1952), *Pickup on South Street* (1953), *Pillow Talk* (1959), and *Birdman of Alcatraz* (1962), though she never won an Oscar. After delivering a warm, wry performance as Stella, the insurance company nurse in REAR WINDOW, she delivered a verdict on Hitchcock's direction that suggested her many sardonic characters may not have been that much of a stretch: "If Hitchcock liked what you did, he said nothing. If he didn't, he looked like he was going to throw up." She returned in one of her few television roles as the imprudently imaginative murder witness Lottie Slocum in the ALFRED HITCHCOCK PRESENTS segment "The Baby Sitter" (1956).

RKO Radio Pictures   The smallest of the five major American studios (along with MGM, PARAMOUNT, WARNER BROS., and TWENTIETH CEN-

TURY-FOX) began in 1931 under the joint auspices of the Radio Corporation of America (later RCA) and the Keith-Orpheum theater circuit. Despite the success of *King Kong* (1933), the studio struggled throughout the thirties and had just emerged from receivership in 1940 when RKO began to seek Hitchcock to direct *Before the Fact* (later SUSPICION) on a loanout by David O. SELZNICK. The director, recalling the example of the free rein RKO production head George J. Schaefer had recently given Orson Welles on *Citizen Kane,* encouraged their overtures, and eventually Selznick agreed to loan him to RKO for two films, *MR. AND MRS. SMITH* and *Suspicion.* Five years later, needing a cash infusion to complete *Duel in the Sun* (1946), Selznick sold the story, stars, and director of *NOTORIOUS* to RKO, where Schaefer allowed Hitchcock to serve as his own producer for the first time. The studio's hopes of attracting Hitchcock for future productions were dashed soon afterward when Howard Hughes, its principal stockholder since 1948, sold it to Desilu Productions, the television company owned by former RKO contract player Lucille Ball and her husband Desi Arnaz, in 1954. Though films under the RKO banner continued to trickle forth for another five years, the studio was the first—and to date the only one—of the majors to go out of business.

Robbins, Richard (1919–1969) American actor whose only film credit is Daniell in *THE WRONG MAN.*

Roberson, Lorraine American hair stylist, in Hollywood for a dozen films and television programs (1959–81), who collaborated with Hal SAUNDERS in designing hair styles for *TORN CURTAIN.*

Roberts, J.H. (1884–1961) British stage actor who came to films through the 1928 adaptation of *The Constant Nymph* and then produced his next film, *A Safe Affair* (1931), himself before settling into a round of 30 roles as variously doddering old gents. He was especially memorable in *YOUNG AND INNO-CENT* as Henry Briggs, the discouraging, disorganized solicitor whose eyeglasses Robert Tisdall purloins in order to escape from police custody.

Robertshaw, Jerrold (1866–1941) Spectrally thin British stage actor who appeared in some 15 silent film roles, from the title character in *Don Quixote* (1923) to Tim Wakeley's minister father in *DOWNHILL.*

Robertson, Peggy (1916–1998) American production assistant, born Peggy Singer, whom Hitchcock hired as script supervisor on *UNDER CAPRICORN* and (uncredited) *STAGE FRIGHT.* Though her non-Hitchcock credits were scant, she returned under her married name as uncredited script supervisor on *VERTIGO* and is billed as "Assistant to Mr. Hitchcock" on all his UNIVERSAL films from *THE BIRDS* through *FAMILY PLOT.* Donald SPOTO maintains that she functioned unofficially as his associate producer, as Herbert COLEMAN had done in the fifties.

Robin, Dany (1927–1995) Attractive, strong-willed French actress, a former ballerina with the Paris Opera who appeared in some 50 French films from 1946. Toward the end of her career she added a handful of roles in international coproductions. The very last of these was *TOPAZ,* in which, as Andre Devereaux's frustrated wife Nicole, she is literally sleeping with the enemy Jacques Granville, completing the pattern established by Andre's own long-term adultery with Juanita de Cordoba.

Robinson, Casey (1903–1979) Veteran American writer of some 70 screenplays whose first Hollywood job was writing intertitles for silent films. He directed seven films at the beginning of the thirties, meanwhile worked his way up to additional dialogue and adaptation credits, and by the end of the decade was writing such accomplished comedies and romances as *Tovarich* (1937), *Dark Victory* (1939), *The Old Maid* (1939), and *All This And Heaven Too* (1940). His reputation as a writer of women's weepies is strikingly at odds with his adaptation of Roald DAHL's story "POISON," which isolates the two male leads in the jungle, far from the woman they both love, for *ALFRED HITCHCOCK PRESENTS.* He also produced eight films between 1944 and 1975.

Robinson, E(dward) R(ay)   American set decorator who worked on some 20 films of the forties, mostly at UNIVERSAL. He served as Russell GAUSMAN's associate on *SHADOW OF A DOUBT* and *The Killers* (1946).

Rogers, Kasey (1926–)   American character actress, born Imogene Rogers, who was given the nickname Casey because of her grade-school baseball prowess and changed the C to a K for her professional career. When she signed with Paramount in 1949, the studio billed her as Laura Elliot, sometimes Elliott, and it was under this last name that she appeared as Guy Haines's unfaithful wife Miriam, the murder victim in *STRANGERS ON A TRAIN*. Soon after, she reclaimed her own name for a series of film and television jobs that culminated in the roles of Julie Anderson on *Peyton Place* (1964–66) and Louise Tate in *Bewitched* (1966–72).

Rogerson, Jack   British sound recordist who worked on five films of the thirties, the last of which was *JAMAICA INN*.

Rohmer, Eric (1920–)   French filmmaker, former journalist and critic, born Jean-Marie Maurice Schérer. Drawn to the cinema as early as 1950, when he began directing a series of short films with *Journal d'un scélérat* and, together with Jean-Luc Godard and Jacques Rivette, founded the short-lived journal *La gazette du cinéma*. In 1957 he succeeded André Bazin as editor of *CAHIERS DU CINÉMA*, where he remained until 1963. Soon thereafter, the success of *La collectioneuse* (1967) and *Ma nuit chez Maud* (1969), the first two feature-length entries in his *Six contes moraux*, established him as one of the key figures of the French New Wave and the one whose conservatism made him most accessible to American audiences. Rounding out the cycle with *Le genou de Claire* (1970) and *L'amour l'aprés-midi* (1972), he continued to such projects as *La marquise d'O* (1976), *Le beau mariage* (1982), *Pauline à la plage* (1983), and a second cycle of *contes* dedicated to the seasons of springtime (1990), winter (1992), summer (1996), and autumn (1998). Just before assuming the editorship of *Cahiers,* he collaborated with Claude CHABROL on *Hitchcock* (1957), a seminal critical study

that rooted the unity of the director's work—still a radical assumption to make on behalf of a Hollywood filmmaker at the time—in his severely unforgiving Jansenist morality, which entangled technically innocent heroes from *THE LODGER* to *THE WRONG MAN* in a "transfer of guilt" from the criminal counterparts with whom they are doubled. Emphasizing Hitchcock's American over his English films and assigning special importance to *SHADOW OF A DOUBT, STRANGERS ON A TRAIN,* and *I CONFESS,* Rohmer and Chabrol argue that Hitchcock's formal inventiveness works through such motivic devices as the gaze, the confession, and the exchange to create a self-contained moral universe that implicates even the most apparently innocent characters in evil. Although the volume had to wait more than 20 years before Stanley Hochman translated it into English as *Hitchcock: The First Forty-Four Films* (Ungar, 1979), its indirect influence on the first generation of Hitchcock criticism has been immeasurable.

Roman, Ruth (1924–1999)   American leading lady of the fifties who later emerged as a character actress. After experience onstage and in a series of unbilled bits in 20 films from *Stage Door Canteen* (1943) to *Gilda* (1946) to *The Big Clock* (1948), she won more substantial roles in three 1949 films, *Champion, Beyond the Forest,* and (most memorably) *The Window,* in which she played the threatening Mrs. Kellerton. In 1950, as a contract player at WARNER BROS., she was assigned to play Anne Morton, the lover of tennis player Guy Haines in *STRANGERS ON A TRAIN*. Curiously, Guy's adulterous love for Senator Morton's daughter, which might have expected to be at the heart of the film, was upstaged by both the barely disguised homosexual overtones of Guy's relation with the killer Bruno Anthony and by Patricia HITCHCOCK's gleefully unnuanced performance as Anne's kid sister Barbara. If Roman's career had not been dramatically promoted by the film, however, it had not been hurt either, and after reprising her role for CBS radio later in 1951, she went on to 20 more films during the following decade, her most notable roles including Rhonda Castle in *The Far Country* (1954) and Lily Macbeth in *Joe Macbeth* (1956). Most of her subsequent work was in television, where she played Addie, the homicidal maid in the *Alfred Hitch-*

cock Hour episode "What Really Happened" (1963), Minnie Littlejohn in the series *The Long Hot Summer* (1965–66), Sylvia Lean in *Knots Landing* (1986), and Loretta Spiegel, her final role, in several episodes of *Murder She Wrote* (1987, 1989).

Romer, Jeanne   American actress who plays Marigold, one of the bickering conjoined twins in *SABOTEUR*.

Romer, Lynn   Jeanne ROMER's conjoined twin, who plays Annette in *SABOTEUR* and also appears with her in *Hitchhike to Happiness* (1945), *Easter Parade* (1948), and *The Great Gatsby* (1949).

Romero, Joseph E.   One of five staff composers for *ALFRED HITCHCOCK PRESENTS*. Although less well known and prolific than Frederick HERBERT, Bernard HERRMANN, Lyn MURRAY, or Stanley WILSON, he wrote music for many episodes of the series, including the Hitchcock-directed "THE HORSEPLAYER" and "BANG! YOU'RE DEAD."

Romm, May E., M.D.   David O. SELZNICK's psychiatrist, who was billed as Psychiatric Advisor on *Since You Went Away* (1944) and *SPELLBOUND*.

Rondel, Ronnie   (1903–1999)   American character actor of the forties who played some three dozen cabdrivers, hotel clerks, and waiters including the Florida Club server in *MR. AND MRS. SMITH* and then became an assistant director on a half-dozen fifties films including *Around the World in 80 Days* and *While the City Sleeps* (both 1956) and on dozens of segments of *ALFRED HITCHCOCK PRESENTS* and *THE ALFRED HITCHCOCK HOUR* from 1956 to 1965.

Roome, Alfred   British editor who worked on more than 40 films from *Dirty Work* (1934) to *Carry on Behind* (1975), and under a supervising editor's direction cut 10 more, including *THE LADY VANISHES*. In 1948–49, he produced four features and directed two more.

Rope   (Alternative titles: *Cocktail für eine Leiche, La corde, Nodo all gola, Cocktail per un cadavere*) Transatlantic,

Warner Bros., 80 minutes, August 1948. **Producers:** Alfred Hitchcock and Sidney Bernstein; **Director:** Alfred Hitchcock; **Screenplay:** Arthur Laurents, based on the play by Patrick Hamilton; **Adaptation:** Hume Cronyn; **Cinematographers:** Joseph Valentine and William V. Skall; **Assistant director:** Lowell J. Farrell; **Lighting technician:** Jim Potevin; **Camera operators:** Edward Fitzgerald, Paul G. Hill, Richard Emmons, Morris Rosen; **Art director:** Perry Ferguson; **Set decoration:** Emile Kuri and Howard Bristol; **Costumes:** Adrian; **Makeup:** Perc Westmore; **Production manager:** Fred Ahern; **Technicolor consultant:** Natalie Kalmus; **Associate:** Robert Browe; **Sound:** Al Riggs; **Editor:** William Ziegler; **Music:** David Buttolph, Francis Poulenc; **Musical direction:** Leo Forbstein; **Cast:** James Stewart (Rupert Cadell), John Dall (Brandon Shaw), Farley Granger (Philip Morgan), Joan Chandler (Janet Walker), Sir Cedric Hardwicke (Mr. Kentley), Constance Collier (Anita Atwater), Edith Evanson (Mrs. Wilson), Douglas Dick (Kenneth Lawrence), Dick Hogan (David Kentley).

Even before he was free of the contractual obligations to David O. SELZNICK that had so come to chafe him, Hitchcock announced that the first production of TRANSATLANTIC PICTURES, his newly formed partnership with Sidney BERNSTEIN, would be based on a favorite play of his: Patrick HAMILTON's 1929 one-set melodrama *Rope,* also known as *Rope's End.* Working first from a screen adaptation by Hamilton and then from a prose treatment by Hume CRONYN, Hitchcock planned to heighten the realism of the film by compressing its single sweep of time from 7:30 to 9:15 P.M. into a single LONG TAKE. But because standard 35 mm magazines held only 10 minutes worth of filmstock, he was restricted to takes lasting 10 minutes or less—in practice, an average of seven to eight minutes for each of the film's 11 shots, several of which ended with pans to the characters' backs (or, in one especially dramatic coup, the dark top of the chest holding David Kentley's body as the lid is thrown open) that would disguise the splices. There were other reasons for Hitchcock to favor long takes as well: to emphasize the claustrophobia of his single set instead of opening it up in orthodox and expensive Hollywood fashion by presenting new scenes outside the main story space, and,

Brandon Shaw (John Dall) exults over the murder of David Kentley, whose body has just been placed in the chest on which his brooding fellow conspirator Philip Morgan (Farley Granger) is sitting in *Rope*. *(National Film Society Archive)*

as Orson Welles and Preston Sturges had demonstrated in *The Magnificent Ambersons* and *The Miracle of Morgan's Creek,* to cut down shooting time by making it unnecessary to rerig studio lighting for successive camera setups. But the unbroken flow of time, space, and incident Hitchcock had wanted to capture bedeviled his long takes from the beginning. The need to produce sunset lighting that would be the same day after day forced the construction of an interior set with a meticulously detailed urban cyclorama, complete with movable spun-glass clouds, variable sun effects, and some 1,200 lights, visible through the window. When the bulky Technicolor camera, which

he was using for the first time, proved too big to fit through the doorways of the set, the walls, mounted on pulleys, had to be raised on its approach to allow it through. The incessant noise of the moving walls and furniture, fitted with wheels so that it too could be moved around the camera, made the live soundtrack the director had hoped to produce impossible, and the film's entire soundtrack, including the dialogue, was postsynchronized. Dick HOGAN, the actor cast as the strangled David Kentley, was too claustrophobic to remain in the chest where he had been placed even for the length of a single long take, so a special release had to be built into the bottom of the chest to allow him to escape. The acrobatics of the moving camera, which was constantly threatening to bump into performers and technicians who did not stay out of its way, made the actors nervous, especially because they were worried about ruining an entire take (and with it a whole day's work) by a miscue seconds before the shot ended; James STEWART, appearing in his first film for Hitchcock, complained that the film's unusually extensive rehearsals had been called for the sake of the camera, not the actors. Finally, Hitchcock, unaccustomed to shooting in color, did not bother to look at the rushes until the film was nearly half completed and then told Joseph VALENTINE that all completed shots would have to be retaken because the light was too orange. Miraculously, the film was shot quickly and inexpensively, requiring only 18 days of shooting after 10 days of rehearsal with the camera, and survived tepid reviews to turn a modest profit. It was enthusiastically greeted by a new generation of viewers on its rerelease on videotape in 1983 after many years of unavailability.

Apart from its value as a never repeated technical experiment (its closest analogues, the long-take experimental films of Andy Warhol and Michael Snow, do not tell stories)—a value its director was the first to disclaim in later interviews in which he said that his flirtation with the long take had been a disastrous failure—the film is notable as an example of Hitchcock's black comedy at its most baleful. The screenplay punctuates Hamilton's story about two college friends who murder a third friend for the thrill of seeing what it felt like and whether they could get away with it (apparently based on the real-life murder conviction of Leopold and Loeb, though Hamilton maintained he had never heard of the case until the play had been completed) with dozens of emphatic laugh lines delivered either by aspiring criminal mastermind Brandon Shaw (asked if he's serving champagne because it's somebody's birthday, he replies, "Actually, it's just the opposite") or the unwitting participants in the dinner party he throws to celebrate his success (as when Mrs. Atwater tells Brandon's conspirator, pianist Philip Morgan, "These hands will bring you great fame"). In turning the breaking of so many taboos about murder and social behavior into a hideously decorous

joke, the film anticipates PSYCHO and FRENZY, which are more graphic and sexually outspoken but no more bleak. The casting of normally genial James Stewart as Rupert Cadell, the schoolmaster whose Nietzschean theories the killers adopted as their justification for murder—a justification Rupert, roused from his diffident aestheticism to turn avenging detective, is swift to deny with self-righteous defensiveness—adds still another layer of subversive jesting to the film. Long regarded because of its connection with Leopold and Loeb, its intended casting (Montgomery CLIFT, offered the role of Brandon, reportedly declined because the character's homosexuality too closely echoed his own; Cary GRANT, Hitchcock's first choice to play Rupert, had conflicting obligations at RKO; Farley GRANGER, who played Philip, was enjoying his own fling with screenwriter Arthur LAURENTS), and its sexual double-entendres ("How cozy," Janet purrs when Brandon tells her the telephone is in his bedroom) as Hitchcock's most explicitly homophobic film, it has come under recent revaluation by such scholars as D.A. Miller, in RAUBICHECK and SREBNICK, and Peter Wollen, in ALLEN and GONZALÈS, for the homoerotic subtext it represses beneath its façade of formal experimentation, Nietzschean philosophizing, and mordant wit.

Rosen, Morris American studio technician whose first Hollywood credit is as one of the four camera operators on ROPE. He was similarly employed on *Massacre River* (1949), and then spent the next 15 years as a grip on films from *High Noon* (1952) to *The Thomas Crown Affair* (1968).

Ross, Herbert (1865–1934) Stage-trained British character actor who appeared toward the end of his life as the Hillcrest tenant farmer Jackman in THE SKIN GAME and took roles in two other 1931 films as well.

Ross, Robert C. (d. 1990) American character actor who appeared in a half-dozen films and television programs from 1956 to 1977, including the ALFRED HITCHCOCK PRESENTS segment "LAMB TO THE SLAUGHTER."

Rothman, William American film scholar, professor of Motion Pictures and of Video-Film at the University of Miami and author of *The "I" of the Camera* (1988), *Documentary Film Classics* (1997), and, with Marian Keane, *Reading Cavell's* The World Viewed: *A Philosophical Perspective on Film* (2000). His first book, *Hitchcock—The Murderous Gaze* (Harvard University Press, 1982), is a shot-by-shot analysis of five films; it focuses on the relation between the camera's view of the characters as externalized yet unknowable and the camera's view of itself as a figure for the limits of perception and the powers of authorship to dramatize its subjects' mysteries and the author's own, while yet leaving them intact. Rothman finds these concerns fully articulated as early as THE LODGER, which emphasizes "the camera's enigmatic bond with the lodger and his double, the Avenger." His reading of MURDER! traces the shifting relations between the film's repeated invocations of theatricality and its declaration of the camera as denying a framing proscenium that could separate viewers from the players whose vicissitudes they are watching, a theme that returns in THE 39 STEPS. SHADOW OF A DOUBT, "a film that aspires to teach its audience what a Hitchcock film really is," is a meditation on the relation between the everyday world and the nihilistic challenge represented by Uncle Charlie's pitiless way of seeing. In PSYCHO, which gives the greatest prominence to the //// figure Rothman identifies as Hitchcock's visual signature of authorship, the camera, previously incorporeal, becomes incarnate in both male and female terms, apparently giving physical, maternal birth to a world that it simultaneously penetrates in a masculine sense as already existing. The films taken together proclaim both the intractability of the world and its creation by the camera eye and the authorial gaze it figures—a premise Rothman has pursued in his essays on NORTH BY NORTHWEST and VERTIGO in *The "I" of the Camera* and his essay comparing Hitchcock's *Psycho* to Gus Van Sant's 1998 remake in ALLEN and GONZALÈS.

Roxborough, Picton (1875–1932) British stage actor, né Picton Gaunt, whose one foray into film was his service as one of the twelve jurors in MURDER!

Rózsa, Miklós (1907–1995) Hungarian film composer, former violinist and composer of concert works. His friendship with compatriot producer Alexander Korda drew him to write the scores for Korda's films *Knight Without Armour* (1936), *The Divorce of Lady X* (1938), *The Four Feathers* (1939), and *The Thief of Baghdad* (1940), for which he received his first Academy Award nomination. By the early forties, he was in Hollywood where he showed his mastery of a wide range of styles, from the flag-waving of *So Proudly We Hail!* (1943) to the doomy, Oscar-nominated atmospherics of *Double Indemnity* (1944) and *The Killers* (1946), whose score introduced the hammering four-note motif that became his most recognizable piece of music when it was recycled for the television series *Dragnet* (1952). He was especially noted, however, for lush, romantically overripe scores, and it was for three of these—for *Quo Vadis* (1951), *Ivanhoe* (1952), and *El Cid* (1961)—that he was again nominated for Academy Awards, and for three more—for SPELLBOUND, *A Double Life* (1947), and *Ben-Hur* (1959)—that he won.

Ruddock, John (b. 1897) Peruvian-born actor in two dozen (mostly British) films from 1944, often as fussy professional men. His most notable film roles were Dr. Wilson in *The Fallen Idol* (1948), the banker Cedric Potter in UNDER CAPRICORN, and Elder Harith in *Lawrence of Arabia*.

Rudley, Sarett American screenwriter who adapted Emily NEFF's story "MR. BLANCHARD'S SECRET" for ALFRED HITCHCOCK PRESENTS.

Russell, John L. American cinematographer, in Hollywood from 1934. He had already shot more than 20 features, from *Moonrise* and *Macbeth* (both 1948) to *The Beast from 20,000 Fathoms* (1953), when he and John F. WARREN became the two staff cinematographers for ALFRED HITCHCOCK PRESENTS in 1955. He lit and photographed more than 100 episodes of the series, including most of those directed by Hitchcock: "REVENGE," "BREAKDOWN," "THE CASE OF MR. PELHAM," "WET SATURDAY," "MR. BLANCHARD'S SECRET," "ONE MORE MILE TO GO,"

"THE PERFECT CRIME," "LAMB TO THE SLAUGHTER," "POISON," "BANQUO'S CHAIR," "ARTHUR," "MRS. BIXBY AND THE COLONEL'S COAT," "THE HORSE-PLAYER," and "BANG! YOU'RE DEAD." He also photographed the "FOUR O'CLOCK" segment of *SUSPICION* and the *FORD STARTIME* episode "INCIDENT AT A CORNER," Hitchcock's only color project for television. When Hitchcock decided to economize on the production of *PSYCHO*, a potentially risky project of dubious box-office appeal that he was financing himself, by shooting it with a television crew, Russell was the obvious choice for cinematographer—the only time between 1951 and 1966 that anyone but Robert BURKS shot one of Hitchcock's theatrical films. The result is a black-and-white visual style that owes at least as much to the look of fifties television as to the FILM NOIR cycle with which critics have persistently linked the film. Although Russell continued as a staff cinematographer when *Alfred Hitchcock Presents* was stretched to THE ALFRED HITCHCOCK HOUR in 1962, he had already accepted a similar position on the series *Thriller* (1960–62) and would do so again on *McHale's Navy* (1962–66). He ended his career with four theatrical films and a single 1968 television film, appropriately titled *Now You See It, Now You Don't.*

Russell, William (G.) American sound technician who worked on 16 films and television programs between 1957 and 1968. In collaboration with Waldon O. WATSON, he recorded and mixed the soundtracks for *PSYCHO, THE BIRDS*, and *MARNIE.*

Ryall, Tom British film historian who teaches film studies in the History of Art, Design and Film Program at Sheffield Hallam University. His first book, *Alfred Hitchcock and the British Cinema* (Croom Helm/University of Illinois Press, 1986; second edition, Athlone, 1996), responds to the prevailing view of Hitchcock as a solitary, independent auteur by urging a return to historical contexts within which his alleged individuality might be demonstrated rather than assumed. Its focus is accordingly less on Hitchcock's relatively neglected British films than on the contexts against which they can most authoritatively be analyzed. The principal contexts Ryall

invokes are the state of film culture in England during the twenties and thirties; the economics of film production at GAINSBOROUGH, BRITISH INTERNATIONAL, and GAUMONT-BRITISH; and the specific popular genres (the crime film, the spy story, the romance) within which Hitchcock's "thriller sextet"—*THE MAN WHO KNEW TOO MUCH* (1934), *THE 39 STEPS, SECRET AGENT, SABOTAGE, YOUNG AND INNOCENT*, and *THE LADY VANISHES*—locate themselves and establish both their distinctiveness and their currency as reliable mass entertainment. He concludes that Hitchcock's later British thrillers repeatedly adopt an analytical, even a disruptive, attitude toward the informing conventions of classical cinema.

This argument about the distance Hitchcock's films mark from their enabling conventions is developed in greater detail in Ryall's monograph *Blackmail* (British Film Institute, 1993), which includes information on the technological and aesthetic challenges of synchronized sound, the attitude of British International head John MAXWELL to the new medium, the production history of the film and its critical reception from its first release to the feminist essays of Tania MODLESKI and Robin WOOD before proceeding to a scene-by-scene critical analysis. Ryall concludes that *BLACKMAIL*, far from dating rapidly as an historical curio, manages to combine conventional visual techniques with a revolutionary approach to sound, invoking the terms of both modernism (in its "'artistic' mode of narration") and postmodernism (in its eclectic range of stylistic devices), and is therefore likely to remain a subject of fascinated study.

Ryan, Edmon (1905–1984) American character actor who lent his reassuring presence to some 40 films and television programs from *Crime Over London* (1936) to *Tora! Tora! Tora!* (1970). He appeared as Dr. Croatman in THE ALFRED HITCHCOCK PRESENTS segment "John Brown's Body" (1956), returned to the series as the peacemaking lawyer John Benson in "The Festive Season" (1958), as Simpson in "I Can Take Care of Myself" (1960), and as Lt. Huntley in THE ALFRED HITCHCOCK HOUR episode "Isabel" (1964), and was featured as McKittreck in *TOPAZ.*

Ryan, Madge (1919–1994) Formidable Australian character actress, on the British stage since the midfifties and in films soon after. During her tenure at London's National Theatre she played the monstrously indomitable Mother Courage, a hint of whom seems to cling to her portrayal of the rapacious widow Mrs. Davison, who saunters down the stairs from the Blaney Bureau with her prey well in hand in *FRENZY*.

Sabotage   (Alternative titles: *The Hidden Power, The Woman Alone* [U.S.], *Agent secret*) Gaumont British, General Film Distribution Ltd., 76 minutes, December 1936. **Producer:** Michael Balcon; **Associate producer:** Ivor Montagu; **Director:** Alfred Hitchcock; **Screenplay:** Charles Bennett, based on *The Secret Agent,* a novel by Joseph Conrad; **Continuity:** Alma Reville; **Dialogue:** Ian Hay and Helen Simpson; **Additional dialogue:** E.V.H. Emmett; **Cinematographer:** Bernard Knowles; **Art director:** O. Werndorff; **Assistant director:** Penrose Tennyson; **Wardrobe:** Marianne; **Sound:** A. Cameron; **Editor:** Charles Frend; **Musical director:** Louis Levy; **Cartoon sequence** [*Who Killed Cock Robin?*] by arrangement with and thanks to Walt Disney; **Cast:** Sylvia Sidney (Mrs. Verloc), Oscar Homolka (her husband, Karl Verloc), Desmond Tester (her young brother, Stevie), John Loder (Ted Spencer), Joyce Barbour (Renee), Matthew Boulton (Superintendent Talbot), S.J. Warmington (Hollingshead), William Dewhurst (the Professor), Clare Greet (Mrs. Jones), Aubrey Mather (greengrocer), Fred Schwartz (tailor), Austin Trevor (Vladimir, Verloc's paymaster), Charles Hawtrey (aquarium visitor), Martita Hunt (Professor's daughter), Peter Bull (Michaelis), Torin Thatcher (Yundt), Frederick Piper (bus conductor), Sam Wilkinson, Pamela Bevan, Frank Atkinson, D.A. Clarke Smith, Hal Gordon.

The choice of Joseph CONRAD's 1907 novel *The Secret Agent,* easily the most distinguished literary source he would ever adapt, as the basis for Hitchcock's 20th film was the director's own. As in adapting the stories from *Ashenden* for *SECRET AGENT* (whose title, which duplicated the Conrad title he would next adopt, required a change of the later project to *Sabotage*) he and Charles BENNETT, working in January and February 1936, lightened the tone of his dark original, which unfolded the catastrophic consequences of a suspected spy's passing a bomb to his retarded brother-in-law near the Greenwich Observatory in a symbolic attempt to "blow up the Prime Meridian." They made the unwitting courier a thoroughly normal English boy who is delayed in planting his deadly package at Piccadilly circus first because he is waylaid by a street salesman who wants to use him as a dummy to demonstrate his products and then by the route of the Lord Mayor Show Day parade; made the principal police investigator rather foolishly good natured and in love with Stevie's sister Mrs. Verloc; changed the saboteur Verloc from a pornographic bookseller to the owner of a cinema; and simplified the anatomy of action adumbrated by Conrad's complex network of official betrayals. Verloc is no longer really a double agent trying to ingratiate himself with the spies whose network he has penetrated, and the police officer who is watching him is no longer contending with the very different loyalties of his higher-ups. The film's tone was lightened still further by the last-minute substitution of John LODER for Robert DONAT, whose asthma made it impossible for him to play Ted Spencer, though the casting of American actress Sylvia SIDNEY, again with an eye toward the international market, gave the closing episodes, particularly Mrs. Verloc's murder of her husband after she learns he has sent her brother to his death, a special pathos. The prevailing tone, even of such witty sequences as Verloc's meeting with his contact at the Regent's Park Zoo aquarium and Verloc's visit to the mad bomber whom Conrad had called the Professor, is grim and fatalistic throughout. But the story is leavened by enough humor to make Stevie's death, when the bomb he is carrying blows up the bus he is riding in presumably, with the little dog he has been playing with and all the other passengers—doubly shocking. Hitchcock's insistence on a realistic setting for the disaster—he spent £3,000 to construct a tram line for a single day's shooting—led to his estrangement from Ivor MONTAGU, who asked to be removed from the project. A larger closing awaited only a few days after the production wrapped because Isidore Ostrer, who had purchased a controlling interest in GAUMONT-BRITISH, disbanded the production side of the studio, leaving only the distribution wing intact and leaving Hitchcock to find work elsewhere.

It was a fitting coda to a film that so concerned itself with the powers of cinema—whether it is providing cover for Verloc's nest of spies (or for Spencer's attempt to eavesdrop on them that convinces Verloc to pass the bomb to the unsuspected Stevie) or Verloc's bomb (hidden in a film canister marked *Bartholomew the Strangler*) or jarring Mrs. Verloc momentarily out of her sense of nightmare when she returns from repeated visions of her dead brother's face in the crowds on the street to stand and laugh at the cartoon *Who Killed Cock Robin?* until the death of the title character rekindles her grief. As these two examples suggest, however, Hitchcock invokes cinema's power only to undercut it as a disguise or deflection rather than a true representation. In the same way, the birds that the film consistently poses as victims—the birds at the Professor's shop; the birds in whose cage he places the bomb with a note "DON'T FORGET THE BIRDS WILL SING AT 1:45" and with whom Verloc clearly identifies his own position as he watches the police officers who have surrounded his house, making it impossible for him to plant the bomb himself; the birds in *Who Killed Cock Robin?*—figure the film's most predatory and aggressive instincts as well, focusing Conrad's anatomy of action (every action, even the most murderous, turns out to be a reaction to something else) just as the images of cinema map a corresponding anatomy of representation (every attempt to represent action is only a cover for a secret that cannot be represented or even acknowledged). C.A. Lejeune's critical review of the film helped persuade Hitchcock that in killing Stevie at the end of a highly suspenseful countdown to, and even a few seconds past, 1:45 he had toyed unconscionably with his audience, and he insisted for the rest of his life that the explosion was "a mistake" he had never repeated, at least not until PSYCHO, that other fable about the fatal power of helpless birds. But it is exactly this uncompromising pursuit of the consequences of suspense, so much in keeping with the Conrad novel the adaptation might seem to oversimplify and betray, that has given the film a renewed fascination for recent critics.

Saboteur (Alternative titles: *Saboteure, Cinquième colonne, Sabotatori, Danger*) Frank Lloyd, Universal, 108 minutes, April 1942. **Producer:** Frank Lloyd; **Associate producer:** Jack H. Skirball; **Director:** Alfred Hitchcock; **Original screenplay:** Peter Viertel, Joan Harrison, and Dorothy Parker; **Cinematographer:** Joseph Valentine; **Assistant director:** Fred Frank; **Second unit director:** Vernon Keays; **Second unit cinematographer:** Charles Van Enger; **Art director:** Jack Otterson; **Associate:** Robert Boyle; **Set decoration:** R.A. Gausman; **Continuity:** Adele Cannon; **Sound director:** Bernard B. Brown; **Sound technician:** William Hedgecock; **Special effects:** John P. Fulton, **Editors:** Otto Ludwig and Edward Curtiss; **Music:** Frank Skinner; **Musical director:** Charles Previn; **Cast:** Robert Cummings (Barry Kane), Priscilla Lane (Pat Martin), Otto Kruger (Charles Tobin), Alan Baxter (Freeman), Clem Bevans (Neilson), Norman Lloyd (Frank Fry), Alma Kruger (Mrs. Sutton), Vaughan Glaser (Philip Martin), Dorothy Peterson (Mrs. Mason), Ian Wolfe (Robert), Frances

Carson (society matron), Murray Alper (truck driver), Kathryn Adams (young mother), Pedro de Cordoba (Bones), Billy Curtis (the Major), Marie Le Deaux (fat lady), Anita Bolster (Lorelei), Jeanne Romer, Lynn Romer (conjoined twins), Virgil Summers (Ken Mason), Jean Trent (blonde aircraft worker), William A. Lee, George Offerman (workers), Gus Glassmire (Mr. Pearl), Lee Phelps (plant security), Will Wright (company official), Pat Flaherty (George), Margaret Moffatt (Mrs. Mason's neighbor), Oliver Blake, Hardie Albright, Jack Cheatam (detectives), Margaret Ann McLaughlin (Susie Brown), Belle Mitchell (Adele, Tobin's maid), Kermit Maynard (cowhand), Matt Willis (sheriff), Rex Lease (deputy), William Ruhl (deputy marshal), Duke York (driver, deputy), Paul E. Burns (farmer), Marjorie Wood (farmer's wife), Nancy Loring (young mother), Norma Drury (refugee mother), Claire Whitney (wife in movie audience), Mary Curtis, Walter Miller (midgets), Hans Conried (Edward), Samuel S. Hinds (foundation leader), Ruth Peterson (society matron), John Eldredge (footman), Paul Everton (bus man), Cyril Ring (party guest), William Gould (stranger), Gene O'Donnell (jitterbug), Ralph Brooks (dance extra), Emory Parnell (husband in movie), Margaret Hayes (wife in movie), Jack Arnold (other man in movie), Veda Ann Borg (actress on movie screen), Milton Kibbee (man killed in movie theater), Carol Stevens (his companion), Kernan Cripps (man in movie audience), Charles Sherlock (Barry's taxi driver), Jack Gardner (Pat's taxi driver), Jimmy Lucas (taxi driver), Ed Foster (saboteurs' driver), Paul Phillips (driver), Frank Marlowe (man in newsreel truck), Gerald Pierce (elevator operator), Alexander Lockwood (Marine), Al Bridge (Marine sergeant), Byron Shores (detective), Harry Strang (police officer), Barton Yarborough (first FBI man), Don Cadell, Dick Midgley (FBI men), Selmer Jackson (FBI chief), Dale Van Sickel (FBI assistant), James Flavin (motorcycle cop), Archie Twitchell (motorcycle cop's voice), Eugene Gericke, Louis Lubin, Torin Thatcher.

Despite his misgivings that the original idea behind Hitchcock's 28th film looked episodic and derivative of his British chase films, David O. SELZNICK assigned producer John HOUSEMAN and screenwriter Peter VIERTEL to help him develop it. When neither provided the narrative or thematic discipline Selznick thought the project needed but Viertel had at least completed a preliminary screenplay that could be shown around, Selznick asked the director to sell it to

After pursuing Frank Fry (Norman Lloyd) through most of *Saboteur*, Barry Kane (Robert Cummings) struggles in vain to rescue him from a fatal plunge off the Statue of Liberty. *(National Film Society Archive)*

another studio, and after TWENTIETH CENTURY-FOX and RKO turned it down, UNIVERSAL purchased it on November 7, 1941, for $130,000 and 10 percent of the gross receipts, offering Hitchcock another 10 percent of the gross if he could stay within the film's $750,000 budget. Just as the film was going into production, the Japanese bombed Pearl Harbor, and Hitchcock—motivated perhaps by a desire to seize the historical moment, perhaps by the likelihood of a larger profit than he realized from his earlier loanouts—finished scripting and shooting it in 15 weeks, the fastest of his American films to date. Unfortunately, none of the leads was cast as he would have liked. Gary Cooper, who had turned down *FOREIGN CORRESPONDENT*, was uninterested in playing Barry Kane, the aircraft worker who is pursued by the police after an explosion at his factory leaves his best friend dead; Barbara Stanwyck was unavailable to play love interest Pat Martin; and

Harry Carey, whose booming all-American manner Hitchcock thought would make him perfect to play the Fifth Columnist Charles Tobin, declined to play so un-American a character. The film proceeded with Robert CUMMINGS, Priscilla LANE, and Otto KRUGER in the leading roles. Although Hitchcock enjoyed working with Dorothy PARKER, who was brought in to punch up the dialogue, he was soon calling Viertel, according to John Russell TAYLOR, to tell him, "You'd better come over here and clear up the mess you've started." Principal photography was completed in January 1942, but one problem still remained. During the final editing in April, Hitchcock had intercut a pair of shots of the saboteur Frank Fry looking out a car window and smiling in satisfaction with a newsreel shot of the French liner *Normandie* that had been disabled in a suspicious fire in February soon after being reflagged by the United States and renamed *Lafayette.* Despite the objections of the War Office, who felt the sequence implied that they had been derelict in allowing the ship to be sabotaged, the sequence remained in the film.

Saboteur, the first film in which Hitchcock was billed above the title (a distinction he was never again to lose except in BON VOYAGE and AVENTURE MALGACHE), was also the first of Hitchcock's American films whose reviewers saw him unequivocally typecast as the master of suspense. "This is Hitchcock at his most Hitchcock, which doesn't necessarily mean at his best," Dilys Powell reported from London. More recent critics have been no kinder, seeing the film as utterly characteristic yet not particularly successful. (It is a textbook refutation of Andrew SARRIS's bromide that the trace of a director's individual personality is a mark of distinction.) The problem with Barry Kane's cross-country odyssey from California to New York—including a scene in Radio City Music Hall, where the film would premiere—is not simply a lack of originality, because NORTH BY NORTHWEST borrows just as much from THE 39 STEPS but borrows it more successfully. It is more fundamentally a failure of pace, variety, and unity. Of pace, because it moves much more slowly than *The 39 Steps;* until the hero and heroine arrive in New York, even the most straightforwardly expository scenes take longer to unfold, and heroes and villains alike cannot resist the temptation to make

speeches about their politics. Of variety, because successive sequences, varied as they are in geography, differ very little in tone; even Parker's vaunted wit, which shows itself in such touches as the bickering conjoined twins and the blind Philip Martin's advice to Barry to "keep practicing that triangle," is too sour and synthetic to be very funny so that the film is much less witty than its British forbear. And of unity, because Barry's adventures neither establish a unified sense of the country he is traversing nor indicate what the journey does for him; he lacks both Hannay's amusingly suave adaptability to circumstance and the comically suave immaturity Roger Thornhill will grow out of in *North by Northwest.* Barry is a nice, earnest young man too callow to hold together a story that lacks any other strong center. What remains are several individually memorable scenes. The opening sequence showing the sabotage at the munitions factory is ruthless in its economy. A scene showing a vulnerable Barry and Pat surrounded by obliviously unhelpful society dancers in a New York mansion expertly melds glamour and menace. The shootout in Radio City, though hardly original in its contrast of fictional and real-life melodrama, effectively contrasts the enormous scale of the movie images with the more intimate scale of the saboteur and his victims. Most enduring of all is the finale atop the Statue of Liberty, from which the dangling saboteur falls when the coat by which Barry is holding him rips before the police can come to his aid. The use of models, angled shots, and natural-seeming sounds creates a masterly sense of eeriness. Even here, though, Hitchcock's comment to Taylor ("the audience would have cared more if it had been the hero dangling instead of the villain") suggests a fundamental carelessness in narrative planning, a mistake Hitchcock was not to correct until the Mount Rushmore finale of *North by Northwest.*

Saint, Eva Marie (1924–) Ethereal blonde American star of stage, screen, and television. She first made an impression on some of the earliest television broadcasts as the presenter of commercials in *Campus Hoopla* (1946–47) and the ingenue of *One Man's Family* (1950–52). Following her Drama Critics Award for *The Trip to Bountiful* (1953), she made her Oscar-winning film debut as the fragile Edie Doyle in *On the Waterfront* (1954)—a role originally offered to Grace KELLY—and followed it with *That Certain Feeling* (1956), *A Hatful of Rain* (1957), and *Raintree County* (1957). Over the objections of the MGM executives who wanted him to feature Cyd Charisse as Eve Kendall in NORTH BY NORTHWEST, Hitchcock fought for Saint and supervised the wardrobe selection of his latest Kelly stand-in, he acknowledged, as closely as "a rich man keeping a woman." Saint later recalled his emphasizing three pieces of direction: "Keep your voice low, sit on your hands so that you don't wave them about, and never take your eyes off Cary GRANT." The resulting performance created the coolest of all Hitchcock's ice goddesses, though the one whose personality is required by the script to undergo the greatest number of changes. This cool image, however, was only a blip on what turned out to be Saint's subsequent run of loyal, matter-of-fact helpmeets in films from *Exodus* (1960) to *The Russians Are Coming, The Russians Are Coming* (1966) and, more recently, television shows from *How the West Was Won* (1977) to *Voyage of Terror: The Achille Lauro Story* (1990).

St. John, Howard (1905–1974) American character actor, onstage from 1925, who made his film debut nearly a quarter-century later in *The Undercover Man* (1949) and then played more than 40 screen roles as bluff, authoritative figures like Captain Turley in STRANGERS ON A TRAIN.

Sala, Oskar (1910–) German-born composer who scored two German-language films before collaborating with Remi GASSMAN to produce the electronic sound effects for THE BIRDS.

Samuels, Robert (1961–) American cultural theorist, lecturer in writing at the University of California, Santa Barbara, and author of *Between Philosophy and Psychoanalysis: Lacan's Reconstruction of Freud* (1993) and *Hitchcock's Bi-Textuality: Lacan, Feminisms, and Queer Theory* (1998). The latter, following Freud and LACAN in defining human desire as irreducibly bisexual, argues that Hitchcock's work has been impoverished by theorists who privilege the operation of male heterosexual desire, figured most prominently in the scopophilic gaze discerned by Laura MULVEY, in reading them. Rejecting the widespread tendency of contemporary feminists to equate masculinity with the Lacanian Symbolic and femininity with the Real, he suggests instead that representation throughout Hitchcock is linked to both murder and the denial or Symbolic murder of the Real. Just as the desires that define the leading subjectivities in THE LADY VANISHES, REBECCA, SPELLBOUND, NOTORIOUS, REAR WINDOW, VERTIGO, PSYCHO, THE BIRDS, and *MARNIE* are radically heterogeneous rather than marked by a single gendered orientation, Samuels finds an analogous "bi-textuality" in these films which, however repressed by linear narrative, returns in those modes of representation—word play, jokes, dreams, symbols, psychosis—that express unconscious desires more directly, modes Hitchcockian narrative strategically emphasizes to champion bitextuality against the Symbolic murders of representation. Samuel's most recent book is *Writing Prejudices* (2001).

Sanders, George (1906–1972) Suave, languid, sometimes sneering British actor born in Russia to English parents. Following work in a textile mill and an advertising firm, he played in revues and cabarets and on radio programs before making his film debut in *Find the Lady* (1936) and his Hollywood debut later the same year in *Lloyds of London*. He had already begun his stint as Simon Templar in *The Saint Strikes Back* (1939)—a role he disliked nearly as much as Gay Lawrence in *The Gay Falcon* (1941) and its three successors—when he was cast as the insinuating bounder Jack Favell in REBECCA and the hero's sidekick Scott ffolliott in FOREIGN CORRESPONDENT. Throughout the war, he alternated between playing such wordly heroes as the Saint and the Falcon and playing such sinister Nazis as Quive-Smith in *Man Hunt* (1941). His Lord Henry Wotton in *The Picture of Dorian Gray* (1945) marked the beginning of a long line of weary roués, of which the best known was his Oscar-winning turn as the acidulous critic Addison De Witt in *All About Eve* (1950). Twelve years after publishing his *Memoirs of a Professional Cad* (1960), he committed suicide, leaving behind a note reading, "Dear World, I am leaving you because I am bored. I feel I have lived long enough. I am leaving you with your worries in this sweet cesspool. Good luck."

Sandys, Oliver Pseudonym of Marguerite Florence Barclay (d. 1964), later Marguerite Evans, prolific British novelist. Her novel *Chappy* was adapted for the screen in 1924; THE PLEASURE GARDEN (1923) became the basis for Hitchcock's first directorial feature; and *Mops* was the basis for *Born Lucky* (1933). Under the name Countess Barcynska, she wrote three more novels and two stories that were adapted as silent films.

Sanford, Erskine (1885–1969) Imperious, sputtering American character actor who made his film debut in *Pop Always Pays* (1940), too late in life to play anything but kindly or short-tempered old gents, most memorably Herbert Carter, the editor of the *New York Inquirer* in *Citizen Kane* (1941). A specialist in family physicians, he can be briefly glimpsed as Dr. Galt in SPELLBOUND.

Sangster, Jim British film reviewer and researcher who has written *Friends Like Us: An Unofficial Guide to* Friends (with David Bailey, 1998) and edited *The Press Gang Programme Guide. The Complete Hitchcock,* the synoptic guide he coauthored with Paul CONDON (Virgin, 1999), includes extensive summaries of each of Hitchcock's sound films—except for *The Lodger,* the silent features are given more cursory treatment—followed by information on their links to other Hitchcock films (familiar performers, incarnations of the "ice maiden," recurring thematic or visual motifs); notable technical innovations, broken taboos, or other historical curiosities; information about publicity lines, quotable bits of dialogue and Hitchcock's cameos; notes on later films echoing or influenced by Hitchcock's; and final evaluations. Occasional sidebars pick out key Hitchcockian performers such as Grace KELLY and James STEWART, and eight pages of illustrations, black-and-white and color, reproduce publicity stills and movie posters. Though it is not designed to be read straight through, it is so engaging and approachable a reference, so obviously a labor of love, that its browsing possibilities are immense.

Sarris, Andrew American film critic, longtime reviewer for the *Village Voice* and the *New York Observer.* His books include *The Films of Josef Von Sternberg* (1966), *The American Cinema: Directors and Directions, 1929–1968* (1968), *The Film* (1968), *Confessions of a Cultist: On the Cinema, 1955–1969* (1970), *The Primal Screen: Essays on Film and Related Subjects* (1973), *The John Ford Movie Mystery* (1975), *Politics and Cinema* (1978), and *"You Ain't Heard Nothing Yet": The American Talking Film, History and Memory, 1927–1949* (1998). A series of articles he wrote in the early 1960s was mainly responsible for introducing and popularizing Francois TRUFFAUT's *politique des auteurs* for American filmgoers. In Sarris's hands, "the AUTEUR theory," as he called it, established the mark of a film director's distinctive personality as an index of quality. Hitchcock, whom Sarris called "the supreme technician of the American cinema," master of "the only contemporary style that unites the divergent classical traditions of [F.W.] MURNAU (camera movement) and [Sergei] Eisenstein (montage)," was his beau ideal of a Hollywood auteur, and his variably critical reviews of the UNIVERSAL films are clearly written more in sorrow than in anger. Attacked by his contemporary Pauline Kael and ignored by many more recent critics, Sarris is nonetheless indispensable to an understanding of how Hitchcock and auteurism were used as interdependent props for taking Hollywood movies seriously and ultimately for the academic study of film.

Saunders, Hal American hair stylist responsible for Julie ANDREWS's hair styles in TORN CURTAIN and *Thoroughly Modern Millie* (1967).

Savory, Gerald (1909–) British actor, screenwriter, and producer. Onstage from 1931, he wrote his first play in 1937, the same year he received his first film credit for contributing dialogue to YOUNG AND INNOCENT. After contributing to two more thirties screenplays, he returned to the stage full time, traveling to America in 1941 and taking time out to write a novel, *Behold This Dreamer* (1943). Beginning in 1972, as head of plays for BBC television, he adapted and often produced television films and the miniseries *Love in a Cold Climate* (1980) and *Mapp and Lucia* (1985).

Schünzel, Reinhold (1886–1954) German actor, director, and screenwriter, otherwise Schuenzel or Schunzel. After business and journalism experience, he made his film debut in 1918 and by 1921 was writing and directing features as well. After appearing in some two dozen films and writing or directing two dozen more—most notably *Viktor und Viktoria* (1933) and *Amphitryon* (1935)—he moved to America, where despite four films he failed to establish himself as a director but enjoyed greater success as an actor with the Hollywood Gestapo. Cast as the kindly Nazi Dr. Anderson in *NOTORIOUS*, he suggested Leopoldine KONSTANTIN for the crucial role of Madame Sebastian. In the fifties he returned to Germany, where he appeared in three final films before his death.

Schwartz, Fred British character actor with a half-dozen film credits in the thirties, the first of them the role of Mr. Kelly in *JUNO AND THE PAY-COCK*.

Scott, Janet American character actress who played Norma in *SPELLBOUND* and two other film roles in the forties.

Scott, Mary Pixieish American character actress whose eight film appearances have spanned the half-century from *Kings Row* (1947) to *Love Me Twice* (1995). Her more frequent television roles have included four for *ALFRED HITCHCOCK PRESENTS*—inquisitive mystery writer Babs Fenton in "MR. BLANCHARD'S SECRET," newlywed Meg Loomis in "Crackpot" (1957), bereaved daughter Janet Wallace in "The Diplomatic Corpse" (1957), and Nurse Copeland in "Safety for the Witness" (1958)—and three for *THE ALFRED HITCHCOCK HOUR*—Wanda Hatfield in "Don't Look Behind You" (1962), Laura in "How to Get Rid of Your Wife" (1963), and a party guest in "The Trap" (1965).

Secret Agent (Alternative titles: *Der Geheimagent, Quatre de l'espionage, L'Agente secreto, Amore e mistero*) Gaumont British, General Film Distributors Ltd., 83 minutes, May 1936. **Producer:** Michael Balcon; **Associate producer:** Ivor Montagu; **Director:** Alfred Hitchcock;

Screenplay: Charles Bennett, based on the play by Campbell Dixon, adapted from [two stories, "The Traitor" and "The Hairless Mexican" in] *Ashenden, or The British Agent,* by W. Somerset Maugham; **Continuity:** Alma Reville; **Dialogue:** Ian Hay; **Additional dialogue:** Jesse Lasky, Jr.; **Cinematographer:** Bernard Knowles; **Art director:** O. Werndorff; **Assistant director:** Penrose Tennyson; **Set director:** Albert Jullion; **Costumes:** J. Strassner; **Sound:** Philip Dorte; **Editor:** Charles Frend; **Musical director:** Louis Levy; **Cast:** John Gielgud (Edgar Brodie, alias Richard Ashenden), Peter Lorre (the General), Madeleine Carroll (Elsa Carrington), Robert Young (Robert Marvin), Percy Marmont (Caypor), Florence Kahn (Mrs. Caypor), Charles Carson ("R"), Lilli Palmer (Lilli), Tom Helmore (Col. Anderson), Andreas Malandrinos (manager), Michael Redgrave (army captain), Michel Saint-Denis (coachman), Howard Marion Crawford (Carl), Michael Rennie.

Michael BALCON chose the property on which Hitchcock's 19th film would be based: Campbell DIXON's play *Ashenden,* based on W. Somerset MAUGHAM's short story "The Hairless Mexican." Although Ivor MONTAGU was unenthusiastic about the project, Hitchcock persuaded him that they might treat the subject as freely as *THE 39 STEPS* had treated John BUCHAN's novel. Certainly the screenplay, a fantasia that freely mingled and transformed elements from Dixon's play (a secret agent travels to Switzerland to execute an enemy agent, kills the wrong man by mistake, and then has to kill the real agent), "The Traitor," another of the stories from Maugham's Ashenden cycle (a spy has to be lured from his wife's side back to England so that he can be arrested), and new material based on Hitchcock's picture-postcard approach to Switzerland in which mountains, cathedrals, village rituals, and chocolate are all made to play a leading role. Story conferences, blocked by the story's lack of momentum, proceeded slowly. John Russell TAYLOR reports that Charles BENNETT did not sketch out the complete treatment until the night before he and Hitchcock left to scout Swiss locations. Though he was as reluctant as Ashenden to take the role, Shakespearean actor John GIELGUD was persuaded by Hitchcock's argument that Ashenden was a modern Hamlet and found himself shuttling between early morning calls to the set and

Richard Ashenden (John Gielgud) tries in vain to comfort Elsa Carrington (Madeleine Carroll), the fellow spy playing his wife, after the death of Caypor in *Secret Agent*. *(National Film Society Archive)*

evening performances in *Romeo and Juliet* every night. He was joined by two stars designed to appeal to the American market, Madeleine CARROLL and Robert YOUNG, and by Peter LORRE, playing a killer even more mercurial than Abbott in THE MAN WHO KNEW TOO MUCH (1934). Distraught by the tension of switching between two roles and two media, resentful of Lorre's scene-stealing and Hitchcock's devoted attention to Carroll's wardrobe and lighting, and ready to doubt his own performance, Gielgud has described the shoot as an ordeal that left him with a lasting distrust of movies, and the press and public, which received the film more coolly than its two immediate predecessors, seems to have echoed his discomfort.

That discomfort stems not from Ashenden's position as an unwilling and deeply flawed antihero with no appetite for his brutal job, but from the misfit between this modern Everyman's disillusionment, faithfully captured in Maugham's measured cadences, and the heroic avidity required by the newly emergent formula of the Hitchcock thriller. The situation revealed by the film's prologue—well-known writer Edgar Brodie is reported dead so that he can go underground in the role of Richard Ashenden and travel to Switzerland, accompanied by another agent who, he later finds, is masquerading as his wife to assassinate an enemy agent—could promise either thrills or disillusionment or the first followed by the second. The film, unlike Maugham's stories, tries to have both in more-or-less regular alternation. The avidity normally associated with the Hitchcock hero is assumed here by the General, the wenching, bloodthirsty assassin sent to assist Ashenden in Switzerland, and by the blathering American Robert Marvin, whose puppy-dog lovemaking to Elsa in a carriage scene largely extemporized for the camera, conceals his identity as the real enemy agent. The screenplay is careful to lift the ultimate guilt for executing the innocent Caypor from Ashenden (who ends up watching through a telescope as the General pushes him off an Alp). Lorre's performance as the General is entertainingly grotesque. Although the confusion of the opening-night audience over a striking innovation during the train-wreck sequence—a brief segment of color film, designed by Len Lye, that made it look as if the actual filmstock was burning and breaking in the projector—led to its prompt removal, the film still abounds in Hitchcockian set pieces—from the discovery of the dead organist in the chapel, his finger still sustaining a single ominous note, to the frenzied comedy of Ashenden and the General shouting warnings at each other over the din of the church bells in whose tower they have taken refuge, from the sequence in which Ashenden follows the General's tip to a chocolate factory concealing the spy ring to the climactic train wreck itself, which solves the characters' moral problems by leaving two of them dead. But the energy behind these set pieces, which made the film one of Hitchcock's own favorites, is never reconciled with the weary moral lassitude of the hero and, eventually, the heroine, who begins the film eager for intrigue before turning on Ashenden to blame him for Caypor's death. Like earlier films from THE LODGER to *The 39 Steps,* this one seems to straddle the thin line between dreaming and waking, especially in the nightmarish scene in which Ashenden's false wife Elsa realizes that he has killed the wrong man. As Elisabeth WEIS has pointed out, the soundtrack throughout is one of Hitchcock's most subjectively distorted. But the sour subjectivities Hitchcock's set pieces and distorted soundtrack reveal impede rather than develop the narrative flow; the film keeps leading the characters to complex moral dilemmas—there is indeed more than a hint of Hamlet in Ashenden—from which the

plot seems obliged to rescue them. In seeking to combine Maugham's hard-won world weariness with the subversive velocity of *The Man Who Knew Too Much* and *The 39 Steps,* the film ends up as one of Hitchcock's least satisfactory adaptations, and his most problematic film for GAUMONT-BRITISH.

Seel, Charles (1898–1980) American character actor, onscreen from 1938. He appeared as the customer in the watch shop in the SUSPICION segment "FOUR O'CLOCK," the court clerk in the ALFRED HITCHCOCK PRESENTS episode "The Kind Waitress" (1959), and in two roles for THE ALFRED HITCHCOCK HOUR: Dr. Chalmont in "You'll Be the Death of Me" (1963) and the barber in "The Return of Verge Likens" (1964). Eventually, having come into his own in *The Horse Soldiers* (1959) and three other John Ford westerns, he settled into the role of telegraph operator Barney Danches in the television series *Gunsmoke* (1965–74).

Selzer, Milton (1918–) Sad-faced American character actor who followed his television debut as Mahatma Gandhi in *You Are There* (1954) with more than 100 supporting roles, mostly for television. In MARNIE, he played the persistent man at the racetrack who recognizes Marnie as Peggy Nicholson.

Selznick, David O. (1902–1965) Legendary Hollywood producer, the quintessential independent studio head. Son of a first-generation movie mogul, he worked in Lewis J. Selznick's production company, then made two short documentaries when his father went bankrupt in 1923, and finally, having lost the profits from these films in other investments, wheedled a job as assistant story editor from Louis B. Mayer, his father's former partner, in 1926. Unsatisfied as associate producer of MGM's B pictures, he left in 1927 to become an associate producer of such films as *The Four Feathers* (1929) at PARAMOUNT. Four years later he moved to RKO as vice president in charge of production. Here his energy blossomed, and he produced some three dozen films, including *A Bill of Divorcement* (1932) and *What Price Hollywood?* (executive producer, 1932), during the next two years. In 1933, Mayer, whose daughter Irene had

David O. Selznick

married Selznick, brought him back to MGM as vice president and producer of such star-studded literary adaptations as *Dinner at Eight* (1933) and *David Copperfield* (1935). He left MGM in 1936 to form SELZNICK INTERNATIONAL, whose hallmark during the next 20 years would be careful, faithful adaptations of such literary properties as *The Garden of Allah* (1936), *The Prisoner of Zenda* (1937), *The Adventures of Tom Sawyer* (1938), and, most notably, *Gone With the Wind* (1939). In 1937, Selznick, impressed by Hitchcock's reviews though he had seen none of his films, opened the negotiations that would bring him to America two years later, under a contract paying $50,000 for each of two films to be completed within a year and four further options of one film a year, with each of the first three options to pay an additional 10 percent. Although Selznick initially planned to have Hitchcock direct *The Titanic,* and the director was amenable, his first assignment turned

out to be REBECCA. It may have been inevitable that Selznick, the most adventurous of studio heads, would have been the one to sign Hitchcock, who was represented in their contract negotiations by the producer's brother Myron SELZNICK; it was certainly inevitable that the two personalities, each so bent on total control of their projects, would clash over casting, budget, shooting schedules, and especially adaptation. Selznick, appalled at the irreverently free treatment of Daphne DU MAURIER's novel originally submitted by Hitchcock, fired off one of his notorious memos demanding a new and more faithful treatment, signaling his intention of fighting his new employee over every aspect of production. The two battled courteously during the nine weeks of the film's production, as Selznick repeatedly nettled Hitchcock by arriving on the set full of energetically expressed opinions that the director preferred to ignore, and it was something of a relief when the producer loaned the director to Walter WANGER for his next assignment, FOREIGN CORRESPONDENT. Throughout the eight years to which his contract eventually ran, in fact, Hitchcock directed only three films for Selznick International—*Rebecca,* SPELLBOUND (based on Selznick's longtime wish to make a film about psychoanalysis), and THE PARADINE CASE (whose screenplay is credited, like those of a half-dozen of Selznick's other films, to the producer himself). Even before his contract was up, Hitchcock was already negotiating with Sidney BERNSTEIN to set up the independent partnership TRANSATLANTIC PICTURES, showing at once how much clout his association with Selznick's access to money, stars, and power had given the immigrant to Hollywood, and how much the experience had made him yearn for the independence of producing his own films. For his part, Selznick, who had divorced Irene Mayer to marry his frequent star Jennifer Jones, was exhausted by his struggles with the epic *Duel in the Sun* (1946) and the regime of drugs that underwrote his 20-hour days; he produced only another handful of films, ending with *A Farewell to Arms* (1957), before his death. The relationship between the two men is chronicled in Leonard J. LEFF's *Hitchcock and Selznick: The Rich and Strange Collaboration of Alfred Hitchcock and David O. Selznick in Hollywood* (1987).

Selznick, Myron

Selznick, Myron (1898–1944)   American producer, production executive, and agent, son of Lewis J. Selznick and brother of David O. SELZNICK. A veteran of his father's production company, he rose through the ranks to become Hollywood's youngest producer before he was old enough to sign his own checks. Forced out of the industry by his father's bankruptcy in 1923, he worked for a few years as an independent producer and then in 1928 became an agent. He represented Hitchcock in the contract he signed with SELZNICK INTERNATIONAL in 1939 and remained active in representing him until his death.

Selznick International Studios

Selznick International Studios   The most famous of American independents during the studio era, founded in 1936 by David O. SELZNICK to release a steady diet of "prestige" (well-made middlebrow) films, usually based on literary properties whose name recognition would both sell the finished product and provide a template for its production. The hallmarks of the studio's product, from *Little Lord Fauntleroy* (1936) to *A Farewell to Arms* (1957)—consistently high production values, aversion to departures from the tone or technique of the original property, a wholehearted allegiance to traditional American values—could be traced to the tight creative control of Selznick, the only important Hollywood producer to immerse himself routinely and unstintingly in the minutiae of film production. The company released three Hitchcock films—*REBECCA, SPELLBOUND,* and *THE PARADINE CASE*—and developed two more, *SABOTEUR* and *NOTORIOUS,* that were sold respectively to UNIVERSAL and RKO.

Sersen, Fred

Sersen, Fred (1890–1962)   American special-effects cinematographer, born Ferdinand Sersen, at 20TH CENTURY–FOX for many more than 100 films. In Hollywood from 1930, he designed the climactic fire for *In Old Chicago* (1938) and won Oscars for *The Rains Came* (1939) and *Crash Dive* (1943). The Sersen tank in which he helped shoot all of *LIFEBOAT* is named after him.

sexuality

sexuality   Despite his well-documented prudishness, sex is everywhere in Hitchcock's films. But it can involve power, violence, disguise, VOYEURISM, GUILT, repression, disavowal, displacement, or FETISHISM. In fact, as the catalogue of icy BLONDES, erotic strangulations, handcuffs, barely closeted HOMOSEXUALS, and priests with a romantic past in his films indicates, sex in Hitchcock *always* involves power, violence, disguise, voyeurism, guilt, repression, disavowal, displacement, or fetishism. Whether because of industry censorship, personal neurosis or an aesthetic of perversion, Hitchcock never shows a romantic couple simply enjoying a sexual situation. Sam Marlowe's abbreviated courtship of Jennifer Rogers in *THE TROUBLE WITH HARRY* is almost entirely devoted to the question of what to do with her first husband's corpse. Francie Stevens wants to seduce John Robie in *TO CATCH A THIEF* because he is a thief, and Mark Rutland wants to rape Marnie Edgar in *MARNIE* for the same reason. Just before Roger Thornhill and Eve Kendall retire to her berth aboard the Twentieth Century Limited in *NORTH BY NORTHWEST,* Hitchcock is careful to show that she is in communication with Thornhill's enemy Philip Vandamm. If intrigue eventually drives a wedge between Thornhill and Eve, or Alice White and Frank Webber in *BLACKMAIL,* or Daisy Bunting and the lodger in *THE LODGER,* or most of the ill-suited pairs in *TOPAZ,* it brings together many more romantic couples in *THE 39 STEPS, SECRET AGENT, YOUNG AND INNOCENT, THE LADY VANISHES, REBECCA, FOREIGN CORRESPONDENT, SABOTEUR, SPELLBOUND, NOTORIOUS, THE PARADINE CASE, STAGE FRIGHT, REAR WINDOW,* and *THE BIRDS.*

Ever since Jean DOUCHET and Raymond BELLOUR, analysts have been interested in specific sexual practices in Hitchcock from voyeurism to enslavement, but they have seldom approached the larger question of why sexuality is represented in such perverse or displaced terms throughout his films. One possible answer is the ubiquitous censors, on whom the director was ready to blame every commercial compromise. Another is a matter of genre because a convention of thrillers is that their intrigue supplies both promising romantic partners and the aphrodisiac of danger. But Hitchcock's representations of sexuality seem focused and energized, not dissipated, by the censorship that he internalized so easily that it became only another formal challenge like those of his one-set films. Apart from THE FARMER'S WIFE, moreover, even Hitchcock's nonthrillers, from THE PLEASURE GARDEN and DOWNHILL to THE MANXMAN and RICH AND STRANGE, seem more interested in sex displaced, fetishized, perverted, thwarted, or shamefully endured than sex blissfully consummated. It therefore seems more likely that Hitchcock's representation of sexuality—which defines it not in terms of a specific physical experience or emotional ideal or even in terms of a discrete zone of desire, but in terms of the inextricable associations with power, violence, disguise, voyeurism, guilt, repression, disavowal, displacement, and fetishism with which it is inevitably bound up, and in particular in terms of the filmmaker's seductive or assaultive relationship to the audience—is strikingly postmodern, perhaps the most socially prophetic aspect of his work.

Shadow of a Doubt   (Alternative titles: *Uncle Charlie* [working title], *Im Schatten des Zweifels, L'Ombre d'un doute, L'Ombra del dubbio*) Skirball, Universal, 108 minutes, January 1943. **Producer:** Jack Skirball; **Director:** Alfred Hitchcock; **Screenplay:** Thornton Wilder, Alma Reville, and Sally Benson, from an original story by Gordon McDonnell; **Cinematographer:** Joseph Valentine; **Assistant director:** William Tummel; **Second assistant director:** Ralph Slosser; **Art director:** John B. Goodman; **Associate:** Robert Boyle; **Set decorator:** R.A. Gausman; **Associate:** E.R. Robinson; **Costumes:** Adrian, Vera West; **Set continuity:** Adele Cannon; **Sound:** Bernard B. Brown; **Sound technician:** Robert Pritchard; **Editor:** Milton Carruth; **Music:** Dimitri Tiomkin; **Musical director:** Charles Previn; **Cast:** Joseph Cotten (Charles Oakley), Teresa Wright (Charlie Newton), Macdonald Carey (Jack Graham), Patricia Collinge (Emma Newton), Henry Travers (Joe Newton), Hume Cronyn (Herb Hawkins), Wallace Ford (Fred Saunders), Edna May Wonacott (Ann Newton), Charles Bates (Roger Newton), Irving Bacon (station master), Clarence Muse (railroad porter), Janet Shaw (Louise), Estelle Jewell (Charlie's girlfriend), Constance Purdy (Mrs. Martin), John McGuire, Byron Shores (detectives), Vaughan Glaser (Dr. Phillips), Virginia Brissac (Mrs. Phillips), Edwin Stanley (Mr. Green), Isabel Randolph (Mrs. Green), Frances Carson (Mrs. Potter), Earle S. Dewey (Mr. Norton), Grandon Rhodes (Rev. MacCurdy), Ruth Lee (Mrs. MacCurdy), Minerva Urecal

(Mrs. Henderson), Eily Malyon (librarian), Edward Fielding (doctor on train), Sarah Edwards (his wife), Shirley Mills (young girl).

Hitchcock's 29th film, his second on his UNIVERSAL loanout, began in an unpublished story idea by the husband of Selznick story editor Margaret McDonnell about a serial killer who, hounded by police officers back east, comes to California to take refuge with his sister's family until his niece surmises his secret but keeps it to herself even after his death. Meeting with Gordon MCDONNELL in May 1942, Hitchcock was immediately attracted to the idea. Although a memo he wrote that month emphasized his eagerness to "avoid the conventional small town American scene" by creating "modern" characters whose "social ambitions could concern themselves possibly with war work" and representing "life in a small town lit by neon signs," his interest in securing Thornton WILDER to help work on the treatment and scout locations soon overrode this desire; there is nothing specifically modern about the small town of Santa Rosa, where the film is set, and it conspicuously avoids any mention of war work except at a few crucial moments. When Wilder left to join the War Office, story and screenplay writer Sally BENSON joined Hitchcock and Alma REVILLE in competing the screenplay, though an unprecedented expression of appreciation in the credits memorialized Wilder's contributions. The director faced one disappointment in casting and another in filming. Denied the opportunity to cast Joan FONTAINE as Charlie Newton by a rift between Fontaine and David O. SELZNICK, Hitchcock borrowed his second choice, Teresa WRIGHT, from Samuel Goldwyn (for whom she had played a similar role in her first film, *The Little Foxes,* alongside Patricia COLLINGE) and Joseph COTTEN from Selznick. His hopes of shooting the entire film on location in Santa Rosa in and around the middle-class house he had selected were dashed by space limitations, requiring studio work and the construction of an exterior set instead. Donald SPOTO has found a deeper cause for concern in the final illness of Hitchcock's mother back in England and his own inability to return to her, leading him to project his anxieties onto the family in his film. But neither

Uncle Charlie (Joseph Cotten) presents a gift to his niece Charlie Newton (Teresa Wright): a ring he has stolen from one of his victims in *Shadow of a Doubt.* *(National Film Society Archive)*

Cotten nor Wright nor Hume CRONYN, in his film debut, nor Collinge (who wrote the scene between Charlie and Jack Graham in the garage herself) seems to have detected them, and filming, which began in August, was completed without incident in the fall. The film, completed for just over $800,000, returned a respectable profit and remained the film Hitchcock most often identified as his own favorite.

Whatever its possible connections to his own family, *Shadow of a Doubt* incontestably brings one of Hitchcock's major themes, the doubling of villain and victim, to its first full blossom. After a prologue introduces her Uncle Charlie in his Philadelphia rooming house, Charlie Newton is introduced by a series of exactly parallel shots outside her own house in a mirror-image pose, lying on her bed in a mood of passive fatalism. Like her uncle, she thinks herself disillusioned with life, and like him, she hits on a remedy: She will ask him to come visit. Before she can get in touch with him, however, word arrives that he already plans to visit. Seeing him as her family's salvation, she joyfully informs him on his arrival that the two of them share a special bond indicated by their names. The rest of the film explores just how terrible that special bond can be, as Charlie soon begins to suspect that her uncle is hiding a sinister secret and then confirms that he is the Merry Widow Murderer police detectives Jack Graham and Fred Saunders, who have invaded the Newton household disguised as polltakers, are seeking. Uncle Charlie, seeing that his niece knows the truth about him, appeals to her in all his old roles—authoritarian father figure, suavely attentive escort, solicitous brother of her fragile mother—but now they are all poisoned, and her obsession with expelling him from the house he has violated makes her increasingly complicit with his past, even as it casts her more and more obviously as his victim, until the moment when, as he prepares to throw her from a train leaving Santa Rosa, she kills him instead, keeping his secret in a sadly decorous epilogue as Graham consoles her by offering one of the film's few discreet references to the war. The duality of the villain and his victim/accomplice is emphasized not only by the profusion of doubles throughout the film (two opening segments, two pairs of two detectives, Charlie's two siblings, two girlfriends, and two suitors, two suspects in the Merry Widow case, two scenes at the train station and in the garage, two more involving a ring, two attempts on Charlie's life before the climax, even a confrontation at a bar called the 'Til Two) but by the stages in Charlie's relationship with her uncle—adoration, bewilderment, suspicion, revulsion, defiance—that mark her entrance to adulthood by her growing awareness of the menace he represents to the life she once yearned to escape and now longs to return to, of her relation to all his earlier victims, to the mother she is fighting to protect, and, in her vow to kill him, to himself. The film's deep-focus compositions make it one of Hitchcock's richest visually, and its unmistakable overtones of incest make it, despite its placid surface and near-avoidance of screen violence, one of his most disturbing.

Shaffer, Anthony (1926–) British playwright and screenwriter, former barrister. The twin of Oscar-winning screenwriter Peter Shaffer, he wrote the screen adaptation of Graham Billings's novel *Forbush and the Penguins* (1971), but his cunning play *Sleuth* (1970, filmed 1972) had already signaled his specialization in mystery stories. After adapting Arthur LA BERN's *Goodbye Piccadilly, Farewell*

Leicester Square to the screen as FRENZY, he rewrote the adaptation of *Murder on the Orient Express* (1974) without screen credit. Approached by Hitchcock to adapt Victor Canning's *The Rainbird Pattern* (1972) to the screen, he dissented from the director's intention of establishing a generally comic tone for the intrigue and was promptly replaced by Ernest LEHMAN. Since then he has adapted three other Agatha Christie novels and written the original story for *Summersby* (1993).

Shamley Productions American company that oversaw the production of ALFRED HITCHCOCK PRESENTS (1955–62) and THE ALFRED HITCHCOCK HOUR (1962–65), named after the country house the Hitchcocks had lived in back in England.

Shannon, Harry (T.) (1890–1964) Craggy American character actor who played more than 100 gruff cops, bartenders, and blue-collar workers, moving up a notch to Doc Horner in the ALFRED HITCHCOCK PRESENTS segment "BREAKDOWN." He is best known, however, for playing the fathers of Charles Foster Kane in *Citizen Kane* (1941), of Katie Holstrum in *The Farmer's Daughter* (1947), and of Mitch Wayne in *Written on the Wind* (1956).

Sharff, Stefan American filmmaker and film theorist who, after working with Sergei Eisenstein, produced and directed more than 60 films, including the feature *Across the River* (1965). Professor emeritus and former head of the film school at Columbia University, he has written *The Elements of Cinema: Toward a Theory of Cinesthetic Impact* (1982), which lays down a grammar of cinematic structure reducible to eight elements—separation, parallel action, slow disclosure, familiar image, moving camera, multiangularity, master shot discipline, orchestration—that govern the ways the cinema remakes the physical world into a world with its own narrative strategies and kinesthetic form. This grammar forms a theoretical basis for his more specialized Hitchcock studies. *Alfred Hitchcock's High Vernacular: Theory and Practice* (Columbia University Press, 1991) is a close examination of NOTORIOUS, FRENZY, and FAMILY PLOT designed to illustrate the "architecture of cinematic elements" that constitute cinema as a signifying system parallel to, but dissimilar from, prose fiction and the theater. Although he emphasizes that his structural analysis should not be confused with interpretation, Sharff takes *Notorious* as marking Hitchcock's "entry into cinema's full expressiveness," especially in its natural-seeming separations of characters in immediately contiguous space into distinct shots whose graphic and rhythmic elements can be expressively combined and contrasted, and his last two films as characteristic, in their different ways, of a similar expressiveness, and therefore of the medium Hitchcock's work represents.

The Art of Looking in Hitchcock's Rear Window (Limelight, 1997) focuses still more narrowly on an extended shot-by-shot analysis of *REAR WINDOW* that emphasizes not only the thematic importance of looking as a metaphor for the experience of watching movies, but also the specific modality of looking in *Rear Window,* whose moving camera, together with Jefferies's resolutely partial views of his neighbors' homes and the systematic parallels between the parallel actions occurring in their homes and his own, is designed to foster a "slow disclosure" that "make[s] the viewers more attentive by sharpening their visual memory" for information most crucially offered without interpretive dialogue. Noting the high proportion of shots without dialogue (35 percent, plus another 15 percent, in which characters in the foreground comment on silent characters in the background), Sharff argues that the film emphasizes both a subjective mode of voyeurism attributable to Jefferies and an objective mode attributable to cinema itself, keeping them distinct until they merge at the end in the long-withheld "fourth-wall shot" of Jefferies hanging over the edge of his balcony.

Shaw, Janet (1919–) Pouting American character actress, born Ellen Clancy, who played nearly 60 waitresses, secretaries, and roommates from 1935 through 1950. As Louise, the emerald-hungry young waitress in the café 'Til Two, she provided Charlie Newton a terrifying vision of her vulnerable alter ego and her adored uncle's homicidal rage in *SHADOW OF A DOUBT.*

Shayne, Konstantin (1888–1974) Russian actor, brother of character actress Tamara Shayne. Barred from the Moscow Art Theatre by World War I and the Russian Revolution, he ended up in Hollywood, where from 1938 he played some three dozen mysterious, often sinister, foreigners. He was especially memorable as Ike Weber in *None But the Lonely Heart* (1944) and as General Konrad Meinike, Franz Kindler's comrade and victim, in *The Stranger* (1946). He appeared twice in *ALFRED HITCHCOCK PRESENTS*—as the customs officer in "Safe Conduct" (1956) and the father of suspected arms dealer "Sasha the Terrible" in "Flight to the East" (1958)—before his final role as Pop Leibl, gossipy owner of the Argosy Book Store, in *VERTIGO*

Sheean, Vincent American newspaperman who supplied the story, "Ambassador from the United States," on which the Will Rogers comedy *Ambassador Bill* (1931) is based. His *Personal History* provided the nominal basis for *FOREIGN CORRESPONDENT.*

Sheffield, Reginald (1901–1957) British actor, born Reginald Sheffield Casson. A child star who made his film debut in 1913, he never made the transition to adult stardom despite his performance in the title role of *David Copperfield* (1923) and by the thirties had settled into a succession of some 50 balding character roles such as Reggie Wetherby, the safe, homely alternative to Johnnie Aysgarth in *SUSPICION.*

Sherwood, Robert E(mmet) (1896–1955) American playwright and screenwriter with editorial background. His earliest work for Hollywood (*The Lucky Lady,* 1926) predates his first notable play, *The Road to Rome* (1927), which was followed by *The Queen's Husband* (1928), *This Is New York* (1929), *Reunion in Vienna* (1931), *The Petrified Forest* (1935), and *Idiot's Delight* (1936), which won the Pulitzer Prize. Further Pulitzers followed for *Abe Lincoln in Illinois* (1938), *There Shall Be No Night* (1940), and the historical work *Roosevelt and Hopkins: An Intimate History* (1948). In addition to supplying raw material for many films, he worked throughout the thirties on such notable projects as *The Ghost Goes West* (1936)

Robert E. Sherwood

and *The Adventures of Marco Polo* (1938) and was credited as lead screenwriter on the adaptation of *REBECCA*, for which he shared an Academy Award nomination. During World War II he headed the Overseas Branch of the Office of War Information, which he had been instrumental in forming, and then returned to win an Oscar for his adaptation of MacKinlay Cantor's verse essay *Glory for Me* (1945) as *The Best Years of Our Lives* (1946) and collaborated in the original screenplay for *The Bishop's Wife* (1947).

Shine, Billy, Jr. (1910–) British stage actor, né Wilfred William Dennis, whose only film role is Carl in *WALTZES FROM VIENNA*.

Short Night, The Hitchcock purchased the rights to Ronald KIRKBRIDE's suspense novel, which tells the story of a British agent on the trail of a terrorist who has escaped from Wormwood Scrubs prison, killed one of the women who aided his escape for resisting his sexual advances, and fled to his family in Finland, as early as 1968. But it was not until after *FAMILY PLOT* that he set about the task of adapting the novel—first with James Costigan, who worked briefly on the project in 1978, and then with Ernest LEHMAN, who produced a draft screenplay that fall; and finally with David FREEMAN, whose screenplay, copyrighted under the title *Alfred Hitchcock's The Short Night,* is reprinted as an addendum to his memoir *The Last Days of Alfred Hitchcock* (1984).

Shourds, Sherry American filmmaker who worked on some 20 properties from *The Iron Mask* (1929), in which he was billed as assistant director, to *I CONFESS*, his final film, on which he served as unit production manager. He returned in 1967 as assistant director on eight episodes of the television series *The High Chapparal.*

Sidney, Sylvia (1910–1999) Winsome, sad-eyed American actress, born Sophia Kosow. Onstage from 1926, she came to Hollywood soon after and shot to early stardom in *City Streets* (1931). Typecast as a downtrodden working girl throughout the Depression years, she projected an almost unbearable vulnerability in *An American Tragedy* (1931), *Jennie Gerhardt* (1933), *Fury* (1936), *You Only Live Once* (1937), *Dead End* (1937), and *You and Me* (1938) and, during a trip to England, was signed by Michael BALCON to play the strikingly similar role of the American-born Mrs. Verloc in *SABOTAGE*. At first hesitant about Hitchcock's methods—"How can we do the end of the scene before we've even rehearsed?" she asked him—she was startled by the force of the sequence in which she murders her husband when she finally saw the completed film. After 1940 she was more active onstage than onscreen, though her Oscar-nominated role as Rita Walden's mother, Mrs. Pritchett, in *Summer Wishes, Winter Dreams* (1973) led to some 30 television roles during the next 25 years. The first of her three husbands was publisher Bennett Cerf, the second, actor Luther Adler.

Silliphant, Stirling (Dale) (1918–1996) American screenwriter and producer, former advertising executive with Disney and Fox. He began as a producer in 1953 and then turned to screenwriting with such films as *5 Against the House* (1955), *Village of the Damned* (1960), and *In the Heat of the Night* (1967), for which his adaptation won an Academy Award. Long active in television, he wrote the ALFRED HITCHCOCK PRESENTS segment "THE CRYSTAL TRENCH" and created the series *Naked City* (1958–63) and *Route 66* (1960–64).

Silvera, Darrell (1900–1983) American set decorator, head of RKO's prop department for 20 years and hundreds of films from *Follow the Fleet* (1936) to *Beyond a Reasonable Doubt* (1957)—including all three of Hitchcock's RKO films, MR. AND MRS. SMITH, SUSPICION, and NOTORIOUS—who, when the studio went under, turned independent for another 20 films through *The Driver* (1978).

Sim, Alastair (1900–1976) Brilliantly eccentric Scottish character actor, a former professor of elocution who left the University of Edinburgh to go onstage in 1930, made his film debut in 1936, and returned to Edinburgh as rector from 1948 to 1951. Widely known for his ferocious twinkle and lugubrious charm, he was by 1950, the year he appeared as the heroine's father Commodore Gill in STAGE FRIGHT, the most popular male star in Britain. But his most memorable roles were still ahead of him: the title character in *Scrooge* (1951), hopeful heir Deniston Russell in *Laughter in Paradise* (1951), ludicrously homely Miss Fritton and her brother Clarence in *The Belles of St. Trinian's* (1954), Inspector Poole in *An Inspector Calls* (1954), and the assassin Hawkins in *The Green Man* (1956). He also starred as Mr. Swallow, the Stipendary Magistrate in the television series *Misleading Cases* (1967–71).

Sim, Gerald (1925–) Distinguished-looking British character actor with a special line on pompous upper-class twits such as the man who holds forth on the necktie murders in the pub where Richard Blaney gulps brandy in FRENZY.

Simone, Sam P(aul) (1945–) American film historian whose 1982 doctoral dissertation at Brigham Young University, published as *Hitchcock as Activist: Politics and the War Films* (UMI Research Press, 1985), argues on the basis of Hitchcock's four films that most explicitly deal with World War II—FOREIGN CORRESPONDENT, SABOTEUR, LIFEBOAT, and NOTORIOUS—that Hitchcock, a British émigré who continued to support Britain actively throughout the war, planned each of these four films as defenses of democratic values whose suspense was generated by the question of whether those values would triumph in a world that challenged them in social and ideological as well as individual terms. Urging his adopted country from isolationism to interventionism in *Foreign Correspondent* and from interventionism to internationalism in *Lifeboat* and *Notorious,* Hitchcock used his wartime films to urge U.S. entry into the war, expose the threat of Fifth Columnists, unite the forces of liberal democracy, and maintain vigilance on an international level when it had ended. Although an introductory chapter provides background information about Hitchcock's earlier espionage films, no mention is made of the wartime films—MR. AND MRS. SMITH, SUSPICION, SHADOW OF A DOUBT, and SPELLBOUND—that do not deal explicitly with the war. In the past several years, Simone's conclusions have been vigorously disputed by Ina Rae Hark.

Simpson, Helen (Deguerry) (1897–1940) Australian novelist who collaborated with Clemence DANE to write *Enter Sir John* (1928), which Hitchcock filmed as MURDER!, and on her own wrote UNDER CAPRICORN (1937), filmed nearly 10 years later. In between, she joined Ian HAY to write the dialogue for SABOTAGE, her only screenwriting credit. She was killed when German bombs struck the London hospital in which she was recuperating from surgery.

Simpson, Peggy (1913–) Prime British character actress who appeared in a dozen films of the thirties. She played the maid who admits Richard Hannay to Professor Jordan's house in THE 39 STEPS and one of the two women who discovers Christine Clay's body on the beach in YOUNG AND INNOCENT and thinks she has been killed by Robert Tisdall, who is running off to fetch the police.

Singer, Peggy   See ROBERTSON, PEGGY.

Sinyard, Neil   British academic and film historian, senior lecturer in Film Studies at Hull University. His many books include *Journey Down Sunset Boulevard: The Films of Billy Wilder* (with Adrian Turner, 1979), *Directors: The All-Time Greats* (1985), *The Films of Richard Lester* (1985), *Classic Movies* (1985), *Filming Literature: The Art of Screen Adaptation* (1986), *The Films of Mel Brooks* (1987), *The Films of Steven Spielberg* (1987), *The Films of Woody Allen* (1987), *The Best of Disney* (1988), *Marilyn* (1989), *Silent Movies* (1990), *The Films of Nicholas Roeg* (1991), *Children in the Movies* (1992), *Classic Movie Comedians* (1992), *Mel Gibson* (1992), and *Clint Eastwood* (1995). He is coeditor with Brian McFarlane of Manchester University Press's British Film Makers series, which includes his own *Jack Clayton* (2000). His *The Films of Alfred Hitchcock* (Multimedia Publications, 1986), like his volumes on Brooks, Spielberg, and Allen, is a heavily illustrated, large-format overview of the director, proceeding chronologically from film to film, providing for each a brief synopsis and critical assessment, with more extended, though still brief, analysis reserved largely for the films from VERTIGO to MARNIE. Its most distinctive feature, compared to similar nonacademic volumes by George PERRY and Robert HARRIS, is a brief final chapter, "Influence and Achievement," which cites films from Francois TRUFFAUT's *Fahrenheit 451* (1965) and Claude CHABROL's *Le boucher* (1970) to Jonathan Demme's *Last Embrace* (1979), Brian DE PALMA's *Obsession* (1975), and Richard Franklin's *Psycho II*. An appendix provides abbreviated cast lists for each of the 53 feature films and 20 television segments Hitchcock directed.

Skall, William V.   (1898–1976)   American cinematographer, a specialist in Technicolor, who moved from studio to studio shooting some three dozen films from 1935. He was nominated for Academy Awards for his work on *Northwest Passage* (1941), *Billy the Kid* (1941), *Arabian Nights* (1942), *Life with Father* (1947), *Quo Vadis* (1951), and *The Silver Chalice* (1954), and shared an Oscar for *Joan of Arc* (1948). That same year, he shared credit with Joseph VALENTINE for photographing *ROPE*.

Skin Game, The   (Alternative titles: *Bis auf's Messer, Fiamma d'amore*) British International, Wardour & F., 89 minutes, February 1931. **Producer:** John Maxwell; **Director:** Alfred Hitchcock; **Adaptation:** Alfred Hitchcock, from the play by John Galsworthy; **Scenario:** Alma Reville; **Cinematography:** J.J. Cox; **Camera operator:** Charles Martin; **Art director:** J.B. Maxwell; **Assistant director:** Frank Mills; **Editors:** A. Cobbett and Rene Marrison; **Sound:** Alec Murray; **Cast:** Edmund Gwenn (Mr. Hornblower), Jill Esmond (Jill Hillcrist), John Longden (Charles Hornblower), C.V. France (Mr. Hillcrist), Helen Haye (Mrs. Hillcrist), Dora Gregory (Mrs. Jackman), Phyllis Konstam (Chloe Honblower), Edward Chapman (Dawker), Frank Lawton (Rolf Hornblower), Herbert Ross (Mr. Jackman), Ronald Frankau (auctioneer), R.E. Jeffrey (first stranger), George Bancroft (second stranger), Wally Patch (van driver).

John Galsworthy's play had been both a notable success on its first West End run (1920–21) and the basis for a 1920 film in which the entire stage cast reprised their roles. Its revival in 1929 presumably gave John MAXWELL the idea of filming it again; certainly the choice was not that of the director, who as usual professed himself impatient with another example of canned theater and unwilling to discuss it in any detail. Although Hitchcock would use several members of the original cast (Ivor BERNARD, Mary CLARE, Malcolm KEEN, J.H. ROBERTS) in later films, his adaptation of Galsworthy's play, which was shot during the winter of 1930–31, included only two members of the original cast, Edmund GWENN and Helen HAYE, both of whom would return in later Hitchcock films. The film follows the play in tracing the tragic consequences of the conflict between two families. The Hillcrists are cash-poor landed gentry who cannot keep the parvenu industrialist Hornblower at a safe distance. The beginning of the film, after a single shot showing three men beginning to chop down a tree, already finds Jill Hillcrist, on horseback, confronted by Rolf Hornblower, driving a noisy car through the bucolic landscape. Rolf's father, a pushy, coarse, but vital figure, is attempting to buy the Centry, a neighboring farm that will ring the Hillcrists' land with his factories. Calling on his neighbors and offering his hand in friendship, Hornblower is briskly rebuffed and his son Charles's wife Chloe publicly snubbed, setting up the auction for the Centry that follows as the first sign of open war. It is a war the Hillcrists cannot win, of course, and their top bid for the land is easily surpassed by Hornblower, active himself in the auction but placing this crucial final bid through an intermediary. Desperate to head off this fait accompli, Mrs. Hillcrist (without the knowledge or approval of her husband, as in the play) blackmails Hornblower with some news uncovered by her agent Dawker: that before her marriage, Chloe was a professional divorce co-respondent. Hornblower agrees to let the Hillcrists have the Centry, but Dawker repeats the secret to Charles. When he abandons her, Chloe throws herself into the Hillcrist pond, killing the baby she is carrying and perhaps herself as well, and denying any possibility of rapprochement between the two families that the tentative romance between Jill and Rolf had offered, and a final shot bookends the film by showing a tree falling heavily to earth.

Although the adaptation by Hitchcock and Alma Reville is less free than Eliot STANNARD's adaptations for Hitchcock's silents had been, Hitchcock's inventiveness shows in his staging of the action for the camera. The adaptation succeeds not only in opening out Galsworthy's interior sets to the outdoors in frequent shots that show the visual and auditory contrast the play hints at but also in establishing a new, specifically cinematic rhythm for the story. In an odd prefiguration of *Citizen Kane,* the film, as Charles BARR has shown, alternates between unusually long takes (the first meeting between Hornblower and the Hillcrists runs $4\frac{1}{2}$ minutes without a cut, and half of the film's total running time is devoted to shots running more than a minute each) and unusually rapidly cut sequences (especially the auction halfway through the film, which cuts rapidly between tightening closeups of Hornblower, Hillcrist, and the auctioneer, coming to a climactic point with a torrent of 15 rapid glances back and forth in just 20 seconds). Having set up Chloe's vulnerability to the blackmail threat in a series of rapid shots, the film can linger over a much longer sequence shot of her announcing her pregnancy but not her scandalous past, to her husband. This is echoed by a parallel scene in which

Jill keeps her distance from Rolf's conciliatory overtures by looking offscreen in the opposite direction toward what is apparently a series of balls she is tossing offscreen before a pan left reveals a dog who has been returning the same ball to her repeatedly. The games the Hillcrists are playing with the Hornblowers end in their treating the interlopers as no better than animals, and they end by corrupting them as well: Mrs. Hillcrist through her classbound cruelty, her husband by his passive acquiescence, their daughter by the reflexive hardening that prevents her from opening herself to the emotional vulnerability that destroys the happiness, and perhaps the life, of her counterpart on the other side of the tracks. In the attempt to preserve their idyllic world from the unseemly noise that the film persistently associates with Hornblower's cars and machines and his booming lower-class voice, it is the Hillcrists and their hireling who have said too much.

Skinner, Frank (1897–1968)   American composer who during his 30-year career at UNIVERSAL worked, often uncredited, on some 400 films, including everything from *Three Smart Girls* (1936) to Abbott and Costello second features to Douglas Sirk melodramas to *SABOTEUR.*

Skirball, Jack H. (1896–1985)   American film executive who was put in charge of production and distribution at Educational Pictures from 1932 to 1939, when he left to set up shop as an independent producer. The most notable of the dozen films he released through 1951 are Hitchcock's two films for UNIVERSAL: *SABOTEUR,* which he coproduced, and *SHADOW OF A DOUBT,* on which he is billed as producer.

Slade, Olga (d. 1949)   British stage actress who played Mary Hearn, the postmistress in *THE FARMER'S WIFE,* during the London runs that began in 1924 and then recreated the role for Hitchcock's film. Her only other recorded film role is an uncredited bit in *One Precious Year* (1933).

Slesar, Henry (1927–)   American suspense writer with radio experience. Even as he was working full-time writing advertising copy, his short stories were repeatedly adapted for *ALFRED HITCHCOCK PRESENTS* and *THE ALFRED HITCHCOCK HOUR*, and he became one of the series' most prolific adapters, writing more than 20 episodes, including two directed by Hitchcock: "THE HORSEPLAYER" and "I SAW THE WHOLE THING." He won an Edgar for his first novel, *The Gray Flannel Shroud* (1959), and a 1974 Emmy for his work as head writer on the television series *The Edge of Night* (1968–79), a period when *TV Guide* described him as "the writer with the biggest audience in America." He has also written occasional film scripts, from *Two on a Guillotine* (1965) to *The Maddening* (1995).

Slezak, Walter (1902–1983) Roly-poly Viennese actor born into a theatrical family and discovered by Michael Kertesz (later Curtiz) while he was working in a bank in 1922. Forced from romantic leads to character parts onstage and onscreen by his advancing weight, he made his Broadway debut in 1931 and began to appear in Hollywood films in 1942 while still pursuing an active stage career. Willy, the U-boat commander he played in *LIFEBOAT*, belongs to his wartime-German-villain period; after the war, he was cast in a broader range of ethnic roles, sometimes menacing, sometimes comical, sometimes—as in *The Pirate* (1948)—both. An accomplished singer, he appeared in several operas and operettas and won a Tony for his work in the Broadway musical *Fanny* (1955). He also served as a regular panelist in three television series, *The Name's the Same* (1951–55), *This Is Show Business* (1956), and *Made in America* (1964), and alternated with Vincent Price in hosting *The Chevy Mystery Show* (1960).

Slifer, Clarence (W.D.) American special-effects cinematographer best known for his contributions to four SELZNICK productions—*Since You Went Away* (1944), *Duel in the Sun* (1946), *THE PARADINE CASE*, and *Portrait of Jennie* (1948)—who returned 20 years later to work on *Ice Station Zebra* (1968).

Sloan, Jane E. (1946–) American scholar and bibliographer, former cinema librarian at the University of Southern California, current women's studies librarian at Rutgers University, and author of

Robert Bresson: A Guide to References and Resources (1983) and *Alfred Hitchcock: A Guide to References and Resources* (G.K. Hall, 1993; 2nd edition, University of California paperback, 1995). Following a substantial introduction surveying different critical approaches to Hitchcock's work from auteurism to feminism, the first two-thirds of this monumental reference comprise detailed scene-by-scene summaries of all Hitchcock's theatrical films. The final 200 pages review, summarize, and comment on published writings by and about Hitchcock in all languages annually from 1919 (the director's one-page story "Gas") through 1990. Supplemental sections list reviews of all Hitchcock's features, give cast and production credits both for films in which Hitchcock was involved but did not direct and television segments he did direct, and describe archival resources around the world for Hitchcock prints, scenarios, and production materials. For serious Hitchcock scholars, Sloan's magisterial book is a truly indispensable reference; for more casual readers, it provides an excellent place to begin research among the 1,500 books, essays, and reviews it cites.

Sloane, Olive (1896–1963) British character actress who followed her film debut in *Greatheart* (1921) with some 50 performances as housewives and maidservants such as Sal in *UNDER CAPRICORN*.

Smit, Howard American makeup artist, in Hollywood from 1948, whose 10 films and television programs through 1974 included *THE BIRDS* and *MARNIE*.

Smith, (Sir) C(harles) Aubrey (1863–1948) Majestically stern British character actor. A former member of England's national cricket team, then a teacher and stockbroker, he made his stage debut at 30 and was soon shuttling between Britain, where he played Professor Henry Higgins in the 1914 production of George Bernard Shaw's *Pygmalion,* and America, where he made his film debut in 1915. He starred in a dozen American and British silents through 1924 but made a far more lasting mark when the coming of sound called him back to the screen in 1930. Although he could play French in *Love Me Tonight* and *Trouble in Paradise* (both 1932), Swedish in *Queen Christina* (1934), and Ruritanian in *The Prisoner of Zenda* (1937), his sepulchral voice, imposing frame, and gray-moustached face more often invoked an England whose time had passed, except in such movies as *Lives of a Bengal Lancer* (1935), *Wee Willie Winkie* (1937), *The Four Feathers* (1939), and *Waterloo Bridge* (1941). As informal head of Hollywood's émigré British community, he was a natural choice to play the benevolent, stiffly righteous Chief Constable Colonel Julyan, the most English of the English types who crowded REBECCA, Hitchcock's first American film.

Smith, Cyril (1892–1963) Unassuming British character actor, onstage as a child, who made his film debut in 1908 and went on to play hundreds of menials, servants, and functionaries such as the secretary in WALTZES FROM VIENNA. A few years before his brief retirement, he played Merlin in the television series *The Adventures of Sir Lancelot* (1956–57).

Smith, George F.J. American author who wrote the 1956 story on which the ALFRED HITCHCOCK PRESENTS episode "ONE MORE MILE TO GO" is based.

Smith, (Frank) Kent (1907–1985) Stalwart, rather bland American actor of stage and screen. His square-jawed blond earnestness served as a useful anchor to the more florid stars of *The Garden Murder Case* (1936), his debut; *Cat People* (1942), in which he had his best-known role as Oliver Reed; *The Spiral Staircase* (1946); and nearly 100 other films and television segments. He appeared as the guilt-ridden murderer Gilbert Hughes in the ALFRED HITCHCOCK PRESENTS episode "Curtains for Me" (1959) and in three roles in THE ALFRED HITCHCOCK HOUR: as Michael Barnes's friend Jerry O'Hara in "I SAW THE WHOLE THING," Dr. Adamson in "Body in the Barn" (1963), and Sally Benner's father in "Thou Still Unravished Bride" (1965).

Smith, Kirby American actor whose four credits in films and television include Tom Mason in the ALFRED HITCHCOCK PRESENTS segment "THE CASE OF MR. PELHAM."

Smith, Susan British film scholar, lecturer at the University of Sunderland's Centre for Research in Media and Cultural Studies and author of *Hitchcock: Suspense, Humour and Tone* (British Film Institute, 2000). Deploring the frequent insensitivity of thematically based Hitchcock commentary to the ways in which shifts of tone inflect emotional reactions and interpretations, Smith rejects both Robin WOOD's choice of VERTIGO and Lesley BRILL's choice of THE TROUBLE WITH HARRY as exemplary Hitchcock films, proposing instead "a cinema based on SABOTAGE." Central to both *Sabotage* and Hitchcock's work in general is a control of suspense through humor (not merely as comic relief, but as a means of intensifying and modulating suspense) and a thematizing of the relationship between the cinema audience and the director (the historical figure, the putative shaper of fictive worlds, the public persona) who poses as a saboteur of viewers' conventional expectations. Subsequent chapters consider suspense and humor in both affective and epistemological terms, examining the construction and inflection of point of view through camera setups, mise-en-scène, music, and Hitchcock's CAMEO APPEARANCES in NOTORIOUS, ROPE, REAR WINDOW, PSYCHO, and especially THE BIRDS.

Smythson, George British actor whose only film credit is as one of the 12 jurors in MURDER!

Snell, George British actor who plays Oscar Hamilton, the lubricious manager of the Pleasure Garden Theater, in THE PLEASURE GARDEN.

Soulé, Olan (1910–1994) American character actor, otherwise known as Alan Soulé, with more than 20 years' radio experience before his 1949 film debut. In some 50 films and 100 television episodes he was typecast by his slight build and worried face as bank and hotel clerks, as the nervous assistant auctioneer in NORTH BY NORTHWEST, and in his five roles for ALFRED HITCHCOCK PRESENTS—the laboratory assistant in "Our Cook's a Treasure" (1955), the shop clerks in "Portrait of Jocelyn" (1956) and "Graduating Class" (1959), Darlene's father in "BANG! YOU'RE DEAD," and Brother Charley Fish in "The Faith of

Aaron Menefee" (1962)—and a sixth in THE ALFRED HITCHCOCK HOUR as Bill in "Ride the Nightmare" (1962). Unseen, he voiced the superhero Batman in six different animated series from 1968 through 1979.

South, Leonard (J.)
American cinematographer who began his career as an uncredited assistant camera on REAR WINDOW; served as camera operator on MARNIE and TORN CURTAIN; assisted Gilbert TAYLOR, again without credit, on FRENZY; and returned as lighting cinematographer on FAMILY PLOT. Most of his other credits have been on such television series as Me and the Chimp (1972), The Rockford Files (1974–80), and Coach (1989–97).

Spanish Jade, The
Famous Players–Lasky, 1922 **Presented by** Adolph Zukor; **Director:** John S. Robertson; **Supervisor:** Thomas J. Geraghty; **Screenplay:** Josephine Lovett, based on the novel by Maurice Hewlett and the play by Louis Joseph Vance; **Cinematographer:** Roy Overbaugh; **Cast:** David Powell (Gil Pérez), Marc MacDermott (Don Luis Ramónez de Alavia), Charles de Rochefort (Esteban), Evelyn Brent (Mañuela), Lionel d' Aragon (Mañuela's stepfather), Frank Stanmore (Tormillo, Don Luis's servant), Roy Byford (Esteban's spy and confidant), Harry Ham (Osvald Manvers).

Tenth of the 12 silent films, 1920–22, for which Hitchcock designed intertitles.

Spellbound
(Alternative titles: The House of Dr. Edwards [working title], Alfred Hitchcock's Spellbound, Ich kämpfe um dich, La maison du Docteur Edwardes, Io ti salverò) Selznick International, United Artists, 111 minutes, October 1945. **Producer:** David O. Selznick; **Director:** Alfred Hitchcock; **Screenplay:** Ben Hecht, suggested by The House of Dr. Edwardes, a novel by Francis Beeding; **Adaptation:** Angus MacPhail; **Cinematographer:** George Barnes; **Assistant director:** Lowell J. Farrell; **Art director:** James Basevi; **Associate:** John Ewing; **Set decoration:** Emile Kuri; **Costumes:** Howard Greer; **Sound:** Richard DeWeese; **Special effects:** Jack Cosgrove; **Dream sequence designs:** Salvador Dali; **Psychiatric adviser:** Ray E. Romm, M.D; **Production assistant:** Barbara Keon; **Supervising film editor:** Hal C. Kern;

Associate: William H. Ziegler; **Music:** Miklós Rózsa; **Orchestrations:** Eugene Zador; **Cast:** Ingrid Bergman (Dr. Constance Peterson), Gregory Peck (John Ballantine), Michael Chekhov (Dr. Alex Brulov), Leo G. Carroll (Dr. Murchison), John Emery (Dr. Fleurot), Rhonda Fleming (Mary Carmichael), Norman Lloyd (Garmes), Bill Goodwin (hotel detective), Wallace Ford (hotel masher), Jean Acker (matron), Steven Geray (Dr. Graff), Donald Curtis (Harry), Art Baker (Lt. Cooley), Regis Toomey (Sgt. Gillespie), Irving Bacon (railroad ticket taker), Paul Harvey (Dr. Hanish), Erskine Sanford (Dr. Galt), Janet Scott (Norma), Constance Purdy (Dr. Brulov's housekeeper), Victor Kilian (sheriff), Addison Richards (police captain), Matt Moore (police officer), Clarence Straight (secretary at police station), George Meader (railroad clerk), Richard Bartell (ticket seller), Harry Brown (gateman), Dave Willock (bellboy), Joel Davis (young John Ballantine), Teddy Infuhr (his brother), Edward Fielding (Dr. Edwards).

Soon after he began psychotherapy in 1943, David O. SELZNICK conceived the idea of a movie about psychoanalysis. Leonard J. LEFF has described how Hitchcock, who had purchased the screen rights to Francis BEEDING'S 1928 novel The House of Dr. Edwardes, persuaded Selznick to buy them for $40,000, and, after agreeing with Selznick that veteran craftsman Ben HECHT would be the primary screenwriter, sat down with his old friend Angus MACPHAIL to work Beeding's wild melodrama about an impostor who has taken over an asylum into the sober treatment Selznick wanted. Successive drafts pruned Hitchcock's set pieces and jokes concerning mental patients in favor of the heroic treatment of psychotherapists, and Hecht's first-draft screenplay, completed in May 1944, placed the romance between Dr. Constance Peterson and the false Dr. Edwards, an amnesiac, at the center of the story and featured an extended dream sequence. To counterbalance the film's talkiness about psychiatry, Selznick urged Hecht and Hitchcock to emphasize the possibility that the false Edwards had murdered his own therapist. Although both Hecht and Hitchcock had envisioned Joseph COTTEN as the false Dr. Edwards, Selznick cast him in I'll Be Seeing You (1945) and instead cast Gregory PECK and—after toying with the possibilities of Dorothy McGuire and Greta Garbo in the role of the psychiatrist who falls in love with him—Ingrid BERGMAN, whom Selznick's story department had been trying to cast in a Hitchcock film for three years. Selznick was forced to give up the casting of Dr. Murchison, the outgoing head of the Green Manors, as a romantic rival when Fredric March and Ralph Bellamy turned down the role, leaving it open for the dryly paternal Leo G. CAR-ROLL. At Hitchcock's request, Selznick paid Salvador DALÍ $4,000 to design the celebrated dream sequence. Principal photography began on July 10, 1944, and was completed—despite the misgivings of the inexperienced Peck, who would have liked more time and more direction—at the end of August. After the usual postproduction maneuvering, which

included Selznick's trimming of 14 minutes from Hitchcock's rough cut and Miklós RÓZSA's introduction of the theremin's weird vibrato to indicate the intensity of mental disorder, the film was previewed on February 16, 1945, but not released until Halloween because of the popularity of long-running summer films. Although several reviewers warned that *Spellbound* was heavy going, especially in small-town markets, Hitchcock's 31st film enjoyed a record-breaking opening in London, garnered worldwide receipts of $6 million, and landed six Academy Award nominations—for Best Picture, Direction, Supporting Actor (Michael CHEKHOV), Black-and-White Cinematography, Special Effects, and Music (the only Oscar it won).

Challenged by Dr. Constance Peterson (Ingrid Bergman), the amnesiac posing as Dr. Anthony Edwardes (Gregory Peck) in *Spellbound* confesses that he does not know who he really is. *(National Film Society Archive)*

Spellbound (the title was suggested by SELZNICK INTERNATIONAL secretary Ruth Rickman) has not worn well. Even reviewers in 1945 often found the story of Dr. Constance Peterson's love for a neurotic new colleague who turns out to be an imposter and her determination to join him, as he is pursued by the police, in proving his innocence by unlocking the past secrets he has repressed, static, talky, and pretentious in its earnest faith in the talking cure. Fifty years later, the film's confidence in the ability of psychoanalysis to drive "the evils of unreason . . . from the human soul" seems even more naïve, the Freudianism of its dream sequence foursquare, its casting of Ingrid Bergman at her most wholesome as everyone's favorite psychiatrist pat, its conflation of the therapeutic dialogue with courtship patronizing. (Interestingly, recent Hitchcock commentary has been more interested in MARNIE, which deals far more skeptically with this conflation.) Yet the film is interesting as more than a collection of striking moments—the doors that magically open over the lovers' heads as they kiss, the long takes of the false Edwards walking around Dr. Brulov's house with a razor, the giant gun in Dr. Murchison's giant hand as he slowly turns it from the departing Dr. Peterson to himself and the screen, and of course the dream sequence itself—or the catalogue of Hitchcock's personal fears Donald SPOTO has found in it. Working with the richest MACGUFFIN of his career—the unconscious memories of the false Dr. Edwards, who serves at once as detective, victim, and chief suspect—may not have ensured the film's success, but it did give Hitchcock a psychological model that helped integrate his trademark set pieces by providing a direction for the story aiming to uncover the truth about the hero. If the film's decision to shift its emphasis from mental patients to mental health professionals makes it ponderous and condescending in the tone it adopts toward psychopathology, it set the stage for the less profound but more dramatic staging of individual and interpersonal pathologies in NOTORIOUS and prepared a return for the still more probing examinations of characters closer to the audience—characters who, lacking the calmly authoritative psychiatrists who dispense wisdom and closure in *Spellbound,* suffer and die in VERTIGO or talk matter-of-factly about

themselves in a locked room in PSYCHO while a psychiatrist paces the office next door explaining away their unspeakable mysteries.

Spelling, Aaron (1923–) Influential American producer who, before becoming rich and famous as godfather of *Beverly Hills 90210* (1990–2000), *Melrose Place* (1992–99), and more than 100 other television series and segments, appeared as an aspiring actor in some 20 film and television roles, one of the earliest as a road worker in the ALFRED HITCHCOCK PRESENTS episode "BREAKDOWN."

Spencer, Dorothy (1909–) American film editor who spent most of her 50-year career (1929–79) at 20TH CENTURY-FOX. More than 20 years after she edited FOREIGN CORRESPONDENT and LIFEBOAT, she was nominated for Oscars for *Cleopatra* (1963) and *Earthquake* (1974).

Spoto, Donald (1941–) American writer whose early work on film includes *Camarado: Hollywood and the American Man* (1978), *Stanley Kramer, Film Maker* (1978), and *The Art of Alfred Hitchcock: Fifty Years of His Motion Pictures* (Doubleday, 1976; 2nd edition, 1992), which after a preliminary survey of the early films before THE 39 STEPS (only BLACKMAIL among these early films comes in for more extensive treatment) then proceeds to a film-by-film analysis whose variable attention to Hitchcock collaborators, Hollywood parallels, and technical information is systematically subordinated to thematic analysis. The two exceptions to this pattern are VERTIGO, the subject of a much longer chapter, and FAMILY PLOT, whose briefer chapter is supplemented by the storyboard for the sequence in which Blanche Tyler and George Lumley hurtle down a mountainside road in a car whose brake lines have been cut. The volume, very well illustrated in black-and-white, includes a detailed filmography and a brief bibliography.

When Spoto returned to Hitchcock in *The Dark Side of Genius: The Life of Alfred Hitchcock* (Little, Brown, 1983), more than his genre had changed. Whereas his earlier study had enshrined Hitchcock as an exemplary filmmaker, his biography, which proposed to read Hitchcock's films in lieu of any considerable correspondence, diaries, or personal papers, as an extended exercise in self-revelation, mingled extensive research (including many interviews with writers, technicians, and performers who had worked with the director) with further analysis of such allegedly revelatory films as SHADOW OF A DOUBT, VERTIGO, and FRENZY and gossip about Hitchcock's sexual desires, particularly his desire to dominate the BLONDE actresses he so often cast as his heroines. Although Hitchcock scholars were quick to attack Spoto's research as undermined by his psychobiographical speculations, in practice it is easy enough to separate the two, and the volume is as useful to Hitchcockians as it has been to its author, whose revelations about Hitchcock's sexual pursuit of Tippi HEDREN guaranteed his book notoriety and launched his career as a show-business and celebrity biographer. His publications since then have included *The Kindness of Strangers: The Life of Tennessee Williams* (1985), *Lenya: A Life* (1989), *Madcap: The Life of Preston Sturges* (1990), *Laurence Olivier: A Biography* (1991), *Blue Angel: The Life of Marlene Dietrich* (1992), *Marilyn Monroe: The Biography* (1993), *A Passion for Life: The Biography of Elizabeth Taylor* (1995), *The Decline and Fall of the House of Windsor: From Queen Victoria to Queen Elizabeth II, the Secret History of the Royal Family* (1995), *Rebel: The Life and Legend of James Dean* (1996), *Notorious: The Life of Ingrid Bergman* (1997), *Diana: The Last Year* (1997), *The Hidden Jesus: A New Life* (1998), and *Jacqueline Bouvier Kennedy Onassis* (2000).

Srebnick, Walter American film scholar, professor of English at Pace University. With Walter RAUBICHECK, he has coedited *Hitchcock's Rereleased Films: From* Rope *to* Vertigo (Wayne State University Press, 1991), a collection of 15 original essays on the five films withheld from circulation from 1968 through 1983: ROPE, REAR WINDOW, THE TROUBLE WITH HARRY, THE MAN WHO KNEW TOO MUCH (1956), and VERTIGO—a small group of films that the editors argue in their general introduction are central to Hitchcock's career. The contributors, participants in a 1986 conference held at Pace, include John BELTON, Lesley BRILL, Thomas M. LEITCH, Robert STAM, and Robin WOOD—most of whom incorporated their essays, or the papers that led to them, into book-

length studies. Most of the essays are on *Rear Window* and *Vertigo,* with three on *Rope,* two on *The Man Who Knew Too Much,* and one on *The Trouble with Harry.* They are bookended by a brief foreword by Andrew SARRIS and the transcript of Samuel TAYLOR's conference talk and question-and-answer session on the screenplay of *Vertigo.* The collection concludes with a brief bibliography of recommended books on Hitchcock.

Stafford, Frederick (1928–1979) Austrian actor, born Friedrich Strobel von Stein. He made his film debut in 1965 and after several years in European international thrillers was chosen for the role of André Devereaux in TOPAZ, his first English-language film. Proficient but colorless, he made little impression in the film and returned soon after to the French and Italian industries for another eight films before his death in a plane crash.

Stafford, Harry British musician whose sole film credit is as cocompiler and arranger, with Hubert BATH, for the musical score of BLACKMAIL.

Stage Fright (Alternative titles: *Die rote Lola, Le grand alibi, Paura in palconscenico*) Warner Bros.–First National, 110 minutes, February 1950. **Producers:** Alfred Hitchcock and Fred Ahern; **Director:** Alfred Hitchcock; **Screenplay:** Whitfield Cook, based on *Man Running,* a novel by Selwyn Jepson; **Adaptation:** Alma Reville; **Additional dialogue:** James Bridie and Ranald MacDougall; **Cinematographer:** Wilkie Cooper; **Set decoration:** Terence Verity, Jr.; **Costumes:** Milo Anderson, Christian Dior; **Makeup:** Colin Garde; **Production manager:** Fred Ahern; **Editor:** E.B. Jarvis; **Music:** Leighton Lucas; **Musical direction:** Louis Levy; **Songs:** Cole Porter ("The Laziest Gal in Town"), Mischa Spoliansky ("When You Whisper Sweet Nothings to Me"); **Cast:** Marlene Dietrich (Charlotte Inwood), Jane Wyman (Eve Gill), Michael Wilding (Wilfred Smith), Richard Todd (Jonathan Cooper), Alastair Sim (Commodore Gill), Sybil Thorndike (Mrs. Gill), Kay Walsh (Nellie Goode), Miles Malleson (Mr. Fortescue), Hector MacGregor (Freddie Williams), Joyce Grenfell (sharpshooting concessionaire), André Morell (Inspector Byard), Patricia Hitchcock (Chubby Bannister), Ballard Berkeley (Sgt. Mellish).

Even before the disastrous reception of *UNDER CAPRICORN*, his second and last film for TRANSAT-LANTIC PICTURES, Hitchcock and Alma REVILLE had been at work since December 1948 on an adaptation of Selwyn JEPSON's novel *Man Running,* first serial-ized in 1947, which several reviewers, presumably drawn by both its plot and its title, had described as ideal Hitchcock material. Whitfield COOK, who had written the second Broadway play in which Patricia HITCHCOCK appeared, wrote the dialogue, and James BRIDIE supplied additional material. The participation of Bridie, who refused to travel outside Britain, may have been the reason Hitchcock returned to his native country for this film, though the ability to shoot on London locations or the proximity of the Royal Academy of Dramatic Art, where Patricia Hitchcock was studying, may have influenced him as well. By the time the film was cast the following

Eve Gill (Jane Wyman), playing the role of suspected killer Charlotte Inwood's maid, holds a mirror up to Charlotte (Marlene Dietrich) as her employer prepares to play a role herself in the garden party in *Stage Fright. (National Film Soci-ety Archive)*

spring, Hitchcock had signed a new financing and distribution deal with WARNER BROS., the studio that had distributed Transatlantic's films. Despite the fail-ure of *Under Capricorn* with Ingrid BERGMAN in the lead, he persuaded Warners that the new film needed a bankable star, and they agreed to cast Jane WYMAN, who had just won an Academy Award for *Johnny Belinda* (1948), as RADA student Eve Gill; Richard TODD, who would be nominated for an Oscar for *The Hasty Heart* (1949), as Jonathan Cooper, the old friend she hides from the police when he is suspected of murder; and evergreen femme fatale Marlene DIETRICH as Charlotte Inwood, the actress whom Jonathan is in turn protecting. The director's attitude toward his two lead actresses was strikingly different: He chided Wyman, who spent most of the film dis-guised as the lower-class maid Doris Tinsdale, for her distress at looking less glamorous than Dietrich, while he gave the older actress the freedom to pick out her own wardrobe and jewelry and instruct cine-matographer Wilkie COOPER in the best way to light her. The film, shot between June and September 1949, proceeded smoothly but did not end Hitch-cock's atypical string of weak financial performers; it was not until his next film, *STRANGERS ON A TRAIN,* that he would return to genuine success.

Even now a prejudice persists that *Stage Fright* is a mere "run for cover," an efficient black-and-white filming (after Hitchcock's first two Technicolor pro-ductions) of a routine whodunit. This description is unfortunate first because it is inaccurate. *Stage Fright* is no more a whodunit than *Psycho* because charac-ters and viewers in both films spend little of their running time wondering whodunit; they think they already know. In *Stage Fright,* the murderer of Char-lotte's inconvenient husband seems clearly to be Charlotte, who confesses to Jonathan in a flashback showing his return to the murder scene to retrieve a dress to replace the bloodstained dress Charlotte is still wearing. Whatever they may suspect, neither Eve (who spends most of the film not only protecting Jonathan but also trying to gather evidence against Charlotte) nor the audience knows until the end of the film that the flashback is a lie designed to support Jonathan's story of Charlotte's guilt. Hitchcock more accurately described the nature of the film when he told François TRUFFAUT that "it was a story about the theater." The lying flashback is only the most spectacular example of the film's many masquerades, disguises, and deceptions.

The film begins with a curtain rising to disclose a long shot of the streets of London and ends shortly after a curtain falls over the murderer trapped onstage, killing him. Jonathan, pretending to be another innocent man on the run, first brings himself to Eve's attention when he grabs a prop and strides onstage in the middle of her rehearsal of *The School for Scandal*. Eve spends most of the film undercover as Doris Tinsdale and most of her remaining scenes trying to fool Inspector Smith into revealing information about his ongoing investigation. Constantly attentive to her appearance and the impression she is making on others and constantly indifferent to their needs, Charlotte is even in her most intimate moments never offstage. Twice—in the scene in the pub in which Eve has to brush off the advances of the sodden Mr. Fortescue to attract Smith's attention, and later at the garden party where she and her father frighten Charlotte into screaming by having her approached by a boy displaying a doll with a bloody skirt and Charlotte's producer Freddie Williams recognizes her as Doris even as Smith is watching her as Eve—the film shows the dangers and hints at the necessity of playing multiple roles at once. As in *MURDER!*, the other Hitchcock film most commonly identified as a whodunit, the director's deepest interest is in the characters' inveterate theatricality, whether they are onstage or off, whether they are playing a discrete role or they are simply playing themselves. The participation of Hitchcock's family members—Alma Reville took her last screen credit for the adaptation, and Patricia Hitchcock appeared in a small role as Eve's friend Chubby Bannister and doubled for Jane Wyman—has prompted Paula Marantz COHEN to describe *Stage Fright* as "culminat[ing] the line of father-daughter plots in the 1940s films" by doubling Hitchcock's real-life daughter with Eve, the RADA student who was playing a role of which her father broadly disapproved—he lectures her about "the folly of transmuting melodrama into real life"—but whom he actively supported in a gesture of "patriarchal indulgence" rather than "patriar-

chal complicity." More broadly, the film marks a fascinating bridge between the understatement of Hitchcock's British thrillers and the fifties successes just around the corner.

Stainer, Alan   British actor who served on the jury in *MURDER!* and in no other film.

staircases   Following the credits that run at the beginning of *THE PLEASURE GARDEN*, the first film Hitchcock directed, the very first shot presents showgirls rushing down a staircase from their dressing rooms to the stage below. It is an apt prophecy of one of the director's most enduring signatures. Though they are less widely noted than his trademark CAMEO APPEARANCES, shots of staircases are nearly as frequent in Hitchcock's work and usually a good deal more important. As early as *THE LODGER* and *BLACKMAIL*, staircases assume central importance both as a stylized pivot of visual interest—the overhead shot of a hand on the banister, the only clear indication of the Lodger's descent to the first floor, which Mrs. Bunting hears from her bed; the unhurried crane up the staircase that follows Alice White and the artist Crewe as they ascend to his top-floor flat—and as a thematically vital space that links two realms, the public world normally associated with downstairs and the outdoors and the private world at the top of the stairs.

Many other films, of course, have included important scenes on staircases, from the climactic quarrel between Scarlett and Rhett in *Gone With the Wind* to the majestic scene around the Amberson staircase (and its ironic echoes later in the film) in *The Magnificent Ambersons*. Yet no filmmaker has returned so often to the dramatic, symbolic, and visual possibilities of staircases as Hitchcock or treated them so lovingly in so many different ways. Even brief glimpses of staircases, like the shots of the terrorist on his way to the dentist's office in *THE MAN WHO KNEW TOO MUCH* (1934), carry a burden of stylish menace. The staircase at the inn both divides and protects Hannay and Pamela from the schemes below in *THE 39 STEPS*, and the entire first half of *NUMBER SEVENTEEN* is set on and immediately around a winding staircase whose different levels hold surprises that Hitchcock exploits with obvious enthusiasm.

It was not until he moved to America, however, that Hitchcock began to develop the possibilities *Number Seventeen* had raised of constructing crucial scenes around staircases instead of merely using them to stage striking transitions. Perhaps the most dramatic scene of his first American film, *REBECCA*, follows the exultant but still tellingly anonymous heroine, unknowingly wearing a copy of the dress her predecessor Rebecca de Winter had worn to her last party, down the broad staircase at Manderley to the grand costume ball she has organized and her husband waiting below, and then indicates her shocked retreat before Max de Winter's wrath moments later with an abruptly foreshortened shot of her disappearing up the same staircase. *FOREIGN CORRESPONDENT* traps Huntley Haverstock, straining to overhear the spies plotting below him, on a staircase inside a sinister windmill as the gears of the mill's machinery pull his telltale raincoat inexorably away and threaten to drop it in the middle of the plotters. *SHADOW OF A DOUBT* returns repeatedly to the staircase leading to Charlie Newton's bedroom, in which her family has installed the homicidal Uncle Charlie, and later shows Uncle Charlie attempting to use the outdoor staircase leading from the same upstairs hallway as a murder weapon against his inquisitive niece.

Hitchcock often uses staircases to slow down the characters, linger over their misgivings about what they are about to do, and inflate the moment before the catastrophe into a tour de force of suspense. In *SPELLBOUND*, Hitchcock uses optical point-of-view shots to indicate Constance Peterson twice mounting the stairs at Green Manors, the first time to confront the newly arrived head, with whom she has fallen in love, the second to confront his immediate predecessor, whom she is about to accuse of murder. A menacing dog waiting halfway up the stairs that lead to Mr. Anthony's bedroom in *STRANGERS ON A TRAIN* gives viewers something to worry about instead of whether Guy Haines, cautiously mounting the stairs, is really likely to shoot Bruno's father. Bob Rusk escorts the unsuspecting Barbara Milligan to his flat in *FRENZY* in an unbroken crane shot, and after they disappear inside, the camera slowly retraces its path down the deserted stairway and outside in one of the most powerful images of desolation in Hitchcock's work. In the most celebrated of all such preparatory sequences, Hitchcock cuts in to tight closeups to show Melanie Daniels's feet climbing the stairs to the attic in *THE BIRDS* where she has heard strange noises, a sequence he echoes in the climactic sequence of *Frenzy*. Even when the stairs outside the hero's apartment are never shown, as in *REAR WINDOW*, the film can use exaggerated sound effects to evoke the threat of the approaching murderer. In *PSYCHO*, he can play with viewers' expectations by shooting the slow ascent of Arbogast to the second floor of the Bates house as if it were the prelude to a murderous attack and then staging the attack at the top of the staircase itself.

All these scenes might suggest that staircases represent a frontier not only between public and private worlds but also more generally between the world of everyday reality and that of fantasies, desires, and nightmares. But Hitchcock's determination to turn so many of these scenes into visual set pieces—an attempt facilitated by the geometric designs of staircases' multiple planes and the way they turn the most purposive human moments into slow contortions—indicates that these transitional moments become increasingly oneiric themselves, as they reveal the nightmarish costs behind any attempt at psychological integration between public and private, external and internal, action and desire. In this connection the crucial staircase sequences in Hitchcock's work are those in *VERTIGO*, at once the most memorable visually and the most important to their film. Both when acrophobic Scottie Ferguson is vainly attempting to follow Madeleine Elster up the staircase of the Mission of San Juan Batista and when he is dragging Judy Barton, the same woman, up the same staircase to recreate Madeleine's apparent suicide, the elongating spirals he seems to see below him—in a series of shots achieved by combining a track-out and a zoom-in—indicate not only his fear of the height that is his destination but also his terror of coming to terms first with his desire for Madeleine and later with his fatal knowledge that she is really Judy. It is a fitting apotheosis for the director's obsession with dividing interior and psychological landscapes into visually discrete areas and then dramatizing the dangers of crossing the boundaries between them.

Stamp–Taylor, Enid (1904–1946) Stage-trained British actress whose 20-year film career was launched with *Land of Hope and Glory* (1927) and *EASY VIRTUE*, in which she played Sarah, the former intended of John Whittaker who turns out to be unexpectedly sympathetic to John's unhappily misfit new wife Larita.

Stanley, Forrest (1889–1969) American actor, a star who made more than 50 silents before essentially retiring with the coming of sound, though he reemerged periodically in such films as *Show Boat* (1936) and such television programs as *ALFRED HITCHCOCK PRESENTS*, in which he appeared as Hubka in the episode "BREAKDOWN."

Stannard, Eliot (1888–1944) British screenwriter who wrote or adapted screenplays for 100 silent films beginning in 1914, 80 of them before he first worked with Hitchcock. If John Russell TAYLOR is correct in reporting that THE RING is based on "an original script by [Hitchcock] and Eliot Stannard (whom he had brought with him from GAINSBOROUGH)," then Stannard wrote or cowrote every one of the silent films Hitchcock directed: *THE PLEASURE GARDEN, THE MOUNTAIN EAGLE, THE LODGER, DOWNHILL, EASY VIRTUE, The Ring* (uncredited), *THE FARMER'S WIFE, CHAMPAGNE* (credited to Stannard and Hitchcock in collaboration), and *THE MANXMAN*— a longer collaboration, as Charles BARR has pointed out in urging closer attention to Stannard's career and contributions to Hitchcock's films, than any other writer save Alma REVILLE. A firm proponent of solid dramatic structure, he evidently served throughout Hitchcock's early career to counterbalance the director's fondness for brilliant but often irrelevant individual shots and sequences whose centrifugal force pulled against the center of each film. His credits dried up soon after he and Hitchcock parted, however, and he died forgotten 10 years after his last film credit (1933).

Stanton, (Harry) Dean (1926–) Intense, uniquely scruffy American character actor who was billed as Dean Stanton until the retirement of character actor Harry Stanton in 1971. As Dean Stanton, he played Bill, one of the toughs who, in the course of robbing the watchmaker in the *SUSPICION* episode "FOUR O'CLOCK," tie him up a few feet from his own ticking bomb; in his much more celebrated life as Harry Dean Stanton, he has made nearly 100 appearances, including such offbeat films as *The Rose* (1979), *Paris, Texas* (1984), *Wild at Heart* (1990), and *She's So Lovely* (1997).

Starkey, Dewey American assistant director at RKO from *Conspiracy* (1930) through *Experiment Perilous* (1944) who assisted Hitchcock on MR. AND MRS. SMITH and SUSPICION.

Stefano, Joseph (William) (1922–) American screenwriter and producer, former song-and-dance man and songwriter. After two earlier film credits—*The Black Orchid* (1958) and *The Naked Edge* (1959)—he adapted Robert BLOCH's novel *PSYCHO* (1959) to the screen. Most of his subsequent work has been for television. He produced the suspense anthology series *The Outer Limits* (1963–64), wrote a half-dozen television films in the seventies and the telefilm *Psycho IV: The Beginning* (1991), and served as executive consultant in the revived *Outer Limits* (1995–97). In 1998 he revised and updated his Hitchcock screenplay for the Gus Van Sant remake of *Psycho*.

Steinbeck, John (Ernst) (1902–1968) American novelist who turned from laboring at odd jobs in his native California to chronicling the adversities of the laborers who could not escape their harsh, beautiful world. His most famous novels mostly appeared in the thirties: *Tortilla Flat* (1935), *In Dubious Battle* (1936), *Of Mice and Men* (1937), and *The Grapes of Wrath* (1939), which won the 1940 Pulitzer Prize for fiction. During the war, he took time out from his duties as a writer for the federal government to write the original story adapted for *LIFEBOAT*. Although Hitchcock, warmly remembering his collaboration with Thornton WILDER on *SHADOW OF A DOUBT*, had urged producer Kenneth MACGOWAN to hire Steinbeck, he was unhappy with his treatment, and hired Jo SWERLING to write the screenplay. The novelist, nothing daunted, returned after the war to fiction, producing among other works *The Pearl* (1947), *East of Eden* (1952), and *The Winter of Our Discontent* (1962), whose publication prompted his award of the Nobel Prize for Literature that same year. Among his other novels that have been adapted by Hollywood are *The Red Pony* (1937), filmed in 1949; *The Moon Is Down* (1942), filmed in 1943; *Cannery Row* (1945), filmed in 1982; and *The Wayward Bus* (1947), filmed in 1956. He was nominated for Academy Awards for the original stories for *A Medal for Benny* (1945) and the story and screenplay for *Viva Zapata!* (1952), as well as for the original story for *Lifeboat* Hitchcock had found so unsatisfactory.

Sterritt, David   American film critic, longtime reviewer for *The Christian Science Monitor,* adjunct professor of film at C.W. Post College, Long Island University, and adjunct associate professor of film at Columbia University. He has written *Mad to Be Saved: The Beats, the '50s, and Film* (1998) and *The Films of Jean-Luc Godard: Seeing the Invisible* (1999) and edited *Jean-Luc Godard: Interviews* (1998) and *Robert Altman: Interviews* (2000). His first book, *The Films of Alfred Hitchcock* (Cambridge University Press, 1993), sandwiches a detailed analysis of six films— BLACKMAIL, SHADOW OF A DOUBT, THE WRONG MAN, VERTIGO, PSYCHO, and THE BIRDS—between an extended introduction that defines "the transcendence of physical conflict over psychological and even moral confrontation with evil" as "the culminating fact of Hitchcock's universe" and a brief epilogue that considers the continuing debate over the merits of *Marnie.* Of the major analyses, the longest and most valuable is the chapter on *The Birds,* which emphasizes the film's logophobia (the film is "*about* the futility of language") as a symbol of the failure of social structures to deal with "physical and spiritual black holes that yawn amid so many of his films," this time threatening the very power of storytelling itself to impose order on a turbulent, chaotic, and violent world. An enlarged second edition is forthcoming.

Stevenson, Edward (1906–1968)   American costume designer. As chief designer at RKO (1936–49), he designed costumes for *Citizen Kane,* SUSPICION, and such films noir as *Murder, My Sweet*

(1944) and *Out of the Past* (1947). In the fifties, he went to 20TH CENTURY–FOX, UNIVERSAL, and the television series *I Love Lucy* (1951–57).

Stewart, H(ugh) St.C. (1910–)   British producer whose first film credit is for editing THE MAN WHO KNEW TOO MUCH (1934). After cutting 10 films, he turned producer in 1946, eventually specializing, beginning with *Man of the Moment* (1955), in nine slapstick comedies starring Norman Wisdom.

Stewart, James (1908–1997)   Irresistibly gawky, self-deprecating American movie star whose loping walk and gentle drawl drew thousands of imitators and millions of fans. He studied architecture at Princeton, but upon graduation his classmate Joshua Logan talked him into joining their friend Henry FONDA and Margaret Sullavan at the University Players in Massachusetts. Although he played the murderer in *After the Thin Man* (1936), the year after making his film debut, he was nearly always cast in his early films as shy, sincere, sweetly boyish types with a unique ability to tap deeper wells of zaniness in *You Can't Take It with You* (1938) and moral outrage in *Mr. Smith Goes to Washington* (1939). When he won an Oscar for playing the newspaperman Macaulay Conner in *The Philadelphia Story* (1940), he sent it back home to his father, who displayed it in the window of his hardware store for 25 years. (He had already been nominated for *Mr. Smith Goes to Washington* and would earn further nominations for *It's a Wonderful Life,* 1946; *Harvey,* 1950; and *Anatomy of a Murder,* 1959.) That same year, Stewart was the first Hollywood star to volunteer for military service; as an air force pilot, he flew 20 missions over Germany and was promoted from private up the line to colonel; he retired as a brigadier general, the highest rank achieved by any actor. After a five-year absence from the screen, he seemed poised to return to the mold of his small-town heroes in *It's a Wonderful Life,* but his screen persona, despite occasional returns to his aw-shucks mode such as in *Harvey,* was darkened and complicated by his collaborations with two directors, Hitchcock and Anthony Mann. For Mann he played a series of tough, physically and psychologically vulnerable western heroes whose emotions often crossed the line to rage in a memorable series beginning with *Winchester '73* (1950). His range in Hitchcock's films was more complicated. The head-master-turned-publisher Rupert Cadell in *ROPE* had originally been intended for Cary GRANT; the casting of Stewart made the character's unwitting fostering of his former students' murderous fantasies especially devious. Throughout the fifties Stewart alternated with Grant as Hitchcock's favorite actor. In *REAR WINDOW* he starred as L.B. Jefferies, the commitment-shy photographer whose obvious charm is constantly undercut by John Michael HAYES's sharp script. The sorely tried paterfamilias Dr. Ben McKenna in *THE MAN WHO KNEW TOO MUCH* (1956) is the most conventional of his Hitchcock roles; yet he brings to it an intriguing and characteristically Hitchcockian mixture of authority and insecurity. His final Hitchcock role, the acrophobic ex-cop Scottie Ferguson in *VERTIGO*, is the richest of all, drawing on virtually every aspect of the star's persona: innocence, idealism, independence, compassion, stubbornness, romantic diffidence, emotional vulnerability, and the capacity for volcanically destructive emotions. Though Stewart had hoped to star in *NORTH BY NORTHWEST* as well, Hitchcock, stung by the financial failure of *Vertigo,* had determined to cast Grant as Roger Thornhill and delayed the start of filming until Stewart was committed to *Bell, Book, and Candle* (1959). Hitchcock's relations with his two most iconic male stars have been memorably summarized by Donald SPOTO's dictum that Grant represented Hitchcock as he would have liked to see himself, Stewart as the person he really was.

Stewart, James G(raham) (1907–1997) American sound recordist, at RKO for three dozen films from 1933, including *Gunga Din* (1939) and *Citizen Kane* (1941). He began to freelance shortly before he worked on *THE PARADINE CASE* and a handful of later films through *L.A. Story* (1991).

Stewart, Kay (1919–) Wholesome American character actress who sold cigarettes to the Soviet envoys in *Ninotchka* (1939) and played Henry Aldrich's sister Mary in *Life with Henry* (1941). Most of her credits, however, were on such television series as *Wagon Train* (1957–65) and *ALFRED HITCHCOCK PRESENTS*, where she appeared in five roles, as Albert Pelham's secretary in "THE CASE OF MR. PELHAM," the woman on the street in "The Older Sister" (1956), Della, the secretary in "Crack of Doom" (1956), and the unidentified women in "Manacled" (1957) and "The Motive" (1958).

Stewart, Marianne American-born actress, daughter of actor Reinhold SCHÜNZEL, whose dozen roles on film and television include Alice West in the *ALFRED HITCHCOCK PRESENTS* segment "THE PERFECT CRIME."

Stewart, Sally British character actress whose handful of film appearances (1932–93) include Iris Henderson's friend Julie in *THE LADY VANISHES*.

Stockford, Philip British set decorator whose only film credit is *UNDER CAPRICORN*.

Stone, Harold J. (1911–) Serious, soft-spoken American character actor whose deliberate manner often cast him in such gritty dramas as *The Harder They Fall* (1956), *The Garment Jungle* (1957), and *THE WRONG MAN*, in which he played Lieutenant Bowers. He appeared three times on *ALFRED HITCHCOCK PRESENTS*—as the prankster reporter Halloran in "The Night the World Ended" (1957), as Lieutenant Noonan in "LAMB TO THE SLAUGHTER" (1958), and as Mac Davis, the mobster who wants to go straight in "Ambition" (1961)—and twice on *THE ALFRED HITCHCOCK HOUR*, as the cabdriver who takes the hero to an address that reveals his unwitting double life in "The Black Curtain" (1962) and as Mr. Osterman in "Second Verdict" (1964).

Story, Jack Trevor (1917–1991) British novelist whose comic novel *THE TROUBLE WITH HARRY* (1949) so intrigued Hitchcock in its cheerfully cold-blooded approach to the problem of its title character's mortal remains that he sought to film it despite a discouraging report from PARAMOUNT's story department. Negotiating through an intermediary, Hitchcock was able to purchase the film rights for only $11,000, much to the chagrin of the author, who worked on a half-dozen screenplays from 1957 to 1962 but saw only one of his 50 other novels, *Mix Me a Person* (1959), adapted to the screen in 1962.

Stradling, Harry (1902–1970) Veteran British-born cinematographer, in Hollywood from 1910, who lit and shot more than 100 films on both sides of the Atlantic. He spent much of the thirties working in European films, then was back in England for a dozen films including *JAMAICA INN*, and, returning to America soon after, shot *MR. AND MRS. SMITH, SUSPICION*, and dozens of others. Equally at home in black-and-white and color, he was nominated for Academy Awards for *The Human Comedy* (1943), *The Picture of Dorian Gray* (1945), *The Barkleys of Broadway* (1949), *A Streetcar Named Desire* (1951), *Hans Christian Andersen* (1952), *Guys and Dolls* (1955), *The Eddy Duchin Story* (1956), *Auntie Mame* (1958), *The Young Philadelphians* (1959), *A Majority of One* (1961), *Gypsy* (1962), *Funny Girl* (1968), and *Hello, Dolly!* (1969) and won an Oscar for *My Fair Lady* (1964). His son, Harry Stradling, Jr., is also an Oscar-nominated cinematographer.

Strangers on a Train (Alternative titles: *Verschwörung in Nordexpress, L'inconnu du Nord-express, L'altro uomo, Delitto per delitto*) Warner Bros.–First National, 101 minutes, June 1951. **Producer:** Alfred Hitchcock; **Director:** Alfred Hitchcock; **Screenplay:** Raymond Chandler, Czenzi Ormonde (and Ben Hecht), based on the novel by Patricia Highsmith; **Adaptation:** Whitfield Cook; **Cinematographer:** Robert Burks; **Art director:** Edward S. Haworth; **Set decorator:** George James Hopkins; **Wardrobe:** Leah Rhodes; **Makeup:** Gordon Bau; **Production associate:** Barbara Keon; **Sound:** Dolph Thomas; **Special effects:** H.F. Koenekamp; **Editor:** William Ziegler; **Music:** Dimitri Tiomkin. **Musical direction:** Ray Heindorf; **Cast:** Farley Granger (Guy Haines), Robert Walker (Bruno Anthony), Ruth Roman (Anne Morton), Leo G. Carroll (Senator Morton), Patricia Hitchcock (Barbara Morton), Laura Elliott (Miriam Haines), Marion Lorne (Mrs. Anthony), Jonathan Hale (Mr. Anthony), Howard St. John (Captain Turley), John Brown (Professor Collins), Norma Varden (Mrs. Cunningham), Robert Gist (Leslie Hennessy), Howard Washington (waiter), Dick Wessel (Bill), Edward Clark (Mr. Hargreaves), Tommy Farrell, Roland Morris (Miriam's boyfriends), Louis Lettieri (boy with balloon), John Butler (blind man), John Doucette (Hammond), Edward Hearne (Sgt. Campbell), Mary Alan Hokanson (secretary), Georges Renavent (M. Darville), Odette Myrtil (Mme. Darville), Edna Holland (Mrs. Joyce), Charles Meredith (Judge Dolan), Laura Tredwell (Mrs. Anderson), Monya Andre, Minna Phillips (dowagers), Ralph Moody (seedy man), Murray Alper (boat concessionaire), Harry Hines (man under merry-go-round), Joel Allen, Roy Engel (police officers), Leonard Carey, J. Louis Johnson (butlers), Sam Flint, Janet Stewart, Shirley Tegge.

Eager to film Patricia Highsmith's novel as soon as it was published in spring 1950, Hitchcock purchased the film rights anonymously for $7,500 on April 20. But although he and Whitfield COOK had completed a treatment by the end of June that kept the focus on two men whose chance meeting changes their lives when one of them proposes to the other that they exchange murders ("your wife—my father") to provide themselves with alibis but switched the story's settings to the New York–Washington corridor, transformed its hero Guy Haines from an architect to a tennis player with political aspirations, and complemented its amusement-park murder with a climactic return to the same fairground, he could not find a writer to work on the screenplay. After his attempt to interest Dashiell Hammett in the property failed, he approached Raymond CHANDLER to write the dialogue. The resulting three drafts, written between July and September 1950, offered a textbook case of the consequences when a director's views fail to mesh with either the original author's or the screenwriter's. Highsmith's novel had been a brooding examination of the guilt that gradually overwhelms Guy Haines after the charming psychopath Charles Anthony Bruno, who has already killed Guy's philandering wife, wears him down to the point of killing Bruno's authoritarian father. The film Hitchcock envisioned would embody this transfer of guilt in a series of dramatic episodes—from the opening intercutting of two pairs of legs approaching a train to the climactic crosscutting between Guy struggling to win a tennis match in time to prevent Bruno Anthony from planting his incriminating cigarette lighter at the murder scene and Bruno straining to

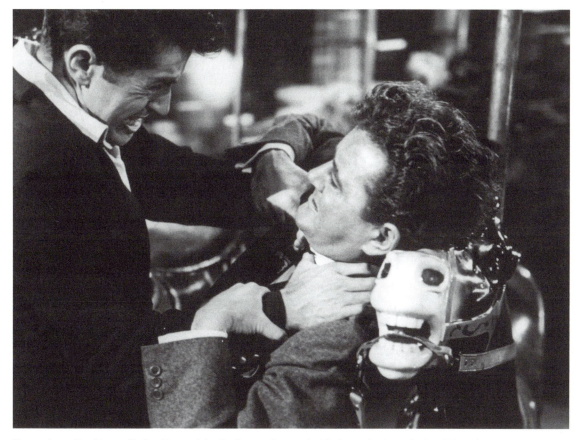

Tennis player Guy Haines (Farley Granger) battles his murderous double Bruno Anthony (Robert Walker) aboard a merry-go-round run mad in the climactic scene of *Strangers on a Train*. *(National Film Society Archive)*

retrieve the lighter from the storm drain into which he has dropped it—while still maintaining Guy's technical innocence (after pretending to agree to Bruno's plan to shoot his father, he would go to his house to warn him about his son). Chandler, concerned above all with the logic of the characters' development, was exasperated by Hitchcock's subordination of character to visual style and was unable to supply dialogue, for example, for the scene in which Guy persuades the audience that he has changed his mind about killing Bruno's father but does not persuade Bruno. The collaboration ended unhappily with Hitchcock's dismissal of Chandler, and the finished script, written during three weeks in September and October after the studio nearly canceled the project, was mostly the product of Ben HECHT's assis-

tant Czenzi ORMONDE, who took over from Chandler when Hecht was unavailable. Hitchcock succeeded in casting boy-next-door Robert WALKER as Bruno, but, unable to secure William Holden for Guy, he signed Farley GRANGER instead and formally screen-tested Patricia HITCHCOCK for her most important screen role. Principal photography began on October 20, 1950, and wrapped just before Christmas. The film previewed in March 1951 and opened across the country to enthusiastic reviews and strong business in June.

Strangers on a Train is not Hitchcock's most searching examination of psychological duality—that honor goes to *PSYCHO*—but it is his most consistently entertaining. If *SHADOW OF A DOUBT* had demonstrated how frequently and rigorously DOUBLES could be introduced into a film, *Strangers on a Train* uses the idea more idiomatically. "Scotch, a pair, doubles," Bruno calls out to the railroad porter moments after meeting Guy and then adds to his companion, "Only kind of doubles I play." In a stroke the film has linked the pairing of the two characters with the obsessive competitiveness that will not let Guy lose his once-in-a-lifetime tennis match, the wistful dissolution that draws Bruno to his beau ideal, and the more general notion, quite remote from *Shadow of a Doubt,* of doubling as a game to be played. Soon thereafter, the crossed tennis racquets on Guy's lighter, along with the inscription "A to G," will invoke Guy's two heterosexual pairings with the estranged wife who "must have played around" and the senator's daughter who gave him the lighter Bruno will shortly pocket. The exhilarating ease behind all this doubling—Guy's marriage is doubled by his romance with Ann Morton, which is in turn doubled by his unwilling intimacy with Bruno—continues in the tensely erotic sequence in which Bruno stalks the errant Miriam Haines (accompanied, naturally, by two young men) through the amusement park, distantly flirting with her, until he comes on her alone and strangles her in a shockingly aestheticized image when the murder is reflected in the distorting lens of the eyeglasses that have fallen off in her struggle. This tableau, which presents Bruno—marked as a Hollywood homosexual by his importunate pursuit of Guy, his readily assumed hatred of Miriam, his silk dressing gown, his care for his manicure, his resentment of his father, and his closeness to his mother—at his most darkly sexual, is balanced by the earlier shot of his puncturing a little boy's balloon with his cigarette. Bruno is not only Miriam's opposite and Ann Morton's but is also Guy's repressed child, who returns with a vengeance to crash Senator Morton's party, invite a pair of society women to share his naughty fantasies, and nearly kill one of them when he sees in Ann's sister Barbara the double of the woman he killed. For all its thematic unity, however—a unity whose emphasis on the dreamlike logic of symbol overshadows the logic of individual character Chandler had vainly defended—the film never feels forced or programmatic because it moves so deftly, aided by the stylish black-and-white visuals

of Robert BURKS, shooting the first of his many Hitchcock films, from one set piece to the next and because Walker's performance as the beguiling murderer Bruno, perhaps the finest portrait of any Hitchcock villain, provides the story with an irresistible momentum. It is no wonder that both Bruno and the film his character dominates figure so prominently in Robert J. CORBER's work as the model for Hitchcock's mixture of suspense and gender politics in his cold-war films.

Strassner, J(oe)   British costume designer who worked on a dozen films of the thirties, including *THE 39 STEPS, SECRET AGENT,* and *SABOTAGE.*

Strauss, Johann (1804–1849) and **Strauss, Johann, Jr.** (1825–1899)   Father-and-son Viennese composers whose rivalry was the subject of *WALTZES FROM VIENNA* and whose music was used throughout the film. In the movies, as in Hitchcock's film, the younger Strauss's victory has been decisive; although Strauss senior's waltzes and marches have been used in another half-dozen films, his son's music, especially *Auf der schönen blauen Donau,* has turned up in nearly 100 as different as *2001: A Space Odyssey* (1969), *Harold and Maude* (1971), and the WARNER BROS. cartoon *A Corny Concerto* (1943).

Stuart, John (1898–1979)   Staunch Scottish leading man, born John Croall, who returned from wartime service with the Black Watch to make his stage debut in 1919 and his film debut a year later in *Her Son.* A top romantic lead throughout the silent era, he starred as Jill Cheyne's faithful suitor Hugh Fielding in *THE PLEASURE GARDEN* and then returned in *NUMBER SEVENTEEN* as Fordyce, the innocent passerby eventually revealed as the master detective Barton. Still later, he developed into a character actor who played more than 100 doctors, military officers, and professional gents with the common touch and was still active in 1978, when he appeared as one of the elders in *Superman.*

subjective camera   "Young directors always come up with the idea, 'Let the camera be someone and let it move as though it's the person, and you put the guy in front of a mirror and then you see him,'" Hitchcock told Peter BOGDANOVICH, and added: "It's a terrible mistake. Bob MONTGOMERY did that in *Lady in the Lake*—I don't believe in it myself." But although, just like every other leading Hollywood director, he never attempted anything like Montgomery's problematic extended experiment with point-of-view shots, Hitchcock was widely known for his strategic use of subjective camera, typically alternating with shots of the subject whose point of view was being represented, as in L.B. Jefferies's neighborly spying in REAR WINDOW, Scottie Ferguson's dreamlike shadowing of Madeleine Elster in VERTIGO, and Lila Crane's approach to the Bates house in PSYCHO. As early as THE LODGER he used a forward tracking shot to the Buntings' door to represent the point of view of the yet-unseen lodger, and although he rarely used optical point-of-view shots, he continued to use shots whose obvious visual distortion was inflected by a specific character's point of view in films as different as EASY VIRTUE and NOTORIOUS. What Hitchcock objects to in *The Lady in the Lake* is not the use of subjective camera but the effacement of the character by the subjective camera, which threatens to become a character itself. As the shot-reversal sequences common to most of his best-known uses of subjective camera suggest, Hitchcock is constantly seeking to encourage viewers to identifications with his characters, but he works most comfortably and distinctively in the zone between apparently objective distance and complete congruence between camera and character because those identifications are always partial, critical, ironic. William ROTHMAN has analyzed the ways Marion Crane's conversation with Norman BATES in the room behind his office, beginning by favoring first her point of view and then his, gradually detaches Norman from anything remotely resembling Marion's point of view to indicate Hitchcock's uncanny affinity with Norman. The closeup of a shower head from Marion's point of view that follows a minute later—perhaps the most undeniably subjective shot in Hitchcock's entire career—establishes viewers' closest identification with Marion exactly as she is about to be killed. The triumph of subjective camera is in Hitchcock a triumph of incomplete, analytical, heuristic identification.

Subor, Michel (1935–) Dark, intense French actor who provided the voiceover narration for *Jules et Jim* (1961) and has since gone on to make some 20 continental films, with occasional English-language appearances as Philippe in *What's New, Pussycat?* (1965) and François Picard, Andre Devereaux's enterprising journalist son-in-law, in TOPAZ.

suspense vs. surprise Perhaps the most enduring canard of Hitchcock commentary is the filmmaker's alleged preference for suspense over surprise—a preference he illustrated in many interviews by the following anecdote he told François TRUFFAUT:

We are now having a very innocent little chat. Let us suppose that there is a bomb underneath this table between us. Nothing happens, and then all of a sudden, "Boom!" There is an explosion. The public is *surprised,* but prior to this surprise, it has seen an absolutely ordinary scene, of no special consequence. Now, let us take a *suspense* situation. The bomb is underneath the table and the public *knows* it, probably because they have seen the anarchist place it there. The public is *aware* that the bomb is going to explode at one o'clock and there is a clock in the décor. The public can see that it is a quarter to one. In these conditions this same innocuous conversation becomes fascinating because the audience is participating in the scene. The audience is longing to warn the characters on the screen: "You shouldn't be talking about such trivial matters. There's a bomb beneath you and it's about to explode!"

In the first case we have given the public fifteen seconds of *surprise* at the moment of the explosion. In the second case we have provided them with fifteen minutes of *suspense.* The conclusion is that whenever possible the public must be informed. Except when the surprise is a twist, that is, when the unexpected ending is, in itself, the highlight of the story.

This anecdote helps explain Hitchcock's aversion to whodunits and his fondness for dramatic irony. But only the closing exception, which would certainly allow whodunits, accounts for the power of the revelation of Norman BATES's guilt in PSYCHO or, on a smaller scale, of the kiss the demure Francie Stevens suddenly plants on John Robie's mouth just before she closes her hotel door on him in TO CATCH A THIEF—a kiss Hitchcock defends to Truffaut on the basis of "the element of *surprise*." Whatever his reasons for insisting on the distinction between suspense and surprise, Hitchcock understood very well a contrary maxim his career as a television producer illustrates: the dependence of seduction, wit, variety, and indeed suspense itself on the possibility of surprise. Without this possibility, all suspense would be merely ritualistic, instead of as inventive as the continually surprising sequence in the Tabernacle of the Sun in THE MAN WHO KNEW TOO MUCH (1934) or the outrageous plot of NORTH BY NORTHWEST. Moreover, Hitchcock surely understood that after a certain point in his career, his reputation as master of suspense would encourage viewers to frame the most innocuous scenes (e.g., the opening 20 minutes of THE BIRDS, which would have been utterly unthinkable anyplace but in a Hitchcock film) in terms of their own suspense because of their expectations about what kinds of things were likely to happen next. Perhaps a more judicious way to restate Hitchcock's bromide, therefore, would be the public must always be kept occupied and amused—perhaps by learning *something* the characters do not know, perhaps by being led to expect a specific development they desire—whether the ultimate goal is the fulfillment, the frustration, or the surprising transformation of their expectations.

Suspicion

(Alternative titles: *Before the Fact* [working title], *Verdacht, Soupçons, Il sospetto*) RKO, 99 minutes, September 1941. **Producer:** Alfred Hitchcock; **Director:** Alfred Hitchcock; **Screenplay:** Samson Raphaelson, John Harrison, and Alma Reville, based on *Before the Fact,* a novel by Francis Iles; **Cinematographer:** Harry Stradling; **Assistant director:** Dewey Starkey; **Art director:** Van Nest Polglase; **Associate:** Carroll Clark; **Set decoration:** Darrell Silvera; **Costumes:** Edward Stevenson; **Special effects:** Vernon L. Walker; **Sound:** John E. Tribby; **Editor:** William Hamilton; **Music:** Franz Waxman; **Cast:** Cary Grant (Johnnie Aysgarth), Joan Fontaine (Lina McLaidlaw), Sir Cedric Hardwicke (General McLaidlaw), Nigel Bruce (Beaky Thwaite), Dame May Whitty (Mrs. McLaidlaw), Isabel Jeans (Mrs. Newsham), Heather Angel (Ethel), Auriol Lee (Isobel Sedbusk), Reginald Sheffield (Reggie Wetherby), Leo G. Carroll (Captain Melbeck), Billy Bevan (ticket taker), Ben Webster (registrar), Lumsden Hare (Inspector Hodgson), Gertrude Hoffman (Mrs. Wetherby), Hilda Plowright (postmistress), Doris Lloyd and Elsie Weller (the Misses Wetherby), Gavin Gordon (Bertram Sedbusk), Kenneth Hunter (Sir Gerald), Carol Curtis-Brown (Jessie Barham), Nondas Metcalf (Phyllis Swinghurst), Rex Evans (Mr. Bailey), Aubrey Mathew (Mr. Webster), Constance Worth (Mrs. Fitzpatrick), Vernon Downing (Benson), Pax Walker (Phoebe, maid), Maureen Roden-Ryan (Winnie, maid), Clyde Cook (photographer), Edward Fielding (antique shop proprietor), Leonard Carey (butler), Alec Craig (Hogarth Club receptionist).

Francis ILES's portrait of a woman so besotted with the irresponsible child-man whom she has married that she hides her knowledge of his swindles, thefts, and murder and eventually allows him to kill her was one of the properties RKO had suggested for Hitchcock's loanout, and he began work on his 27th film as soon as he had finished MR. AND MRS. SMITH for the studio. Although the film had been planned as a modest B picture, its problems continued to expand. Hitchcock was eager to sign Cary GRANT in the role of impecunious Johnnie Aysgarth, but Grant's screen image made it impossible to accept him as a killer; although Joan FONTAINE had been so taken with the role of the spinsterish Lina McLaidlaw, the bride Johnnie entrances, that she offered to waive her salary, she was no more comfortable with Grant than she had been with Laurence OLIVIER in REBECCA. The real difficulties, however, came in the writing. A draft screenplay the studio had commissioned from Nathanael West and Boris Ingster was decreed unusable, and Alma REVILLE set to work on a new treatment that served as a basis for Hollywood veteran Samson RAPHAELSON's screenplay. But Raphaelson could not solve the problem of the story's ending. The materials on the ending Dan AUILER has collected in *Hitchcock's Notebooks* show that at different times Lina kills Johnnie in self-defense (the West-Ingster screenplay), allows him to poison her (in a memorable touch, Hitchcock

As Johnnie Aysgarth (Cary Grant) tries to reassure his ailing wife Lina (Joan Fontaine) in *Suspicion,* she is framed between him and the most alarming glass of milk in cinema history.   *(National Film Society Archive)*

placed a light bulb in the fatal glass of milk, imparting to it a spectral glow), gets him to describe his early life to her, listens to his confession of his wrongdoings, and watches him from afar as he expiates his earlier sins by piloting an RAF plane. Studio head George Schaefer wanted Johnnie to take the poison he had intended for Lina, which would then be revealed as a harmless narcotic. Hitchcock himself told François TRUFFAUT that his preferred ending would have left Lina dead of Johnnie's poison and Johnnie going off whistling to the mailbox to post the letter in which Lina told her mother what he had done. After principal photography, which lasted from February 10 to July 24, 1941, was finally completed, Hitchcock left on vacation, only to find on his return that producer Sol Lesser, after weighing the prospect of withholding the film from release, had cut every mention of murder from it, boiling it down to 55 minutes. Insisting that his original cut be restored, the director made a futile last-ditch plea to change its title from *Suspicion* to *Johnnie* and waited for the inevitable pans. But the film, which earned Fontaine the Oscar she had been denied for *Rebecca,* was successful with both the press and the public despite the ambiguous ending on which Hitchcock had finally settled.

It is precisely this ambiguity that has made the film intriguing to more recent critics. The film is structured by several competing logics. The Production Code stipulates that Johnnie cannot get away with murder. The dramatic logic of the film requires him to try to kill Lina to accentuate her status as victim. The curve of Lina's development as a character demands that sooner or later she stand up to Johnnie. But Johnnie's character is given no corresponding curve; he simply alternates repeatedly between one more impish apology for his bad behavior (which ranges from toying with Lina's affections to borrowing money for an extravagant honeymoon to passing bad checks to perhaps murdering his simple old friend Beaky Thwaite) and one more irrepressible return to that behavior. So the heroine must change enough to stop the hero, but the hero cannot change enough to stop. To put it differently, Lina's suspicions about Johnnie must turn out to be true; otherwise not only her reactions but also the occasions that provoke them (the word game in which she idly forms the word *MURDER,* the glowing glass of milk) would degenerate in retrospect into an intolerable series of red herrings. But they must be false as well because they coalesce into something like certainty so early on that there must be some dramatic reversal in store. The ending as it stands tries to solve this problem in the same terms as THE LODGER, by rationalizing its hero's suspicious behavior in terms of a new revelation: Johnnie has been planning to kill himself. But Johnnie makes such an unconvincing suicide that it makes more sense to read the ending as a blackly comic return to form as Johnnie tenders still another confession to his suspicious wife, puts his arm around her, and leads her back home in preparation for his next scheme. The clash of logics that so exercised the director and his screenwriters (though evidently not viewers on the film's first release) appears to postmodern critics as an indication of the exemplary obscurity that led Stephen Heath to feature one of two shots of the police officer staring at the abstract painting hanging in the Aysgarth house, accompanied both times by a discordant piano phrase heard nowhere else in the film, on the dust jacket of his *Questions of Cinema* as a figure for the undecidability of cinematic representation.

Suspicion NBC television series created in the mold of *ALFRED HITCHCOCK PRESENTS.* Though it borrowed the same anthology format and emphasis on suspense, it offered two innovations: Each episode would air for a full hour, and half of the episodes would be taped live in New York, the other half filmed in Hollywood either by SHAMLEY PRODUCTIONS, with Hitchcock billed as executive producer and Joan HARRISON as associate producer, or by REVUE PRODUCTIONS, under the supervision of Alan Miller. The series premiered on September 30, 1957, with "FOUR O'CLOCK," an episode directed by Hitchcock about a watchmaker trapped in his basement together with the bomb he has planted to punish his unfaithful wife. Although Dennis O'Keefe, who introduced "Four O'Clock," left the series after this initial installment, Shamley contributed nine more episodes: "Rainy Day," (December 2, 1957), "Lord Arthur Saville's Crime" (January 13, 1958), "Heartbeat" (February 3, 1958), "Meeting in Paris" (February 10, 1958), "The Eye of Truth" (March 17, 1958), "The Bull Skinner" (April 7, 1958), "The Way Up to Heaven" (April 28, 1958), "The Voice in the Night" (May 26, 1958), and "The Woman Who Turned to Salt" (June 16, 1958). Several of the 40 episodes NBC first ordered were rebroadcast in the summer of 1959 with Walter Abel as host, but no new episodes were added, and the series soon came to an end.

Swanton, Harold American screenwriter who adapted Margery VOSPER's story "BANG! YOU'RE DEAD" and 10 other stories for *ALFRED HITCHCOCK PRESENTS.* Most of his other credits are for television westerns: *Bonanza* (1971), *Heck Ramsey* (1972–74), and *Little House on the Prairie* (1974–76).

Sweeney, Bob (1918–1992) Balding American character actor, former standup comedian. When his comedy partnership with Hal March ended in the early fifties, he moved over to television, where his humorous testiness made him much in demand as the star of such series as *My Favorite Husband* (1953–55) and *Fibber McGee and Molly* (1959–60). He appeared as bank president William Spengler in the *ALFRED HITCHCOCK PRESENTS* episode "Letter of Credit" (1960), as Janey Medwick's Uncle Jeffrey in the *FORD STARTIME* segment "INCIDENT AT A CORNER," and as Mark Rutland's disapproving cousin Bob in *MARNIE.*

Swenson, Karl (1908–1978) American character actor, a fixture of television westerns of the fifties and sixties. He appeared in three episodes of ALFRED HITCHCOCK PRESENTS: as Ed in "On the Nose" (1958), John Thompson in "A Very Moral Theft" (1960), and George Sherston in "House Guest" (1962), and returned as the doomsaying diner in the Tides Café in THE BIRDS. From 1974 to 1983 he was featured as Mr. Hanson in the television series *Little House on the Prairie.*

Swerling, Jo(seph) (1897–1964) Russian-born playwright and screenwriter who came to American in childhood. He quit newspaper work for Hollywood in 1930, eventually writing or cowriting more than 60 films, from *Dirigible* and *The Miracle Woman* (both 1931) to *The Westerner* (1940) and *Pride of the Yankees* (1942), a collaboration that was nominated for an Academy Award. A master at evoking sentiment from ordinary characters and situations such as those in *Man's Castle* (1933), he was equally comfortable in comedies such as *The Whole Town's Talking* (1935) and melodramas like LIFEBOAT, which he took over from John Steinbeck.

Swift, Clive (1936–) Stage-trained British character actor, former director of the Royal Academy of Dramatic Art, who has appeared in some 40 screen roles, mostly on television. His work runs the gamut from such old-school twits as Johnny Porter in FRENZY to such solemn-eyed dignitaries as Bishop Proudie in the BBC miniseries *The Barchester Chronicles* (1984) and King George II in the BBC's *Aristocrats* (1999).

Sylos, Ralph (d. 1981) American set decorator, in Hollywood from 1945 for eight films and hundreds of television segments. As a regular staffer for ALFRED HITCHCOCK PRESENTS, he dressed the sets for the Hitchcock-directed "BACK FOR CHRISTMAS" and "ONE MORE MILE TO GO," among many others. His later television work included stints on *M Squad* (1957–60), *McHale's Navy* (1962–66), *Dragnet 1967* (1967–71), and *M★A★S★H* (1972–83).

Talton, Alix (1919–1992)   American actress, a former Miss Georgia who came to Hollywood for some 20 film and television roles, sometimes as Alice Talton, beginning in 1941. Shortly after her run as the snobbish neighbor Myra Cobb on the television series *My Favorite Husband* (1953–55) came to an end, she was cast as Jo McKenna's London friend Helen Parnell in THE MAN WHO KNEW TOO MUCH (1956). She retired from the screen after *The Devil's Brigade* (1968).

Tandy, Jessica (1909–1994)   Fragile yet tough British actress whose considerable stage success was eventually overshadowed by her reputation as a film star. Onstage at 16, she made her New York stage debut in 1930. Although she won a Tony Award for her best-known role, Blanche Dubois in Tennessee Williams's *A Streetcar Named Desire* (1948), the film role went to Vivien Leigh. But Tandy won further Tonys for *The Gin Game* (1978), in which she stared with her husband, Hume CRONYN, and *Foxfire* (1982). Onscreen in some 30 sporadic film and television roles from 1932 through 1980, she appeared in three episodes of ALFRED HITCHCOCK PRESENTS, as maternal recluse Edwina Freel in "Toby" (1956), smitten spinster Julia Lester in "The Glass Eye" (1957), and psychic Mrs. Bowlby in "The Canary Sedan" (1958), before returning as grief-stricken, possessive widow Lydia Brenner in THE BIRDS. Ironi-

cally, the dependent neurotics she created in these roles gave no hint of the late blooming of her film career. In her seventies and eighties she appeared in 20 films—as many as her previous total—playing such indomitable survivors as the title character of *Driving Miss Daisy* (1989), for which she won an Academy Award, and Ninny Threadgoode in *Fried Green Tomatoes* (1991), for which she was nominated for another Oscar.

Target for Tonight   Crown Film Unit, British Ministry of Information, Warner Bros., 1941. **Director:** Harry Watt; **Screenplay:** Harry Watt and B. Cooper.

According to Jane SLOAN, Hitchcock supervised the reediting and dubbing of American release prints for this wartime documentary about a bombing run at a German oil refinery. His name does not appear on extant credits.

Taylor, Gil(bert) (1914–)   British cinematographer who worked as a camera operator on *Brighton Rock* (1947) and then plowed through a series of routine assignments as a lighting cinematographer in the fifties to emerge with a strikingly varied list of credits including *Dr. Strangelove* (1963), *A Hard Day's Night* (1964), *The Omen* (1976), *Star Wars* (1977), *Meetings with Remarkable Men* (1979), and *Dracula* (1979). He worked with Roman Polanski on

Repulsion (1965), *Cul-de-sac* (1966), and *Macbeth* (1971) and shot FRENZY, Hitchcock's first British film in more than 20 years.

Taylor, John Russell British writer and biographer, film reviewer for the *Times* of London from 1962 to 1973, more recently professor of film at the University of Southern California. He has written *The Angry Theater: New British Drama* (1962; 2nd edition, 1969), *Cinema Eye, Cinema Ear: Some Key Film Makers of the Sixties* (1964), *The Penguin Dictionary of the Theater* (1966; 3rd edition, 1993), *The Rise and Fall of the Well-Made Play* (1967), *the Art Nouveau Book in Britain* (1967), *The Art Dealers* (with Brian Brooke, 1969), *Harold Pinter* (1969), *The Second Wave: British Drama for the Seventies* (1971), *The Hollywood Musical* (with Arthur Jackson, 1971), *David Storey* (1974), *Peter Shaffer* (1974), *Directors and Directions: Cinema for the Seventies* (1975), *Strangers in Paradise: The Hollywood Émigrés, 1933–1950* (1983), *Ingrid Bergman* (1983), *Alec Guinness: A Celebration* (1984), *Orson Welles: A Celebration* (1986), *Impressionist Dreams: The Artists and the World They Painted* (1990), and *The Sun Is God: The Life and Work of Cyril Mann (1911–80)* (1999), and edited *John Osborne:* Look Back in Anger: *A Casebook* (1968). His *Hitch: The Life and Times of Alfred Hitchcock* (1978), the authorized biography of the director, is chatty, confiding, and discreet, as would be expected of any life written with the full cooperation of the subject and his family. Taylor, who sees Hitchcock at once as "the most sophisticated of film-makers" and "one of the great primitives, allowing himself with extraordinary lack of self-consciousness to be totally known through his films," relies on Hitchcock's memory in the absence of letters and memos, and so tends to take the director's assessment of his colleagues, his conflicts, and his career at face value. His maidenly reserve makes a fascinating counterpoint to Donald SPOTO's gossipy tell-all *The Dark Side of Genius,* which gave a whole new meaning to the term *critical biography.*

Taylor, Rod(ney Sturt) (1929–) Manly Australian actor who studied art but turned to acting instead, first on his native stage and screen and then, beginning in 1955, in Hollywood, where he rose through the ranks to star as the time traveler George in *The Time Machine* (1960); voice Pongo, father figure of the cartoon *One Hundred and One Dalmatians* (1961); and play Mitch Brenner, the mama's-boy lawyer who shuttles between San Francisco and Bodega Bay, in THE BIRDS. His good nature and air of easy authority led to his pairing with Doris DAY in *Do Not Disturb* (1965) and *The Glass-Bottom Boat* (1966) and his casting as hotel executive Peter McDermott in *Hotel* (1967), but his lack of a strong or distinctive personality or a genuinely comic sensibility has limited his roles. He is best known to television audiences as *Falcon Crest*'s Frank Agretti, a role he played from 1988 through 1990.

Taylor, Samuel (A.) (1912–2000) American playwright and screenwriter, born Samuel Albert Tanenbaum. His play *The Happy Time* (1950) was filmed in 1952, but his Hollywood reputation dates from 1954, when he worked with Billy Wilder in adapting his play *Sabrina Fair* (1953) as *Sabrina.* Soon after he was writing directly for the screen, and when Alec COPPEL's work on VERTIGO ran aground, Hitchcock's old friend Kay Brown recommended Taylor, a San Francisco native, as a replacement. The new writer saw his brief as providing narrative continuity and three-dimensional characters who could motivate particular scenes to which the director was committed; his greatest contribution to the film, he later maintained, was the invention of Midge Wood as Scottie Ferguson's confidante and the reassuringly rooted foil to his wildly romantic dreams of the possessed Madeleine Elster. The two men became friends. Taylor worked on the abortive *No Bail for the Judge,* and Hitchcock sought him in vain for THE BIRDS. But the next collaboration for the two, Taylor's rewrite of Leon URIS's adaptation of his own novel TOPAZ, was far less satisfying. Taylor had by this time become an established screenwriter whose credits included *The Pleasure of His Company* (1961), *Aimez-vous Brahms?* (1961), and *Three on a Couch* (1966)—a list that would ultimately expand to *The Love Machine* (1971) and *Avanti!* (1972), Wilder's adaptation of his 1968 play. Both *Avanti!* and *Sabrina* were remade, the first for television, the second for theatrical release, in the nineties.

Taylor, Vaughn (1910–1983) Dapper, retiring American character actor, in Hollywood from 1933 for more than 100 roles, mostly in the fifties and sixties, in films and television, where he played a wide variety of milquetoasts, professional men, and businessmen such as George Lowery, the realtor boss whom Marion Crane robs of $40,000 in PSYCHO, and Dr. Babcock in THE ALFRED HITCHCOCK HOUR segment "The Long Silence" (1963).

Teal, Ray (E.) (1902–1976) American character actor. A former saxophone player with stage experience, he made his Hollywood debut in 1938 and spent the rest of his life playing outdoorsmen, often sheriffs, in nearly 200 films and 50 television programs. He appeared as the police lieutenant unable to track down the man who identified Elsa Span in "REVENGE," the premiere episode of ALFRED HITCHCOCK PRESENTS, and returned in seven more episodes: as Warden Jacobs in "You Got to Have Luck" (1956), the police sergeant in "The Baby Sitter" (1956), Sheriff Briggs in "My Brother Richard" (1957), the chief of detectives in "Number Twenty-Two" (1957), the fire chief in "Total Loss" (1959), bartender Ben Tulip in "Road Hog" (1959), and Jim Hale in "A Jury of Her Peers" (1961). He remains best known for still another television role, Sheriff Roy Coffee in *Bonanza* (1960–72).

Tearle, (Sir) Godfrey (1884–1953) Reserved British stage actor who also appeared in some 30 film roles, beginning with the lead in *Romeo and Juliet* (1908). As Professor Jordan in THE 39 STEPS, he was the very model of the gentlemanly, treacherous enemy agent.

Tedrow, Irene (1907–1995) American actress who made her Hollywood debut in 1941 but whose greatest success came on television, where she appeared in the regular casts of *Meet Corliss Archer* (1952), *Dennis the Menace* (1959–63), *Mr. Novak* (1965), *The Young Marrieds* (1965), and *The Amazing Spider-Man* (1978–79). Three of her many television guest appearances were on ALFRED HITCHCOCK PRESENTS as Lucy in "Don't Come Back Alive" (1955), Mrs. Hewitt in "BACK FOR CHRISTMAS," and Lady

Musgrove in "The Hero" (1960). She returned as Ethel in THE ALFRED HITCHCOCK HOUR segment "The Paragon" (1963).

Tell Your Children International Artists (Gaumont), 1922. **Producer:** Martin Sabine; **Director:** Donald Crisp; **Screenplay:** Leslie Howard Gordon, based on *Lark's Gate,* a novel by Rachel Macnamara; **Cast:** Doris Eaton (Rosny Edwards), Walter Tennyson (John Haslar), Margaret Halstand (Lady Sybil Edwards), Warwick Ward (Lord Belhurst), Mary Rorke (Susan Haslar), Cecil Morton York (Reuben Haslar), Adeline Hayden Coffin (Nancy Dyson), Gertrude McCoy (Maudie), A. Harding Steerman (Vicar).

Eleventh of the 12 silent films, 1920–22, for which Hitchcock designed intertitles.

Tennyson, Pen(rose) (1912–1941) British writer-director who left Oxford in 1932 to work with Michael BALCON in films. He served as uncredited assistant director on THE MAN WHO KNEW TOO MUCH (1934), THE 39 STEPS, SECRET AGENT, SABOTAGE, and YOUNG AND INNOCENT, married Nova PILBEAM, the star of the last film who had also appeared as a child in the first, then moved with Balcon to MGM British, where he was billed as assistant director on *The Citadel* (1938), and wrote and directed three films for Balcon at Ealing: *There Ain't No Justice* (1939), *The Proud Valley* (1940), and *Convoy* (1940). When war broke out, he joined the navy to make training films but died in a plane crash shortly after.

Terry, Harry British character actor who made his film debut as the showman in THE RING, played a wedding guest in THE MANXMAN, and went on to another 20 minor roles through 1946.

Terry Lewis (or Terry-Lewis), Mabel (1872–1957) British stage actress who also appeared in eight films from 1921 to 1943. She played Sir Humphrey Pengallan's aristocratic friend Lady Beston in JAMAICA INN.

Tester, Desmond (1919–) British child actor who had already appeared in four films before SABOTAGE, in which he played Mrs. Verloc's brother

Stevie, the luckless boy who takes what he thinks is a canister of film labeled *Bartholomew the Strangler* aboard a London bus and is blown up along with the conductor, the other passengers, and a friendly dog. After making four more films in the thirties, he went to Australia; his subsequent film appearances are few.

Tetzel, Joan (Margaret) (1924–1977) Delicate, down-to-earth American actress with extensive stage experience who created the role of Nurse Ratched in the stage version of *One Flew Over the Cuckoo's Nest*. After making her film debut as Helen Langford in *Duel in the Sun* (1946), she appeared in a dozen film and television roles, including sympathetic, gossipy Judy Flaquer in THE PARADINE CASE and battling housewife Eve Ross in the ALFRED HITCHCOCK PRESENTS episode "Guest for Breakfast" (1958). Her second husband was actor Oscar HOMOLKA.

Tetzlaff, Ted (1903–1995) American cinematographer-turned-director who began as a performer, playing himself as a race car driver in *The Speed Kings* (1913). He then worked as a lab and camera assistant before becoming a lighting cinematographer in 1926, first with Columbia, where he shot *The Criminal Code* (1931), and then with PARAMOUNT, where his dozens of films included *Hands Across the Table* (1935), *My Man Godfrey* (1936), *True Confession* (1937), and *Easy Living* (1937). Soon after making his directorial debut with *World Premiere* (1941) and earning an Oscar nomination for shooting *Talk of the Town* (1942), he enlisted in the armed forces, returning to a few more photographic assignments, of which the last was NOTORIOUS, before establishing himself as a full-time director of a dozen features, of which the most notable is *The Window* (1949).

Tey, Josephine Pseudonym of Elizabeth Mackintosh (1896–1952), Scottish playwright and mystery novelist. A former teacher of physical education—a background she put to good use in *Miss Pym Disposes* (1946)—she first turned to the whodunit under the name Gordon Daviot with *The Man in the Queue* (1929), which introduced wealthy Scotland Yard detective Alan Grant, who continued through six of her eight mysteries. The second Grant novel, *A*

Shilling for Candles (1936), served as the basis for YOUNG AND INNOCENT, shorn of its detective and its original killer, and with a supporting character, an inventive young nuisance of a girl, transformed into its romantic heroine. Tey's best-known novel is *The Daughter of Time* (1951), in which a bedridden Grant, fascinated by a painting of Richard III, sets out to prove against the weight of historical consensus that Richard did not murder the two nephews he was holding in the Tower of London.

39 Steps, The (Alternative titles: *Die neununddreissig Stufen, Les trente-neuf marches, Il Club dei trentanove*) Gaumont-British, General Film Distributors Ltd., 86 minutes, June 1935. **Producers:** Michael Balcon and Ivor Montagu; **Screenplay:** Charles Bennett, based on the novel by John Buchan; **Continuity:** Alma Reville; **Dialogue:** Ian Hay; **Cinematographer:** Bernard Knowles; **Art director:** O. Werndorff; **Set director:** Albert Jullion; **Costumes:** J. Strassner; **Wardrobe:** Marianne; **Sound:** A. Birch; **Editor:** D.N. Twist; **Music:** Hubert Bath; **Musical director:** Louis Levy; **Cast:** Robert Donat (Richard Hannay), Madeleine Carroll (Pamela), Lucie Mannheim (Annabella Smith), Godfrey Tearle (Professor Jordan), John Laurie (crofter, John), Peggy Ashcroft (crofter's wife, Margaret), Helen Haye (Mrs. Jordan), Frank Cellier (sheriff), Wylie Watson (Mr. Memory), Jerry Verno, Gus McNaughton (commercial travelers), Peggy Simpson (maid), Frederick Piper (milkman), John Turnbull (police inspector), Ivor Bernard (chair of political meeting), Matthew Boulton (fake police officer), S.J. Warmington (detective), Det.-Sgt. Bishop (police sergeant), Vida Hope (usher), Miles Malleson (Palladium manager).

As soon as principal photography ended on THE MAN WHO KNEW TOO MUCH (1934), Hitchcock began story conferences with Charles BENNETT on a project that would fulfill his longtime dream of adapting the work of John BUCHAN, a best-selling acquaintance whose novel *The Thirty-Nine Steps* (1915) was still regularly reprinted. Attracted as he was to the source novel's tale of a man unjustly accused of murder on the run from both enemy agents and the police, however, Hitchcock, urged by Bennett, approached it with a freedom undreamed of by the director of THE SKIN GAME and RICH AND STRANGE. The contemporary setting, the

Leaving behind the murdered Annabella Smith, Richard Hannay (Robert Donat)—asking the milkman (Frederick Piper) if he can borrow his uniform to escape the spies who have killed her and staked out his flat—sets out on the first of his many disguises in *The 39 Steps*. *(Literature/Film Society Archive)*

framing scenes at the music hall and the London Palladium, the pair of stories the hero Richard Hannay tells the milkman, his comic adventures aboard the train, the somber episode of the crofter and his wife, the enemy agent missing half a finger, Hannay's escape from the false police handcuffed to Pamela, the use of Mr. Memory to smuggle a military secret out of the country—none of them appear in the novel, just as there is no staircase numbering 39 steps in the film. Indeed, all of the film's prominent female characters who define Hannay's adventures—the seductive spy Annabella Smith whom he takes home only to find

her murdered in his flat, the wives of the crofter and of Professor Jordan, the pertly skeptical Pamela—are the film's inventions. But partisans of the novel cannot have been any more bemused than the film's leads. Only two days after the English-born Hollywood star Madeleine CARROLL, whom Michael BALCON had escorted home from America, had agreed to play Pamela, the director introduced her to Robert DONAT on the morning of the first day of shooting, January 11, 1935, then handcuffed them together for the scene at the bridge, and then allegedly misplaced the key until the end of the day. Whether he wanted to break through Carroll's reserve as a performer or simply take one of his most high-profile stars to date down a peg, he evidently succeeded; filming proceeded smoothly, and when the film had wrapped, she satisfied the two-picture contract Balcon had offered her by working on SECRET AGENT. Despite the obligatory disapproval of C.M. WOOLF, *The 39 Steps* extended the success of *The Man Who Knew Too Much* still further, providing Hitchcock with his first truly international fame.

For all its departures from Buchan's novel, Hitchcock's 18th film follows it in one important respect: Both stories are highly episodic, unrolling almost like collections of self-contained short stories: The main difference structurally is that Buchan's episodes, enshrined in long, discrete chapters, have a beginning, a middle, and an end, whereas Hitchcock hurtles from one episode to the next with scarcely more warning of his abrupt changes in time and place and tone than in *The Man Who Knew Too Much*. Hence Hannay, having made his way one step ahead of the police to Alt-Ne-Shellach to warn Professor Jordan that the military secret Annabella wanted to protect is on its way out of the country, suddenly finds himself sipping champagne at a Sunday morning party before the Professor pulls a gun on him and reveals, rather illogically, that he is the ringleader whose plans Annabella was trying to thwart. Not even the sudden interruption of Mrs. Jordan to call her husband for lunch can prevent Jordan from impassively shooting Hannay—although an abrupt cutaway to the crofter's cottage sets up the revelation the Hannay is still alive, saved by a hymnal in his borrowed coat that stopped Jordan's bullet. Nor is this resurrection halfway through the film the end of the story's dizzying alternation of tones because only a few minutes later, telling his story to a sympathetic-seeming sheriff, Hannay is crashing through the window of the sheriff's office with the police again in pursuit as he marches off in a Salvation Army parade and suddenly finds himself addressing a political rally on behalf of a candidate whose name he does not know (an episode suggested by Buchan but much brisker and wittier in the film) before he is led off from a cheering crowd by police officers who turn out to be more spies. Even the opening riot in the music hall is played for humor until a pistol shot sud-

denly sends the panicked crowd scurrying into the streets and Hannay into the arms of Annabella Smith, who drops hints about the plot in the spookily shrouded flat he has rented during the slow, tense, yet erotic sequence preceding her death. Unlike Buchan's novel, in which Hannay's frank, manly narrative tone is echoed by his repeated unburdenings of himself to important characters who believe his story, the film marks Hannay's progress by a constant string of disguises—the few characters he tells the truth to either disbelieve or betray him—and its sexual fetishism, culminating in the famous sequence in which Hannay, handcuffed to a woman who thinks him a murderer, pretends to hold a gun on her while he persuades a Scottish innkeeper and his wife that they are a runaway couple in love. Hitchcock transforms Buchan's adventure yarn for grownup boys into a coolly modernist exercise in manipulation whose political propaganda is systematiclly trumped not by psychological realism (because Hitchcock's Hannay remains a man without a past or, except for Pamela, a future) but by the sexualizing of the story's power relationships, a potent image for the deftly shifting relations between filmmaker and audience.

Thomas, Dolph (1891–1966)   American sound recordist, at WARNER BROS. for some 50 films from *Tovarich* (1937) to *The Music Man* and *Gypsy* (both 1962). One of his last projects was STRANGERS ON A TRAIN.

Thomas, Jameson (1889–1939)   Stage-trained British actor, on the boards from his teens, who made his film debut in 1924. Although he played Samuel Sweetland, the widowed farmer in THE FARMER'S WIFE, with an appealing combination of dignity and comic vulnerability, and returned in a mock-dramatic role in a completely different key in ELSTREE CALLING, his journey to Hollywood in 1930 won few leads among his 40 roles. Instead, he is best remembered as King Westley, the forbidden new husband Clark Gable is plotting to help Claudette Colbert reach in *It Happened One Night* (1934).

Thorndike, (Dame Agnes) Sybil (1882–1976)   Dominant British stage actress, a former pianist whose broken wrist changed her career plans. She made her stage debut in 1904 and won particular praise for her classical Greek heroines and her performance in the title role of *Saint Joan* (1923), a part George Bernard Shaw is said to have written especially for her, She had already made her film debut two years earlier and had starred as the multiple heroines of the 1922 *Tense Moments from Great Plays.* Though her 40 films were clearly secondary to her work onstage, she gave memorable performances as Nurse Edith Cavell in *Dawn* (1928), the Salvation Army general in *Major Barbara* (1941), Mrs. Squeers in *Nicholas Nickleby* (1947), and Eve Gill's fluttery, self-absorbed mother in STAGE FRIGHT. She was married to actor Lewis Casson from 1908 to his death in 1969.

3-D process Stereoscopic devices for the projection of still images like the stereopticon, popularized as the children's toy the View-Master, had antedated the invention of cinema itself. But the imprecise registry and inconvenience associated with all of them, whether based on red and green images designed to be viewed through red- and green-filtered glasses or on polarized images designed to be viewed through polarized glasses, had kept them from achieving lasting popularity until 1952, when Hollywood's panic over the rising threat of television led studio heads to revisit such technologies as CinemaScope, Cinerama, and 3-D that television could not readily imitate. The first feature to be filmed in 3-D, United Artists' *Bwana Devil* (1952), advertised "a lion in your lap"; it was soon followed by similar projects at all the major studios. Once Jack L. Warner chose DIAL M FOR MURDER as WARNER BROS.' contribution to the cycle, it became the only film under production after the studio had closed down for five months. Despite the long rehearsals and visual limitations imposed by the 3-D camera's gargantuan size, immobility, and inability to bring tight closeups into focus, the film, which was shot in just 36 days, is generally agreed to be the most successful of all fifties films to use the process. Even though Hitchcock disclaimed any interest in the 3-D process, it posed the sorts of technical challenges he delighted in addressing, and his approach to its possibilities was unique. Instead of barraging the audience with unexpected

movements toward the camera (and hence apparently toward them), Hitchcock not only shoots virtually the entire film within a single stage set but also, as in his one-set film *Rope,* emphasizes the staginess of the action. Characters seldom move directly toward the camera but are repeatedly framed behind objects and furnishings that loom ominously before them. When Margot Wendice, who is being strangled by the hired killer Swann, stabs Swann to death with a pair of scissors, Hitchcock shows her straining toward the foreground to reach the scissors, but forgoes the opportunity to thrust the scissors toward the camera, showing Swann's body falling toward the camera instead. The most emphatic movement toward the camera in the entire film is therefore the quietly climactic moment when a hand, in impossibly tight closeup, holds out a latchkey whose provenance is central to the plot. The film was never widely released in 3-D, and within a year the studios' craze for stereoscopic projection had ended, leaving extant 3-D prints of *Dial M for Murder* to be shown as curiosities in film festivals and retrospectives.

thrillers Hitchcock did not invent the thriller—the term was already in common use to describe sensationalistic plays before movies were ever invented—but his greatest commercial success was to place himself so completely at its center that it is often defined in terms of him, rather than the other way around, as in Charles DERRY's *The Suspense Thriller: Films in the Shadow of Alfred Hitchcock* (1988). Unlike the literary thrillers of E. Phillips Oppenheim and Edgar Wallace, the Hitchcock thriller, taking its model from the tales of John BUCHAN, typically aims to combine a wider range of tones with a greater concentration of suspense. Hence the comedy of THE MAN WHO KNEW TOO MUCH (1934) and the romance of NORTH BY NORTHWEST do not interrupt the suspense but intensify it; the most heartfelt thrills in NOTORIOUS come not from the conflict of Nazi and American agents but from the romance between T.R. Devlin and Alicia Huberman. Martin Rubin's *Thrillers* implies one reason why Hitchcock has been so central to the thriller: The term is otherwise "impossibly broad and vague," ranging as it does over crime dramas, adventure yarns, horror films, science-fiction tales, and stories about spies and the police—though by no means including every entry in any of these categories. Rubin's useful survey of earlier attempts by G.K. Chesterton, John G. Cawelti, Pascal Bonitzer, Lars Ole Sauerberg, and Noël Carroll to define the genre emphasizes several crucial dialectics—anxiety/pleasure, sadism/masochism, identification/ detachment, vulnerability/control, not knowing/ knowing—that further suggest Hitchcock's centrality. By the time he left Britain, Hitchcock's films from *The Man Who Knew Too Much* through THE LADY VANISHES had established both a thematic structure and a standard for the thriller that guaranteed certain kinds of pleasure (the pleasure of being puzzled while anticipating a definitive revelation, the pleasure of sharing the ordeals of sympathetic characters, the pleasure of seeing ordinary fears transformed into stylized nightmares, the pleasure of knowing that justice would prevail, the pleasure of seeing terror aestheticized in startling and revealing ways) for viewers who could thenceforth take Hitchcock's name as both a criterion of value for his own films and a containing term for genre entries besides his own that would balance the lack of control, knowledge, and comfort implied by the very label "thriller."

Thurman, Lois American script supervisor whose eight credits include four Hitchcock films: *THE BIRDS, MARNIE, TORN CURTAIN*, and *TOPAZ*.

Tiomkin, Dimitri (1899–1979) Russian-American composer, with Max Steiner, Miklós RÓZSA, and Alfred NEWMAN the best-known provider of film music in his day. Trained in both music and law, he introduced George Gershwin's music to Europe in the twenties and then immigrated to the United States, where, beginning in 1929, he turned out some 150 impressively various scores from the expressionism of *Mad Love* (1935) to the flag-waving patriotism of *Mr. Smith Goes to Washington* (1939). His gift for melodic ideas that could be transposed into different modes made him especially adept in scoring films that covered a broad emotional gamut, such as *Only Angels Have Wings* (1939) and *It's a Wonderful Life* (1946). He was Hitchcock's favorite com-

Dimitri Tiomkin

poser in the years between Louis LEVY and Bernard HERRMANN, composing the music for SHADOW OF A DOUBT and returning for Hitchcock's three films at WARNERS BROS.: *STRANGERS ON A TRAIN, I CONFESS*, and *DIAL M FOR MURDER*. Nominated for Academy Awards for *Lost Horizon* (1937), *Mr. Smith Goes to Washington* (1939), *The Corsican Brothers* (1942), *The Moon and Sixpence* (1943), *The Bridge of San Luis Rey* (1944), *Champion* (1949), *Giant* (1956), the song "Wild Is the Wind" (from *Wild Is the Wind* [1957], the song "Strange Are the Ways of Love" (from *The Young Land,* 1959), the song "The Green Leaves of Summer" and the score for *The Alamo* (1960), the song "Town Without Pity" (from *Town Without Pity,* 1961), the song "So Little Time" and the score for *55 Days at Peking* (1963), *The Fall of the Roman Empire* (1964), and the music adaptation for *Tchaikovsky*

(1971), Tiomkin won two Oscars, Best Song and Best Dramatic Score, for *High Noon* (1952), and two more for *The Old Man and the Sea* (1958) and *The High and the Mighty* (1954). On the latter occasion his acceptance speech extending his thanks to those to whom he owed the most—"Brahms, Bach, Beethoven, Richard Strauss, and Johann Strauss"—brought the house down.

To Catch a Thief   (Alternative titles: *Über den dächern von Nizza, La main au collet, Caccia al ladro*) Paramount, 97 minutes, July 1955. **Producer:** Alfred Hitchcock; **Director:** Alfred Hitchcock; **Screenplay:** John Michael Hayes, based on the novel by David Dodge; **Cinematographer:** Robert Burks; **Assistant director:** David McCauley; **Second unit director:** Herbert Coleman; **Second unit cinematographer:** Wallace Kelley; **Art directors:** Hal Pereira and Joseph MacMillan Johnson; **Set decoration:** Sam Comer and Arthur Crams; **Costumes:** Edith Head; **Makeup:** Wally Westmore; **Dialogue coach:** Elsie Foulstone; **Sound:** Harold Lewis and John Cope; **Special effects:** John P. Fulton and Farciot Edouart; **Technicolor consultant:** Richard Mueller; **Editor:** George Tomasini; **Music:** Lyn Murray; **Cast:** Cary Grant (John Robie), Grace Kelly (Frances Stevens), Jessie Royce Landis (Jessie Stevens), John Williams (H.H. Hugheson), Charles Vanel (Bertani), Brigitte Auber (Danielle Foussard), Jean Martinelli (Foussard), Georgette Anys (Germaine), René Blancard (Inspector Lepic), Jean Hébey (Mercier), Dominique Davray (Antoinette), Frank Chelland (chef), Aimee Torriani (woman in kitchen), Lewis Charles (man with milk in kitchen), William "Wee Willie" Davis (big man in kitchen), Edward Manouk (kitchen help), Paul Newlan (vegetable man), Roland Lesaffre (Claude), Stephen Geray (desk clerk), Philip Van Zandt (jewelry clerk), Louis Mercier (croupier), Gladys Holland (elegant woman), Russell Gaige (Mr. Sanford), Marie Stoddard (Mrs. Sanford), John Alderson, Guy De Vestel, Bela Kovacs, Don Megowan, Alberto Morin (detectives), Michael Hadlow, Leonard Penn (Monaco police officers), Martha Bamattre.

The history of Hitchcock's 41st film is closely bound up with that of his 40th. Bill KROHN reports that David DODGE's 1952 novel, whose adaptation rights Hitchcock had purchased on its first publication, was the first film Hitchcock planned to make at PARA-MOUNT, with Cary GRANT as reformed cat thief John Robie. Even though REAR WINDOW took its place as Hitchcock's first Paramount film, the director was planning it as he shot *Rear Window* early in 1954. John Michael Hayes, who had written the screenplay for *Rear Window* with little ongoing input from Hitchcock, told Donald Spoto that the director flew Hayes and his wife to the Riviera so that he could get a sense of the location and worked closely and rapidly with him in daily story conferences, and the screenplay was finished in April. Grace KELLY was quickly cast opposite Grant, although Grant, returning from an 18-month retirement at 50, was twice as old as his romantic partner (older indeed than Jessie Royce LANDIS, who played her endearingly parvenu mother), and although Hitchcock had to wait until Kelly had completed the three intervening films for which she was contracted for filming to begin—even then bad weather in Cannes caused the cancellation of a Mardi Gras parade that was to have been one of its set pieces. The shoot proceeded, however, in a relaxed, holiday atmosphere, with the director unbending to the extent of allowing his stars to ad-lib three completely different takes of the picnic scene (though the scene in the finished film closely follows Hayes's screenplay).

Principal photography was completed by August, just as *Rear Window* was opening. Hayes's screenplay, whose scenes pairing American heiress Francie Matthews with Robie or with his admirer Danielle Foussard, the daughter of one of his Resistance comrades, were spiked with genial double-entendres, was one of the wittiest of his four scripts for Hitchcock at Paramount, and Robert BURKS's scintillating traversal of the Riviera in Technicolor and VISTAVISION (it was Hitchcock's first film in Paramount's new widescreen process) won an Academy Award for Best Color Cinematography. Despite the lukewarm response of reviewers, the film's commercial success, immediately following the even greater success of *Rear Window,* consolidated Hitchcock's independence at his new studio and freed him to choose his own projects. But it also marked his final collaboration with Kelly, who met Prince Rainier of Monaco during filming, married him in 1956, and retired from Hollywood, despite Hitchcock's urging that she return for *MARNIE.*

Francie Stevens (Grace Kelly) and John Robie (Cary Grant) tussle playfully over her seductive accusation that he is the cat burglar responsible for the rash of thefts on the French Riviera in *To Catch a Thief. (National Film Society Archive)*

Because it was the only one of Hitchcock's five films for Paramount whose ownership the studio retained, the film remained for 10 years the sole measure of his midfifties work with Hayes. In some ways it is not truly representative of the period because, buoyant as the others are, *To Catch a Thief* is lighter than any of them except for *THE TROUBLE WITH HARRY*. Its enduring popularity despite its featherweight and often illogical plot is a testimonial to Hitchcock's belief in imagery and mood over the logic of plot and motivation. The film is essentially a nonstop series of chases and masquerades whose motivation does not stand up to close scrutiny. The police, convinced that Robie has not really reformed despite his pardon for his wartime activities, follow him incessantly in the hope of proving that he is responsible for a new rash of cat burglaries; he does everything he can to keep ahead of them. But his repeated failures cost him nothing; he is arrested only to be released. Similarly, he offers no convincing reason for his masquerade as lumberman Conard Burns to meet wealthy potential target Jessie Stevens and her daughter Francie; Francie struggles to trap him in an admission of duplicity that she might have confirmed with a few transatlantic phone calls; and her interest in him becomes even more predatory when she thinks he is up to his thieving habits again, though she is inexplicably outraged when she thinks he has chosen her mother's jewels (a bit of sexual innuendo whose source Ken MOGG traces to Patricia HITCHCOCK's performance in a 1953 radio adaptation of *The Moonstone*). An incongruously gratuitous murder late in the film sends Robie into hiding, even though it helps confirm his innocence; when he appears soon after in the prefect's office, the officials take no action against him. The film is an example of precisely the sort of whodunit Hitchcock affected to disdain; indeed, viewers who believe Robie innocent will find more detective-story elements in it than in STAGE FRIGHT, which is commonly classified as a whodunit. Yet the film's good-natured wit effaces its logical flaws even as it transmutes its signature chases from high-stakes pursuits to romantic rituals memorializing the perverse glamour of courtship among beautiful people in beautiful places. Even the American Grace Kelly's persistent attempts to unmask the English-born American Cary Grant as French come across as slyly self-referential instead of simply inept or absurd. The film marks Hitchcock's most remarkable success in making something out of airy nothing.

Todd, Ann (1909–1993)   Cool BLONDE British movie star of the forties. Onstage from 1928, she made her film debut in 1931, but it was not until her performance as the romantically torn pianist Francesca Cunningham in *The Seventh Veil* (1946) that she emerged as a major star and was cast in her first American film as barrister Anthony Keane's loyal but sorely tried wife Gay in THE PARADINE CASE. Although Todd fits seamlessly into the pantheon of Hitchcock BLONDES, her performance in the film, is overshadowed by that of the truly arctic Alida VALLI. Two years after completing the film, Todd married David Lean, who directed her in three films—*The Passionate Friends* (1949), *Madeleine* (1950), *The Sound Barrier* (1952)—before her carrer petered out. After her divorce from Lean, she appeared as the title character, a suicidal heiress, in the ALFRED HITCHCOCK PRESENTS segment "Sylvia" (1958) and wrote, directed, and produced several travel documentaries in the sixties.

Todd, Richard (1919–)   Handsome, callow British leading man, born Richard Andrew Palethorpe-Todd in Dublin to a British officer. His stage career was interrupted by distinguished service as a paratrooper in World War II, but he returned to more prominent roles onstage and, beginning in 1948, onscreen. Soon after his Oscar-nominated performance as Lachie MacLachlan, a recreation of his stage role, in *The Hasty Heart* (1949), Hitchcock cast him as Jonathan Cooper, the most surprising of all his men on the run, in STAGE FRIGHT. He went on to success in the title roles of *The Story of Robin Hood and His Merrie Men* (1952), *Rob Roy, the Highland Rogue* (1953), and *A Man Called Peter* (1955), but his favorite of his later character roles was in *The Longest Day* (1962), in which he appeared as Major John Howard, his own commanding officer during the D-day invasion.

Tomasini, George (1909–1964)   American film editor at PARAMOUNT from 1947, who became Hitchcock's most frequent collaborator outside his family circle in the fifties. Beginning with REAR WINDOW, he cut all Hitchcock's films except for THE TROUBLE WITH HARRY through his death: TO CATCH A THIEF, THE MAN WHO KNEW TOO MUCH, THE WRONG MAN, VERTIGO, NORTH BY NORTHWEST (for which he was nominated for an Academy Award), PSYCHO (on which he worked without cinematographer Robert Burks), THE BIRDS (on which he worked with no more than token participation by Bernard Herrmann), and MARNIE. His other credits include *The Time Machine* (1960), *The Misfits* (1961), *Cape Fear* (1962), and *In Harm's Way* (1965), his final film.

Toomey, Regis (1902–1991)   Likeable, dependable American character actor, everyone's favorite sidekick in more than 200 film and television roles from 1929. He played dozens of cops, including Sergeant Gillespie in SPELLBOUND and Bernie Ohls in *The Big Sleep* (1946), and provided good-humored support as one of the newshounds in *His Girl Friday* (1940), one of the family in *Mighty Joe Young* (1949), and one of the Salvation Army officers in *Guys and Dolls* (1955) before settling into continuing roles in the television series *Burke's Law* (1963–65) and *Petticoat Junction* (1968–69).

Topaz (Alternative titles: *Topas, L'étau*) Universal, 126 minutes, December 1969. **Producer:** Alfred Hitchcock; **Associate Producer:** Herbert Coleman; **Director:** Alfred Hitchcock; **Screenplay:** Samuel Taylor, based on the novel by Leon Uris; **Cinematographer:** Jack Hildyard; **Consultant:** Karl Mohr; **Camera operators:** William Dodds (and Sherman Kunkel); **Assistant directors:** Douglas Green and James Westman; **Production designer:** Henry Bumstead; **Set decorator:** John Austin; **Costumes:** Edith Head and Peter Saldutti, fashioned by Pierre Balmain; **Makeup:** Bud Westmore and Leonard Engelman; **Hairstyles:** Larry Germain and Nellie Manly; **Sound:** Waldon O. Watson and Robert R. Bertrand; **Script supervisor:** Trudy Von Trotha; **Production assistant:** Peggy Robertson; **Unit production manager:** Wallace Worsley; **Technical advisers:** J.P. Mathieu (Cuban), Odette Ferry (French); **Special effects:** Albert Whitlock; **Editor:** William Ziegler; **Assistant:** Jeff Gourson; **Music:** Maurice Jarre; **Cast:** Frederick Stafford (André Devereaux), John Forsythe (Michael Nordstrom), Dany Robin (Nicole Devereaux), Karin Dor (Juanita de Cordoba), John Vernon (Rico Parra), Claude Jade (Michéle Picard), Michel Subor (François Picard), Michel Piccoli (Jacques Granville), Philippe Noiret (Henri Jarre), Roscoe Lee Browne (Philippe Dubois), Per-Axel Arosenius (Boris Kusenov), Sonja Kothoff (Mrs. Kusenov), Tina Hedström (Tamara Kusenov), Edmon Ryan (McKittreck), George Skaff (Rene d' Arcy), Don Randolph (Luis Uribe), Carlos Rivas (Hernandez), Roberto Contreras (Munoz), John Roper (Thomas), Anna Navarro (Carlotta Mendoza), Lewis Charles (Pablo Mendoza), John Van Dreelen (Claude Martin), Roger Til (Jean Chabrier), Sándor Szabó (Emile Redon), Lew Brown (American official), Rita Conde (Dolores), Al Lewis (old man with bags at St. Regis).

UNIVERSAL had purchased the rights to Leon URIS's best-selling espionage novel in the fall of 1967, and when Hitchcock could not come up with another property for his 51st film, he agreed to tackle it, even though he had rarely had good luck with authors adapting their own work to the screen (the happiest exception had been *DIAL M FOR MURDER*, a claustrophobic play rewritten as an even more claustrophobic film by Frederick KNOTT). In the end, he threw out Uris's screenplay as the shooting was about to begin in June 1969 and asked first Arthur LAURENTS and then Samuel TAYLOR to prepare a new one. Responding to the director's urgent plea, Taylor flew to London to find that Hitchcock was unwilling even to let him see Uris's screenplay—and that casting remained incomplete. As the crew traveled from one European location to the next, shooting scenes in Copenhagen, Paris, and Wiesbaden, new performers were signed: Claude JADE, Dany ROBIN, Karin DOR, John FORSYTHE, Frederick STAFFORD. The film's large budget precluded any delay long enough for Taylor to prepare a wholly new screenplay, and he was often forced to write individual scenes only hours before they went before the camera. The experience wore down both the writer and the director and virtually guaranteed that the film—one of the few Hitchcock films without an obvious main character or a single pivotal relationship—would be even more disjointed than Uris's sprawling novel. The problems with the evolving screenplay and the hasty shooting, so antithetical to Hitchcock's preferred approach to filming, did not come to a head until after principal photography was completed in August and Hitchcock realized he still had no satisfactory ending for a story that he could barely remember himself. As with *SUSPICION* nearly 30 years earlier, ending after ending was proposed, and three different endings were filmed: a scene in which a pair of spies working for opposite sides go their separate ways in businesslike peace; a duel between André Devereaux and Jacques Granville, the Soviet agent who has seduced his wife, which ends when Granville is executed by a sniper; and a stock exterior shot of Granville's Paris apartment (although the actor entering is actually Philippe NOIRET rather than Michel PICCOLI), with a gunshot added to indicate Granville's suicide. After the second of these endings left a preview audience confused, this third ending was used in release prints of the film, although the other endings are available on the film's DVD release.

Despite a massive publicity push by Universal, including an unprecedented number of interviews by the director himself, and despite the National Board of Review's naming Hitchcock Best Director of 1969 for his work on the film, *Topaz* flopped with both the press and the public, losing more money than any other Hitchcock film. It has never been

The wound to François Picard (Michel Subor, seated) momentarily brings together the shattered family of his wife Michele (Claude Jade, second from right) in *Topaz,* as she tends him along with her parents, Nicole Devereaux (Dany Robin) and André Devereaux (Frederick Stafford). *(National Film Society Archive)*

rereleased by the studio, and it is virtually unknown except to Hitchcock scholars. For all the problems in its writing and casting, however, its plan is authentically Hitchcockian. From its opening scene, the film systematically explores the toll social culture takes on the capacity to love. The mise-en-scène is full of books, paintings, sculptures, and (especially) flowers designed to cover the grubby tasks of professional eavesdroppers and professional betrayers by gilding them with the trappings of a culture worth saving. As the imperious behavior of the Soviet defector Boris Kusenov indicates, however, the political and cultural affiliations for which the characters here so readily betray each other are relatively superficial and mutable, even though the authentic natures that ought to lie beneath have long since been hollowed out by the wearisome game of politics. Despite the excitement generated by an early sequence in which an undercover agent penetrates the New York headquarters of visiting Cuban president Rico Parra, a Fidel Castro lookalike, and the warmth of the Cuban sequence reuniting Devereaux with his not-so-secret love Juanita de Cordoba, the film continues and deepens the cynicism TORN CURTAIN displays toward politics. Even its fragmentation, which works against the empathy Hitchcock had created with such apparent ease in his earlier thrillers, heightens the mood of disillusionment and despair. Set alongside Hitchcock's very first spy story, THE MAN WHO KNEW TOO MUCH (1934), *Topaz* offers both a quietly frightening view of the bankruptcy of all the values—family, romance, personal loyalty, political idealism—that had made Hitchcock's stories of international intrigue not only thrilling but also uplifting and a strikingly prescient view of both cold-war politics and cultural analysis in general. Its sour retreat from the glamour of international politics would be complemented three years later by Hitchcock's equally bleak account of private crime and punishment in FRENZY.

Torn Curtain (Alternative titles: *Der Zerrissene Vorhang, Le rideau déchiré, Il sipario strappato*) Universal, 120 minutes, July 1966. **Producer:** Alfred Hitchcock; **Director:** Alfred Hitchcock; **Original screenplay:** Brian Moore; **Cinematographer:** John F. Warren; **Camera operator:** Leonard South; **Assistant director:** Donald Baer; **Production designer:** Hein Heckroth; **Art director:** Frank Arrigo; **Set decorator:** George Milo; **Costumes:** Edith Head and Grady Hunt; **Makeup:** Jack Barron; **Hairstyles:** Hal Saunders and Lorraine Robertson; **Script supervisor:** Lois Thurman; **Production assistant:** Peggy Robertson; **Unit production manager:** Jack Corrick; **Special effects:** Albert Whitlock; **Editor:** Bud Hoffman; **Music:** John Addison; **Cast:** Paul Newman (Professor Michael Armstrong), Julie Andrews (Sarah Sherman), Lila Kedrova (Countess Luchinska), Hansjörg Felmy (Heinrich Gerhard), Tamara Toumanova (ballerina), Wolfgang Kieling (Hermann Gromek), Ludwig Donath (Professor Gustav Lindt), Günter Strack (Professor Karl Manfred), David Opatoshu (Jakobi), Gisela Fischer (Dr. Koska), Mort Mills (farmer), Carolyn Conwell (farmer's wife), Arthur Gould-Porter (Freddy), Gloria Gorvin (Fräulein), Mischa Hausserman (idealistic young man), Jan Malmsjö (Swedish photographer), Maurice Doner.

Once MARNIE was completed, Hitchcock toyed with several possible subjects for his 50th film. He considered starring Tippi HEDREN in *Mary Rose,* an adaptation of J.M. Barrie's play he had dreamed of for 40 years. He worked briefly on an adaptation of John BUCHAN's *The Three Hostages* and more seriously on *R.R.R.R.,* a comedy about an émigré Italian

hotelkeeper taxed by the attempt to keep his relatives from robbing a guest in his hotel. In May 1965, however, he fell back on an idea he had conceived when British diplomats Guy Burgess and Donald Maclean defected to the Soviet Union in 1951: What would the drama feel like from Mrs. Maclean's point of view, especially given the homosexual overtones of her husband's betrayal? The idea did not interest William Goldman or, at first, Brian MOORE; but when UNIVERSAL doubled the promised payment to $50,000, Moore agreed, and despite his misgivings about Hitchcock's lack of interest in character, worked until the end of the year on the story, fleshing it out with the MACGUFFIN of a scientific secret

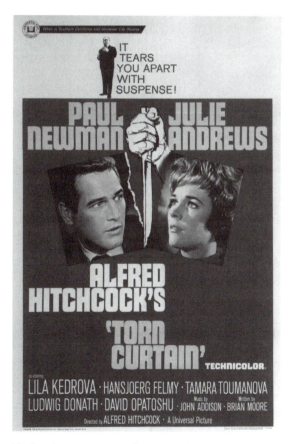

Hitchcock manages to sneak a personal appearance into the advertising poster for *Torn Curtain* featuring Paul Newman and Julie Andrews as physicist Michael Armstrong and his fiancée Sarah Sherman. *(National Film Society Archive)*

that must be wormed out of a professor's head, the idea of a murder that would show just how hard it is to kill someone, and the appearance of a character who would batten on the hero and heroine in the hope of escaping with them on their departure. At the same time, the original impetus for the story—the woman's perspective on her husband's treachery—ebbed nearly to the vanishing point, largely because Professor Michael Amstrong, the defecting hero, was now a double agent who was only pretending to defect to trick his opposite number in Leipzig into revealing the knowledge that is the basis of a nuclear project. When Moore voiced reservations about the completed script, Hitchcock replaced him with Keith Waterhouse and Willis Hall and then asked him to share screen credit with them. The Writers Guild settled the dispute in Moore's favor, but the conflict indicated the trouble that still lay ahead. UNIVERSAL, eager for the PARAMOUNT-sized hit that had eluded the studio with THE BIRDS and MARNIE, pressed Hitchcock to accept Paul NEWMAN and Julie ANDREWS, the biggest box-office stars in America, as the two nuclear physicists at the heart of the intrigue. Soon after shooting began on the Universal backlot in November—it was hardly likely that East Germany would allow the project to be shot on location—Hitchcock was repeatedly clashing with the Method-trained Newman over his performance and pronouncing the wholesome Andrews flatly unbelievable as a scientist. But the gravest blow did not come until postproduction, when Hitchcock, urged by the studio to seek a light score including a title song with the chart-climbing potential of "Whatever Will Be," rejected the somber no-violins score Bernard HERRMANN completed in March 1966, and Herrmann, never one to walk away from a quarrel, responded by ending perhaps Hitchcock's single most fruitful collaboration. When the film opened in July with a new score (but no hit single) by John ADDISON, some of the reviews were as downbeat as Herrmann's abortive score, although the film earned more in American rentals than any other Hitchcock film after PSYCHO and ended up turning a profit.

Shorn of Herrmann's discarded score, *Torn Curtain* is still Hitchcock's chilliest film. Even its jokes are chilly, like the opening sequence showing (or not quite showing) Michael Armstrong in bed with his fiancée Sarah Sherman not only because they are in love, but also because the heating on their cruise ship has failed and they are trying to keep warm—a joke that will be echoed in the very last shot of the film, when after all their betrayals, revelations, and escapes, they are still simply trying to keep warm. Immersing a loving couple in a political situation guaranteed to drive them apart had of course been the recipe behind NOTORIOUS, but this time there seems less at stake in the threats to the couple because there is less heat between them. The lack of warmth can be traced partly to the absence of chemistry between Newman and Andrews but more fundamentally to the way their characters are conceived. Michael Armstrong is as remote as T.R. Devlin but far more petulant throughout the first half of the film, first because he is trying to keep his impending defection secret from his fiancée and then because he is trying to keep his status as a double agent secret. The film, unable or unwilling to suggest a stronger romantic current between the leads, methodically builds the pervasive chill into the mise-en-scène, dressing the East Germans in gray, photographing the exteriors representing East Berlin and Leipzig through gray filters that bleach the skies, and emphasizing the drab uniformity of the monumental postwar architecture. The film's grayness is punctuated by flashes of bright color planted throughout: Andrews's red hair standing out from the white bedclothes in her stateroom (and the earthtones she consistently wears thereafter), the flowers in the Leipzig garden where Michael reveals his real mission to her, the brilliant scarf worn by the floridly aspiring defector Countess Luchinska, the fiery sets for the infernal ballet *Francesca da Rimini,* at which the fugitive Michael and Sarah are at the point of being unmasked, not for the last time, by a prima ballerina jealous of the press coverage accorded Michael's defection when Michael has THE 39 STEPS–inspired idea of yelling, "Fire!" This opposition between occasional warmth and habitual torpor ironically comes to life only in the sequence in which Michael is forced to excruciating lengths in his attempt to kill the East German watchdog who has learned his double-agent status and is about to turn him in. Apart from this scene, the film, more programmatic than passionate, has won few enthusiasts, though its cool remoteness from both partisan politics and romance has won the respect of poststructuralist analysts from Jean Narboni to Christopher MORRIS.

Toumanova, Tamara (1917–1996) Russian ballerina who made her professional debut in 1924. Between 1942 and 1970, she appeared in eight scattered films. Perhaps her least taxing assignment was in TORN CURTAIN, in which she played an Iron Curtain ballerina. She was married to screenwriter Casey ROBINSON.

Tovey, George (1913–1982) Short, shy British character actor whose dozen film and television roles include Mr. Salt, whose interest in beekeeping seems a pitifully inadequate preparation for the marriage the Blaney Bureau has launched him into in FRENZY.

Tracy, William (1917–1967) Boyish American character actor, in Hollywood for 30 films beginning with *Brother Rat* (1938), who played Sammy, the hapless messenger from David Smith's law office in MR. AND MRS. SMITH.

Transatlantic Pictures Short-lived independent production company formed by Hitchcock and Sidney BERNSTEIN in 1946. Even before his eight-year association with David O. SELZNICK had concluded, Hitchcock was eager to establish an independent corporation to release his own films. He had always been too opinionated and dictatorial to welcome producers' interference with his shoots, and Selznick, the most hands-on producer in Hollywood, had often disagreed sharply with his ideas about casting, script, and camera and, Hitchcock felt, exploited him financially as well by loaning him out to other studios at sizeable profits that he did not share with the director. For several years Hitchcock negotiated with businessman Bernstein over the formation of an independent company, and in 1946, the trade papers announced the formation of Transatlantic Pictures as a company that would make films alternately in London and Hollywood and distribute them through WARNER BROS. The company's first announced production was UNDER CAPRICORN; its second was to be a modern-dress *Hamlet*. In the instance, ROPE preceded *Under Capricorn,* and Hitchcock declined to compete with Laurence OLIVIER's acclaimed period *Hamlet* (1948). When *Rope* returned only a modest profit and *Under Capricorn* turned into an unmitigated flop, Transatlantic folded after only two films, and Jack L. Warner extended his distribution agreement with the company to Hitchcock's next three films, leaving the director as a quasi-independent producer-director (with studio financing and distribution, but a minimum of studio interference)—a status he maintained for the rest of his career.

Travers, Henry (1874–1965) Lantern-jawed British character actor, born Travers Heagarty, who after long stage experience went in 1933 to Hollywood, where he played more than 50 twinkling, slightly befuddled old gents. He was a kindly doctor in *Dark Victory* (1939), a kindly neighbor in *Mrs. Miniver* (1942, in an Oscar-nominated performance), the heroine's kindly oblivious father in SHADOW OF A DOUBT, and, most memorably, the kindly Clarence Oddbody, "angel second class," in *It's a Wonderful Life* (1946).

Travers, Linden (1913–2001) Kittenish British actress of the thirties and forties, born Florence Linden-Travers. Onstage from 1931, she made her screen debut in *Children of the Fog* (1935) and played creamy, dark-eyed brunettes in both lead and character roles for two dozen films. She was paired with stiffly uncomfortable Cecil PARKER in THE LADY VANISHES, in which she played the mistress who is travelling with him as his wife, and again in *The Stars Look Down* (1939).

Tremaine, Kathleen British actress whose second and last film credit is Anna, the hotel Bandrikan maid whose room is taken over by Caldecott and Charters in THE LADY VANISHES.

Tremayne, Les (1913–) Mild-mannered British character actor who since making his debut on American television in 1950 has appeared in more than 100 films and television episodes, typically as unflappable politicians (*A Man Called Peter,* 1955), military officers (*The War of the Worlds,* 1953), or professional types (*The Angry Red Planet,* 1959). He appeared twice in ALFRED HITCHCOCK PRESENTS, as the deceived but not outwitted husband Dr. Fred Bixby in "MRS. BIXBY AND THE COLONEL'S COAT" and the equally ineffectual husband Peter Talbot in "Deathmate" (1961); returned as Ryder and Mr. Selby in THE ALFRED HITCHCOCK HOUR segments "Day of Reckoning" (1962) and "Isabel" (1964); and was especially effective as the harried auctioneer dueling the disruptive Roger Thornhill in NORTH BY NORTHWEST.

Tribby, John E. American sound recordist. Soon after joining RKO in 1929, he was nominated for an Academy Award for *The Case of Sergeant Grischa* (1930). Among his 70 later credits through 1951 are serving as recording director on MR. AND MRS. SMITH and sound recordist on SUSPICION.

Triesault, Ivan (1898–1980) Estonian-born character actor, onstage in his native land from 14, who immigrated to America in 1914, appeared as dancer and mime on both sides of the Atlantic, and traveled in 1943 to Hollywood where his precise gestures and accented English typecast him as a Nazi in such roles as the cold-blooded Eric Mathis in NOTORIOUS. During the following 20 years, he played more than 50 film and television roles, specializing in sinister Europeans but occasionally playing as far outside his type as King George in *The Lady and the Bandit* (1951).

Tripp, June (1901–1985) British actress of the twenties. Billed only as June, she made her film debut in *The Yellow Claw* (1920) and after one other film starred as the first of the malleable Hitchcock BLONDES, model Daisy Bunting in THE LODGER. In 1929, she married Lord Inverclyde and effectively retired.

Trouble with Harry, The (Alternative titles: *Immer Ärger mit Harry, Mais qui a tué Harry, La congiura della innocenti*) Paramount–Alfred Hitchcock, 99 minutes, October 1955. **Producer:** Alfred Hitchcock; **Associate producer:** Herbert Coleman; **Director:** Alfred Hitch-

cock; **Screenplay:** John Michael Hayes, based on the novel by Jack Trevor Story; **Cinematographer:** Robert Burks; **Assistant director:** Howard Joslin; **Art directors:** John Goodman and Hal Pereira; **Set decoration:** Sam Comer and Emile Kuri; **Costumes:** Edith Head; **Makeup:** Wally Westmore; **Sound:** Harold Lewis and Winston Leverett; **Special effects:** John P. Fulton; **Technicolor consultant:** Richard Mueller; **Editor:** Alma Macrorie; **Music:** Bernard Herrmann; **Cast:** Edmund Gwenn (Captain Albert Wiles), John Forsythe (Sam Marlowe), Shirley MacLaine (Jennifer Rogers), Mildred Natwick (Ivy Gravely), Mildred Dunnock (Mrs. Wiggs), Jerry Mathers (Arnie Rogers), Royal Dano (Calvin Wiggs), Parker Fennelly (millionaire), Barry Macollum (tramp), Dwight Marfield (Dr. Greenbow), Leslie Wolff (art critic), Philip Truex (Harry Warp), Ernest Curt Bach (Ellis, the chauffeur).

Hitchcock was so eager to adapt Jack Trevor STORY's 1950 comedy of manners about a closed community whose routines are interrupted by the sudden appearance of a corpse in their midst that he asked John Michael HAYES to begin work on a screenplay even before he began shooting TO CATCH A THIEF— and before purchasing the rights, as he did anonymously in 1954 for $11,000. Suspecting that Story's archly grotesque tale might lack popular appeal, even transplanted from England to New England for an American audience, Hitchcock avoided the big stars who had helped make his earlier films so successful and prepared a budget of $1 million, far less than *Rear Window* and *To Catch a Thief.* The top billing was shared by newcomer John FORSYTHE and 79-year-old Edmund GWENN, appearing in his fourth Hitchcock role since 1931. The cast was completed by stage-trained veterans Mildred NATWICK and Mildred DUNNOCK and by Shirley MACLAINE, an ingenue Herbert COLEMAN had discovered when, as a Broadway understudy, she took over the lead from Carol Haney the night he saw *The Pajama Game.* Determined to shoot the film's exteriors on location to take advantage of the autumn foliage, Hitchcock arrived in East Craftsbury, Vermont, in October 1954 just in time to see fierce week-long rains lashing the leaves from the trees, forcing the shoot inside an interior cover set in nearby Morrisville, where the rain

The comic conspirators of *The Trouble with Harry*—Captain Wiles (Edmund Gwenn), Miss Gravely (Mildred Natwick), Jennifer Rogers (Shirley MacLaine), and Sam Marlowe (John Forsythe) – wait anxiously for Harry Warp's body to be discovered for the last time by Jennifer's son Arnie. *(National Film Society Archive)*

pinging on the tin roof of the gymnasium in which the set had been built made it impossible to record a live soundtrack. Although the skies lifted for long enough to allow some exterior shots that were used as backgrounds in process work and as framing shots to the main action, that action itself was filmed entirely indoors, either in Morrisville or back in California, on a PARAMOUNT set festooned with autumn leaves carefully packed by the technicians who had remained behind for that purpose. Because contractual agreements had taken Philip TRUEX on to other projects, he had to be doubled on the studio set by an actor whose face was obscured by an elaborately

casual branch. Postproduction in November and December required extensive rerecording—like *ROPE*, much of the film relies on a postsynchronized soundtrack—but yielded one lasting reward: After repeated attempts to sign Bernard HERRMANN, Hitchcock was finally able to obtain him to compose the film's alternately bucolic and astringent music, from which Herrmann, who was to become one of Hitchcock's most highly regarded collaborators during the next 10 years, extracted a suite he called "A Portrait of Hitch."

Hitchcock's premonitions about the limited box-office appeal of the film proved all too accurate: *The*

Trouble with Harry was the only one of his Paramount films to lose money. Despite the rise in the film's reputation over the years, it is one of Hitchcock's least studied films; the only presentation on it at the 1986 Pace conference on the rereleased films was Lesley BRILL's paper, which became the crowning chapter of *The Hitchcock Romance*. It is easy to dismiss the posthumous adventures of Harry Warp—who has died in pursuit of Jennifer Rogers, the bride (and one-time sister-in-law) who left him years ago after he abandoned her on their wedding night because his horoscope promised trouble—as a single brittle joke, a progenitor to the coarser humor of *Weekend at Bernie's* (1989) and its 1993 sequel. Yet no two films could differ more. Unlike the murdered Bernie, Harry does not party, sunbathe, or go hang gliding; he does nothing but be repeatedly interred and exhumed. The film's black comedy arises not from the attempt to persuade anyone that Harry is alive but from the matter-of-fact attempts of Sam Marlowe and Captain Wiles to protect Jennifer, Miss Gravely, and Captain Wiles himself from implication in Harry's death—alternately by burying him to conceal the crime and by digging him up to check the evidence or to allow Jennifer to marry Sam by proving that Harry is dead. As Brill has noted, the film is the deepest social affirmation of Hitchcock's maturity, linking Harry's death to the natural cycles of the single day and night within which the story unfolds and the season of autumn that every shot invokes. But the affirmation is voiced in the driest possible tone. More than that of any other Hitchcock film, *The Trouble with Harry* depends on ensemble acting, especially on a gravely arch performance style most successfully maintained by Natwick and Gwenn, as in her opening greeting to him as he is lugging Harry's corpse by its feet off the trail where he has found it: "What seems to be the trouble, Captain?"—a line Hitchcock once identified as his favorite speech in all his films. Despite the film's box-office failure and its subsequent neglect by Hitchcock scholars, it has left an indelible legacy. When James ALLARDICE, the writer engaged to write the introductions and conclusions by which Hitchcock framed every episode of *ALFRED HITCHCOCK PRESENTS* and *THE ALFRED HITCHCOCK HOUR*, asked what

tone he should strike in these speeches, Hitchcock asked him to watch *The Trouble with Harry,* whose clipped comedy (Hitchcock called it the most English of his American films) thereby became the single most important model for the director's television persona, and indeed for his public persona until his death and beyond.

Truex, Philip (1911–   )   Occasional American actor who made his film debut in *This Is the Army* (1943) as Sergeant Philip Truek, appeared as the Timid Guy in a 1950 episode of the television series *Actor's Studio,* and, in his final role, played the late Harry Warp in THE TROUBLE WITH HARRY. Despite the relatively undemanding requirements of the role, additional shooting back in Hollywood, where Truex was unavailable, forced Hitchcock to use a stunt double, his face strategically obscured, in some shots of the corpse.

Truffaut, François (1932–1984)   Key French New Wave filmmaker who spent years attacking the Tradition of Quality and developing the *politiques des auteurs* under the banner of *Cahiers du cinéma* before following the debut of the short films *Une visite* (1954) and *Les mistons* (1958) with a series of groundbreaking features he directed, often wrote, and occasionally starred in: *Les quatre cent coups* (*The 400 Blows*, 1959), *Tirez sur le pianiste* (*Shoot the Piano Player,* 1960), *Jules et Jim* (1961), *L'amour à vingt ans* (*Love at Twenty* [French episode], 1962), *La peau douce* (*The Soft Skin,* 1964), *Fahrenheit 451* (1966), *La mariée était en noir* (*The Bride Wore Black* 1967), *Baisers volés* (*Stolen Kisses,* 1968), *La sirène du Mississippi* (*Mississippi Mermaid,* 1969), *L'enfant sauvage* (*The Wild Child,* 1970), *Domicile conjugale* (*Bed and Board,* 1970), *Les deux anglaises et le continent* (*Two English Girls,* 1971), *Une belle fille comme moi* (*Such a Gorgeous Kid Like Me,* 1972), *La nuit américaine* (*Day for Night,* 1974), *L'histoire d'Adèle H* (*The Story of Adele H,* 1975), *L'argent du poche* (*Small Change,* 1976), *L'homme qui amait les femmes* (*The Man Who Loved Women,* 1977), *La chambre verte* (*The Green Room,* 1978), *L'amour en fuite* (*Love on the Run,* 1979), *Le dernier métro* (*The Last Metro,* 1980), and *Vivement dimanche* (*Confidentially Yours,* 1983). A longtime champion of Hitchcock, whose work he

François Truffaut

the sumptuously illustrated, large-format volume is rivaled only by Sidney GOTTLIEB's *Hitchcock on Hitchcock* as a portrait of the director as raconteur—and pressing him most closely on technical matters (the glass ceiling in THE LODGER, the Shuftan shots in BLACKMAIL, the plane crash William Cameron MENZIES designed for FOREIGN CORRESPONDENT, the track-out/zoom-in down the staircase in VERTIGO), least closely on thematic questions and the nature of the relationship he cultivated with his audience. The enlarged and updated third edition (1983) includes information on TOPAZ, FRENZY, and FAMILY PLOT. For all the limitations of Truffaut's uncritical stance, his volume remains unrivaled in importance by his other, mostly posthumous books—*Les films de ma vie* (1978), *The Early Film Criticism of François Truffaut* (1993), *Truffaut by Truffaut* (1987), *Correspondance 1945–1984* (1988), and *Le plaisir des yeux* (1990)—as one of the three or four essential books on Hitchcock, one that represented a generation of students' ideas of what a film book ought to be.

Truman, Ralph (1900–1977) British stage actor who has appeared in some 70 films since 1937 in supporting roles of ever more weighty authority as in *Mrs. Fitzherbert* (1947), *Quo Vadis* (1951), and *Le carosse d'or* (1952). By the time of THE MAN WHO KNEW TOO MUCH (1956), his surprisingly sympathetic Inspector Buchanan was a distinct step down from the lords and admirals he habitually played.

Tummel, William (F.) (1892–1977) American assistant director on some three dozen films, 1925–46, including *Sadie Thompson* (1928), *Cavalcade* (1933), *The Little Foxes* (1941), and, among the last, SHADOW OF A DOUBT.

Tuttle, Lurene (1906–1986) American character actress with radio background. Hitchcock directed her as the landlady in THE LODGER (1940), his first live RADIO broadcast, and she voiced Effie Perrine and many other characters in *The Adventures of Sam Spade* (1946–51). After two earlier bits, her film career began in earnest with *Heaven Only Knows* (1947), and she played variously fluttery wives and mothers in some 50 films, including *Don't Bother to*

echoes in *Tirez sur le pianiste, La mariée était en noir,* and *La sirène du Mississippi,* he had interviewed him with Claude CHABROL on the completion of TO CATCH A THIEF in 1955, though the interview had to be postponed for several hours when the two journalists fell through the ice into a pond. In June 1962, he asked Hitchcock to grant him a series of extended chronological interviews about his films, with sidelights on their background and the general issues they raised for filmmaking, whose text would become the basis of a book. Hitchcock agreed, and the initial series of interviews from August 1962, facilitated by the translator Helen G. Scott and supplemented by later interviews on MARNIE and TORN CURTAIN, became *Le cinéma selon Hitchcock* (Robert Laffont, 1966), published in America as *Hitchcock* (Simon and Schuster, 1967). Truffaut rarely departs from an admiring, often devotional tone, allowing Hitchcock to retell most of his favorite anecdotes—

Knock (1952), *Niagara* (1953), and *The Fortune Cookie* (1965). In 1960, the year she played Sheriff Chambers's wife in PSYCHO, she was rather less fluttery as the title character in *Ma Barker's Killer Brood.* But her greatest success was on such television series as *Life with Father* (1953–55), *Pete and Gladys* (1960–62), and *Julia* (1968–71).

Tweedsmuir, Lord   See BUCHAN, JOHN.

Twentieth Century–Fox Pictures   American production company formed in 1935 by the merger of Nicholas Schenck's Twentieth Century Pictures with William Fox's Film Corporation, which had pioneered the Movietone system for synchronized sound. Darryl F. Zanuck, production chief from 1935 to 1952, quickly gained a reputation for ruthless cost cutting and for liberal use of the casting couch. The company's biggest star through the thirties was Shirley Temple, its most prestigious contract director in the forties John Ford, and its most notable discoveries in the fifties Marilyn Monroe and CinemaScope, which it introduced in *The Robe* and *How to Marry a Millionaire* (both 1953). After Hitchcock had produced FOR-EIGN CORRESPONDENT on loanout from David O. SELZNICK to Walter WANGER, Fox sought him in vain for *How Green Was My Valley* (1941) but turned down SABOTEUR when he offered it to them. In November 1942 the director went to Fox as part of package loanout that included Ingrid BERGMAN, Joan FONTAINE, Gene Kelly, Dorothy McGuire, cinematographers George BARNES and Stanley Cortez, and the properties *Claudia, Jane Eyre,* and *The Keys of the Kingdom* and eventually settled on a story that would become LIFEBOAT. The film lost more than a million dollars, and Hitchcock never worked at Fox again.

Twist, D(erek) N. (1905–1979)   British director who began as an editor on nine films of the thirties, from THE 39 STEPS to *The Edge of the World* (1937), before turning screenwriter with *They Drive by Night* (1938) and director with *End of the River* (1947). He also produced one film, *Angels One Five* (1953).

Tyner, Charles (1925–)   American character actor who since his debut in the telefilm *Ethan Frome* (1960), has appeared in mostly minor roles in more than 60 films and television segments, from *Cool Hand Luke* (1967) to *Planes, Trains, and Automobiles* (1987). He played Wheeler in FAMILY PLOT.

Ulric, Lenore (1892–1970) American stage actress, born Lenore Ulrich, who also appeared in sporadic films, first as a femme fatale in Essanay silents, then as a character actress in the thirties and forties. One of her last roles was an uncredited bit in NOTORIOUS.

Under Capricorn (Alternative titles: *Sklavin des Herzens, Les amants du Capricornem, Il peccato di Lady Considine, Sotto il Capricorno*) Transatlantic, Warner Bros., 117 minutes, September 1949. **Producers:** Alfred Hitchcock, Sidney Bernstein; **Director:** Alfred Hitchcock; **Screenplay:** James Bridie, based on the novel by Helen Simpson (and the dramatic adaptation by Margaret Linden and John Colton); **Adaptation:** Hume Cronyn; **Cinematographer:** Jack Cardiff; **Assistant director:** C. Foster Kemp; **Camera operators:** Paul Beeson, Ian Craig, David MacNeilly, Jack Haste; **Production designer:** Thomas Morahan; **Set dresser:** Philip Stockford; **Costumes:** Roger Furse; **Makeup:** Charless Parker; **Sound:** Peter Handford (and A.W. Watkins); **Continuity:** Peggy Singer; **Production manager:** Fred Ahern; **Unit manager:** John Palmer; **Technicolor consultant:** Natalie Kalmus; **Associate:** Joan Bridge; **Editor:** A.S. Bates; **Music:** Richard Addinsell; **Musical direction:** Louis Levy; **Cast:** Ingrid Bergman (Lady Henrietta Flusky), Joseph Cotten (Sam Flusky), Michael Wilding (Charles Adare), Margaret Leighton (Milly), Jack Watling (Winter), Cecil Parker (Governor), Denis O'Dea (Corrigan), John Ruddock (Mr. Potter), Ronald Adam (Mr. Riggs), G.H. Mulcaster (Dr. McAllister), Francis De Wolff (Major Wilkins), Bill Shine (Mr. Banks), Victor Lucas (Rev. Smiley), Harcourt Williams (coachman), Olive Sloane (Sal), Maureen Delaney (Flo), Julia Lang (Susan), Betty McDermot (Martha).

SELZNICK story editor Margaret McDonnell had brought Helen SIMPSON's 1937 novel, as well as an unpublished dramatic adaptation by Margaret LINDEN and John COLTON, to Hitchcock's attention as early as 1944, but although he was indeed eager to star Ingrid BERGMAN in a film version, he was not eager to make it under Selznick's thumb. It was not until after establishing TRANSATLANTIC PICTURES and finishing ROPE in 1948, when Bergman was free of other contractual obligations, that he traveled to England for the filming. Discussing the film with later interviewers, Hitchcock invariably told the same story: He was so infatuated by the idea of snagging Bergman, who had just begun her liaison with Roberto Rossellini, that he paid no attention to the rest of the production or to the fact that his star's generous salary made profits unlikely. For whatever reason, the film, a costume drama set in the Australia of 1831 (and therefore exactly the sort of property Hitchcock normally took the greatest pains to avoid), was both written and cast like a labor of love. When Arthur LAURENTS declined to work on the film, Hitchcock turned, in lieu of a strong storyteller

Hitchcock casts an eye over cinematographer Jack Cardiff's shoulder during the filming of *Under Capricorn*. *(National Film Society Archive)*

stemmed from a most unlikely source: friction between the director and his star. For the first time Bergman rebelled against Hitchcock's strict allegiance to decoupage, wondering why she had to hit her marks when she was playing an incapacitated alcoholic and refusing to give her climactic confession of guilt in a single LONG TAKE. But if his star had changed, Hitchcock had not, and a few minutes after she launched into a tirade against the tyranny of his long takes, his horror of public scenes led him to leave the set, where she raged on for 20 minutes before she noticed his absence. Reviewers, when the film was released in September 1949, were no kinder, and it ended up losing so much money—more than any other Hitchcock film between *The Paradine Case* and *TOPAZ*—that its failure sent Transatlantic into receivership and ended Hitchcock's brief career as an independent producer.

Critics seeking to salvage the reputation of neglected Hitchcock films from THE PLEASURE GARDEN to *TORN CURTAIN* commonly describe them as more interesting in their parts than as a whole. Hitchcock's 35th film traces the course of a young visitor's infatuation with a noblewoman who had left Ireland years ago to be with her husband, the family groom, who murdered her brother when he pursued them after their elopement, up to the moment when she acknowledges that she herself, not Sam Flusky, had shot him. The film is by and large not even interesting in its parts; apart from the frankly comic MR. AND MRS. SMITH and THE TROUBLE WITH HARRY, it is the least thrilling of Hitchcock's American films. What is interesting is the idea behind the story's visualization: the attempt to breach the borders between one space and the next, outside and inside, and ultimately the characters' façades and their hidden natures by a series of elaborate, often unrelenting long takes. *Under Capricorn* uses the long take more interestingly and far more romantically than the better-known *Rope* because both its camera movements and its mise-en-scène are more ambitious and varied, because Hitchcock does not attempt to mask the cuts between successive takes, and because he routinely cuts within as well as between scenes. (The film contains about 170 shots, still well below the industry standard of 400–700.) The intricate shot that takes Charles Adare

who could supplement his own visual imagination, to two friends—Hume CRONYN, whose work on *Rope* had been his first adaptation, and James BRIDIE, whom he had lured into THE PARADINE CASE but who had soon left the project—and paired Bergman not with an earthy actor like Burt Lancaster but with the relaxed, genteel Joseph COTTEN. Struggling with the effort to translate a substantial novel into a two-hour film, Hitchcock consulted experts as different as Peter Ustinov and Marjorie Bowen, but the script remained ungainly and inert, lacking either any compelling narrative momentum or the kinds of memorable set pieces that might compensate for its absence. Principal photography began in August 1948 with a budget of $2.5 million, but as usual, problems in the adaptation heralded problems in the production, and this time many of the problems from the grounds of the house Sam shares with Lady Hetty past a window that gives him his first glimpse of his intoxicated hostess to the abortive dinner party to which Sam has invited him is a particularly dazzling example of suspenseful composition, and Lady Hetty's climactic confession (presented, over Bergman's objections, in a single ten-minute take) is riveting. But one feature remains from the long takes of *Rope:* by their very nature, such indefinitely prolonged moments tend to compete with dramatic structure rather than accentuating it. But the writing and acting never bring the intrigue, with its obvious echoes of REBECCA, to life, and for every moment the camera reveals a telling truth about the characters, there are a half-dozen moments when it upstages them—not such a difficult job, considering that most of their secrets seem to make little difference in their moral experience. Despite Hitchcock's dismissal of *The Lady in the Lake,* Robert MONTGOMERY's 1947 exercise in subjective camera, *Under Capricorn,* like *Rope,* closely resembles it as a technical experiment that was so revealing no one has felt the need to repeat it. The fact that the film remains more memorable for individual shots than for any correspondingly dramatic moments suggests that Bergman may have been onto something after all.

United Artists Pictures   The only Hollywood production company to be founded by filmmakers (hence its name) was formed in 1919 by Charles Chaplin, Douglas Fairbanks, D. W. Griffith, and Mary Pickford. Its greatest glory came early on, in the days when it produced and distributed silent films by its stars and, after Joseph Schenck arrived in the midtwenties, Buster Keaton, Gloria Swanson, and Rudolph Valentino. Because it functioned as an independent production company with no studios or contract stars of its own, its list of projects had dwindled by the time it released Walter WANGER's production of FOREIGN CORRESPONDENT and David O. SELZNICK's SPELLBOUND, the first incurring a small loss, the second earning sizable profits. Although it later recovered some of its former prosperity with the James Bond franchise, the company was ultimately merged into MGM following the disastrous losses of *Heaven's Gate* (1981).

Universal Pictures   The studio where Hitchcock ended his career had one of the oldest pedigrees in Hollywood; it was founded in 1912 by Carl Laemmle. A major producer of silent films, it survived the thirties mostly courtesy of vehicles for monsters and Deanna Durbin. Soon after releasing SABOTEUR and SHADOW OF A DOUBT, the studio merged in 1946 with International Films and was known as Universal-International until 1952. Ten years later, the studio was absorbed by the Music Corporation of America, whose president, Lew WASSERMAN, had been managing Hitchcock's career for many years. Hitchcock had already renewed his ties to the studio through ALFRED HITCHCOCK PRESENTS and THE ALFRED HITCHCOCK HOUR, which were shot, like PSYCHO, at REVUE, the television production facility at Universal City. After the success of *Psycho,* Wasserman brokered a deal that not only brought Hitchcock to Universal to direct his last six films—THE BIRDS, MARNIE, TORN CURTAIN, TOPAZ, FRENZY, and FAMILY PLOT—but also allowed the director to trade his share of the film's negative for a block of MCA stock that made him the corporation's third-largest shareholder. Although he never produced the runaway financial hit the studio hoped for, the rights to release his Universal films in different video formats, coupled with Hitchcock's residual interest in his PARAMOUNT films, also released on video by Universal, have brought the studio millions since his death.

unrealized projects   In addition to the 53 features he completed, Hitchcock considered directing a substantial number of other films. Some of these never got beyond the dreaming stage, others went into preproduction before their cancellation, and one important project was aborted at a still later stage. Although Hitchcock mentioned several of these projects to François TRUFFAUT, from a day in the life of a city to a suspense feature that was filmed entirely in a phone booth to *Mary Rose,* the supernatural fantasy that his UNIVERSAL contract specifically forbade him from filming, the most complete and reliable accounts of these projects are those by Dan AUILER, in Ken MOGG's *The Alfred Hitchcock Story,* and Sidney GOTTLIEB, in a more detailed forthcoming essay. Gottlieb distinguishes between several levels of Hitchcock's commitment to unfilmed projects. Some are no more than story ideas by writers he had worked with or admired, such as Sean O'CASEY (whose screenplay for *The Park* was eventually turned into the play *Within the Gates*), Francis ILES (whose *Malice Aforethought* he directed not as a movie but as a radio play), and John BUCHAN (whose *The Three Hostages* he considered filming in the sixties), or projects for which some producer sought him (as David O. SELZNICK did for *The Titanic,* or Walter WANGER, according to John Russell TAYLOR, for *Cleopatra* [1963]). More revealing are projects for which there is more substantial evidence of the director's interest or involvement: *Perjury,* a 1938 screenplay based on Marcel Auchard's novel *The False Witness,* in which a woman is killed after recanting the false alibi she had given a murderer; an early forties remake of THE LODGER, which ended up at 20TH CENTURY–FOX when Hitchcock sold his rights in the property; a modern-dress version of *Hamlet,* to star Cary GRANT, announced as TRANSATLANTIC's first feature; *The Knave of Newgate,* an 18th-century costume drama still under consideration in the midfifties; Margaret Wilson's *The Dark Duty,* a novel about a prison governor who refuses to execute a convicted prisoner, announced in 1949 as Hitchcock's next film after UNDER CAPRICORN; David Duncan's *The Bramble Bush,* which Hitchcock worked on with George TABORI in 1952, years before Michelangelo Antonioni used its central idea in *The Passenger* (1975); *Flamingo Feather,* Laurens Van Der Post's adventure based on African political intrigue, which he dropped in favor of VERTIGO; *Blind Man,* an original 1960 script by Ernest LEHMAN about a blind man whose recent corneal transplant allows him to see his hero for the first time; and *Dead Run,* a 1964 Richard Condon script intended for television.

Three projects stand apart from all the others. For several years, Hitchcock had been interested in adapting Henry CECIL's novel *No Bail for the Judge,* in which a respected jurist falsely accused of killing a prostitute is rescued when his daughter turns detective, and in 1959, after he and Samuel TAYLOR had prepared a visual treatment and had begun to scout London locations, Taylor completed a draft screenplay. But when Audrey Hepburn, who had agreed to star in the film, saw that her character would be required not only to befriend a gentleman burglar and an upper-class pimp but also to masquerade as a prostitute, she pulled out of the film, which promptly collapsed. Eight years later, Hitchcock worked first with his former colleague Benn W. LEVY, then with novelist Howard Fast, and finally with Hugh Wheeler on successive drafts of a film based on the crimes of British psychopath Neville Heath, who had been hanged in 1946 after raping and murdering two women. Between story conferences, storyboards preserved on hundreds of slides, and 10 minutes of test sequences using unknown actors, the film, alternately called *Frenzy* and *Kaleidoscope,* occupied Hitchcock for an entire year. But Universal summarily rejected the project and prevailed on Hitchcock to take on TOPAZ instead. Finally, there is the last project Hitchcock worked up in detail: *The Short Night,* Ronald KIRKBRIDE's novel about a police officer's obsessive pursuit of a figure based on the British spy George Blake, a criminal who raped and killed one of the sympathizers who had helped him escape from prison. In 1978 he worked with three writers—James Costigan, Ernest Lehman, and David FREEMAN—on the film, but ill-health forced him to put it aside. Freeman's published screenplay, together with the slides and test footage for *Kaleidoscope,* provides the closest look most fans are likely to get at the Hitchcock that never was.

Uris, Leon (M.) (1924–)

Best-selling American novelist who first came to Hollywood to adapt his World War II novel *Battle Cry* (1953) for the screen in 1955 and then stayed to adapt *Gunfight at the O.K. Corral* (1957). Among his other works adapted for the cinema are *The Angry Hills* (1959), *Exodus* (1960), and TOPAZ.

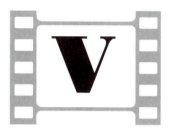

Vachell, H(orace) A(nnesley) (1861–1955). British playwright whose adaptation of *The Lodger* into the stage success *Who Is He?,* which Hitchcock saw in 1915, dates from the same year as his original play *The Case of Lady Camber.* This last was adapted in 1920 to the silent screen and again in 1932 as LORD CAMBER'S LADIES, the one film Hitchcock produced but did not direct.

Valentine, A.D. British sound recordist whose film credits include NUMBER SEVENTEEN and three later films, 1936–43.

Valentine, Joseph (A.) (1900–1949) Italian-American cinematographer, born Giuseppe Valentino. Arriving in Hollywood in 1920, he became a lighting cinematographer at Fox in 1924 and during the thirties developed a glossy style for UNIVERSAL that served him well in such Deanna Durbin vehicles as *Three Smart Girls* (1936) and *One Hundred Men and a Girl* (1937). Among his dozens of other assignments were *The Wolf Man* (1941) and the Abbott and Costello film *In the Navy* (1941). He shot two Hitchcock films at Universal: SABOTEUR and SHADOW OF A DOUBT, the latter in a deep-focus style, presumably influenced by William Wyler, that made the most of its suburban California locations. He was signed to shoot Hitchcock's first independent film, ROPE, but found the technical demands of lighting the one-set film and the demand for eight-minute retakes of a sunset that the director, shooting his first color film, pronounced "like a lurid postcard," so taxing that he ended up sharing credit with William V. SKALL. He shared an Oscar with Skall and Winton Hoch, however, for *Joan of Arc* that same year (1948).

Valentine, Val (1898–1971) British screenwriter, at British International (later Associated British) for nearly 50 films from *The Rocket Bus* (1929) to *A Weekend with Lulu* (1962). He came to Hitchcock's attention as one of the writers on the studio's musical showcase, ELSTREE CALLING, and collaborated with Alma REVILLE on the scenario for RICH AND STRANGE. That same year he directed his only film, based on his screenplay for *Pyjamas Preferred* (1932). His later work included several films with Frank LAUNDER and Sidney GILLIAT, most notably *The Belles of St. Trinian's* (1954) and two sequels.

Valli, Alida (1921–) Glamorous, mysterious Italian leading lady, born Alida Maria Altenberger. Although she had appeared in some 30 European films from 1934, Hitchcock and SELZNICK "introduced" her to the English-language cinema in THE PARADINE CASE simply as "Valli." Her portrayal of Maddalena Paradine, the widow suspected of killing her husband, a blind, much older war veteran, was alternately frigid and flashing with anger and contempt for her would-be savior, Anthony Keane. But the role did not launch her on a successful American career, and after her costarring role in the British production *The Third Man* (1949), she returned to work largely in the Italian industry, where she has made more than 100 films.

Valli, Virginia (1898–1968) American silent star, born Virginia McSweeney. She began film work with Essanay in Chicago in 1917 and three years later found herself in Hollywood, where she starred in more than 50 films, mostly in the midtwenties, when she played Patsy Brand, the good-girl chorine to Carmelita GERAGHTY's inconstant, gold-digging Jill Cheyne in THE PLEASURE GARDEN. The coming of sound, which brought hundreds of stage-trained hopefuls to town, made her salary seem excessive, and after a few sound features, she married actor Charles Farrell and retired in 1932.

Vanel, Charles (1892–1989) Flinty, inscrutable French actor, born Charles-Marie Vanel. In films for 80 years, beginning in 1908, he played hundreds of French military officers, judges, and police commissioners and was especially memorable as the fanatical Inspector Javert in *Les misérables* (1934). Following his success as Jo, one of the doomed truck drivers in *Le salaire de la peur* (1953), and the imperturbable Inspector Fichet in *Les diaboliques* (1955), he made his English-language debut as the restaurateur Bertani in TO CATCH A THIEF and then returned to the French industry for nearly 50 more films through 1988. He also directed two films, *Dans la nuit* (1929) and *Affaire classée (1931).*

Van Hessen, Richard American sound recordist at RKO for some 50 films from *Swing Time* (1936). When David O. SELZNICK arranged to shoot THE PARADINE CASE on the RKO lot, Van Hessen recorded the sound, as he had for Liberty Productions' *It's a Wonderful Life* (1946). One of his last projects before retirement was the television series *The Lone Ranger* (1949–57).

Varden, Norma (1898–1989) British-born character actress who made her most lasting mark as a comically snobbish society matron. A veteran of nearly 30 British films from 1931, she went to Hollywood in 1940 and made nearly 70 more. Even when uncredited, she is easily spotted in *Casablanca* (1942) and *The Senator Was Indiscreet* (1947), and she steals her one scene as Mrs. Cunningham, the naughty party guest who chats with Bruno Anthony about murder in STRANGERS ON A TRAIN and nearly ends up dead.

Vas Dias, Zelma Italian actress whose only film credit is Signora Doppo, the magician's wife in THE LADY VANISHES.

Ventimiglia, Baron (Gaetano di) Titled Italian cinematographer whose credits include *L'Incognita* (1922), *Toilers of the Sea* (1923), *Die Stadt der Versuchung* (1925), and Hitchcock's first three films: THE PLEASURE GARDEN, THE MOUNTAIN EAGLE, and THE LODGER.

Verity, Terence, Jr. (1913–) British art director who worked on some 16 films from *One Night with You* (1948) to *The Long and the Short and the Tall* (1960). His most notable films in between were *The Hasty Heart* (1949), STAGE FRIGHT, and *The Devil's Disciple* (1959).

Verno, Jerry (1895–1975) British character actor who appeared in some three dozen comic supporting roles, mostly during the thirties. He is one of the commercial travelers whose trainboard chatter haunts the escaping Richard Hannay in THE 39 STEPS, and he returns as the lorry driver in YOUNG AND INNOCENT.

Vernon, John (1932–) Stentorian Quebecois actor, né Adolphus Vernon Agopsowicz, who won a scholarship to the Royal Academy of Dramatic Art; first made his mark as the voice of the omnipresent but unseen Big Brother in *1984* (1956); starred in several Shakespearean productions for Canadian television and produced one of them, *Julius Caesar* (1964); supplied the voices for the television cartoon heroes Submariner and Iron Man (both 1966); starred as the title character in the Canadian television series *Wojeck* (1966); and finally made his

Hollywood debut as the treacherous Mal Reese in *Point Blank* (1967). After his casting as the sad-eyed Fidel Castro lookalike Rico Parra in TOPAZ, he went on to 150 film and television credits. He has been especially adept as such slick, self-justifying weasels as the San Francisco mayor in *Dirty Harry* (1971), Maynard Boyle in *Charley Varrick* (1973), and Dean Wormer in *Animal House* (1978).

Vertigo (Alternative titles: *From Among the Dead, Darkling I Listen* [working titles], *Aus dem Reich des Toten, Sueurs froides, La donna che visse due volte*) Paramount—Alfred Hitchcock, Paramount, 128 minutes, May 1958. **Producer:** Alfred Hitchcock; **Associate producer:** Herbert Coleman; **Director:** Alfred Hitchcock; **Screenplay:** Samuel Taylor and Alec Coppel, based on *D'entre les morts,* a novel by Pierre Boileau and Thomas Narcejac; **Cinematographer:** Robert Burks; **Assistant director:** Daniel McCauley; **Art directors:** Hal Pereira and Henry Bumstead; **Set decorators:** Sam Comer and Frank McKelvey; **Costumes:** Edith Head; **Makeup:** Wally Westmore; **Hairstyles:** Nellie Manley; **Sound:** Harold Lewis and Winston Leverett; **Special effects:** John P. Fulton; **Process photography:** Farciot Edouart and Wallace Kelley; **Technicolor consultant:** Richard Mueller; **Editor:** George Tomasini; **Music:** Bernard Herrmann; **Cast:** James Stewart (Scottie Ferguson), Kim Novak (Madeleine Elster/Judy Barton), Barbara Bel Geddes (Midge Wood), Tom Helmore (Gavin Elster), Konstantin Shayne (Pop Leibl), Raymond Jones (coroner), Raymond Bailey (doctor), Ellen Corby (manager of McKittrick Hotel), Lee Patrick (older mistaken identity), Buck Harrington (Elster's gateman), June Jocelyn (Miss Woods), Fred Graham (death fall officer), Ed Stevlingson (inquest attorney), William Remick (jury foreman), Paul Bryar (Captain Hansen), Joanne Genthon (Carlotta Valdez), Nina Shipman (younger mistaken identity), Dori Simmons (middle-aged mistaken identity), Jack Richardson (escort), Roland Got (maitre d' at Ernie's), Carlo Cotto (Ernie's bartender), Bruno Santina (Ernie's waiter), Julian Petruzzi (flower seller), John Benson, Don Giovanni (salesmen), Margaret Brayton (Ransohoff's saleswoman), Roxann Delman (Ransohoff's model), Miliza Milo (saleswoman), Mollie Dodd (beautician), Sara Taft (nun), Isabel Analla, Jack Ano, Bess Flowers.

Hitchcock's most profound meditation on possession was provoked, ironically enough, by his sense of competition with Henri-Georges Clouzot, whose *Les diaboliques* (1955), based on a thriller by Pierre BOILEAU and Thomas NARCEJAC, had given him a reputation as the French Hitchcock. Determined to outdo Clouzot on his own ground, Hitchcock kept an eye out for the next appearance of the novelists, who were meantime engaged in creating the sort of story they thought most likely to appeal to him for a lucrative film sale. Although PARAMOUNT promptly bought the rights to *D'entre les morts* for Hitchcock, however, the screenplay had a long and troubled gestation. Hitchcock dismissed Maxwell ANDERSON, the writer assigned to the project in October 1956, soon after Anderson submitted a script titled *Darkling I Listen;* and Angus MACPHAIL removed himself from the project shortly afterwards (though not before submitting a brief outline, beginning with a new rooftop chase, that would become the armature for the next version of the script). Nor was the work of Alec COPPEL, who toiled on the project while Hitchcock was ill with colitis and then hospitalized for gall bladder surgery, any more satisfactory. But Samuel TAYLOR, the San Francisco playwright on whom Hitchcock called after he had decided that his hometown provided the likeliest atmosphere for the otherworldly story, proved uncommonly gifted at providing compelling psychological motivations that strung together the tableaux the director envisioned; he deleted the boyfriend whom Anderson and Coppel, following Boileau and Narcejac, had given Judy Barton; instead, he invented Midge Wood, a more down-to-earth counterpart to Madeleine Elster, who provided the hero, Scottie Ferguson, with a sounding board that opened up the story. A final change proved crucial: Instead of preserving Madeleine's mystery to the end, Taylor ended the scene in which Scottie first talked to Judy with a flashback in which Judy revealed that she had played the part of the allegedly suicidal Madeleine as part of Gavin Elster's plot to kill his wife, letting viewers in on this secret before Scottie realized it. (Taylor also provided a final scene never filmed, in which Midge hears on the radio that Elster has been arrested and then turns it off upon Scottie's haunted entrance.) New difficulties arose when Vera MILES, for whom Hitchcock had always intended the role, announced a pregnancy that would make it impossible to cast her.

Just as Gavin Elster had coached Judy Barton to play the role of Madeleine Elster, Hitchcock coaches Kim Novak to play Judy Barton on the Empire Hotel set of *Vertigo*. *(National Film Society Archive)*

After a long delay, Hitchcock accepted Lew Wasserman's suggestion that he cast Kim NOVAK opposite James STEWART instead, though by the time Novak was ready to begin filming, Miles had had her baby and might well have taken the role after all—if Hitchcock had returned it to her. Production finally began in September 1957, nearly a year after Anderson had begun work on the screenplay, and wrapped shortly before Christmas, although *Vertigo,* as the project had finally been titled, was not released until May. Reviewers were generally cool; so was the public, which found the film's languorous rhythms puzzling and unexpected. Because the film was kept out of release from 1973 to 1983, its reputation grew slowly as Hitchcock's unseen masterpiece.

Masterpiece the film certainly is; although it has never achieved the widespread popularity of lower-impact thrillers like THE 39 STEPS, NOTORIOUS, STRANGERS ON A TRAIN, REAR WINDOW, NORTH BY NORTHWEST, or PSYCHO, it has no serious rival in the hearts of most Hitchcockians. Raymond DURGNAT has remarked that the most interesting part of most Hitchcock films is the middle third, when will-o'-the-wisp suspicions thicken before dissolving into the satisfying but straightforwardly melodramatic chases or shootouts of his finales. But *Vertigo,* after establishing a nightmare atmosphere with a prologue that breaks off as the helplessly acrophobic Scottie is dangling impossibly over a drop that has already killed the policeman who tried to help him, turns into a dream whose complications steadily thicken until the very last moment. When Scottie follows Madeleine's car around the hills of San Francisco in the film's wordless, magically extended third sequence, it is obvious from her gravely obsessive behavior that she is possessed, but he mistakes the agent of possession, as he has been set up to do, as the ghostly Carlotta Valdes; instead, Madeleine is possessed by one man, Elster, who is paying her to impersonate the wife he plans to kill, and is looking forward, though she does not know it, to being possessed by another, Scottie himself. This second possession is not consummated when Scottie rescues Madeleine from her plunge into San Francisco Bay or even when Scottie and Madeleine embrace near the shadow of the giant redwoods that remind her of death, but when Scottie, recovering from the nervous breakdown into which Madeleine's death has sent him spiraling, encounters Judy on the street and begins a relationship that will not be complete until he has followed in Elster's footsteps by remaking her into Madeleine himself. Of the two unequal parts, then, the longer first part is essentially a prologue to its richer, crueler second part, a prophecy in which the characters are trapped in a time warp that captures their most characteristic pose—Scottie eternally in pursuit of an impossible romantic ideal desirable precisely because she is impossible, because it is in the nature of both his gaze and her manufacture to ensure that she remain forever unavailable—without either of them understanding that this pursuit will be repeatedly replayed as their only possible pose. Bernard HERRMANN's score, which everywhere recalls *Tristan und Isolde,* conveys the lure of Madeleine's treacherous sexuality, the romantic power of Scottie's longing for her, and the catastrophic destructiveness of his rage with all the fairytale force of a modern opera. The film's presentation of Scottie has been widely taken as the self-portrait of the director as Svengali, and a merciless self-portrait it is because Hitchcock, even as he brings out the tenderness and pathos of Scottie's yearning, does not shrink from its fatal consequences. His hero's vertigo—the fear of falling crossed with an unappeasable longing to fall—provides Hitchcock with the richest metaphor of his career, one that links love, death, and

the perverse pleasures of film spectatorship in the only one of his films that can without reservation be called beautiful.

Vest, James M. (1947–) American literary scholar, professor of French at Rhodes University, author of *The French Face of Ophelia from Belleforest to Baudelaire* (1989) and translator of *The Poetic Works of Maurice de Guerin* (1992). He has published several essays on Hitchcock's cameo appearances; his study of Hitchcock's French connections will be published by Praeger/Greenwood in 2003.

Vetchinsky, Alexander (1907–1980) British art director. Under a variety of credits (Alec Vetchinsky, Alex Vetchinsky, A. Vetchinsky, or simply Vetchinsky), he worked on more than 80 British films from *The Lucky Number* (1932) to *Kidnapped* (1971), sometimes as production designer or set decorator, or credited, as in THE LADY VANISHES, with "settings." He directed one film, *Night Without Stars* (1951).

VistaVision A nonanamorphic wide-screen process introduced by PARAMOUNT in *White Christmas* (1954) in the wake of Hollywood's anxiety about the competition provided by freely available television programming in the academy aspect ratio—a crisis that also produced films in 3-D, Cinerama, and CinemaScope. The chief advantages of the new process, which was used in TO CATCH A THIEF (for which cinematographer Robert BURKS won an Academy Award), THE TROUBLE WITH HARRY, THE MAN WHO KNEW TOO MUCH (1956), VERTIGO, and NORTH BY NORTHWEST, were its ability to achieve greater depth of field than CinemaScope and its flexibility in projection because showing the image unmasked produced an academy-ratio image, while using projection plates masking the top and bottom of the image, where important screen action was proscribed, allowed it to be exhibited in a 2:1 widescreen ratio that closely resembled CinemaScope.

Von Alten, Theo (1885–1933) Russian-born actor active throughout the twenties as Ferdinand von Alten in German-language cinema, where he made his debut in Lubitsch's *Anna Boleyn* (1920). Following a dozen German films from *Othello* (1922) to *Der Student von Prag* (1926), he appeared as the mysterious man ("The Man") who is watching the heroine in CHAMPAGNE, where he is billed even more mysteriously as Theo von Alten. After making eight more German-language films, he died at 48.

Von Trotha, Trudy American script supervisor whose dozen films have included assignments with Stanley Kubrick (*Paths of Glory,* 1957), Hitchcock (TOPAZ), and Sam Peckinpah (*Bring Me the Head of Alfredo Garcia,* 1974; *Cross of Iron,* 1977). She served as assistant director on *La Mort en direct* (1980).

Von Zerneck, Peter (1908–1992) Hungarian-born character actor in occasional European roles in Hollywood films from NOTORIOUS, in which he plays Rossner.

Vosper, Frank (1899–1937) Stiffly aloof British stage actor and playwright who appeared in some 15 films of the thirties. He played the Prince in WALTZES FROM VIENNA and the assassin Ramon in THE MAN WHO KNEW TOO MUCH (1934). His own plays served as the basis for the films *Murder on the Second Floor* (1932) and *Shadows on the Stairs* (1941), and *Love from a Stranger* (1936); his stage adaptation of Agatha Christie's 1934 story "Philomel Cottage" was filmed in 1937 and again in 1947.

Vosper, Margery American author who wrote the story on which the ALFRED HITCHCOCK PRESENTS episode "BANG! YOU'RE DEAD" is based.

voyeurism Hitchcock is fascinated with voyeurism from the very beginning of his career. The first scene in his first film, THE PLEASURE GARDEN, shows a man with opera glasses scanning the line of chorus girls and even adopts his point of view to tilt upward from Patsy Brand's legs, the first object of his attention, to her face, which frowns in return. The segment combines three elements of Hitchcock's scenes of voyeurism described by Laura MULVEY—the male watcher's frankly sexual interest in the woman who is the object of his GAZE (when women watch

men in Hitchcock, their gaze rarely becomes an important action or visual motif), the ease with which the camera adopts his point of view and so encourages viewers to share his scopophilic pleasure, and the persistent fetishizing of the female object, in this case by reducing her body to its parts—with a fourth noted by Tania MODLESKI: the use of satiric elements, in this case the returned gaze, to comment more severely on him than on the object of his desire. All these elements remain important throughout Hitchcock's films, but they undergo several vital changes in the course of his career. The most obvious is Hitchcock's identification with the thriller, which complicates the question of voyeurism by thematizing the gaze as spying (so that in watching through a telescope as the General pushes Caypor off a cliff in SECRET AGENT, Ashenden is indulging Elsa's most melodramatic fantasy, but feeling only revulsion, self-loathing, and impotence). Even before this development, however, Hitchcock had already begun to explore inversions of the gaze in EASY VIRTUE, which persistently conveys the sense of being looked at, and not all pleasurably, rather than looking. These tendencies naturally double each other in such paranoid moments as the train rides in THE 39 STEPS, when Richard Hannay becomes convinced the nattering commercial travelers sharing his compartment have seen his photograph in the newspaper and will recognize him, and in THE LADY VANISHES, when Iris Henderson sees the face of the vanished Miss Froy that she is projecting onto one seat after another dissolving into the impassive faces of the fellow travelers riding with her who have denied ever seeing Miss Froy.

The voyeuristic moments in *The Pleasure Garden* and *Easy Virtue* undermine whatever voyeurism they solicit by straightforward appeals to identification with the object of the gaze. In NOTORIOUS, however, two further complications emerge. The film adopts a new attitude toward men who would rather watch women than be with them: Instead of ridiculing them as conventional butts of satire, it probes their pathology. At the same time, *Notorious* establishes a more complex system of gazes whereby identification is shared, however unequally, by T.R. Devlin and Alicia Huberman. When they meet at the race track, Devlin, the spy whose nominal job is to keep an eye on Alicia, is as much an object of Alexander Sebast-ian's gaze (he has been watching the two of them through binoculars and presses her to marry him largely because of what he has seen) as Alicia. Just as Charlie Newton, after getting over the uncritical infatuation she had shown her Uncle Charlie as he squired her around town in SHADOW OF A DOUBT, comes to watch him in a new way that is both devoid of pleasure and increasingly aware of the fact that he is directing his more powerful, even annihilating, gaze on her as well, the hope of simple voyeuristic pleasure dwindles to the vanishing point after *Notorious:* The watchful or worshipful heroes and heroines of THE PARADINE CASE and STAGE FRIGHT know, or will soon learn, how expensive the pleasures of looking can be. Guy Haines, in STRANGERS ON A TRAIN, squirms under the gaze not only of the police detectives who suspect him of killing his wife but also of Bruno Anthony, whose look he finds intolerable largely because he cannot accept its voyeuristic motive.

Hitchcock's fifties films take a crucial final step in thematizing voyeurism as emblematic of spectatorship itself. Just as *Stage Fright* frames its nested games of spying and masquerading by the rise and fall of a stage curtain, REAR WINDOW's action is framed by the raising and lowering of the blinds that turn the courtyard outside L.B. Jefferies's window into the equivalent of a proscenium stage (because for most of the film's running time, as Stefan SHARFF points out, the camera is forbidden to cross the proscenium or display the fourth wall) or a series of movie or television screens framed by the individual windows that mirror Jeff's. When Jeff sees Lars Thorwald finally staring back at him, the anatomy of Jeff's voyeurism turns into an indictment of the viewers who, like Jeff, had sought the satisfactions of entertainment without commit-ment. After Manny Balestrero's ordeal in the first half of THE WRONG MAN, Hitchcock's most baleful and extended plunge into the world of being-looked-at, the director returns to the specifically sexual gazes of VERTIGO, PSYCHO, and MARNIE, explicitly critical not only of the death-seeking viewers who watch the spectacle but also of the death-dealing entrepreneurs who stage it, anatomizing himself as ruthlessly as his audience. Hitchcock does not become more critical of his voyeurs as his career unfolds, but he does become more thoughtfully critical: Scottie Ferguson's romantically obsessive gaze in *Vertigo,* as annihilating as any gaze from *The Pleasure Garden* to *The Wrong Man,* is more anguished than any of them, perhaps because the director is acknowledging the impossibil-ity of his audience or himself looking away.

Wagenheim, Charles (1896–1979) American character actor, in Hollywood from 1931, who played bits in a hundred films and 20 television programs. Though most of his roles gave him even less screen time than the minor, albeit pivotal, part as the assassin in FOREIGN CORRESPONDENT and Henline in the ALFRED HITCHCOCK PRESENTS episode "Specialty of the House" (1959), he appeared in such important films as *The Song of Bernadette* (1943), *The Spiral Staircase* (1946), *Monsieur Verdoux* (1947), *Joan of Arc* (1948), *A Streetcar Named Desire* (1951), *The Diary of Anne Frank* (1959), and *Hello, Dolly!* (1969). But he was best known as the rancher Halligan in the television series *Gunsmoke* (1966–75).

Wakefield, Gilbert (Edward) (1892–1963) British playwright and screenwriter who collaborated on the screenplays of LORD CAMBER'S LADIES and three other 1932 films and then saw two of his own plays made into films: *Counsel's Opinion* (1933) and its remake *The Divorce of Lady X* (1938) and *Room for Two* (1940).

Wakefield, Hugh (1888–1971) Comically stiff British character actor. Onstage from childhood, he made his film debut as Algernon Sprigg in *The Sport of Kings* (1931) and followed in three dozen roles as titled fops and fools. It is never clear whether Clive, his mild-mannered sidekick to Bob Lawrence

in THE MAN WHO KNEW TOO MUCH (1934), is Betty Lawrence's uncle or simply a friend of her parents. He directed himself in one of his last films, *Love's a Luxury* (1952).

Waldis, Otto (1901–1974) Austrian-born actor who made his film debut in *M* (1931). He made only one other German film that same year and then turned up in Hollywood after the war filling out the casts of some 40 such films as *Letter from an Unknown Woman* (1948), *Five Fingers* (1952), and *Judgment at Nuremberg* (1961). Among his 15 television roles are two for ALFRED HITCHCOCK PRESENTS: a police officer in "LAMB TO THE SLAUGHTER" and Mr. Koslow in "Little White Frock" (1958).

Walker, Robert (Hudson) (1918–1951) Boyish American actor who left the American Academy of Dramatic Arts to marry fellow student Phyllis Isley in 1939 and then departed with her for a honeymoon in Hollywood. When their initial search for film work produced only a few uncredited bits, they returned to New York, where he secured a part on a radio series. By the time they returned to the West Coast in 1942, Phyllis, her name now changed to Jennifer Jones, was under contract to David O. SELZNICK, and Walker to MGM. A year after her Oscar-winning performance in *the Song of Bernadette* (1943), Selznick costarred them in *Since You Went Away* (1944), but they were already separated; they divorced in 1945, and she married Selznick in 1949. In the meantime, Walker had been modestly successful as the fresh-faced lead of *See Here, Private Hargrove* (1944), *What Next, Corporal Hargrove?* (1945), and *The Clock* (1945); he also played the composers Jerome Kern in *Till the Clouds Roll By* (1946) and Johannes Brahms in *Song of Love* (1947). Following his brief second marriage to director John Ford's daughter Barbara, a recurrence of his old problems with alcoholism, and a year-long hospitalization for a nervous breakdown, he returned in the role of his career, the psychopathic Bruno Anthony in STRANGERS ON A TRAIN. Cast stunningly against type as the relentlessly ingratiating murderer, he was the most disturbingly charming of all Hitch-cock's villains, and the role seemed to promise a new maturity in his acting. But his next role, the all-American Communist John Jefferson in *My Son John* (1952), proved to be his last; sedated after the latest of his emotional outbursts, he died of an adverse reaction to the medication before filming had been completed.

Walker, Vernon L. (1894–1948)   American special-effects cinematographer, in Hollywood from 1920. Soon after his co-credit for photographing *King Kong* (1933), he was named head of RKO's special effects department and in that capacity supervised the special effects on more than 150 films, from the Astaire-Rogers musicals to the exotic adventures *She* (1935) and *Gunga Din* (1939) and from the visual showcases *The Hunchback of Notre Dame* (1939) and *Citizen Kane* (1941) to the Hitchcock films MR. AND MRS. SMITH, SUSPICION, and NOTORIOUS. He was nominated for Academy Awards for *Swiss Family Robinson* (1940), *The Navy Comes Through* (1942), *Bombardier* (1943), and *Days of Glory* (1944).

Walsh, Kay (1914–)   Stage-trained British actress who entered films in 1934, establishing herself in such leading roles as Freda Lewis in *In Which We Serve* (1942) and Nancy in *Oliver Twist* (1948), both under the direction of her then-husband David Lean, for whom she also collaborated on the adaptation of *Great Expectations* (1946). Her turn as Charlotte Inwood's thin-lipped, calculating servant Nellie

Goode in STAGE FRIGHT might have been a blueprint for her 30 later character roles in films from *The Horse's Mouth* (1958) to *Tunes of Glory* (1960), and as Mrs. Morgan, the wife whose husband suspects her of adultery in the ALFRED HITCHCOCK PRESENTS segment "I Spy" (1961).

Walters, James (M.) (1913–1982)   American set decorator whose 40 years of Hollywood credits date back to *The Blue Dahlia* and *To Each His Own* (both 1946). At Universal for 20 years, he served as a staff decorator on ALFRED HITCHCOCK PRESENTS and is credited on many episodes, including the Hitch-cock-directed "MR. BLANCHARD'S SECRET."

Waltzes from Vienna   (Alternative titles: *Strauss's Great Waltz* [U.S.], *The Great Waltz*) A Tom Arnold Production for Gaumont-British, GFD, 80 minutes, February 1934. **Producer:** Tom Arnold: **Director:** Alfred Hitchcock; **Screenplay:** Alma Reville and Guy Bolton, based on the play by Dr. A.M. Willner, Heinz Reichert, and Ernst Marischka; **Cinematographer:** Glen McWilliams; **Art director:** Oscar Werndorff; **Editor:** Charles Frend; **Sound:** Alfred Birch; **Music:** Johann Strauss, father and son, adapted by Hubert Bath; **Musical direction:** Louis Levy; **Cast:** Jessie Matthews ("Rasi" [Therese Ebeseder]), Edmund Gwenn (Johann Strauss the Elder), Fay Compton (Countess Helga von Stahl), Esmond Knight (Schani Strauss), Frank Vosper (the Prince), Robert Hale (Ebeseder), Charles Heslop (valet), Hindle Edgar (Leopold), Marcus Barron (Dreschler), Betty Huntley Wright (lady's maid), Sybil Grove (Madame Fouchet), Billy Shine, Jr. (Carl), Bertram Dench (engine driver), B.M. Lewis (Domeyer), Cyril Smith (secretary).

When Alexander Korda withdrew in 1933 from a new contract with Hitchcock, recently released by BRITISH INTERNATIONAL after LORD CAMBER'S LADIES, Hitchcock contracted with theatrical impresario Tom ARNOLD to direct musical star Jessie MATTHEWS in an adaptation of a stage musical in which she had not appeared. Initially intrigued by the prospect of making a musical, Hitchcock soon cooled toward the project, especially as it was budgeted on a shoestring and cast with performers who found him as antipathetic as he found them. Esmond KNIGHT, the one cast member recruited from the play, recalled that Hitchcock was aggressively critical of the cast during rehearsals, so that by the time filming began they were all cowed. Matthews told her biographer Michael Thornton that Hitchcock "was out of his depth" and the film "perfectly dreadful." Their lack of enthusiasm was wholeheartedly shared by the director. Long before shooting ended on Hitchcock's 16th film, he was announcing, "I hate this sort of stuff. Melodrama is the only thing I can do," and he continued for the rest of his life to disown the film, describing it to François TRUFFAUT as his "lowest ebb." Rarely included in retrospectives of Hitchcock's work, the film has never been released on videotape, LaserDisc, or DVD.

Yet the few commentators who have seen the film are much less severe in their criticism. Maurice YACOWAR finds it charming, and Charles BARR notes that Hitchcock's distaste for the film cannot have been fueled by his preference for melodrama, for both the story here—a highly fictionalized account of how Johann Strauss, Jr., came to achieve fame, independence from his daunting father, and romantic fulfillment by the composition and premiere of the Blue Danube waltz—is nothing if not melodramatic in both its story and its treatment. Once the greater number of the Alhambra show's musical numbers had been removed, the screenplay had room for numerous new incidents—the fire at the Ebeseder bakery that opens the film, Schani Strauss's inspiration for the waltz by the working rhythms of the bakery, its gradual composition during the course of the film—and an important new character, the Count, with whom Schani's threateningly romantic patron, the Countess, could eventually reconcile, freeing Schani to pair off with his true love, Rasi Ebeseder. Despite the thematic continuities with later Hitchcock films that Barr remarks, the film's most important innovations, as he points out, concern its use of sound (especially in a dazzling long take of nearly three minutes that climaxes with a pair of onscreen servants interrupting their own romantic dalliance to act as emissaries for the conversation that passes between the offscreen Count and the offscreen Countess). Hitchcock's use of music, if not nearly as original as he claimed in a contemporaneous interview "On Music in Films" that Sidney GOTTLIEB has reprinted, is consistently

thoughtful. The different stages of the waltz, like the corresponding sound effects in SECRET AGENT, offer insight into Schani's thoughts while providing a dramatic armature to the film, an experiment to which Hitchcock returned 20 years later with the song "Lisa" in REAR WINDOW. The promotion of both music and quasi-musical sounds from the fire alarm that opens the film to the routine of baking and packing bread at Ebeseder's, from an accompaniment to the visual to an equally important, and often more important, element in grounding the characters' psychologies and relationships—an experiment reflecting Pare Lorentz's assessment that in the Paramount musical *Love Me Tonight* (1932), Rouben Mamoulian had "illustrated a musical score"—looks forward to his use of Bernard HERRMANN's music to substitute for dialogue that would be far less complexly expressive in THE WRONG MAN, VERTIGO, and PSYCHO. *Waltzes from Vienna* does not so much show that Hitchcock had no affinity for musicals (though it did confirm his lack of affinity for costume pictures) as provide a glimpse of his success years later in constructing films as different as *Rear Window, Vertigo,* and THE BIRDS on musical principles.

Wanger, Walter (1894–1968) American producer, born Walter Feuchtwanger. A veteran production chief at PARAMOUNT, Columbia, and MGM, he is best remembered as an independent producer releasing through UNITED ARTISTS and his own company. Although many of his 60 films were routine vehicles or misfires, he produced an impressive array of important films: *The Cocoanuts* (1929), *Queen Christina* (1934), *The Trail of the Lonesome Pine* (1936), and, as an independent, *Stagecoach* (1939), *The Long Voyage Home* (1940), and FOREIGN CORRESPONDENT. He served as president of the Academy of Motion Picture Arts and Sciences from 1939 to October 1941 and took over from Bette Davis when she abruptly resigned, serving from December 1941 to 1945, and he was nominated for an Academy Award himself for *Stagecoach*.

Wanger Productions A short-lived independent production company formed by Hollywood producer Walter WANGER in 1937. Among the films it released in its first year were *History is Made at Night, Stand-In, You Only Live Once,* and *Vogues of 1938.* By 1941 its productions included *Stagecoach* (1939), *The Long Voyage Home* (1940), and FOREIGN CORRESPONDENT. But by the following year the corporation had folded and Wanger was back working for the studios he had left five years earlier.

Ward, Edward (1900–1971) American composer, in Hollywood from 1928, who bounced from studio to studio—WARNER BROS., MGM, UNITED ARTISTS, RKO—for more than 200 films, many uncredited. His credits include *Kind Lady* (1935), *Wife vs. Secretary* (1936), *Saratoga* (1937), and MR. AND MRS. SMITH, much of whose music grows out of two motifs, a sprightly pennywhistle tune and a yearning rising phrase, in a manner that portends Bernard HERRMANN's later Hitchcock scores.

Warmington, S.J. (1884–1941) Stage-trained British character actor in occasional film roles from 1919, many of them for Hitchcock. He played Sir John's secretary Bennett in MURDER!, an uncredited member of Abbott's gang in THE MAN WHO KNEW TOO MUCH (1934), the police officer (also uncredited) who tries to cajole Hannay out of the London Palladium just before he confronts Mr. Memory in THE 39 STEPS, and Hollingshead in SABOTAGE.

Warner Bros.–First National Pictures American production company incorporated in 1923 by Harry, Albert, Sam, and Jack L. Warner, nickelodeon owners who had been producing films since 1912. In 1925 the company absorbed Vitagraph and First National Pictures, an independent company founded in 1917, and the following year launched Vitaphone, a subsidiary devoted to pioneering a synchronized sound system with Western Electric. The system debuted in a series of short films and the feature *Don Juan* (1926), but it was *The Jazz Singer* (1927), the first part-sound film that used synchronized dialogue to tell a story, that put the surviving brothers (Sam had died earlier that year) on the map and effectively ended the silent era. Through 1956, Harry remained the company's president, Albert its treasurer, and Jack the iron-willed head of production. Location shoot-

ing, often intended to keep set-construction budgets down, gave the studio a long-standing reputation for a proletarian touch as against the cosmopolitanism of PARAMOUNT and the middle-class kitsch of MGM. Hitchcock first signed a distribution arrangement with Warners when he and Sidney BERNSTEIN formed TRANSATLANTIC PICTURES. When Transatlantic folded after only two films, Hitchcock signed a contract to direct and produce four films for $999,000. Halfway through this string of films, which turned out to be STAGE FRIGHT, STRANGERS ON A TRAIN, I CONFESS, and DIAL M FOR MURDER, Hitchcock offered to return to the studio to direct one more film for a percentage of the profits in lieu of salary, and he interrupted his work at Paramount to return to Warners to make THE WRONG MAN on this basis.

Warren, John F. (1909–2000) American cinematographer who worked his way up from slate boy at Metro Pictures in New York to lighting cinematographer on *The Country Girl* (1954) and *The Seven Little Foys* (1955). As a staff cinematographer on ALFRED HITCHCOCK PRESENTS and THE ALFRED HITCHCOCK HOUR, he shot dozens of episodes, including the Hitchcock-directed "DIP IN THE POOL" and "THE CRYSTAL TRENCH," and went on to shoot TORN CURTAIN as well.

Warren, Katherine (1905–1965) American character actress chosen to play Jack Burden's mother in *All the King's Men* (1949). Over the next 12 years, she took some 40 supporting roles in movies and television, appearing in three roles in ALFRED HITCHCOCK PRESENTS: as Mrs. Wallingford in "BACK FOR CHRISTMAS," Mrs. Edwards in "The Hidden Thing" (1956), and the older babysitter in "Silent Witness" (1957).

Warth, Theron (B.) (1911–1973) American editor who, by the time he cut NOTORIOUS, the last of his two dozen films from 1939, had already begun to work as a producer whose eight credits would include *Having Wonderful Crime* (1945) and *Blood on the Moon* (1948).

Wasserman, Lew (1913–) American film executive who rose from usher in a Cleveland theater to talent agent to become vice president of the Music Corporation of America's motion picture division in 1940 and eventually assume the MCA presidency. Shortly after Myron SELZNICK's death, he became Hitchcock's exclusive agent in 1945, one of the director's closest friends, and the principal business adviser who helped him achieve wealth and independence as a quasi-independent. In 1955 he suggested putting Hitchcock on television; the resulting programs, ALFRED HITCHCOCK PRESENTS and THE ALFRED HITCHCOCK HOUR, were a financial success that also provided weekly confirmation of Hitchcock's status as the most famous filmmaker in the world. In 1962 he gave up MCA's agency interest in Hitchcock when the director moved over to UNIVERSAL, MCA's own studio, where he continued, as chairman of the board and chief executive officer of MCA, to play an equally powerful role in directing Hitchcock's fortunes, even though his name never appeared on the credits of a single film.

Watling, Jack (1923–) Versatile British character actor, a veteran of some 70 films and television episodes from *Young Mr. Pitt* (1942) to *Dr. Who* (1963) and its television and video spinoffs through 1995. He played Winter, the convict freed to work at Sam Flusky's home in UNDER CAPRICORN.

Watson, Justice (1908–1962) American character actor with Broadway experience who made sporadic appearances on film and television throughout the fifties, for example in the ALFRED HITCHCOCK PRESENTS episode "THE CASE OF MR. PELHAM" as Albert Pelham's butler Peterson, and in "Santa Claus and the Tenth Avenue Kid" (1956) as Mr. Shaw.

Watson, Lucile (1879–1962) Canadian-born actress who left her convent school for the American Academy of Dramatic Arts. Onstage from 1900, she appeared in two 1919 silents and a bit in *The Royal Family of Broadway* (1930) but did not establish herself in Hollywood until 1934. Her combination of gentility, starch, and moral force often cast her as mothers, She played Mary Haines's mother in *The Women* (1939), Jeff Custer's mother in MR. AND MRS. SMITH, and Sara Muller's mother in *Watch on the Rhine* (1943),

in an Oscar-nominated performance. She retired from the screen in 1951 after some three dozen roles.

Watson, Waldon O. (1907–1986) American sound recordist, at Republic from 1934, who moved to UNIVERSAL in 1948. After becoming sound director at Universal in 1959, he supervised the sound for *Spartacus* (1960), PSYCHO, and many of the studio's showcase projects: *To Kill a Mockingbird* (1962), *The List of Adrian Messenger* (1963), *Gambit* (1966), *Thoroughly Modern Millie* (1967), and *Airport* (1970). In addition, he recorded the soundtracks for THE BIRDS, MARNIE, TORN CURTAIN, and TOPAZ. In all, he worked on nearly 100 films before retiring in 1973. He was nominated for Oscars five consecutive years, for *Flower Drum Song* (1961), *That Touch of Mink* (1962), *Captain Newman, M. D.* (1963), *Father Goose* (1964), *Shenandoah* (1965), and then in 1967 for *Gambit*. He won a technical achievement award in 1968 for his work in the redesign of musical scoring stages and shared a scientific and engineering award in 1975 for the development of Sensurround.

Watson, Wylie (1889–1966) British character actor, born John Wylie Robertson. After extensive music-hall experience, he made his film debut in *For the Love of Mike* (1932) and went on to play nearly 50 mustached, inoffensive midges through *The Sundowners* (1960). He appeared as Joss Merlin's religious-minded henchman Salvation Watkins in JAMAICA INN but is far better known as Mr. Memory in THE 39 STEPS.

Watt, Harry (1906–1987) Scottish film director. He first came to prominence as the director of such documentary classics as *Song of Ceylon* (1934), *Night Mail* (1936), and the wartime propaganda pieces *Dover Front Line* (1940) and TARGET FOR TONIGHT (1941); later, he traveled to exotic lands to make such lightly plotted fictional films as *Where No Vultures Fly* (1951) and *West of Zanzibar* (1954). He took a break from directing to supervise the special effects for one film, JAMAICA INN.

Wattis, Richard (1912–1975) Stage-trained British character actor who appeared in nearly 100 films, most often as a mild-mannered clerk, secretary, or attendant such as Seaton, Algernon Moncrieff's butler in *The Importance of Being Earnest* (1952), or the assistant manager in THE MAN WHO KNEW TOO MUCH (1956). He was a regular on the BBC comedy series *Dick and the Duchess* (1957–58) and *Sykes* (1972–74).

Watts, Haward   British stage actor whose only film credit is Dick Coaker in THE FARMER'S WIFE.

Waxman, Franz (1906–1967)   Prolific German composer of hundreds of movie scores, born Franz Wachsmann, who trained at the Dresden Music Academy and the Berlin Music Conservatory. After scoring some 15 films for UFA, he left Germany in 1934, arriving the following year in Hollywood, where he scored an immediate hit with his moody music for *The Bride of Frankenstein* (1935). The workhorse soon demonstrated his range with such films as *Magnificent Obsession* (1935), *Fury* (1936), and *Captains Courageous* (1937) and was nominated for an Academy Award for *The Young in Heart* (1938). By the time he scored REBECCA, his second Oscar nomination, he was one of the most sought-after composers in Hollywood. He was subsequently nominated for *Dr. Jekyll and Mr. Hyde* (1941), *Objective, Burma!* (1945), *Humoresque* (1946), *The Silver Chalice* (1954), *The Nun's Story* (1959), and *Taras Bulba* (1962), and he won back-to-back Oscars for *Sunset Boulevard* (1950) and *A Place in the Sun* (1951). A master at translating psychological conflicts into lush orchestrations, he returned to collaborate with Hitchcock on SUSPICION, THE PARADINE CASE, and REAR WINDOW, in which his entirely diegetic score melds radio performances from PARAMOUNT's backlist with the jazz riff heard over the film's main credits and the embryonic theme, "Lisa," heard in its fully orchestrated version only in the film's final sequence.

Wayne,   David (1914–1995)   Sandy-haired American character actor, born Wayne McMeekan. A former statistician, he made his Broadway debut in 1938, rising to stardom in such vehicles as *Finian's Rainbow* (1947), *Mister Roberts* (1952), and *The Teahouse of the August Moon* (1953). The year after his first Hollywood film, *Portrait of Jennie* (1948), he made a

memorable impression as the insouciant composer Kip Lurie in *Adam's Rib* (1949) and was cast throughout the fifties in a wide variety of comic and dramatic roles, from Horace, the New York cop in *O. Henry's Full House* (1952) to the psychotic child-killer Martin Harrow, the old Peter Lorre role in *M* (1951). His first television role was Sam Jacoby, the hapless wife-killer in the ALFRED HITCHCOCK PRESENTS segment "ONE MORE MILE TO GO," and he returned as hapless widower Andy Anderson in the ALFRED HITCHCOCK HOUR episode "The 31st of February" (1963). From the sixties on, most of his work was in television, most notably as a regular on series from *The Good Life* (1971–72) to *House Calls* (1979–82). He played Inspector Queen in *Ellery Queen* (1975–76) and Digger Barnes in *Dynasty* (1978), always with a ready smile or his trademark smirk.

Wayne, Naunton (1901–1970)   Welsh character comedian, born Henry Wayne Davies, who made his film debut in 1931. Teamed with Basil RADFORD as Caldicott and Charters, Englishmen abroad in THE LADY VANISHES, he was reunited with Radford in similarly oblivious roles in 10 later films, including *Crooks Tour* (1939), *Night Train to Munich* (1940), *Millions Like Us* (1943), *Dead of Night* (1945), and *Passport to Pimlico* (1949). After Radford's death, he costarred in the television series *John Brown's Body* (1969).

Weaver, Doodles (1911–1983)   American character actor, born Winstead Sheffield Weaver. A radio comedian who made his film debut in 1937, he was most popular as the antic narrator of musical numbers as if they were sporting events. From 1946 through 1951, as a member of Spike Jones's comedy troupe, he created the tongue-tied Professor Feitlebaum and recorded his classic horse-race voiceover routines to Rossini's *William Tell Overture* and Ponchielli's *Dance of the Hours*. In Hollywood, in the meantime, he played nearly 100 rustic rubes and hicks in movies and on television, often in "Day with Doodles" segments of his own design or in walk-on roles such as the piano players in *Our Gang Follies of 1938* (1937) and *Kitty Foyle* (1940), the fisherman in

THE BIRDS, or Gregg in THE ALFRED HITCHCOCK HOUR segment "Body in the Barn" (1963).

Webber, Peggy American character actress who made her film debut in 1946, appeared in some 10 Hollywood roles—including Lady Macduff in the Orson Welles *Macbeth* (1948) and Miss Dennerly, the clerk in THE WRONG MAN—and 20 television roles. She finally found a niche as the voice of Farmer Smurf in the television series *The Smurfs* (1981–89).

Webster, Ben (1864–1947) British character actor with long stage experience who appeared in more than two dozen films from 1916. His specialty was the stiff or courtly self-righteousness of such Dickens roles as the Marquis d'Evremonde in *The Only Way* (1926) and Little Nell's grandfather in *The Old Curiosity Shop* (1934), the British ambassador in *The Prisoner of Zenda* (1937), and Dr. Dowson, the stern headmaster of DOWNHILL. He also played the registrar in SUSPICION, one of his last films.

Webster, Charles (1906–1983) American character actor of the midfifties whose handful of film and television credits include a reporter in the ALFRED HITCHCOCK PRESENTS segment "THE PERFECT CRIME" and the gasman, Chuck Webster, in the "FOUR O'CLOCK" episode of SUSPICION.

Wehmeyer, Ernest B. American production manager, at Universal from *Come September* (1961) and *To Kill a Mockingbird* (1962) for some 20 films, including *The Andromeda Strain* (1971), *The Sting* (1973), and, as unit production manager, FAMILY PLOT.

Weis, Elisabeth American film scholar, professor and head of Film Studies at Brooklyn College and professor of theater at the City University of New York's Graduate Center. A founding editor of *Persistence of Vision,* she has edited *The National Society of Film Critics on the Movie Star* (1981) and coedited *The National Society of Film Critics on Movie Comedy* (with Stuart Byron, 1977) and *Film Sound: Theory and Practice* (with John BELTON, 1985). *The Silent Scream: Alfred Hitchcock's Sound Track* (Fairleigh Dickinson University Press, 1982) is a pioneering study of Hitchcock's use of sound that has two goals: to illustrate the importance of sound to a cinematic medium that is often analyzed in purely visual terms, and to trace the development of expressive sound in Hitchcock's career. Weis uses this second project to attack her first by demonstrating how Hitchcock systematically distorts the sounds of dialogue, music, and auditory effects to evoke subjective states within a predominantly realistic mode that prevents subjective sounds from calling attention to themselves. Contrasting the "classical style" of the essentially musicless soundtrack in THE MAN WHO KNEW TOO MUCH (1934) with the extreme expressionism of SECRET AGENT's eerily sustained organ tone, clanging bells, and distorted village dance, she proceeds to examine the connections between songs and psychological states, the use of auditory intrusions to disempower characters in Hitchcock's one-set films, the use of a subjective soundtrack in REAR WINDOW to align viewers subtly with L.B. Jefferies's fallible point of view, the auditory associations of bird attacks with film direction in THE BIRDS, and the importance of silence as a dramatic element in Hitchcock's sound films. The volume concludes with a brief filmography and an extensive bibliography.

Weldon, Jim (1923–) American television personality who hosted the series *Funny Boners* (1954–55) and appeared as a convict in the ALFRED HITCHCOCK PRESENTS episode "BREAKDOWN" but found his greatest success more than 20 years later as Jimmy Weldon voicing cartoon characters on the series *Fred Flintstone and Friends* (1977), *Scooby and Scrappy-Doo* (1979–83), and *Challenge of the GoBots* (1984).

Welles, Halsted American screenwriter of the fifties and sixties who, shortly after *3:10 to Yuma* (1957) and *The Hanging Tree* (1959), adapted Roald Dahl's story "MRS. BIXBY AND THE COLONEL'S COAT" for ALFRED HITCHCOCK PRESENTS.

Wells, Billy (1887–1967) Stage-trained British character actor, onscreen from 1918 to 1944, often in uncredited roles, as in THE RING.

Werndorff, O(scar Friedrich) (1886–1938) German-born art director whose first film credit is *Variety* (1925). In the thirties he came to England, where, billed variously as O. Werndorff, O.F. Werndorff, O.P. Werndorff, or Otto Werndorff, he designed the visuals for THE 39 STEPS, SECRET AGENT, SABOTAGE, and a dozen other films.

West, Martin (1934–) American actor, onscreen from 1960 but best known for his television work. In between his stints as Dr. Phil Brewer in *General Hospital* (1967–75) and Don Hughes in *As the World Turns* (1977–78), he played Sanger in FAMILY PLOT. His final role, on the telefilm *Manhunt: Search for the Night Stalker* (1989), was Los Angeles police chief Daryl Gates.

West, Vera (1900–1947) American costume designer, at UNIVERSAL from 1927, sometimes billed simply as Vera. Her credits include *Show Boat* (1936), *Destry Rides Again* (1939), SHADOW OF A DOUBT and more than 100 second features.

Westman, James A. American production manager whose first Hollywood credit was as assistant director on TOPAZ. He has served as unit production manager on a dozen films and (mostly) television programs from the seventies on, and as a producer on the Vietnam War series *Tour of Duty* (1987–90).

Westmore, Ern(est Henry) (1904–1968) American makeup artist, son of the Hollywood British wigmaker George Westmore (1879–1931) and twin brother of Perc WESTMORE. His 40 films on both sides of the Atlantic include JAMAICA INN, *Blood on the Moon* (1945), *Angel on My Shoulder* (1946), *The Private Affairs of Bel Ami* (1947), and *He Walked by Night* (1948).

Westmore, Perc(ival Harry) (1904–1970) American makeup artist, twin brother of Ern WESTMORE; at WARNER BROS. for hundreds of films from 1930, including *The Public Enemy* (1931), *A Midsummer Night's Dream* (1935), *The Letter* (1940), *Sergeant York* (1941), *The Maltese Falcon* (1941), *Yankee Doodle Dandy* (1942), *Casablanca* (1942), and ROPE.

Westmore, Wally (1906–1973) American makeup artist, younger brother of Ern and Perc WESTMORE, born Walter James Westmore. At PARAMOUNT for hundreds of films, he worked with Preston Sturges from *The Great McGinty* (1940) to *Hail the Conquering Hero* (1944), with Billy Wilder from *The Major and the Minor* (1942) to *Sabrina* (1954), and with Hitchcock on REAR WINDOW, THE TROUBLE WITH HARRY, TO CATCH A THIEF, THE MAN WHO KNEW TOO MUCH (1956), and VERTIGO.

"Wet Saturday" 40th episode of *Alfred Hitchcock Presents,* broadcast September 30, 1956. **Associate producer:** Joan Harrison; **Director:** Alfred Hitchcock; **Assistant director:** Jack Corrick; **Teleplay:** Marian Cockrell, based on the short story by John Collier; **Cinematographer:** John L. Russell; **Art director:** Martin Obzina; **Set designer:** James S. Redd; **Costumes:** Vincent Dee; **Editors:** Richard G. Wray and Edward W. Williams; **Music:** Stanley Wilson; **Cast:** Sir Cedric Hardwicke (Mr. Princey), John Williams (Captain Smollet), Kathryn Givney (Mrs. Princey), Tita Purdom (Millicent Princey), Jerry Barclay (George Princey), Irene Lang (maid).

The opening episode of the program's second season presents the archly dysfunctional family of stuffy Mr. Princey, who is so devoted to Millicent, the daughter who has just killed the village schoolmaster when he announced that he loved someone else, that he resolves to conceal her involvement and incidentally to protect the family name. When Captain Smollet, the unsuccessful suitor of the schoolmaster's fiancée, obligingly blunders onto the scene, Princey threatens to kill him unless he helps Princey concoct new evidence that points to Smollet. Reluctantly agreeing to go along with the scheme, Smollet helps Princey dispose of the body and then leaves on Princey's assurances of conspiratorial silence. But Princey immediately phones the police after calling his family together for one last council, ensuring that their stories will leave Smollet odd man out.

Wheeler, Lyle (R.) (1905–1990) Noted American art director, former industrial designer, and magazine illustrator. He began with SELZNICK INTERNATIONAL in *The Garden of Allah* (1936) and remained through *Gone With the Wind* (1939), during which period he won his first Academy Award and worked with Hitchcock on REBECCA, earning him one of his 22 Oscar nominations. In 1944 he was appointed supervising art director at 20TH CENTURY–FOX and became head of the art department in 1947. At Fox his name appeared on hundreds of films, and he won or shared further Academy Awards for *Anna and the King of Siam* (1946), *The Robe* (1953), *The King and I* (1956), and *The Diary of Anne Frank* (1959).

White, Ethel Lina (1884–1944) British author, formerly with the Ministry of Pensions, who published 15 mystery novels, focusing most often on sturdy English damsels in distress, between 1931 and her death. Three of them have been memorably filmed: *Some Must Watch* (1933) as *The Spiral Staircase* (1946); *The Wheel Spins* (1936) as THE LADY VANISHES; and *Her Heart in Her Throat* (1942) as *The Unseen* (1945).

Whitelaw, Billie (1932–) Strong-willed, incisive British actress. In radio from age 11, she made her West End debut in 1950 and her film debut three years later. Though better known for her work onstage, where she has been particularly associated with the plays of Samuel Beckett, and in television, where she has headlined series from *Time Out for Peggy* (1958) to *Born to Run* (1997), she has appeared in more than 50 films. Her performance in *Charlie Bubbles* (1968) as Lottie won a British Film Academy Award. In addition to playing Johnny Porter's hostile wife Hetty in FRENZY, she has played the Empress Josephine in the 1974 miniseries *Napoleon and Love,* Mrs. Blaylock in *The Omen* (1976), Madame Defarge in the telefilm *A Tale of Two Cities* (1980), and Mary Yellan's Aunt Patience in the 1985 television remake of JAMAICA INN.

White Shadow, The (Alternative title: *White Shadows*) Balcon-Saville-Freedman, Wardour & F., 1923. **Producer:** Michael Balcon; **Director:** Graham Cutts; **Screenplay:** Alfred Hitchcock, based on *Children of Chance,* a novel by Michael Morton; **Cinematographer:** Claude L. McDonnell; **Assistant director:** Alfred Hitchcock; **Art director:** Alfred Hitchcock; **Editor:** Alfred Hitchcock; **Cast:** Betty Compson (Nancy Brent/Georgina Brent), Clive Brook (Robin Field), Henry Victor (Louis Chadwick), Daisy Campbell (Elizabeth Brent), Olaf Hytten (Herbert Barnes), A.B. Imeson (Mr. Brent), Bert Darley, Maresco Marisini, Donald Searle, Muriel Gregory.

Balcon's second commercial feature (following WOMAN TO WOMAN) and the second completed film on which Hitchcock combined the roles of assistant director, art director, and screenwriter.

Whitlock, Albert (1915–1999) British special-effects artist whose first credit was *The Bad Lord Byron* (1949). He worked on a half-dozen films of the fifties, but his painstaking matte paintings for THE BIRDS marked a turning point in his work. Hitchcock engaged him as pictorial designer on MARNIE and TORN CURTAIN; he was nominated for an Oscar for his work on *Tobruk* (1967); and he began to take on between two and six assignments a year in the seventies. He headed the special-effects team on TOPAZ, FRENZY, and FAMILY PLOT and won successive Academy Awards for his work on *Earthquake* (1974) and *The Hindenburg* (1975). By 1980 he had slowed down considerably but still executed the matte paintings for *Psycho II* (1983). The last of his 84 films was *Millenium* (1989).

Whitty, (Dame) May (1865–1948) Invincible British character actress, born Mary Whitty. Onstage as a ballerina at 16 and in the London theater the following year, she enjoyed a long string of stage successes, with time out for the occasional silent film, before she was created a Dame Commander of the British Empire in 1918 for her war service. In 1936 she departed for Hollywood, where the first of her 30 featured roles, Mrs. Bramson in *Night Must Fall* (1937), won her an Oscar nomination. She extended her series of velvet-and-steel spinsters and dowagers with Laetitia Bonaparte in *Conquest* (1937), the missing schoolteacher Miss Froy in THE LADY VANISHES, Mrs. McLaidlaw in *Suspicion,* Madame Eugene Curie in *Madame Curie* (1943), and Miss Thwaites in *Gaslight* (1944).

Wieth, Mogens (1919–1962) Danish actor who made his film debut in 1940 but did not appear in an English-language role until 1956, when he played the ambassador threatened with assassination, a virtually speechless role, in *THE MAN WHO KNEW TOO MUCH.*

Wikstrom, Patrik Swedish project manager of cable television networks and longtime fan of *ALFRED HITCHCOCK PRESENTS* and *THE ALFRED HITCHCOCK HOUR.* He is coauthor with Martin J. GRAMS, Jr., of *The Alfred Hitchcock Presents Companion* (Morris, 2001), an authorized, illustrated survey of Hitchcock's television work including a history of the series, sidelights on its producers and leading contributors, and an extensive episode-by-episode guide featuring transcripts of Hitchcock's opening and closing remarks, summaries and cast credits, and information about performers' and writers' other non-Hitchcock work. These chapters, interspersed with essays by other contributors on the episodes Hitchcock directed, are bracketed by Patricia HITCHCOCK O'Connell's introduction and briefer summaries of *THE NEW ALFRED HITCHCOCK PRESENTS,* Hitchcock's publishing ventures, Hitchcock collectibles, and an appendix listing ratings, awards, and Hitchcock marathons.

Wild, Thomas American actor whose credits are limited to one low-budget film, *Space Master X-7* (1958), and two television roles as doctors in the *ALFRED HITCHCOCK PRESENTS* segments "Disappearing Trick" (1958) and "LAMB TO THE SLAUGHTER."

Wilder, Thornton (Niven) (1897–1975) American playwright and novelist. Although he first came to critical notice when his novel *The Bridge of San Luis Rey* (1927) won the 1928 Pulitzer Prize, it is for his plays *Our Town* (1938) and *The Skin of Our Teeth* (1942), both Pulitzer winners as well, that he is likely to be longest remembered. Struck by his ability to tease universalistic intimations from the small-town evocation of *Our Town,* Hitchcock asked producer Jack SKIRBALL to engage him to work on the screenplay for *SHADOW OF A DOUBT* and grew so attached to Wilder during their weeks of preliminary work that months after Wilder had departed for the War Office and the screenplay had been transformed by Sally BENSON, Alma REVILLE, Patricia COLLINGE, and Hitchcock himself, he attached an unprece-

dented credit to the film expressing his gratitude for Wilder's contributions. Most of Wilder's other film credits are based on his sources. *Our Town* has been filmed three times, once (1940) with the playwright's participation, twice (1977, 1989) for television. *The Skin of Our Teeth* has been presented as a television film twice, once (1955) with the playwright's collaboration, once (1983) without. *The Bridge of San Luis Rey* has been filmed twice (1929, 1944) for Hollywood and once (1958) for television. Wilder's play *The Merchant of Yonkers* (1938), revised as *The Matchmaker* (1954), has been the basis for the film *The Matchmaker* (1958), the stage musical *Hello, Dolly!,* and its 1969 film version; his *Shadow of a Doubt* has been remade theatrically as *Step Down to Terror* (1958) and for television (1994).

Wilding, Michael (1912–1979) Polished British leading man of the forties. A former commercial artist whose first film job was with the art department, he switched to acting on stage and screen and by 1940 was much in demand for his chiseled good looks and upper-class delivery in such films as *Kipps* (1941), *In Which We Serve* (1942), *English Without Tears* (1944), and *An Ideal Husband* (1947). Hitchcock cast him twice as romantic leads—Charles Adare, the slightly bumptious visitor in *UNDER CAPRICORN,* and the more subdued Inspector Wilfred Smith in *STAGE FRIGHT*—and again as David Saunders, the vacationing father whose daughter gets into the wrong car and disappears in the *ALFRED HITCHCOCK HOUR* segment "Last Seen Wearing Blue Jeans" (1963). But he was better known, at least in America, for his own real-life marriage to the actress Elizabeth Taylor, who became his second wife in 1952. Even after they divorced in 1957, his film work was largely overshadowed by his status as her ex-husband. His fourth wife, from 1964 to her death in 1976, was actress Margaret LEIGHTON.

Wiles, S(ydney) British sound recordist who worked on a dozen films during the 20 years from 1937 to 1957. His second film was *THE LADY VANISHES;* his subsequent credits included *Ask a Policeman* (1939), *Night Train to Munich* (1940), and *Charlie's Big-Hearted Aunt* (1940).

Williams, Adam (1929–) Stocky blond American character actor, in Hollywood from 1951 for some 30 films and another 30 television programs, often in proletarian roles of indeterminate ethnicity. He played Lt. Malotke in *Flying Leathernecks* (1951) and Larry Gordon, the hoodlum who planted the bomb that killed Sgt. Dave Bannion's wife in *The Big Heat* (1953). In between his two roles in ALFRED HITCHCOCK PRESENTS—Lt. King in "Listen, Listen!" (1958) and Dr. Collen, the prison psychiatrist in "What Frightened You, Fred?" (1962)—he appeared as Valerian, the gardener/assassin in NORTH BY NORTH-WEST. Since his last role before the cameras in 1977, he has worked as a driver and electrician on several films.

Williams, Arthur (pseudonym of **Peter Barry Way)** (1917–1969) American storyteller who wrote "Being a Murderer Myself," the 1948 story whose nameless narrator became the title character of the ALFRED HITCHCOCK PRESENTS segment "ARTHUR."

Williams, Edward W. American film editor, in Hollywood from 1945. After eight film credits, he was appointed a staff editor on ALFRED HITCHCOCK PRESENTS and its successor THE ALFRED HITCHCOCK HOUR and collaborated in cutting scores of episodes of both programs, including every episode Hitchcock directed: "REVENGE," "BREAKDOWN," "THE CASE OF MR. PELHAM," "BACK FOR CHRISTMAS," "WET SATUR-DAY," "MR. BLANCHARD'S SECRET," "ONE MORE MILE TO GO," "THE PERFECT CRIME," "LAMB TO THE SLAUGHTER," "DIP IN THE POOL," "POISON, BANQUO'S CHAIR," "ARTHUR, THE CRYSTAL TRENCH," "MRS. BIXBY AND THE COLONEL'S COAT," "THE HORSE-PLAYER," "BANG! YOU'RE DEAD," and "I SAW THE WHOLE THING," as well as the "FOUR O'CLOCK" seg-ment of SUSPICION and the FORD STARTIME episode "INCIDENT AT A CORNER."

Williams, (George) Emlyn (1905–1987) Welsh playwright, screenwriter, director, and charac-ter star. Scholarships took him away from his coal-mining community, and he made his stage debuts in London and New York in 1927. By 1933 he was cowriting and costarring in the Thornton WILDER–inspired film *Friday the Thirteenth*. The fol-lowing year he contributed additional dialogue to THE MAN WHO KNEW TOO MUCH, his suspense tour de force *Night Must Fall* (1935) was filmed in 1937, and shortly after the London opening of his autobio-graphical play *The Corn Is Green* (1938)—but before it won the New York Drama Critics Award for best foreign play of 1941—he played Joss Merlyn's side-kick Harry the Pedlar in JAMAICA INN. In addition to acting in some 40 films and contributing the screen-plays of 15 more, he directed himself in his own screenplay for *The Last Days of Dolwyn* (1948). In his later years, he reached a new worldwide audience in his one-man touring shows based on the works of Dickens, Dylan Thomas, and Saki.

Williams, Eric Bransby (b. 1900) British silent actor who made some 10 movies. In one of the last, EASY VIRTUE, he plays the artist named as core-spondent in Larita Filton's divorce case.

Williams, J. Terry American film editor who worked on some 20 films in the 20 years from *Send Me No Flowers* (1964). His subsequent projects included *The Russians Are Coming, the Russians Are Coming* (1966), *The Secret War of Harry Frigg* (1968), and FAMILY PLOT. Most of his more recent work has been for television.

Williams, John (1903–1983) Stage-trained British actor whose arched eyebrow raised under-statement to high art. He made his London stage debut at 13 and his Broadway debut at 21 playing juveniles and then leads, while gradually adding films during the thirties and forties. But he is best remem-bered for the character roles of his maturity. He had already appeared as a barrister in THE PARADINE CASE, his first American film, when his success as Inspector Hubbard in Frederick KNOTT's play DIAL M FOR MUR-DER (1952) led Hitchcock to choose him for the film (the only cast member he selected). His dry upper-class inflections as the imperturbable Hubbard, as the title character's chauffeur father in *Sabrina* (1954), and as the inoffensive insurance executive H. H. Hugheson in TO CATCH A THIEF revealed a sensibility that precisely matched Hitchcock's own public image, and he was a favorite of ALFRED HITCHCOCK

PRESENTS, where he was cast in eight roles: British courier Walker Hendricks in "The Long Shot" (1955), methodical wife-killer Herbert Carpenter in "BACK FOR CHRISTMAS" (1956), murdered mystery writer Arthur Arlington in "Whodunit" (1956), framed innocent Captain Smollet in "WET SATURDAY," suspicious publisher Alexander Vinton in "The Rose Garden" (1956), Scotland Yard Inspector Davidson in "I Killed the Count" (1957), henpecked husband Ernest Findlater in "The Three Dreams of Mr. Findlater" (1957), and wily Inspector Brent in "BANQUO'S CHAIR." His later roles, which stayed comfortably inside his iconic range, included Brogan-Moore in *Witness for the Prosecution* (1957), Inspector Briscoe in the television series *The Rogues* (1964–65), and Niles French in the television series *Family Affair* (1967).

Williams, John (Towner) (1932–) American composer who turned from jazz piano to film scores of many kinds before emerging as the successor to the Steiner-RÓZSA epic school of film music. Educated at the Juilliard School of Music, he began to compose in the early fifties for such television programs as *General Electric Theater* (1953–62), *Bachelor Father* (1957–62), *Gilligan's Island* (1964–67), and, as Johnny Williams, *Lost in Space* (1965–68). He began to score films, sometimes as John Williams, sometimes as Johnny, in 1959. In 1971 he received an Academy Award for his adaptation and orchestration of the music to *Fiddler on the Roof.* Four other Oscars followed for his original scores for *Jaws* (1975), *Star Wars* (1977), *E.T.—the Extraterrestrial* (1982), and *Schindler's List* (1993). He has been nominated for 31 other Oscars as well. In light of his apocalyptic reputation as Hollywood's least subtle manipulator of audiences' emotions, particularly in action spectaculars, Williams's score for FAMILY PLOT, composed between the blockbusters *Jaws* and *Star Wars,* is revelatory: dry and droll, with a particularly stately part for solo harpsichord.

Willis, Constance American script supervisor. Ten years after her acting credit in *The Mikado* (1939), she became the continuity supervisor on such films as *Goldfinger* (1964), *A Man for All Seasons*

(1966), *A Touch of Class* (1973), and *A Bridge Too Far* (1977). She is also credited as technical adviser—her only such credit—on THE MAN WHO KNEW TOO MUCH (1956).

Willis, Norman (1903–1988) American character actor, sometimes credited as Jack Norman, seen mainly in westerns from *The Trail of the Lonesome Pine* (1936) to *The Bounty Killer* (1965). His rare appearances without his chaps include four roles for ALFRED HITCHCOCK PRESENTS: the police sergeant in "REVENGE," the bartender in "THE CASE OF MR. PELHAM," the desk officer in "Santa Claus and the Tenth Avenue Kid" (1955), and the police officer in "Fog Closing In" (1956).

Willman, Noel (1918–1988) British actor and stage director, a specialist in impassive officials whose range nonetheless extended to Lord Byron in *Beau Brummell* (1954), Woburn in THE MAN WHO KNEW TOO MUCH (1956), and Razin in *Doctor Zhivago* (1965).

Willock, Dave (1909–1990) American character actor who played more than 100 sidekicks, menials, and walk-ons in films and television from 1939. He played the uncredited bellboy in SPELLBOUND and later graduated to the hero's father in *The Buster Keaton Story* (1957), Ray Hudson in *Whatever Happened to Baby Jane?* (1962), and many roles in television series, including one in the ALFRED HITCHCOCK PRESENTS episode "Total Loss" (1959) as insurance agent Frank Voss and another as the salesman in THE ALFRED HITCHCOCK HOUR segment "Wally the Beard" (1965).

Wills, Drusilla (1884–1951) Stage-trained British actress, onscreen from 1921. As one of the few members of the jury in MURDER! to enjoy a significant film career, she appeared in the 1932 remake of *The Lodger* and rounded off her two dozen film roles with Mrs. Crudden in *Nicholas Nickleby* (1947) and the Countess's servant in *The Queen of Spades* (1949).

Wilson, Elizabeth (1921–) American character actress. Though she has played some 50 film and television roles, from Christine Schoenwalder in *Picnic* (1955) to Deke Carter's wife Helen, of the Tides Café in THE BIRDS, to Dorothy Van Doren in *Quiz Show* (1994), and has been a series regular in television programs from *East Side/West Side* (1963–64) to *Doc* (1975–76), she will probably be best remembered as Benjamin Braddock's mother in *The Graduate* (1967).

Wilson, James   British cinematographer who shot more than 100 films between 1930 and 1966, including LORD CAMBER'S LADIES, *The Tell-Tale Heart* (1962), and 10 second features about Old Mother Riley (1939–51). He returned to direct and photograph one final film, *Death Riders,* in 1976.

Wilson, Josephine (1904–1990)   British character actress whose film debut as Madame Kummer, the replacement for Miss Froy in THE LADY VANISHES, led to eight other films, from *South Riding* (1938) to *The End of the Affair* (1955).

Wilson, Paul   British camera operator on FRENZY and eight other films, 1960–73; more recently a miniature and visual effects photographer for *Superman II* (1980), *Superman III* (1983), *Supergirl* (1984), and James Bond films from *Moonraker* (1979) to *The World Is Not Enough* (1999).

Wilson, Stanley (1917–1970)   American composer, former Dixieland trumpeter, who scored, orchestrated, or conducted the music for nearly 100 Hollywood films, mostly B-westerns, before going into television, first composing the main theme and additional music for *General Electric Theater* (1953–62), then working as staff composer and music supervisor for ALFRED HITCHCOCK PRESENTS and THE ALFRED HITCHCOCK HOUR. He is credited with composing or arranging the music for dozens of episodes of both programs, including the Hitchcock-directed "REVENGE," "BREAKDOWN," "THE CASE OF MR. PELHAM," "BACK FOR CHRISTMAS," "WET SATURDAY," "MR. BLANCHARD'S SECRET," "ONE MORE MILE TO GO," "THE PERFECT CRIME," "LAMB TO THE SLAUGHTER," and "DIP IN THE POOL," as well as the SUSPICION segment "FOUR O'CLOCK." As head of creative activi-

ties at UNIVERSAL's music department, he continued to work until his death on television episodes and series.

Winston, Irene (1920–1964)   American character actress and writer. Her radio play *Bury Me Dead* was adapted to the movies in 1947, and she had a half-dozen small roles in fifties films, several of them uncredited, before returning to writing on the television series *Maverick* (1957–62). When she died of complications from pneumonia, she was little older than Anna Thorwald, the ill-fated character she played in REAR WINDOW.

Winter, Philip   British actor whose film career was limited to playing Robert, a member of the Manderley staff in REBECCA, and two other uncredited roles, all in 1940.

wit   Every commentator on Hitchcock has referred in passing to his wit, but it has never been the subject of sustained study even though an enabling paradox of his films is their knack of making situations that would be unpleasantly trying or threatening in real life pleasurably suspenseful by the witty way in which they are presented. In STRANGERS ON A TRAIN, for example, Bruno Anthony's murderous obsession with Guy Haines and Guy's resulting paranoia are no laughing matter, but Hitchcock makes Bruno's obsession perversely amusing even at particularly tense moments by framing his carousel horse in ritual pursuit of the doomed Miriam Haines's, by showing his shadow engulfing hers in the tunnel of love only to have her scream prove a false alarm, by zooming in on Bruno looking steadily at Guy during a tennis match whose every other spectator is turning back and forth to watch the play, and by staging the climactic showdown between the two men on a carousel running dangerously out of control. Hitchcock's wit is often comic, but it is not the same as COMEDY: The tableau of Miriam's murder reflected in the eyeglasses whose distorting lens makes Bruno's hands loom enormous as "The Band Plays On" is heard in the background is witty but not funny. Although Hitchcock was legendary for indulging his wit at the expense of other colleagues by means of practical jokes or the narrative line of his films by means of episodic interruptions, his wit has a communal as well as a disruptive function. Just as he could express his affection for Carole LOMBARD, one of the few actresses who stood up to him, by trading jokes with her, the wittiest moments in his films tend to develop the narrative rather than interrupting it, like the auditory cut from Richard Hannay's landlady discovering the body in Hannay's flat to the scream of the whistle on the train carrying Hannay safely out of London in THE 39 STEPS. One key to Hitchcock's distinctive wit is his statement to François TRUFFAUT à propos THE TROUBLE WITH HARRY: "Nothing amuses me so much as understatement." Just as PRACTICAL JOKES have two audiences, the butts who are ridiculed and the onlookers who are invited to appreciate the joker's malicious humor, Hitchcock's wit postulates two audiences, the uninitiate who take understated words and images at face value, and the connoisseurs who can appreciate their true significance. Because both these audiences typically coexist within each viewer, Hitchcock's wit, in addition to its self-aggrandizing aspect, is both sadistic and solicitous, his every IRONY designed not only to display an olympian aloofness toward his often macabre subjects but to invite viewers into an ambivalent relationship—not only feeling both threatened and amused but also reacting both emotionally and analytically—toward his cinematic representations themselves.

Withers, Googie (1917–) Ebullient, down-to-earth British leading actress, born Georgette Lizette Withers in Karachi. Onstage from 12, she took over the second lead in her second film, *Girl in the Crowd* (1935), when director Michael Powell fired the actress who had originally been cast. The 50 film roles that followed included Iris Henderson's friend Blanche in THE LADY VANISHES, trial-marriage experimenter Helen Hale in *On Approval* (1944), the frightened Joan Cortland in *Dead of Night* (1945), and David Helfgott's encouraging patron Katharine Prichard in *Shine* (1996).

Wolfe, Ian (1896–1992) Durable American character actor who despite a late start appeared in more than 200 films and television episodes from *The Barretts of Wimpole Street* (1934) to *Dick Tracy* (1990). He played noblemen, clergymen, judges, and servants with equal aplomb and was equally at home in *Julius Caesar* (1953) and *Witness for the Prosecution* (1957), the upright Stiles in FOREIGN CORRESPONDENT and the menacing butler Robert in SABOTEUR.

Woman to Woman Balcon-Saville-Freedman, Wardour & F., 1923. **Producer:** Michael Balcon; **Director:** Graham Cutts; **Screenplay:** Graham Cutts and Alfred Hitchcock, based on the play by Michael Morton; **Cinematographer:** Claude L. McDonnell; **Assistant director:** Alfred Hitchcock; **Art director:** Alfred Hitchcock; **Editor:** Alma Reville; **Cast:** Betty Compson (Louise Boucher/Deloryse), Clive Brook (David Compton/David Anson-Pond), Josephine Earle (Mrs. Anson-Pond), Marie Ault, M. Peter, A Harding Steerman, Victor McLaglen (Nubian slave).

Michael BALCON's first feature production and the first film on which Hitchcock served as assistant director, art director, and coscenarist was such a success that Balcon rushed into a second film, THE WHITE SHADOW, with the same costars, writers, and crew, only to meet rejection later the same year. Nontheless, the film encouraged Balcon, Hitchcock, and Graham CUTTS in burgeoning careers.

Wonacott, Edna May (1932–) American child actress who debuted as Charlie Newton's unflappable kid sister Ann in SHADOW OF A DOUBT and made five more films before retiring in 1951.

Wood, Robin (1931–) Pioneering English-born film scholar, retired professor of Film Studies at York University's Atkinson College. His books include *Antonioni* (with Ian Cameron, 1968; revised edition, 1971), *Howard Hawks* (1968), *Arthur Penn* (1970), *Claude Chabrol* (1970), *The Apu Trilogy* (1971), *Personal Views: Explorations in Film* (1976), *Hollywood from Vietnam to Reagan* (1986), and *Sexual Politics and Narrative Film: Hollywood and Beyond* (1998). Although he has written on subjects as diverse as F.R. Leavis and the American horror film, he is best known for his work on Hitchcock. His first book, *Hitchcock's Films* (Tantivy/Barnes, 1965), began with the challenging question, "Why should we take Hitchcock seriously?" It proceeded to a defense of Hitchcock's work, particularly his films from STRANGERS ON A TRAIN through MARNIE, as aesthetically rich and morally challenging. Grounding his auteurism in Leavis's literary criticism and repeatedly invoking literary analogies from Shakespeare to CONRAD and Lawrence to bolster his arguments against dismissing Hitchcock as a mere entertainer, technician, or master of a single genre, Wood contended that suspense was not an end of Hitchcock's films but a means toward involving viewers in the characters' moral development as they struggle to relinquish their obsessions and trust in love. For the second edition of the book (1977), Wood contributed a new chapter on TORN CURTAIN, which he found less successful than any of the films he had discussed in detail, and an afterword apologizing for his earlier excesses (especially his neglect of Hitchcock's British films) and emphasizing two limitations in Hitchcock's work: the frequent dependence of "Hitchcock the artist" on "Hitchcock the showman-entertainer," and "the relative weakness . . . of the normative impulse" in films routinely concerned with extreme experiences. The third edition, retitled *Hitchcock's Film Revisited* (Columbia University Press, 1989), reprinted the second edition in full but added a long new introduction and seven substantial essays on such diverse topics as paradigmatic plots, homophobia, and Hitchcock's collaboration with Ingrid BERGMAN. The signature question of this new edition—"Can Hitchcock be saved for feminism?"—showed how far Wood had come from his earlier aestheticism to a Marxist analysis of power, which continued, however, to insist on the relevance of Leavis. *Hitchcock's Films Revisited,* the single most important critical analysis of the director's work, shows how Wood's development as a critic has been virtually coeval with the evolution of Hitchcock studies itself.

Woolf, C(harles) M(oss) (1879–1942)

British film financier and distributor who, as director of the distribution company Wardour & F., bankrolled Michael BALCON's early films WOMAN TO WOMAN and THE WHITE SHADOW. His relationship with Hitchcock, who worked as assistant director, art director, and coscenarist on these films, was persistently adversarial once Hitchcock began to direct on his own. He held up the distribution of THE PLEASURE GARDEN for nearly a year because he thought its Germanic visuals too arty and adventurous for all but a small coterie of British audiences, and he refused to distribute THE LODGER until Ivor MONTAGU, working with Hitchcock, drastically cut its intertitles. When Hitchcock returned from BRITISH INTERNATIONAL seven years later to work once more with Balcon, Woolf, in charge of distribution for GAUMONT-BRITISH since 1929, again refused to release one of his films, this time THE MAN WHO KNEW TOO MUCH (1934), relenting only far enough to distribute it as a second feature, before his disapproval was buried under critical plaudits. He left Gaumont-British in 1935, but soon thereafter his company, General Film Distributors, acquired a major stake in UNIVERSAL and became the sole Universal distributor in Britain.

Woolrich, Cornell (1903–1968)

American mystery writer, born Cornell George Hopley-Woolrich. A child of divorce, he traveled widely with his father, dropped out of Columbia University, published six Jazz Age novels, and spent a brief period around 1928 in Hollywood writing movie titles under the pseudonym William Irish. He found his true voice as the paranoid chronicler of urban nightmares beginning with *The Bride Wore Black* (1940), *The Black Curtain* (1941), and, as Irish, *Phantom Lady* (1942). His many novels and stories regularly served as the basis for such noir-shaded movies as *Street of Chance* (1942), *The Leopard Man* (1943), *Phantom Lady* (1944), *Black Angel* (1946), *The Night Has a Thousand Eyes* (1948), *The Window* (1949). His short story originally titled "It Had to Be Murder" (1942) became the basis for REAR WINDOW, and his 1938 story "Four O'Clock," adapted for the television series SUSPICION, was followed by three more adaptations for ALFRED HITCHCOCK PRESENTS and a fourth for THE ALFRED HITCHCOCK HOUR. A neurotic recluse, Woolrich spent most of his adult life living in a series of anonymous hotel rooms with his mother; after she died in 1957, his fear of going out led him to leave a leg infection untended until gangrene set in and amputation was necessary. A $1 million legacy on his death established a scholarship fund at Columbia.

Worsley, Wallace (Jr.) (d. 1991) American production manager, son of Hollywood director Wallace Worsley, who began as uncredited script clerk on *The Wizard of Oz* (1939), served as assistant director on *The Barkleys of Broadway* (1949) and the ALFRED HITCHCOCK PRESENTS episode "BANG! YOU'RE DEAD," and became unit production manager on some 20 film and television productions beginning in 1964, including TOPAZ, *Deliverance* (1972), *Coal Miner's Daughter* (1980), and *E.T.—the Extraterrestrial* (1982).

Wray, Fay (1907–) Canadian actress, born Vina Fay Wray, who shot to stardom in the lead of *The Wedding March* (1928) after five years of work as an extra and then became the best-known scream queen of the thirties in such films as *Doctor X* (1932), *The Mystery of the Wax Museum* (1933), *The Vampire Bat* (1933), and most indelibly, *King Kong* (1933), which made her one of the most recognized women in the world without extending the range or prestige of her film roles. Retiring in 1942 to marry screenwriter Robert Riskin, she returned to the screen in 1953 in character roles, soon appearing in two episodes of ALFRED HITCHCOCK PRESENTS, as the unimpressed wife of William Botibol's boss Renshaw in "DIP IN THE POOL" and as Ben Nelson's deceived and briefly outraged wife in "The Morning After" (1959).

Wray, Richard G. (1912–1981) Canadian-born film editor of the thirties and forties, brother of Fay Wray. A former editor with Britain's Office of War Information, he spent 25 years at UNIVERSAL, eventually leaving the big screen behind to take a job with the television series *The Lone Ranger* (1949–57). As a supervising editor for ALFRED HITCHCOCK PRESENTS, he coedited dozens of episodes of the program, including the Hitchcock-directed "REVENGE," "BREAKDOWN," "THE CASE OF MR. PELHAM," "BACK FOR CHRISTMAS," "WET SATURDAY," "MR. BLANCHARD'S SECRET," "ONE MORE MILE TO GO," "THE PERFECT CRIME," "LAMB TO THE SLAUGHTER," "DIP IN THE POOL," "POISON," "BANQUO'S CHAIR," "ARTHUR," and "THE CRYSTAL TRENCH," as well as the SUSPICION segment "FOUR O'CLOCK" and the FORD STARTIME episode "INCIDENT AT A CORNER." As editorial supervisor at Universal, he also served as supervising editor on the series *M Squad* (1957–60) and 15 telefilms of the sixties and seventies.

Wright, Betty Huntley See HUNTLEY WRIGHT, BETTY.

Wright, Teresa (1918–) Wholesome, vivacious American actress, born Muriel Teresa Wright. Apprenticed to the Provincetown Players, she made her Broadway debut understudying Martha Scott in the Broadway production of *Our Town* (1938) and was soon spotted by a scout for Samuel Goldwyn. She was nominated for an Academy Award for her first film role as Alexandra Giddens in *The Little Foxes* (1941) and the following year was nominated twice more for her second and third films, as Best Actress for her role as Eleanor Gehrig in *Pride of the Yankees* and as Best Supporting Actress for her Carol Beldon in *Mrs. Miniver,* an Oscar she won. Her performance in SHADOW OF A DOUBT as fresh-faced Charlie Newton, the small-town girl forced to come to terms with the unfathomable evil of her beloved uncle, marked the first time she gave a film performance that was not nominated for an Oscar. Though her later vehicles were often routine, she shined in *The Best Years of Our Lives* (1946), *The Men* (1950), and *Track of the Cat* (1954). She starred in two episodes of THE ALFRED HITCHCOCK HOUR, as Marion Brown, the wife who takes a murderous revenge on her bigamous husband in "Three Wives Too Many" (1964), and as Stella Emory, the farm wife terrorized by a drifter her husband has hired in "Lonely Place" (1964).

Wright, Thomas J. American artist and illustrator who began his Hollywood career as property master on *The Pawnbroker* (1965) and sketch artist on *The Russians Are Coming, the Russians Are Coming* (1966). Although most of his subsequent credits have been in the property department, he has worked as continuity illustrator on *The Hindenburg* (1975), as production illustrator on FAMILY PLOT, and as storyboard illustrator on *Terms of Endearment* (1983).

Wrong Man, The

Wrong Man, The (Alternative titles: *Der falsche Mann, La faux coupable, Il ladro*) Warner Bros.–First National, 105 minutes, December 1956. **Producer:** Alfred Hitchcock; **Associate producer:** Herbert Coleman; **Director:** Alfred Hitchcock; **Screenplay:** Maxwell Anderson and Angus MacPhail, based on "The True Story of Christopher Emmanuel Balestrero," a story by Anderson (and on "A Case of Identity," a *Life* magazine article by Herbert Brean); **Cinematographer:** Robert Burks; **Additional photography:** Frank J. Calabria; **Assistant director:** David J. McCauley; **Art director:** Paul Sylbert; **Set decorator:** William J. Kuehl; **Makeup:** Gordon Bau; **Sound:** Earl Crain, Sr.; **Editor:** George Tomasini; **Technical advisers:** Frank D. O'Connor, District Attorney, New York, and Sgt. George Groves, NYPD; **Music:** Bernard Herrmann; **Cast:** Henry Fonda (Christopher Emmanuel Balestrero), Vera Miles (Rose Balestrero), Anthony Quayle (Frank O'Connor), Harold J. Stone (Lt. Bowers), John Heldabrand (Tomasini), Doreen Lang (Ann James), Norma Connolly (Betty Todd), Lola D'Annunzio (Olga Conforti), Robert Essen (Gregory Balestrero), Dayton Lummis (Judge Groat), Charles Cooper (Detective Matthews), Esther Minciotti (Mrs. Balestrero), Laurinda Barrett (Constance Willis), Nehemiah Persoff (Gene Conforti), Kippy Campbell (Robert Balestrero), Richard Robbins (Daniell), Peggy Webber (Miss Dennerly), Rhodelle Heller, Oliver Stacey, John Stephen (Stork Club customers), Helen Shields (receptionist), Donald May (arresting patrolman), John Vivyan (Detective Holman), John C. Becher (liquor store proprietor), Mary Boylan (curious customer), Dallas Midgette (customer at Bickford's), Don Turner (detective), Ray Bennett, Clarence Straight (police officers), Gordon Clark, John R. McKee (police attendants), Paul Bryar (interrogation officer), William Hudson (police lieutenant from 110th Precinct), Daniel Ocko (Felony Court judge), Walter Kohler (Manny's Felony Court attorney), Richard Durham, Chris Gampel, Mike Keene, Frank Schofield, Maurice Wells (Department of Correction officers), Charles Aidman (jail medical attendant), Silvio Minciotti (Mr. Balestrero), Barry Atwater (Mr. Bishop), Michael Ann Barrett (Miss Daily), Olga Fabian (Mrs. Mank), Will Hare (McKaba), Anna Karen (Miss Duffield), William LeMassena (Sang), Alexander Lockwood (Emmerton), Marc May (Tomasini's assistant), Dan Stanton (Mr. Ferraro), Rossana San Marco (Mrs. Ferraro), Otto Simánek (Mr. Mank), Emerson Treacy (Mr. Wendon), Frances Reid (Mrs. O'Connor), Werner Klemperer (Dr. Bannay), Maurice Manson (district attorney), Henry Beckman (prisoner), Spencer Davis (prisoner's lawyer), Harold Berman (court stenographer), Leonard Capone (court clerk), Ed Bryce, Charles J. Guiotta, Thomas J. Murphy (court officers), William Crane, Josef Draper, Barney Martin (jurors), Earl George (delicatessen proprietor), Natalie Priest (his wife), Sammy Armaro, Allan Ray, John Truax (suspects), M'el Dowd (nurse), Maria Reed, Penny Santon (Spanish women), Don McGovern (waving man), Cherry Hardy, Elizabeth Scott (waving women), Barbara Karen, Tuesday Weld (giggly girls), Paul Carr, Bonnie Franklin, Pat Morrow, Harry Stanton.

Almost as soon as he finished work on THE MAN WHO KNEW TOO MUCH (1956), Hitchcock returned to WARNER BROS. in August 1955 to honor the offer he had made to Jack L. Warner two years earlier to make a fifth film at Warners, waiving his salary in return for a percentage of the profits. He was particularly intrigued by an unusual Warners property: Herbert Brean's screen treatment of his 1953 *Life* article "A Case of Identity," the story of a Stork Club musician mistaken for a thief and arrested, arraigned, and tried for robbery, as his wife slowly disintegrated under the strain, before the real thief was caught in the act. When John Michael HAYES, whom Hitchcock had hoped would follow him on the same terms, told the director his financial circumstances made it impossible for him to waive his own salary, Hitchcock asked Angus MACPHAIL, who had worked on *The Man Who Knew Too Much,* to write the screenplay. When Maxwell ANDERSON joined MacPhail, Hitchcock told him that he envisioned the story as a domestic counterpart to *The Man Who Knew Too Much* that would track the intolerable strain on another American couple—the husband's mounting apprehension, the wife's breakdown—in everyday settings that would make the situation less glamorous but more powerful. The first draft of the screenplay was completed in October, and by January 1956 Hitchcock was examining the New York locations on which he had decided to shoot the entire film in a black-and-white semidocumentary style, poles apart from the lush Technicolor visuals of his PARAMOUNT films. Before shooting began, he flew his leads—Henry FONDA, the veteran star he had long

Hitchcock and his new discovery Vera Miles arrive in New York to visit locations for *The Wrong Man*. *(National Film Society Archive)*

admired, and his new discovery Vera MILES, whom he told the press was about to become the new Grace KELLY—to Florida so that they could meet Manny and Rose Balestrero, who, as the film faithfully reports, had retreated there when their ordeal in New York was over. Despite Hitchcock's reservations about Anderson's contributions to the screenplay, which led to another round of rewrites by MacPhail, principal photography began in March and was completed by May, just as *The Man Who Knew Too Much* premiered. Shorn of a cameo the director had filmed when he decided it was out of keeping with the tone of the film, it was released in December with a prologue showing Hitchcock directly addressing the audience and describing the unique nature of the film.

Hitchcock told François TRUFFAUT that he was drawn to the project because of his lifelong fear of the POLICE, and much of the first half of the film—from the initial detention of Manny, whose suggestive ges-

ture in pulling an insurance policy from his pocket as if it were a gun has led a clerk in the office to misidentify him as the thief who recently held her up, to his release on bail the following day—is heavy with a paranoia and despair focused specifically on the police. The arresting officers do not treat Manny unkindly or brutally; yet their imperturbable dedication to a routine designed to rob him of freedom and their mild imperviousness to his need to notify his wife that he has been detained dehumanize him in a hundred chilling ways, from the moment they first approach him, calling his name as "Chris," to their insistence on his walking through the scenes of previous robberies without looking at or talking to the people he is supposed to have robbed, to their warehousing of him as one more jailed prisoner in a scene elaborating the opening sequence of *Blackmail*. Although Manny, in Fonda's remarkable performance, maintains his temper and his dignity throughout this ordeal, the camera intimates his shame when it frames his manacled wrist without showing the fellow prisoner to whom he is handcuffed. In the second half of the film, however, the fear of the police recedes along with the police themselves, who become minor players in the Balestreros's nightmare, before a more general paranoia focusing on Rose Balestrero's mental breakdown when the deaths of Manny's two alibi witnesses persuade her that "it doesn't do any good to care." When Truffaut suggested that "the dramatization of authentic events actually served to detract from their reality," which a more straightforwardly documentary style might have preserved—in the whole sequence of Truffaut's interviews, this is the only moment at which the two differ sharply—Hitchcock defended his dramatization, blaming the deficiencies of the story's construction on its faithfulness to actual events. Yet the two-part structure of the film as it stands illustrates perhaps more clearly than any other the transfer of guilt Eric ROHMER and Claude CHABROL had pronounced as central to Hitchcock's work: a transfer not only of legal guilt from the real criminal to the innocent suspect Manny but also of a moral guilt amounting to self-annihilation from Manny to Rose, who is last shown greeting Manny's news of his exculpation with the toneless response, "That's fine for you." The closing title, which assures viewers that the Balestreros are now living happily in Florida, produces the most radically equivocal ending in Hitchcock because its long-shot vista of a palm-lined street does nothing to dispel the horror of Rose's disintegration and even trivializes it by implying that it was cured offscreen. In its descent from American normalcy to Manny's nightmare and Rose's despair, the film offers the first installment of the anatomy of identity Hitchcock would develop still more profoundly in VERTIGO, NORTH BY NORTHWEST, and PSYCHO.

Wyllie, Meg (1919–) American character actress who, soon after her film debut in 1961, played Mrs. Turpin, who boards Forio in MARNIE. Most of her many later appearances have been on television, from *Mad About You,* in which she appeared as Aunt Lolly in six episodes (1994–95), to *General Hospital,* on which she played Nurse Doris Roach in 1975 and returned, filling in for Anna Lee, as Lila Quartermaine in 1994.

Wyman, Jane (1914–) American actress, born Sarah Jane Mayfield, who adopted the name Faulks when she was adopted by neighbors of her single mother. She sang on the radio as Jane Durrell and then toiled in Hollywood for 10 years as a brassy blonde before her role as Ray MILLAND's loyal girlfriend in *The Lost Weekend* (1945) showed her dramatic talent. She was nominated for an Oscar for *The Yearling* (1946) and won the Best Actress award for her performance as the deaf-mute Belinda McDonald in *Johnny Belinda* (1948) shortly after she divorced her second husband, actor Ronald Reagan. She received two later nominations for *The Blue Veil* (1951) and *Magnificent Obsession* (1954). The same year that she played Laura Wingfield in the film version of *The Glass Menagerie* (1950), Hitchcock cast her in STAGE FRIGHT as acting student Eve Gill, who takes in her friend Jonathan Cooper when he is suspected of murder by the police. But Hitchcock was annoyed when she complained about her distress at

being upstaged by the glamorous Marlene DIETRICH. A veteran of television from the fifties, she enjoyed a stint as *Falcon Crest* matriarch Angela Channing that lasted longer (1981–90) than her ex-husband's corresponding tenure in the White House.

Wyndham, Denis (b. 1887) Stage-trained Irish actor who after a single silent film returned to the studios with the advent of sound, playing Murphy in *The Informer* (1929) and the Mobiliser in JUNO AND THE PAYCOCK, and then proceeded to three dozen more proletarian roles through *Ramsbottom Rides Again* (1956).

Wyndham Lewis, D. B. (1894–1969) British journalist, humorist, and screenwriter brought in after two 1933 film credits to write additional dialogue for THE MAN WHO KNEW TOO MUCH (1934). Although Charles Bennett, the film's principal screenwriter, told Patrick MCGILLIGAN that none of his dialogue was used, the 1956 remake credits him as a collaborator both on the original story and on Arthur BENJAMIN's *Storm Cloud Cantata*. His six later film credits are all from the thirties.

Wynn, Keenan (1916–1986) Stage-trained American character actor, born Francis Xavier Aloysius Wynn to the vaudevillian (and later movie actor) Ed Wynn. After serving as Joan Crawford's stunt double in *Chained* (1934), he began his Hollywood career in earnest in 1942. He appeared in more than 200 film and television supporting roles, often as irritable comic butts. He was a spluttering comic villain in *The Absent-Minded Professor* (1961) and *Son of Flubber* (1963) and a creditable dramatic villain in *Stagecoach* (1966), a hilariously deadpan army bureaucrat in *Dr. Strangelove* (1964) and a touchingly bereaved husband in *Nashville* (1975). He appeared twice in ALFRED HITCHCOCK PRESENTS, as the ineffectual schemer William Botibol, a man out wildly past his depth in "DIP IN THE POOL," and as the equally ill-fated escape artist Joe Ferlini in "The Last Escape" (1961).

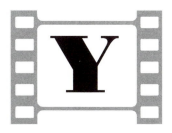

Yacowar, Maurice Canadian film scholar, professor of film studies and dean of the faculty of fine arts at Calgary University and author of *Tennessee Williams and Film* (1977), *Loser Take All: The Comic Art of Woody Allen* (1979; expanded edition, 1991), *Method in Madness: The Comic Art of Mel Brooks* (1983), and *The Films of Paul Morrissey* (1993). His critical study *Hitchcock's British Films* (Archon, 1977), the first book-length study of Hitchcock's early work, is clearly intended as a response to their neglect by Robin WOOD and others. Disclaiming any single interpretive schema, it is divided into self-contained essays on each film from THE PLEASURE GARDEN through JAMAICA INN, proceeding from brief plot summaries to formal and thematic readings that isolate leading symbols—the vertigo of DOWNHILL, the interlocking rings in THE RING, the threatening eyes in SABOTAGE—to intertextual analyses that compare most of them (usually favorably) to their literary sources. The scope is modest and the analyses usually as uncritical as they are nontechnical. Such is the continued neglect of Hitchcock's British films, however, that with a few obvious exceptions—William ROTHMAN's readings of THE LODGER, and MURDER!, Tania MODLESKI's of BLACKMAIL, and Charles BARR's reconsideration of the nature of Hitchcock's authorship in *English Hitchcock*—most of Yacowar's readings, particularly of the silent films, have remained the last word on the subject. A conclusion defends the British films as a group and notes their continuity with Hitchcock's American films, and an appendix speculates on the thematic patterns behind Hitchcock's CAMEO APPEARANCES in his U.S. as well as his British films.

Young, Robert (George) (1907–1998) Untroubled American light leading man whose 100 movies will forever be eclipsed by his work on television. Before he starred as Jim Anderson in *Father Knows Best* (1954–62) or the title character in *Marcus Welby, M.D.* (1969–76), however, he had enjoyed a Hollywood career stretching back to the silent era. He was cast most often in debonair roles like Rudolph Pal in *The Bride Wore Red* (1937) but sometimes combined comedy and drama, as with Elsa Carrington's companion Robert Marvin in SECRET AGENT or tenderfoot Richard Blake in *Western Union* (1941), and handled occasional dramatic roles in *Journey for Margaret* (1942) and *Crossfire* (1947) capably. When his Robert MONTGOMERY phase had reached an end, he aged in the most graceful way imaginable, by becoming everyone's favorite television father figure.

Young and Innocent (Alternative titles: *A Shilling for Candles* [working title], *The Girl Was Young* [U.S.], *Jung und unschuldig, Jeune et innocent*) Gaumont British, General Film Distributors Ltd., 80 minutes, November 1937. **Producer:** Edward Black; **Screenplay:** Charles Bennett,

Edwin Greenwood, and Anthony Armstrong, based on *A Shilling for Candles,* a novel by Josephine Tey; **Continuity:** Alma Reville; **Dialogue:** Gerald Savory; **Cinematographer:** Bernard Knowles; **Art director:** Alfred Junge; **Assistant director:** Penrose Tennyson; **Costumes:** Marianne; **Sound:** A. O'Donoghue; **Editor:** Charles Frend; **Musical director:** Louis Levy; **Song:** "No One Can Like the Drummer Man": (Samuel) Lerner, (Al) Goodheart, and (Al) Hoffman; **Cast:** Nova Pilbeam (Erica Burgoyne), Derrick de Marney (Robert Tisdall), Percy Marmont (Colonel Burgoyne), Edward Rigby (Old Will), Mary Clare (Erica's aunt), John Longden (Inspector Kent), George Curzon (Guy), Basil Radford (Erica's uncle), Pamela Carme (Christine [Clay]), George Merritt (Sergeant Miller), J.H. Roberts (solicitor Henry Briggs), Jerry Verno (lorry driver), H.F. Maltby (Police Sergeant Ruddock), John Miller (police constable), Peggy Simpson and Anna Konstam (young women on beach), Richard George (police constable), Beatrice Varley (courtroom wife), William Fazan (chief magistrate), Frank Atkinson (garage man), Bill Shine (manager of Tom's Hat), Torin Thatcher (manager of Nobby's), Clive Baxter, Pamela Bevan, Albert Chevalier, Syd Crossley, Gerry Fitzgerald, Richard George, Fred O'Donovan, Frederick Piper, Jack Vyvian, and Humberston Wright.

With the closing of GAUMONT-BRITISH's production wing, Hitchcock signed a two-picture contract with GAINSBOROUGH and spent autumn of 1936 working with Charles BENNETT on a treatment based on Josephine TEY's recent detective story *A Shilling for Candles.* The treatment, as had now become Hitch-

During a children's birthday party in *Young and Innocent,* Erica Burgoyne's aunt (Mary Clare, second from left) begins to suspect the real relationship between Erica (Nova Pilbeam, right) and Robert Tisdall (Derrick de Marney, left), the suspect she is helping elude the police. *(National Film Society Archive)*

cock's habit, was exceptionally free, with little remaining of the novel beyond the name of its victim, its first two chapters, and a relatively minor character now promoted to the status of heroine. Erica Burgoyne was played by Nova PILBEAM, the kidnapped child of THE MAN WHO KNEW TOO MUCH (1934), now at the age of 18 essaying her first adult role under the watchful eye of her fiancé, assistant director Penrose TENNYSON. Opposite her Hitchcock cast sleepy-eyed Derrick DE MARNEY as the young fop accused of killing Christine Clay. Percy MARMONT, who had played Emily Hill's gentlemanly suitor Commander Gordon in RICH AND STRANGE and the doomed Caypor in SECRET AGENT, was featured as Erica's father, and Mary CLARE and Basil RADFORD, both of whom would return in THE LADY VANISHES, her aunt and uncle. At first it seemed that the shutdown of Gaumont-British would change little in Hitchcock's filmmaking routine, because Gainsborough rented production space in Lime Grove and released through Gaumont-British. But a reorganization at Lime Grove forced shortly after shooting began obliged the production to move to Pinewood Studios. It is no wonder that the shoot, which lasted from late March to early May, was by all accounts untroubled because Hitchcock was not dealing with any established temperamental stars, bullying executives, or unusual technical challenges. But postproduction was delayed first by the Hitchcocks' annual vacation, then by the chaotic state of affairs at Gainsborough, and finally by a trip to America that pushed the final editing of the film back to September 1937; it was not shown commercially until the following February. It marked another success for the director, even though he was rankled that the American distributor, finding it too slow, cut it down to 70 minutes by removing Erica's visit to Tisdall with her uncle and aunt—a sequence extraneous to the action, like the baggage-car scene in THE LADY VANISHES, but one equally essential to the mood of the film.

Shorn of spies, politics, and strongly established personalities, *Young and Innocent,* as its title suggests, is the sunniest and most beguiling of the six thrillers Hitchcock released through Gaumont-British. The brusque nighttime prologue setting up flirtatious Christine Clay to be murdered seems worlds apart from the scene the following morning, when her body is discovered by two young women who take Tisdall, run off in a different direction to fetch the police, as the killer. Thereafter the film is practically devoid of violence or malice; of all Hitchcock's man-on-the-run films it is the least concerned with what Eric ROHMER and Claude CHABROL call the transfer of guilt. It is structured more purely along the lines of romantic comedy, with Christine and the furiously jealous husband who kills her replaced by the sympathetic, helpful Erica and the gently authoritarian father whose position on the police force constantly makes Erica question herself legally and morally in her attempts to help Tisdall—who escapes from police custody after realizing that his myopic lawyer is ready to throw in the towel—hide from the police and find the evidence that will clear himself. Donald SPOTO has emphasized the film's emphasis on *imperfect seeing* (the eyeglasses Tisdall steals from his lawyer to make his escape, the game of blindman's bluff played at the child's birthday party that Erica and Tisdall interrupt, the twitching eyes that give the murderer away, even the tiny camera Hitchcock, in one of his most memorable cameos as a press photographer, is wearing around his neck as the criminal he has come to photograph escapes under his nose); the lightness of Hitchcock's treatment might be emphasized by contrasting this pattern with the image of *being seen* that runs through PSYCHO, a far graver concern that is virtually absent here because the murderer is not watching Tisdall or Erica. The most baleful, albeit providential, gaze is given to an extraordinary camera movement that pointedly fails to correspond to any character's point of view. As Erica and Old Will, a tramp who can identify the killer and has already alerted her to the clue of his twitching eyes, sit at tea in the Grand Hotel, where a telltale matchbook presumably carried by the murderer has brought them, she says in frustration, "He must be here somewhere!" Hitchcock cuts on the line not to the police surrounding the hotel to apprehend Erica and Old Will but to an impossibly high crane shot that skims the ceiling of the dining room, passes over a dividing wall into the ballroom next door, and travels 145 feet to the far end of the room before coming to rest on an extreme closeup of the blackfaced drummer on the bandstand—whose eyes obligingly twitch as if in response to the withering gaze that prophesies his imminent discovery by the heroine (who, characteristically, will identify him only when he collapses from the medication he is dosing his nerves with and she bends over him to administer first aid). It is the most remarkable shot in Hitchcock's entire British career and one that coun-terpoints the essential lightness of the film without entangling it in any of the moral complexities of the preceding cloak-and-dagger thrillers.

Yount, John   American child actor whose only known film or television role is an altar boy in the *ALFRED HITCHCOCK PRESENTS* segment "THE HORSE-PLAYER."

Zaremba, John (1908–1986)   American character actor in some 80 film and (mainly) television roles since 1952. He appeared in seven roles for *ALFRED HITCHCOCK PRESENTS*—the newspaper photographer in "THE PERFECT CRIME," Dr. Maxwell in "The Kind Waitress" (1959), Talbot Collins in "The Doubtful Doctor" (1960), the supermarket manager in "BANG! YOU'RE DEAD," Lt. Morgan in "The Big Score" (1962), Dr. Chaff in "The Kerry Blue" (1962), and the tax investigator in "Most Likely to Succeed" (1962)—and four more for *THE ALFRED HITCHCOCK HOUR*—as Richard Anderson in "I SAW THE WHOLE THING," Mr. Meecham in "Final Vow" (1962), the coroner in "The Dark Pool" (1963), and the judge in "Starring the Defense" (1963).

Ziegler, William (1909–1977)   American film editor who put in several years on Our Gang shorts at the Hal Roach lot, worked on a dozen features, and then joined David O. SELZNICK for *I'll Be Seeing You* (1944), *SPELLBOUND* (on which he served as associate editor), and *Duel in the Sun* (1946). When Hitchcock struck out on his own, Ziegler was engaged to edit *ROPE*—perhaps the least demanding editorial job in the history of feature films—and later returned for *STRANGERS ON A TRAIN* and, after George TOMASINI, Hitchcock's favorite editor, had died, *TOPAZ*. Among his 90 films are *Auntie Mame* (1958), *The Music Man*

(1962), and *My Fair Lady* (1964), all of which won him Oscar nominations.

Žižek, Slavoj (1949–   )   Slovenian psychoanalyst and cultural theorist, senior researcher in Philosophy at the University of Ljubljana. A self-described "Pauline materialist," he has achieved a formidable reputation in the United States through his application of the later theories of Jacques LACAN, particularly Lacan's theory of a Real beyond individual subjectivity or cultural history, and presenting them into popular culture. Hitchcock films crop up to provide illustrative anecdotes in many of his books, which include *The Sublime Object of Ideology* (1989), *For They Know Not What They Do: Enjoyment as a Political Factor* (1991), *Enjoy Your Symptom! Jacques Lacan in and out of Hollywood* (1992), *Tarrying with the Narrative: Kant, Hegel, and the Critique of Ideology* (1993), *The Metastases of Enjoyment: Six Essays on Women and Causality* (1994), *The Indivisible Remainder: An Essay on Schelling and Related Matters* (1996), *The Plague of Fantasies* (1997), *The Ticklish Subject: The Absent Center of Political Ontology* (1999), *The Reader* (1999), *The Art of the Ridiculous Sublime: On David Lynch's Lost Highway* (2000), and *The Fragile Absolute; or, Why Is the Christian Legacy Worth Fighting For?* (2000). In addition, he has edited *Mapping Ideology* (1994), *Gaze and Voice as Love Objects* (with Renata Salecl, 1996), and *Cogito and the Unconscious* (1998).

His more extended discussions of Hitchcock in *Looking Awry: An Introduction to Jacques Lacan Through Popular Culture* (1991) and *Everything You Always Wanted to Know About Lacan . . . But Were Afraid to Ask Hitchcock* (Verso, 1992), which he edited and to which he contributed an introduction and two essays, treat Hitchcock as paradigmatic in his status as a realist master of classic narrative whose stories focus on the Oedipal initiation of the romantic couple (in the Gaumont-British thrillers from THE 39 STEPS to THE LADY VANISHES), the modernist proponent of the long take whose psychological portraits focus on the heroine traumatized by a father figure (in the SELZNICK period from REBECCA to UNDER CAPRI-

CORN), and the postmodern allegorist of the male hero blocked from "a 'normal' sexual relation" by a maternal superego (in the films from STRANGERS ON A TRAIN through THE BIRDS). Crucial to Hitchcock's relation to the Real is the Hitchcockian "stain" or "blot," the telltale detail that calls attention to the falseness of appearances by sticking out (like the windmill whose vanes rotate the wrong way in FOREIGN CORRESPONDENT). The intertextual equivalent of these blots are "sinthoms" like the unglamorous woman who knows too much or the glass full of a white drink, "characteristic details which persist and repeat themselves without implying a common meaning" and so "designate the *limit of interpretation*."

BIBLIOGRAPHY

As a comprehensive list of books about Hitchcock published in English, this bibliography omits books published in other languages unless they have been translated (in which case the bibliographic data given are for the English translation) and shorter essays unless they have been collected in an anthology.

A rudimentary Hitchcock bookshelf of a dozen titles might include Donald Spoto's biography (indispensable, though always to be taken with a grain of salt), François Truffaut's historic series of interviews, the interviews and essays collected by Sidney Gottlieb, the anthologies edited by Richard Allen and Sam Ishii-Gonzalès and by Marshall Deutelbaum and Leland Poague—both of which include bibliographies considerably more extensive than this one—the oversized volumes of Bill Krohn and Ken Mogg, a judicious selection from the specialized literature—perhaps including Charles Barr, Robert J. Corber, Leonard J. Leff, Tania Modleski, and certainly Robin Wood—and Dan Auiler's selection of production materials in *Hitchcock's Notebooks.*

BIOGRAPHIES

Spoto, Donald. *The Dark Side of Genius: The Life of Alfred Hitchcock.* Boston: Little, Brown, 1983.

Taylor, John Russell. *Hitch: The Life and Times of Alfred Hitchcock.* New York: Pantheon, 1978.

BIBLIOGRAPHY

Sloan, Jane E. *Alfred Hitchcock: A Guide to References and Resources.* New York: G. K. Hall, 1993.

INTERVIEWS

Bogdanovich, Peter. *The Cinema of Alfred Hitchcock.* New York: Museum of Modern Art, 1963.

Gottlieb, Sidney. *Hitchcock on Hitchcock: Selected Writings and Interviews.* Berkeley: University of California Press, 1995.

Truffaut, François. *Hitchcock.* Revised ed. New York: Simon & Schuster, 1984.

ANTHOLOGIES AND COLLECTIONS OF ESSAYS

Allen, Richard, and S. Ishii-Gonzalès, eds. *Alfred Hitchcock: Centenary Essays.* London: British Film Institute, 1999.

Boyd, David, ed. *Perspectives on Alfred Hitchcock.* New York: G. K. Hall, 1995.

Deutelbaum, Marshall, and Leland Poague, eds. *A Hitchcock Reader.* Ames: Iowa State University Press, 1986.

Freedman, Jonathan, and Richard Millington, eds. *Hitchcock's America.* New York: Oxford University Press, 1999.

LaValley, Albert J., ed. *Focus on Hitchcock.* Englewood Cliffs, N.J.: Prentice-Hall, 1972.

Raubicheck, Walter, and Walter Srebnick, eds. *Hitchcock's Rereleased Films: From Rope to Vertigo.* Detroit: Wayne State University Press, 1991.

Žižek, Slavoj, ed. *Everything You Always Wanted to Know About Lacan (But Were Afraid to Ask Hitchcock).* London: Verso, 1992.

GENERAL SURVEYS

Condon, Paul, and Jim Sangster. *The Complete Hitchcock.* London: Virgin, 1999.

Haley, Michael. *The Alfred Hitchcock Album.* Englewood Cliffs, N.J.: Prentice-Hall, 1981.

Harris, Robert A., and Michael S. Lasky. *The Complete Films of Alfred Hitchcock.* Revised and updated ed. New York: Carol, 1999.

Humphries, Patrick. *The Films of Alfred Hitchcock.* London: Hamlyn/Bison, 1986.

Mogg, Ken. *The Alfred Hitchcock Story.* London: Titan, 1999.

Perry, George. *Hitchcock.* New York: Dutton, 1975.

Phillips, Gene D., S.J. *Alfred Hitchcock.* Boston: Twayne, 1984.

Sinyard, Neil. *The Films of Alfred Hitchcock.* New York: Gallery, 1986.

Spoto, Donald. *The Art of Alfred Hitchcock: Fifty Years of His Motion Pictures.* Second ed. New York: Doubleday, 1992.

SPECIALIZED CRITICAL STUDIES

Barr, Charles. *English Hitchcock.* Moffat, Scotland: Cameron & Hollis, 1999.

Bellour, Raymond. *The Analysis of Film.* Ed. Constance Penley. Bloomington: Indiana University Press, 2000.

Brill, Lesley. *The Hitchcock Romance: Love and Irony in Hitchcock's Films.* Princeton: Princeton University Press, 1988.

Cohen, Paula Marantz. *Alfred Hitchcock: The Legacy of Victorianism.* Lexington: University of Kentucky Press, 1995.

Conrad, Peter. *The Hitchcock Murders.* London: Faber and Faber, 2000.

Corber, Robert J. *In the Name of National Security: Hitchcock, Homophobia, and the Political Construction of Gender in Postwar America.* Durham: Duke University Press, 1993.

Derry, Charles. *The Suspense Thriller: Films in the Shadow of Alfred Hitchcock.* Jefferson, N.C.: McFarland, 1988.

Durgnat, Raymond. *The Strange Case of Alfred Hitchcock; or, the Plain Man's Hitchcock.* Cambridge: MIT Press, 1974.

Finler, Joel W. *Hitchcock in Hollywood.* New York: Continuum, 1992.

Grams, Martin, Jr., and Patrik Wikstrom. *The Alfred Hitchcock Presents Companion.* Churchville, Md.: OTR Publishing, 2001.

Hurley, Neil P. *Soul in Suspense: Alfred Hitchcock's Fright and Delight.* Metuchen, N.J.: Scarecrow, 1993.

Kapsis, Robert E. *Hitchcock: The Making of a Reputation.* Chicago: University of Chicago Press, 1992.

Kindem, Gorham Anders. *Toward a Semiotic Theory of Communication in the Cinema: A Reappraisal of Theories for a Cinematic Perspective and a Semiotic Analysis of Color Signs and Communication in the Color Films of Alfred Hitchcock.* New York: Arno/New York Times, 1980.

Krohn, Bill. *Hitchcock at Work.* London: Phaidon, 2000.

Leff, Leonard J. *Hitchcock and Selznick: The Rich and Strange Collaboration of Alfred Hitchcock and David O. Selznick in Hollywood.* London: Weidenfeld & Nicolson, 1987.

Leitch, Thomas M. *Find the Director and Other Hitchcock Games.* Athens: University of Georgia Press, 1991.

McCarty, John, and Brian Kelleher. *Alfred Hitchcock Presents: An Illustrated Guide to the Ten-Year Television Career of the Master of Suspense.* New York: St. Martin's, 1985.

Modleski, Tania. *The Women Who Knew Too Much: Hitchcock and Feminist Theory.* New York: Methuen, 1988.

Price, Theodore. *Hitchcock and Homosexuality: His 50-Year Obsession with Jack the Ripper and the Superbitch Prostitute: A Psychoanalytic View.* Metuchen, N.J.: Scarecrow, 1992.

Rohmer, Eric, and Claude Chabrol. *Hitchcock: The First Forty-Four Films.* Trans. Stanley Hochman. New York: Ungar, 1979.

Rothman, William. *Hitchcock—The Murderous Gaze.* Cambridge: Harvard University Press, 1982.

Ryall, Tom. *Alfred Hitchcock and the British Cinema.* Revised ed. London: Athlone, 1996.

Samuels, Robert. *Hitchcock's Bi-Textuality: Lacan, Feminism, and Queer Theory.* Albany: State University of New York Press, 1998.

Sharff, Stefan. *Alfred Hitchcock's High Vernacular: Theory and Practice.* New York: Columbia University Press, 1991.

Simone, Sam P. *Hitchcock as Activist: Politics and the War Films.* Ann Arbor: UMI Research Press, 1985.

Smith, Susan. *Hitchcock: Suspense, Humour and Tone.* London: British Film Institute, 2000.

Sterritt, David. *The Films of Alfred Hitchcock.* Cambridge: Cambridge University Press, 1993.

Weis, Elisabeth. *The Silent Scream: Alfred Hitchcock's Sound Track.* Rutherford, N.J.: Fairleigh Dickinson University Press, 1982.

Wood, Robin. *Hitchcock's Films Revisited.* New York: Columbia University Press, 1989.

Yacowar, Maurice. *Hitchcock's British Films.* Hamden, Conn.: Archon, 1977.

BOOKS ON INDIVIDUAL FILMS

Anobile, Richard J. *Alfred Hitchcock's* Psycho. New York: Darien House, 1974.

Auiler, Dan. *Vertigo: The Making of a Hitchcock Classic.* New York: St. Martin's, 1998.

Belton, John, ed. *Alfred Hitchcock's* Rear Window. Cambridge: Cambridge University Press, 2000.

Fawell, John. *Hitchcock's* Rear Window: *The Well-Made Film.* Carbondale: Southern Illinois University Press, 2001.

Launder, Frank, and Sidney Gilliat. The Lady Vanishes, *Directed by Alfred Hitchcock.* London: Lorrimer, 1984.

Lehman, Ernest. *North by Northwest.* New York: Viking, 1972.

Naremore, James. *Filmguide to* Psycho. Indiana University Press Filmguide Series, 4. Bloomington: Indiana University Press, 1973.

Naremore, James, ed. North by Northwest: *Alfred Hitchcock, Director.* New Brunswick, N.J.: Rutgers University Press, 1993.

Paglia, Camille. *The Birds.* London: British Film Institute, 1998.

Rebello, Stephen. *Alfred Hitchcock and the Making of* Psycho. New York: Dembner, 1990.

Ryall, Tom. *Blackmail.* London: British Film Institute, 1993.

Sharff, Stefan. *The Art of Looking in Hitchcock's* Rear Window. New York: Limelight, 1997.

MEMOIRS AND BIOGRAPHICAL REMINISCENCES

Freeman, David. *The Last Days of Alfred Hitchcock.* Woodstock, N.Y: Overlook, 1984.

Hunter, Evan. *Me and Hitch.* London: Faber and Faber, 1996.

Leigh, Janet, with Christopher Nickens. *Psycho: Behind the scenes of the Classic Thriller.* New York: Harmony, 1995.

PRODUCTION RESOURCES

Auiler, Dan. *Hitchcock's Notebooks.* New York: Avon, 1999.

MISCELLANEOUS

Bouzereau, Laurent. *The Alfred Hitchcock Quote Book.* New York: Citadel, 1993.

Brown, Bryan. *The Alfred Hitchcock Movie Quiz Book.* New York: Perigee, 1986.

Kaska, Kathleen. *The Alfred Hitchcock Triviography & Quiz Book.* Los Angeles: Renaissance, 1999.

INDEX